Mastering Enterprise JavaBeans™

and the Java™ 2 Platform, Enterprise Edition

Ed Roman

Wiley Computer Publishing

John Wiley & Sons, Inc.

NEW YORK • CHICHESTER • WEINHEIM • BRISBANE • SINGAPORE • TORONTO

Publisher: Robert Ipsen
Editor: Robert M. Elliott
Managing Editor: Brian Snapp
Electronic Products, Associate Editor: Mike Sosa
Text Design & Composition: Rob Mauhar

Designations used by companies to distinguish their products are often claimed as trademarks. In all instances where John Wiley & Sons, Inc., is aware of a claim, the product names appear in initial capital or all capital letters. Readers, however, should contact the appropriate companies for more complete information regarding trademarks and registration.

Sun, Sun Microsystems, the Sun Logo, Enterprise JavaBeans, Java, and JNDI are trademarks or registered trademarks of Sun Microsystems, Inc. in the United States and other countries.

This book is printed on acid-free paper.

Published by John Wiley & Sons, Inc.

Published simultaneously in Canada.

This publication is designed to provide accurate and authoritative information in regard to the subject matter covered. It is sold with the understanding that the publisher is not engaged in professional services. If professional advice or other expert assistance is required, the services of a competent professional person should be sought.

Library of Congress Cataloging-in-Publication Data:

0-471-33229-1

Printed in the United States of America.

10 9 8 7 6

What People Are Saying about Ed Roman's
Mastering Enterprise JavaBeans and the Java 2 Platform, Enterprise Edition...

"Ed Roman has done a great job of explaining a complex topic: how to build Java applications for the middle tier. Not only does he explain how to program with EJB, he explains how to design applications so that they can use EJB intelligently. This is a great starting place for programmers who are trying to move from simplistic client/server applications to true multi-tier development using the official Java middle-tier platform."

—Roger Sessions, President, Objectwatch
Author, "ObjectWatch Newsletter"

"This book is a must-have for developers who want to jumpstart their EJB development process. Ed Roman shows the right way to use the J2EE technology with in-depth examples and coding patterns from the real world. We recommend this book as part of our education materials for both in-house staff and customer engagements."

—William W. Lee, Chief Technology Officer, The Theory Center

"Enterprise JavaBeans and the J2EE are among the most important technologies in enterprise computing. Organizations that are exploring or implementing mission-critical, Web-based, and distributed systems should understand the role that the Enterprise Java platform can play. Ed Roman has done an excellent job of taking this complex subject and explaining it in a clear and practical manner. I recommend this book to anyone who wants to increase their knowledge and expertise in building robust, 'real-world' computing systems."

—Doug Hibberd, Chief Technology Officer, iMARK.COM

"This book explains all fundamentals of EJB wrapped up in an easy to follow set of examples. It is easy enough for the beginner and covers enough for more experienced users to like it. It also provides the reader with a guide to what you should consider when buying an EJB server, as well as a brief look into the future and what's coming next in this exciting new technology."

—Rickard ÖBerg, Software Architect, DreamBean

"This book starts off innocently enough with the idea of explaining Enterprise JavaBeans. However, by the end, you realize that Ed Roman has effectively unwrapped the onion that is today's multi-tier architecture and shown how J2EE can revolutionize how systems are architected. I highly recommend this book to anyone who wishes to keep up with the latest in Java technology and internet systems architecture."

—Mike Perham, Senior Web Developer, living.com

To my family:
Mom, Dad, and Mike

CONTENTS

v

As I write these words, I can't help but think back to an inflection point that occurred in my life almost a year and half ago. I remember sitting in my cubicle at Trilogy Software Inc., an e-commerce company down in Austin, TX, lost in deep middleware thoughts. My challenge was to devise an interesting load-balancing strategy for our in-house application server, which we called the backbone.

The backbone was a superb software system. It was cleanly written, easy to use, and boasted some very high-end features. Features such as distributed object support, object-relational mapping, and extensible domain object modeling. It had almost anything you needed for Internet development. It was a worthy investment for Trilogy to have.

I was part of a task force to add enterprise features to this backbone. Features such as transaction control, security, and load-balancing. Our goal was to improve the backbone into a product worthy of large-scale deployments.

So that day, after hours of racking my brain, I finally finished crafting what I believed to be a highly creative and optimal load-balancing strategy. Looking for feedback, I decided to walk down to my friend Court Demas' office. Court is one of those developers that can really pick apart almost any design and expose its flaws. He has a unique quality that only a few developers I know have.

Walking into Court's office, I was expecting a typical developer-level conversation, and that's what I received. We turned the design inside and out, marking up my freshly printed hard-copy with scribbles and other unintelligible comments that only we could understand. Finally, satisfied that we had reached a conclusion, I thanked Court and walked toward the door, prepared to implement the changes we had agreed upon.

But I didn't make it that far. Court said something to me that would change my way of thinking. He said something that baffled and confused me at first, but would eventually result in a complete paradigm shift and career move for me. What did Court say? Nothing profound. But simply, "You know Ed, this stuff is really what Enterprise JavaBeans is for."

At first, I had no idea what he was talking about. Enterprise JavaBeans? What's that? Something like regular JavaBeans? I had no idea. Eventually, Court managed to explain to me what EJB was. And once he explained it, I knew that Trilogy had to do a 180-degree turn, or Trilogy would lose their competitive advantage.

You see, EJB is a specification for a server-side component marketplace. EJB enables you to purchase off-the-shelf components from one vendor, combine them with components from another vendor, and run those components in an application server written by yet a third vendor. This means companies could collaborate on the server-side. EJB enables you to buy, rather than build, elements of server-side applications.

The EJB value proposition had strong ramifications for Trilogy. EJB represented a way for Trilogy to get out of this middleware business, and concentrate on their e-commerce strategic efforts. This would mean discarding the backbone completely in favor of a third party vendor's architecture. Not only would this reduce Trilogy's maintenance costs, but it would solidify their software suite, since their middleware would now be written by professionals who had been in the business for twenty years. This proposition would eventually lead to an entirely new business unit forming at Trilogy.

So I decided to start researching EJB and pushing for Trilogy to adopt it. I went to the Sun Microsystems Web page and downloaded the EJB 1.0 specification in PDF form and printed it out. Back then, the specification was about a third of the size it's grown to today.

Understanding the specification turned out to be much more challenging than downloading it. The specification was written for system-level vendors, and was not meant to be a tutorial for end developers. The section on entity beans, for example, took me a good two months to really grasp, as the notion of persistent components was new to me.

This arduous struggle with understanding the EJB specification is what eventually lead me to write this book for you. This book represents everything I wish I had when I first started a year and a half ago. So what is this book about? This is not a book on EJB propaganda. Well, it may be more accurate to tell you what this book is *not* about. This is not a book on how to write EJB code on any single application server. This is not a nice book that paints a perfect picture of the EJB world. This is not an advertisement for any particular EJB product, nor a campaign to rid the world of Microsoft.

The goal of this book is to help you. I want you to be able to craft solid, secure, and scalable server-side deployments. As you read this book, you'll learn how to design, implement, and deploy EJB solutions. This book covers both the vision and the reality of EJB, and is written from an independent developer's perspective. I hope it will prepare you for the challenges you will face.

I wish the grass was greener and I could write a book on how clean and portable EJB is, but the truth is that this technology is not perfect, and you should know exactly what the imperfections are. I will expose you to the gruesome and incompatible parts of EJB, and also explain how the industry is solving these problems.

Indeed, the newer specifications (especially EJB 1.1) improve portability and incompatibilities tremendously. I hope that by the time you're done reading this book, you are convinced that the vision of EJB is solid, and the future is very bright.

To give you as much exposure to EJB as possible, almost every new concept in this book is complemented by a brand-new enterprise bean. This is not a book with a single code example that flows for the entire text, because that would give you a very narrow view of the kinds of domain models you can build with EJB. So prepare yourself, because together we will develop *thirteen* enterprise beans over the course of this book. We'll also write other small modules, such as servlet code, JNDI code, RMI code, XML code, and more, to give you a taste for the Java 2 Platform, Enterprise Edition (J2EE) suite.

My hope is that I can save you time and energy, and aid you in designing well-crafted server-side deployments. But this is merely the beginning. The EJB marketplace is just getting started, and there's a whole lot more work ahead to do. I encourage you to take an active role in the middleware industry, and to work with me taking EJB to the next level. Feel free to e-mail me your experiences, tips, and design strategies, and I'll post them on the book's accompanying Web site to share with others. Our goal is to increase our knowledge of EJB as a community, and together we can do it.

Sincerely,

Ed Roman

On an airplane home from the PLoP (Pattern Languages of Programming) conference, 1999

Ed Roman is one of the world's leading authorities on high-end middleware technologies. He has been actively involved with Sun Microsystems' enterprise Java solutions from their inception, and has designed, built, and deployed a variety of enterprise applications, including architecting and developing complete application server products. He routinely devotes a significant amount of time towards influencing and refining Sun's enterprise specifications, is a regular contributor to middleware interest mailing lists, and regularly speaks at middleware-related conferences.

Ed is the CEO of The Middleware Company (www.middleware-company.com). Via on-site training courses, The Middleware Company educates developers and managers on the latest server-side technologies. They also aid in the development of custom middleware solutions. This includes making an application server purchase decision (EJB/COM+), integration paths for migrating legacy systems, and working with Internet-based e-commerce deployments.

This book is a tutorial on *Enterprise JavaBeans (EJB)*. It's about EJB concepts, methodology, and development. You'll see many, many examples of Enterprise JavaBeans throughout this book, giving you a practical understanding of the subject. This book is also about *Java 2, Enterprise Edition (J2EE)*, a software platform for developing robust enterprise applications, of which EJB is an essential component. By reading this book, you will acquire a *deep* understanding of EJB and J2EE.

Make no mistake about it—what you are about to read is *not* an easy subject. EJB and J2EE incorporate concepts from a wealth of areas, including distributed computing, databases, security, component-driven software, and more. Combining them together is a magnificent stride forward for the Java community, but with that goes a myriad of concepts to learn and understand. This book will teach you the concepts and techniques for authoring reusable components in Java, and it will do so from the ground up. You only need to understand Java in order to understand this book.

While you're reading this book, you may want to download the appropriate specifications, such as the EJB and J2EE specifications, available on the Sun Microsystems Web site. See the book's accompanying Web site for links to these specifications, as they complement this book nicely.

Technologies Covered in This Book

The Java 2 Platform, Enterprise Edition (J2EE) is a sophisticated suite of enterprise APIs that enable you to write robust, scalable, and multiuser secure deployments. J2EE is huge, and it spawns a multitude of concepts. The major parts of the J2EE platform that we cover are everything you need to begin advanced programming with EJB. This means you only need to approach this book with understanding of the Java language because we will teach you everything you need beyond that.

We cover the following J2EE technologies:

- Enterprise JavaBeans (EJB) version 1.0, found throughout the book.

- The latest information about programming with the new EJB version 1.1, covered in Appendix D.

- How to use Java Database Connectivity (JDBC) with enterprise beans, covered in Chapter 8.

- The Java Transaction API (JTA), covered in Chapter 10, with a real-world example in Chapter 14.

- CORBA and RMI-IIOP, covered in Chapter 11.

- Servlets and EJB, covered as part of a large e-commerce example in Chapter 15.

- Java Remote Method Invocation (RMI), covered in Appendix A.

- The Java Naming and Directory Interface (JNDI), covered in Appendix B.

- The Extensible Markup Language (XML), an ancillary technology that is used in J2EE, covered in Appendix C.

Technologies Not Covered in This Book

This book does not cover several enterprise Java technologies. For one, we do not cover the Java Message Service (JMS). JMS allows for asynchronous distributed object communications. Unfortunately, the current EJB specification (revision 1.1) does not include support for JMS. Sun Microsystems is promising that EJB 2.0 will include JMS support.

We also do not cover Java Server Pages (JSPs). JSPs enhance your enterprise deployment with a Web-based presentation layer. The closest technology to JSPs that we cover are Java servlets in Part IV (JSPs are compiled into servlets at runtime).

Finally, we do not cover the JavaMail API in this book. JavaMail is part of the Java 2 Platform, Enterprise Edition architecture, and is useful for performing mail operations in Java. JavaMail is useful in e-commerce deployments for sending a confirmation e-mail when purchasing goods online. See the book's accompanying Web site for links to JavaMail resources.

Organization of the Book

The text is organized into the following five parts.

Part I begins with a tour of enterprise computing. We'll talk about components, distributed frameworks, multitier deployments, and the various competing architectures out there, including the *Java 2, Enterprise Edition (J2EE)* platform. We'll have a look at where J2EE fits into the grand scheme of things, and we'll explore the role that EJB plays within the J2EE platform. We'll also take a whirlwind tour of EJB, which serves as a great overview for people in a hurry. While Part I is essential information to EJB newcomers, veterans will also find nuggets of useful knowledge as well. There are two chapters in Part I.

Part II devotes exclusive attention to programming with EJB. We'll see how to write both kinds of enterprise beans: session beans and entity beans. We'll cover the basics of writing each type of bean, including extensive examples. We'll see both types of session beans (stateful and stateless), as well as both types of entity beans (bean-managed persistent and container-managed persistent). There are seven chapters in Part II.

Part III covers advanced concepts that are related to EJB and J2EE. We'll learn the fundamentals of transactions and understand why they are necessary for a robust deployment. We'll also take a look at the *Common Object Request Broker Architecture (CORBA)* and study how it related to EJB and the J2EE platform. There are two chapters in Part IV.

Part IV shows how to use EJB and the J2EE platform in the real world. We'll develop an extensive e-commerce deployment that illustrates how to build an e-commerce Web site using the J2EE platform. We'll begin with an analysis of our deployment's requirements, and from there we'll design a set of enterprise beans and Java servlets that fulfill those requirements. We'll then implement each of these components and show you how to put it all together to make the deployment go live. By the time you're done reading Part IV, you should have a firm grasp on how EJB and the J2EE platform can be used to solve real-world problems. There are four chapters in Part IV.

The Appendices plunge into the concepts and APIs that form the building-blocks for the J2EE platform. EJB is put aside to introduce *Java Remote Method Invocation (RMI)*, the *Java Naming and Directory Interface (JNDI)*, and the *Extensible Markup Language (XML)*. Each appendix is devoted to one of these technologies. Within each appendix, we first introduce the technology's core concepts, quickly moving from basic concepts to advanced development. Each appendix concludes by relating the knowledge you've just learned to EJB programming. Depending on your background, you may not need to read all of the appendices. I encourage all readers to review the latter half of each appendix, so that you understand how each technology is related to EJB. Appendix D moves on to cover what's new in the EJB 1.1 specification, and Appendix E is a guide for making an EJB product purchase decision. Finally, Appendix F is a quick reference for programmers to use during EJB development. It includes diagrams illustrating what's really going on in an EJB system, a guide to the core EJB API, and a transaction reference.

Illustrations in the Text

Almost all of the illustrations in this book are written in the *Unified Modeling Language (UML)*. UML is the de facto standard methodology for illustrating software engineering concepts in an unambiguous way. If you don't know UML, pick up a copy of *The Unified Modeling Language's Users Guide*, which illustrates how to effectively use UML in your everyday software. UML is a highly important achievement in Object-Oriented Methodology. It's a common mechanism for engineers to communicate and design, and it forces you to abstract your object model and object prior to implementation. I cannot stress its use enough.

Examples Used

While writing this book, I asked some developer friends what they hate most in technical books. Other than obvious things, such as source code not working, the biggest complaint I found is that the books do not go deep enough. Specifically, many people feel that the canonical "Hello, World!" examples, while they may have their merit, are insufficient for revealing the intricacies of the technology being explained.

In this book, I have tried to keep the examples as robust and relevant as possible. The examples start out simple, so that first-time users as well as veterans will have simple templates to use to write their code. But as each chapter progresses, the examples become more complex, exercising a significant portion of each API that's introduced. I've also tried to develop useful utilities from the examples that you can use in practice. For example, Appendix A (which covers Java Remote Method Invocation) introduces a simplified message queue that's based on RMI. Appendix B (which covers the Java Naming and Directory Interface) walks you through a browser that you can use to interact with different kinds of directory structures. Part IV (multiple chapters illustrating how to deploy an e-commerce solution with the J2EE platform) has several reusable enterprise beans that you can extend for your own purposes.

The goal of these efforts is to give you a breadth of understanding beyond just "Hello, World!" despite the newness of EJB. I hope you find this to be the case.

The Included CD-ROM

On the accompanying CD-ROM, you will find all the source code you see in this book. The code comes complete with makefiles, ready to build and run with the BEA *WebLogic* server. Note that the code has been built from the ground-up, adhering to the EJB specification, and contains nothing specific to WebLogic. With minor changes, you should be able to run this book's code on the application server of your choice, assuming it fully implements the EJB specification. The one major step that will change between application servers is the deployment step. Be sure to consult with your vendor's documentation for details on this.

In addition to the code, you'll also find on the CD-ROM:

- An evaluation copy of the BEA WebLogic EJB application server
- An evaluation copy of the BEA WebLogic Commerce Server 1.7.1
- ObjectSpace™ JGL 3.1
- Complete ready-to-use sample code

The Accompanying Web Site

This book would not be complete without a way to keep you in touch after the book was published. In addition to the CD-ROM, there is a Web site available for resources related to this book. There you'll find:

- Error corrections from the text
- Links to EJB resources
- Any updates to the source code examples

Before reading on, I would go to this Web site immediately to get any changes or updates that have happened since the book was first published. The Web site is at:

- www.wiley.com/compbooks/roman

Feedback

When you begin your EJB programming, I'm sure you'll have many experiences to share with other readers as well. Feel free to e-mail me examples, case studies, horror stories, or tips that you've found helpful in your experiences, and I'll post them on the Web site.

Acknowledgments

This book has been over a year in the making, and I am proud to say it is the finest work I have produced in my life. What made the book a reality, however, were the many people that aided in its development.

First, hats off to my review panel, including Anne Thomas, Rickard ÖBerg, Mike Perham, Doug Hibberd, Simon North, William Lee, Roger Sessions, Mike Roman, Charles Erickson, the folks at Net.Quotient, and anyone else I may have left off. You have simply been awesome, and I couldn't have done it without you.

Thanks to my love, Youn Hi, who endured the rough times when I was holding down a job and writing this book simultaneously, and lived through the hardship when I quit my job to work on this book full-time, giving the book the attention it deserved.

Thanks to my friends: Jonah Probell, Luke Benes, Henry Tran, Mike Uzquiano, DJ Piglet, Todd Snyder, Bryan Vandrovec, Maurice Garfinkel, Katie, Adit, James Kao, Lawrence Eng, José Gonzales, Dave Frank, Charles Erickson, Ahmed Gheith, Shawn Smith, Bindu and Richard Rao, Jian Song, Will Ballard, Doug Hibberd, Sean Hoffman, Daan DeBrouckere, Charles Erickson, Mike Perham, Alex Bentley, Jeff Ragusa, Sammy Wu, TU97.5, Scott Merriam, Galvin, Jeremy Deutsch, and V.

Thanks to the great folks over at John Wiley & Sons publishing. They have been absolutely outstanding throughout this book's evolution. In particular, I'd like to thank Bob Elliott, Brian Snapp, and Emilie Herman for their incredible efforts.

## PART ONE

Overview

I n Part I, we introduce the server-side development platform that is the *Java 2 Platform, Enterprise Edition (J2EE)*, of which the *Enterprise JavaBeans (EJB)* component architecture is a vital piece. J2EE is a conglomeration of concepts, programming standards, and innovations—all written in the Java programming language. With J2EE, you can rapidly construct distributed, scalable, reliable, and portable secure server-side deployments.

Chapter 1 begins by exploring the need for a server-side development platform such as J2EE. You'll see the rich needs of server-side computing, such as scalability, high availability, resource management, and security. You'll also see the need for a rapid application development component architecture such as EJB and COM+. We'll wrap up by surveying Sun Microsystems' J2EE, a complete server-side development platform.

Chapter 2 moves on to the Enterprise JavaBeans component model. We'll take a look at how EJB empowers heterogeneous vendors to collaborate to solve a business problem, and we'll study the roles of each party in an EJB deployment. We'll also look at the different functional software modules in an EJB deployment and how they relate.

## CHAPTER 1

Server-side Component Architectures

nterprise JavaBeans (EJB) is a server-side component architecture that enables and simplifies the process of building enterprise-class distributed object applications in Java. By using EJB, you can write scalable, reliable, and secure applications without writing your own complex distributed object framework. EJB is about rapid application development for the server side; you can quickly and easily construct server-side components in Java by leveraging a prewritten distributed infrastructure provided by the industry. EJB is designed to support application portability and reusability across any vendor's enterprise middleware services.

If you are new to enterprise computing, these concepts will be made very clear shortly. EJB is a complicated subject and thus deserves a thorough explanation. In this chapter, we'll discusses the main concepts surrounding Enterprise JavaBeans. This starts with a discussion about what's involved in writing enterprise software and why a prepackaged distributed object architecture such as Enterprise JavaBeans simplifies your life. From this discussion, we'll have a greater insight into why a server-side component architecture makes sense, as well as a feature list of what we'd like to see when we choose an architecture for developing server-side distributed object applications.

We'll then examine several endeavors by the industry to address these enterprise needs. The highlight of this discussion—as well as this book—is Sun's *Java 2 Platform, Enterprise Edition (J2EE)*. J2EE is a collection of enterprise technologies, of which EJB is an integral part. By understanding and using J2EE properly, you can build portable, object-oriented, enterprise-class applications in Java.

The Need for a Server-Side Component Architecture

To understand the value EJB brings to the table, we first must examine the needs that developers commonly have when authoring and deploying components in a server-side environment. As we uncover the issues surrounding server-side development, we'll begin to see the need for a standardized architecture such as EJB.

Software Components

We begin our discussion with a look at software components. A software component is code that implements a set of well-defined interfaces. It is a manageable, discrete chunk of logic. Components are not entire applications—they cannot run alone. Rather, they can be used as puzzle pieces to solve some larger problem.

The idea of software components is very powerful. A company can purchase a well-defined module that solves a problem and combine it with other components to solve larger problems. For example, consider a software component that computes the price of goods. We'll call this a *pricing component*. You hand the pricing component information about a set of products, and it figures out the total price of the order.

The pricing problem can get quite hairy. For example, let's assume we're ordering computer parts, such as memory and hard drives. The pricing component figures out the correct price based on a set of *pricing rules* such as:

Base prices of a single memory upgrade or a single hard disk

Quantity discounts that a customer receives for ordering more than 10 memory modules

Bundling discounts that the customer receives for ordering *both* memory and a hard disk

Preferred customer discounts that you can give to big-name customers

Locale discounts depending on where the customer lives

Overhead costs such as shipping and taxes

These pricing rules are in no way unique to ordering computer parts. Other industries, such as health care, appliances, airline tickets, and others need the same pricing functionality. Obviously, it would be a huge waste of resources if each company that needed complex pricing had to write its own sophisticated pricing engine. Thus, it makes sense that a vendor provides a generic pricing component that can be reused over and over again for different customers. For example:

1. The U.S. Postal Service can use the pricing component to compute shipping costs for mailing packages. This is shown in Figure 1.1.

2. An automobile manufacturer can use the pricing component to discriminate prices for cars. For example, the manufacturer can set up a Web site that allows customers to get price quotes for cars over the Internet. Figure 1.2 illustrates this scenario.

3. An online grocery store can use the pricing component as a discrete part of a complete *workflow* solution. When a customer purchases groceries over the Web, the pricing component first computes the price of the groceries. Next, a different vendor's component bills the customer with the generated price. Finally, a third component fulfills the order, setting things in motion for the groceries to be delivered to the end user. We depict this in Figure 1.3.

Reusable components are quite enticing because components promote rapid application development. An IT shop can quickly assemble an application from prewritten components, rather than writing the entire application from scratch. This means:

The IT shop needs less in-house expertise. The IT shop can consider the pricing component to be a black box, and it does not need experts in complex pricing algorithms.

The application is assembled faster. The component vendor has already written the tough logic, and the IT shop can leverage that work, saving development time.

There is a lower total cost of ownership. The component vendor's cash cow is its components, and therefore it must provide top-notch documentation, support, and maintenance if it is to stay in business. Because the component vendor is an expert in its field, the component generally has fewer bugs and higher performance than an IT shop's home-grown solution. This reduces the IT shop's maintenance costs.

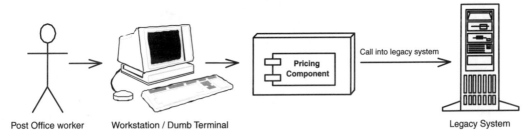

Post Office worker   Workstation / Dumb Terminal   Call into legacy system   Legacy System

Figure 1.1   Reusing a pricing component for the U.S. Postal Service.

Thus, once the rules of engagement have been laid down for how components should be written, a *component marketplace* is born, where vendors can sell re-usable components to companies.

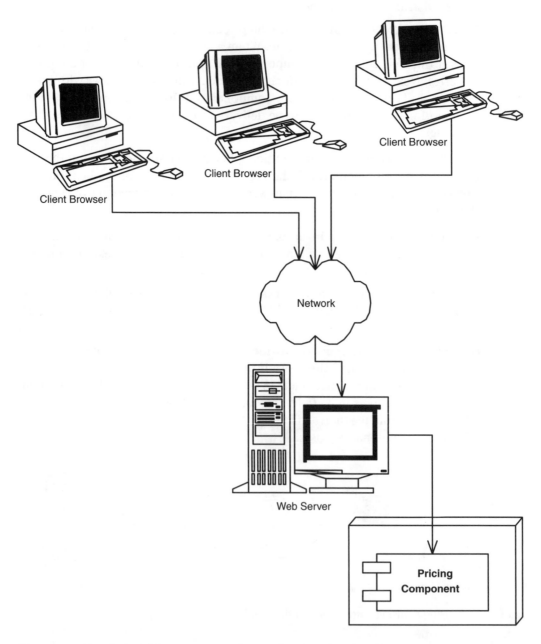

Figure 1.2   Reusing a pricing component for quoting car prices over the Internet.

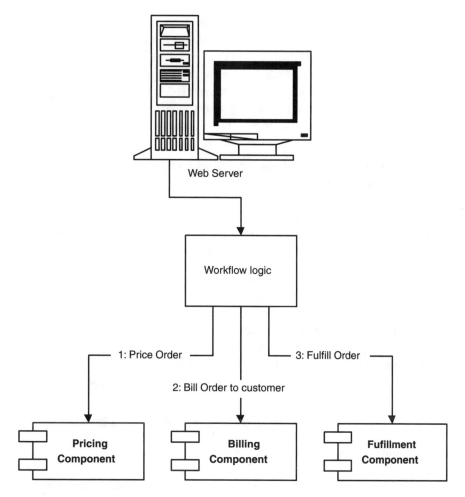

Figure 1.3 Reusing a pricing component as part of an e-commerce workflow solution.

Component Architectures

To facilitate the component development process, there should be a standard-ized way to build, manage, and maintain components. This approach consists of the following:

Tools for developing components. The process of building components should be streamlined, allowing the component developer to focus on writ-ing the core logic behind the component. This promotes rapid application development and is essential for any component standard to succeed. For example, an *Integrated Development Environment (IDE)*, such as Symantec's *Visual Cafe*, IBM's *VisualAge for Java*, or Inprise's *JBuilder 2*, assists Java developers in rapidly building and debugging components. Other vendors, such as Inline Software, provide enhanced EJB-specific development tools.

A container that manages your deployed components. This component container provides a runtime environment for your components to play in. It also provides a set of common services that most components will need. For example, the container could automatically instantiate new components as necessary, thus removing that burden from the component developer. To combine any container with any component, you must have a well-defined contract between containers and components. This contract allows any container to manage any component.

Tools for deploying and maintaining components. When an organization purchases components from component vendors, there must be a set of tools to aid in the deployment and maintenance of those components. For example, there should be a way to customize the components for a particular environment. In our pricing component example, we could have a tool that assists us in customizing the products we are pricing.

Each of these features is essential in a mainstream component marketplace. And, of course, as a component developer, you would like to focus on writing the components themselves, rather than the ancillary products that are common to all components: the container and the tools. A well-defined *component architecture* supplies the standards necessary for different vendors to write the components, component containers, and tools. Thus, by having a component architecture standard, developers can employ a "divide-and-conquer" approach to programming.

Java: An Ideal Language for Component Architectures

For a component to succeed in solving a business problem, both the component developer and the customer using the component must agree on the syntax and semantics of calling the component's methods. Thus, the component vendor must publish the *contract* (or rules) for calling the component, and the client code must adhere to these rules.

As the vendor releases new versions of the component, that vendor's customers will want to upgrade. This raises a number of issues. Will the new component work with the IT shop's code that called the old component? Do the IT shops need to recompile their client code? Or, even worse, has the component contract changed, necessitating that IT shops modify their client code to map to the new component contract?

Thankfully, object-oriented design introduced a great programming practice to help solve this problem by separating the *interface* of a component from its *implementation*:

A component's interface defines the component's contract with the code that calls it. For example, the interface defines methods and parameters that the component accepts. The interface masks the implementation from clients of the component, so clients deal only with the end result: the methods the component exposes.

A component's implementation is the core programming logic that an object provides. It has some very specific algorithms, logic, and data. This data is private to the component, and it should be hidden from all client code that calls the component.

For interface/implementation separation to be effective, developers must write client code to a component's interface only (this is called *interface-based programming*). If you're writing components, you can force developers into this paradigm by publishing only the interfaces to your components, not your implementations.

By separating interface from implementation, you can vary a component's proprietary logic without changing any client code. For example, you can plug in a different implementation that performs the same task more efficiently. This is possible because the actual implementation is not needed at compile time—only the interface is needed. Hence, there is no specific implementation tied to the client code. This is shown in Figure 1.4.

The Java language supports interface/implementation separation at a syntactic level via the *interface* keyword and *class* keyword. And because Java is an interpreted language, the separation of code into discrete class files ensures that clients do not have to recompile their code if you ship a new version of your component.

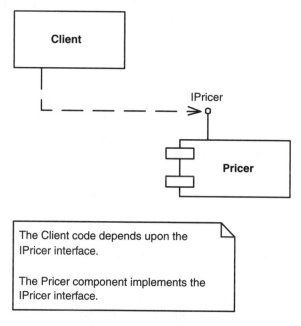

Figure 1.4   Interface-based programming on our pricing component.

In addition to the interface/implementation separation, Java is an object-oriented language that has been built from the ground-up as a cross-platform development language and that has wide industry support. This makes the Java language an ideal technology on which you can base components.

Component Architectures in Java

Now that you've seen what a component architecture is, let's look at what component architectures exist in the Java world. The first one you may have heard of is *JavaBeans*. JavaBeans components are small-grained application bits. You can use JavaBeans to assemble larger-grained components or to build entire applications. JavaBeans, however, are *development components* and are not *deployable components*. You typically do not deploy a JavaBean because a JavaBean is not a complete application; rather, JavaBeans help you construct larger software that *is* deployable. And because they cannot be deployed, JavaBeans do not need a runtime environment in which to live. JavaBeans do not need a container to instantiate them, to destroy them, and to provide other services to them because the application itself is made up of JavaBeans.

By way of comparison, the *Enterprise JavaBeans* (*EJB*) standard defines a component architecture for *deployable components* called *enterprise beans*. Enterprise beans are larger, coarser-grained application components that are ready to be deployed. They can be deployed as is, or they can be assembled with other components into larger application systems. Deployable components must be deployed in a container that provides runtime services to the components, such as services to instantiate components as needed.

Enterprise beans are very similar to two other types of Java components: applets and servlets. Applets can be deployed in a Web page, where the browser's applet viewer provides a runtime container for the applets. Servlets can be deployed in a Web server, where the Web server's *servlet engine* provides a runtime container for the servlets. Enterprise beans are deployed in an *application server*, where the application server provides a runtime container for the Enterprise JavaBeans. This is shown in Figure 1.5.

The real difference between applets, servlets, and enterprise beans is the domain of which each component type is intended to be a part.

Applets are portable Java programs that can be downloaded on the fly and can execute in an untrusting environment. For example, an applet can be downloaded from a Web server into a Web browser, and it typically displays a user interface to the end user.

Servlets are networked components that you can use to extend the functionality of a Web server. Servlets are request/response oriented, in that they take requests from some client host (such as a Web browser) and issue a response

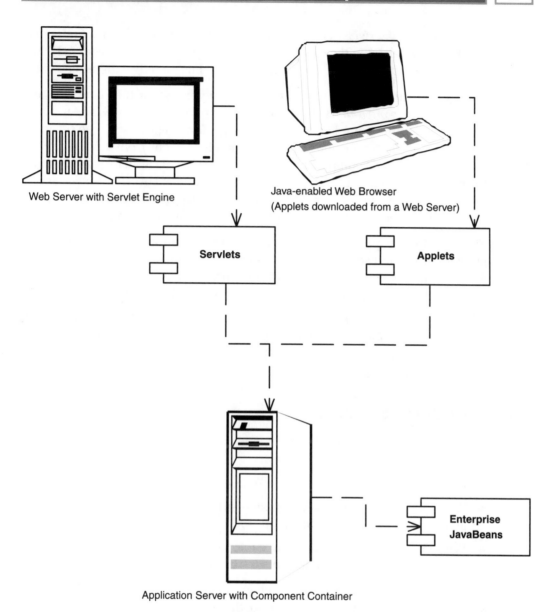

Web Server with Servlet Engine

Java-enabled Web Browser
(Applets downloaded from a Web Server)

Servlets

Applets

Enterprise
JavaBeans

Application Server with Component Container

Figure 1.5 Applets, servlets, and Enterprise JavaBeans.

back to that host. This makes servlets ideal for performing Web tasks, such as rendering an HTML interface to an e-commerce catalog.

Both applets and servlets are well suited to handle *client-side* operations, such as rendering graphical user interfaces (GUIs) (although they don't necessarily need to have one), performing other presentation-related logic, and lightweight business logic operations. The client side could be a Web browser, in the case of applets that render user interfaces using the Java Foundation Classes. The client side could also be a Web server, in the case of servlets that render user interfaces in HTML. In both these situations, the components are dealing directly with the end user.

Enterprise beans, on the other hand, are not intended for the client side, but are *server-side components*. They are meant to perform *server-side* operations, such as executing complex algorithms or performing high-volume business transactions. The server side has different kinds of needs from a rich GUI environment. Server-side components need to run in a highly available (24x7), fault-tolerant, transactional, and multiuser secure environment. An *application server* provides this high-end server-side environment for the enterprise beans, and it provides the runtime containment necessary to manage enterprise beans.

Finally, note that applets, servlets, and enterprise beans are not "either-or" technologies. You can use JavaBeans as development component building blocks for constructing deployable enterprise beans. You can also provide a user interface to your enterprise beans with applets or servlets (shown in Figure 1.5).

Now that you've seen where EJB fits in with other technologies, let's take a look at the class of problems that EJB addresses. EJB is meant for server-side programming; to appreciate what EJB brings to the table, we must first understand what makes server-side programming difficult.

The Needs of the Server Side

As we've mentioned, a complete component architecture paves the way for the following:

- Developers to write reusable components
- Vendors to write component containers that provide a runtime environment and services to components
- Vendors to provide development, deployment, and maintenance tools, which are necessary complements to the components themselves

This divide-and-conquer approach allows vendors to provide a set of common services that most components will need, thus saving precious development and deployment time. Rather than reimplement the wheel, the component developer can simply outsource the services he needs to other products. Professionals who are experts in providing these services write these products. When harnessed properly, users save time by buying rather than building. Additionally, the overall deployment is strengthened because domain experts are writing these common products.

As we'll see, server-side software opens up a whole new set of problems that require some very high-end services. If you choose to home-grow these services yourself, you'll likely encounter a development and maintenance nightmare. Being able to outsource server-side services is one of the key benefits of a server-side distributed object architecture like EJB.

Multi-tier Architectures

A server-side deployment is software written to support concurrent users performing operations simultaneously, securely, reliably, and efficiently. Examples of server-side deployments include the following:

Banks where many ATM machines connect to a central bank server

Retail outlets such as the Wal-Mart chain of stores, where many Wal-Mart stores send shopping information to a central Wal-Mart server

Support centers where support engineers have terminals that can bring up customer data from a central server

Insurance agencies where insurance sales staff have terminals that connect to a central server

Web sites where thousands or millions of users connect to Web servers and those Web servers need to connect with a central server for data and logic

Robust server-side deployments are not easy to build. Many issues arise, such as scalability, maintainability, security, reliability, and more. With so many clients depending on your central server-side deployment, it would be a catastrophe if your central servers went down, slowed to a crawl, or allowed a hostile party to gain access to the systems. Therefore, server-side deployments need to be well written from the ground up and well tested, and they need to run in a robust environment.

Any well-written deployment has a logical software partitioning into *layers*. Each layer has a different responsibility in the overall deployment, and within each layer there can be one or more components. Note that these layers are purely abstractions, and they may not correspond to physical distribution. A layered system is a well-designed system because each layer is responsible for a separate task. Here is a typical layer partitioning:

A presentation layer contains components dealing with user interfaces and user interaction. For example, the presentation layer of a stand-alone application could be written in Visual Basic. The presentation layer of a Web-based deployment could use Java servlets, Java server pages, and/or Java applets.

A business logic layer contains components that work together to solve business problems. These components could be high-performance engines, such as catalog engines or pricing engines. Typically, these components are written in a type-safe language such as Java or C++.

A data layer is used by the business logic layer to persist state permanently. Central to the data layer is one or more databases that house the stored state.

The advantage to partitioning an application into these logical layers is to isolate each layer from the others. For example, it should be possible to plug in a different view (i.e., change the presentation layer) while minimizing impacts on the business logic or data layers. It should similarly be possible to plug in a different set of business rule component implementations within your business logic layer, or to plug in a different database in your data layer, with relatively minor effects on the other layers. In some ways, this is analogous to how the classic model-view-controller separation allows the developer to vary the model, view, and controller independently of one another.

The physical separation of these layers is another story. In a *two-tier architecture*, two of these layers are physically separated from the third, forming two physically separated *tiers*. On the other hand, a *three-tier architecture* separates each of these three abstract, logical layers into three physically distributed tiers. In each of these architectures, the tiers are separated from one another by some physical boundaries, such as machine boundaries, process boundaries, or corporate boundaries. In the discussion that follows, we don't really care what the boundary is—it could be a process boundary, a machine boundary within a local area network, or a boundary across the Internet. And for clarity, we will refer to all deployments with three tiers or more as *N-tiered*, which is used interchangeably with three-tiered occasionally.

So what are the advantages to separating your application into two tiers verses N tiers? There are a number of compelling reasons for both sides, which we'll soon uncover. From this debate, you will begin to see the needs of the server side and why a distributed server-side architecture such as Enterprise JavaBeans is necessary.

Two-Tier Architectures

Traditionally, most high-end deployments have been two-tiered. Two-tier deployments combine the business logic layer with one of the other two layers. There are two combinations possible: combining the presentation layer with the business logic layer, and pushing some of the business logic layer into the data layer. Let's take a look at each scenario.

Combining the Presentation Layer with the Business Logic Layer

Your presentation layer and business logic layer can be coupled together in a single tier, pushing the data access layer into a tier by itself. This draws a tier boundary between the business logic layer and the data layer (Figure 1.6). If you think of the first tier as a "client" and the second tier as a "server," this architecture effectively makes the client "fat" and the server "thin."

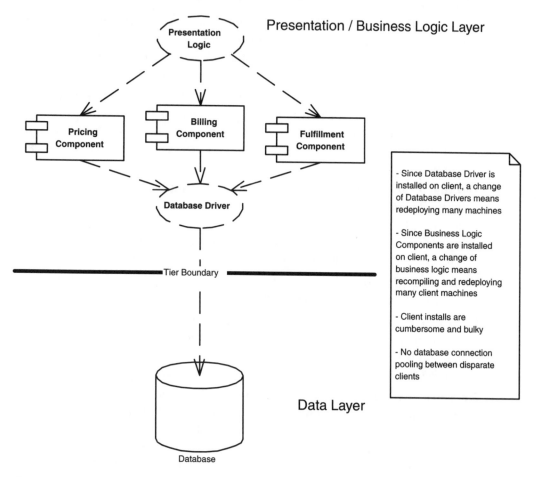

Figure 1.6 Combining presentation with business logic in a two-tier architecture.

In a two-tier architecture, the client application typically communicates with the data layer through a database bridge API such as Open Database Connectivity (ODBC) or Java Database Connectivity (JDBC). This decouples the client from the particular database being used. So that each vendor's proprietary database will conform to the database bridge, each database vendor must supply a database driver that is called from the database bridge API, such as an ODBC driver or JDBC driver.

Two-tier architectures have the following characteristics:

Deployment costs are high. Database drivers must be installed and configured on each of the client tiers, which may mean hundreds or thousands of machines.

Database driver switching costs are high. Switching one database driver with another now requires a reinstallation of every client machine's database drivers. This is very costly from a maintenance perspective because the client tier could reside on the desktops of hundreds or thousands of client machines. For example, the size and mobility of a sales force could make uniform upgrades on all the individual laptops virtually impossible.

Database schema switching costs are high. The fat clients directly access the database via JDBC, SQL/J, or ODBC. This means that the clients are dealing directly with the underlying database schema. If you ever decide to migrate the schema to handle new business processes, you need to redeploy each client.

Database type switching costs are high. The fat clients are bound to a database API, such as a relational database API or an object database API. If you ever decide to switch between database types (such as switching from a relational database to an object database), you must not only redeploy each client, but you must drastically change the client code to suit the new database type.

Business logic migration costs are high. Changing the business logic layer involves recompiling and redeploying the client tier.

Database connection costs are high. Every database client needs to establish its own database connection. These connections are limited in number and costly to establish. When clients are not using the database, the connection is often still held and cannot be used by others.

Network performance suffers. Each time your business logic performs a database operation, you need to make a number of roundtrips across the physical boundary separating the business logic layer and the data layer. If this barrier is a network boundary, it could severely hamper the total time a database operation takes—and it could clog the network, reducing the amount of bandwidth other users have.

Pushing Some of the Business Logic Layer into the Data Layer

More recently, deployments have begun to combine parts of the business logic layer with the data layer into a separate tier. This is illustrated in Figure 1.7. If you think of the first tier as a "client" and the second tier as a "server," this architecture effectively makes the client "thin" and the server "fat."

To actualize this scenario, you push some of your business logic (usually your persistence-related data logic) *within the database*. Databases allow you to execute logic within the database's context by writing a suite of modules known as *stored procedures*. By pushing select parts of your logic into stored procedures, you gain a number of scalability and performance enhancements. For one, because you are pushing some logic inside of the database, the network round trip from the logic to the database is minimized. Rather than performing n database queries, you can call one procedure kept inside the database, which performs n queries for you. This saves you many round trips, increasing the speed

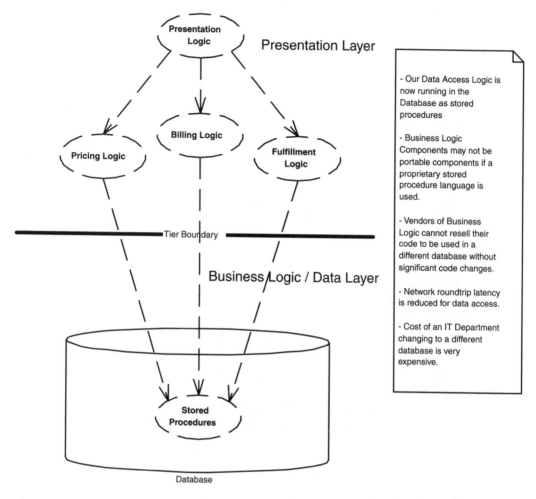

Presentation Layer

- Our Data Access Logic is now running in the Database as stored procedures

- Business Logic Components may not be portable components if a proprietary stored procedure language is used.

- Vendors of Business Logic cannot resell their code to be used in a different database without significant code changes.

- Network roundtrip latency is reduced for data access.

- Cost of an IT Department changing to a different database is very expensive.

Tier Boundary

Business Logic / Data Layer

Database

Figure 1.7 Pushing data access logic into the second tier in a two-tier architecture.

of database operations. It also reduces total network traffic, enabling other clients to perform network operations more speedily.

Thus, having database-specific logic within the database does enhance performance and increases the overall deployment scalability. Most of the other problems with two-tiered approaches listed previously, however, still apply. And while the development of stored procedures is an important step forward, they do not solve every problem. In fact, they add some problems of their own. For example, stored procedure languages are often proprietary, which ties clients to a particular database. The whole point of having a database bridge such as ODBC or JDBC, allowing any database to plug in, was defeated. Now it becomes even harder to plug in a database of a different genre, such as an object database. It should be noted, however, that Java is being used more and more as a stored procedure language, which enhances the portability of stored procedures.

N-Tier Architectures

An N-tier architecture adds one or more tiers to the two-tier model. In N-tier deployments, your presentation layer, business logic layer, and data layer are separated into respective physical tiers. With four or more tiers, you decompose each of these layers even further to allow various parts of your system to scale independently.

A concrete example of an N-tier architecture is a three-tiered Web-based deployment, as illustrated in Figure 1.8. A three-tiered Web-based deployment is typically broken down as follows:

Your presentation tier runs within the address space of one or more Web servers. It consists of Java servlets, scripts to customize look-and-feel (such as Active Server Pages, Java Server Pages, etc.), and workflow logic that ties things together.

Your business logic tier runs within the address space of one or more *application servers*. Application servers are necessary to provide a suitable containment environment for the business logic components to run in. The application server also manages these components efficiently and provides a number of services to the components. For example, the application server provides a database access layer for the business components, allowing the business components to persist data to and load data from the data tier. The application server is also responsible for making the business components available to be used, instantiating them as necessary.

Your data tier consists of one or more databases and may contain data-related logic in the form of stored procedures.

Note that a single-company Web deployment is only one example of a viable N-tier deployment. Another example is a banking system that has many tiers, with each tier representing a department of a bank. Another example is a control system that does not have a graphical user interface, yet also requires several tiers. Yet another example is a distributed deployment that spans company boundaries, where several companies work together to provide enhanced value (such as an online purchasing store that involves UPS for shipping logic and VISA for credit card logic).

N-tier architectures have the following characteristics:

Deployment costs are low. Database drivers are installed and configured on the server-side, rather than on client machines. It is much cheaper to deploy and configure software in a controlled server-side environment than to deploy

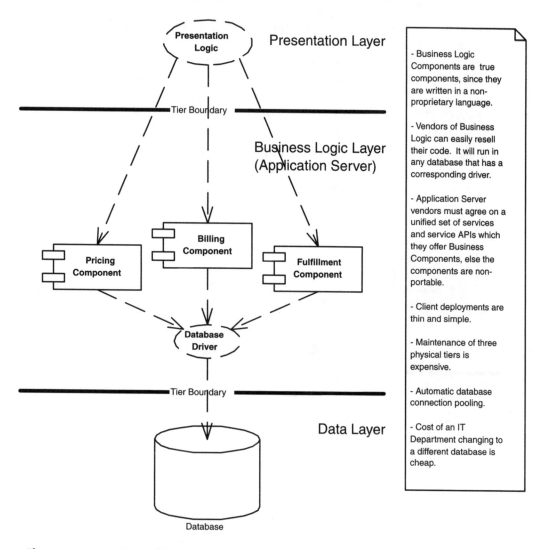

Figure 1.8 An N-tier architecture.

software on (for example) thousands of salesmen's laptops, or on thousands of end user terminals.

Database switching costs are low. Clients no longer access the database directly, but rather go through the middle tier for data access. This enables you to migrate database schemas, change to different database drivers, or even change your persistent storage type without re-deploying clients.

Business logic migration costs are low. Changing the business logic layer may not necessitate recompiling and redeploying the client tier.

You can secure parts of your deployment with firewalls. Many businesses are sensitive about protecting their data, yet they do not want to hamper a deployed application. For example, in a Web-based deployment, businesses may not want to expose their business layer directly to outside users. Yet the deployment must expose the presentation layer to outside users so that they can hit the Web site. A solution is to place a firewall in between the presentation and business logic tiers, as shown in Figure 1.9

Resources can be efficiently pooled and re-used. With an N-tier architecture, connections to external resources can be managed very efficiently. *Resource pooling* exploits the fact that clients are often doing other things

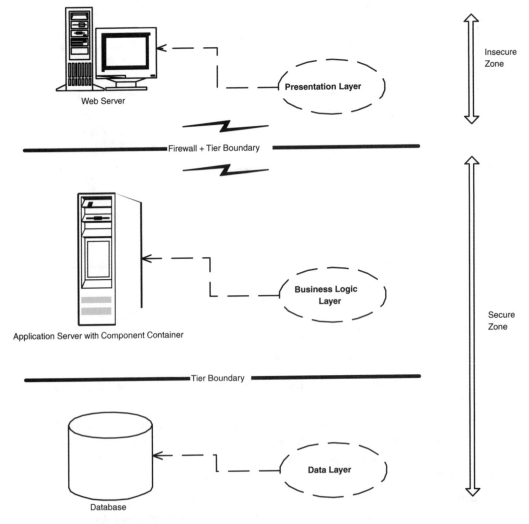

Figure 1.9 Security reasons often necessitate three-tier divisions.

besides using resources, such as rendering a graphical user interface. Rather than your business components acquiring and releasing connections to resources (such as databases), the resources can be pooled and re-used for different client requests. The resulting set of database connections required is often far less than the total number of components in a deployed system. Because database connections are very expensive, this paradigm increases the overall scalability of the deployment. Furthermore, connections to resources do not need to be re-established continuously, improving application performance. Resource pooling can be applied to other resources as well, such as socket connections and threads. In fact, with an N-tier architecture, the business components themselves can be pooled and reused by multiple clients. Pooling of components means you don't need a dedicated component for each client, as is true with two-tier thick clients. The pooling of resources is illustrated in Figure 1.10.

Each tier can vary independently. For example, you can add database images while minimizing changes and recompilations of the other tiers.

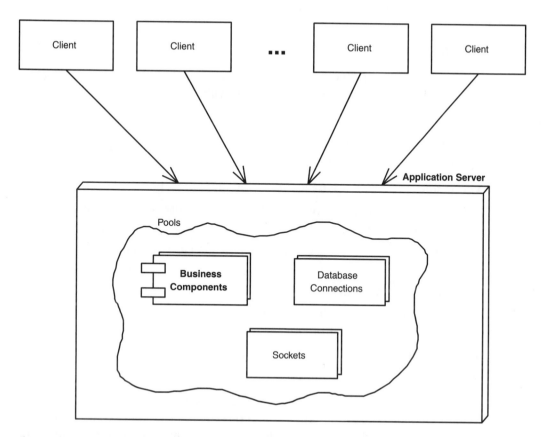

Figure 1.10 Pooling of resources in an N-tier deployment.

Performance slowdown is localized. If one tier is overloaded, the other tiers can still function properly. In a Web deployment, users may able to view your front page even though the application server is overburdened.

Errors are localized. If a critical error occurs, it is localized to a single tier. The other tiers can still function properly, gracefully dealing with the situation. For instance, if your application server crashes, your Web server could report a "site down" page to client browsers.

Communication performance suffers. Since the tiers are physically separate, they must communicate across process boundaries, across machine boundaries, or across enterprise domain boundaries. This results in high communications overhead. Only by designing your distributed object application properly can you have an efficient deployment. Unfortunately, this often necessitates being very aware of tier boundaries and reduces the location transparency of your application code.

Maintenance costs are high. You are deploying in three or more physically separate tiers. Software installation costs, software upgrade costs, redeployment costs, and administration costs increase significantly.

Making Multi-tier a Reality

The benefits of multi-tier deployments do not come for free. Someone, at some point in time, needs to write the code that will:

- Broker method requests
- Perform resource pooling
- Handle the lifecycle of your components
- Handle the logic to load-balance communications between each tier
- Deal with the ramifications of two or more clients concurrently accessing the same component
- Reroute client requests to other machines in case of failure
- Provide a secure environment so that unauthorized clients cannot sabotage the system state
- Provide monitoring software that might page a system administrator in case of catastrophic problems
- Authorize users to perform secure operations
- And much, much, *much* more.

Each of these issues is a separate service that needs to be addressed for serious server-side computing. And each of these services requires a lot of thought and a lot of network middleware plumbing to resolve. Often times, companies build in-house proprietary frameworks that give some of these services. Those companies are setting themselves up for failure, because high-end application servers are hideously complicated to build and maintain, require expert-level knowledge of middleware, gain support of industry-standard tools, and are completely orthogonal to most companies' core business. Why not build instead of buy?

The *application server* was born to let you buy these middleware services, rather than build them yourself. Application servers provide a runtime environment for server-side components. They provide component developers with common middleware services, such as resource pooling, networking, and more. Application servers allow you to focus on your application, and not worry about the middleware you need for a robust server-side deployment.

Server-Side Component Architecture Solutions

It has been a number of years now since the idea of multi-tier server-side deployments surfaced. Since then, multitudes of application servers have begun to appear on the market. These application servers provide a usable runtime environment in which components can execute and provide the needed middleware services (such as resource pooling and security) for reliability and scalability. But unfortunately, up until now there has not been a definition of what a middle-tier component really is. Because of this, each application server has been providing component services in a non-uniform, proprietary way. This means that once you bet on an application server, your code is locked into that vendor's solution. This greatly reduces portability and is an especially tough pill to swallow in the Java world, which promotes portability. It also hampers the commerce of components because a customer cannot combine a component written to one application server with another component written to a different application server.

From this, the need for a standard architecture for server-side components has arisen. This architecture needs to craft a well-formed interface between the application server, which contains the components, and the components themselves. These interfaces allow the components to be managed in a portable way, rather than a proprietary one. The component vendors should be able to focus on the business logic of the problems being solved and not worry about external overhead such as resource pooling, networking, security, and so on. These necessary elements of enterprise-class deployments should be externalized to application server vendors, which should provide these common services to all component developers. The goal here is rapid application development of server-side deployments, allowing developers to leverage preexisting network middleware while still writing portable server-side components. This will allow components to be switched in and out of various application servers, without having to change code or potentially even recompile the components themselves.

To address the need, technology advances have been made to compensate for the lack of server-side component architectures. The most popular standards have emerged from Microsoft, Sun Microsystems, and the Object Management Group (OMG). We now outline each of these architectures.

Microsoft's Distributed interNet Applications Architecture

Microsoft has recently consolidated its multi-tier vision into the Windows Distributed interNet Applications Architecture (DNA). This architecture combines the following:

Windows NT, the underlying operating system that provides a runtime environment for all Microsoft technology

Distributed COM, a core technology that promotes interface/implementation separation and language independence and that allows for distributed components

Microsoft Message Queue (MSMQ), a message-queuing product for asynchronous communications between components

Microsoft Transaction Server (MTS), an application server product that manages components

Microsoft Wolfpack, software for server clustering

Microsoft SQL Server, a relational database store

Microsoft Internet Information Server, its Web server, which includes *Active Server Pages (ASP)* scripts, which can be used to coordinate interactions with client browsers

Microsoft Management Console, a tool for deployment and administration

Windows DNA is a server-side development platform that incorporates all these products and more. Note that these technologies are also evolving as we speak— specifically, Distributed COM, MTS, and parts of MSMQ are evolving into a new, combined technology called *COM+*. COM+, along with the ancillary Windows DNA services, allows vendors to build and deploy server-side components with Microsoft technology. Needs such as resource pooling, database transactions, asynchronous communications, and security are all handled implicitly by the underlying distributed object infrastructure.

Microsoft's N-tier vision is quite compelling because it's a one-vendor distributed object framework. Rather than assembling products from competing vendors, developers can work with tools written by a single source. But unfortunately, developers who integrate to Microsoft's N-tier vision must tie themselves to a particular vendor (Microsoft), which allows only the Microsoft platform as a deployment scenario. This makes it difficult if not impossible to perform deployments on mainframes or high-end UNIX machines, which have a significant amount of services available for high-reliability deployments, as well as much higher processor and resource scalability. And while the number of server-side Win32-based workstations is climbing incredibly fast, Windows NT is scalable to only four processors (or reportedly 16 processors with NT 5.0). This means a Windows-based deployment has a very high machine maintenance cost due to the sheer number of machines required. Hopefully, this will change in the future.

Sun Microsystems's Java 2 Platform, Enterprise Edition (J2EE)

Sun Microsystems has also realized the need for a server-side component architecture. Many Java component vendors have been clamoring for a full server-side N-tier story that is Java-based; the Java language itself is well suited for the server. Client-side Java has many problems, such as inconsistency with user interfaces between platforms, slow speed of these user interfaces, and wrong versions of Java Virtual Machines running on client machines. But for the server side, Java is the ideal language. Server-side deployments run in a controlled environment, which means that the correct version of the Java programming language will always be used. The speed of Java is also a less significant issue on the server because often typically 80 percent or more of an N-tier application's time is spent at the database or networking level.

Java is also a very convenient language to write server-side components in, if for one reason alone: The server-side market is dominated by UNIX machines and mainframes. This means a cross-platform language for writing server-side components adds huge value because a developer can write a component once and deploy it on any customer's existing server-side environment. This means that customers with legacy applications (such as programs written in COBOL on mainframe systems) have a well-defined migration path to e-commerce and other modern business processes.

Thus, to enable server-side computing in Java, Sun has produced a complete development platform called the *Java 2 Platform, Enterprise Edition (J2EE)*. The mission of J2EE is to provide a platform-independent, portable, multiuser, secure, and standard enterprise-class platform for server-side deployments written in the Java language. The cornerstone of J2EE is Enterprise JavaBeans (EJB), a standard for building server-side components in Java.

J2EE simplifies many of the complexities surrounding the construction of a scalable, component-based server-side application, and it is very analogous to Windows DNA. The most notable exception is that J2EE is a specification, whereas Windows DNA is a product. J2EE specifies the rules of engagement that people must agree on when writing enterprise software. Vendors then *implement* the J2EE specifications with their J2EE-compliant products.

Because J2EE is a specification (meant to address the needs of many companies), it is inherently not tied to one vendor; it also supports cross-platform development. This encourages vendors to compete, yielding best-of-breed products. As we will see in this book, though, incompatibilities between vendor products will arise— some problems due to ambiguities with specifications, other problems due to the human nature of competition.

The Object Management Group's CORBA Standard

The Object Management Group (OMG) is an open standards body whose mission is to standardize on industry guidelines and build object management standards to provide a common framework for application development and to promote a software component marketplace. The OMG's two most notable achievements have been the Common Object Request Broker Architecture (CORBA), as well as the Internet Inter-ORB Protocol (IIOP). We will cover these technologies in Chapter 11. For now, you should know that CORBA/IIOP are standards that promote portable distributed objects. If you write your objects to use CORBA/IIOP, you can leverage prewritten middleware supplied by vendors. For example, a vendor could provide a security service, a transaction service, or a persistence service, and you can use those services in your applications without writing that middleware yourself.

Like J2EE, CORBA is a specification, not a product. Vendors (such as Inprise, Iona, and IBM) implement the CORBA specification with their products. The big distinction between CORBA and J2EE is that (until now) CORBA has had only the notion of an object and had no notion of a deployable server-side component that is automatically managed by an application server. The OMG, however, has recently addressed this need by bolstering CORBA with a *CORBA Components* proposal. This proposal defines the notion of a component in CORBA—an entity that is deployable within an application server, is managed by the application server, and is sellable in a component marketplace, resulting in rapid application development through the divide-and-conquer strategy.

 CORBA Components is still in its infancy at the time of this writing. In fact, there is great debate within the OMG over whether CORBA Components should even be standardized at all. The main reason behind this is that J2EE contains built-in support for CORBA (as we will see). The real danger is if the OMG creates yet a third server-side component standard beyond Windows DNA and J2EE. This is definitely a specification to keep an eye on in the future.

The Java 2 Platform, Enterprise Edition

Now that you have seen the three major server-side architectures out there, let's turn our attention to the Java 2 Platform, Enterprise Edition (J2EE), of which EJB is an integral part.

Why J2EE?

To understand why J2EE is necessary, we need to take a look back in time and chart the evolution of the Java platform.

JDK Efforts

Sun Microsystems first focused on building a robust Java Development Kit (JDK). The JDK became the de facto reference implementation of the Java platform. Not much exciting development was happening here for server-side middleware support.

Enterprise API Efforts

Sun Microsystems then recognized the power of Java on the server and began to develop several Enterprise APIs that provided enterprise-level services for server-side deployments. These services include naming and lookup services, transaction services, and the Enterprise JavaBeans (EJB) 1.0 API. Sun also began to develop elements of Consumer Java, which provide functionality for consumer devices to interoperate.

Several months after EJB 1.0 was finalized, the first EJB-based application servers began to arrive on the market (BEA's *WebLogic* was the first). These application servers took advantage of the other Enterprise APIs as well, such as the ones for naming and lookup services, for transactions, and for database operations. The early application servers served as a great feedback device to Sun because they highlighted many problems with the Enterprise APIs. These include the following:

Ambiguities. The unspecified sections of the Enterprise API specifications (particularly EJB 1.0) hampered portability of components. This is unacceptable due to the "Write Once, Run Anywhere" paradigm of Java.

Poor synchrony between Enterprise APIs. Each of Sun's Enterprise APIs was related, yet each was being developed independently. Sun was not communicating the typical purpose of the enterprise APIs together as a suite, and the specifications themselves were not very intertwined.

A moving target. Each of Sun's Enterprise APIs was evolving separately and had new version numbers coming out all the time. This made it somewhat difficult to program using EJB because EJB depends on those Enterprise APIs. What versions of each API should be used? This was unspecified, leading to nonportable code between application server vendors.

No way to test application server compatibility. When a vendor wrote a product to the EJB 1.0 standard, there was no way to test whether this product was compatible with Sun's specification. Similarly, a consumer had no information about whether a vendor was compliant with EJB 1.0.

No reference implementation. The Enterprise APIs were simply specifications; Sun did not provide a default reference implementation. Thus, application developers had no low-end enterprise platform against which to test code. By way of comparison, programmers who did not leverage the Enterprise APIs could simply use Sun's JDK reference implementation. Thus, the Enterprise APIs needed an analog to the JDK.

Platform Separation

Realizing the problems with the Enterprise APIs, Sun Microsystems has recently taken a major leap forward in solving the problems we alluded to previously by issuing *three different* Java platforms. Each platform is a superset of the next smaller platform.

The Java 2 Platform, Micro Edition (J2ME) is a development platform for Java-enabled devices, such as Palm Pilots, pagers, watches, and so-on. This is a very restricted form of the Java language due to the inherent performance and capacity limitations of small devices.

The Java 2 Platform, Standard Edition (J2SE) contains standard Java services for applets and applications, such as input/output facilities, graphical user interface facilities, and more. This platform contains what most people use in standard JDK programming.

The Java 2 Platform, Enterprise Edition (J2EE) takes Java's Enterprise APIs and bundles them together in a complete development platform for enterprise-class server-side deployments in Java.

The arrival of J2EE is significant because it addresses all the problems raised when Sun developed the Enterprise APIs, including the following:

Fewer ambiguities. Sun has addressed a great deal of the incompatibilities in EJB 1.0 with the EJB 1.1 specification (covered in Appendix D). This specification corrects bugs and other ambiguities that had been restricting portability.

Enterprise API synchrony. Each of the Enterprise APIs has a clear role in J2EE, as defined by Sun's *J2EE Application Programming Model* document.

This should clear up any confusion about how you can use the Enterprise APIs together to enable a server-side deployment. Similarly, the Enterprise APIs are evolving in harmony, as the specifications leverage each other in an intertwined fashion.

Locked-down revisions. Enterprise Java is no longer a moving target, as Sun has locked down versions of each Enterprise API specification and bundled them together as the de facto versions to use when developing with J2EE. This increases code portability across vendors' products because each vendor supports exactly the same API revision.

Test suite. As we mentioned above, there is no way for a vendor to know if he or she is implementing EJB 1.0 properly. Sun has fixed this with J2EE, as it provides a test suite for vendors to test their products against. If a product passes the tests, Sun will issue a compliance brand, alerting customers that the vendor's product is indeed J2EE-compliant.

Reference implementation. To enable developers to write code against J2EE as they have been doing with the JDK, Sun is providing its own free reference implementation of J2EE. Sun is positioning it as a low-end reference platform, as it is not intended for commercial use.

The J2EE Technologies

The Java 2 Platform, Enterprise Edition is a robust suite of middleware services that make life very easy for server-side application developers. The technologies included with J2EE are shown in Figure 1.11; they include the following:

Enterprise JavaBeans (EJB). EJB defines how server-side components are written and provides a standard contract between components and the application servers that manage them. EJB promotes the spawning of a component marketplace, where vendors can sell reusable components that can be purchased to help solve business problems. EJB is the cornerstone for J2EE and is covered throughout this book.

Java Remote Method Invocation (RMI) and RMI-IIOP. RMI allows for interprocess communication and provides other communication-related services. RMI-IIOP is a portable extension of RMI that can use the Internet Inter-ORB Protocol (IIOP) and can be used for CORBA integration. RMI is covered in Appendix A. RMI-IIOP is covered in Chapter 11.

Java Naming and Directory Interface (JNDI). JNDI identifies the locations of components or other resources across the network. JNDI is covered in Appendix B.

Java Database Connectivity (JDBC). JDBC is a relational database bridge that allows for relatively portable database operations. JDBC is used in Chapter 8.

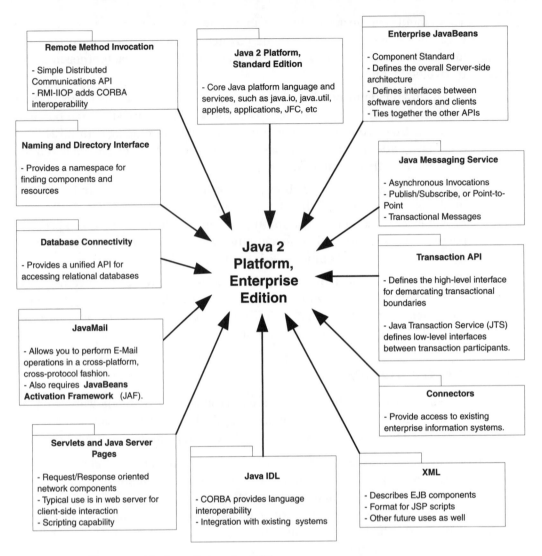

Figure 1.11 The Java 2 Platform, Enterprise Edition.

Java Transaction API (JTA) and Java Transaction Service (JTS). The JTA and JTS specifications allow for components to be bolstered with reliable transaction support. JTA and JTS are explained in Chapter 10.

Java Messaging Service (JMS). JMS allows for asynchronous distributed object communications. We do not cover JMS in this book, as Sun Microsystems has not integrated JMS with EJB yet.

Java Servlets and Java Server Pages (JSPs). Servlets and JSPs are networked components which are ideally suited for request/response oriented computing, such as interacting with clients over HTTP. We illustrate using servlets with EJB in Chapters 12 and 15.

Java IDL. Java IDL is Sun Microsystem's Java-based implementation of CORBA. Java IDL allows for integration with other languages. Java IDL also allows for distributed objects to leverage CORBA's full range of services. Thus, J2EE is fully compatible with CORBA, rounding out the Java 2 Platform, Enterprise Edition completely. Java IDL is explained in Chapter 11.

JavaMail. The JavaMail service allows you to send e-mail messages in a platform-independent, protocol-independent manner from your Java programs. For example, in a server-side J2EE deployment, you can use JavaMail to confirm a purchase made on your Internet e-commerce site by sending an e-mail to the customer. Note that JavaMail depends on the *JavaBeans Activation Framework (JAF)*, which makes JAF part of J2EE as well. We do not cover JavaMail in this book.

Connectors. Connectors make J2EE well suited to integrate with mainframe systems running high-end transactions (such as those deployed with IBM's CICS), as well as Enterprise Resource Planning (ERP) systems. Connectors will be included in a future release of J2EE.

The Extensible Markup Language (XML). Several J2EE technologies (such as EJB 1.1 and JSP) depend on XML as a meta-markup language for describing content. We cover XML in Appendix C, and we cover how XML and EJB are related in Appendix D.

The Java 2 Platform, Enterprise Edition (J2EE) builds on the existing technologies in the Java 2 Platform, Standard Edition (J2SE). J2SE includes the base Java support and the various libraries (.awt, .net, .io) with support for both applets and applications. Because J2EE builds on J2SE, a J2EE-compliant product must not only implement all of J2EE, but must also implement all of J2SE. This means that building a J2EE product is an absolutely *huge* undertaking. This barrier to entry will likely result in significant industry consolidation in the Enterprise Java space, with a few players emerging from the pack as leaders.

 At the time of this writing (May 1999), Sun Microsystems had not finalized the Java 2 Platform, Enterprise Edition (J2EE) specifications. Sun expects to complete them by Fall 1999. This means you are likely to see J2EE products emerging in the marketplace sometime in the year 2000.

To understand more about the real value of J2EE, we now explore each API in more detail.

Enterprise JavaBeans (EJB)

EJB is a component architecture that allows developers to quickly create scalable enterprise applications. It provides complex middleware enterprise features at no cost to application developers. With EJB, you can now focus your energies on writing the applications that solve real-world problems, rather than on all the overhead that goes with distributed server-side systems. You can think of EJB almost as a suite of common functionality that most applications need. Through the EJB model, you won't need to reinvent those wheels.

To this, EJB adds legacy integration flexibility. You can rewrite your components from scratch to be EJB-compliant, or you can wrap an existing component; there's no need to build your enterprise system from the ground up. Many vendors of EJB products (IBM and BEA come to mind) provide well-defined migration paths for existing legacy system customers to jump aboard the EJB bandwagon without abandoning their existing enterprise information system. This is critical for companies that may have their entire business running in millions of lines of COBOL running off CICS systems.

EJB also offers "plug-and-play" enterprise features. With EJB, you barely need to know anything at all about middleware to construct components designed to run in a scalable, multi-tier architecture. Rather than writing to middleware APIs (which is the old CORBA style of distributed object computing), your components gain middleware services *implicitly and transparently* from the EJB server, without writing one line of middleware code yourself. The application server implicitly handles transactions, persistence, security, state management, component lifecycle, threading, and more.

The cross-platform, cross-vendor nature of the EJB standard is another extremely important benefit that EJB brings to the table. It means that there's now a common standard for distributed component architectures to which all vendors can integrate. It also means that there's going to be intense competition in the EJB market. EJB levels the playing field by defining one standard component API. This means you can expect the new EJB-compliant products that emerge in the market to be both reliable and high-performing because middleware vendors can be compared in the same light. There is one standard, allowing the vendors to focus on the quality of their EJB products. The standard also allows application developers to focus on writing best-of-breed applications, rather than supporting every brand of middleware out there. This is the promise of EJB.

Remote Method Invocation (RMI) and RMI-IIOP

The EJB standard depends on several other APIs in J2EE; the most visible of these is Java Remote Method Invocation (RMI). RMI is a mechanism for invoking methods remotely on other machines. It is tightly integrated with the Java language itself; if you know Java, it won't take much to learn RMI. EJB relies on RMI as a communications API between components and their clients.

RMI is seamless—you almost don't even know you're using it when you program your distributed application. RMI allows Java programmers to communicate in a distributed object fashion using an almost identical programming style to coding a standalone Java applet or application. That is the beauty in RMI—it abstracts networking issues away from you, such as marshalling parameters, handling machine byte-order, and so on, which are all necessary for network communications. RMI also contains other niceties such as dynamic class downloading, automatic activation of remote objects, and a distributed garbage collector to clean up unused remote objects. Because many Java programmers already know RMI, we cover it in Appendix A.

RMI-IIOP

Sun Microsystems (in a joint venture with IBM and others) has more recently developed a more portable version of RMI as well, which can use the Object Management Group's (OMG's) Internet Inter-ORB Protocol (IIOP) as a communications protocol. IIOP is a very robust protocol, and it adds several qualities of service than RMI can support in its native protocol. IIOP is also necessary for J2EE deployments to integrate with CORBA systems. We explain RMI-IIOP in Chapter 11.

Java Naming and Directory Interface (JNDI)

The Java Naming and Directory Interface (JNDI) is a standard for *naming and directory services*. Enterprise JavaBeans relies on JNDI for looking up distributed components across the network. JNDI is a key technology required for client code to connect to an EJB component.

JNDI hinges on the notion of a *directory service*. A directory service stores information about where resources (such as components) reside, as well as other information such as username and passwords. In EJB, when client code requests access to a component, directory services are used to locate and retrieve a component to service that client (see Figure 1.12). You can think of the directory service as a matchmaker that connects clients to components.

Historically, there are many types of directory services, as well as protocols to access them. Some examples include Novell's NDS and the Internet standard LDAP. These are all competing standards, so each type of directory service is accessed differently. And each directory service stores information in a proprietary way. If you write an application that accesses a particular directory service, it becomes a real mess if you want to switch to a different directory service.

The Java Naming and Directory Interface (JNDI) solves this problem by bridging the gap between different directory services. With JNDI, you can write portable naming and directory service code, rather than writing nonportable code that works only with a particular directory service or standard. You can do this because JNDI abstracts your code from any particular directory service, enabling

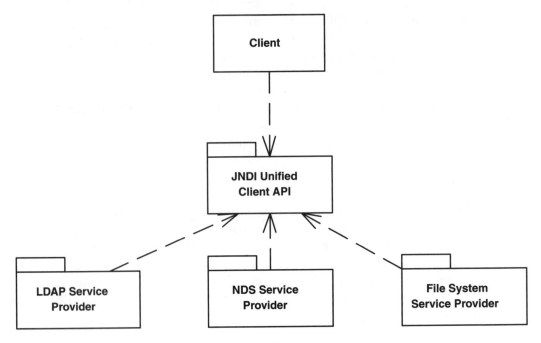

Figure 1.12 The Java Naming and Directory Interface.

you to simply plug in a different kind of directory service without changing your code. In the future, if new directory service standards emerge, JNDI will most probably be updated to reflect those changes.

EJB strictly depends on JNDI, so we've devoted a section to it, but we've left it as Appendix B because some of you may already be familiar with JNDI.

Java Database Connectivity (JDBC)

The Java Database Connectivity (JDBC) 2.0 package is a standard Java extension for data access that allows Java programmers to code to a unified relational database API. By using JDBC, Java programmers can represent database connections, issue SQL statements, process database results, and more in a relatively portable way. Clients program to the unified JDBC API, which is implemented by a *JDBC Driver*, an adapter that knows how to talk to a particular database in a proprietary way (see Figure 1.13). JDBC is similar to the Open Database Connectivity (ODBC) standard, and the two are quite interoperable through JDBC-ODBC bridges. JDBC 2.0 contains built-in support for database connection pooling, further enhancing the database independence of your application code.

Because EJB does not strictly depend on JDBC, we do not cover JDBC explicitly in this book. We do show how to use JDBC in the EJB world; see Chapter 8 for that information.

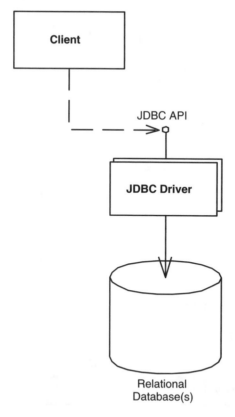

Figure 1.13 Java Database Connectivity.

Java Transaction API (JTA) and Java Transaction Service (JTS)

A *transaction* is a unit of work that makes a set of guarantees about its execution. For example, one guarantee that transactions give you is that any code executing within the scope of a transaction is guaranteed either to all be executed or to not execute at all. Transactions are one of the most useful constructs EJB brings to the table, and they are required to maintain a consistent system state. Transactions allow for multiple users to be modifying the same data, yet each to be isolated from one another—in essence, a very sophisticated form of synchronization.

To facilitate transactions, Sun Microsystems has produced two APIs: the *Java Transaction API* (*JTA*) and the *Java Transaction Service* (*JTS*). These two products embody how transactions can be performed in Java (see Figure 1.14).

JTA is a high-level transaction interface that your applications use to control transactions. You need to understand how the JTA works in order to perform transactions in Java.

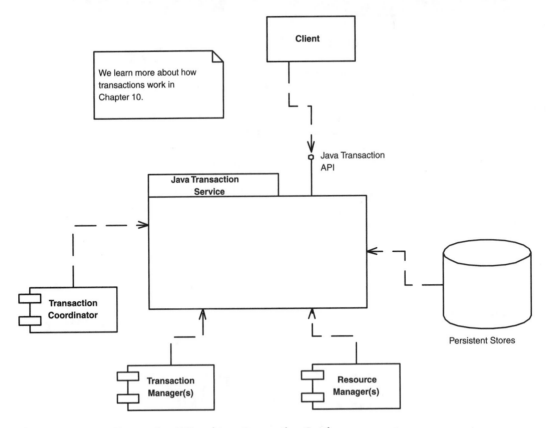

Figure 1.14 Java Transaction API and Java Transaction Service.

JTS is a set of low-level transaction interfaces that EJB uses behind the scenes (your client code doesn't directly interact with JTS). JTS makes it possible for multiple vendors to collaborate when performing transactions in a distributed, heterogeneous environment. JTS is based on the *Object Transaction Service* (*OTS*), which is part of CORBA.

Enterprise JavaBeans strictly depends on JTA, but it does not depend on JTS. As an application programmer, you may need to learn the JTA for performing advanced transaction control. We'll go into more detail about the JTA, as well as touch on the JTS, in Chapter 10.

Java Messaging Service (JMS)

A *messaging service* allows for distributed objects to communicate in an asynchronous, reliable manner. By passing messages asynchronously rather than synchronously, the overall system scalability is increased. Processes can respond to messages at their leisure, and they could potentially be offline when a message is initially sent.

You can perform asynchronous messaging by using an *Enterprise Messaging Product* (these are grouped together under the title *Message Oriented Middleware*, or *MOM*). These messaging systems are very proprietary. As with directory services, choosing a MOM vendor often entails binding yourself to a particular vendor.

Sun Microsystems has released an API called the *Java Messaging Service* (*JMS*) that can be used as a portable messaging service. By using a common API, distributed objects can communicate in a scalable, transactional, fault-tolerant, asynchronous, and, most important, vendor-independent manner. The JMS is illustrated in Figure 1.15.

Unfortunately, the EJB 1.1 specification does not define the integration points necessary to fully leverage JMS in EJB components, so we do not explicitly cover JMS in this book. The EJB 2.0 specification is expected to address this outstanding issue.

Java Servlets and Java Server Pages (JSPs)

Servlets are networked components that you can use to extend the functionality of a Web server. Servlets are request/response oriented in that they take

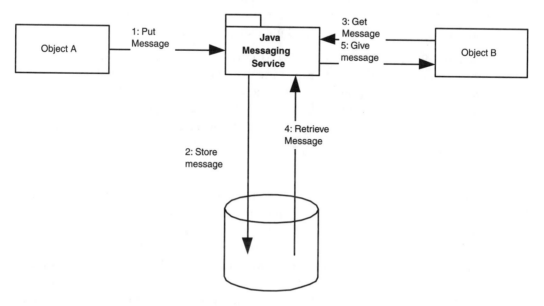

Figure 1.15 Java Messaging Service.

requests from some client host (such as a Web browser) and issue a response back to that host. This makes servlets ideal for performing Web tasks, such as rendering an HTML interface to an e-commerce catalog. Note, however, that servlets are not necessarily tied to Web servers, and they can be used as generic request/response-oriented components. Servlets differ from EJB components in that the breadth of server-side component features that EJB offers is not readily available to servlets. Servlets are much better suited to handling simple request/response needs, and they do not require sophisticated management by an application server.

Java Server Pages (JSPs) are very similar to servlets. In fact, JSP scripts are compiled into servlets. The largest difference between JSP scripts and servlets is that JSP scripts are not pure Java code, but they are much more centered around look-and-feel issues. You would use JSP when you want the look and feel of your deployment to be physically separate and easily maintainable from the rest of your deployment. JSPs are perfect for this, and they can be easily written and maintained by non-Java savvy staff members (JSPs do not require a Java compiler).

We illustrate connecting servlets with EJB components in Chapters 12 and 15.

Java IDL

As we've mentioned, CORBA is a massive middleware effort developed by the Object Management Group (OMG). The OMG represents hundreds of companies that have invested in this cross-platform architecture. CORBA is language independent; it doesn't matter what you code your programs in with CORBA, so long as CORBA supports the language in which you're developing.

Java IDL is an implementation of the CORBA specification in Java, and it allows for connectivity and interoperability with heterogeneous objects. Java IDL is one specific implementation of CORBA; there are many such implementations. And while Java IDL does not implement everything that is specified in CORBA, Java IDL ships free with the Java 2 platform. We cover Java IDL briefly in Chapter 11.

JavaMail

Sun's *JavaMail API* allows your applications to use e-mail capabilities. The JavaMail object model is quite simple to use, and it is easy to pick up if you've been programming with Java (it follows similar methodologies, such as exception handling and event handling). Like most of the other J2EE APIs (JNDI comes to mind), JavaMail defines a set of interfaces to which you write your application code, and those interfaces shield your code from the specific protocols or mail service implementations used. Your Internet mail code effectively becomes portable across platforms, as well as across mail protocols. JavaMail also ships

CORBA and EJB

EJB and CORBA share much functionality—many of the qualities of service that EJB offers are also in CORBA. In fact, you can think of EJB as CORBA plus standards for how your components should be written and managed, increasing productivity.

A massive amount of development effort has gone into CORBA. It would be a shame if Enterprise JavaBeans did not integrate with CORBA. Fortunately, Sun Microsystems and the OMG are both supporting EJB/CORBA interoperability, and they have produced standards that will allow that to happen.

The EJB/CORBA mapping specification, along with RMI-IIOP, lifts the restriction that EJB must be solely Java-based. You can expose EJB components as CORBA objects, which generalizes EJB and makes it well suited for cross-language interoperability. This is a very powerful idea, which we'll examine further in Chapter 11.

with a set of *convenience classes* to simplify application development, and it also ships with a few *service providers* that implement the most popular mail protocols. JavaMail depends on the *JavaBeans Activation Framework (JAF)* to encapsulate message data and to handle interactions with that data. This makes J2EE depend on JAF, meaning that a vendor that provides a J2EE product must provide JAF as well.

Connectors

J2EE is being enhanced to include integration with existing information systems via *connectors*. A connector is a vendor-specific bridge that links an existing system to the Java 2 Platform, Enterprise Edition. Using connectors, you can write cross-platform, cross-vendor J2EE code that leverages existing investments. These existing investments could be Enterprise Resource Planning (ERP) systems, message-oriented middleware (MOM) systems, mainframe systems such as IBM's CICS and IMS, BEA's Tuxedo, or existing legacy databases.

Connectors are useful because they will automatically manage the hairy details of middleware navigation to existing systems, such as handling transaction and security concerns. Sun's connector specification should also provide standard interfaces that vendors can write to, enabling you to plug any connector into any J2EE product, which means your legacy access code should be portable across application servers. Note that connectors are different from the other J2EE APIs because connectors are very vendor-specific (the API for an IBM CICS connector would most certainly be different from an SAP R/3 connector).

When Sun Microsystems completes the connector specification (most likely not until well into the year 2000), you should see a *connector marketplace* emerge, where *connector providers* such as IBM, BEA, SAP, Baan, Peoplesoft, or other companies provide J2EE connectors to specific existing systems. Until then, you have several choices for connecting to existing information systems, such as using a proprietary connector solution (SAP will likely ship one before J2EE connectors are finalized), using CORBA to integrate with existing systems, or growing an in-house solution.

The Extensible Markup Language (XML)

The Extensible Markup Language (XML) is a universal standard for structuring content in electronic documents. XML is extensible in that businesses can use XML to craft new structure to their documents as needed. The XML standard does not suffer the version control problems of other markup languages such as HTML because there are no predefined tags in XML—rather, you define your own tags for your business needs. This makes XML the ideal document format for transferring business data electronically, and it has a wide variety of other applications as well. We cover XML in Appendix C.

J2EE uses XML in several ways. Java Server Pages (JSPs) use XML as a data document format for authoring Web script. EJB 1.1 uses XML to describe components, which we cover in Appendix D. Sun may also mandate that J2EE products make APIs available for applications to parse and interpret XML documents as well.

Summary

By now, you should have a solid idea about the issues involved in server-side computing. You should also understand why a server-side component architecture is needed and why it provides the ability to rapidly develop applications without having to write complex middleware services. You've also seen why the J2EE was invented, what the J2EE value proposition is, and the technologies behind J2EE.

So far, we've taken a snapshot of the various APIs that J2EE encompasses. We're just getting started, so hang in there! There are many more interesting concepts to learn ahead.

## CHAPTER 2

Enterprise JavaBeans Overview

C hapter 1 introduced the motivation behind creating the EJB component architecture and the J2EE development platform for multi-tier deployments. In this chapter, we'll dive into EJB in detail, including the specific benefits EJB products offer to server-side components. This chapter will remain at a fairly high level, reserving the programming details of EJB for Part II.

As we alluded to in Chapter 1, Enterprise JavaBeans takes a *divide-and-conquer* approach to server-side computing. In fact, the EJB standard contracts allow for a collaboration of *six* different parties. Each of these parties is an expert in its own field and is responsible for a key part of a successful Enterprise JavaBeans deployment. Because each party is a specialist, the total time required to build an enterprise-class deployment is significantly reduced. This chapter begins with a discussion of the distinct role that each of these parties undertakes.

You'll then learn about the physical parts of an EJB deployment, including the following:

- What is an enterprise bean? You'll see the types of beans available, and you'll learn about the appropriate times to use them.

- What are the responsibilities of an EJB server and container? You'll learn about the specific middleware services the EJB server and container provide to EJB components.

This is a perfect chapter for people in a hurry who want to know some details about how EJB works. Whether you're a developer, an IT manager, or simply someone who's curious about EJB, this chapter is applicable. It provides a solid background on EJB, without getting into the programming details.

Because EJB is such a huge subject, you can expect to encounter many new concepts here. You may need to read this chapter twice to fully grasp the material. And, of course, everything we cover here will be explained in further detail as the book unfolds.

Who's Who in Enterprise JavaBeans

In the world of Enterprise JavaBeans, business solutions are developed in four stages:

1. Vendors of business logic, such as sales force automation vendors, enterprise resource planning vendors, financial services vendors, and e-commerce vendors, can modularize their products into reusable EJB components. Each component has a well-known but limited duty. These components adhere to the EJB specification, which means anyone with knowledge of EJB and Java 2 Enterprise Edition programming should be able to use the components.

2. The business components need to run in a distributed multi-tier fashion for a scalable, enterprise-class deployment. To achieve this, the components need a variety of tricky middleware, such as connection pooling, security, and life-cycle management. Rather than explicitly writing these middleware services over and over again, EJB enables middleware vendors to provide these system-level services in an application server. How do the components leverage these middleware services? In traditional server-side programming, you as a component developer would need to explicitly write to middleware APIs, such as persistence APIs, security APIs, or transaction APIs. In the EJB world, however, things are much easier. An application server provides middleware services for you in a *transparent* way, without your explicitly coding to middleware APIs. This is possible because the EJB specification lays out the rules governing middleware that both components and application servers must follow. For example, your components can get automatic persistence by setting *attributes* on your component that describe the component's need for persistence. The application server understands these attributes because the EJB specification defines them, and the application server complies with the specification. As a component developer, this means your life is simplified greatly because you can rapidly develop persistent components without coding to, debugging, or even understanding persistence APIs. Transparent middleware is a significant achievement because it allows developers to concentrate on application logic, rather than system-level middleware issues.

3. With application servers and reusable components for sale in a marketplace, a customer can purchase these and combine them to solve a business

problem in a server-side deployment. Purchased components, though, won't magically work together—especially if different vendors write the components. To address the customer's business needs, a third party (such as a systems integrator) combines these components into a workflow environment. The party makes recommendations for which components need to be purchased and hooks the components together, adding some custom code to the equation. During this process, coding efforts focus on integrating the business logic of the purchased components, rather than dealing with the overhead of the proprietary middleware that each component may use. Each of the components has adhered to the same EJB contracts and so can make use of the same underlying middleware.

4. The entire system is finally deployed, distributed among multiple machines across a network in a multi-tier environment. The system must be maintained and upgraded as it evolves over time.

As EJB matures, this scenario will become more and more of a reality. Assuming vendors stick to the EJB contracts, a world of true plug-and-play Enterprise features can be actualized. And even though it may not be entirely true today, the vision of portable EJB components deployable across heterogeneous application servers will solidify over the next few years.

The Six Parties

The foundations for EJB portability are the contracts and roles that each party must follow. Going with the divide-and-conquer theme, EJB partitions the responsibility of an EJB deployment to up to six different parties. Here is a brief overview of those parties:

The bean provider provides reusable business components that companies can purchase and use to help solve business problems. Beans are not complete applications, but rather are deployable components that can be assembled into complete solutions. An example of a bean provider that ships reusable components today is BEA, which provides the WebLogic Commerce Server 1.7.1 for building e-business applications. In the future, traditional enterprise software vendors (such as SAP and Trilogy) will offer their software as enterprise beans or will provide connectors to their current technology.

The container provider supplies the low-level runtime execution environment needed to run EJB applications.

The server provider supplies the application server logic to contain, manage, and deploy components. Currently there is no distinction between EJB container providers and EJB server providers. Examples of EJB container/server products are BEA's *WebLogic*, Sun Microsystems' *NetDynamics*, IBM's *WebSphere*, Oracle's *Oracle 8i*, Persistence Software's *PowerTier*, and Inprise's *Inprise Application Server*.

The application assembler is the overall application architect, perhaps for a specific deployment. He or she is responsible for understanding how various components fit together and writes the applications that use components. He or she may even author a few components along the way. An example of an application assembler is a systems integrator, a consulting firm, or an in-house programmer.

The deployer takes prewritten components, usually chosen by the application assembler, and applies his or her deployment expertise to install the components in one or more application servers.

The system administrator oversees the well-being of a deployed system.

These parties interact as shown in Figure 2.1.

You may be wondering why so many different participants are needed to provide an EJB deployment. The answer to this is that EJB enables companies or individuals to become experts in roles and that division of labor leads to best-of-breed deployments. For example, an EJB deployer does not need to be an expert at *developing* (designing and implementing) enterprise software but does need to be an expert at *deploying* an already developed EJB solution into a particular domain. This empowers EJB deployers to master deploying solutions, and it enables other parties (such as bean providers and application assemblers) to worry about developing solutions.

The EJB specification makes each role very clear and distinct, enabling experts in different areas to participate in a deployment without loss of interoperability. Note that there is also room for some of these roles to be combined as well. For example, the EJB server and EJB container may indeed come from the same vendor. For some of the parties, EJB merely suggests the possible duties that

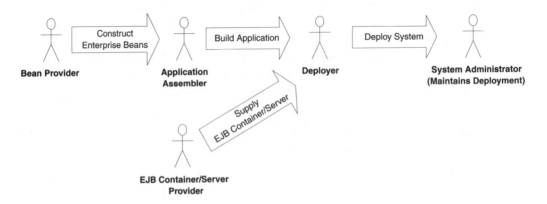

Figure 2.1 The six parties of EJB.

the party might assume, such as the system administrator overseeing the well-being of a deployed system. For other parties, such as the bean provider and container provider, EJB defines a set of strict interfaces and guidelines that must be followed or the entire model will break down. By clearly defining the roles of each party, EJB lays a foundation for a distributed, scalable component architecture where multiple vendors' products can interoperate.

We will now examine the responsibilities of each of the players in the Enterprise JavaBeans realm in more detail.

The Bean Provider

The bean provider is the party who supplies *enterprise beans*—components that expose methods for performing application logic. The bean provider might be a vendor of components that can be resold over and over again on the market—possibly through an indirect sales channel. The bean provider might be an in-house developer as well.

Enterprise beans are distributed, server-side components. They provide useful functionality that can be assembled to form larger applications. Enterprise beans *may* also be reusable components, but this is not guaranteed. Don't believe anyone who tells you that enterprise beans are reusable by definition because that is *false*. You need to design your beans correctly if you want them to be reusable. You need to consider the different applications, domains, and users of your enterprise beans, and you need to develop your beans with as much flexibility as possible. Developing a truly reusable set of beans will likely require many iterations of feedback from customers using your beans in real-world situations.

Roughly speaking, bean reusability can fall into three different levels:

Reuse as given. The application assembler uses the acquired bean as it is to build an application. The bean functionality cannot be tailored to fit the application. This is typically what bean providers are offering in the market.

Reuse by customization. The application assembler configures the acquired bean by modifying the bean properties to fit the specific needs of the application. Bean customization typically occurs during development time. To allow for a more flexible maintenance environment, some bean providers allow runtime bean customization.

Reuse by extension (subclass). The application assembler creates custom application-specific beans by subclassing the prebuilt acquired beans. The behavior of the resulting bean is tailored for the application. This level of reusability is generally more powerful but difficult to achieve. Reuse by extension is made available by only a few bean providers.

The more reusability levels that a bean provides, the more useful a bean is. By leveraging prebuilt beans, organizations can potentially lower the development time of building enterprise applications.

Enterprise beans can also range in size and scope. Smaller-grained enterprise beans typically have very concrete, but limited, scoped duties. Larger-grained, fuller-featured enterprise beans have a wider business scope, and they typically interact with other smaller-grained enterprise beans.

For example, imagine you go to a music store to purchase a compact disc. The cashier takes your credit card and runs it through a scanner. The scanner has a small Java Virtual Machine running within it, which acts as a client of enterprise beans. It contacts American Express, which has an EJB-compliant application server containing a number of beans. The beans are responsible for conducting the credit card transaction on behalf of that client.

Once the scanner has a reference to a credit card transaction bean, the bean must first verify that your credit is good before billing your card. At that point, the bean itself acts as a client and contacts another bean—a verifier bean—to verify your credit rating. Once your credit is verified, the original bean can complete the transaction. So beans can indeed be clients of other beans. This is a very powerful, flexible model, and it allows for large-grained components to be composed of smaller ones in a hierarchical fashion.

The EJB Server and EJB Container Providers

If you'll recall, an application server provides middleware services to your applications, such as transaction services, security services, and others. These services are needed for your application to be scalable, robust, and secure for multiple concurrent users. EJB takes the notion of application servers and partitions them into two distinct parts:

The EJB container. The EJB container provides a playground where your enterprise beans can run. There can be many beans running within a container. Bean containers are responsible for managing the beans running within them. They interact with the beans by calling a few required methods that the bean must expose. Containers may also provide access to a legacy system.

The EJB server. The EJB server provides a runtime environment for one or more containers. EJB servers manage low-level system resources, allocating resources to containers as they are needed. The relationship between the EJB server and container is depicted in Figure 2.2.

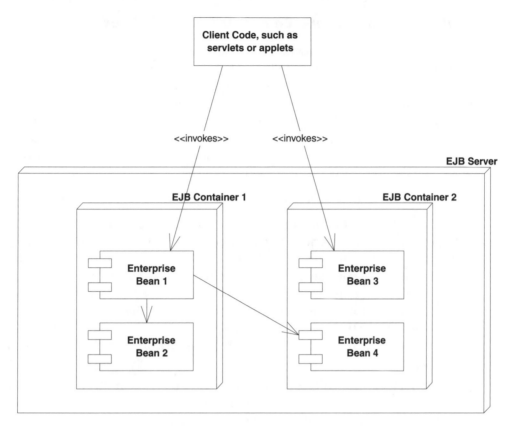

Figure 2.2   The relationship between EJB servers and EJB containers.

No Clear Separation Between Container and Server

Unfortunately, the EJB specification does not explicitly define the separation of roles between EJB servers and EJB containers yet. There is no concrete interface between the two entities. Until EJB addresses this issue, one vendor's EJB container will be not be installable within another vendor's EJB server. For now, you may be tied to one vendor for both the container and server.

   To deal with the lack of a good EJB server/container contract, EJB server vendors are publishing proprietary APIs for custom EJB containers to run within their servers, such as BEA's WebLogic EJB server.

Highlights of Server and Container Responsibilities

In traditional server-side programming (such as with CORBA), you needed to write to complex middleware APIs to gain an application server's middleware services. But in the EJB world, you can harness complex middleware in your enterprise applications without writing to middleware APIs—instead, you can simply *declare* the middleware services that your application needs, and the application server will provide that middleware *transparently* to your application code. You can focus away from the middleware and concentrate on your application's business code.

Here are just some of the services that containers/servers must provide for you.

Implicit distributed transaction management. Transactions allow for you to perform robust, deterministic operations in a distributed environment by setting attributes on your enterprise beans. We'll get into the details of transactions and how you can use them effectively in Chapter 10. For now, know that the EJB server provides a *transaction service*—a low-level implementation of transaction management and coordination. The transaction service must be exposed through the *Java Transaction API (JTA)*. The JTA is a high-level interface that you can use to control transactions, which we also cover in Chapter 10.

Implicit security. Security is a major consideration for multi-tier deployments. The Java 2 Platform, Standard Edition yields a robust security service that can authorize and authenticate users, securing deployments from unwanted visitors. EJB adds to this the notion of transparent security, allowing components to reap the benefits of a secure deployment without necessarily coding to a security API.

Implicit resource management and component life cycle. The EJB server implicitly manages resources for your components, such as threads, sockets, and database connections. The life cycle of the components themselves are also managed, allowing for components to be reused by the EJB server as necessary.

Implicit persistence. Persistence is a natural requirement of any deployment that requires permanent storage. EJB offers assistance here by automatically saving persistent object data to an underlying storage and retrieving that data at a later time.

Implicit remote accessibility. EJB products will automatically convert your stand-alone, network-less components into distributed, network-aware beings.

Implicit multiclient support. EJB servers automatically route concurrent requests from clients. EJB servers provide built-in thread support, instantiating multiple copies of your component as necessary and channeling client requests to those instances.

Implicit component location transparency. Clients of components are decoupled from the specific whereabouts of the component being used.

In addition to these implicit services, the EJB server provides a number of explicit services. For example, the EJB server must provide a *naming and directory service*, allowing components to be located across the network. The EJB server also ships with a set of *deployment tools* that allow the EJB deployer to deploy components into the EJB server and customize those components as needed.

Finally, EJB servers may go above-and-beyond the bare requirements, providing additional value-adds that are not required by the EJB specification. This could be intelligent load balancing, transparent fail-over, server clustering, and connectors for integration to legacy systems (such as BEA Tuxedo, IBM TXSeries, SAP R/3, and so on).

The Application Assembler

As we've mentioned, the bean provider supplies reusable, deployable server-side components. But when these components are purchased by a customer and put to actual use, who actually assembles them to solve a business problem? The answer is the *application assembler*.

The application assembler is the person, whether on staff or as an outside consultant, who understands the complete application system and understands how the various components fit together. He or she is the application architect—the person who understands what the components do. His or her job is to build an application from those components—an application that can be deployed in a number of settings.

The application assembler could perform any or all of the following tasks:

1. Write the code that calls on components purchased from vendors.
2. Provide a workflow solution between a number of disparate components, mapping between them.
3. Supply a user interface (perhaps using JFC, JSP, or servlets).
4. Write new enterprise beans to solve domain-specific problems. For example, you might need to model a business process or business entity that is specific to your business. This task will often fall into the hands of the application assembler.

Note that EJB allows for distributed components (versus the traditionally rigid client/server paradigm). Therefore, the application assembler could be involved in the design and implementation of logic residing in several tiers in a multi-tier architecture. Perhaps the code the application assembler writes is local to the components, perhaps it is remote. EJB does not dictate the physical placement of things.

The EJB Deployer

We've described how the container/server provider supplies the runtime management of the components and how the application assembler builds the specific applications. That is not enough, though, for a successful deployment. The applications must still be *deployed* in a running operational environment. And unfortunately, the application assembler (who is usually a developer or systems analyst) may not be familiar with the specific operational environment that the application must run in.

This is where the EJB deployer comes into play. EJB deployers are aware of specific operational environments. They understand how to deploy beans within servers and how to customize the beans for a specific environment (such as a multi-tier deployment involving a firewall). The EJB deployer has the freedom to adapt the beans, as well as the containers and servers, to the environment in which the beans are to be deployed. He or she also has knowledge of a customer's existing naming and directory services and understands how to customize enterprise beans for that scenario.

Another concrete role of the deployer is mapping security settings. Most businesses store lists of their employees and their security levels in some directory service structure, and the EJB deployer may be required to adapt the access level of the beans to fit that particular environment. That way, the multi-tier application developed by the application assembler is usable in the specific deployment scenario.

To facilitate this process, EJB deployers must be aware of the differences between the various beans, servers, and containers on the market. An EJB deployer can be a staff person or an outside consultant.

The System Administrator

Once the deployment goes live, the system administrator steps in to oversee the stability of the operational solution. The system administrator is responsible for the upkeep and monitoring of the deployed system and may make use of runtime monitoring and management tools that the EJB server and containers provide.

For example, a sophisticated deployment might page a system administrator if a serious error occurs that requires immediate attention. Note that EJB servers and containers may not provide this explicit monitoring (and it is not required by the EJB specification). Some EJB products, however, are developing hooks into professional monitoring products, such as Tivoli and Computer Associates, to aid with this. The Java 2 Platform, Enterprise Edition may in the future contain specification rules that govern management as well.

Now that you've seen the EJB players, let's move on to the business components themselves—the *enterprise beans*.

Enterprise Beans

An enterprise bean is a server-side software component that can be deployed in a distributed multi-tier environment. An enterprise bean can comprise one or more Java objects because a component may be more than just a simple object. Regardless of an enterprise bean's composition, the clients of the bean deal with a single exposed component interface. This interface, as well as the enterprise bean itself, must conform to the Enterprise JavaBeans specification. The specification requires that your beans expose a few required methods; these required methods allow the EJB container to manage beans uniformly, regardless of which container your bean is running in.

Note that the "client" of an enterprise bean could be anything—perhaps a servlet, an applet, or even another enterprise bean. In the latter case, a client request to a bean can result in a whole chain of beans being called. This is a very powerful idea because you can subdivide a complex bean task, allowing one bean to call on a variety of prewritten beans to handle the subtasks. This hierarchical concept is quite extensible.

Types of Beans

EJB 1.0 and 1.1 defines two different kinds of enterprise beans: *session beans* and *entity beans*. Let's take a look at how they compare.

Session Beans

A session bean represents work being performed for client code that is calling it. Session beans are business process objects. They implement business logic, business rules, and workflow. For example, a session bean could perform price quoting, order entry, video compression, banking transactions, stock trades, database operations, complex calculations, and more. They are reusable components that contain logic for business processes.

Session beans are called session beans because they live for about as long as the *session* (or lifetime) of the client code that's calling the session bean. For example, if client code contacted a session bean to perform order entry logic, the application server (that is, the EJB container/server) is responsible for creating an instance of that session bean component. When the client later disconnects, the application server may destroy the session bean instance.

Session beans are usable by one client at a time—that is, they are not shared between clients. When a client is using a session bean, that client is the only client dealing with that session bean. This is in stark contrast to entity beans, whose state is shared among many clients.

The EJB server is responsible for managing the lifetime of beans. That is, the client does *not* directly instantiate beans—the EJB container does this automatically. The EJB container similarly destroys session beans at the appropriate times. This allows beans to be pooled and reused for multiple clients.

There are two subtypes of session beans—*stateful session beans* and *stateless session beans*.

Stateful Session Beans

As we have said, session beans represent business processes. Some business processes can be performed in a single method request, such as computing the price of goods or verifying a credit card account. Other business processes are more drawn out and can last across multiple method requests and transactions.

One example of a business process that lasts for multiple method calls is an e-commerce Web store. As the user peruses an online e-commerce Web site, he or she can add products to the online shopping cart. This implies a business process that spans multiple method requests. The consequence of such a business process is that the components must track the user's state (such as a shopping cart state) from request to request.

Another example of a drawn-out business process is a banking application. In a bank, you may have code representing a bank teller that deals with a particular client for a long amount of time. That teller may perform a number of banking transactions on behalf of that client, such as checking the account balance, depositing funds, and making a withdrawal.

A *stateful session bean* is a bean that's designed to service business processes that span multiple method requests or transactions. To accomplish this, stateful session beans *retain state* on behalf of an individual client. If a stateful session bean's state is changed during a method invocation, that same state will be available to that same client upon the following invocation.

Stateless Session Beans

Some business processes naturally lend themselves to a single request paradigm. A single request business process is one that does not require state to be maintained across method invocations. Stateless session beans are components that can accommodate these types of single request business processes. They are anonymous method providers—anonymous because they are not aware of any client history.

For instance, a stateless session bean could be a high-performance engine that solves complex mathematical operations on a given input, such as compression of audio or video data. The client could pass in a buffer of uncompressed data, as well as a compression factor. The bean would return a compressed buffer and would then be available to service a different client. The business process has spanned one method request. The bean does not retain any state from previous requests.

Another example of a stateless session bean is a credit card verification component. The verifier bean would take a credit card number, an expiration date, a cardholder's name, and a dollar amount as input. The verified would then return a yes or no answer depending on whether the card holder's credit is valid.

EJB Design Strategies

Stateful or Stateless?

When deciding to use stateful session beans, you must first ask yourself whether the business process you're modeling inherently requires a stateful model. If it does, a stateful session bean may be the ideal component to use. When using stateful session beans, however, your inherent statefulness may limit your fault tolerance. For example, what happens if an unexpected system-level error occurs, such as a bean crashing, the network dying, or a machine rebooting? In a stateless model, the request could be transparently rerouted to a different component because any component can service the client's needs. In stateful models, there is little that can be done to reroute the client's request because the client's state is lost when the failure occurs (the state was kept within the lost bean). Note, however, that some high-end EJB container implementations are adding on stateful recovery services as an optional value feature. These services allow for even stateful components to be transparently recovered, by continually persisting the bean's active state and recovering from permanent storage in case of failure.

If you have a drawn-out business process, there is another alternative to using stateful session beans. You can go with a stateless model and pass the entire client state as parameters to the stateless bean during method invocations. Passing of state in such a way could lead to severe performance degradation. This is especially true if the client is remotely located from the bean and if the state passed over the network is large. Thus, you may achieve lightweight fault tolerance, but the overall scalability of your system may be compromised by the added network latency expense.

We'll explore the trade-offs between stateful and stateless models in more detail in Chapter 6.

Once the bean completes this task, it is available to service a different client and retains no past knowledge from the original client.

Entity Beans

Another fundamental part of a business is the permanent data that the business processes use. This is illustrated in the following examples:

- A bank teller component performs the business process of banking operations. But the data used by the teller is the bank account data.

- An order-entry component performs the business process of submitting new orders for products, such as submitting an order for a new computer to be delivered to a customer. But the data generated by the order-entry component is the order itself, which contains a number of order line-items describing each part ordered.

- A stock portfolio manager component performs the business process of updating a stock portfolio, such as buying and selling shares of stock. But the data manipulated by the portfolio manager is the portfolio itself, which might contain other data such as account and stock information.

In each of these scenarios, business process components are manipulating data in some underlying data storage, such as a relational database. An *entity bean* is a component that represents such persistent data. Entity beans model bank accounts, orders, order line items, stock portfolios, and so on. Entity beans represent real data objects, such as customers, products, or employees.

Entity beans do not contain business process logic—they model data. Session beans handle the business processes. Session beans might use entity beans to represent the data they use, similar to how a bank teller uses a bank account.

 An EJB 1.0 container/server is not required to support entity beans. An EJB 1.1 container/server is required to support them fully.

The value that entity beans provide is an object-oriented in-memory view of data in an underlying data store. The traditional way for applications to deal with data is to work with relational tables in a database, reading and writing that data as needed. Entity beans, on the other hand, are object representations of this underlying data. You can treat data in a relational store as real objects. You can read an entire set of data out of a database at once into an in-memory entity bean component. You can then manipulate this entity bean in memory by calling methods on it. For example, you could call a *withdraw()* method on a bank account entity bean, which would subtract money from a bank account by reducing the value of a private member variable called *balance*. Once that bank account entity bean object is persisted, the database will contain the new bank account balance. Thus, entity beans allow you to combine the functionality of persistent data with the convenience of object encapsulation. In essence, an entity bean implements the data access logic layer in multi-tier architectures. This is shown in Figure 2.3.

Because they model permanent data, entity beans are long lasting. They survive critical failures, such as application servers crashing, because entity beans are just representations of data in a permanent, fault-tolerant underlying storage. If a machine crashes, the entity bean can be reconstructed in memory again by simply reading the data back in from the permanent database. Because the database survives crashes, the components that represent them do as well. This is a huge difference between session and entity beans—entity beans have a life cycle much longer than a client's session, perhaps years long, depending on how long the data sits in the database.

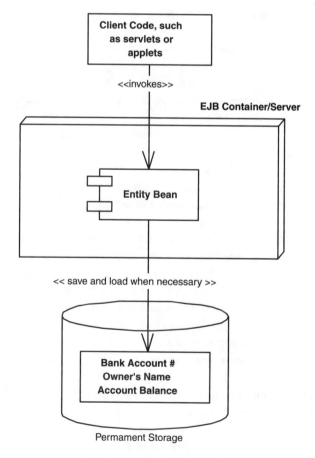

Figure 2.3 Entity beans are a view into an underlying data store.

Session Beans versus Entity Beans

Now that you've seen the different types of enterprise beans, how do you decide what logic to put in a session bean and what to put in an entity bean? The key differences between the two are that session beans represent business *processes* and typically contain business logic, and entity beans, on the other hand, embody permanent business *entities*, such as business data, and typically contain data-related logic.

As a concrete example of this, consider an application that is responsible for generating prices of products for customers. If a customer wants to order 15 workstations, with a certain bundle of memory and processors, the pricer would display a price detailing the products and listing the price of each item.

A pricer component is well represented by a session bean: The pricer is having a business process conversation with the client. The client code interacts with the pricer, asking for prices of products that the customer has indicated, and then the client code disconnects from the pricer component. After the conversation is over, the pricer is free to service another client.

Later, when the customer wants to place an order, an order entity bean could represent the customer's permanent request for goods to be delivered. The order bean would represent database data that detailed the customer's purchase. The order can then be fulfilled by another application—perhaps another session bean that contains the logic to do so. This is shown in Figure 2.4.

Notice the theme here: Session beans are performing application logic, which uses persistent entity beans behind the scenes as the data that they're manipulating. This is very similar to the *façade* design pattern. A façade is a high-level interface that masks lower-level subsystems. In the EJB distributed object architecture, session beans can be used to provide a high-level interface façade to business processes, masking the lower-level entity bean subsystems used behind the scenes.

Because entity beans model permanent business entities, entity beans typically achieve a higher level of reuse than session beans. For instance, consider our banking example, with a session bean that acts as a bank teller. This session bean knows how to withdraw and deposit by calling methods on a bank account entity bean. One day, you may decide to replace your session bean teller with a different teller bean. But you'd still want all your customers' bank accounts to remain the same.

Now consider our order-entry example. Here, your company's product line, as well as the purchase orders themselves, are data. Therefore, they are well represented as entity beans—objects that are saved over time and are forever part of the database. The components that generate and manipulate the products and the purchase orders are very well modeled as session beans. You'd probably want to fine-tune and change these session beans over time, as user requirements change.

Thus, in practice you can expect the reuse of session beans to be a bit lower than that of entity beans. Session beans model a current business process, which can be tweaked and tuned with different algorithms and approaches. Entity beans, on the other hand, define your core business. Data such as purchase orders, customers, and bank accounts do not change very much over time, and in practice entity beans achieve a higher level of reuse.

Note that what we've presented here are merely guidelines, not hard-and-fast rules. Indeed, a session bean can contain data-related logic as well, such as a session bean performing a bulk database read via JDBC or SQL/J. The key to remember is that session beans never *embody* permanent data, but merely provide access to data. Session beans are not persistable; they represent business processes. By comparison, entity beans embody data and are persistable. If you have a business process that you'd like to run in a transactional, distributed, and secure environment, you can use session beans to model that business process. If you have a permanent business entity, you can access that entity as a distributed component by representing it as an entity bean.

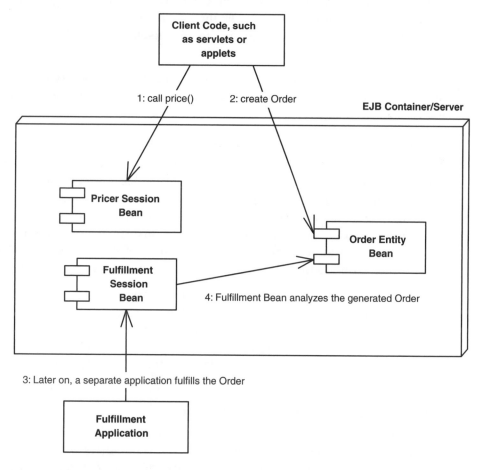

Figure 2.4   Combinations of beans in a pricing application.

Entity beans are distinct from session beans in another respect as well—multiple clients can use entity beans simultaneously. Think of this as multiple clients manipulating the same data in a database simultaneously. You can isolate these clients from one another by using *transactions*. When used properly, transactions guarantee that multiple clients who perform persistent operations act completely independently of one another. We'll find out more about transactions in Chapter 10.

Entity beans are very useful when you have a legacy database with data already inside. They are great for providing access to existing persistent data. In this manner, the data that entity beans model could exist in a database before a company decided to employ Enterprise JavaBeans.

In fact, the database records representing an object could have existed before the company even decided to go with a Java-based solution because a database structure can be language-independent. Database records can be read in and interpreted as objects in almost any language. EJB takes advantage of this and allows for the transformation of a database's data into a Java object. The burden of this transformation can fall on the bean itself or the EJB container can perform the transformation automatically.

This brings us to the next topic. There are two subtypes of entity beans available: *bean-managed persistent* entity beans and *container-managed persistent* entity beans.

Bean-Managed Persistent Entity Beans

As we have seen, entity beans are persistent components because their state is saved to a secondary storage such as a relational database. For example, by using *object-relational mapping* technology, you can take an in-memory *object* and *map* that object into a persistent series of *relational* database records. You can then retrieve those records at a later time to reconstruct the object in-memory and use it again. Another scheme is to use an *object database* as your persistent store, which stores actual objects rather than relational records.

A bean-managed persistent entity bean is an entity bean that must be persisted by hand. In other words, you as the component developer must write code to translate your in-memory fields into an underlying data store, such as a relational database or an object database. You handle the persistent operations yourself—including saving, loading, and finding data—within the entity bean. Therefore, you must write to a persistence API, such as JDBC or SQL/J.

Container-Managed Persistent Entity Beans

The good news is that EJB allows entity bean developers to not worry about coding persistence logic. One service that EJB 1.0 containers *may* provide, and EJB 1.1 containers *must* provide, is automatic persistence for your entity beans.

The container/server performs every function of your component's data access layer for you, including saving, loading, and finding component data. You do not have to hard-code to a relational database API or an object database API, saving much coding time. Rather, you simply describe what you want persisted upfront to the container, and it persists it for you, using whatever storage it happens to have. This gives you theoretical database independence, allowing you to switch one data store for another, since you don't write any code to a database API. The EJB container/servers on the market today perform a wide variety of mapping functionality and tools—some simple, some complex. For example, BEA's *WebLogic* server performs fairly simple object/relational mapping. But BEA also supports the Object People's *TOPLink*, an enhanced persistence module that allows for complex mapping.

When choosing between container-managed persistence and bean-managed persistence, many issues are at stake. We'll contrast the promises and realities of automatic persistence fully in Part II.

Motivation for Multiple Bean Types

You may be wondering why the EJB paradigm is so robust in offering the various kinds of beans. Why couldn't Sun come up with a simpler model? Microsoft's N-tier vision, for example, does not include the equivalent of entity beans—components that represent data in a permanent storage.

The answer is that Sun is not the only company involved in constructing the Enterprise JavaBeans standard. In fact, many companies have been involved, each with customers that have different kinds of distributed systems. To accommodate the needs of different enterprise applications, Sun decided to allow users the flexibility of each kind of bean.

Admittedly, this increases the ramp-up time to learn EJB. But it also pays off in the long run with increased functionality. By including session beans, Sun has provided a mechanism to model business processes without writing middleware in a distributed multi-tier environment. By including entity beans in the EJB specification, Sun has taken the first steps toward persistent, distributed objects usable by those business processes.

Overview of EJB Container and EJB Server Responsibilities

Earlier in this chapter, we mentioned that EJB containers provide the implicit services to your EJB components and that containers live within the runtime environment of an EJB server. Because the EJB specification has not drawn the

Single-Threaded versus Multithreaded Session Beans

One great benefit of EJB is you don't need to write thread-safe code. You design your enterprise beans as single-threaded components, and you never need to worry about thread synchronization when concurrent clients access your component. Your EJB container will automatically instantiate multiple instances of your component to service concurrent client requests.

The container's thread services can be both a benefit and a restriction. The benefit is that you don't need to worry about race conditions or deadlock in your application code. The restriction is that some problems lend themselves very well to multithreaded programming, and that class of problems cannot be easily solved in an EJB environment.

So why doesn't the EJB specification allow for multithreaded beans? The answer is that EJB is intended to relieve component developers from worrying about threads or thread synchronization. The EJB container handles those issues for you by load-balancing client requests to multiple instances of a single-threaded component. An EJB server provides a highly scalable environment for single-threaded components, and adding the abillity for beans to control threads opens up a Pandora's box of problems. For example, the ability for an EJB container to control a transaction (discussed in Chapter 10) becomes a *very* complicated problem if threads are being started and stopped randomly by beans.

One alternative to threading is to use a transactional messaging API such as the Java Messaging Service (JMS) that allows for asynchronous actions to occur in a distributed object environment. JMS enables you to safely and reliably achieve multitasking, without the beans themselves messing around with threads. JMS support is expected to be in the 2.0 EJB specification, due out in late 2000.

The bottom line here is that EJB was not meant be a swiss-army knife, solving every problem in existence. It was designed to assist with server-side *business problems*, which are largely single-threaded. For applications that absolutely must be multithreaded, EJB may not be the correct choice of distributed object architectures.

line between a container and a server, we will use the words interchangeably in this book.

EJB containers are responsible for managing your beans. Containers can interact with your beans by calling your beans' required management methods as necessary. These management methods are your bean's callback methods that the container, and only the container, invokes. The management methods allow the container to alert your bean when middleware events take place, such as when an entity bean is about to be persisted to storage.

The most important responsibility of an EJB container is to provide an environment in which enterprise beans can run. EJB containers house the enterprise beans and make them available for clients to invoke remotely. In essence, EJB containers act as invisible middlemen between the client and the beans. They are responsible for connecting clients to beans, performing transaction coordination, providing persistence, managing a bean's life cycle, and other tasks. The EJB container-bean relationship is depicted in Figure 2.5.

The key to understanding EJB containers is to realize that they are *abstract entities*. Neither the beans nor the clients that call beans ever explicitly code to the API of an EJB container. Rather, the container implicitly manages the overhead of a distributed component architecture. The container is analogous to a 'behind the scenes' stage manager in a theatre, providing the lighting and backdrop necessary for a successful stage performance by the actors on stage. But neither the actors nor the audience directly interact with the stage manager. The same is true for EJB containers. Neither the beans nor the clients that call the beans ever code directly to an EJB container API.

EJB containers are a huge challenge to write because they are so complex and perform so many tasks. As of the time of this writing, there are 27 EJB containers in development, varying widely in implementation. For example, BEA makes

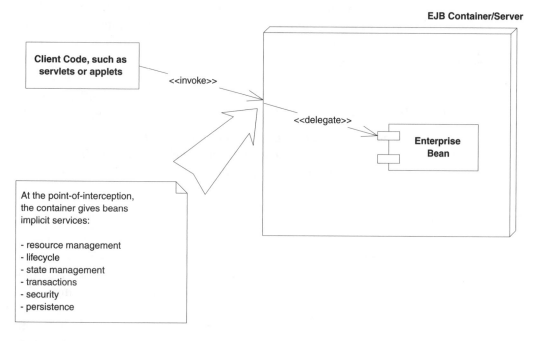

Figure 2.5 An EJB container housing a bean.

an EJB container that is written entirely in Java, managing your Java-based enterprise beans. Sybase, on the other hand, makes an EJB container written in C++, which interacts with beans via the Java Native Interface. Oracle provides a container that physically runs within the context of a database. As you can see, a container can be manifested in a number of functional environments.

We now present an architectural overview of the features an EJB container provides.

Resource Management and Bean Life Cycle Management

As we've mentioned in Chapter 1, a multi-tier architecture's overall scalability is enhanced when an application server intelligently manages needed resources across a variety of deployed components. The resources could be threads, socket connections, database connections, and more. For example, database connections could be pooled by application servers and reused across heterogeneous components. In the EJB realm, the container is responsible for providing all resource management services behind the scenes.

In addition to resource management, the EJB container is responsible for controlling the life cycle of the deployed enterprise bean components. As bean client requests arrive, the EJB container dynamically instantiates, destroys, and reuses beans as appropriate. For example, if a client requests a certain type of bean that does not exist in memory yet, the EJB container may instantiate a new in-memory instance on behalf of the client. On the other hand, if a bean already exists in memory, it may not be appropriate to instantiate a new bean—especially if the system is low on memory. Instead, it might make more sense to re-assign a bean from one client to another. It might also make sense to destroy some beans that are not being used anymore. This is called *instance pooling*.

The take-away point here is that the EJB container is responsible for coordinating the entire effort of resource management as well as managing the deployed beans' life cycle. Note that the exact scheme used is EJB container-specific.

State Management

State management is another value that containers bring to the table. To explain the need for state management, we first must observe that users, as well as client code, often take a lot of time to "think" in between method calls to a component. The classic example of this is an HTML (Web) client interacting with a human being. Web users often will click on a button that executes some business logic in a component, but then they wait around and read text before initiating another action. While the user is doing this, the application server could reuse that component to service other clients.

This is exactly what happens in EJB. If a bean is stateless, it can be reassigned to other clients dynamically by the EJB container. This is possible because there is no state lost from the primary client. This reuse of beans results in incredible resource gains—often only a few beans need to be instantiated to handle a multitude of clients. If a client times out (for example, because of a crash), the EJB container can destroy the bean or perhaps reuse it. This is all possible because the EJB container is constantly monitoring bean invocation activity.

On the other hand, if the bean is stateful, things get a little more complicated. The EJB container must provide transparent *state management* for stateful components. State management is necessary when you want to reuse a stateful component to service multiple clients.

Consider the scenario where a client hasn't used a stateful bean for a long time. This stateful bean could be a stateful session bean or an entity bean (entity beans are inherently stateful because they represent data). When a new client connects and requests a component, the container may have reached its limit of instantiated components. In this case, the container can take a component that hasn't been used in a while, then *serialize* (convert to a binary stream—see Appendix A) the bean's conversational state, and write the state out to disk. Now that the original client's state has been preserved, the bean can be reassigned to a different client, and it can retain state for that new client exclusively. Later on, if the original client makes a request, the original client's bean state can be read back in from disk and used again, perhaps in a different in-memory bean object.

The management of state is a responsibility of the EJB container, and it is mostly masked from component vendors. It is an implicit service provided by the EJB architecture.

Transactions

Transactions are a safe way to have multiple components participate in distributed object operations. A *transaction* is a series of operations that appear to execute as one large, atomic operation. Transactions allow multiple users to share the same data, and they guarantee that any set of data they update will be completely and wholly written, with no interleaving of updates from other clients. In a sense, transactions are a very sophisticated form of concurrency control.

When properly used, transactions ensure that database data is kept consistent. Transactions also ensure that two components' database operations are isolated from one another. Transactions prevent disaster from striking if your database crashes, too. Without transactions, your database could easily become corrupt, which is unacceptable for such mission-critical applications as banking applications.

The EJB server/container handles the underlying transaction operations, coordinating efforts behind the scenes between transaction participants. The value-add of EJB here is that transactions can be performed implicitly and automatically. This allows beans to leverage transactions in deployments without writing to an explicit transaction API. We cover transactions more thoroughly in Chapter 10.

Security

In any critical deployment, security is always going to be an issue. The role of EJB containers in security is to handle the validation of users for tasks they wish to accomplish. This is done via *Access Control Lists* (*ACLs*). An ACL is a list of users and their rights. If the user has the correct rights, he or she can perform the desired operation. The Java Development Kit 1.2 provides a robust security model that allows for authentication (identifying that the user is who he or she claims to be) and authorization (identifying that the user is of the correct role to perform the desired operation).

EJB containers add transparent security to this. Rather than programmatically accessing a security API, enterprise beans can automatically run as a certain security identity. Alternatively, enterprise beans can programmatically ensure that clients are authorized to perform desired operations.

Persistence

As we've mentioned earlier in the chapter, entity beans are persistent objects that represent data in an underlying storage. EJB containers can provide the transparent persistence of container-managed persistent entity beans. Note that while the EJB 1.0 specification does not require that containers manage persistence for beans, it is required in the 1.1 specification. We'll see more about how EJB persistence works in Part II.

Remote Accessibility and Location Transparency

Remote accessibility is the conversion of a network-naive component into a fully networked component that can be invoked remotely. Enterprise JavaBeans insulates the bean provider from all networking issues. Beans are written as stand-alone, nonnetworked components. But once they are deployed in the EJB realm, they become distributed components, deployable across multiple tiers.

EJB containers use the Java Remote Method Invocation (RMI) interfaces to specify remote accessibility, which you can learn about by reading Appendix A. The benefit of distributed communication technologies such as RMI is that your client code is unaware of the physical location of the component it is calling. The component could be located across the world, on a local area network right next door to you, or on the client's machine itself. It could even reside in the client code's address space (such as an application server that supports Java servlets and enterprise beans in a single JVM). Whatever is the case, the client should be totally unaware of where the component really is—whether the component is local or remote should be *transparent* to the client. This is known as *location transparency*.

Why is location transparency beneficial? Well, for one thing, you aren't writing your bean's client code to take advantage of a particular deployment configuration because you're not hard-coding machine locations. This is an essential part of reusable components that can be deployed in a wide variety of multitier situations.

Location transparency also enables container vendors to provide additional value-adds, such as the ability to take a machine on the network down temporarily to perform system maintenance, to install new software, or to upgrade the components on that machine. During maintenance, location transparency allows for another machine on the network to serve up components for a component's client because that client is not dependent on the hard locations of any components. If a machine that has components on it crashes due to hardware or software error, you may be able to reroute client invocations to other machines without the client even knowing about the crash, allowing for an enhanced level of fault-tolerance.

Glue-Code and Bean Installation Tools

Each EJB container ships with a suite of *glue-code tools*. These tools are meant to integrate beans into the EJB container's environment. The tools generate helper Java code, such as stubs, skeletons, data access classes, and other classes that this specific container requires. Bean providers do not have to think about the specifics of how each EJB container works because the container's tools generate its own proprietary Java code automatically.

The container's glue-code tools are responsible for transforming an enterprise bean into a fully managed, distributed server-side component. This involves logic to handle resource management, life cycle, state management, transactions, security, persistence, and remote accessibility—every service we've mentioned so far. The automatic code generated handles these services in the container's proprietary way.

Specialized Container Features

Beyond the normal duties of a container, *specialized containers* can provide additional qualities of service that are not required by the EJB 1.0 specification. Most vendors have several different versions of their containers for sale, allowing customers to pay for what they get. These services help differentiate EJB container vendors, allow for innovation, and foster best-of-breed products. They also add an element of danger. If a bean depends on particular qualities of service, it may not run in other containers.

For example, let's take the case of a load-balancing service. Load-balancing is the fair selection of components on behalf of their clients. These components may reside in many containers, housed in multiple EJB servers, distributed across the network. Given the fact that N-tier deployments can vary widely in the actual physical locations of components, the actual load-balancing algorithm is implementation dependent. This allows a lot of creativity for the EJB container provider. For example, some containers may provide a way to perform customized load balancing between distributed components. The customized load-balancer might be tunable for particular deployments and might make the overall system more scalable.

A high-end EJB container may also provide dynamic resizing of managed resources and components. For example, if clients are less active at night than during the day, perhaps a smaller pool of resources is necessary at night. Some EJB containers may be intelligent enough to allow for this dynamic resizing of pools, yielding precious machine resources to be used for other purposes.

Other examples of specialized container functions could include the following:

- Integration to mainframe systems
- COM+ integration
- Transparent fail-over
- Stateful recovery
- Web server, servlet, and JSP support within the container
- Server clustering
- Dynamic redeployment of components in a running system
- Support for a variety of persistence mechanisms, including relational and object databases
- Shared object caches to improve the number of times a database needs to be accessed
- Sophisticated monitoring support
- Distributed transactions
- Resolution of the transactional distributed diamond problem
- Complex database persistence services
- Visual development environment integration

- Integrated XML facilities
- CORBA integration and support

These are merely examples of the variety of services that a vendor could choose to add. The key idea to keep in mind when choosing to use services such as these is whether the services lock you into a particular vendor. If so, you need to ask yourself if that's a safe bet and if you want your components to be deployable across a variety of middleware vendor products.

Summary

In this chapter, we've taken a whirlwind tour of Enterprise JavaBeans. We started by looking at how EJB promotes a divide-and-conquer approach to server-side computing by defining the roles of six parties in a successful EJB deployment. We then went into what an enterprise bean is, and we looked at the different kinds of beans, including session and entity beans, and their subtypes. We analyzed the trade-offs of when it was appropriate to use each kind of bean.

Finally, we took a look at the responsibilities of the EJB container and server. We examined the services containers provide to distributed server-side components, such as resource management, state management, and location transparency.

And congratulations—you've made it to the end of Part I! In these two chapters, you've taken the first steps necessary to understanding and mastering Enterprise JavaBeans. Now that you understand the high-level concepts, let's move on and begin programming with EJB.

Developing Beans

For a successful server-side deployment, typically six major steps must be undertaken. Each of these steps can be a collaboration between several individuals, perhaps from different companies.

1. **Get the application requirements down.** Before embarking full-steam on writing a multi-tier distributed application, you should always spend a significant amount of time in a design phase. You should learn who will use your application, what its purpose is, and what the application requirements are. Are you or your customers running on Microsoft's platform, UNIX, or mainframe systems? Do you need to integrate with existing application servers that are already deployed and running? Is there legacy middleware, such as CICS or Tuxedo that you need to support? Which application vendors do you need to support, such as SAP or Peoplesoft? How compatible are their products with server-side development platforms such as Windows DNA or J2EE? All of this information is necessary before you can finally make a decision on a server-side development platform.

2. **Decide on a distributed object architecture, and design your application.** Once you've settled on your application requirements, you should choose the server-side development platform that best fits your needs. Once you've done this, you can begin designing your application. This includes breaking up your application into components, designing your object model, specifying the interfaces between your major subsystems, and whiteboarding your application's interactions. *The Unified Modeling Language (UML)* is an excellent language for this type of object modeling (the diagrams in this book are written mostly in UML). You should also look at what other vendors are building reusable components in your vertical market, as it may save you development time to buy rather than build.

69

3. **Develop or purchase reusable components.** Assuming you choose the J2EE platform, you can then decide on developing your own beans or purchasing them. If you choose to build your own components, you can either develop them from scratch or wrap existing legacy systems. You can also buy prewritten enterprise beans supplied by third parties.

4. **Assemble the application.** Once you've developed a core set of components, you can start putting them to use in specific applications. This stage involves writing client code that calls your components, making them useful for a specific business or workflow. Your client code can be inside a Java applet, servlets running within a Web server, or elsewhere. They can be Java-based clients or CORBA-based clients. When you assemble your application, you can also develop custom components that your specific application needs.

5. **Deploy the beans.** Now that a specific application has been developed, you can physically deploy your beans inside of an EJB container/server. At this stage, you should be customizing your components for this specific deployment, such as mapping security roles to existing users in an LDAP server.

6. **Oversee the deployment.** Once the deployment has gone live, a system administrator should be appointed to oversee the stability of the deployed system.

In Part II, we'll focus on the development details for implementing an EJB application. We'll see how to write both major types of enterprise beans: *session beans* and *entity beans*. Session beans represent a business process, such as computing the price of an order, transferring funds from one bank account to another, performing statistical analysis, and so on. Entity beans are persistent business objects, and they are an object-oriented view into an underlying data store.

We'll also see how to assemble applications using enterprise beans. You'll learn about how to write client code that calls into enterprise beans to solve a business problem. This entails understanding the contract that clients must abide by to use EJB.

Part II is great for those of you who are ready to get down-and-dirty with EJB programming fundamentals. The more advanced topics, such as transactions and CORBA, are reserved for future chapters.

## CHAPTER 3

Introduction to Session Beans

I n this chapter, we'll take our first look at enterprise bean development concepts. This chapter covers the following topics:

1. What an enterprise bean component is composed of, including the enterprise bean class, the remote interface, the EJB object, the home interface, the home object, the deployment descriptor, the manifest, and the Ejb-jar file.

2. The characteristics of session beans. We'll see what makes session beans unique, and we'll introduce the differences between stateful and stateless session beans.

3. The rules for writing session bean classes.

4. How to write client code to call session beans.

This chapter lays the necessary conceptual framework for you to begin EJB programming. We'll see complete code examples in Chapters 4, 5, and 6.

 EJB depends on several other technologies in the Java 2 Platform, Enterprise Edition suite. If you're having difficulty understanding this chapter, you may find it helpful to read several of the appendices first—in particular, Appendix A (covering Java Remote Method Invocation) and Appendix B (covering the Java Naming and Directory Interface).

What Constitutes an Enterprise Bean?

Enterprise beans are distributed, deployable server-side components that can be assembled into larger applications. Enterprise beans can be partitioned across multiple tiers, can be transactional, can be multiuser secure, and can be deployed in any EJB-compatible container/server product.

Enterprise beans currently have two flavors: session beans and entity beans. Session beans represent a business process, whereas entity beans represent permanent business data. Sun Microsystems may introduce other bean types in the future as well.

This section examines exactly what constitutes an enterprise bean. As we will see, an enterprise bean component is not a single monolothic file—a number of files work together to make up an enterprise bean.

The Enterprise Bean Class

In Part I, we learned that the Enterprise JavaBeans specification defines the *contracts* between the different parties involved in a deployment. In order for a bean to work in any container, and to work with any client of that bean, the bean must adhere to a well-defined interface. In EJB, you provide your enterprise bean component implementation in an *enterprise bean class*. This is simply a Java class that conforms to a well-defined interface and obeys certain rules.

An enterprise bean class contains implementation details of your component. And although there are no hard-and-fast rules in EJB, a session bean implementation will be very different from an entity bean implementation. For session beans, an enterprise bean class typically contains business-process-related logic, such as logic to compute prices, transfer funds between bank accounts, or perform order entry. For entity beans, an enterprise bean class typically contains data-related logic, such as logic to change the name of a customer, reduce the balance of a bank account, or modify a purchase order.

The EJB specification defines a few standard interfaces that your bean class can implement. These interfaces force your bean class to expose certain methods that all beans must provide, as defined by the EJB component model. The container calls these required methods to manage your bean and alert your bean to significant events.

The most basic interface that *all* bean classes must implement (both session and entity) is the *javax.ejb.EnterpriseBean* interface, shown in Source 3.1.

```
public interface javax.ejb.EnterpriseBean extends java.io.Serializable
{
}
```

Source 3.1   The javax.ejb.EnterpriseBean interface.

This interface serves as a *marker* interface; implementing this interface indicates that your class is indeed an enterprise bean class. The interesting aspect of *javax.ejb.EnterpriseBean* is that it extends *java.io.Serializable*. This means that all enterprise beans can be converted to a bit-blob and share all the properties of serializable objects (described in Appendix A). This will become important later, so keep it in mind.

Both session beans and entity beans have more specific interfaces that *extend* the *javax.ejb.EnterpriseBean* interface. All session beans must implement *javax.ejb.SessionBean*, while all entity beans must implement *javax.ejb.EntityBean*. We'll see the details of these interfaces a bit later. For now, know that your enterprise bean class never needs to implement the *javax.ejb.EnterpriseBean* interface directly—rather, your bean class implements the interface corresponding to its bean type.

The EJB Object

When a client wants to use an instance of an enterprise bean class, the client never invokes the method directly on an actual bean instance. Rather, the invocation is *intercepted* by the EJB container and then *delegated* to the bean instance. This happens for many reasons:

- Your enterprise bean class can't be called across the network directly because an enterprise bean class is not network-enabled. Your EJB container handles networking for you by wrapping your bean in a network-enabled object. The network-enabled object receives calls from clients and delegates these calls to instances of your bean class. This saves you from having to worry about networking issues (the container provides networking as a free service to you).

- By intercepting requests, the EJB container can automatically perform some necessary management. This includes transaction logic, security logic, bean instance pooling logic, and any other logic that the container may require.

- The EJB container can track which methods are invoked, display a real-time usage graph on a system administrator's user interface, gather data for intelligent load balancing, and more. There is no requirement that an EJB container perform these tasks. But because the EJB container intercepts all method calls, there is an opportunity for containers to perform them.

Thus, the EJB container is acting as a layer of indirection between the client code and the bean. This layer of indirection manifests itself as a single network-aware object, called the *EJB object*. The EJB object is a surrogate object that knows about networking, transactions, security, and more. It is an intelligent object that knows how to perform intermediate logic that the EJB container requires before a method call is serviced by a bean class instance. An EJB object acts as glue between the client and the bean, and it exposes every business method that the bean itself exposes. EJB objects delegate all client requests to beans. We depict EJB objects in Figure 3.1.

You should think of EJB objects as physical parts of the container; all EJB objects have container-specific code inside of them (each container handles middleware differently and provides different qualities of service). Because each bean's EJB object is different, your container vendor supplies glue-code tools that *generate* the class file for your EJB objects automatically.

The Remote Interface

As we mentioned previously, bean clients invoke methods on EJB objects, rather than the beans themselves. To perform this, EJB objects must clone every business method that your bean classes expose. But how do the tools that auto-generate EJB objects know which methods to clone? The answer is in a special interface that a bean provider writes. This interface duplicates all the business logic methods that the corresponding bean class exposes. This interface is called the *remote interface.*

Remote interfaces must comply with special rules that the EJB specification defines. For example, all remote interfaces must derive from a common interface that is supplied by Sun Microsystems. This interface is called *javax.ejb.EJBObject,* and it is shown in Source 3.2.

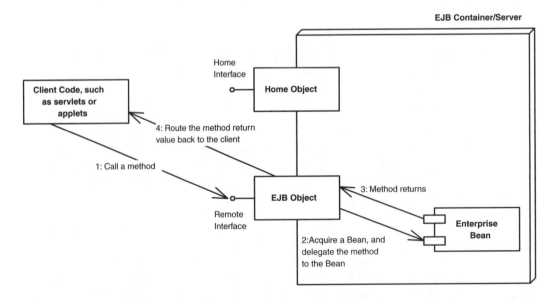

Figure 3.1 EJB objects.

```
public interface javax.ejb.EJBObject
extends java.rmi.Remote
{
    public abstract javax.ejb.EJBHome getEJBHome()
        throws java.rmi.RemoteException;

    public abstract java.lang.Object getPrimaryKey()
        throws java.rmi.RemoteException;

    public abstract void remove()
        throws java.rmi.RemoteException,
        javax.ejb.RemoveException;

    public abstract javax.ejb.Handle getHandle()
        throws java.rmi.RemoteException;

    public abstract boolean isIdentical(javax.ejb.EJBObject)
        throws java.rmi.RemoteException;
}
```

Source 3.2   The javax.ejb.EJBObject interface.

javax.ejb.EJBObject lists a number of interesting methods. Their explanations are previewed in Table 3.1. For now, don't worry about fully understanding the meanings—just know that these methods are required methods that all EJB objects must implement. And remember that *you* don't implement the methods—the EJB container does when it auto-generates the EJB objects for you.

Table 3.1   Required Methods That All EJB Objects Must Expose

METHOD	EXPLANATION
getEJBHome()	Retrieves a reference to the corresponding *home object* (we describe home objects later).
getPrimaryKey()	Returns the primary key for this EJB object. A primary key is used only for entity beans (see Chapters 7-9).
remove()	Destroys this EJB object. When your client code is done using an EJB object, you should call this method. The system resources for the EJB object can then be reclaimed. *Note: For entity beans, remove() also deletes the bean from the underlying persistent store.*
getHandle()	Acquires a *handle* for this EJB object. An EJB handle is a persistent reference to an EJB object that the client can stow away somewhere. Later on, the client can use the handle to reacquire the EJB object and start using it again.
IsIdentical()	Tests whether two EJB objects are identical.

The client code that wants to work with your beans calls the methods in *javax.ejb.EJBObject*. This client code could be stand-alone applications, applets, servlets, or anything at all—even other enterprise beans.

In addition to the methods listed in Table 3.1, your remote interface duplicates your beans' business methods. When a bean's client invokes any of these business methods, the EJB object will delegate the method to its corresponding implementation—which resides in the bean itself.

Java RMI and EJB Objects

You may have noticed that *javax.ejb.EJBObject* extends *java.rmi.Remote*. The *java.rmi.Remote* interface is part of Java Remote Method Invocation (RMI). Any object that implements *java.rmi.Remote* is a *remote object* and is callable from a different Java Virtual Machine. This is how remote method invocations are performed in Java (we fully describe this in Appendix A).

Because the EJB object—provided by the container—implements your remote interface, it also indirectly implements *java.rmi.Remote* as well. This means that your EJB objects are fully networked objects, able to be called from other Java Virtual Machines or physical machines located elsewhere on the network. Thus, EJB remote interfaces are really just Java RMI remote interfaces—with the exception that EJB remote interfaces must also be built to conform to the EJB specification.

EJB remote interfaces must conform to Java RMI's remote interface rules. For example, any method that's part of a remote object callable across virtual machines must throw a special *remote exception*. A remote exception is a *java.rmi.RemoteException* (or a superclass of it in Java 2). A remote exception indicates that something unexpected happened on the network while you were invoking across virtual machines, such as a network, process, or machine failure. Every method shown in Table 3.1 for *javax.ejb.EJBObject* throws a *java.rmi.RemoteException*.

Remote interfaces must conform to Java RMI's parameter-passing conventions as well. Not everything can be passed over the network in a cross-VM method call. The parameters you pass in methods must be valid types for Java RMI. This includes primitives, serializable objects, and Java RMI remote objects. The full details of what you can pass are given in Appendix A.

EJB also inherits a very significant benefit from Java RMI. In RMI, the physical location of the remote object you're invoking on is masked from you. This feature spills over to EJB. Your client code is unaware of whether the EJB object it's using is located on a machine next door or a machine across the Internet. It also means the EJB object could be located on the *same* Java VM as the client.

Thus, EJB guarantees location transparency of distributed components. Location transparency is a necessary feature of multi-tier deployments. It means your client code is portable and not tied to a specific multi-tier deployment configuration. It also allows EJB containers to perform interesting optimizations behind the scenes when everything is running locally.

The EJB specification mandates that you use a more portable version of Java RMI, called *RMI-IIOP*, rather than standard Java RMI. RMI-IIOP is a standard Java extension that allows your deployment to harness more robust distributed communications and provides for interoperability with CORBA systems.

Unfortunately for EJB, RMI-IIOP was still in beta as of May 1999. This means all EJB 1.0-based application servers are based on the standard Java RMI package, not RMI-IIOP (and hence our code examples in this book rely on standard Java RMI). This should change over time, and so it's important that you understand how RMI-IIOP works. See Chapter 11 for a tutorial on RMI-IIOP.

The Home Object

As we've seen, client code deals with EJB objects and never with beans directly. The next logical question is, how do clients acquire references to EJB objects?

The client cannot instantiate an EJB object directly because EJB objects could exist on a different machine than the one the client is on. Similarly, EJB promotes location transparency, so clients should never be aware of exactly where EJB objects reside.

To acquire a reference to an EJB object, your client code *asks* for an EJB object from an EJB object *factory*. This factory is responsible for instantiating (and destroying) EJB objects. The EJB specification calls such a factory a *home object*. The chief responsibilities of home objects are to do the following:

- Create EJB objects
- Find existing EJB objects (for entity beans—we'll learn about that in Chapter 7)
- Remove EJB objects

Just like EJB objects, home objects are proprietary and specific to each EJB container. They contain interesting container-specific logic, such as load-balancing logic, logic to track information on a graphical administrative console, and more. And just like EJB objects, home objects are physically part of the container and are auto-generated by the container vendor's tools.

The Home Interface

We've seen that home objects are factories for EJB objects. But how does a home object know how you'd like your EJB object to be initialized? For example, one EJB object might expose an initialization method that takes an integer as a parameter, while another EJB object might take a String instead. The container needs to know this information to generate home objects. You provide this information to the container by specifying a *home interface*. Home interfaces simply define methods for creating, destroying, and finding EJB objects. The container's home object *implements* your home interface. We show this in Figure 3.2.

As usual, EJB defines some required methods that all home interfaces must support. These required methods are defined in the *javax.ejb.EJBHome* interface—an interface that your home interfaces must extend. We show *javax.ejb.EJBHome* in Source 3.3.

Notice that the parent *javax.ejb.EJBHome* derives from *java.rmi.Remote*. This means your home interfaces do as well, implying that home objects are also fully networked Java RMI remote objects, which can be called across VMs. The types of the parameters passed in the home interface's methods must be valid types for Java RMI.

If you'd like a preview of the methods of *EJBHome*, refer to Table 3.2.

Deployment Descriptors

The next file that you must include with your enterprise bean component is a *deployment* descriptor. Deployment descriptors enable EJB containers to provide *implicit middleware services* to enterprise bean components. An implicit

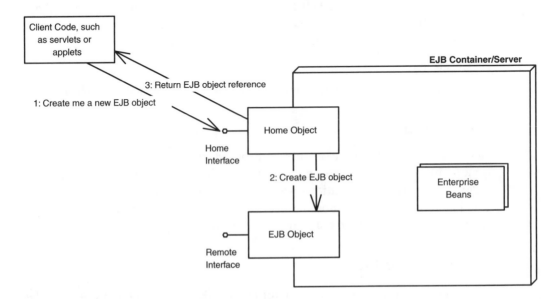

Figure 3.2 Home objects.

```
public interface javax.ejb.EJBHome
extends java.rmi.Remote
{
    public abstract EJBMetaData getEJBMetaData()
        throws java.rmi.RemoteException;

    public abstract void remove(Handle handle)
        throws java.rmi.RemoteException
        javax.ejb.RemoveException;

    public abstract void remove(Object primaryKey)
        throws java.rmi.RemoteException,
        javax.ejb.RemoveException;
}
```

Source 3.3   The javax.ejb.EJBHome interface.

middleware service is a service that your beans can gain without coding to any middleware API—the beans gain the services automatically.

To inform the container about your middleware needs, you as a bean provider must *declare* your components' middleware service requirements in a *deployment descriptor* file. For example, you can use a deployment descriptor to declare how the container should perform life-cycle management, persistence, transaction control, and security services. The container inspects the deployment descriptor and fulfills the requirements that you lay out.

Table 3.2   Required Methods That All Home Objects Expose

METHOD	EXPLANATION
getEJBMetaData()	Used to access information about the enterprise beans you're working with—for example, whether a bean is a session bean or an entity bean. This information is encapsulated in an *EJBMetadata* object, which this method returns. EJBMetadata is primarily useful for development tools, to find out information about your beans, and for scripting languages. Most likely, you won't need to deal with EJBMetadata at all.
remove()	This method destroys a particular EJB object. You can call remove() in one of two ways: 1. By passing a *javax.ejb.Handle* object, which removes an EJB object based on a previously retrieved EJB handle. We'll learn about handles in Chapter 6. 2. By passing a *primary key*. This is only applicable to entity beans, which we'll learn about in Chapters 7-9.

You can use a deployment descriptor to specify the following requirements of your bean:

Bean management and life-cycle requirements. These deployment descriptor settings indicate how the container should manage your beans. For example, you specify the name of the bean's class, whether the bean is a session or entity bean, and the home interface that generates the beans.

Persistence requirements (entity beans only). Authors of entity beans use the deployment descriptors to inform the container about whether the bean handles its persistence on its own or delegates the persistence to the EJB container in which it's deployed.

Transaction requirements. You can also specify transaction settings for beans in deployment descriptors. These settings control what the bean requirements are for running in a transaction. By specifying your transactional needs declaratively in a deployment descriptor, your beans may not have to code to a transaction API at all, yet still benefit from sophisticated online transaction processing concepts.

Security requirements. Deployment descriptors contain *access control entries*, which the beans and container use to control access control to certain operations. For example, you can specify who is allowed to use which beans, and even who is allowed to use each method on a particular bean. You can also specify what security roles the beans themselves should run in, which is useful if the beans need to perform secure operations.

In EJB 1.0, a deployment descriptor is a *serialized* object (see Appendix A for an explanation of Java serialization). The creation of EJB 1.0 deployment descriptors is automated for you by EJB tools supplied by parties such as EJB container vendors, EJB server vendors, or Java Integrated Development Environment (IDE) vendors. For example, you might simply need to step through a wizard in a Java IDE to generate a deployment descriptor.

As a bean provider, you are responsible for creating a deployment descriptor. Once your bean is used, other parties can modify its deployment descriptor settings. For example, when an application assembler is piecing together an application from beans, he or she can tune your deployment descriptor. Similarly, when a deployer is installing your beans in a container in preparation for a deployment to go live, he or she can tune your deployment descriptor settings as well. This is all possible because deployment descriptors *declare* how your beans should use middleware, rather than your writing code that uses middleware. Declaring rather than programming enables people without Java knowledge to tweak your components at a later time. This paradigm becomes an absolute necessity when purchasing EJB components from a third party because third-party source code is typically not available. By having a separate customizable deployment descriptor, you can very easily fine-tune components to a specific deployment environment without changing source code.

Bean-Specific Properties

Finally, you can include a Java-based properties file with your bean. Your bean can read these properties in at runtime and use the properties to tune how the bean functions. For example, a computation bean can use properties to enable selection of an algorithm to use. A pricing bean could use properties to customize pricing rules (as shown in Part IV of this book).

Ejb-jar File

Once you've generated your bean classes, your home interfaces, your remote interfaces, your deployment descriptors, and your bean's properties, it's time to package them up into one entity. This entity is called the *Ejb-jar file*. It is a compressed file that contains everything we have described, and it follows the .ZIP compression format. Jar files are convenient, compact modules for shipping your Java software. The Ejb-jar file creation process is shown in Figure 3.3.

By the time you read this, there should be a number of tools available to autogenerate Ejb-jar files, such as Java IDEs. You can also generate these files yourself—we'll show you how in Chapter 4.

Once you've made your Ejb-jar file, your enterprise bean is complete, and it is a deployable unit within an application server. When they are deployed (perhaps after being purchased), the tools that EJB container vendors supply are responsible for decompressing and reading and extracting the information contained

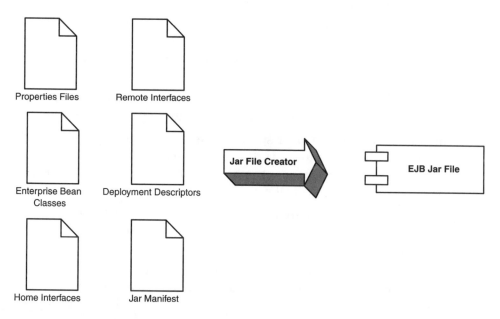

Figure 3.3 Creating an Ejb-jar file.

within the Ejb-jar file. From there, the deployer has to perform vendor-specific tasks, such as generating EJB objects, generating home objects, importing your bean into the container, and tuning the bean. Support for Ejb-jar files is a standard, required feature that all EJB tools support.

Summary of Terms

For your convenience, we now list the definitions of each term we've described so far. As you read future chapters, refer back to these definitions whenever you need clarification (you may want to bookmark this page).

The enterprise bean instance is a Java object instance of an enterprise bean class. It contains business method implementations of the methods defined in the remote interface. The enterprise bean instance is "network-less" in that it contains no networked logic.

The remote interface is a Java interface that enumerates the business methods exposed by the enterprise bean class. In EJB, client code always goes through the remote interface and never interacts with the enterprise bean instance. The remote interface is "network-aware" in that the interface obeys the rules for Java RMI.

The EJB object is the container-generated implementation of the remote interface. The EJB object is a network-aware intermediary between the client and the bean instance, handling necessary middleware issues. All client invocations go through the EJB object. The EJB object delegates calls to enterprise bean instances.

The home interface is a Java interface that serves as a factory for EJB objects. Client code that wants to work with EJB objects must use the home interface to generate them. The home interface is network-aware because it is used by clients across the network.

The home object is the container-generated implementation of the home interface. The home object is also network-aware, and it obeys Java RMI's rules.

The deployment descriptor specifies the middleware requirements of your bean. You use the deployment descriptor to inform the container about how to manage your bean, your bean's life-cycle needs, your transactional needs, your persistence needs, and your security needs.

The bean's properties are attributes that your bean uses at runtime. You use properties to allow people to customize how your bean's logic works internally.

The Ejb-jar file is the finished, complete component containing the enterprise bean class, the remote interface, the home interface, the bean's properties, and the deployment descriptor.

Now that you've covered the required ground for general enterprise bean concepts, let's spend the remainder of this chapter looking at our first major bean type: the session bean.

What Is a Session Bean?

Session beans are enterprise beans that represent work performed for a client. Session beans are intended to represent business processes. A business process is any task involving logic, algorithms, or workflow. Examples of business processes include billing a credit card, fulfilling an order, performing calculations, and trading stock. All of these processes are well represented by session beans.

Session Bean Lifetime

A chief difference between session beans and entity beans is the scope of their lives. A session bean is a relatively short-lived component. Roughly, it has the lifetime equivalent of a client's *session*. A client's session duration could be as long as a Netscape Navigator window is open, perhaps connecting to an e-commerce site with deployed session beans. It could also be as long as your Java applet is running, as long as a stand-alone application is open, or as long as another bean is using your bean.

The length of the client's *session* generally determines how long a session bean is in use—that is where the term *session bean* originated. The EJB container is empowered to destroy session beans if clients time out. If your client code is using your beans for 10 minutes, your session beans might live for minutes or hours, but probably not weeks, months, or years. Typically, session beans do not survive application server crashes, nor do they survive machine crashes. They are in-memory objects that live and die with their surrounding environments.

In contrast, entity beans can live for months or even years because entity beans are *persistent objects*. Entity beans are part of a durable, permanent storage, such as a database. Entity beans can be constructed in memory from database data, and they can survive for long periods of time.

Session beans are *nonpersistent*. This means that session beans are not saved to permanent storage, whereas entity beans are. Note that session beans *can* perform database operations, but the session bean *itself* is not a persistent object.

All session beans (as well as entity beans) must expose required *management callback methods*. The container uses the management methods to interact with the bean, calling them periodically to alert the bean to important events. For example, the container will alert the bean when it is being initialized and when it is being destroyed. These callbacks are not intended for client use, so you will never call them directly—only your EJB container will. We'll learn about the specifics of these management methods in the pages to come.

Conversational versus Nonconversational Session Beans

All enterprise beans hold *conversations* with clients at some level. A conversation is an interaction between a client and a bean, and it is composed of a number of method calls between the client and the bean. A conversation spans a business process for the client, such as configuring a frame-relay switch, purchasing goods over the Internet, or entering information about a new customer.

A *stateless session bean* is a bean that holds conversations that span a single method call. They are stateless because they do not hold multimethod conversations with their clients. After each method call, a stateless session bean clears itself out of all information pertaining to past invocations. Stateless session beans store no conversational state from method to method.

Because stateless session beans hold no state, all instances of the same stateless session bean enterprise class are equivalent and indistinguishable to a client. It does not matter who has called a stateless session bean in the past, since a stateless session bean retains no state knowledge about its history. This means that *any* stateless session bean can service *any* client request because they are all exactly the same. This also means that stateless beans can be easily reused by multiple clients, rather than destroyed and re-created per client. This is depicted in Figure 3.4.

A *stateful session bean* is a much more interesting beast. Stateful session beans are components that hold conversations with clients that may span many method

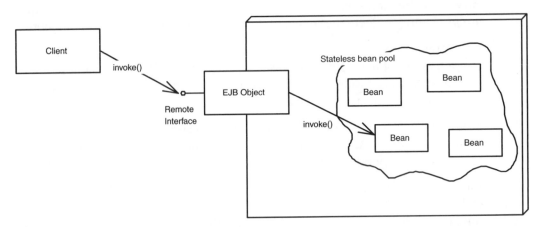

Figure 3.4 Stateless session bean pooling.

calls. During a conversation, the bean holds conversational state for that client and that client alone. Thus, stateful session beans are more functional than stateless session beans because they retain conversational state. As we will see when we explore stateful session beans, this functionality can come at a performance cost.

All Session Beans' Methods Are Serialized

When you call a method on a session bean instance, your EJB container guarantees that no other clients are using that instance. The container exclusively holds that bean instance and directs concurrent clients to other instances or makes them wait until you're done with that instance. Thus, if multiple clients simultaneously invoke methods on a session bean, the invocations are *serialized*, or performed in lock-step. This means that the container automatically makes clients line up one by one to use a bean instance (behind the scenes, the container might use Java thread synchronization to aid with this). Note that this is in no way a performance bottleneck because the container can provide other instances of the bean to service multiple simultaneous clients.

Because client requests are serialized, you do not need to code your beans as *re-entrant* (thread-safe); only one thread for a client can be executing within the bean at any time.

Understanding How to Write Session Beans

To write a session enterprise bean class, your class must implement the *javax.ejb .SessionBean* interface. This interface defines a few required methods that you must fill in. These are management methods that the EJB container calls on your bean to alert it about important events. Clients of your bean will never call these methods because these methods are not made available to clients via the EJB object. The *javax.ejb.SessionBean* interface is shown in Source 3.4.

Notice that the *javax.ejb.SessionBean* interface extends the more generic *javax.ejb.EnterpriseBean* interface that we saw earlier. Entity beans have their own interface, called *javax.ejb.EntityBean*, which also inherits from the *javax.ejb.EnterpriseBean* interface.

Sometimes you can simply provide empty implementations of the methods required by *javax.ejb.SessionBean*, and sometimes it's necessary to put logic in them. We'll spend a good amount of time looking at what the implementations should be in this book.

Let's take a detailed look at each method in the *SessionBean* interface.

```
public interface javax.ejb.SessionBean
extends javax.ejb.EnterpriseBean
{
    public abstract void setSessionContext(SessionContext ctx)
throws java.rmi.RemoteException;

    public abstract void ejbPassivate()
throws java.rmi.RemoteException;

    public abstract void ejbActivate()
throws java.rmi.RemoteException;

    public abstract void ejbRemove()
throws java.rmi.RemoteException;

}
```

Source 3.4   The javax.ejb.SessionBean interface.

setSessionContext(SessionContext ctx)

The container calls this method to associate your bean with a *session context*. A session context is your bean's gateway to interact with the container; your bean can use session contexts to query the container about your current transactional state, your current security state, and more.

A typical bean implementation would store the context away in a member variable so the context can be queried later. For example:

```
import javax.ejb.*;

public class MyBean implements SessionBean {
    private SessionContext ctx;

    public void setSessionContext(SessionContext ctx) {
    this.ctx = ctx;
    }

    ...
    }
```

In Chapter 6, we'll take a more detailed look at what you can do with session contexts.

ejbCreate(...)

ejbCreate(...) methods initialize your session bean. You can define several *ejbCreate(...)* methods, and each can take different arguments. This allows clients to initialize your bean in different ways. Because you define your own *ejbCreate(...)* method signatures, there is no *ejbCreate(...)* method listed in the *javax.ejb.SessionBean* interface. Note that you must provide at least one *ejbCreate()* method in your session bean, and thus you have at least one way for your bean to be initialized.

Your implementation of *ejbCreate(...)* should perform any initialization your bean needs, such as setting member variables to the argument values passed in. For example:

```
import javax.ejb.*;

public class MyBean implements SessionBean {
    private int memberVariable;

    public void ejbCreate(int initialValue) {
        this.memberVariable = initialValue;
    }

    ...
}
```

ejbCreate(...) methods are callback methods that your container will invoke. Client code never calls your *ejbCreate(...)* methods because clients never deal with beans directly—they must go through the container. But clients must have some way of passing parameters to your *ejbCreate(...)* methods because clients supply your initialization parameters. And if you'll recall, a home interface is the factory interface that clients call to initialize your bean. Therefore, you must duplicate each e*jbCreate()* method in your home interface. For example, if you have the following *ejbCreate()* method in your bean class:

```
public void ejbCreate(int i) throws ...
```

you must have this *create()* in your home interface (you leave off the "ejb" part of the signature):

```
public void create(int i) throws ...
```

The client calls *create()* on the home interface, and the parameters are then passed to your bean's *ejbCreate()*.

ejbPassivate()

If too many beans are instantiated, the EJB container can *passivate* some of them, which means writing the beans to a temporary storage such as a database or file system. The container can then release the resources the beans had claimed. Immediately before your beans are passivated, the container calls your *ejbPassivate()* method.

Your bean's implementation of *ejbPassivate()* should release any resources your bean may be holding. For example:

```
import javax.ejb.*;

public class MyBean implements SessionBean {

    public void ejbPassivate() {
        <close socket connections, etc...>
    }

    ...

}
```

We'll learn more about passivation in Chapter 5.

 Passivation does not apply to stateless session beans because stateless session beans do not hold state and can simply be created/destroyed rather than passivated/activated.

ejbActivate()

When a client needs to use a bean that's been passivated, the reverse process automatically occurs: The container kicks the bean back into memory, or *activates* the bean. Immediately after your bean is activated, the container calls your *ejbActivate()* method.

Now that your bean is back in memory again, your bean's implementation of *ejbActivate()* should acquire any resources your bean needs. This is typically every resource you released during *ejbPassivate()*. For example:

```
import javax.ejb.*;

public class MyBean implements SessionBean {

    public void ejbActivate() {
        <open socket connections, etc...>
    }

    ...

}
```

We'll learn more about activation in Chapter 5.

 Activation does not apply to stateless session beans because stateless session beans do not hold state and can simply be created/destroyed rather than passivated/activated.

ejbRemove()

When the container is about to remove your session bean instance, it calls your bean's *ejbRemove()* callback method. *ejbRemove()* is a clean-up method, alerting your bean that it is about to be destroyed and allowing it to end its life gracefully. *ejbRemove()* is a required method of all beans, and it takes no parameters. Therefore, there is only one *ejbRemove()* method per bean. This is in stark contrast to *ejbCreate()*, which has many forms. This makes perfect sense—why should a destructive method be personalized for each client? (This is an analogous concept to destructors in C++.)

Your implementation of *ejbRemove()* should prepare your bean for destruction. This means you need to free all resources you may have allocated. For example:

```
import javax.ejb.*;

public class MyBean implements SessionBean {

    public void ejbRemove() {
        <prepare for destruction>
    }

    ...
}
```

Your container can call *ejbRemove()* at any time, including if the container decides that the bean's life has expired (perhaps due to a very long timeout). Note that the container may *never* call your bean's *ejbRemove()* method, such as if the container crashes or if a critical exception occurs. You must be prepared for this contingency. For example, if your bean represents an e-commerce shopping cart, it might store temporary shopping cart data in a database. Your application should provide a utility that runs periodically to remove any abandoned shopping carts from the database.

Business Methods

In addition to the required callback methods we just described, you should define zero or more business methods in your bean. These methods actually solve business problems. For example:

```
import javax.ejb.*;

public class MyBean implements SessionBean {

    public int add(int i, int j) {
        return (i + j);
    }
```

. . .
}

For clients to call your business methods, you must list your business methods
in your bean's remote interface.

Understanding How to Call Session Beans

We now take a look at the other half of the world—the client side. We are now
customers of the beans' business logic, and we are trying to solve some real-
world problem by using one or more beans together. Clients can exist in any
scenario:

- On a stand-alone machine communicating with beans deployed locally.

- In a stand-alone application communicating over the network with remote
  beans.

- In a Java-based applet running inside a Web browser, communicating over
  the network with remote beans.

- Behind a Web server, communicating over a LAN with remote beans. The
  end user might be using an HTML-based user interface, communicating
  over the Internet, bound to the bean client with glue-code such as *Java
  Server Pages (JSPs)* or Java servlets (our e-commerce deployment in Part
  IV shows how to use servlets as EJB clients).

- As other enterprise beans, perhaps as part of a workflow to solve a larger
  business problem.

Note that in any of these scenarios, there are two different kinds of clients:

Java RMI-based clients. These clients use the *Java Naming and Directory
Interface (JNDI)* to look up objects over a network, and they use the *Java
Transaction API (JTA)* to control transactions.

CORBA clients. Clients can also be written to the CORBA standard. This yields
a fuller suite of distributed object services and allows for legacy integration.
CORBA clients use the *CORBA Naming Service (COS Naming)* to look up
objects over the network, and they use the CORBA's *Object Transaction Service (OTS)* to control transactions.

Whether you're using CORBA or RMI, your client code typically looks like this:

1. Look up a home object.

2. Use the home object to create an EJB object.

3. Call business methods on the EJB object.

4. Remove the EJB object.

Let's go through each of these steps with Java RMI-based clients. See Chapter 11 for CORBA.

Looking Up a Home Object

To look up a home object, your client code must use the JNDI. We now provide a brief overview of the role JNDI plays in deployments; feel free to read Appendix B for the full details of how JNDI works.

The Role of Naming and Directory Services in J2EE

One of the goals of the Java 2 Platform, Enterprise Edition (J2EE) is that your application code should be "write once, run anywhere." Any Java code running in an enterprise deployment should be independent of a particular multi-tier configuration. How you choose to distribute your beans, your servlets, and other logic across multiple tiers should not affect your code. This is called location transparency—the physical locations of entities across a deployment are transparent to your application code.

J2EE *achieves* location transparency by leveraging *naming and directory services*. Naming and directory services are products that store and look up resources across a network. Some examples of directory service products are Netscape's *Directory Server*, Microsoft's *Active Directory*, and IBM's *Lotus Notes*.

Traditionally, corporations have used directory services to store usernames, passwords, machine locations, printer locations, and so on. J2EE products exploit directory services to store location information for resources that your application code uses in an enterprise deployment. These resources could be EJB home objects, enterprise bean environment properties, database drivers, message service drivers, and other resources. By using directory services, you can write application code that does not depend on specific machine names or locations. This is all part of EJB's location transparency, and it keeps your code portable. If later you decide that resources should be located elsewhere, your code will not need to be rebuilt because the directory service can simply be updated to reflect the new resource locations. This greatly enhances maintenance of a multi-tier deployment that may evolve over time. This becomes absolutely necessary when purchasing prewritten software (such as enterprise beans), because your purchased components' source code will likely not be made available to you to change.

Unless you're using CORBA, the de facto API used to access naming and directory services is JNDI. JNDI adds value to your enterprise deployments by providing a standard interface for locating users, machines, networks, objects, and services. For example, you can use the JNDI to locate a printer on your corporate intranet. You can also use it to locate a Java object or to connect with a database. In J2EE, JNDI is used extensively for locating resources across an enterprise deployment, including home objects, environment properties, database resources, and more.

There are two common steps that must be taken to find any resource in a J2EE deployment:

1. Associate the resource with a "nickname" in your deployment descriptor. Your J2EE product will bind the nickname to the resource.

2. Clients of the resource can use the nickname with JNDI to look up the resource across a deployment.

How to Use JNDI to Locate Home Objects

To achieve location transparency, EJB containers mask the specific locations of home objects from your enterprise beans' client code. Clients do not hard-code the machine names that home objects reside on, but rather they use JNDI to *look up* home objects. Home objects are physically located "somewhere" on the network—perhaps in the address space of an EJB container, perhaps in the address space of the client, or perhaps elsewhere on the network. As a developer who writes client code to use beans, you don't care.

For clients to locate a home object, you must provide a *nickname* for your bean's home object. Clients will use this nickname to identify the home object it wants. For example, if you have a bean called *MyBean*, you may specify a nickname *MyHome* in the deployment descriptor. The container will automatically *bind* the nickname *MyHome* to the home object. Then any client on any machine across a multi-tier deployment can use that nickname to find home objects, without regard to physical machine locations. Clients use the JNDI API to do this. JNDI goes over the network to some directory service to look for the home object, perhaps contacting one or more directory services in the process. Eventually the home object is found, and a reference to it is returned to the client. This is shown in Figure 3.5.

More concretely, your client code must execute the following steps to acquire a reference to a home object via JNDI:

Set up your environment. You must specify which directory service you're using, specify the network location of the directory service you desire, and specify any usernames and passwords that may be required for authentication.

Form the initial context. The initial context is a local starting point for connecting to directory structures. You need to pass the initial context to the environment properties you just set up.

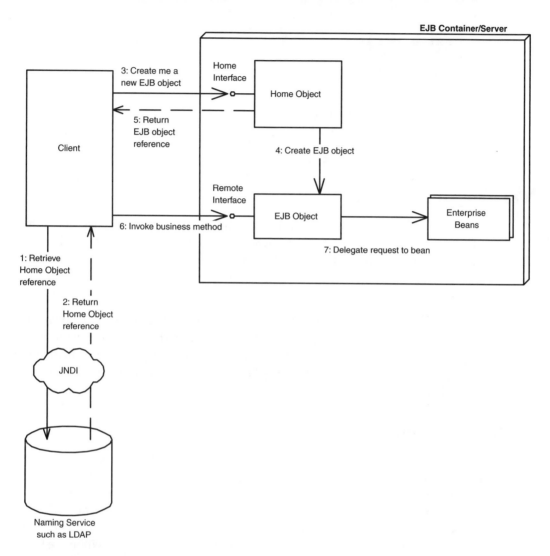

Figure 3.5 Acquiring a reference to a home object.

> **Retrieve the home object.** To retrieve the home object, you must perform a JNDI *lookup()* operation on the remote directory. The returned object is an RMI remote object that you must cast to a home object.
>
> The following code segment illustrates these steps:
>
> ```
> /*
>  * Get System properties for JNDI initialization
>  */
> Properties props = System.getProperties();
> ```

```
/*
 * Form an initial context
 */
Context ctx = new InitialContext(props);

/*
 * Get a reference to the home object - the
 * factory for EJB objects
 */
MyHome home = (MyHome) ctx.lookup("MyHome");
```

Creating an EJB Object

Once your client code has a reference to a home object, you can use that home object as a factory to create EJB objects. To create an EJB object, call one of the *create()* methods on the home. The following line illustrates this:

```
MyRemoteInterface ejbObject = home.create();
```

We pass no parameters to *create()* because stateless session beans never take initialization parameters (they would never remember the parameter values later because they are stateless). Note that when we call *create()*, the bean instance's *ejbCreate()* method may not be called because the container can pool and re-use existing beans.

Calling a Method

Now that the bean's client has an EJB object, it can start calling one or more of the methods that the bean exposes through the EJB object. When the client calls a method on the EJB object, the EJB object must choose a bean instance to service the request. The EJB object may need to create a new instance or reuse an existing instance. The actual scheme of when pooling and reusing beans is performed is proprietary to each EJB container implementation. When the bean instance is done, the EJB object takes the return value from the bean's method and ships it back to the bean's client. This process is shown in Figure 3.5.

The following line illustrates calling an *add()* business method through the EJB object:

```
ejbObject.add();
```

Destroying the EJB Object

Finally, when you want to destroy an EJB object, call a *remove()* method on the EJB object or home object. This enables the container to destroy the EJB object.

The following line illustrates removing our hello EJB object:

```
ejbObject.remove();
```

 As with creating a bean, destroying a bean might not necessarily correspond with literally destroying in-memory bean objects because the EJB container controls their life cycles to allow for pooling between heterogeneous clients.

Summary

In this chapter, we learned the fundamental concepts behind session beans. We started off by looking at the general enterprise bean—the fundamental component in an EJB system. We then looked at session beans—enterprise beans that represent a business process—and saw the characteristics that make session beans unique. We surveyed the rules for writing a session bean class, and we also stepped through a client interaction with a session bean.

In the next chapter, we'll learn about *stateless session beans*. We'll also write our first enterprise bean, complete with an enterprise bean class, remote interface, home interface, deployment descriptor, manifest file, and Ejb-jar file.

## CHAPTER 4

The Basics of Stateless Session Beans

I n this chapter, we'll learn how to write stateless session beans. Stateless session beans are components that model business processes that can be performed in a single method call.

This chapter begins with a look at the characteristics that stateless session beans share. We'll then show an example of a stateless bean and write sample client code to access it.

Characteristics of Stateless Session Beans

Before we get into the programming details, we begin with an overview of the characteristics that make stateless session beans different from other enterprise beans.

No Conversational State

Stateless sessions hold no conversational state on behalf of clients. Although they can contain internal state, their state is not *customized* for a particular client. This means all stateless beans appear identical to clients; clients cannot tell them apart. For a stateless session bean to be useful for a client, the client must pass all client data that the bean needs as parameters to business logic methods. Alternatively, the bean can retrieve the data it needs from an external source, such as a database.

Only One Way to Initialize Stateless Sessions

We've learned that session beans are initialized with *ejbCreate()* methods. And since stateless session beans cannot retain state between method calls, they also cannot retain state after a client passes data to an *ejbCreate()* call. It therefore doesn't make sense for a stateless session bean to support fancy *ejbCreate()* methods because on subsequent calls to the bean instance, the instance would have no record of previous *ejbCreate()* calls. Thus, all stateless session beans may expose only a single *ejbCreate()* method, which takes no parameters. The home object also exposes a matching *create()* method which takes no parameters.

Containers Can Pool and Reuse Stateless Sessions

Because stateless session beans' *ejbCreate()* methods take no parameters, clients never supply any critical information that bean instances need to start up. EJB containers can exploit this and precreate instances of your stateless session beans. Thus, EJB containers can *pool* stateless session bean instances before your clients connect. When a client calls a method, the container can retrieve an instance from the pool, have it service the method, and then return it to the pool. This enables the container to dynamically assign instances of your bean to different clients.

A side effect of this is that every time requests come in from a client, a different stateless session bean instance can service that request. This is because stateless sessions hold conversations spanning a single method request and are free of client-specific state *after each method call*. All stateless session beans think they are in the same state after a method call; they are effectively unaware that previous method calls even happened. Therefore, the container can dynamically reassign beans to client requests at the *per-method* level. A different stateless session bean can service *each* method call from a client. Of course, the actual implementation of reassigning beans to clients is container-specific.

The benefit of bean instance pooling is that the pool of beans can be much smaller than the actual number of clients connecting. This is due to client "think time," such as network lag or human decision time on the client side. While the client is thinking, the container can use the bean instances to service other clients, saving previous system resources.

Note that bean pools do not need to be statically sized. Advanced containers support dynamically resizable pools over time, allowing pool sizes to change as load demands fluctuate. For example, if more clients connect to your deployment during the day than at night, your container might allow you to have a large pool during the day and a small pool at night. This frees system resources to be used for other tasks during off-peak hours.

When Are My Beans Created?

We've learned that the container is responsible for pooling stateless session beans. The container creates and destroys beans when the container decides it's the right time to resize its pool. Your client code is absolutely not responsible for creating beans. A client deals with the networked bean wrapper, called the EJB object. The EJB object is part of the container, and it is responsible for retrieving beans from a pool to service client requests.

But if the container is responsible for bean life cycle, then why does the home interface specify *create()* and *remove()* methods? What you must remember is that these methods are for creating and destroying *EJB objects*. This may not correspond to the actual creation and destruction of beans. The client shouldn't care whether the actual bean is created or destroyed—all the client code cares about is that the client has an EJB object to invoke. The fact that beans are pooled behind the EJB object is irrelevant.

So, when debugging your EJB applications, don't be alarmed if your bean isn't being created or destroyed when you call *create()* or *remove()* on the home object. Depending on your container's policy, your stateless session beans may be pooled and reused, with the container creating and destroying at will.

EJB Object Decoupling

Because the beans are pooled and reused, they are decoupled from EJB objects. The beans can be reassigned at any time to another EJB object, depending on the container's strategy. Therefore, a new bean does not necessarily have to be created at the same time an EJB object is created. Rather, a bean can be taken from the available pool. If client load suddenly increases, more beans can be instantiated by the EJB container at any time. Similarly, the EJB container can destroy beans at any time.

The decoupling of stateless session beans from EJB objects is very important to know when debugging EJB applications. We expand on this idea in the sidebar.

Writing a "Hello, World!" Stateless Session Bean

Now that we've learned the theory behind stateless session beans, let's apply our knowledge and construct a simple bean. Our stateless session bean, a component running in a distributed object framework, will be responsible for the mighty task of returning the string "Hello, World!" to the client.

While this may not be the most functional demonstration of the power of EJB, this is a great example for illustrating the basics of EJB programming, and it is a useful template for building more complex beans.

Constructing the "Hello, World!" Remote Interface

We begin by coding our bean's remote interface. The remote interface duplicates every business method that our beans expose. The container will implement the remote interface; the implementation is the EJB object. The EJB object will delegate all client requests to actual beans. The code is shown in Source 4.1.

Things to notice about our remote interface include the following:

- We extend *javax.ejb.EJBObject*. This means the container-generated EJB object, which implements the remote interface, will contain every method that the *javax.ejb.EJBObject* interface defines. This includes a method to compare two EJB objects, a method to remove an EJB object, and so on.

- We have one business method—*hello()*—which returns the String "Hello, World!" back to the client. We'll need to implement this method in our enterprise bean class. Because the remote interface is a Java RMI remote interface (it *extends java.rmi.Remote*), it must throw a remote exception.

```
package com.wiley.compBooks.roman.session.helloworld;

import javax.ejb.*;
import java.rmi.RemoteException;
import java.rmi.Remote;

/**
 * This is the HelloBean remote interface.
 *
 * This interface is what clients operate on when
 * they interact with EJB objects.  The container
 * vendor will implement this interface; the
 * implemented object is the EJB object, which
 * delegates invocations to the actual bean.
 */
public interface Hello extends EJBObject {

  /**
   * The one method - hello - returns a greeting to the client.
   */
  public String hello() throws java.rmi.RemoteException;

}
```

Source 4.1 Hello.java.

This is really the only difference between the remote interface's *hello()* signature and our bean's *hello()* signature. The exception indicates a networking or other critical problem.

Implementing the "Hello, World!" Bean

Next, let's create the bean itself. We'll implement our one business method, *hello()*. We'll also add the required container callback methods. The code is shown in Source 4.2.

This is about the most basic bean you can have. Notice the following:

- Our bean implements the *javax.ejb.SessionBean* interface (shown in Chapter 3), which makes it a session bean.

```java
package com.wiley.compBooks.roman.session.helloworld;

import javax.ejb.*;

/**
 * Demonstration stateless session bean.
 */
public class HelloBean implements SessionBean {

    //
    // EJB-required methods
    //
    public void ejbCreate() {
        System.out.println("ejbCreate()");
    }

    public void ejbRemove() {
        System.out.println("ejbRemove()");
    }

    public void ejbActivate() {
        System.out.println("ejbActivate()");
    }

    public void ejbPassivate() {
        System.out.println("ejbPassivate()");
    }

    public void setSessionContext(SessionContext ctx) {
        System.out.println("setSessionContext()");
    }
```

Source 4.2 HelloBean.java *(continues)*.

```
//
// Business methods
//
public String hello() {
    System.out.println("hello()");
    return "Hello, World!";
}
}
```

Source 4.2 HelloBean.java *(continued).*

EJB Design Strategies

Don't Implement That Remote Interface!

Our *HelloBean.java* enterprise bean implementation did not implement its own remote
interface. Why not? Doesn't the remote interface seem like a natural fit for the interface
to your bean? After all, the remote interface defines every business method of the bean.
Implementing your remote interface would be a nifty way to perform compile-time
checking to make sure your bean's method signature matches your remote interface's
signature.

There are two good reasons not to implement your bean's remote interface:

Reason #1
Remote interfaces extend *javax.ejb.EJBObject*. Since *javax.ejb.EJBObject* defines additional methods intended for client use, you'd have to implement those methods in your
bean. Those methods have no place in your bean class.

Reason #2
Let's assume your enterprise bean wants to call a method on a *different* enterprise
bean, and you want to pass a reference to your bean as a parameter to the other bean's
method (similar to passing the *this* parameter in Java). How can you do this in EJB?

Remember that all clients call methods on EJB objects, not beans. Thus, if your bean
calls another bean, you must pass a reference to your bean's EJB object, rather than a
reference to your bean. The other bean should operate on your EJB object, and not your
bean, because the other bean is a client, just like any other client, and all clients must
go through EJB objects.

The danger here is if your enterprise bean class implements your EJB object's remote
interface. You could accidentally pass a reference to the bean itself, rather than pass a
reference to the bean's EJB object. Because your bean implements the same interface as

- Our bean does *not* implement its own remote interface (you should avoid doing this—see the sidebar).

- The bean is stateless and does not contain any client-specific state that spans method calls. Therefore, each bean is identical and has an identical initialization method—a simple *ejbCreate()* that takes no paramaters.

- When we destroy the bean, there's nothing to clean up, so we have a very simple *ejbRemove()* method.

- The *setSessionContext()* method associates a bean with an environment. We don't provide any implementation, however, since our bean never has to query information about its environment. We'll explore session contexts in Chapter 6.

---

the EJB object, the compiler would let you pass the bean itself as a *this* parameter, which is an error.

A Solution
Fortunately, there is a clean alternative way to preserve compile-time checks of your method signatures. The design pattern is to contain your bean's business method signatures within a common superinterface that your remote interface extends and your bean implements. You can think of this superinterface as a *business interface* that defines your business methods and is independent of EJB. The following example illustrates this concept:

```
// Business interface
public interface HelloBusinessMethods {
    public String hello() throws java.rmi.RemoteException;
}


// EJB remote interface
public interface HelloRemoteInterface extends javax.ejb.EJBObject,
HelloBusinessMethods {
}


// Bean implementation
public class HelloBean implements SessionBean, HelloBusinessMethods {
    public String hello() {
        return "Hello, World!";
    }

    <...define other required callbacks...>
}
```

- The *ejbActivate()* and *ejbPassivate()* methods are used when beans are activated and passivated, respectively. These concepts do not apply to stateless session beans, and so we leave these methods empty. We'll see what these methods mean and what to use them for when we examine stateful session beans.

Constructing the "Hello, World!" Home Interface

Our home interface specifies mechanisms to create and destroy EJB objects. The code is shown in Source 4.3.

Notice the following about our home interface:

- Our home interface extends *javax.ejb.EJBHome* (shown in Chapter 3). This is required for all home interfaces. *EJBHome* defines a way to destroy an EJB object, so we don't need to write that method signature.

- Our home interface exposes one method to create an EJB object and takes no arguments. This is correct because we're dealing with stateless session beans, and stateless sessions have empty *create()* methods.

```java
package com.wiley.compBooks.roman.session.helloworld;

import javax.ejb.*;
import java.rmi.RemoteException;

/**
 * This is the home interface for HelloBean.  This interface
 * is implemented by the EJB Server's glue-code tools - the
 * implemented object is called the Home Object and serves
 * as a factory for EJB Objects.
 *
 * One create() method is in this Home Interface, which
 * corresponds to the ejbCreate() method in HelloBean.
 */
public interface HelloHome extends EJBHome {

    /*
     * This method creates the EJB Object.
     *
     * @return The newly created EJB Object.
     */
  Hello create() throws RemoteException, CreateException;
}
```

Source 4.3 HelloHome.java.

- Our home interface's *create()* method throws a *java.rmi.RemoteException* and a *aavax.ejb.CreateException*. Remote exceptions are necessary side effects of Java RMI because the home object is a networked RMI remote object. The *CreateException* is also required in all *create()* methods. We explain this further in the following sidebar.

Writing the Deployment Descriptor

Next, we need to generate a *deployment descriptor*, which describes our bean's middleware requirements to the container. Deployment descriptors are one of the key features of EJB because they allow you to *declaratively* specify attributes on your beans, rather than programming this functionality into the bean itself.

In EJB 1.0, a deployment descriptor is a *serialized* (see Appendix A) Java object that you store as a file on disk. In EJB 1.1, a deployment descriptor is an XML document (see Appendix D for more details). Your EJB container or IDE environment should supply tools to help you generate such a deployment descriptor. The application server we tested against, BEA's *WebLogic*, ships with a deployment descriptor generation wizard. Major Integrated Development Environments (IDEs) such as Inprise's *JBuilder*, Symantec's *VisualCafe*, or IBM's *VisualAge for Java* are beginning to provide such tools as well. Consult your specific product documentation for more details.

Deployment Descriptor Settings

There are many different settings that make up a deployment descriptor. We'll touch on some of them now and reveal others as we explore other topics later in this book (we cover entity bean settings in Chapters 7–9 and transaction settings in Chapter 10).

Let's take a quick look at some of the deployment descriptor settings that are relevant to session beans:

Bean home name. The nickname that clients use to look up your bean's home object.

Enterprise bean class name. The fully qualified name of the enterprise bean class.

Home interface class name. The fully qualified name of the home interface.

Remote interface class name. The fully qualified name of the remote interface.

Re-entrant. Whether the enterprise bean allows re-entrant calls. This setting must be false for session beans (it applies to entity beans only).

Exceptions and EJB

Every networked object in EJB conforms to the RMI standard and must throw a remote exception. Thus, every method in an EJB object and home object (such as our *hello()* method) must throw a remote exception. When such an exception is thrown, it indicates a special error condition—that a network failure, machine failure, or other catastrophic failure occurred.

But how can your beans throw exceptions that indicate regular, run-of-the-mill problems, such as bad parameters passed to a business method? EJB comes with some built-in exceptions to handle this, and it also allows you to define your own exception types.

More formally, EJB defines the following exception types:

1. A *system-level exception* is a serious error that involves some critical failure, such as a database malfunction.

2. An *application-level exception* is a normal, run-of-the-mill exception, such as an indication of bad parameters to a method or a warning of an insufficient bank account balance to make a withdrawal. For example, in our "Hello, World!" home interface, we throw a standard *javax.ejb.CreateException* from home interface's *create()* method. This is an example of a required application-level exception, indicating that some ordinary problem occurred during bean initialization.

Why must we separate the concepts of system-level and application-level exceptions? The chief reason is that system-level exceptions are handled quite differently from application-level exceptions.

For example, system-level exceptions are not necessarily thrown back to the client. Remember that EJB objects—the container-generated wrappers for beans—are middlemen between a bean's client and the bean itself. EJB objects have the ability to *intercept* any exceptions that beans may throw. This allows EJB objects to pick and choose which exceptions the client should see. In some cases, if a bean fails, it may be possible to salvage the client's invocation and redirect it to another bean. This is known as *transparent fail-over*—a quality of service that some EJB container/server vendors provide. This is a very easy service to provide for stateless beans because there is no lost state

Stateful or stateless. Whether the session bean is a stateful or stateless session bean.

Session timeout. The length of time (in seconds) before a client should time out when calling methods on your bean.

On the CD-ROM we include a sample deployment descriptor text file that works with BEA's *WebLogic* product. The values of these deployment descriptor settings for our "Hello, World!" bean are shown in Table 4.1.

when a bean crashes. Some high-end EJB products even provide transparent fail-over for stateful beans by routinely checkpointing the stateful bean's conversational state. In case of a critical, unrecoverable problem, your EJB container may support professional monitoring systems, alerting a system administrator in the event of a catastrophic error.

By way of comparison, application-level exceptions should always be thrown back to the client. Application-level exceptions indicate a routine problem, and the exception itself is valuable data that the client needs. For example, we could notify a client that there are insufficient funds in a bank account by throwing an application-level exception. The client would always want to know about this because it is an application-level problem, not a systems-level problem.

Besides correctly routing system-level and application-level exceptions, the EJB object is responsible for catching all *unchecked* exceptions (flavors of *java.lang.RuntimeException*) that your bean may throw, such as a NullPointer exception. These are typically not caught by code. Exceptions that are unchecked in the bean could leave the bean in an abnormal state because the bean is not expecting to handle such an exception. Under this kind of scenario, the EJB container intercepts the exception and can perform some action, such as throwing the exception back to the client as a remote exception. It also will probably stop using that bean because the bean is in an undefined state.

The following two rules of thumb should help you with exceptions:

1. Application-level exceptions are always thrown back to the client. This includes any exception the bean defines. It also includes the *javax.ejb.CreateException* for creating beans (and the *javax.ejb.FindException* for entity beans, which we'll see in Chapters 7–9).

2. When system-level exceptions occur, the EJB container can do anything it wants to: page a system administrator with an alert, send an e-mail to a third party, or throw the exception back to the client. Your bean can throw a system-level exception as either a Java RMI remote exception or an unchecked *RuntimeException*. If the exception is thrown to the client, it is always thrown as a remote exception or a subclass of it.

Exceptions also have an impact on transactions. We'll learn more about this effect in Chapter 10.

The Environment Properties

Finally, you can include an environment properties file with your bean to specify business logic customization. Your bean can use this information to adapt itself to a particular environment.

For example, if you have a bean that employs a variety of algorithms (using different strategies to solve a problem or the strategy design pattern), you could specify the particular algorithm to use on deployment with environment properties.

Table 4.1 Deployment Descriptor Settings for HelloBean

DEPLOYMENT DESCRIPTOR SETTING	VALUE
Bean home name	HelloHome
Enterprise bean class name	com.wiley.compBooks.roman.session.helloworld.HelloBean
Home interface class name	com.wiley.compBooks.roman.session.helloworld.HelloHome
Remote interface class name	com.wiley.compBooks.roman.session.helloworld.Hello
Environment properties	<empty>
Re-entrant	false
Stateful or stateless	STATELESS_SESSION
Session timeout	10 seconds

Note the difference of function here—the container uses the deployment descriptor to aid in managing your bean, while your bean can use the environment properties file to customize its internal logic.

Because our "Hello, World!" bean is very simple, we do not need to define properties. If you'd like to see environment properties in action, see Chapter 6.

The Ejb-jar File

There's one last step before deploying our bean. Now that we've written all the necessary files for our component, we need to package the files together in an *Ejb-jar* file. This is a compressed file that contains everything we've written above, following the .ZIP compression format. Jar files are convenient, compact modules in which to wrap our beans. Note that you can have more than one bean in an Ejb-jar file, allowing you to ship an entire product set of beans in a single jar file.

The following files must be included in an Ejb-jar file:

- Enterprise bean(s)
- Remote interface(s)
- Home interface(s)
- Deployment descriptor(s), including properties to customize your beans' logic

If you're developing with EJB 1.0, you can also include a *manifest* file containing a list of what's in the Ejb-jar file.

The Manifest

Manifests are simple text files that can be part of a jar file. Usually you put information in the manifest detailing what's in the jar. In EJB 1.0, the manifest file identifies which enterprise beans are inside your Ejb-jar file. In EJB 1.1, manifests are not necessary because the XML deployment descriptor contains all the necessary descriptive information.

Manifests are organized into several *sections*. You *must* separate one section from another with a blank line. Within each section you can put one or more *headers*. Each header is similar to a Java properties file, of the form *<tag>* : *<value>*.

There are two header tags that are relevant to EJB:

Name whose value is the location of a bean's deployment descriptor in the Ejb-jar file. This name must be a "relative" name, meaning the location relative to the root of the jar file.

Enterprise-Bean whose value must be "True."

For example, the manifest that follows identifies the locations of two beans, whose serialized deployment descriptors are named *Bean1DD.ser* and *Bean2DD.ser*:

```
Name: Bean1/deployment/manifest/Bean1DD.ser
Enterprise-Bean: True

Name: Bean2/deployment/manifest/Bean2DD.ser
Enterprise-Bean: True
```

Here's the manifest that goes with our "Hello, World!" example:

```
Name: com/wiley/compBooks/roman/session/helloworld/deployment/
HelloBeanDD.ser
Enterprise-Bean: True
```

The EJB container will look for this manifest in a well-known location in the jar, and it will use the manifest to acquire information about the beans inside the jar. The previous example contains the following information in the manifest:

- The first line locates our serialized deployment descriptor within the jar. Remember, the deployment descriptor tells everything about our bean, so this is the only real locator information we need to supply in our manifest.

- The second line simply indicates to the container that we are indeed supplying an enterprise bean. This is a reality check so the container knows it is dealing with an enterprise bean.

Generating the Ejb-jar

Once we have all the ingredients, we generate the Ejb-jar with the following statement:

```
jar cmf ..\manifest HelloWorld.jar *
```

This command assumes that the manifest file is one directory below the current one. The asterisk indicates the files to include in the jar—this means all the necessary classes, properties files, and deployment descriptors. They must be in properly named subdirectories of the current directory. For example, our *Hello.class* file is located in *com\wiley\compBooks\roman\session\helloworld\ Hello.class*, below the current directory. You must store your classes in a directory corresponding to the package that the class belongs to or the JVM will be unable to locate your classes when it searches your jar.

If you're using a development environment supporting EJB, the development environment may contain an automated way to generate the Ejb-jar file for you.

Deploying the Bean

Finally, we're ready to deploy our bean in an EJB container. This step will vary from container to container. When you reach this point, you should consult your container's documentation on how to deploy a bean. For an example using the BEA *WebLogic* server, see the included CD-ROM.

When deploying an Ejb-jar file into a container, the following steps are usually performed:

- The Ejb-jar file is verified. The container checks that the enterprise bean class, the remote interface, and other items are valid. Any commercial tool should report intelligent errors back to you, such as "You need to define one *ejbCreate()* method in a stateless session bean."

- The container tool generates an EJB object and home object for you.

- The container tool generates any necessary RMI stubs and skeletons (see Appendix A for more information about stubs and skeletons).

Once you've performed these steps, start up your EJB container/server product. Most products will output a server log or have a GUI to view the beans that are deployed. Make sure that your container is indeed making your bean available. For example, when we start the BEA *WebLogic* server, the server yields the following output:

```
...
Tue Feb 23 05:20:07 CST 1999:<I> <EJB> Reading Enterprise JavaBean
descriptor: d:/apps/weblogic/classes/com/wiley/compBooks/roman/session/
helloworld/deployment/HelloBeanDD.ser
```

```
Tue Feb 23 05:20:08 CST 1999:<I> <EJB> EJB home interface
'com.wiley.compBooks.roman.session.helloworld.HelloHome' bound to the
JNDI name 'HelloHome'

Tue Feb 23 05:20:08 CST 1999:<I> <EJB> Deployed d:/apps/weblogic/
classes/com/wiley/compBooks/roman/session/helloworld/deployment/
HelloBeanDD.ser
...
```

As you can see, the server recognized our deployed bean and made it available for clients to call.

Writing Client Code for Our Stateless Bean

Next, let's write a sample client to call our enterprise bean. The complete client source code illustrating the previous steps is shown in Source 4.4.

```java
package com.wiley.compBooks.roman.session.helloworld;

import javax.ejb.*;
import javax.naming.*;
import java.rmi.*;
import java.util.Properties;

/**
 * This class is an example of client code that invokes
 * methods on a simple stateless session bean.
 */
public class HelloClient {

    public static void main(String[] args) {

        try {
            /*
             * Get System properties for JNDI initialization
             */
            Properties props = System.getProperties();

                /*
                 * Form an initial context
                 */
                Context ctx = new InitialContext(props);

            /*
             * Get a reference to the home object
             * (the factory for EJB objects)
             */
```

Source 4.4 HelloClient.java *(continues)*.

```
        HelloHome home = (HelloHome) ctx.lookup("HelloHome");

    /*
     * Use the factory to create the EJB Object
     */
    Hello hello = home.create();

    /*
     * Call the hello() method, and print it
     */
    System.out.println(hello.hello());

    /*
     * Done with EJB Object, so remove it
     */
    hello.remove();
  } catch (Exception e) {
    e.printStackTrace();
  }
 }
}
```

Source 4.4 HelloClient.java *(continued)*.

The client code performs the following tasks:

1. Looks up a home object

2. Uses the home object to create an EJB object

3. Calls *hello()* on the EJB object

4. Removes the EJB object

Each of these steps was described fully in Chapter 3.

Running the System

To try out the deployment, you first must bring up the application server. This step will vary depending on your vendor. For BEA's *WebLogic*, we type the following (assuming a correct CLASSPATH):

```
t3server
```

Next, run the client application. When running the client, you need to supply the client with JNDI environment information. As we explain in Appendix B, JNDI requires at a minimum two properties to retrieve an initial context:

- The name of the initial context factory. An example is *com.sun.jndi.ldap .LdapCtxFactory*.

- The provider URL, indicating the location of the directory structure to use. An example is *ldap://louvre:389/o=Airius.com*.

The actual parameters you need should be part of your EJB container's documentation. For example, with BEA's *WebLogic* application server, we launched our client program with the following JNDI initialization properties:

```
java -Djava.naming.factory.initial=
     weblogic.jndi.TengahInitialContextFactory
    -Djava.naming.provider.url=
     t3://localhost:7001

com.wiley.compBooks.roman.session.helloworld.HelloClient
```

 For your EJB client code to work, you must take care to distribute the correct class files on the right machines. Because client code uses home interfaces and remote interfaces, you must deploy those class files in your client environment. And because clients never directly access your bean implementation, you don't need to (nor should you) deploy your bean classes in your client environment.

The Server-Side Output

When we run the client, our container shows the following debug log (debug logs are great for seeing what your enterprise beans are doing):

```
setSessionContext()
ejbCreate()
hello()
ejbRemove()
```

As you can see, the container associated our bean with a session context, called *create()*, delegated a business method to the bean, and then called *remove()*. Note that because bean pooling algorithms are proprietary, you may see different output for other containers—it's all implementation-specific and part of EJB product differentiation. Keep this in mind when debugging your beans.

The Client-Side Output

After running the client, you should see the following output:

```
Hello, World!
```

Congratulations—it took awhile, but you've successfully completed your first Enterprise JavaBeans deployment!

Summary

In this chapter, we learned how to program stateless session beans. We saw the theory behind programming each of the beans, as well as examples of the beans in action. We also looked at how deployment descriptors work and how EJB client code is written.

In the next chapter, we'll learn how to code *stateful session beans*.

## CHAPTER 5

The Basics of Stateful Session Beans

S tateful session beans are conversational beans because they hold conversations with clients that span multiple method invocations. Stateful session beans store conversational state within the bean. That conversational state is specific to a particular client. This chapter will teach you the basics of writing stateful session beans. We'll begin at the conceptual level and quickly move into a code example illustrating session bean development. We'll wrap up with a comparison of the stateful and stateless programming models.

Characteristics of Stateful Session Beans

Let's begin with a look at the characteristics that all stateful session beans share.

Achieving the Effect of Pooling with Stateful Beans

Imagine a scenario where thousands of clients are having conversations with different stateful session beans running within a container. Let's assume that the clients are typical clients and take a long time to "think" between method calls. Perhaps a client is far away, connecting from another country, and the network lag is high. Or perhaps the client represents a human interacting with a Java applet, and the human is deciding on the next button to click.

Thousands of clients imply thousands of stateful session beans, each holding conversational state on behalf of a specific client. And, of course, our EJB container/server has only a finite amount of resources available, such as memory, database connections, and socket connections. If the conversational state that the beans are holding is large, the container/server could easily run out of resources. This was not a problem with stateless session beans because the container could pool only a few beans to service thousands of clients.

With stateful session beans, pooling is not as simple. When a client invokes a method on a bean, he or she is starting a *conversation* with the bean, and the conversational state stored in the bean must be available for that same client's next method request. Therefore, the container cannot easily pool beans and dynamically assign them to handle arbitrary client method requests, since each bean is storing state on behalf of a particular client. But we still need to achieve the effect of pooling for stateful session beans, so that we can conserve resources and enhance the overall scalability of the system.

This problem should sound quite familiar to operating systems gurus. Whenever you run an application on a computer, you have only a fixed amount of physical memory in which to run. The operating system still must provide a way for many applications to run, even if the applications take up more aggregate memory than is available physically. To provide for this, operating systems use your hard disk as an extension of physical memory. This effectively extends the amount of *virtual memory* that your system has. When an application goes idle, its memory can be *swapped out* from physical memory and onto the hard disk. When the application becomes active again, any needed data is *swapped in* from the hard disk and into physical memory. This type of swapping happens very often when switching between applications (called *context switching*).

EJB containers exploit this very paradigm to conserve stateful session bean resources. To limit the number of stateful session bean instances in memory, the container can *swap out* a stateful bean, saving its conversational state to a hard disk or other storage. This is called *passivation*. After passivating a stateful bean, the conversational state is safely stored away, allowing resources such as memory to be reclaimed. When the original client invokes a method, the passivated conversational state is *swapped in* to a bean. This is called *activation*. This bean now resumes the conversation with the original client. Note that the bean that receives the activated state may not be the original bean instance. But that's all right because the instance is resuming its conversation from the point where the original instance was passivated.

Thus, EJB does indeed support the *effect* of pooling stateful session beans. Only a few instances can be in memory when there are actually many clients. But this pooling effect does not come for free—the passivation/activation steps could entail an I/O bottleneck. Contrast this to stateless session beans, which are easily pooled because there is no state to save.

So how does the container decide which beans to activate and which beans to passivate? The answer is specific to each container. Most containers will employ a *Least Recently Used* (*LRU*) passivation strategy, which simply means to passivate the bean that has been called the least recently. This is a good algorithm because remote clients have the habit of disconnecting from the network, leaving beans stranded without a client, ready to be passivated. If a bean hasn't been invoked in a while, the container will write it to disk.

Passivation can occur at any time, so long as a bean is not involved in a method call. It's up to the container to decide when passivation makes sense. Note that there is one exception to this rule: Any bean involved in a *transaction* (see Chapter 10) cannot be passivated until the transaction completes.

To activate beans, most containers will usually use a *just-in-time* algorithm. Just in time means that beans should be activated on demand, as client requests come in. If a client request comes in but that client's conversation has been passivated, the container will activate the bean on demand, reading the passivated state back into memory.

In general, passivation and activation are not useful for stateless session beans. Stateless beans do not have any state to passivate/activate, and so stateless beans can simply be destroyed arbitrarily by the container. Passivation/activation also applies to entity beans, which we'll learn about in Chapters 7–9.

The Rules Governing Conversational State

As we have said, stateful session beans hold conversational state on behalf of one client. Let's define that state a bit more rigorously. It's important to know the rules for specifying conversational state, so that the container will passivate and activate properly.

The *conversational state* of a bean follows the rules laid out by *Java object serialization* (see Appendix A). When a container passivates a bean, it uses object serialization (or an equivalent protocol) to convert the bean's conversational state into a bit-blob. It can then write that blob out to storage. Once the bean is written to storage, the memory is available to be freed by the garbage collector.

Activation reverses the process—a serialized blob that had been written to storage is read back into memory and converted to in-memory bean data. What makes this whole process work is the *javax.ejb.EnterpriseBean* interface *extends java.io.Serializable*, and every enterprise bean class indirectly implements this interface.

More concretely, every member variable in a bean is considered to be part of the bean's conversational state if the following apply:

- The member variable is a nontransient primitive type, or
- The member variable is a nontransient Java object (extends java.lang.Object).

For every Java object that's part of a bean's conversational state, the previous algorithm is reapplied recursively on those objects. Thus, object serialization constructs an entire graph of data referred to by the main bean. You should note that while your beans must follow the rules for object serialization, the EJB container itself does not necessarily need to use the default serialization protocol; it could use a custom protocol for this, to allow flexibility and differentiation between container vendors.

Activation/Passivation Callbacks

Let's now look at what actually happens to your bean during passivation and activation. When an EJB container passivates a bean, the container writes the bean's conversational state to secondary storage, such as a file or database. The container informs the bean that it's about to perform passivation by calling the bean's required *ejbPassivate()* callback method. *ejbPassivate()* is a warning to the bean that its held conversational state is about to be swapped out.

It's important that the container inform the bean using *ejbPassivate()* so that the bean can relinquish held resources. These held resources include database connections, open sockets, open files, or other resources that do not make sense to be saved to disk or cannot be transparently saved using object serialization. The EJB container calls the *ejbPassivate()* method to give the bean a chance to release these resources or deal with the resources as the bean sees fit. Once the container's *ejbPassivate()* callback method into your bean is complete, your bean must be in a state suitable for passivation. This is shown in Figure 5.1.

The exact opposite process occurs during the activation process. Here, the serialized conversational state is read back into memory, and the container reconstructs the in-memory state using object serialization or the equivalent. The container then calls the bean's required *ejbActivate()* method. *ejbActivate()* gives the bean a chance to restore the open resources it released during *ejbPassivate()*. This entire process is shown in Figure 5.2.

Do you have to worry about implementing *ejbPassivate()* and *ejbActivate()*? Probably not, unless you are using open resources, such as socket connections or database connections, that must be reestablished after activation. In most cases, you can simply leave these methods empty.

A Simple Stateful Session Bean

Let's put our stateful session bean knowledge to use by programming a simple stateful bean. Our bean will be a counter bean, and it will simply be responsible for counting up one by one. The current count will be stored within the bean, and it will increment as client requests arrive. Thus, our bean will be stateful, and it will hold a multimethod conversation with a particular client.

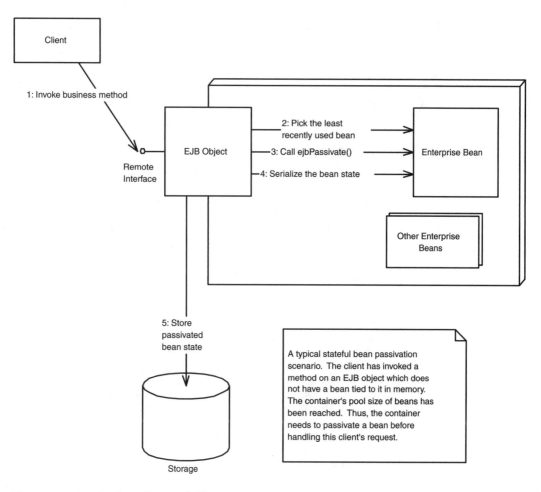

Figure 5.1 Passivation of a stateful bean.

The Count Bean's Remote Interface

First, let's define our bean's remote interface. The code is shown in Source 5.1.

Our remote interface defines a single business method—*count()*—which we will implement in the enterprise bean class.

The Count Bean

Our bean implementation has one business method, *count()*, which is responsible for incrementing an integer member variable, called *val*. The conversational state is the *val* member variable. We show the code for our counter bean in Source 5.2.

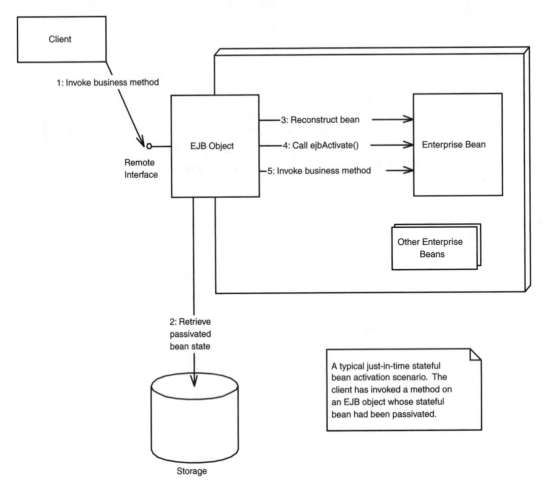

Figure 5.2 Activation of a stateful bean.

```
package com.wiley.compBooks.roman.session.count;

import javax.ejb.*;
import java.rmi.RemoteException;

/**
 * These are CountBean's business logic methods.
 *
 * This interface is what clients operate on when they
 * interact with EJB objects. The container vendor will
 * implement this interface; the implemented object is
```

Source 5.1 Count.java *(continues).*

```
 * the EJB Object, which delegates invocations to the
 * actual bean.
 */
public interface Count extends EJBObject {

  /**
   * Increments the int stored as conversational state
   */
  public int count() throws RemoteException;
}
```

Source 5.1 Count.java *(continued)*.

```
package com.wiley.compBooks.roman.session.count;

import javax.ejb.*;

/**
 * Demonstration Stateful Session Bean.  This bean is
 * initialized to some integer value and has a business
 * method that increments the value.
 *
 * This example shows the basics of how to write a stateful
 * session bean and how passivation/activation works.
 */
public class CountBean implements SessionBean {

    private SessionContext ctx;

    // The current counter is our conversational state.
    public int val;

    //
    // Business methods
    //

    /**
     * Counts up
     */
    public int count() {
        System.out.println("count()");
        return ++val;
    }

    //
    // EJB-required methods
    //
```

Source 5.2 CountBean.java *(continues)*.

```
    public void ejbCreate(int val) throws CreateException {
        this.val = val;
        System.out.println("ejbCreate()");
    }

    public void ejbRemove() {
        System.out.println("ejbRemove()");
    }

    public void ejbActivate() {
        System.out.println("ejbActivate()");
    }

    public void ejbPassivate() {
        System.out.println("ejbPassivate()");
    }

    public void setSessionContext(SessionContext ctx) {
    }
}
```

Source 5.2   CountBean.java *(continued)*.

Here are some things to notice about our bean:

- The bean implements *javax.ejb.SessionBean* (defined in Chapter 3). This means the bean must define all methods in the *SessionBean* interface. Indeed, by looking at the bean, you can see we've defined them but kept them fairly trivial.

- Our *ejbCreate()* initialization method takes a parameter, *val*. This is in stark contrast to stateless session beans, which never take parameters in *ejbCreate()*. Our initialization method is responsible for beginning a conversation with the client. It uses *val* as the starting state of the counter.

- The *val* member variable obeys the rules for conversational state because it is serializable. Thus, it will last across method calls, and it will automatically be preserved during passivation/activation.

The Count Bean's Home Interface

To complete our stateful bean code, we must define a home interface. The home interface will detail how to create and destroy our Count EJB object. The code for our home interface is in Source 5.3.

Because we implement *javax.ejb.EJBHome*, our home interface gets the *remove()* destroy method for free.

```
package com.wiley.compBooks.roman.session.count;

import javax.ejb.*;
import java.rmi.RemoteException;

/**
 * This is the home interface for CountBean.  This interface
 * is implemented by the EJB Server's glue-code tools - the
 * implemented object is called the Home Object and serves
 * as a factory for EJB Objects.
 *
 * One create() method is in this Home Interface, which
 * corresponds to the ejbCreate() method in the CountBean file.
 */
public interface CountHome extends EJBHome {

  /*
   * This method creates the EJB Object.
   *
   * @param val Value to initialize counter to
   *
   * @return The newly created EJB Object.
   */
  Count create(int val) throws RemoteException, CreateException;
}
```

Source 5.3 CountHome.java.

The Count Bean's Deployment Descriptor

Now that we've got all our Java files for our bean, we need to define the deployment descriptor to identify the bean's settings to the container. The deployment descriptor settings we use are listed in Table 5.1.

Notice that we've added a container-specific deployment descriptor setting, "Max beans loaded at any time." Not all containers will support this (the BEA *WebLogic* server we tested against does). We are restricting the maximum number of beans loaded so that we can force the EJB container to passivate and activate our beans. Our strategy will be to load three beans at once, thus forcing the container to passivate in order to reduce the number of beans in memory.

Also notice that our bean's stateful nature is defined declaratively in the deployment descriptor. We never introduce the notion of a bean being stateful in the bean code itself. This allows us to easily switch from the stateful to stateless paradigm and back.

Table 5.1 Deployment Descriptor Settings for CountBean

DEPLOYMENT DESCRIPTOR SETTING	VALUE
Bean home name	CountHome
Enterprise bean class name	com.wiley.compBooks.roman.session.count.CountBean
Home interface class name	com.wiley.compBooks.roman.session.count.CountHome
Remote interface class name	com.wiley.compBooks.roman.session.count.Count
Environment properties	<empty>
Re-entrant	false
Stateful or stateless	STATEFUL_SESSION
Session timeout	10 seconds
Max beans loaded at any time (EJB container-specific)	2

The Count Bean's Environment Properties

This demonstration bean is quite simple, so we do not use environment properties to customize the bean on deployment. Chapter 6 demonstrates beans with properties files.

The Count Bean's Manifest File, Ejb-jar File, and Deployment

To complete our component, we need to write a manifest file for the Ejb-jar file. The jar's manifest is straightforward and no different really from the one we used for our "Hello, World!" bean in Chapter 4. The generation of an Ejb-jar file is similar to our "Hello, World!" example.

Once we generate the Ejb-jar file, we must deploy our bean in an EJB container to test it out. This step varies widely from container to container. If you're using the BEA's *WebLogic* server, take a look at the makefile on the included CD-ROM for this deployment step. If you have a different preferred container vendor, consult your vendor's product documentation.

To save space, in future examples we'll consider that manifest generation, Ejb-jar file generation, and bean deployment are implied steps.

The Count Bean's Client Code

Now that our bean is deployed, we can write some Java code to test our beans. Our client code performs the following steps:

1. We acquire a JNDI initial context.

2. We locate the home object using JNDI.

3. We use the home object to create three different Count EJB objects. Thus, we are creating three different conversations and are simulating three different clients.

4. Our deployment descriptor limits the bean pool size to two beans, so during the previous step some of the three beans must have been passivated. We print out a message during the *ejbPassivate()* callback to illustrate this.

5. Next, we call *count()* on each EJB object. This forces the container to activate the instances, restoring the conversations to memory once again. We print out a mesasge during the *ejbActivate()* callback to illustrate this.

6. Finally, all the EJB objects are removed.

The code appears in Source 5.4.

```
package com.wiley.compBooks.roman.session.count;

import javax.ejb.*;
import javax.naming.*;
import java.util.Properties;

/**
 * This class is a simple example of client code that invokes
 * methods on a simple Stateless Enterprise Bean.
 *
 * We create 3 EJB Objects in this example, but we allow
 * the container to have only 2 in memory.  This illustrates how
 * beans are passivated to storage.
 */
public class CountClient {

    public static void main(String[] args) {

        try {
            /*
             * Get System properties for JNDI initialization
             */
            Properties props = System.getProperties();

            /*
             * Get a reference to the Home Object - the
             * factory for EJB Objects
             */
```

Source 5.4 CountClient.java *(continues).*

```
            Context ctx = new InitialContext(props);
            CountHome home = (CountHome) ctx.lookup("CountHome");

            /*
             * An array to hold 3 Count EJB Objects
             */
            Count count[] = new Count[3];

            int countVal = 0;

            /*
             * Create and count() on each member of array
             */
            System.out.println("Instantiating beans...");
            for (int i=0; i < 3; i++) {
                /*
                 * Create an EJB Object and initialize
                 * it to the current count value.
                 */
                count[i] = home.create(countVal);

                /*
                 * Add 1 and print
                 */
                countVal = count[i].count();

                System.out.println(countVal);

                /*
                 * Sleep for 1/2 second
                 */
                Thread.sleep(500);
            }

            /*
             * Let's call count() on each EJB Object to
             * make sure the beans were passivated and
             * activated properly.
             */
            System.out.println("Calling count() on beans...");
            for (int i=0; i < 3; i++) {

                /*
                 * Add 1 and print
                 */
                countVal = count[i].count();

                System.out.println(countVal);
```

Source 5.4 CountClient.java *(continues)*.

```
            /*
             * Sleep for 1/2 second
             */
            Thread.sleep(500);
        }

        /*
         * Done with EJB Objects, so remove them
         */
        for (int i=0; i < 3; i++) {
            count[i].remove();
        }
    } catch (Exception e) {
        e.printStackTrace();
    }
  }
}
```

Source 5.4 CountClient.java *(continued)*.

Running the Client

To run the client, you need to know the parameters your JNDI service provider uses. This should also be part of your container's documentation. With the BEA *WebLogic* server, we typed the following:

```
java -Djava.naming.factory.initial=
     weblogic.jndi.TengahInitialContextFactory
     -Djava.naming.provider.url=
     t3://localhost:7001
     com.wiley.compBooks.roman.session.count.CountClient
```

The Client-Side Output

After running the client, we see the following output:

```
Instantiating beans...
1
2
3
Calling count() on beans...
2
3
4
```

We first created three beans and then called *count()* on each. As expected, the beans incremented their values by one each during the second pass, so output is as expected. But were our beans really passivated and activated? Let's check the server log.

The Server-Side Output

The container log yields the following results:

```
ejbCreate()
count()
ejbCreate()
count()
ejbCreate()
ejbPassivate()
count()
ejbPassivate()
ejbActivate()
count()
ejbPassivate()
ejbActivate()
count()
ejbPassivate()
ejbActivate()
count()
ejbPassivate()
ejbActivate()
ejbRemove()
ejbActivate()
ejbRemove()
ejbRemove()
```

As you can see from the passivation/activation messages in the log, the container is indeed passivating and activating beans to conserve system resources. Because the client-side output is correct, each of our beans' conversational state was retained properly.

Stateful or Stateless?

Now that we've gone through a few examples, you may be wondering when stateful beans should be used and when stateless beans can get the job done. There are advantages and drawbacks to both stateless and stateful design.

Myths and Facts about Statelessness

Lately, there's been a lot of fuss over statelessness. The limitations of statelessness are often exaggerated, as well as its benefits. Many statelessness proponents blindly declare that statelessness leads to increased scalability, while

---

◄ EJB Design Strategies

What If My Stateful Bean Dies?

Bean failure is an important factor to consider. Because a stateful session bean caches a client conversation in memory, a bean failure may entail losing your conversation. This was not a problem with statelessness—there was no conversation to be lost. Unless you are using an EJB product that routinely checkpoints (i.e., persists) your conversations, your conversations will be lost if an application server fails.

Losing a conversation has devastating impacts. If you have very large conversations that span over time, then you've lost important work. And the more stateful session beans that you use in tandem, the larger the existing network of interconnected objects that each rely on the other's stability. This means that if your code is not prepared for a failure, you may have a very grim situation on your hands. Not an exciting prospect for mission-critical computing, is it?

When designing your stateful beans, you should use the following guidelines:

1. Make sure your problem lends itself to a stateful conversation.

2. Keep your conversations short.

3. If the performance is feasible, consider using an EJB product that checkpoints stateful conversations, to minimize the impacts of bean failure (unfortunately, if you're selling beans, you may not have the luxury of choosing an EJB server).

4. Write "smart" client code that anticipates a bean failure and reestablishes the conversational state with a fresh stateful session bean.

---

stateful backers argue about having to rearchitect entire systems to accommodate statelessness. What's the real story?

Designed right, statelessness has two virtues:

- With stateless beans, the EJB container is able to easily pool and reuse beans, allowing a few beans to service many clients. While the same paradigm applies to stateful beans, the bean state must be passivated and activated between method calls, possibly resulting in I/O bottlenecks. So one practical virtue of statelessness is the ability to easily pool and reuse components at little or no overhead.

- Because a stateful session bean caches a client conversation in memory, a bean failure may entail losing your conversation. This can have severe repercussions if you don't write your beans with this in mind or if you don't use an EJB product that provides stateful recovery.

The largest drawback to statelessness is that you need to push client-specific data into the stateless bean for each method invocation. Most stateless session beans will need to receive some information that is specific to a certain client, such as a bank account number for a banking bean. This information must be resupplied to stateless beans each time a client request arrives because the bean cannot hold any state on behalf of a particular client.

One way to supply the bean with client-specific data is to pass the data as parameters into the bean's methods. This can lead to performance degradation, however, especially if the data being passed is large. This also clogs the network, reducing available bandwidth for other processes.

Another way to get client-specific data to a stateless bean is for the bean to store data persistently on behalf of a client. The client then does not need to pass the entire state in a method invocation, but simply needs to supply an identifier to retrieve the data from persistent storage. The trade-off here is, again, performance—storing conversations persistently could lead to storage I/O bottlenecks, rather than network I/O bottlenecks.

Yet another way to work around the limitations of statelessness is for a bean to store client-specific data in a directory structure using JNDI. The client could later pass the bean an identifier for locating the data in the directory structure. This is quite similar to storing data in a database. The big difference is that a JNDI implementation could be an in-memory implementation (this would give a similar effect to a shared property manager, familiar to MTS/COM+ readers). If client data is stored in memory, there is no database hit.

When choosing between stateful and stateless, you should ask yourself what type of business process your session beans are attempting to emulate. Does the business process span multiple invocations, requiring a conversation? If so, the stateful model fits very nicely because client-specific conversations can be part of the bean state. On the other hand, if your business process lasts for a single method call, the stateless paradigm will better suit your needs.

In reality, most sophisticated deployments are likely to have a complex and interesting combination of stateless and stateful beans. The choice between stateful or stateless may also pale in comparison to other factors in your EJB deployment, such as proper use of transactions. We'll find out how to appropriately use transactions in Chapter 10.

Summary

In this chapter, we learned how to program with stateful session beans. We began with a look at the concepts behind stateful session beans and how they are different from stateless session beans. We then coded up a simple counting program that illustrated stateful session bean programming. We wrapped up with a comparison of the stateful and stateless models.

In the next chapter, we'll take our session bean knowledge and probe deeper. We'll show how to use EJB session contexts, how properties files are used in EJB, and how beans can call other beans. We've just skimmed the surface of EJB programming—there are many interesting concepts ahead.

## CHAPTER 6

Adding Functionality to Your Beans

I n Chapters 3–5, we scratched the surface of EJB with an introduction to session bean programming. Now that you've seen the bare-bones examples, let's put a bit more meat on our beans. In this chapter, you'll see the following:

- How to query the container with EJB contexts
- How to use environment properties to customize your beans, and access those environment properties at runtime
- How to use the EJB security model
- How to use EJB object handles
- How to call beans from other beans
- A non-trivial example illustrating each of these concepts, using both stateless and stateful session beans

Let's begin with a look at EJB contexts.

EJB Contexts: Your Gateway to the Container

As you'll see once you begin your EJB development, non-trivial enterprise beans need to determine information about their current status at runtime. This can include the following:

- Information about the bean's home object or EJB object.
- Information about any transaction the bean is currently involved in. For example, if the current transaction is going to fail, the bean can skip unnecessary computation steps.

■ Security information for client authorization. A bean can query its environment to determine if a client has the required security access level to perform a desired operation.

■ Environment properties that the bean was deployed with.

The container houses all of this information in one object, called an *EJB context object*. An EJB context object is your gateway to the container. EJB contexts are physical parts containers, and can be accessed from within your beans. Thus, a context represents a way for beans to perform callbacks to the container. These callbacks help beans both ascertain their current status and modify their current status.

The motivation behind a context is to encapsulate the bean's domain in one compact object. Note that a bean's status may change over the bean's life cycle, and thus this context object can dynamically change over time as well. At runtime, the container is responsible for changing the context to reflect any status changes, such as the bean becoming involved in a new transaction. Thus, you can think of the context as a middleman for storing status information about a bean—a middleman that is part of the container and is queried by the bean.

Here is what the EJB 1.0 *javax.ejb.EJBContext* interface looks like:

```
public interface javax.ejb.EJBContext
{
    public javax.ejb.EJBHome getEJBHome();
    public java.util.Properties getEnvironment();
    public java.security.Identity getCallerIdentity();
    public boolean isCallerInRole(java.security.Identity);
    public javax.jts.UserTransaction getUserTransaction();
    public void setRollbackOnly();
    public boolean getRollbackOnly();
}
```

We summarize the methods in *javax.ejb.EJBContext* in Table 6.1.

Session Bean Contexts

An EJB context contains callbacks useful for both session beans and entity beans. In comparison, a *session context* is a specific EJB context used only for session beans. Entity beans have their own EJB context, too, called an *entity context*. Both session and entity contexts define extra methods specific to the corresponding kind of bean.

Table 6.1   javax.ejb.EJBContext

METHOD	DESCRIPTION
getHome()	Your bean should call *getHome()* when it needs to access its own home object. The bean can then use its home object to create, destroy, or find EJB objects.
getEnivronment()	Returns a list of environment properties that were deployed with the bean. These properties can be used to set arbitrary information that a bean may need, such as locations of files.
getCallerIdentity()	Returns the *security identity* of the client that is invoking methods on the bean instance's EJB object. You can use the client's identity for many things. For example, you can retrieve the caller's distinguished name, and use it as a key to unlock secured information in a database.
isCallerInRole()	Returns whether the authenticated client is authorized to perform an operation. The client must be in the correct *security role*, which is a group authorized to perform certain operations.
setRollbackOnly()	Allows the instance to mark the current transaction such that the only outcome of the transaction is a rollback.
getRollbackOnly()	Returns a boolean indicating whether the current transaction has been marked for rollback. If it's going to abort, you may be able to bypass logic in your bean, saving valuable computation time.
getUserTransaction() *Note: This method is only supported for beans that perform their own transactions. We'll learn more about this method in Chapter 10.*	Use this method if you want to write code in your bean to control transactions. Once you call this method, your bean can control transactions using the returned *javax.transaction.UserTransaction* object. You can then begin, commit, and rollback transactions explicitly.

Here is what the session context interface looks like:

```
public interface javax.ejb.SessionContext
      extends javax.ejb.EJBContext
{
    public javax.ejb.EJBObject getEJBObject();
}
```

Notice that the *SessionContext* interface extends the *EJBContext* interface, giving session beans access to all the methods that we defined above in *EJBContext*. The one extra method is *getEJBObject()*.

As we saw in Chapter 3, all session beans (and entity beans) must expose a method that the container will call to associate the bean with a particular context. For session beans, this method is called *setSessionContext(SessionContext ctx)*. This method is defined in the *javax.ejb.SessionBean* interface that we showed you in Chapter 3. As we will see in Chapter 7, entity beans have a similar method called *setEntityContext(EntityContext ctx)*.

SessionContext.getEJBObject()

In EJB, beans can act as clients of other beans. The *getEJBObject()* method is useful if your bean needs to call another bean and if you want to pass a reference to your own bean. In Java, an object can obtain a reference to itself with the *this* keyword. In EJB, though, a bean cannot use the *this* keyword and pass it to other beans because all clients invoke methods on beans indirectly through beans' EJB object. Thus, a bean can refer to itself by using a reference to its EJB object, rather than the *this* keyword.

Understanding EJB Security

The next topic we cover is adding security to your enterprise beans. Let's get right down to the meat. There are two security measures that clients must pass when you add security to an EJB system:

First, the client must be *authenticated*. Authentication verifies that the client is who he claims to be. For instance, the client may enter a username/password in a Web browser, and those credentials are checked against a permanent client profile stored in a database or LDAP server. Once the client is authenticated, he is associated with a *security identity* for the remainder of his session.

Then, the client must be *authorized*. Once the client has been authenticated, he must have permission to perform desired operations. For example, in a procurement application, you'd want to ensure that while anyone can submit purchase orders, only supervisors can approve purchase orders.

There is a very important difference here—*authentication* verifies that the client is who he claims to be, whereas *authorization* checks to see if an already authenticated client is allowed to perform a task. Authentication must be performed sometime before an EJB method is called. If the client has an identity, then it has been authenticated. Authorization, on the other hand, occurs during an EJB method call.

Step 1: Authentication

EJB does not help you with authentication. The specific way your client code becomes associated with a security identity is left to the discretion of your application and your EJB container. This means each EJB container may handle authentication differently. For example, with BEA *WebLogic* your client code can specify its username and password when it uses JNDI to look up home objects, as shown in the following code:

```
Properties props = System.getProperties();

props.put(Context.SECURITY_PRINCIPAL, "EmployeeA");
props.put(Context.SECURITY_CREDENTIALS, "myPassword1");

Context ctx = new InitialContext(props);

// Use the initial context to lookup home objects...
```

Since the EJB specification does not specify how to perform authentication, this code is not portable to other application servers. Check your container's documentation for authentication instructions.

When you run this code, the application server must map your username and password to a security identity. Again, this step is application server specific. Some application servers allow you to set up usernames and passwords in the application server's properties file that the application server reads in at runtime. More advanced servers support complex integration with existing security systems, such as a list of usernames and passwords stored in an LDAP server.

As an academic example, here is how to specify usernames and passwords using BEA *WebLogic*'s *weblogic.properties* file. Note that this is insufficient for real deployments that need to map to real security systems, such as an IT shop's existing list of employee usernames/passwords.

```
weblogic.password.EmployeeA=myPassword1
weblogic.password.EmployeeB=myPassword2
...
```

Step 2: Authorization

Once the client has been authenticated, it must then pass an authorization test to call methods on your beans. There are two ways to perform authorization with EJB: declaratively or programmatically.

With *declarative authorization*, the container performs all authorization checks for you. Effectively you are delegating authorization to the EJB container. This keeps your bean code lean and allows you to focus on your business logic, rather than focus on writing security checks.

With *programmatic authorization*, **you hard-code security checks into your bean code.** Your business logic is interlaced with security checks, bloating your bean code.

Security Roles

Authorization in EJB relies on *security roles*. A security role is a collection of client identities. For a client to be authorized to perform an operation, its security identity must be in the correct security role for that operation. The EJB deployer is responsible for associating the identities with the correct security roles *after* you write your beans.

The advantage to using security roles is you do not hard-code specific identities into your beans. This is necessary when you are developing beans for deployment in a wide variety of security environments, because each environment will have its own list of identities. This also allows you to modify access control without recompiling your bean code.

Specifying security roles in EJB is again application server-specific. The following demonstrates how to do it with BEA's *WebLogic* server in the *weblogic.properties* file:

```
weblogic.security.group.employees=EmployeeA, EmployeeB
weblogic.security.group.managers=ManagerA
weblogic.security.group.administrators=AdminA
...
```

The application server queries these groups at runtime when performing authorization.

Declarative Authorization

With declarative authorization, you *declare* your bean's authorization requirements in your deployment descriptor. The container will fulfill these requirements at runtime. For example, take the following sample deployment descriptor entry using BEA's *WebLogic* server:

```
(accessControlEntries
    submitPurchaseOrder    [employees]
    approvePurchaseOrder   [managers]
    DEFAULT                [administrators]
  ); end accessControlEntries
```

The first entry specifies that all identities authorized as *employees* can submit purchase orders, but the second entry specifies that only identities authorized as *managers* can approve purchase orders. The last entry specifies that *administrators* have access to call all other methods on this bean. The EJB container will automatically perform these security checks on your bean's methods at runtime, and throw a *java.lang.SecurityException* back to the client code if the client identity is not authenticated or authorized.

Programmatic Authorization

To perform explicit security authorization checks in your enterprise beans, you must query the EJB context to retrieve information about the current client. There are two relevant methods: *isCallerInRole(Identity role)* and *getCallerIdentity()*.

isCallerInRole()

isCallerInRole(Identity role) checks whether the current caller is in a particular security role. When you call this method, you pass the security role that you want the caller compared against. The difference between *isCallerInRole(Identity role)* and declarative security is *isCallerInRole(Identity role)* does not check the security roles you've defined in the deployment descriptor at all, but rather checks the security role you define in your code. For example:

```
import java.security.Identity;

...

public class MyBean implements SessionBean {

    private SessionContext ctx;

    ...

    public void foo() {
        Identity id = new MyIdentity("administrators");
        if (ctx.isCallerInRole(id)) {
            System.out.println("An admin called me");
            return;
        }
        System.out.println("A non-admin called me");
    }
}
```

The above code demonstrates how to perform different actions based upon the security role of the client. Only if the caller is in the role defined by *MyIdentity* does the caller have administrator access.

Note that we must also define the *MyIdentity* class—it is a concrete implementation of the *java.security.Identity* abstract class. For demonstration purposes this is quite simple, and is shown below.

```
import java.security.Identity;
```

```
public class MyIdentity extends Identity {

 public MyIdentity(String id) {
    super(id);
 }
}
```

getCallerIdentity()

getCallerIdentity() retrieves the current caller's security identity. You can then use that identity for many purposes, such as using the caller's distinguished name in a database query. Here is sample code that uses *getCallerIdentity()*:

```
import java.security.Identity;

...

public class MyBean implements SessionBean {

    private SessionContext ctx;

...

    public void bar() {
        Identity id = ctx.getCallerIdentity();
        String name = id.getName();
        System.out.println("The caller's name is " + name);
    }
}
```

Declarative or Programmatic?

As with persistence and transactions, security is a middleware service that you should strive to externalize from your beans. By using declarative security, you decouple your beans' business purpose from specific security policies, enabling others to modify security rules without modifying bean code.

In the ideal world, we'd code all our beans with declarative security. But unfortunately, the EJB 1.0 specification does not provide adequate facilities for this; specifically, there is no portable way to declaratively perform *instance-level authorization*. This is best illustrated with an example.

Let's say you have an enterprise bean that models a bank account. The caller of the enterprise bean is a bank account manager who wants to withdraw or deposit into that bank account. But this bank account manager is only responsible for bank accounts with balances below $1000, and we don't want him modifying bank accounts with balances larger than that. With EJB security, there is no way to declare in your deployment descriptor that bank account managers can only modify certain bean instances. You can only specify security roles on the enterprise bean class, and those security rules will apply for all instances of that class. For these situations, you should resort to programmatic security.

Security Propagation

Behind the scenes, all security checks are made possible due to *security contexts*. Security contexts encapsulate the current caller's security state. You never see security contexts in your application code, because the container uses them behind the scenes. When you call a method in EJB, the container can propagate your security information by implicitly passing your security context within the stubs and skeletons.

You can control how security information is propagated in your deployment descriptor via the *runAsMode* and the *runAsIdentity* entries. Let's examine each of these.

runAsMode and runAsIdentity

Your bean's *runAsMode* specifies the security identity your bean assumes when it performs operations (such as calling other beans). There are three settings you can specify for *runAsMode*:

CLIENT_IDENTITY: The bean propagates the client's security context. Whatever security identity the client was associated with is the security identity that the bean will use when it executes.

SYSTEM_IDENTITY: The bean runs as with system-level authority.

SPECIFIED_IDENTITY: The bean runs as the identity specified by *runAsIdentity* deployment descriptor setting.

Your EJB container is responsible for intercepting all method calls and ensuring that your bean is running in the *runAsMode* and *runAsIdentity* settings you specify. For example, if you set the *runAsMode* to "SPECIFIED_IDENTITY", and you set the *runAsIdentity* to "admin", then the container must enforce that your bean runs as the "admin" identity when calling other beans.

Security Context Propagation Portability

Unfortunately, the EJB 1.0 and EJB 1.1 specifications do not specify how containers should propagate security contexts. What this means to you is that any two EJB containers are likely to be incompatible in how they deal with security. If you call a method from container A into container B, container B will not understand how to receive the security context sent by container A. There has been discussion of a new EJB/IIOP protocol that defines security context propagation in a portable way as part of EJB 2.0, but that is not likely to emerge until well into the year 2000.

Understanding EJB Object Handles

Many EJB applications require the ability for clients to disconnect from beans, and then reconnect again later to resume using that bean. For example, if you have a shopping cart that you'd like to save for a later time, and that shopping cart is manifested by a stateful session bean, you'd want your shopping cart state maintained when you reconnect later.

EJB provides for this need with *EJB object handles*. An EJB object handle is a long-lived proxy for an EJB object. If for some reason you disconnect from the EJB container/server, you can use the EJB object handle to reconnect to your EJB object, so that you don't lose your conversational state with that bean. An EJB object handle is an essentially persistent reference to an EJB object. The following code demonstrates using EJB object handles:

```
// First, get the EJB object handle from the EJB object.
javax.ejb.Handle myHandle = myEJBObject.getHandle();

// Next, serialize myHandle, and then save it in
// permanent storage.
ObjectOutputStream stream = ...;
stream.writeObject(myHandle);

// time passes...

// When we want to use the EJB object again,
// deserialize the EJB object handle
ObjectInputStream stream = ...;
Handle myHandle = (Handle) stream.readObject();

// Convert the EJB object handle back into an EJB object
MyRemoteInterface myEJBObject =
    (MyRemoteInterface) myHandle.getEJBObject();

// Resume calling methods again
myEJBObject.callMethod();
```

If you're using an EJB container based on Java RMI-IIOP (see Chapter 11) rather than plain vanilla RMI (see Appendix A), you need to use the following statement to convert the EJB object handle into an EJB object instead:

```
// Convert the EJB object handle into an EJB object
MyRemoteInterface myEJBObject = (MyRemoteInterface)
```

```
javax.rmi.PortableRemoteObject.narrow(
myHandle.getEJBObject(), MyRemoteInterface.class);
```

Unfortunately, EJB object handles have a strong domain limitation: Handles cannot be saved in one environment and then re-stored in a different environment. This means handles are not portable across EJB containers. It also means you cannot save a handle on one machine and then re-use it on a different machine.

Example: The Puzzle Game "Fazuul"

Let's put the concepts we've just explored to concrete use. This bean deployment will be a bit more advanced than the ones we've seen so far, as it will illustrate the new concepts we've learned in this chapter, building on our knowledge from Chapters 4 and 5. This example will also show you how to use both stateful and stateless session beans together.

In this example, we're going to have some fun and write a simple puzzle game using EJB. This game is called *Fazuul* and is based on an old Bulletin Board System (BBS) game written by Tim Stryker and Galacticomm, Inc.

What Is Fazuul?

Our Fazuul game puts you in a strange world of *components*—funny-looking objects that are on the ground. You have an infinite supply of these components because you can create them at will. You create components by pushing a button on a machine—whenever you push the button, three new components pop out. This is shown in Figure 6.1.

Your objective is to *combine* these basic components into new, more advanced components. These advanced new components can be combined with other components, yielding even more interesting devices. Whenever you combine two components, they are destroyed and a brand new one is born. Your job is to continue to combine components until you've reached the final, ultimate component, at which point you've won the game.

The three basic components our Fazuul machine generates are called *Snarfs*, *Vrommells*, and *Rectors*. These are definitely strange names, and they are part of the mysterious world that is Fazuul. These three components can be combined to form greater objects, such as *Lucias* and *Subberts*, as shown in Figure 6.2.

How do you know which components to combine? You must look at each component's description, which give you hints. Use the hints properly, and you'll combine the correct components and ultimately win the game. Combine components haphazardly, and you could generate a more primitive component. This is a very simple concept, and it makes for an interesting, challenging game.

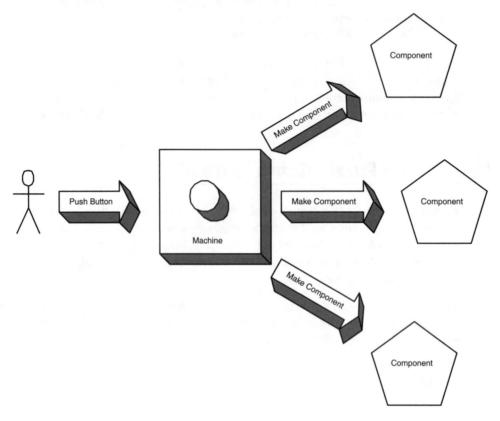

Figure 6.1 The Fazuul Machine.

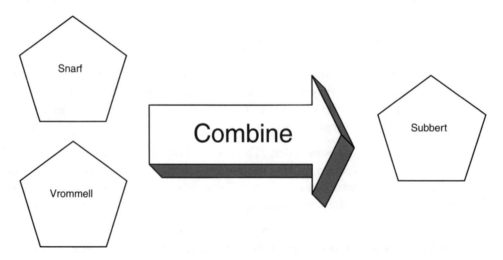

Figure 6.2 Some basic components in Fazuul.

Specifying Fazuul in EJB

Our Fazuul game is broken up into the following parts:

- A *Component* session bean. Components are the objects in the Fazuul world, such as a *Snarf* component or a *Vrommell* component. Components are owned by a particular client, and they are thus modeled well by *stateful* session beans. Our component bean will support the following methods:

  ejbCreate( ) initializes a component to a certain name, such as *Snarf*.

  attachTo( ) tries to attach this component to another component. If successful, the new component will be returned.

  getName( ) returns the string name of this component, such as "Snarf."

  getDescription( ) returns the long description of this component. The long description gives hints about how to combine it with other components.

- A *Machine* session bean, responsible for making new components. Because this machine simply generates components, there is no state associated with it—it is hence best modeled as a stateless session bean. The following method is supported:

  makeComponent( ) generates a new, random component.

- Security functionality. The user should not be able to create components directly, but must use the machine as a facade. Otherwise, the user could create the winning component right away.

- The ability to save and restore the game state. The user should be able to quit the game and later resume where he left off. We'll accomplish this using EJB object handles.

- A text-based client application that interacts with the user. This application has a simple main game loop that calls the appropriate bean methods to perform the game.

Making the Game Data-Driven through Environment Properties

Our game supports a single enterprise bean for representing components in our Fazuul world—the *Component* bean. This bean can represent any kind of component, such as a *Snarf* or a *Vrommell*. Components know what kind of objects they are by examining their name string (e.g., "Snarf"), which is passed in during *ejbCreate()*. But how do they know which components they can attach to, in order to form a new component? And how do the components know what their long descriptions are?

We'll provide this functionality in the application-specific environment properties that will ship with our component bean. Our environment properties will provide a mapping from component names, such as "Snarf," to their long descriptions, such as "This is a Snarf. Snarfs can attach to Vrommells, but don't like Fwiffos."

We'll also make use of the environment properties to keep our list of which components can combine with other components. For example, we'll add the line, "Snarf+Vrommell=Subbert." When the client code calls a component's *attachTo()* method, the component will check the available combinations and throw a *ComponentException* if the two components can't be attached together. Otherwise, the newly generated component will be returned.

Finally, remember that our machine is responsible for generating components. We'll need to supply it with a list of creatable components. This list will be in separate environment properties deployed with the machine bean. By having a separate list, we can control which components our machine creates; after all, we don't want our machine to generate the final, "winning" component—that would make the game too easy!

Implementing Fazuul

Our Fazuul deployment will consist of the following files:

Component.java. The remote interface for ComponentBean.

ComponentBean.java. The enterprise bean class implementation of our components, such as Snarfs.

EJB Design Strategies

Making Your Beans Data-driven

We are using a completely data-driven model in this chapter's example. All of our game-specific logic is being externalized into environment properties. Data-driven models make your applications easily extensible and evolutionary. For example, we can add new components, new descriptions, and new solution paths to our game without recompiling a single line of code. All we'd have to do is change the environment properties. We could easily build on a GUI to allow nontechnical end users to customize our beans as well. The data-driven paradigm is extremely beneficial when you're selling enterprise beans to other companies because you can protect your beans' source code yet still provide a way for the customer to tune your beans. Of course, environment properties aren't the most extensible way to have a data-driven model—a more sophisticated mechanism is to use a resource such as a database. For our game, environment properties will suffice.

ComponentHome.java. The home interface for ComponentBean.

ComponentException.java. Application-level exceptions that our Component-Bean throws when trying to attach to another bean.

The ComponentBean deployment descriptor and environment properties. The deployment descriptor lists the middleware requirements of our bean. The container reads in the deployment descriptor at deployment time. The environment properties allow users of our component bean to customize our bean logic. Our component bean will read the environment properties in at runtime.

Machine.java. The remote interface for MachineBean.

MachineBean.java. The bean implementation of our machine that generates components.

MachineHome.java. The home interface for MachineBean.

MachineException.java. Application-level exceptions that our *MachineBean* throws. Remember that application-level exceptions are "regular, run-of-the-mill exceptions," whereas system-level exceptions are serious problems, such as a database crash.

The MachineBean deployment descriptor and environment properties. The deployment descriptor lists the middleware requirements of our bean. The container reads in the deployment descriptor at deployment time. The environment properties allow users of our machine bean to customize our bean logic. Our machine bean will read the environment properties in at runtime.

Client.java. The client code that calls our beans and provides a text-based interface.

Let's take a look at each of these in detail.

The Component Remote Interface

Component.java is the remote interface for our components. Our interface exposes three business methods. The EJB container will implement this interface; the implementation is the EJB object. The EJB object has container-specific logic for delegating method calls to our enterprise bean implementation. The code is shown in Source 6.1.

The key method of this interface is:

```
Component attachTo(Component other)
```

This method will try to attach two components together and return the resulting component.

```
package com.wiley.compBooks.session.Fazuul;

import javax.ejb.*;
import java.rmi.RemoteException;
import java.rmi.Remote;

/**
 * These are the business logic methods exposed publicly
 * byComponentBean.
 */
public interface Component extends EJBObject {

  /**
   * Attaches this component to another component.  If
   * attach is successful, the Bean will call remove()
   * on the two EJB objects and generate a new,
   * combined Component.
   *
   * @return newly formed Component if successful
   * @exception ComponentException thrown if two
   *  Components can't fit together
   */
  public Component attachTo(Component other) throws RemoteException,
ComponentException;

  /**
   * Returns the short name of this component
   */
  public String getName() throws RemoteException;

  /**
   * Returns the long description of this component
   */
  public String getDescription() throws RemoteException;
}
```

Source 6.1   Component.java.

The Component Bean Implementation

The implementation of our component bean is in *ComponentBean.java*. Our ComponentBean is a stateful session bean. The *conversational state* consists of the name and description of the component. This state will be automatically saved if our component bean is passivated by the EJB container. The code is shown in Source 6.2.

```java
package com.wiley.compBooks.session.Fazuul;

import javax.ejb.*;
import java.util.*;
import java.rmi.*;

/**
 * Stateful Session Bean.
 */
public class ComponentBean implements SessionBean {

  // Constants used for reading properties object
  public static final String ENV_MATCHES = "MATCHES";
  public static final String ENV_DESCRIPTION = "DESCRIPTION_";

  // Conversational state
  public String name;
  public String description;

  private SessionContext ctx;

  public void ejbCreate(String name) {
    this.name = name;

    /*
     * Get the description of our Bean by querying
     * the SessionContext and retrieving the
     * application-specific properties.
     */
    Properties props = ctx.getEnvironment();
    description = (String) props.get(ENV_DESCRIPTION + name);
  }

  public void ejbRemove() {
  }

  public void ejbActivate() {
  }

  public void ejbPassivate() {
  }

  public void setSessionContext(SessionContext ctx) {
    this.ctx = ctx;
  }
```

Source 6.2 ComponentBean.java *(continues)*.

```
/**
 * Attaches this component to another component. If
 * attach is successful, the Bean will call remove()
 * on the two EJB objects and generate a new,
 * combined Component.
 *
 * @return newly formed Component if successful
 * @exception ComponentException thrown if two
 * Components can't fit together
 */
public Component attachTo(Component other) throws RemoteException,
ComponentException {

    /*
     * Retrieve the application-specific environment
     * properties from the current context.
     */
    Properties props = ctx.getEnvironment();

    /*
     * Get the list of matching components from the properties
     */
    String matchString = (String) props.get(ENV_MATCHES);
    Enumeration matches = new StringTokenizer(matchString, ",");

    /*
     * Loop through each match listing. Match listings
     * are of the form x+y=z, such as Snarf+Vrommell=Subbert.
     * Check to see if any of the matches involve our
     * components.
     */
    while (matches.hasMoreElements()) {
        String equationString = (String) matches.nextElement();

        Enumeration equation = new StringTokenizer(equationString, "+=");
        String nameA  = (String) equation.nextElement();
        String nameB  = (String) equation.nextElement();
        String result = (String) equation.nextElement();

        /*
         * If there's a match, make the new, combined component
         */
        if (( nameA.equals(this.getName())
            && nameB.equals(other.getName()) ) ||
              ( nameB.equals(this.getName())
            && nameA.equals(other.getName()) ) ) {
```

Source 6.2 ComponentBean.java *(continues)*.

```
            /*
             * Get my Home Object from Session Context.
             */
            ComponentHome home = (ComponentHome) ctx.getEJBHome();

            /*
             * Create a new Component, and return it
             */
            try {
                return home.create(result);
            }
            catch (Exception e) {
                throw new ComponentException(e.toString());
            }
        }
    }

    /*
     * Two components don't fit together, so throw an exception
     */
    throw new ComponentException("Those components do not fit together!");
}

/**
 * Returns the short name of this component
 */
public String getName() throws RemoteException {
  return name;
}

/**
 * Returns the long description of this component
 */
public String getDescription() throws RemoteException {
  return description;
}
}
```

Source 6.2 ComponentBean.java *(continued).*

Notice our *ejbCreate()* method. It illustrates a session bean retrieving its environment properties from the session context. Our bean can access its environment during *ejbCreate()* because *setSessionContext()* is always called prior to *ejbCreate()*. In fact, you can access the session context any time between *ejbCreate()* and *ejbRemove()*, including within *ejbCreate()* and *ejbRemove()*.

Now take a look at the following segment in the *attachTo()* method, which illustrates how to create an enterprise bean from another bean:

```
ComponentHome home = (ComponentHome) ctx.getEJBHome();
...
return home.create(result);
```

When we call *attachTo()* on a component, the component combines itself with another component, making a new, combined component. In order to create a component, the bean needs to retrieve *its own home object* from the session context. The bean then can call *create()* on the home object, which generates a fresh component EJB object, and can return that to the client.

The Component Home Interface

Next, we have the home interface for our components, shown in Source 6.3.

The home interface has a *create()* method that initializes our component to a certain name, such as "Snarf." This *create()* method gets called in two places:

- When the Machine bean wants to make a component, it calls *create()* to generate a basic component.
- When the Component bean merges two components, it calls *create()* to generate a new, merged component.

The Component Custom Exception Class

The final Java file for our component bean is the custom exception class that it throws, shown in Source 6.4.

```java
package com.wiley.compBooks.session.Fazuul;

import javax.ejb.*;
import java.rmi.RemoteException;

/**
 * This is the home interface for ComponentBean.
 */
public interface ComponentHome extends EJBHome {

    /*
     * This method creates the EJB object for a Component whose Name is name.
     *
     * @return The newly created EJB object.
     */
    Component create(String name) throws RemoteException, CreateException;
}
```

Source 6.3 ComponentHome.java.

```
package com.wiley.compBooks.session.Fazuul;

/**
 * Exceptions thrown by Components
 */
public class ComponentException extends Exception {

    public ComponentException() {
        super();
    }

    public ComponentException(Exception e) {
        super(e.toString());
    }

    public ComponentException(String s) {
        super(s);
    }
}
```

Source 6.4 ComponentException.java.

ComponentException simply delegates all method calls to its parent, *java.lang .Exception*. It's nice to have a custom Exception class as a way of distinguishing the nature of certain exceptions. For example, because we have a *Component-Exception,* we can use it as a way of generating application-level exceptions, rather than using the stock *java.rmi.RemoteException* that all EJB objects throw—remote exceptions are intended for system-level problems, such as machines going down, application servers crashing, or networks failing.

The Component Deployment Descriptor

We now have our component's deployment descriptor. It's shown in Table 6.2.

The two important deployment descriptor settings to notice are the last two, which are related to security. We specify that the component's *ejbCreate()* method may only be called by a client who is assuming the security role of *creators.* We define the *creators* role in the *weblogic.properties* file as follows:

```
weblogic.password.creator=foobarbaz
weblogic.security.group.creators=creator
```

This creates an identity *creator* with password *foobarbaz,* and creates a security role called *creators* which contains a single user, *creator.*

Table 6.2 Deployment Descriptor Settings for ComponentBean

DEPLOYMENT DESCRIPTOR SETTING	VALUE
Bean home name	ComponentHome
Enterprise bean class name	com.wiley.compBooks.roman.session.fazuul .ComponentBean
Home interface class name	com.wiley.compBooks.roman.session.fazuul .ComponentHome
Remote interface class name	com.wiley.compBooks.roman.session.fazuul.Component
Environment properties	See Table 6.3
Re-entrant	False
Stateful or stateless	STATEFUL_SESSION
Session timeout	10 seconds
Declarative security on methods	*ejbCreate* requires client to be in security role *creators*
runAsMode	SPECIFIED_IDENTITY
runAsIdentity	*creator*

The runAsMode is set to SPECIFIED_IDENTITY, with a runAsIdentity equal to *creator*. This means all methods in our component bean run as the *creator* user. We need this access level because components can create other components, and thus need the *creator* level of authorization to create other components.

We also have a number of environment properties that we use for our component. They are shown in Table 6.3.

A component bean queries the DESCRIPTION properties to get its long description. The MATCHES property lists a set of equations, indicating which two components can be combined to form a new, combined component.

The Machine Remote Interface

Now let's move on to our second bean—a Machine bean, used to generate components. We'll start with our remote interface, shown in *Machine.java* in Source 6.5.

Our remote interface is very simple—it has one method, *makeComponent()*, that creates a random component.

Table 6.3 Environment Properties for ComponentBean

ENVIRONMENT PROPERTY SETTING	VALUE
DESCRIPTION_Snarf	"This is a snarf. It came all the way from snarfland. It looks like a large peanut with a hole in the side of it. The hole looks big enough to fit a Vrommell inside."
DESCRIPTION_Vrommell	"This Vrommell is a funny banana-shaped thing. It looks like it will fit snugly into a Snarf."
DESCRIPTION_Rector	"Oh no, it's Rector! Rectors are dangerous, disease-spreading devices. You don't want to hold on to this one for very long. Perhaps if you fed the Rector a peanut or disc, it would be pacified." ... there are more descriptions as well ...
MATCHES	Snarf+Vrommell=Subbert Snarf+Rector=Lucia ... there are more matches as well ...

```
package com.wiley.compBooks.session.Fazuul;

import javax.ejb.*;
import java.rmi.RemoteException;
import java.rmi.Remote;

/**
 * These are the business logic methods exposed publicly by MachineBean.
 */
public interface Machine extends EJBObject {

  /**
   * Makes a new, random Component
   */
  public Component makeComponent() throws RemoteException;
}
```

Source 6.5 Machine.java.

The Machine Bean Implementation

Next, we have our machine's enterprise bean class implementation in *MachineBean .java*, shown in Source 6.6. This is a stateless session bean, and thus it has blank *ejbPassivate()* and *ejbActivate()* methods. We also have a no-argument initializer, *ejbCreate()*—this is required for all stateless session beans.

```java
package com.wiley.compBooks.session.Fazuul;

import javax.ejb.*;
import java.util.*;
import javax.naming.*;

/**
 * Stateless Session Bean.  Simple factory for generating random Components.
 */
public class MachineBean implements SessionBean {

  // Constants used for properties file reading
  public static final String COMPONENT_LIST = "COMPONENT_LIST";

  private SessionContext ctx;

  //
  // EJB-required methods
  //

  public void ejbCreate() {
  }

  public void ejbRemove() {
  }

  public void ejbActivate() {
  }

  public void ejbPassivate() {
  }

  public void setSessionContext(SessionContext ctx) {
    this.ctx = ctx;
  }

  //
  // Business methods
  //

  /**
   * Makes a new, random component
   */
  public Component makeComponent() throws MachineException {
    /*
     * Get properties from Session Context, and retrieve
     * app-specific property that lists the available
     * components for creation.
     */
```

Source 6.6 MachineBean.java *(continues).*

```
    Properties props = ctx.getEnvironment();
    String componentString = (String) props.get(COMPONENT_LIST);
    StringTokenizer components = new StringTokenizer(componentString, ",");

    /*
     * Find a random component name
     */
    int componentNumber = (new Random().nextInt() % components.countTokens());
    if (componentNumber < 0) {
        componentNumber *= -1;
    }

    String componentName = null;
    for (int i=0; i <= componentNumber; i++) {
        componentName = (String) components.nextToken();
    }

    try {
        /*
         * Get a reference to the ComponentHome Object
         * via JNDI.  We need the Component's Home Object
         * to create Components.
         *
         * We rely on app-specific properties to define
         * the Initial Context params which JNDI needs.
         */
        Context ctx = new InitialContext(props);
        ComponentHome home = (ComponentHome) ctx.lookup("ComponentHome");

        /*
         * Use the factory to create the new,
         * merged component, and return it.
         */
        return home.create(componentName);
    }
    catch (Exception e) {
        throw new MachineException(e);
    }
  }
}
```

Source 6.6 MachineBean.java *(continued)*.

Notice the *makeComponent()* method. Here we are using JNDI from *within* a bean. Specifically, we are looking up the bean's home object using JNDI in order to create a new, random component EJB object.

Our approach first queries the session context to get the environment properties. These environment properties specify the necessary startup parameters required by JNDI (see Appendix B for a full review of JNDI). We use those environment properties to form a JNDI initial context, and then use that to retrieve our home object.

The JNDI initialization parameters are part of the application-specific properties deployed with our *MachineBean*, which we'll see later. Thus, our *MachineBean*, as well as our client, needs to have JNDI initialization parameters, such as the location of the directory structure (e.g., *ldap://louvre:389/o=Airius.com*).

There are several alternatives to this approach:

- Have the client pass in the JNDI initialization properties to the MachineBean's *makeComponent()* method.
- Have the client retrieve the component home object, and pass in the home object as a parameter to our MachineBean's *makeComponent()*.

Both of these alternative approaches would rid us of the need to duplicate-code JNDI initialization parameters in both the client and the bean, reducing maintenance. In a production environment, however, you may want to keep the approach we've shown. When your beans look up other beans, the beans you look up may be hosted in a different application server, which may have a different directory protocol.

The Machine Home Interface

Next, we have the home interface for our MachineBean's EJB object—*MachineHome.java*. It's shown in Source 6.7.

Our home interface has a simple, blank *create()* method, which corresponds to our MachineBean's empty *ejbCreate()* method.

The Machine Custom Exception Class

Our last MachineBean Java file is our custom Exception class, shown in Source 6.8. This exception is virtually identical to our ComponentException shown earlier.

The Machine Deployment Descriptor

Finally, we have the MachineBean deployment descriptor (DD). It's shown in Table 6.4.

The only difference between this and the component's DD is that the machine is a stateless session bean, rather than stateful. We also have a number of environment properties, shown in Table 6.5.

```java
package com.wiley.compBooks.session.Fazuul;

import javax.ejb.*;
import java.rmi.RemoteException;

/**
 * This is the home interface for MachineBean. This interface is implemented
 * by the EJB Server's glue-code tools - the implemented object is called
 * the Home Object and serves as a factory for EJB objects.
 *
 * One create() method is in this Home Interface, which corresponds to the
 * ejbCreate() method in the MachineBean file.
 */
public interface MachineHome extends EJBHome {

   /*
    * This method creates the EJB object.
    *
    * @return The newly created EJB object.
    */
   public Machine create() throws RemoteException, CreateException;
}
```

Source 6.7   MachineHome.java.

```java
package com.wiley.compBooks.session.Fazuul;

/**
 * Exceptions thrown by Machine
 */
public class MachineException extends Exception {

    public MachineException() {
        super();
    }

    public MachineException(Exception e) {
        super(e.toString());
    }

    public MachineException(String s) {
        super(s);
    }
}
```

Source 6.8   MachineException.java

Table 6.4 Deployment Descriptor Settings for MachineBean

DEPLOYMENT DESCRIPTOR SETTING	VALUE
Bean home name	MachineHome
Enterprise bean class name	com.wiley.compBooks.roman.session.fazuul.MachineBean
Home interface class name	com.wiley.compBooks.roman.session.fazuul.MachineHome
Remote interface class name	com.wiley.compBooks.roman.session.fazuul.Machine
Environment properties	See Table 6.5
Re-entrant	false
Stateful or stateless	STATELESS_SESSION
Session timeout	10 seconds
Declarative security on methods	none
runAsMode	SPECIFIED_IDENTITY
runAsIdentity	*creator*

Table 6.5 Environment Properties for MachineBean

ENVIRONMENT PROPERTY SETTING	VALUE
java.naming.factory.initial	"weblogic.jndi.TengahInitialContextFactory"
java.naming.provider.url	"t3://localhost:7001"
COMPONENT_LIST	"Snarf,Vrommell,Rector"

The *java.naming.factory.initial* and *java.naming.provider.url* settings are used for JNDI initialization. The ones shown in the table are for the BEA WebLogic JNDI implementation. The EJB container you use should have documentation detailing which settings to use here.

Our machine bean can query the COMPONENT_LIST setting to see which components it can create.

Client.java

The final piece of code we have is the client application that calls our beans. This is shown in Source 6.9.

```java
package com.wiley.compBooks.roman.session.fazuul;

import javax.ejb.*;
import javax.naming.*;
import java.rmi.*;
import java.util.*;
import java.io.*;

/**
 * Client for Fazuul Game.
 */
public class Client {

    public static void main(String[] args) {

        new Client().start();
    }

    // Current list of Component EJB Objects I own
    private Vector components = new Vector();

    // A Machine which dispenses Component EJB Objects
    private Machine machine;

    /**
     * Starts the game.  The main game loop is here.
     */
    public void start() {

        try {
            /*
             * Get System properties for JNDI initialization
             */
            Properties props = System.getProperties();

            /*
             * Get a reference to the MachineHome Object - the
             * factory for Machine EJB Objects
             */
            Context ctx = new InitialContext(props);
            MachineHome home = (MachineHome) ctx.lookup("MachineHome");

            /*
             * Use the factory to create the Machine EJB Object
             */
            machine = home.create();
        }
        catch (Exception e) {
            e.printStackTrace();
```

Source 6.9 Client.java *(continues).*

```
        System.exit(-1);
}

/*
 * Start reading input from standard input
 */
String line = null, command = null, args = null;
StringTokenizer tokens = null;
        BufferedReader reader = new BufferedReader(new
            InputStreamReader (System.in));

        while (true) {

    /*
     * Print prompt, read next input line, and get command
     */
    try {
        System.out.println();
        System.out.print("> ");
        line = reader.readLine();
        System.out.println();
        tokens = new StringTokenizer(line, " ", false);

        // Get command.  e.g. "attach" or "inv"
        command = tokens.nextToken();

        // Get arguments to command.
        args = null;
        if (tokens.hasMoreElements()) {
            args = line.substring( command.length()+1, line.length());
        }
    }
    catch (Exception e) {
        continue;
    }

    /*
     * Do case analysis based upon command.
     */
    try {
        /*
         * If the user wants to examine a component
         */
        if (command.equals("examine")) {
            examine(args);
        }

        /*
         * If user wants to attach 2 components,
```

Source 6.9 Client.java *(continues).*

```
       * then extract the 2 component names from
       * the argument string, and call attach()
       */
      else if (command.equals("attach")) {
          String item1 = null, item2 = null;
          try {
              StringTokenizer argtokens = new StringTokenizer(args,
                  " ");
              item1 = argtokens.nextToken();
              argtokens.nextToken();
              item2 = argtokens.nextToken();
          }
          catch (Exception e) {
              throw new Exception("Syntax: attach <item1> to
                  <item2>");
          }

          attach(item1, item2);
      }
      /*
       * If the user wants to discard an object
       */
      else if (command.equals("drop")) {
          drop(args);
      }
      /*
       * If the user needs more components
       */
      else if (command.equals("gimme")) {
          gimme();
      }
      /*
       * If the user wants to list the components
       * he has.
       */
      else if (command.equals("inv")) {
          inv();
      }
      /*
       * If the user wants to end the game
       */
      else if (command.equals("quit")) {
          quit();
      }
      /*
       * If the user wants to suspend the game
       */
      else if (command.equals("suspend")) {
          if (args == null) {
```

Source 6.9 Client.java *(continues).*

```
                          System.out.println("Please specify a filename.");
                    }
                    else {
                        suspend(args);
                    }
                }
                /*
                 * If the user wants to resume a suspended
                 * game.
                 */
                else if (command.equals("resume")) {
                    if (args == null) {
                        System.out.println("Please specify a filename.");
                    }
                    else {
                        resume(args);
                    }
                }


                else {
                    System.out.println("Syntax: [attach <item1> to <item2> |
                        examine <item> | inv | gimme | drop <item> | suspend
                        <filename> | resume <filename> | quit]");
                }
            }
            catch (Exception e) {
                e.printStackTrace();
            }
        }
    }


    /**
     * Suspends the game.  Writes the current game state to disk
     * via EJB object handles.
     */
    private void suspend(String filename) {

        ObjectOutputStream stream = null;

        try {
            stream = new ObjectOutputStream(
                new FileOutputStream(filename));

            for (int i=0; i < components.size(); i++) {
                Component comp = (Component) components.elementAt(i);
                Handle handle = comp.getHandle();
                stream.writeObject(handle);
            }
```

Source 6.9   Client.java *(continues)*.

```java
        stream.flush();

        System.out.println("Game saved.");
    }
    catch (Exception e) {
        e.printStackTrace();
    }
    finally {
        if (stream != null) {
            try { stream.close(); } catch (Exception e) {}
        }
    }

    System.exit(0);
}


/**
 * Resumes a suspended game via EJB object handles.
 */
private void resume(String filename) {

    clearComps();

    ObjectInputStream stream = null;

    try {
        stream = new ObjectInputStream(
            new FileInputStream(filename));

        while (true) {
            Handle handle = (Handle) stream.readObject();

            components.addElement(
                (Component) handle.getEJBObject());
        }
    }
    catch (EOFException e) {
        System.out.println("Game loaded.");
    }
    catch (Exception e) {
        e.printStackTrace();
    }
    finally {
        if (stream != null) {
            try { stream.close(); } catch (Exception e) {}
        }
    }
}
```

Source 6.9   Client.java *(continues).*

```java
/*
 * Removes all components the user has.
 */
private void clearComps() {

    System.out.println("Clearing game state...");

    for (int i=0; i < components.size(); i++) {
        try {
            Component comp =
                (Component) components.elementAt(i);

            comp.remove();
        }
        catch (Exception e) {
            e.printStackTrace();
        }
    }

    components = new Vector();
}

/**
 * Quits the game, cleaning up all EJB Objects.
 */
private void quit() {

    /*
     * 1: Remove all components
     */
    clearComps();

    /*
     * 2: Remove machine
     */
    try {
        machine.remove();
    }
    catch (Exception e) {
        e.printStackTrace();
    }

    System.exit(0);
}

/**
 * Gets more components from the machine
 */
```

Source 6.9 Client.java *(continues)*.

```java
private void gimme() throws Exception {
    for (int i=0; i < 3; i++) {
        Component comp = machine.makeComponent();
        components.addElement(comp);
        System.out.println("The machine pops out a " + comp.getName());
    }
}


/**
 * Drops a component.
 */
private void drop(String componentName) throws Exception {
    for (int i=0; i < components.size(); i++) {
        Component comp = (Component) components.elementAt(i);
        if (comp.getName().equals(componentName)) {
            // Call remove() on EJB Object
            comp.remove();

            components.removeElement(comp);
            System.out.println("You dropped your " + componentName);
            return;
        }
    }
}


/**
 * Lists the inventory of components I currently have.
 */
private void inv() throws Exception {
    for (int i=0; i < components.size(); i++) {
        Component comp = (Component) components.elementAt(i);
        System.out.println(comp.getName());
    }
}


/**
 * Prints out the description of component with name componentName.
 */
private void examine(String componentName) throws Exception {
    /*
     * Loop through all the components.  Get the names of each
     * component.  If the name matches, then print out that
     * component's description.
     */
    for (int i=0; i < components.size(); i++) {
        Component comp = (Component) components.elementAt(i);
        if (comp.getName().equals(componentName)) {
            System.out.println(comp.getDescription());
```

Source 6.9 Client.java *(continues)*.

```
                return;
            }
        }
    }


    /**
     * Attempts to attach components with names A and B together.
     */
    private void attach(String componentNameA, String componentNameB) throws
        Exception {
        Component componentA = null, componentB = null;

        /*
         * Loop through all the components.  Get the Names of each
         * component.  If the name matches, then that's our Component A.
         */
        for (int i=0; i < components.size(); i++) {
            Component comp = (Component) components.elementAt(i);
            if (comp.getName().equals(componentNameA)) {
                componentA = comp;
            }
        }

        /*
         * Print out some error codes if we didn't find any matches
         */
        if (componentA == null) {
            System.out.println("You don't have a " + componentNameA);
            return;
        }

        /*
         * Loop through all the components.  Get the Names of each
         * component.  If the name matches, AND it's not the same
         * as the Component A above, then that's our Component B.
         */
        for (int i=0; i < components.size(); i++) {
            Component comp = (Component) components.elementAt(i);
            if (comp.getName().equals(componentNameB)
                && (!comp.equals(componentA))) {
                componentB = comp;
            }
        }

        /*
         * Print out some error codes if we didn't find any matches
         */
        if (componentB == null) {
            System.out.println("You don't have a " + componentNameB);
```

Source 6.9 Client.java *(continues).*

```
            return;
        }


        /*
         * Try to attach the two components.  If they attach,
         * 1) Remove the old Component EJB Objects
         * 2) Remove the old Components from our list of components
         * 3) Add the new, combined component to our list
         */
        try {
            Component newComp = componentA.attachTo(componentB);

            // Remove the two old Components' EJB Object
            componentA.remove();
            componentB.remove();

            components.removeElement(componentA);
            components.removeElement(componentB);
            components.addElement(newComp);

            System.out.println("Fitting the " + componentNameA + " into the "
                + componentNameB + ", out pops a " + newComp.getName() + "!");
        }
        /*
         * If an application-level exception occurs (i.e. if
         * the two components won't attach) then handle it.
         * Let the main loop handle system-level exceptions.
         */
        catch (ComponentException e) {
            System.out.println(e.toString());
        }
    }
}
```

Source 6.9 Client.java *(continued)*.

The client app illustrates looking up a bean via JNDI, calling business methods on beans, removing beans, and using EJB object handles.

The program itself consists of a main game loop in its *start()* method. Depending on what the user inputs, the main game loop calls one of the following methods:

gimme(). Asks the machine EJB object for three more components.

inv(). Lists the current components EJB objects I have in my inventory.

attach(). Tries to attach two components together.

examine(). Prints out the long description of a component.

drop(). Removes a component (if my inventory gets too big).

suspend( ). Suspends the game, allowing the user to quit to the command prompt. The user's game state is saved using EJB object handles.

resume( ). Resumes a suspended game.

quit( ). Quits the game.

The Manifest

The final piece of our deployment equation is the manifest file. Because we have two beans, we need to list two serialized deployment descriptors, as shown in the following code snippet. Note that the actual names of your serialized deployment descriptors may vary depending on which EJB tool you use to generate your deployment descriptors.

```
Name: com/wiley/compBooks/roman/session/fazuul/deployment/
ComponentBeanDD.ser
Enterprise-Bean: True

Name: com/wiley/compBooks/roman/session/fazuul/deployment/
MachineBeanDD.ser
Enterprise-Bean: True
```

Running the Client

Let's try the game out. To run the game (assuming the BEA *WebLogic* server), type:

```
java
  -Djava.naming.factory.initial=
   weblogic.jndi.TengahInitialContextFactory
  -Djava.naming.provider.url=
   t3://localhost:7001
  com.wiley.compBooks.roman.session.fazuul.Client
```

Note that your machine's network must be properly set up for the *localhost:7001* to resolve properly. If you can't get the client to connect with the EJB server, try using your IP address instead.

The following is a typical game interaction. The commands the user types are in **bold**:

```
> help

Syntax: [attach <item1> to <item2> | examine <item> | inv | gimme | drop
<item> | suspend <filename> | resume <filename> | quit]

> inv
```

```
> gimme
```

The machine pops out a Snarf
The machine pops out a Rector
The machine pops out a Snarf

```
> gimme
```

The machine pops out a Rector
The machine pops out a Snarf
The machine pops out a Vrommell

```
> inv
```

Snarf
Rector
Snarf
Rector
Snarf
Vrommell

```
> drop Rector
```

You dropped your Rector

```
> inv
```

Snarf
Snarf
Rector
Snarf
Vrommell

```
> examine Snarf
```

This is a snarf. It came all the way from snarfland. It looks like a
large peanut, with a hole in the side of it. The hole looks big enough
to fit a Vrommell inside.

```
> examine Vrommell
```

This Vrommell is a funny banana-shaped thing. It looks like it will fit
snugly into a Snarf.

```
> attach Snarf to Vrommell
```

Fitting the Snarf into the Vrommell, out pops a Subbert!

```
> inv
```

Snarf
Rector

```
Snarf
Rector
Subbert

> examine Subbert

Subberts are small discs and smell funny.  There's a small, banana-
shaped hole in this Subbert.

> gimme

The machine pops out a Rector
The machine pops out a Vrommell
The machine pops out a Rector

> attach Vrommell to Subbert

Fitting the Vrommell into the Subbert, out pops a Fwiffo!

> examine Fwiffo

It's a Fwiffo!  Fwiffos are cute, furry little creatures.  This Fwiffo
has lost some fur on his head, though, and needs something to cover it
up.

> examine Rector

Oh no, it's Rector!  Rectors are dangerous, disease-spreading devices.
You don't want to hold on to this one for very long.  Perhaps if you fed
the Rector a peanut or disc, it would be pacified.

> attach Snarf to Rector

Fitting the Snarf into the Rector, out pops a Lucia!

> examine Lucia

Lucias are peaceful, harmless components.  This Lucia is brown.  Lucia
wants something furry to play with or someone to sing to her.

> attach Lucia to Fwiffo

Fitting the Lucia into the Fwiffo, out pops a Simpthat!

> quit
```

As you can see, typing "gimme" gets three components from the machine. Dropping a component removes it from our inventory, and combining components replaces two components in our inventory with a new merged component.

We examine each component as we get it, and we look for clues as to what the components should attach. For example, the Snarf has a hole inside that can fit a Vrommell, so we attach the Vrommell to the Snarf to generate a Subbert. The Subbert has a banana-shaped hole in it. What should we attach it to? Well, its long description indicates that our Vrommell looks like a banana, so the two naturally fit together. And so we continue. At the end of our interaction, we notice that the Rector can be pacified by feeding it peanuts. The Snarf is peanut-shaped, so we "feed" it to the Rector by attaching the two, and magically a Lucia is born.

Try the game out yourself—you may become addicted. You can modify the game parameters (or cheat!) by modifying the deployment descriptor.

Experimenting with Handles

Let's check out how EJB object handles work in our game.

```
> inv

Vrommell
Rector
Vrommell

> suspend myGame

Game saved.


// At this point, the game exits to the command line
// and the client JVM quits.
//
// Later, when we're ready to start playing again, we
// re-run the client..

> inv

> resume myGame

Clearing game state...
Game loaded.

> inv

Vrommell
Rector
Vrommell
```

As you can see, the EJB object handles served as persistent component references across the client JVM lifecycle.

Experimenting with Security

Just for fun, let's see what happens when we try to create a component directly from the client:

```
ComponentHome home = (ComponentHome) ctx.lookup("ComponentHome");
Component comp = home.create("Snarf");
```

Running this code yields the following output:

```
java.rmi.RemoteException:
java.lang.SecurityException:
User 'guest' not allowed access to method ejbCreate_S in EJB class
'com.wiley.compBooks.roman.session.fazuul.ComponentBean'
```

As you can see, the container is enforcing the correct security policies we out-lined in the deployment descriptor. Client code is not allowed to directly instan-tiate our component bean.

Summary

In this chapter, we stepped up and learned how to make our beans more robust. We learned how to use EJB contexts, how to access environment properties, how to use EJB security, how to use EJB object handles, and how to call beans from other beans. You also saw a non-trivial example illustrating these concepts in action.

In the following chapters, you will gain insight into the sister of the session bean—the persistent entity bean.

## CHAPTER 7

Introduction to Entity Beans

In Chapters 3–6, you learned how to code session beans—distributed components that represent business processes. But session beans are only half of what Enterprise JavaBeans has to offer. One of the key benefits of EJB is the power to create *entity beans*. Entity beans are *persistent objects* that can be stored in permanent storage. This means you can model your business's fundamental, underlying data as entity beans. We'll see exactly what this means in the pages to come.

In this chapter, we'll cover these topics:

- The basic concepts of persistence
- A definition of entity beans, from a programmer's perspective
- The features that entity beans have to offer
- How entity beans compare with session beans
- Entity bean programming concepts

 Entity beans are an *optional* part of Enterprise JavaBeans 1.0. Even if your EJB container is compliant with EJB 1.0, the EJB container may not be able to handle entity beans. If you need entity beans, make sure you choose a container capable of deploying them. EJB 1.1, which is part of Java 2 Platform, Enterprise Edition (J2EE), mandates entity bean support.

This chapter is relatively theoretical, and it is meant to give you a deep foundation in entity bean programming concepts. For those of you with a traditional procedural programming background, entity beans can be a very tough topic to grasp. You may need to reread this chapter a few times to really understand how things work. Make sure you've read and understood the previous chapters in this book; our discussion of entity beans will build on the knowledge you've acquired so far. We'll use these concepts with hands-on code in Chapters 8 and 9.

Persistence Concepts

Because entity beans are persistent objects, our discussion begins with a quick look at popular ways to persist objects.

Java Object Serialization

When you work with Java objects, in many cases you would like to capture the state of the object you're currently working with and save it to a permanent storage. One way to do this, as covered in Appendix A, is to use *object serialization*. Object serialization is an easy way to marshal an object graph into a compact representation. When you serialize an object graph, you convert the graph into a byte stream. You can then do anything you want to with that stream, such as push the data over the network (which is how Java RMI passes parameters over the network), or you can save the stream to a storage, such as a file system, database or JNDI tree. For sophisticated persistence, however, object serialization falls short in many areas.

For example, let's say we store a million serializable bank account objects onto a file system. We do this by converting the objects to their bit-blob representation and then storing the bytes on disk. Let's say we then want to retrieve all bank accounts that have balances over $1000. To do this with serialization, we'd have to load each and every bank account serialized bit-blob from the disk, construct the corresponding object, and then execute a method query on the object to determine if the balance is over $1000. We might want to perform more advanced queries as well, such as retrieving all checking accounts that have been inactive for six months. There is no efficient way to do this with object serialization.

In general, querying objects stored using object serialization is very expensive and cumbersome. Submitting queries against business data is an absolute necessity for large-scale applications, which makes simple object serialization unsuitable for persistent storage. While object serialization has its purpose, it is best used in restricted domains, such as for network communications and simple persistence. For EJB, we'll need a more robust persistence mechanism to address more complex querying operations.

Object-Relational Mapping

Another popular way to store Java objects is to use a traditional relational database, such as Oracle or Microsoft SQL Server. Rather than serialize each object, we could decompose each object into its constituent parts and store each part separately. For example, for a bank account object, the bank account number could be stored in one relational database row, while the bank account balance could be stored in another row. When you save your Java objects, you would use JDBC or SQL/J to *map* the object data into a relational database. You could also store the name of the Java class that this data corresponds to, so that you know which class to instantiate when reading the object back from the database. When you want to load your objects from the database, you'd first instantiate an object from that class, read the data in from the database, and then populate that object instance's fields with the relational data read in. This is shown in Figure 7.1.

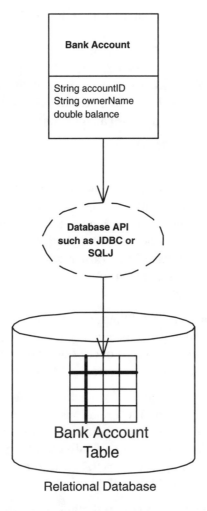

Figure 7.1 Object-relational mapping.

This mapping of objects to relational databases is a technology called *object-relational mapping*. It is the act of converting and unconverting in-memory objects to relational data. An object-relational (O/R) mapper could use any kind of underlying database schema (for example, it could translate a Java object into a single relational record. It could then retrieve that record at a later time to reconstruct an object in memory for you to use).

Object-relational mapping as a persistence mechanism is a much more sophisticated mechanism of persisting objects than simple object serialization. By decomposing your Java objects as relational data, you can issue arbitrary queries for information. For example, you can search through all the database records that have an account balance entry greater than $1000 and load only the objects that fulfill this query. More advanced queries are also possible.

Mapping of objects to relational data can be done in two ways. You can either hand-craft this mapping in your code or use an object-relational mapping product such as ObjectPeople's *TOPLink* or Sun's *JavaBlend* to automate or facilitate this mapping. Today, most users hand-craft the mapping using a database access API such as JDBC or SQL/J. Because the cost of developing and maintaining an object-relational mapping layer is significant, it is likely that the object-relational mapping products will be adopted as they mature.

Object Databases

An *object database management system* (*ODBMS*) is a persistent store that holds entire objects. In an object database, your objects are first-class citizens in the database. This means there is no O/R mapping layer—your Java objects themselves are stored as whole objects. Because of this, you don't need to program to a relational database API—rather, you program to the object database's API. This means you can sidestep object/relational mapping, resulting in simplified data access code.

Most object databases (and O/R mapping products) provide facilities to *query* persisted objects by using an *object query language* (*OQL*). OQL is a nice high-level interface that allows you to query object properties for arbitrary characteristics. It also adds a layer of abstraction from relational database queries.

In addition to OQL-based queries, object databases support *relationships* between objects. You could define a relationship between a Bank Account object and a Customer object and transparently navigate between them. The transparent navigation makes it easy to navigate the object model and has excellent performance when compared to SQL-based joins that are needed to perform equivalent operations in relational databases.

Object databases also have very predictable performance and scalability. They offer very strong integrity and security, and they provide an excellent store for complex persistent objects. There are certain applications that go really well with object databases (geospatial or CAD/CAM, for example) that are complete misfits for relational databases. There are other applications that map easily to relational databases, such as most business applications. For simple high-volume business transactions, relational databases typically scale better than object databases.

ObjectStore, Versant, and POET are a few of the current vendors who provide object database technology. Unfortunately, object database products have not yet been fully embraced by the industry. Although they are very useful for certain applications, object databases are currently limited because they don't have very many associated tools, such as reporting, tuning, and management tools.

Now that we've whetted your appetite with persistence mechanisms, let's take a look at how entity bean persistent objects are used in an EJB multitier environment.

What Is an Entity Bean?

In any sophisticated, object-oriented multitier deployment, we can draw a clear distinction between two different kinds of components deployed:

Application logic components. These components are method providers that perform common tasks. Their tasks might include the following:

- Computing the price of an order
- Billing a customer's credit card
- Computing the inverse of a matrix

Notice that these components represent actions (they're verbs). They are well suited to handle business processes.

Session beans model these application logic components very well. They often will contain interesting algorithms and logic to perform application tasks. Session beans represent work being performed for a user. They represent the user session, which includes any workflow logic.

Persistent data components. These are objects (perhaps written in Java) that know how to render themselves into persistent storage. They use some persistence mechanism, such as serialization, O/R mapping to a relational database, or an object database. These kinds of objects represent *data*—simple or complex information that you'd like saved. Examples here include the following:

- Bank account information, such as account number and balance
- Human resources data, such as names, departments, and salaries of employees

- Lead tracking information, such as names, addresses, and phone numbers of prospective customers that you want to keep track of over time

Notice that these components represent people, places, and things (they're nouns). They are well suited to handle business data.

You might question the need for such persistent data components. Why should we deal with our business data as objects, rather than dealing with raw database data, such as relational rows? The answer is that it is very handy to treat data as objects because they can be easily handled and managed and because they are represented in a compact manner. We can group related data together in a unified object. We associate some simple methods with that data, such as compression or other data-related activities. We can also gain implicit middleware services from an application server, such as transactions, network accessibility, and security.

Entity beans are these persistent data components. Entity beans are enterprise beans that know how to persist themselves permanently to a durable storage such as a database. They are physical, storable parts of an enterprise. Entity beans store data as fields, such as bank account numbers and bank account balances. They also have methods associated with them, such as *getBankAccountNumber()* and *getAccountBalance()*. Entity beans can also be used to integrate with existing legacy enterprise applications.

In some ways, entity beans are analogous to serializable Java objects. Serializable objects can be rendered into a bit-blob and then saved into a persistent store; entity beans can persist themselves in many ways, including serialization, O/R mapping, or object database persistence. There is nothing in the EJB specification that dictates any particular persistence mechanism.

Entity beans are very different from session beans. Session beans model a process or workflow (actions that are started by the user and that go away when the user goes away). Entity beans, on the other hand, contain core business data, such as product information, bank accounts, orders, lead tracking information, customer information, and more. An entity bean does not perform complex tasks or workflow logic, such as billing a customer. Rather, an entity bean *is* the customer itself. Entity beans represent persistent state objects (things that don't go away when the user goes away).

For example, you might want to read bank account data into an entity bean instance, thus loading the stored database information into the in-memory entity bean instance's fields. You can then play with the Java object and modify its representation in memory because you're working with convenient Java objects, rather than bunches of database records. You can increase the bank account balance in-memory, thus updating the entity bean's in-memory bank account balance field. Then you can save the Java object, pushing the data back into the underlying store. This would effectively deposit money into the bank account.

In general, you should use entity beans for modeling data and session beans for modeling business processes. If you design them right, you should be able to reuse your entity beans as your business processes change over time.

 The term *entity bean* is grossly overused. Sometimes it refers to an in-memory Java object instance of an entity bean class, and sometimes it refers to database data that an in-memory Java object instance represents. To make the distinction clear, we introduce two new terms:

- **The entity bean instance is the in-memory view into the database. It is an instance of your entity bean class.**
- **The entity bean data (or data instance) is the physical set of data, such as a bank account record, stored in the database.**

In summary, you should think of an entity bean instance as the following:

- An in-memory Java representation of persistent data
- Smart enough to know how to read itself from a storage and populate its fields with the stored data
- An object that can then be modified in-memory to change the values of data
- Persistable, so that it can be saved back into storage again, thus updating the database data

Files Included with Entity Beans

Let's take a look at the files that make up an entity bean component:

The entity bean class is a Java class that models persistent data. An entity bean class maps to an entity definition in a database schema. For example, an entity bean class could map to a relational table definition. In this case, an entity bean instance of that class would map to a row in that table. Your entity bean class can expose simple methods to manipulate or access that data, such as a method to decrease a bank account balance. Like a session bean class, EJB also requires that an entity bean class must fill in some standard callback methods. The EJB container will call these methods appropriately to manage the entity bean.

The entity bean's remote interface is the interface to your beans on which clients invoke. In it, you should place each of your entity bean's business method signatures. Your EJB container vendor provides tools to implement this remote interface; the implementation is the entity bean's EJB object. The EJB object represents a layer of indirection between the client and the bean. Clients invoke directly on the EJB object, rather than on the entity bean itself.

Because the EJB object is part of the container, it contains logic to intercept method calls and perform management tasks on the bean instance as needed. This is exactly the same concept that we learned for session beans.

The entity bean's home interface is the interface clients use to create, find, and destroy entity bean EJB objects. In it, you should put the different possible methods you'd like available to create new entity bean EJB objects, and to find or destroy old ones. Your EJB container vendor provides tools to implement this home interface; the implementation is the entity bean's home object. This home object is the factory for your EJB objects. To find the home object, your clients must perform a JNDI lookup. This is exactly the same concept that we learned for session beans.

The entity bean's primary key class is a unique identifier for your entity bean. Primary keys make every entity bean different. For example, if you have one million different bank account entity beans, each bank account needs to have a unique ID (such as a bank account ID string) that can never be repeated in any other bank account. A primary key is an object that may contain any number of attributes. This could be whatever data necessary to uniquely identify an entity bean data instance. In some advanced cases, when the entity bean represents a complex relationship, the primary key might be an entire object. EJB gives you the flexibility to define what your unique identifier is by including a primary key class with your entity bean. The one rule is that your primary key class must be serializable and follow the rules for Java object serialization. We present the rules for object serialization in Appendix A.

The entity bean's deployment descriptor contains a list of properties that should be used by the container on deployment. Deployment descriptors inform your container about your bean. There are some new deployment descriptor entries that are particular to entity beans; we'll find out about them later.

The entity bean's environment properties allow end users to customize your entity bean on deployment. Environment properties are optional and are used in the same manner as for session beans.

In order to ship your entity beans, you should package these files in an Ejb-jar file, which is a simple Java archive. Include a manifest file in the Ejb-jar for locating your bean within the jar, and you've got a shippable entity bean component.

Features of Entity Beans

Let's now take a look at the features that entity beans sport. We'll use our understanding of session beans from Chapters 3–6 as a frame of reference for learning entity beans.

Entity Beans Are Long-Lived

In Chapter 3, we pointed out that session beans have a lifetime of a client session. This means that session beans live and die for about the same amount of time that a client is around. When the client leaves, the session bean may be destroyed.

Entity beans, in comparison, can last for days, months, or even years. For example, you definitely would want your bank account to last for a few years, wouldn't you? This is what entity beans are meant to model.

Entity Beans Survive Failures

Because session beans are short-lived and have the lifespan of a client's session, they are typically destroyed in a catastrophic event, such as a JVM crash.

In contrast, because entity beans are part of persistent storage, a crash of the Java Virtual Machine (or database) does not affect the life cycle of an entity bean. As soon as things come back online, the entity bean instances can be created once more, simply by rereading the data from the database and instantiating entity bean instances to represent that data in memory.

Entity Bean Instances Are a View into a Database

When you load entity bean data into an in-memory entity bean instance, you read in the data stored in a database so that you can manipulate the data within a Java Virtual Machine. However, *you should think of the in-memory object and the database itself as really being one and the same.* This means if you update the in-memory entity bean instance, the database should automatically be updated as well. You should *not* think of the in-memory entity bean as a separate version of the data in the database. The in-memory entity bean is simply a *view* or *lens* into the database.

Of course, in reality there are multiple physical copies of the same data. There is the in-memory entity bean instance, and there is the entity bean data itself stored in the database. Therefore, there must be a mechanism to transfer information back and forth between the Java object and the database. This data transfer is accomplished with two special methods that your entity bean class must implement, called *ejbLoad()* and *ejbStore()*.

ejbLoad() reads the data in from the persistent storage into the entity bean's in-memory fields.

ejbStore() saves your bean instance's current fields to the underlying data storage. It is the complement of *ejbLoad()*.

So who decides when to transfer data back-and-forth between the in-memory bean and the database? That is, who calls *ejbLoad()* and *ejbStore()*? The answer is your EJB container. *ejbLoad()* and *ejbStore()* are callback methods that the container invokes. They are management methods required by EJB. The container worries about when is the proper time to call *ejbLoad()* and *ejbStore()*— this is one of the value-adds of the container. Your beans should be prepared to accept an *ejbLoad()* or *ejbStore()* call at almost any time (but not during a business method). The container automatically figures out when each of your instances needs to be refreshed depending on the current transactional state (see Chapter 10). This means that you don't ever explicitly call your own *ejbLoad()* or *ejbStore()* methods. This is one of the advantages of EJB: You don't have to worry about synchronizing your objects with the underlying database. Rather, the EJB black box handles it for you.

Several Entity Bean Instances May Represent the Same Underlying Data

Let's consider the scenario where many threads of execution want to access the same database data simultaneously. In banking, interest might be applied to a bank account, while at the same time a company directly deposits a check into that same account. In E-Commerce, many different client browsers may be simultaneously interacting with a catalog of products.

To facilitate many clients accessing the same data, we'll need to design a high-performance access system to our entity beans. One possibility is if we allow many clients to share the same entity bean instance. That way, an entity bean could service many client requests simultaneously. While this is an interesting idea, it is not very appropriate for EJB. The reason for this is twofold. First, if we'd like an entity bean instance to service many concurrent clients, we'd need to make that instance thread-safe. Writing thread-safe code is difficult and error-prone. Remember that the EJB value proposition is rapid application development. Mandating that component vendors produce stable thread-safe code does not encourage this. Second, having multiple threads of execution makes transactions almost impossible to control by the underlying transaction system. Because of these reasons, EJB dictates that only a single thread can ever be running within a bean instance. With session beans, as well as entity beans, all bean instances are single-threaded.

Mandating that each bean can service only one client at a time could result in performance bottlenecks. Because each instance is single-threaded, clients need to effectively run in lock-step, each waiting their turn to use a bean. This could easily grind performance to a halt in any large enterprise deployment.

To boost performance, we could allow containers to instantiate multiple instances of the same entity bean class. This would allow for many clients to concurrently interact with separate instances, each representing the same underlying entity data. Indeed, this is exactly what EJB allows containers to do. Thus, client requests do not necessarily need to run independently—they can now run simultaneously in several different bean instances.

Having multiple bean instances represent the same data now raises a new problem: data corruption. If many bean instances are representing the same underlying data, then we're dealing with multiple in-memory cached replicas. Some of these replicas could become stale, representing data that is not current.

To achieve entity bean instance cache consistency, each entity bean instance needs to be routinely synchronized with the underlying storage. The container synchronizes the bean with the underlying storage by calling the bean's *ejbLoad()* and *ejbStore()* callbacks, as described in the previous section.

The frequency with which beans are synchronized with an underlying storage is dictated by *transactions*, a topic we cover in Chapter 10. Transactions allow each client request to be isolated from every other request. Transactions enable clients to *believe* they are dealing with a single in-memory bean instance, when in fact there are many instances behind the scenes. They give clients the illusion that they have exclusive access to data when in fact there are many clients all touching the same data.

Entity Bean Instances Can Be Pooled

Let's say you've decided to author your own EJB container/server. Your product is responsible for instantiating entity beans as necessary, with each bean representing data in an underlying storage. As clients connect and disconnect, you could create and destroy beans as necessary to service those clients.

Unfortunately, this is not a very scalable way to build an application server. Creation and destruction of objects is very expensive, especially if client requests come frequently. How can we save on this overhead?

One thing to remember is that an entity bean class describes the fields and rules for your entity bean, but it does not dictate any specific data. For example, an entity bean class may specify that all bank accounts have the following fields:

- The name of the bank account owner
- An account ID
- An available balance

That bean class can then represent any distinct instance of database data, such as a particular bank account record. The class itself, though, is not specific to any particular bank account.

Thus, to save precious time instantiating objects, entity bean instances are re-cyclable objects and may be pooled depending on your container's policy. The container may pool and reuse entity bean instances to represent different in-stances of the same type of data in an underlying storage. For example, a con-tainer could use a bank account entity bean instance to represent different bank account records. Thus, when you're done using an entity bean instance, that instance may be assigned to handle a different client's request and may repre-sent different data. The container performs this by dynamically assigning the entity bean instance to different client-specific EJB objects. Not only does this save the container from unnecessarily instantiating bean instances, but this scheme saves on the total amount of resources held by the system. We show this in Figure 7.2.

Instance pooling is an interesting optimization that containers may provide, and it is not at all unique to entity beans. As we saw in Chapter 3, stateless session beans can also be recycled.

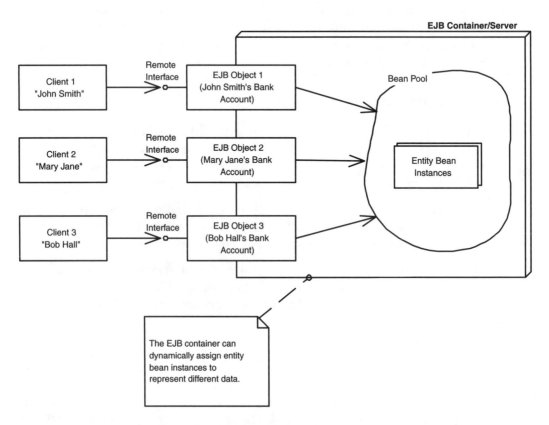

Figure 7.2 EJB container pooling of entity beans.

But as with stateful session beans, there are complications when reassigning entity bean instances to different EJB objects. When your entity bean is assigned to a particular EJB object, it may be holding resources such as socket connections. But when it's in the pool, it may not need that socket. Thus, to allow the bean to release and acquire resources, your entity bean class must implement two callback methods:

ejbActivate() is the callback that your container will invoke on your bean instance when transitioning your bean *out of* a generic instance pool. This process is called *activation*, and it indicates that the container is associating your bean with a specific EJB object and a specific primary key. Your bean's *ejbActivate()* method should acquire resources, such as sockets, that your bean needs when assigned to a particular EJB object. This is the same activation concept that we saw for stateful session beans in Chapter 5.

ejbPassivate() is the callback that your container will invoke when transitioning your bean *into* a generic instance pool. This process is called *passivation*, and it indicates that the container is disassociating your bean from a specific EJB object and a specific primary key. Your bean's *ejbPassivate()* method should release resources, such as sockets, that your bean acquired during *ejbActivate()*. This is the same passivation concept that we saw for stateful session beans in Chapter 5.

When an entity bean instance is passivated, it must not only release held resources but also save its state to the underlying storage—that way, the storage is updated to the latest entity bean instance state. To save the instance's fields to the database, the container invokes the entity bean's *ejbStore()* method prior to passivation. Similarly, when the entity bean instance is activated, it must not only acquire any resources it needs but also load the most recent data from the database. To load data into the bean instance, the container invokes the entity bean's *ejbLoad()* method after activation. This is shown in Figure 7.3.

If you think about it, entity beans are actually quite similar to stateful session beans. Both stateful session beans and entity beans can undergo passivation/activation. The big difference between the two is that entity beans have a separate *ejbStore()* callback for saving state during passivation and a separate *ejbLoad()* callback for loading state during activation. We did not need these callbacks for stateful session beans because the container simply uses object serialization (or the equivalent) to persist stateful session bean fields. Entity beans are more complex, bonafide persistent objects—and naturally, they may need more complex ways of saving state than object serialization. An entity bean instance might use object/relational mapping via a relational database API, or it might persist itself to an object database using an object database API. That's why passivation/activation needs to rely on separate *ejbLoad()* and *ejbStore()* callbacks to deal with state persistence.

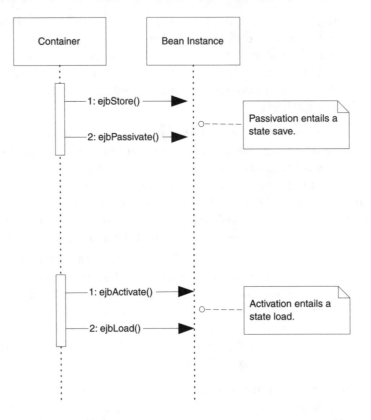

Figure 7.3 Passivation of entity beans entails a state save, and activation entails a state load.

There Are Two Ways to Persist Entity Beans

As should be clear by now, entity beans are persistent objects that know how to render themselves into a data store, such as a relational database via O/R mapping or an object database. One way to do this is to implement a set of database calls within your bean. For example, with a relational database, your entity bean could perform an SQL INSERT statement via JDBC to stick some data into a relational database. You could also perform an SQL DELETE statement via JDBC to remove data from the underlying store. This mechanism of persistence is called *bean-managed persistence* because the bean itself is managing all of its storage.

EJB offers an alternative to bean-managed persistence: You can have your EJB container perform your persistence for you. In this case, you'd usually strip your bean of any persistence logic. Rather than hard-coding persistence into your bean class, you simply tell your EJB container which public fields of your bean are *persistent fields*. You tell the container this via your entity bean's deployment descriptor. Once you've informed the container about what fields to persist, the

---

EJB Design Strategies

Partitioning Your Resources

When programming with EJB, I've found it very handy to separate the kinds of resources your beans use into two categories: *bean-specific resources* and *bean-independent resources.*

Bean-specific resources are resources that your bean uses that are tied to a specific data instance in an underlying storage. For example, a socket connection is a bean-specific resource if that socket is used only when particular bank account data is loaded. That is, the socket is used only when your bean instance is bound to a particular EJB object. Such a resource should be acquired when a bean instance is activated and released when the instance is passivated.

Bean-independent resources are resources that can be used over and over again, no matter what underlying data your instance represents. For example, a socket connection is a bean-independent resource if my bean can reuse that socket no matter what bank account my bean represents (that is, no matter what EJB object your bean instance is assigned to). Global resources such as these should be acquired when your bean is first created, and they can be used across the board as your bean is assigned to different EJB objects. The callback that the container invokes when first creating your bean instance is called *setEntityContext()*, and you should acquire your bean-independent resources here. Similarly, the *unsetEntityContext()* method is called directly before your bean instance is destroyed, and thus you should release bean-independent resources there. Combined, these two methods demarcate the lifetime of a particular entity bean instance—we'll see how to use them in the pages to come.

Because acquiring and releasing resources may be costly operations, categorizing your resources as outlined is a vital step that you must take. Of course, the most stingy way to handle resources is to acquire them on a *just-in-time* basis and release them directly after use. For example, you could acquire a database connection only when you're about to use it and release it when you're done. Then there would be no resources to acquire/release during activation/passivation. In this case, you'd let the container pool your resources and thus manage the resources for you. The disadvantage to this is you need to code resource requests/releases over and over again in your bean code.

---

container will automatically handle your data access logic for you. For example, if you're using a relational database, the container may automatically perform SQL INSERT statements to create database data. Similarly, it will automatically perform SQL DELETE statements to remove database data, and it will handle any other necessary persistent operations. Even if you are not working with a relational database, you can have your container persist for you. If your container supports a nonrelational persistent store, such as an object database or a VSAM file, the container will generate the appropriate logic as necessary. This automatic persistence of entity beans is called *container-managed persistence*. It is up to the EJB deployer to specify exactly how your entity bean should map to an underlying data storage, such as a customer ID Java object field mapping to a customer ID column in a relational database table. This is a huge benefit of entity beans, because you can write storage-independent data objects and re-use them in a variety of enterprise environments.

Container-managed persistence reduces the size of your beans tremendously because you don't need to write JDBC code—the container handles all the persistence for you. Needless to say, this is a huge value-add feature of EJB. Of course, it still has a long way to go, as most things do in the EJB world. Once we've written a few entity beans, we'll review the trade-offs of bean-managed versus container-managed persistence (see Chapter 9).

Entity Beans Can Be Created, Removed, or Found

When you learned about session beans, you saw that session beans support methods for initialization as well as destruction. To initialize a session bean, the container calls session bean's *ejbCreate()* method, allowing the bean to prepare itself for use. Similarly, when a session bean is about to be destroyed, the container calls the bean's *ejbRemove()* method, allowing the bean to prepare itself for destruction.

With entity beans, initialization and destruction work a bit differently. Entity beans are a view into a database, and you should think of an entity bean instance and the underlying database as one and the same (they are routinely synchronized). Because they are one and the same, the initialization of an entity bean instance should entail initialization of database data. Thus, when an entity bean is initialized in memory during *ejbCreate()*, it naturally makes sense to create some data in an underlying database that correlates with the in-memory instance. That is exactly what happens with entity beans. When a bean-managed persistent entity bean's *ejbCreate()* method is called, the *ejbCreate()* method is responsible for creating database data. Similarly, when a bean-managed persistent entity bean's *ejbRemove()* method is called, the *ejbRemove()* method is responsible for removing database data. If container-managed persistence is used, the container will modify the database for you, and you can leave these methods empty of data access logic.

Because entity bean data is uniquely identified in an underlying storage, entity beans can also be *found* rather than created. Finding an entity bean is analogous to performing a SELECT statement in SQL. With a SELECT statement, you're searching for data from a relational database store. When you find an entity bean, you're searching a persistent store for some entity bean data. This differs from session beans because session beans cannot be found—they are not permanent objects, and they live and die with the client's session.

You can define many ways to find an entity bean. You list these ways as methods in your entity bean home interface. These are called *finder* methods. Your home interface exposes finder methods in addition to methods for creating and destroying entity beans. This is the one big difference between an entity bean's home interface and a session bean's home interface—session bean home interfaces do not have finder methods.

Entity Beans Can Represent Legacy Data and Legacy Systems

There can even be entity beans that in effect were around *before* EJB. This means you can take an existing legacy database or existing legacy system and represent it as a suite of entity beans. For example, IBM is working on an EJB facade to CICS systems. Some EJB product vendors should provide tools to map entity beans to MVS systems using IMS or VSAM, as well as to packaged application systems such as SAP R/3 and PeopleSoft.

Mapping to legacy systems is no simple task. Typically, a specialized EJB container vendor will provide the tools necessary to map EJB to legacy systems. There are also emerging tools to assist the user in mapping complicated database structures or complex legacy object-relational mapping schemas.

 You may be wondering why entity beans can be used to represent both database data as well as existing legacy systems. Why are entity beans the right abstraction to be using for legacy integration? Indeed, they may not be, as there are many problems with hooking into an existing system such as an SAP R/3 or CICS system. Sun is aware of this and has tentative plans to provide a separate abstraction for legacy integration. In the future, there will be special *connectors* that know how to access existing systems, as well as *access beans* to access those connectors. This should in turn spawn a separate market of EJB connector providers.

Unfortunately, at the time of this writing, connectors and access beans are still a whiteboard idea, so it may be awhile before deployments really get to make use of these constructs

Entity Beans Can Be Modified without Going through EJB

Usually, you will create, destroy, and find entity bean data by using the entity bean's home object. But you can interact with entity beans another way, too: by directly modifying the underlying database where the bean data is stored. For example, if your entity bean instances are being mapped to a relational database, you can simply delete the rows of the database corresponding to an entity

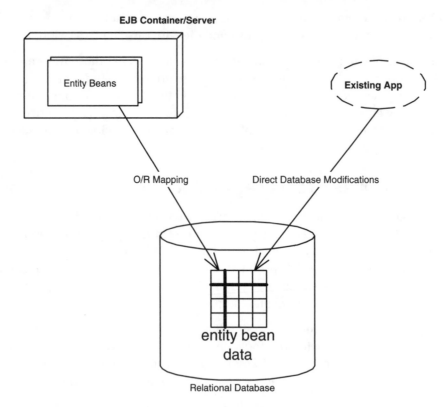

Figure 7.4 Modifying an entity bean's database representation manually.

bean instance (see Figure 7.4). You can also create new entity bean data and modify existing data by directly touching the database. This may be necessary if you have an investment in an existing system that touches a database directly.

Developing and Using Entity Beans

Now that you've got a background in entity bean theory, let's see what's involved in writing and using entity beans. To write an entity bean class, your class must implement the *javax.ejb.EntityBean* interface. This interface defines a number of required methods that your entity bean class must implement. Most of these methods are management methods that are called by your EJB container. The following code details *javax.ejb.EntityBean*, as well as its parent, *javax.ejb.EnterpriseBean*:

The *javax.ejb.EnterpriseBean* interface (Source 7.1) defines no methods (it is simply a marker interface). The *javax.ejb.EntityBean* interface (Source 7.2)

```
public interface javax.ejb.EnterpriseBean implements java.io.Serializable {
}
```

Source 7.1   The javax.ejb.EnterpriseBean interface.

```
public interface javax.ejb.EntityBean implements javax.ejb.EnterpriseBean {
    public abstract void setEntityContext(javax.ejb.EntityContext);
    public abstract void unsetEntityContext();
    public abstract void ejbRemove();
    public abstract void ejbActivate();
    public abstract void ejbPassivate();
    public abstract void ejbLoad();
    public abstract void ejbStore();
}
```

Source 7.2   The javax.ejb.EntityBean interface.

defines callback methods that your bean must implement. The container will call these methods whenever it wishes.

In addition to the methods shown, you would typically define a few *ejbCreate()* methods to create new entity bean data and a few *ejbFind()* methods to find existing bean data.

Creation of Entity Beans: ejbCreate()

An entity bean instance's *ejbCreate()* method is used to initialize a bean for a particular client and to create underlying database data. Each *ejbCreate()* method you define gives clients a different way to create your entity beans.

Here are some of the rules about *ejbCreate()*:

You *do not* need to write any *ejbCreate()* methods with entity beans. Session beans require *ejbCreate()* methods, but they're optional for entities. You'd define an *ejbCreate()* method if you want to provide a way to create some underlying data through EJB. But remember that EJB does allow for you to create data indirectly, via direct database inserts or legacy systems. Thus *ejbCreate()* is optional.

The parameters to ejbCreate() can vary. This allows for multiple ways to initialize an entity bean instance and thus allows for different ways to create entity bean data in a database. For example, one *ejbCreate()* method might create a checking account, while another might create a savings account.

You must duplicate your *ejbCreate()* methods in your home interface. In EJB, remember that clients don't directly invoke on beans—they invoke an EJB object proxy. The EJB object is generated through the home object. Therefore, for each *ejbCreate()* method signature you define in your bean, you must define a corresponding *create()* in the home interface. The client calls the home object's *create()*, which delegates to your bean's *ejbCreate()*.

For example, let's say you have a bean-managed persistent bank account entity bean class called *AccountBean*, with a remote interface *Account*, home interface *AccountHome*, and primary key class *AccountPK*. Given the following *ejbCreate()* method in *AccountBean*:

```
public AccountPK ejbCreate(String accountID, String owner) ...
```

you must have this *create()* in your home interface (notice there is no "ejb" prefix):

```
public Account create(String accountID, String owner) throws ...
```

Notice that there are two different return values here. The bean instance returns a primary key (*AccountPK*), while the home object returns an EJB object (*Account*). This makes sense—the bean returns a primary key to the container (that is, to the home object) so that the container can identify the bean. Once the home object has this primary key, it can generate an EJB object and return that to the client. We show this process more rigorously with the sequence diagram in Figure 7.5.

Finding Existing Entity Beans: ejbFind()

Your entity bean class's *finder* methods are used to find an existing entity bean in storage. Finder methods do not create any new database data—they simply load some old entity bean data. You can have many different finder methods, which all perform different operations:

```
/**
 * Finds the unique bank account indexed by primary key key
 */
public AccountPK ejbFindByPrimaryKey(AccountPK key)

/**
 * Finds all the product entity beans.  Returns an Enumeration
 * of primary keys.
 */
public Enumeration ejbFindAllProducts()
```

```
/**
 * Finds all Bank Accounts that have at least a minimum balance.
 * Returns an Enumeration of primary keys.
 */
public Enumeration ejbFindBigAccounts(int minimum)

/**
 * Finds the most recently placed order
 */
public OrderPK ejbFindMostRecentOrder()
```

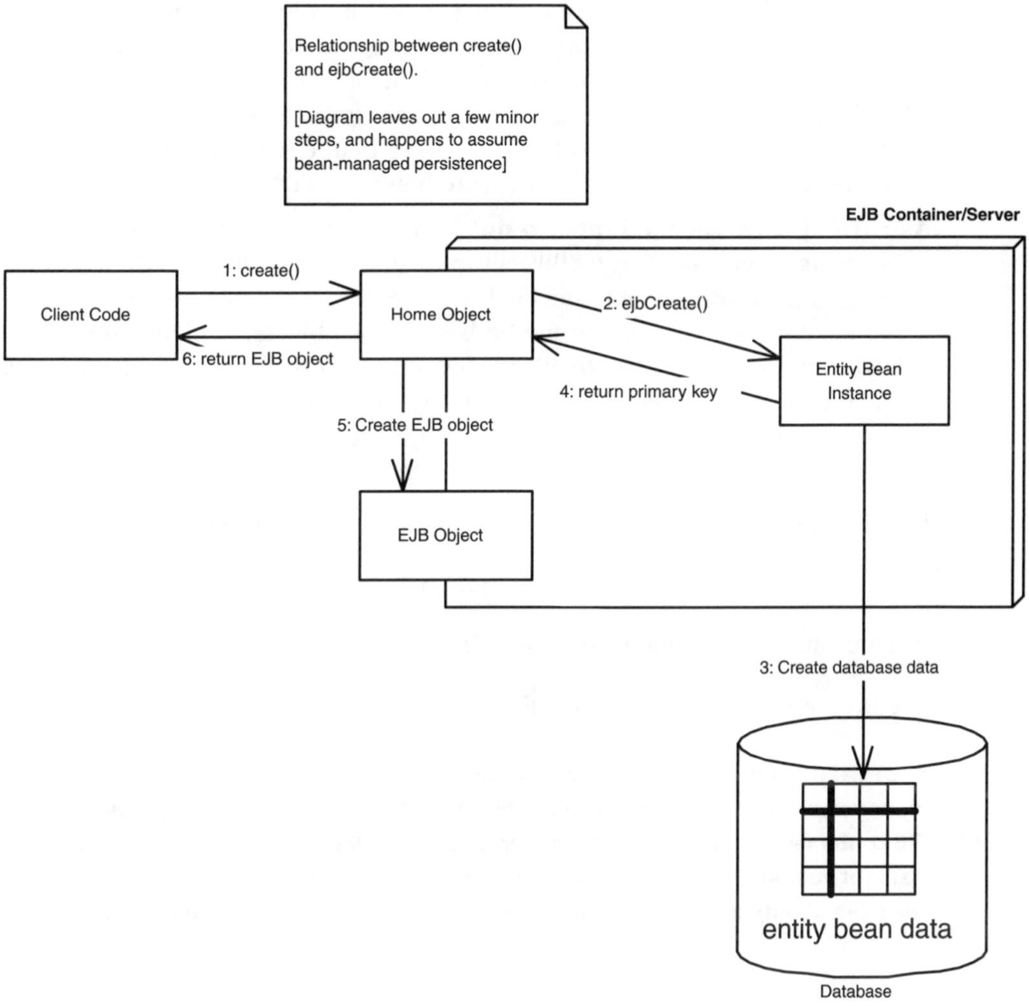

Relationship between create()
and ejbCreate().

[Diagram leaves out a few minor
steps, and happens to assume
bean-managed persistence]

EJB Container/Server

Client Code

1: create()

Home Object

2: ejbCreate()

6: return EJB object

Entity Bean
Instance

4: return primary key

5: Create EJB object

EJB Object

3: Create database data

entity bean data

Database

Figure 7.5 Creating a bean-managed persistent entity bean and EJB object.

Here are some of the rules about finder methods:

All finder methods must begin with "ejbFind." This is simply a syntactic rule.

You must have at least one finder method, called ejbFindByPrimaryKey. This method finds one unique entity bean instance in the database based on its unique primary key. Because every entity bean has an associated primary key, it makes sense that every entity bean class supports this method.

You can have many different finder methods, with different names and different parameters to each method. This allows you to find using different semantics, as illustrated by the previous examples.

A finder method must return either the primary key for the entity bean it finds or an enumeration of primary keys if it finds more than one. Because you could find more than one data instance in the database, finder methods can return enumerations of primary keys. Note that EJB 1.1 allows finder methods to return collections rather than enumerations. Collections are much more powerful to work with than enumerations.

As with ejbCreate( ), clients do not invoke your finder methods on the bean instance itself. A finder method is just like any other method on your entity bean class—clients never directly call any of your bean's methods. Rather, clients invoke finder methods on home objects, implemented by the EJB container, that delegate to your bean. Therefore, for each finder method you define in your bean class, you must define a corresponding finder in the home interface. Clients call your home object's finder methods, which delegate to your bean's finders.

For example, given the following finder method in *AccountBean*:

```
public Enumeration ejbFindAllProducts() ...
```

you must have this finder in your home interface (notice there is no "ejb" prefix):

```
public Enumeration findAllProducts() ...
```

 A special rule about finder methods is that *you implement finders only for bean-managed persistent entities*. If you're using container-managed persistence, your EJB container will implement the finder methods in the EJB object (or somewhere else) for you. After all, the container is responsible for all data access logic. You'll see more about this when we discuss container-managed persistence in Chapter 9.

As with *ejbCreate()*, you must define your finder methods in your home interface and implement your finder methods in your entity bean class. For example, if you have the following finder implementation signature in your entity bean class:

```
public AccountPK ejbFindBigAccounts(int minimum) throws ...
```

you must have this finder signature in your home interface (notice there is no "ejb" prefix):

```
public Account findBigAccounts(int minimum) throws ...
```

Notice that (as with *ejbCreate()*) our method signatures have two different return values: the entity bean instance returns a primary key to the container, whereas the home object returns an EJB object to the client.

Destruction of Entity Beans: ejbRemove()

To destroy an entity bean's data in a database, the client must call *remove()* on the EJB object or home object. This method causes the container to issue an *ejbRemove()* call on the bean. We show this in Figure 7.6.

Note that *ejbRemove()* does not mean the in-memory entity bean instance is going to be destroyed—*ejbRemove()* destroys only database data. The bean instance can be recycled to handle a different database data instance, such as a bank account bean representing different bank accounts.

ejbRemove() is a required method of all entity beans, as it is of session beans, and it takes no parameters. There is only one form of *ejbRemove()*. With entity beans, *ejbRemove()* is not called if the client times out because the lifetime of an entity bean is longer than the client's session.

Entity Contexts

As you learned in Chapter 6, all enterprise beans have a *context object* that identifies the environment of the bean. These context objects contain environment information that the EJB container sets. Your beans can access the context to retrieve all sorts of information, such as transaction and security information.

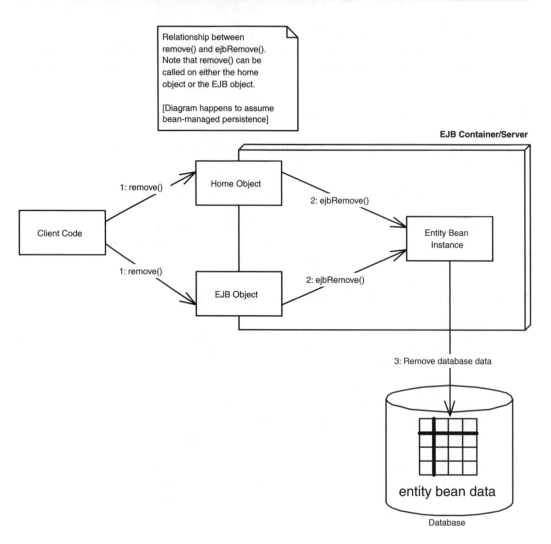

Figure 7.6 Destroying an entity bean's data representation.

For session beans, this context's interface is *javax.ejb.SessionContext*. For entity beans, the interface is *javax.ejb.EntityContext*. Both session contexts and entity contexts extend the more generic *javax.ejb.EJBContext* interface.

We provide a refresher of the *javax.ejb.EJBContext* methods in Source 7.3. Table 7.1 explains the meaning of each method.

Entity contexts add two new methods on top of the generic EJB context, shown in Source 7.4.

Let's look at each of these methods in more detail.

```
public interface javax.ejb.EJBContext {
    public abstract javax.ejb.EJBHome getEJBHome();
    public abstract java.util.Properties getEnvironment();
    public abstract java.security.Identity getCallerIdentity();
    public abstract boolean isCallerInRole(java.security.Identity);
    public abstract javax.jts.UserTransaction getUserTransaction();
    public abstract void setRollbackOnly();
    public abstract boolean getRollbackOnly();
}
```

Source 7.3 The javax.ejb.EJBContext interface.

getEJBObject()

Call this to retrieve the current, client-specific EJB object that is associated with the entity bean. Remember that clients invoke on EJB objects, not on entity beans directly. Therefore you can use the returned EJB object as a way to pass a reference to yourself, simulating the *this* argument in Java. *getEJBObject()* has the same functionality as session beans.

getPrimaryKey()

getPrimaryKey() is new to entity beans. It retrieves the primary key that is currently associated with this entity bean instance. Primary keys uniquely identify an entity bean. When an entity bean is persisted in storage, the primary key can be used to uniquely retrieve the entity bean because you can never have two entity bean database data instances that have the same primary key.

Why would you ever want to call *getPrimaryKey()*? You'd call it whenever you want to figure out with which database data your instance is associated. Remember that entity bean instances can be reused and pooled, as we saw in Figure 7.3. When the container wants to switch an entity bean instance from one data instance to another, the container needs to passivate and activate that entity bean instance. When this happens, your bean instance may switch to a different data instance and thus a different primary key. But your entity bean instance is never told this explicitly when it's activated. Rather, your entity bean must perform a *getPrimaryKey()* callback to the entity context to figure out what data it should be dealing with.

Thus, when you have an entity bean that's performing any persistent work (with bean-managed persistence), you should be calling *getPrimaryKey()* whenever you need to figure out what data you're bean is associated with. This is very useful, for example, in the following methods:

Table 7.1 The javax.ejb.EJBContext Interface's Methods

METHOD	DESCRIPTION	USEFULNESS
getHome()	Returns a reference to the home object for that enterprise bean's class.	Useful if your bean needs to access its own home object factory. You can use the home object to create, destroy, or find EJB objects.
getEnvironment()	Returns a list of environment properties that were deployed with the bean. These properties can be used to set arbitrary information that a bean may need, such as locations of files.	*getEnvironment()* is useful when you deploy your beans with environment properties, and you need to access those environment properties.
getCallerIdentity()	Returns the identity of the client that is invoking methods on the bean instance's EJB object.	Useful for getting the caller's identity. You can use this identity for many things. For example, you can retrieve the caller's distinguished name and use it as a key to information in a database.
isCallerInRole()	Tests if a bean's client is in a particular security role.	This method is useful for querying whether the authenticated client is authorized to perform an operation. It relies on the concept of a *security role*, which is a group authorized to perform certain operations. Note that this method is useful for *authorization*, which is entirely different from *authentication*. Authentication verifies that the client is who he or she claims to be. This must be performed sometime before this method is called—such as when the client gets his or her identity. If the client has an identity, then it has been authenticated.
setRollbackOnly()	Allows the instance to mark the current transaction such that the only outcome of the transaction is a rollback.	Useful for forcing a transaction to abort and roll back.
getRollbackOnly()	Returns a Boolean indicating whether the current transaction has been marked for rollback.	This method will tell you if the current transaction is going to abort. If it's going to abort, you may be able to bypass logic in your bean, saving valuable computation time.

Table 7.1 *(Continued)*

METHOD	DESCRIPTION	USEFULNESS
getUserTransaction() *Note: This method is supported only if the bean performs its own transactions and is hence deployed with the TX_BEAN_MANAGED transaction attribute. See Chapter 10 for more details on this method.*	Returns the *javax.transaction.UserTransaction* interface that the bean can use for explicit transaction demarcation.	Use this method if you want to perform your own transactions programmatically in your bean. For some beans, the transparent, automatic transactions that EJB containers offer may be insufficient. This method allows you to control the transaction explicitly yourself. Once you call this method, your bean can demarcate transactional boundaries using the returned *javax.transaction.UserTransaction* object. You can then begin, commit, and rollback transactions explicitly.

ejbLoad(). If you recall, *ejbStore()* and *ejbLoad()* are bean callbacks to synchronize a bean instance with an underlying storage. *ejbStore()* saves data to storage, and *ejbLoad()* reads data from storage. When the container calls *ejbStore()*, your bean knows exactly what data to save because the bean instance has the data in memory. But when the container calls *ejbLoad()*, how does your bean know what data to load? After all, bean instances are pooled and can be dynamically assigned to different data. The answer is to use *getPrimaryKey()*; it will tell you what primary key you should be looking for in the underlying storage when loading database data.

ejbRemove(). If you recall, *ejbCreate()* and *ejbRemove()* are callbacks for creating and removing data from an underlying storage, respectively. When the container calls *ejbCreate()*, your bean knows exactly what data to create in the database because your bean has received information in the parameters of *ejbCreate()*. But when the container calls *ejbRemove()*, how does your bean know what data to remove? Because bean instances are pooled and dynamically assigned to handle different data instances, you might be deleting the wrong data. Thus you must call *getPrimaryKey()* to figure out what data, keyed on the primary key, your bean should remove from the database.

```
public interface javax.ejb.EntityContext implements javax.ejb.EJBContext {
    public abstract javax.ejb.EJBObject getEJBObject();
    public abstract java.lang.Object getPrimaryKey();
}
```

Source 7.4 The javax.ejb.EntityContext interface.

Thus, it's always important to consider bean pooling when writing your enterprise beans, and *getPrimaryKey()* is the key to always knowing what data your bean is representing.

Putting It All Together: Walking through an Entity Bean Life Cycle

Throughout this chapter, we've touched on various moments in the life cycle of an entity bean instance—when it's created, when it's destroyed, and how it's used. Now that you've seen all the elements, let's wrap up this chapter by examining the big picture and defining this process more concretely. The state machine diagram in Figure 7.7 illustrates the life cycle of an entity bean.

Here is what's going on in this diagram:

1. The *does not exist* state represents entity bean instances that have not been instantiated yet.

2. To create a new instance, the container calls the *newInstance()* method on the entity bean class. This calls your entity bean's default constructor, bringing a new instance into memory. Next, the container associates your entity bean with an entity context object—this is done via a callback that you implement, called *setEntityContext(EntityContext ctx)*. Note that this step occurs only when the container wants to increase the available pool of entity bean instances—this is not necessarily done when a client connects.

3. After step 2, your entity bean is in a pool of other entity beans. At this point your entity bean does not have any entity bean database data loaded into it, and it does not hold any bean-specific resources, such as socket connections. Your bean instance can be used in this mode to find entity data in the database, by servicing a *finder* method on behalf of a client. If the container wants to reduce its pool size, it can destroy your bean. The container signals your bean instance that it is about to be destroyed by calling the *unsetEntityContext()* method on your bean. Once this is done, the container releases any references to your bean, and eventually, the Java garbage collector will clean up the memory your instance had been using. Therefore, your *unsetEntityContext()* method should prepare your bean to be cleaned up, perhaps by releasing any bean-independent resources your bean had claimed.

4. When the client wants to create some new database data (say, a new order for goods placed over the Internet), it calls a *create()* method on your entity bean's home object. The container then grabs an entity bean instance from the pool, and the instance's *ejbCreate()* method is called. *ejbCreate()* initializes the entity bean to a specific data set. For example, if a client calls

a *create()* method to create a bank account, it might pass the bank account holder's name and the initial balance as parameters. Your entity bean's *ejbCreate()* method would populate its member variables with these parameters. It would also create the corresponding database representation (if you're using bean-managed persistence). Now your bean is in the "ready" state.

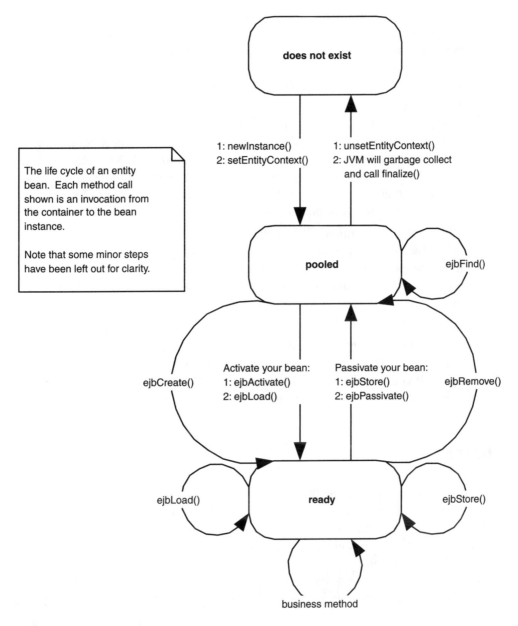

The life cycle of an entity bean. Each method call shown is an invocation from the container to the bean instance.

Note that some minor steps have been left out for clarity.

Figure 7.7 The entity bean life cycle.

5. While your bean is in the ready state, it is tied to specific data and hence a specific EJB object. If there are other entity bean instances that are views into the same database data, the container may occasionally need to synchronize your bean instance with the underlying database, so that you will always be working with the most recent data. The *ejbLoad()* and *ejbStore()* methods do this; the container calls them as appropriate, based on how you define your transactions (see Chapter 10).

6. There are two ways for your entity beans to be kicked back into the pool. If a client calls *remove()* on the home object, then the container will call your instance's *ejbRemove()*. The underlying database data is destroyed, and so, of course, your entity bean instance will become disassociated with the client's EJB object to which it was bound.

7. The second way your bean can return to the pool is if the EJB container decides that your client has timed out, if the container needs to use your bean to service a different client, or if the container is simply running out of resources. At this point, your bean is passivated, and the container calls your *ejbStore()* method to ensure the database has the most recent version of your in-memory data. Next, the container calls your *ejbPassivate()* method—allowing your bean instance to release all bean-specific resources. Your bean instance then enters the pool.

8. When the container wants to assign you to an EJB object again, your bean instance must be activated. The container calls your bean's *ejbActivate()* method, allowing your bean to acquire bean-specific resources. The container then calls your instance's *ejbLoad()* method to load the database data into your bean.

Note that there are a few other minor steps in this process, such as transactional synchronization. Overall, these stages are the essence of an entity bean instance's life cycle. If you've made it this far, then congratulations! You are ready to move on from theoretical concepts to the concrete entity bean programming.

Summary

In this chapter, we've taken the first steps toward developing with entity beans. We started by learning about various persistence mechanisms, including object serialization, object/relational mapping, and persistence to pure object databases. We then looked at exactly what an entity bean is, and we saw the files included with an entity bean component. Next, we used our knowledge of session beans as a basis for learning entity beans. After surveying their features, we took a look at the interfaces that EJB provides for entity bean components, such as the entity bean interface and the entity context interface. Finally, we stepped through the life cycle of a typical entity bean instance.

But the best is yet to come—in the next two chapters, we'll learn hands-on about entity bean programming. Chapter 8 starts off by explaining bean-managed persistent entity beans, and it guides you through the steps in developing them using JDBC. Chapter 9 then continues with container-managed persistent entity beans. Not only will we see how the programming styles differ, but we'll do a full comparison of the promises and realities of the two entity bean programming models. By the time you're through, you'll be armed to create your own entity beans in enterprise deployments.

## CHAPTER 8

Writing Bean-Managed Persistent Entity Beans

I n Chapter 7, we covered some basic entity bean concepts. We learned that there are two kinds of entity beans—*bean-managed persistent* and *container-managed persistent*.

In this chapter, we'll demonstrate how to program bean-managed persistent entity beans. When you code these types of entity beans, you must provide your own data access logic. You are responsible for providing the implementation to map your entity bean instances to and from storage. To do this, you'd typically use a database API such as JDBC or SQL/J. This is in stark contrast to container-managed persistent entity beans, which have their data access handled for them by the EJB container. This chapter will teach you the basics of bean-managed persistence and show you how to build a simple bean-managed entity bean using JDBC.

Implementation Guidelines for Bean-Managed Persistence

In Chapter 7, we saw that all entity bean classes—both bean-managed persistent and container-managed persistent—must implement the *javax.ejb.EntityBean* interface. This interface defines callback methods that the container invokes on your beans. What you should put in these methods depends in part on whether you are using bean-managed persistence or container-managed persistence. Table 8.1 is a summary of what you should implement in each method, assuming your entity bean's persistence is bean-managed. Take a quick glance at the

Table 8.1 Descriptions and Implementation Guidelines for Bean-Managed Persistent Entities

METHOD	EXPLANATION	TYPICAL
setEntityContext()	If the container wants to increase its pool size of bean instances, it will instantiate a new entity bean instance. Following this, the container calls the instance's *setEntityContext()*. This method associates a bean with *context information—* information about the bean's environment. Once this method is called, the bean can access information about its environment.	Stick the entity context somewhere, such as in a member variable. You can then access the context later to acquire environment information, such as security information, from the container. You should also request any resources your instance will need regardless of what data the bean represents. *The bean is now in a pool, does not have any specific database data inside of it, and is not bound to any particular EJB object.*
ejbFind<...>(<...>) (also called *finder* methods)	While your bean instance is still in the pool, the container can use your bean to service a *finder* method. Finder methods locate one or more existing entity bean data instances in the underlying persistent store. You must define at least one finder method— *ejbFindByPrimaryKey()*.	Search through a data store using a storage API such as JDBC or SQL/J. For example, you might perform a relational query such as "SELECT id FROM accounts WHERE balance > 0." When you've found some data, you should return the primary keys for that data back to the container by creating one or more primary key Java object instances. The container will then create EJB objects for the client to invoke on and possibly associate some entity bean instances with those EJB objects. *Those entity bean instances are then no longer in the pool—they now have specific database data inside of them, and they are bound to particular EJB objects.*
ejbCreate(<...>) *Note: You do not need to write any ejbCreate() methods if you don't want EJB clients to be able to create new database data. Instead, you could mandate*	When a client calls *create()* on a home object, the container then calls *ejbCreate()* on a pooled bean instance. *ejbCreate()* methods are responsible for creating new database data and for initializing your bean.	Make sure the client's initialization parameters are valid. Explicitly create the database representation of the data via a storage API such as JDBC or SQL/J. *Your entity bean instance is then no longer in the pool—it now has specific database data inside of it. The container will bind your instance to a particular EJB object.*

Table 8.1 *(Continued)*

METHOD	EXPLANATION	TYPICAL
that all data is created through other means, such as via direct database inserts or through batch files.		
ejbPostCreate(<...>) ejbPostCreate()	Your bean class must define one *ejbPostCreate()* for each *ejbCreate()*. Each pair must accept the same parameters. The container calls *ejbPostCreate()* right after *ejbCreate()*.	The container calls after it has associated your bean instance with an EJB object. You can now complete your initialization, by doing anything you need to that requires that EJB object, such as passing your bean's EJB object reference to other beans. You might also use this method to reset certain transaction-related parameters—for example, you could keep a data status flag in the bean to indicate whether a field has been changed. Because the bean instance may have been used before, these fields might have dirty data.
ejbActivate()	When a client calls a business method on an EJB object but there is no entity bean instance bound to the EJB object, the container needs to take a bean from the pool and transition it into a ready state. This is called *activation*. Upon activation, the *ejbActivate()* method is called by the EJB container. *Note: ejbActivate() is never called during a transaction.*	Acquire any bean-specific resources, such as socket connections, that your bean needs to service a particular client when it's moved into the ready state. Note that you should *not* read the entity bean data from the database in this method. That is handled by a separate method, *ejbLoad()*, which is called right after *ejbActivate()*.
ejbLoad()	The EJB container calls this to load database data into your bean instance, based on the current transactional state.	First, your bean instance must figure out what data it should load. Call the *getPrimaryKey()* method on the entity context; that will tell your bean what data it should be loading. Next, read database data into your bean via a storage API such as JDBC or SQL/J.

continues

Table 8.1 (Continued)

METHOD	EXPLANATION	TYPICAL
ejbStore()	The EJB container calls this to update the database to the new values of your in-memory fields, thus synchronizing the database. The current transactional state dictates when this method is called. Also, this method is called during passivation, directly before *ejbPassivate()*.	Explicitly update the database representation of the data via a storage API such as JDBC. Typically, you'll write a number of your member variable's fields out to disk.
ejbPassivate()	The EJB container will call this method when it wants to return your entity bean to the pool. This is called *passivation* and is the opposite of activation. On passivation, the ejbPassivate() method is called by the EJB container. Note: *ejbPassivate() is never called during a transaction.*	Release any resources, such as socket connections, that you allocated in ejbActivate() and that your bean was holding during the ready state for a particular client. You should not save the entity bean data into the database in this method. That is handled by a separate method, ejbStore(), which is called right before ejbPassivate().
ejbRemove()	Destroys database data. It is not used to destroy the Java Object; the object can be pooled and reused for different data.	First, figure out what data you should be destroying via getPrimaryKey() on the EntityContext. Then explicitly delete the database representation of the data via a storage API such as JDBC.
unsetEntityContext()	This method disassociates a bean from its environment. The container calls this right before your entity bean instance is destroyed (when it wants to reduce the pool size).	Release any resources you allocated during *setEntityContext()*, and get ready to be garbage collected.

chart for now. You should refer back to the chart when reading through the code in this chapter or when programming your own entity bean classes. The order of methods listed very roughly models the flow of control of an entity bean instance's life cycle that we saw at the end of Chapter 7.

Bean-Managed Persistence Example: A Bank Account

Our first example will be a simple bank account entity bean. This bank account bean can be used to represent and manipulate real bank account data in an underlying relational database.

The object model for our bank account is detailed in Figure 8.1.

Let's take a look at each of the files that we must create for our entity bean component.

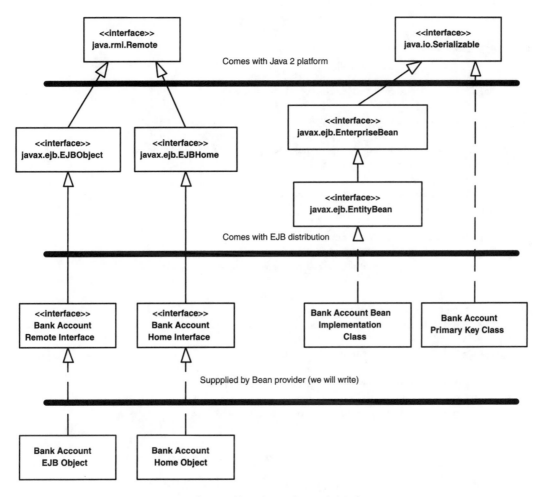

Figure 8.1 The bank account object model.

Account.java

Account.java is our entity bean's remote interface—what the client sees. It's shown in Source 8.1.

Notice that the account remote interface extends *javax.ejb.EJBObject*, which all remote interfaces must do. Our interface exposes a number of methods for manipulating entity beans, such as for making deposits and withdrawals. All of our methods throw remote exceptions to facilitate system-level catastrophic

```java
package com.wiley.compBooks.roman.entity.account;

import javax.ejb.*;
import java.rmi.RemoteException;

/**
 * This is the remote interface for AccountBean.
 *
 * This interface is what clients operate on when they interact with
 * beans. The container will implement this interface; the
 * implemented object is called the EJB object, which delegates
 * invocations to the actual bean.
 */
public interface Account extends EJBObject {

    /**
     * Deposits amt into account.
     */
    public void deposit(double amt) throws RemoteException;

    /**
     * Withdraws amt from bank account.
     * @throw AccountException thrown in amt < available balance
     */
    public void withdraw(double amt) throws AccountException, RemoteException;

    // Getter/setter methods on Entity Bean fields

    public double getBalance() throws RemoteException;

    public String getOwnerName() throws RemoteException;
    public void setOwnerName(String name) throws RemoteException;

    public String getAccountID() throws RemoteException;
    public void setAccountID(String id) throws RemoteException;
}
```

Source 8.1 Account.java.

failures. Notice that in our withdrawal method, we also throw our own custom application-level exception, *AccountException*. We'll define that exception bit later.

AccountHome.java

Our home interface is specified by *AccountHome.java*, shown in Source 8.2.

```
package com.wiley.compBooks.roman.entity.account;

import javax.ejb.*;
import java.rmi.RemoteException;
import java.util.Enumeration;

/**
 * This is the home interface for Account.  This interface is
 * implemented by the EJB Server's glue-code tools - the
 * implemented object is called the Home Object and serves as
 * a factory for EJB Objects.
 *
 * We define a single create() method is in this home interface,
 * which corresponds to the ejbCreate() method in AccountBean.
 */
public interface AccountHome extends EJBHome {

    /**
     * This method creates the EJB Object.
     *
     * Notice that the Home Interface returns a Remote Interface,
     * whereas the Bean returns a PK.
     *
     * @param accountID The number of the account (unique)
     * @param ownerName The name of the person who owns the account
     *
     * @return The newly created EJB Object.
     */
    Account create(String accountID, String ownerName) throws CreateException,
        RemoteException;

    /**
     * Finds an Account by its primary Key (Account ID)
     */
    public Account findByPrimaryKey(AccountPK key) throws FinderException,
        RemoteException;
```

Source 8.2 AccountHome.java *(continues)*.

```
/**
 * Finds an Account by its owner's name (assume there is only one)
 */
public Enumeration findByOwnerName(String name) throws FinderException,
    RemoteException;
}
```

Source 8.2 AccountHome.java *(continued)*.

We provide one method to create a new account. This will create new database data representing a bank account. It returns an EJB object to the client so that the client can manipulate that newly created account. Notice that we throw the application-level *javax.ejb.CreateException*, which all *create()* methods must throw.

We also have two finder methods. *findByPrimaryKey()* searches the database for a bank account that already exists; it searches by the account ID, which we will define below in *AccountPK.java*. We also have a custom finder method, *findByOwnerName()*, which searches the database for all bank accounts that have the same owner's name. Because we're using bean-managed persistence, we'll need to implement both of these finder methods in our entity bean implementation (if we were using container-managed persistence, the container would search the database for us). As with our *create* method, both finders return EJB objects so that the client can manipulate the newly found bank accounts. We throw the application-level *javax.ejb.FinderException*, which all finders must throw.

AccountPK.java

Our entity bean's primary key class is defined by *AccountPK.java*, detailed in Source 8.3.

Our primary key is a simple string—the account ID string. For example, an account ID string could be "ABC-123-0000." This string must be unique to its bank account—we rely on the client code that constructs our account ID to make sure it's unique. The primary key is used to identify each bank account uniquely.

AccountBean.java

Next, we have our entity bean implementation class, *AccountBean.java*. Our bean implementation code is quite lengthy, and it is divided into several sections:

Bean-managed state fields. These are the persistable fields of our entity bean class. Our bean instance will load and store the database data into these fields.

```
package com.wiley.compBooks.roman.entity.account;

import java.io.Serializable;

/**
 * Primary Key class for Account.
 */
public class AccountPK implements java.io.Serializable {
  public String accountID;

  public AccountPK(String id) {
    this.accountID = id;
  }

  public AccountPK() {
  }

  public String toString() {
    return accountID;
  }
}
```

Source 8.3   AccountPK.java.

Business logic methods. These methods perform services for clients, such as withdrawing or depositing into an account. They are exposed by the remote interface, *Account*.

EJB-required methods. These are EJB-required methods that the container will call to manage our bean. They also include our creator and finder methods defined in the home interface.

The code is presented in Source 8.4. Notice how cumbersome the code is—just for a simple bank account. This is an unfortunate drawback of bean-managed persistence because you must provide all data access code.

Notice that most of the logic in our bean is JDBC code. Our *withdraw* and *deposit* methods simply modify the in-memory fields of the entity bean instance. If the client tries to withdraw from a negative account, we throw our custom application-level exception, *AccountException*. Whenever we perform persistent operations, we retrieve a JDBC connection via the *getConnection()* method.

We acquire our environment information from the *EntityContext* by calling *getEnvironment()*. We then use that environment as a parameter to the JDBC *DriverManager's getConnection()* method. This environment specifies the JDBC drivers to load, via the *jdbc.drivers* property. We specify this property in the

```java
package com.wiley.compBooks.roman.entity.account;

import java.sql.*;
import javax.naming.*;
import javax.ejb.*;
import java.util.*;
import java.rmi.RemoteException;


/**
 * Demonstration Bean-Managed Persistent Entity Bean.
 * This Entity Bean represents a Bank Account.
 */
public class AccountBean implements EntityBean {

    protected EntityContext ctx;

    // Bean-managed state fields
    public String accountID;     // PK
    public String ownerName;
    public double balance;

    // Environment properties the bean was deployed with
    public Properties env;

    public AccountBean() {
        System.out.println("New Bank Account Entity Bean Java Object created
            by EJB Container.");
    }

    //
    // Business Logic Methods
    //

    /**
     * Deposits amt into account.
     */
    public void deposit(double amt) {
        System.out.println("deposit(" + amt + ") called.");

        balance += amt;
    }

    /**
     * Withdraws amt from bank account.
     * @throw AccountException thrown in amt < available balance
     */
    public void withdraw(double amt) throws AccountException {
        System.out.println("withdraw(" + amt + ") called.");
```

Source 8.4 AccountBean.java *(continues)*.

```
        if (amt > balance) {
            throw new AccountException("Your balance is " + balance +
                "!  You cannot withdraw " + amt + "!");
        }

        balance -= amt;
    }

    // Getter/setter methods on Entity Bean fields

    public double getBalance() {
        System.out.println("getBalance() called.");
        return balance;
    }

    public void setOwnerName(String name) {
        System.out.println("setOwnerName() called.");
        ownerName = name;
    }

    public String getOwnerName() {
        System.out.println("getOwnerName() called.");
        return ownerName;
    }

    public String getAccountID() {
        System.out.println("getAccountID() called.");
        return accountID;
    }

    public void setAccountID(String id) {
        System.out.println("setAccountID() called.");
        this.accountID = id;
    }

    //
    // EJB-required methods
    //

    /**
     * Called by Container.  Implementation can acquire
     * needed resources.
     */
    public void ejbActivate() throws RemoteException {
        System.out.println("ejbActivate() called.");
    }

    /**
     * Removes entity bean data from the database.
```

Source 8.4 AccountBean.java *(continues)*.

```
   * Corresponds to when client calls home.remove().
   */
 public void ejbRemove() throws RemoteException {
     System.out.println("ejbRemove() called.");

     /*
      * Remember that an entity bean class can be used to
      * represent different data instances.  So how does
      * this method know which instance in the database
      * to delete?
      *
      * The answer is to query the container by calling
      * the entity context object.  By retrieving the
      * primary key from the entity context, we know
      * which data instance, keyed by the PK, that we
      * should delete from the DB.
      */
     AccountPK pk = (AccountPK) ctx.getPrimaryKey();
     String id = pk.accountID;

     PreparedStatement pstmt = null;
     Connection conn = null;
     try {
        /*
         * 1) Acquire a new JDBC Connection
         */
        conn = getConnection();

        /*
         * 2) Remove account from the DB
         */
        pstmt = conn.prepareStatement(
             "delete from accounts where id = ?");
        pstmt.setString(1, id);

        /*
         * 3) Throw a system-level exception if something
         * bad happened.
         */
        if (pstmt.executeUpdate() == 0) {
            throw new RemoteException("Account " + pk +
            " failed to be removed from the database");
        }
     }
     catch (SQLException ex) {
        throw new RemoteException(ex.toString());
     }
     finally {
        /*
```

Source 8.4 AccountBean.java *(continues).*

```
     * 4) Release the DB Connection
     */
    try {
        if (pstmt != null) pstmt.close();
    }
    catch (Exception e) { }
        try {
            if (conn != null) conn.close();
        }
        catch (Exception e) { }
    }
}

/**
 * Called by Container.  Releases held resources for
 * passivation.
 */
public void ejbPassivate() throws RemoteException {
    System.out.println("ejbPassivate () called.");
}

/**
 * Called by the container.  Updates the in-memory entity
 * bean object to reflect the current value stored in
 * the database.
 */
public void ejbLoad() throws RemoteException {
    System.out.println("ejbLoad() called.");

    /*
     * Again, query the Entity Context to get the current
     * Primary Key, so we know which instance to load.
     */
    AccountPK pk = (AccountPK) ctx.getPrimaryKey();
    String id = pk.accountID;

    PreparedStatement pstmt = null;
        Connection conn = null;
    try {
        /*
         * 1) Acquire a new DB Connection
         */
        conn = getConnection();

        /*
         * 2) Get account from the DB, querying
         *    by account ID
         */
```

Source 8.4   AccountBean.java *(continues).*

```
            pstmt = conn.prepareStatement("select ownerName, balance from
                accounts where id = ?");
            pstmt.setString(1, id);
            ResultSet rs = pstmt.executeQuery();
            rs.next();
            ownerName = rs.getString("ownerName");
            balance = rs.getDouble("balance");
        }
        catch (SQLException ex) {
            throw new RemoteException("Account " + pk +
                " failed to load from database", ex);
        }
        finally {
            /*
             * 3) Release the DB Connection
             */
            try {
                if (pstmt != null) pstmt.close();
            }
            catch (Exception e) { }
            try {
                if (conn != null) conn.close();
            }
            catch (Exception e) { }
        }

    }

    /**
     * Called from the Container.  Updates the database
     * to reflect the current values of this in-memory
     * entity bean instance.
     */
    public void ejbStore() throws RemoteException {
        System.out.println("ejbStore() called.");

        PreparedStatement pstmt = null;
                Connection conn = null;
        try {
            /*
             * 1) Acquire a new DB Connection
             */
            conn = getConnection();

            /*
             * 2) Store account in DB
             */
            pstmt = conn.prepareStatement(
                "update accounts set ownerName = ?, balance = ? where id = ?");
```

Source 8.4 AccountBean.java *(continues)*.

```
                pstmt.setString(1, ownerName);
                pstmt.setDouble(2, balance);
                pstmt.setString(3, accountID);
                pstmt.executeUpdate();


        }
        catch (SQLException ex) {
            throw new RemoteException("Account " + accountID +
            " failed to save to database", ex);
        }
        finally {
            /*
             * 3) Release the DB Connection
             */
            try {
                if (pstmt != null) pstmt.close();
            }
            catch (Exception e) { }
            try {
                if (conn != null) conn.close();
            }
            catch (Exception e) { }
        }
    }


    /**
     * Called by the container.  Associates this bean
     * instance with a particular context.  We can query
     * the bean properties that customize the bean here.
     */
    public void setEntityContext(EntityContext ctx) throws RemoteException {
        System.out.println("setEntityContext called");
        this.ctx = ctx;

        env = ctx.getEnvironment();
    }


    /**
     * Called by Container.  Disassociates this bean
     * instance with a particular context environment.
     */
    public void unsetEntityContext() throws RemoteException {
        System.out.println("unsetEntityContext called");
        this.ctx = null;
        this.env = null;
    }


    /**
     * Called after ejbCreate().  Now, the Bean can retrieve
```

Source 8.4 AccountBean.java *(continues)*.

```java
 * its EJBObject from its context, and pass it as
 * a 'this' argument.
 */
public void ejbPostCreate(String accountID, String ownerName) throws
    RemoteException {
}

/**
 * This is the initialization method that corresponds to the
 * create() method in the Home Interface.
 *
 * When the client calls the Home Object's create() method,
 * the Home Object then calls this ejbCreate() method.
 *
 * @return The primary key for this account
 */
public AccountPK ejbCreate(String accountID, String ownerName) throws
    CreateException, RemoteException {

  PreparedStatement pstmt = null;
  Connection conn = null;
  try {
    System.out.println("ejbCreate() called.");
    this.accountID = accountID;
    this.ownerName = ownerName;
    this.balance = 0;

    /*
     * Acquire DB connection
     */
    conn = getConnection();

    /*
     * Insert the account into the database
     */
    pstmt = conn.prepareStatement("insert into accounts (id, ownerName,
        balance) values (?, ?, ?)");
    pstmt.setString(1, accountID);
    pstmt.setString(2, ownerName);
    pstmt.setDouble(3, balance);
    pstmt.executeUpdate();

    /*
     * Generate the Primary Key and return it
     */
    return new AccountPK(accountID);
  }
  catch (Exception e) {
```

Source 8.4 AccountBean.java *(continues)*.

```
            throw new CreateException(e.toString());
      }
      finally {
        /*
         * Release DB Connection for other beans
         */
        try {
            pstmt.close();
        }
        catch (Exception e) { }
        try {
            conn.close();
        }
        catch (Exception e) { }
      }
}

/**
 * Finds a Account by its primary Key
 */
public AccountPK ejbFindByPrimaryKey(AccountPK key) throws
      FinderException, RemoteException {
      PreparedStatement pstmt = null;
      Connection conn = null;
    try {
      System.out.println("ejbFindByPrimaryKey(" + key + ") called");

      /*
       * Acquire DB connection
       */
      conn = getConnection();

      /*
       * Find the Entity in the DB
       */
      pstmt = conn.prepareStatement("select id from accounts where id = ?");
      pstmt.setString(1, key.toString());
      ResultSet rs = pstmt.executeQuery();
      rs.next();

      /*
       * No errors occurred, so return the Primary Key
       */
      return key;
    }
    catch (Exception e) {
      throw new FinderException(e.toString());
    }
```

Source 8.4 AccountBean.java *(continues)*.

```
      finally {
        /*
         * Release DB Connection for other beans
         */
        try {
            pstmt.close();
        }
        catch (Exception e) { }
        try {
            conn.close();
        }
        catch (Exception e) { }
    }
}

/**
 * Finds a Account by its Name
 */
public Enumeration ejbFindByOwnerName(String name) throws
    FinderException, RemoteException {
  PreparedStatement pstmt = null;
  Connection conn = null;
  Vector v = new Vector();

  try {
    System.out.println("ejbFindByOwnerName(" + name + ") called");

    /*
     * Acquire DB connection
     */
    conn = getConnection();

    /*
     * Find the primary keys in the DB
     */
    pstmt = conn.prepareStatement(
        "select id from accounts where ownerName = ?");
    pstmt.setString(1, name);
    ResultSet rs = pstmt.executeQuery();

    /*
     * Insert every primary key found into a vector
     */
    while (rs.next()) {
        String id = rs.getString("id");
        v.addElement(new AccountPK(id));
    }
```

Source 8.4 AccountBean.java *(continues)*.

```
      /*
       * Return an enumeration of found primary keys
       */
      return v.elements();
    }
    catch (Exception e) {
      throw new FinderException(e.toString());
    }
    finally {
      /*
       * Release DB Connection for other beans
       */
      try {
          pstmt.close();
      }
      catch (Exception e) { }
      try {
          conn.close();
      }
      catch (Exception e) { }
    }
}

public static final String JDBC_URL = "JDBC_URL";

/**
 * Gets current connection to the connection pool.
 *
 * Note: In the future, once vendors have adopted JDBC 2.0,
 * the preferred method for retrieving a JDBC Connection is
 * through JNDI.
 *
 * Assumes that environment properties contain a property
 * named "user" and "password" if authentication is desired.
 * These environment properties are retrieved from the
 * EntityContext object during setEntityContext().
 *
 * @return                 Connection
 * @exception              java.sql.SQLException
 *
 */
public Connection getConnection() throws SQLException {
    String jdbcURL = (String) env.get(JDBC_URL);

    // For debugging...
    // String drivers = (String) env.get("jdbc.drivers");
    // System.out.println(jdbcURL + ", " + drivers);
    // DriverManager.setLogStream(System.out);
```

Source 8.4 AccountBean.java *(continues).*

```
        return DriverManager.getConnection(jdbcURL, env);
    }
}
```

Source 8.4   AccountBean.java *(continued)*.

application-specific environment properties that ship with our bean, as we'll see very shortly. We also specify the particular database to connect to via a property we call *JDBC_URL*. This property is passed to the *DriverManager* as well, so it knows with which database to hook up.

In our bank account example, we retrieve our JDBC connections via the JDBC call *DriverManager.getConnection()*. We also close each connection after every method call. This allows our EJB container to pool JDBC connections. When the connection is not in use, another bean can use our connection.

Although this works with BEA *WebLogic* server, it is not a standard, portable way for connection pooling. *WebLogic* performs pooling directly beneath the JDBC 1.0 driver shell, but other EJB vendors may require different mechanisms for pooling database connections. Connection pooling is unfortunately not specified by JDBC 1.0, which means that any enterprise beans that use JDBC 1.0 are not very portable.

There is a light at the end of the tunnel. The new JDBC 2.0 specification, which has been finalized, supports a portable mechanism of database connection pooling. Already vendors are beginning to support JDBC 2.0, and by the time you read this, most every serious relational database vendor should have a JDBC 2.0 driver. The Java 2 Platform, Enterprise Edition (J2EE) specification mandates support of JDBC 2.0 as well, which is good news for anyone writing to J2EE and the EJB 1.1 specification. Furthermore, EJB 1.1 specifies a portable way to retrieve a JDBC driver through the *Java Naming and Directory Interface* (*JNDI*), which we detail in Appendix D.

Our finder methods use JDBC to perform SELECT statements on the relational database to query for bank account records. We create a new primary key class for the data we find, and we return the primary key to the container. The container will then instantiate EJB objects that match each primary key, so that the clients can start working with the data.

To create a new bank account, the client calls *create()* on the home object, which calls our *ejbCreate()* and *ejbPostCreate()* methods. Notice that we insert some data into the database using JDBC in *ejbCreate()*. We also assign our member variables the data passed in from the client. We don't need to use *ejbPostCreate()* for anything. Our entity bean is now associated with some specific database data and is associated with a client-specific EJB object.

Notice that we don't hold any bean-independent resources, so our *setEntity-Context()* and *unsetEntityContext()* methods are fairly bare-boned. We also don't hold any bean-specific resources, so our *ejbPassivate()* and *ejbActivate()* methods are empty.

When the container synchronizes our bean with the database, the *ejbLoad()* and *ejbStore()* methods perform JDBC persistence, thus keeping everyone's data in synch. Notice that *ejbLoad()* acquires the primary key via a *getPrimaryKey()* call to the Entity Context. This is how it figures out what data to load.

 JDBC can be very tough to debug due to incompatibilities between databases. It's much easier to debug JDBC if you log what JDBC is doing behind the scenes. To do this, see the commented code in the *getConnection()* method of *AccountBean.java*. Simply uncomment those lines to enable logging.

AccountException.java

Our custom exception class is *AccountException.java*, displayed in Source 8.5. It simply delegates to the parent *java.lang.Exception* class. It's still useful to define our own custom exception class, however, so that we can distinguish between a problem with our bank account component, and a problem with another part of a deployed system.

```
package com.wiley.compBooks.roman.entity.account;

/**
 * Exceptions thrown by Accounts
 */
public class AccountException extends Exception {

    public AccountException() {
        super();
    }

    public AccountException(Exception e) {
        super(e.toString());
    }

    public AccountException(String s) {
        super(s);
    }
}
```

Source 8.5 AccountException.java.

Client.java

Our last Java file is a simple test client to exercise our bean's methods. It's shown in Source 8.6.

The client code is fairly self-explanatory. We perform some bank account operations in the try block. We have a finally clause to make sure our bank account is properly deleted afterward, regardless of any exceptions that may have been thrown.

```java
package com.wiley.compBooks.roman.entity.account;

import javax.ejb.*;
import javax.naming.*;
import java.rmi.*;
import java.util.Enumeration;

/**
 * Sample client code that manipulates a Bank Account Entity Bean.
 */
public class Client {

    public static void main(String[] args) {

        Account account = null;

        try {
            /*
             * Get a reference to the Account Home Object - the
             * factory for Account EJB Objects
             */
            Context ctx = new InitialContext(System.getProperties());
            AccountHome home =
            (AccountHome) ctx.lookup("AccountHome");

            /*
             * Use the factory to create the Account EJB Object
             */
            home.create("123-456-7890", "John Smith");

            /*
             * Find an account
             */
            Enumeration e = home.findByOwnerName("John Smith");
            if (e != null) {
                account = (Account) e.nextElement();
            }
```

Source 8.6 Client.java *(continues)*.

```
                else {
                    throw new Exception("Could not find account");
                }

                /*
                 * Call the balance() method, and print it
                 */
                System.out.println("Initial Balance = " + account.getBalance());

                /*
                 * Deposit $100 into the account
                 */
                account.deposit(100);

                /*
                 * Retrieve the resulting balance.
                 */
                System.out.println("After depositing 100, account balance = " +
                    account.getBalance());

                /*
                 * Retrieve the Primary Key from the EJB Object
                 */
                AccountPK pk = (AccountPK) account.getPrimaryKey();

                /*
                 * Release our old EJB Object reference.  Now call
                 * find() again, this time querying on Account ID
                 * (i.e. the Primary Key).
                 */
                account = null;
                account = home.findByPrimaryKey(pk);

                /*
                 * Print out current balance
                 */
                System.out.println("Found account with ID " + pk + ".  Balance = "
                    + account.getBalance());

                /*
                 * Try to withdraw $150
                 */
                System.out.println(
                    "Now trying to withdraw $150, which is more than is " +
                    "currently available.  This should generate an exception..");
                account.withdraw(150);

        }
        catch (Exception e) {
```

Source 8.6   Client.java *(continues)*.

```
            System.out.println("Caught exception!");
            e.printStackTrace();
      }
      finally {
            /*
             * Destroy the Entity permanently
             */
            try {
                System.out.println("Destroying account..");
                if (account != null) {
                    account.remove();
                }
            }
            catch (Exception e) {
                e.printStackTrace();
            }
      }
   }
}
```

Source 8.6 Client.java *(continued)*.

The Deployment Descriptor

Now, let's take a look at our deployment descriptor. The deployment descriptors for entity beans are slightly different from those for their sister session beans. Our deployment descriptor is shown in Table 8.2.

Table 8.2 Deployment Descriptor Settings for AccountBean

DEPLOYMENT DESCRIPTOR SETTING	VALUE
Bean home name	AccountHome
Enterprise bean class name	com.wiley.compBooks.roman.entity.account.AccountBean
Home interface class name	com.wiley.compBooks.roman.entity.account.AccountHome
Remote interface class name	com.wiley.compBooks.roman.entity.account.Account
Environment properties	see Table 8.3.
Re-entrant	false
Primary key class name	com.wiley.compBooks.roman.entity.account.AccountPK
Container-managed fields	<empty>

Table 8.2 illustrates a typical deployment descriptor for a bean-managed persistent entity bean. Notice that we have two new fields that we do not have for session beans:

The primary key class name identifies the Java class for our primary key. Session beans do not have primary keys because they are not persistent.

The container-managed fields entry specifies what fields of your entity bean class are persistent fields. This applies only to container-managed persistent entity beans (described in Chapter 9), and it should be left blank when using bean-managed persistence.

Environment Properties

Next, we have our bean's custom environment properties. These environment properties allow consumers of your bean to tune your bean's functionality without touching your bean's source code (shown originally in Chapter 6). Our bean class retrieves these properties via *EntityContext.getEnvironment()*. The properties are shown in Table 8.3.

Notice that we're using enterprise bean environment properties to specify JDBC initialization information. This enables a consumer of our bean to use the database of his or her choice without modifying our bean code. The particular JDBC settings you use will vary depending on your configuration. Consult your database documentation or JDBC driver documentation for more details.

The JDBC_URL setting is passed to the DriverManager to locate the proper database. The jdbc.drivers setting is passed to the DriverManager to locate the proper JDBC driver.

Setting Up the Database

Lastly, you need to create the appropriate database table and columns for our bank accounts. You can do this through your database's GUI or command-line interface. The book's included CD-ROM comes with a preconfigured sample database that you can use right away. If you're using a different database, you

Table 8.3 Environment Properties for AccountBean

ENVIRONMENT PROPERTY SETTING	VALUE
jdbc.drivers	Your database's JDBC driver goes here. For example: "com.sun.jdbc.odbc.JdbcOdbcDriver."
JDBC_URL	Your database's JDBC URL goes here. For example: "jdbc:odbc:ejbdatabase."

should enter the following SQL *Data Definition Language (DDL)* statements in your database's SQL interface:

```
drop table accounts;
create table accounts (id varchar(64), ownername varchar(64), balance
    numeric(18));
```

This creates an empty table of bank accounts. The first column is the bank account id (the primary key), the second column is the bank account owner's name, and the third column is the bank account balance.

Running the Client Program

To run the client program, type a command similar to the following (depending on what your EJB container's Java Naming and Directory Interface (JNDI) connection parameters are—see your container's documentation):

```
java
-Djava.naming.factory.initial=weblogic.jndi.TengahInitialContextFactory
-Djava.naming.provider.url=t3://localhost:7001
com.wiley.compBooks.entity.Account.Client
```

The initialization parameters are required by JNDI to find the home object, as we learned in Chapter 4.

Server-Side Output

When you run the client, you should see something *similar* to the following on the server side. Note that your particular output may vary, due to variances in EJB container behavior.

```
New Bank Account Entity Bean Java Object created by EJB Container.
setEntityContext called
ejbCreate() called.
New Bank Account Entity Bean Java Object created by EJB Container.
setEntityContext called
ejbFindByOwnerName(John Smith) called
ejbLoad() called.
getBalance() called.
ejbStore() called.
ejbLoad() called.
deposit(100.0) called.
ejbStore() called.
ejbLoad() called.
getBalance() called.
```

```
ejbStore() called.
ejbLoad() called.
getBalance() called.
ejbStore() called.
ejbLoad() called.
withdraw(150.0) called.
ejbRemove() called.
```

Notice what's happening here:

- When our client code called *create()* on the home object, the container created an entity bean instance. The container first called *newInstance()* and *setEntityContext()* to get the entity bean into the available pool of entity beans. The container then serviced our client's *create()* method by taking that bean out of the pool. It called the bean instance's *ejbCreate()* method, which created some new database data, and returned control back to the container. Finally, the container associated the bean instance with a new EJB object and returned that EJB object to the client.

- To service our *finder* method, the container instantiated another entity bean. The container called *newInstance()* and then *setEntityContext()* to get that new bean instance into the available pool of entity beans. It then used the bean in the pool to service our finder method. Note that the bean instance is still in the pool and could service any number of finder methods.

- In addition to the methods that the client calls, our EJB container inter-leaved a few *ejbStore()* and *ejbLoad()* calls to keep the database in synch.

Testing JDBC Database Work

Probably the most frustrating part of an application is doing the database work. Often you will have punctuation errors or misspellings, which are tough to debug when performing JDBC. This is because your JDBC queries are not compiled—they are interpreted at runtime, so you don't get the nifty things like type checking that the Java language gives you. You are basically at the mercy of the JDBC driver. It may or may not give you useful feedback.

You might consider using SQL/J instead of JDBC. SQL/J precompiles your SQL code, and you don't have to write all the prepares and JDBC connection code—you just write embedded SQL code. SQL/J is available with Oracle Corporation's Oracle database and with IBM's DB2 database.

When performing any kind of database work, the best way to debug is to set up a simple test database. If your queries are not functioning properly, try duplicating and running them against your database using your database's direct interface. This should help you track down your database problems much more quickly.

Client-Side Output

Running the client program yields the following client-side output:

```
Initial Balance = 0.0
After depositing 100, account balance = 100.0
Found account with ID 123-456-7890.  Balance = 100.0
Now trying to withdraw $150, which is more than is currently available.
This should generate an exception..
Caught exception!
com.wiley.compBooks.roman.entity.account.AccountException: Your balance
is 100.0!  You cannot withdraw 150.0!
Destroying account..
```

We created an entity bean, deposited into it, and tried to withdraw more than we had. The entity bean correctly threw an application-level exception back to us indicating that our balance had insufficient funds.

Summary

In this chapter, you've seen how to write bean-managed persistent entity beans. Bean-managed persistent entity beans are useful if you need to control the underlying database operations yourself. EJB's real advantage comes from *container-managed persistent* entity beans. Container-managed persistent entity beans can be developed much more rapidly because the container handles all data access logic for you. The next chapter covers container-managed persistence.

## CHAPTER 9

Writing Container-Managed Persistent Entity Beans

I n Chapter 8, we wrote a bean-managed persistent entity bean representing a bank account. In this chapter, we'll see how things change when we move to a container-managed model. With container-managed persistence, you don't implement any persistence logic in the entity bean itself—rather, the EJB container performs storage operations for you. As you will see, this greatly simplifies bean development.

Before reading this chapter, you should be familiar with the entity bean concepts we covered in Chapter 7.

Container-Managed Fields

A container-managed persistent entity bean allows the container to handle some or all of its data access logic. Rather than coding JDBC or SQL/J operations in your bean class, your container implicitly performs all database operations behind the scenes.

With container-managed persistence, you must make some of your entity bean class's fields public so that the container can set the fields when it performs database operations on behalf of your bean. The fields that you want to be persistent are called *container-managed fields*. You don't have to worry about setting these fields—the EJB container will automatically manipulate them for you behind the scenes when it performs storage operations.

One restriction of container-managed fields is that every field you want to be managed by the container must follow the rules for Java object serialization (we describe these rules in full in Appendix A). This means that primitive types such as doubles and Booleans, as well as serializable classes such as primary key classes or EJB handles to other entity beans, can be container-managed fields.

For example, the following is a snippet of code from our bank account entity bean class that we wrote in Chapter 8:

```
public class AccountBean implements EntityBean {
    public String accountID;     // PK
    public String ownerName;
    public double balance;
...
}
```

With container-managed persistence, the container can persist each of these fields for you behind the scenes. When saving your bean instance's fields, the container is responsible for querying your bean instance for these field values. When loading data into your bean instance, the container sets these fields. This is possible because each of the fields is declared as public.

Of course, you still must inform the container about which fields it should manipulate. You specify this in your bean's deployment descriptor. The EJB container will inspect the deployment descriptor to figure out which of your entity bean's fields to manipulate.

Note that not all fields within the bean have to be managed by the container. You might be pulling data manually from a secondary source, or you might have calculated fields. The EJB container will automatically notify your bean class during persistent operations, allowing you to manage these fields.

Primary Key Class

As with bean-managed persistence, container-managed persistence dictates that your primary key class must be serializable. Because the EJB container will work with your primary key, there are new restrictions for how you write your primary key class. The most important restriction is that the fields you have in your primary key must come from the container-managed fields of your entity bean, which we described previously. This restriction allows the EJB container to set, as well as extract, your entity bean's primary key fields.

For example, take our primary key class from our Chapter 8's bank account:

```
public class AccountPK implements java.io.Serializable {
  public String accountID;
...
}
```

This is a valid primary key class for container-managed persistence because it's serializable and because its public fields come from our bean class's container-managed fields.

Implementation Guidelines for Container-Managed Persistence

The method implementations of your entity beans should be different for container-managed persistent entities. No longer are you controlling the routine persistent operations of your beans, and so many of the methods can be left empty—the container will do it for you. Table 9.1 is a summary of what you should implement in each method, assuming your entity bean's persistence is container managed. Take a quick glance at the chart for now. As you can see from the table, many of the database-intensive operations have been reduced in scope significantly. You should refer back to the chart when reading through the code in this chapter or when programming your own entity bean classes. The order of methods listed very roughly models the flow of control of an entity bean instance's life cycle that we saw at the end of Chapter 7.

Table 9.1   Descriptions and Implementation Guidelines for Container-Managed Persistent Entities

METHOD	EXPLANATION	TYPICAL IMPLEMENTATION
setEntityContext() (same as bean-managed persistence)	If the container wants to increase its pool size of bean instances, it will instantiate a new entity bean instance. Following this, the container calls the instance's *setEntityContext()*. This method associates a bean with *context information—*information about the bean's environment. Once this method is called, the bean can access information about its environment.	Stick the entity context somewhere, such as in a member variable. You can then access the context later to acquire environment information, such as security information, from the container. You should also request any resources your instance will need regardless of what data the bean represents. *The bean is now in a pool, does not have any specific database data inside of it, and is not bound to any particular EJB object.*

continues

Table 9.1 *(Continued)*

METHOD	EXPLANATION	TYPICAL IMPLEMENTATION
ejbFind<...>(<...>) (new for container-managed persistence)	*You do not write finder methods for container-managed beans.* The EJB container will handle *all* issues relating to finding data for you. But how does the EJB container know what kinds of finder methods you want in your bean? After all, there are an infinite variety of ways to find data in a database. The answer is that your EJB container ships with tools for this purpose. You use the container tools to tell the container what logic to execute when the client performs a finder method on the home object. You'll see how BEA's WebLogic does this in the next example.	You should not implement these methods for container-managed persistent entity beans.
ejbCreate(<...>) (new for container-managed persistence) *Note: You do not need to write any ejbCreate() methods if you don't want EJB clients to be able to create new database data. Some systems may allow creation of data to occur via direct database inserts, through batch files or other means.*	When a client calls *create()* on a home object, the container then calls *ejbCreate()* on a pooled bean instance. *ejbCreate()* methods are responsible for creating new database data and initializing your bean.	*Do not create database data in this method.* Rather, simply check that the client parameters are correct, and set your container-managed fields to the parameters passed in. After the EJB container calls your *ejbCreate()* method, it will extract the container-managed fields from your bean and create the database representation of the data for you. If you'll recall, with bean-managed persistence, your *ejbCreate()* method returns a primary key class to the container. With container-managed persistence, you don't need to return a primary key class. The EJB container can simply extract data from your public fields and create a primary key object by itself. *Your entity bean instance is then no longer in the pool—it now has specific database data inside it. The container will bind your instance to a particular EJB objects.*

METHOD	EXPLANATION	TYPICAL IMPLEMENTATION
ejbPostCreate(<...>) (new for container-managed persistence)	There is one *ejbPostCreate(...)* for each *ejbCreate(...)*. Each pair has the same parameters. The container calls your bean instance's *ejbPostCreate(...)* method following *ejbCreate(...)*.	The container calls *ejbPostCreate()* after it has associated your bean instance with an EJB object. You can now complete your initialization, by doing anything you need to that requires that EJB object, such as passing your bean's EJB object reference to other beans. You might also use this method to reset certain transaction-related parameters—for example, you could keep a data status flag in the bean to indicate whether a field has been changed. Because the bean instance may have been used before, these fields might have dirty data. *Note: By now the EJB container will have created your primary key object, so you can now retrieve it and use it.*
ejbActivate() (same as bean-managed persistence)	When a client calls a business method on an EJB object, but there is no entity bean instance bound to the EJB object, the container needs to take a bean from the pool and transition it into a ready state. This is called *activation*. On activation, the *ejbActivate()* method is called by the EJB container. *Note: ejbActivate() is never called during a transaction.*	Acquire any bean-specific resources, such as socket connections, that your bean needs to service a particular client when it's moved into the ready state.
ejbLoad() (new for container-Managed Persistence)	The EJB container calls this to load database data into your bean instance, based on the current transactional state.	*Do not read data from the database in this method.* Rather, the EJB container will read in data from the database for you automatically right *before* calling your *ejbLoad()* method. It does this by setting your container-managed fields to the data it reads from the database. In this method, you should perform any utilities you need to work with the read-in data, such as decompressing a text field.

continues

Table 9.1 (Continued)

METHOD	EXPLANATION	TYPICAL IMPLEMENTATION
ejbStore() (new for container-managed persistence)	The EJB container calls this to update the database to the new values of your in-memory fields, thus synchronizing the database. The current transactional state dictates when this method is called. Also, this method is called during passivation, directly before *ejbPassivate()*.	*Do not update the database in this method.* Rather, the EJB container will update the database for you automatically right *after* calling your *ejbStore()* method. It does this by extracting your container-managed fields and writing them to the database. In this method, you should prepare your container-managed fields to be written to the database. For example, you can compress the text of your fields if necessary.
ejbPassivate() (same as bean-managed persistence)	The EJB container will call this method when it wants to return your entity bean to the pool. This is called *passivation* and is the opposite of activation. On passivation, the *ejbPassivate()* method is called by the EJB container. Note: *ejbPassivate() is never called during a transaction.*	Release any resources, such as socket connections, that you allocated in *ejbActivate()* and that your bean was holding during the ready state for a particular client.
ejbRemove() (new for container-managed persistence)	The client calls the home object's *remove()* method to destroy database data *remove()*, which then calls your *ejbRemove()*. Note that this does not destroy the Java Object because the object can be pooled and reused for different data.	*Do not destroy database data in this method.* Rather, simply perform any operations that must be done before the data in the database is destroyed. The EJB container will destroy the data for you right after *ejbRemove()* is called.
unsetEntityContext() (same as bean-managed persistence)	This method disassociates a bean from its environment. The container calls this right before your entity bean instance is destroyed (when it wants to reduce the pool size).	Release any resources you allocated during *setEntityContext()*, and get ready to be garbage collected.

Container-Managed Persistence Example: A Product Line

Let's see a quick demonstration of container-managed persistence in action, applied to the concept of a product line.

If you're working for a product-based company, your company's product line is the suite of products your company offers. For example, if you're an appliance company, you might offer a dishwasher, a stove, and a dryer. If you're a computer hardware company, you might offer memory, hard disks, and processors. We're going to model a generic product as an entity bean that uses container-managed persistence.

The object model for our product line is detailed in Figure 9.1.

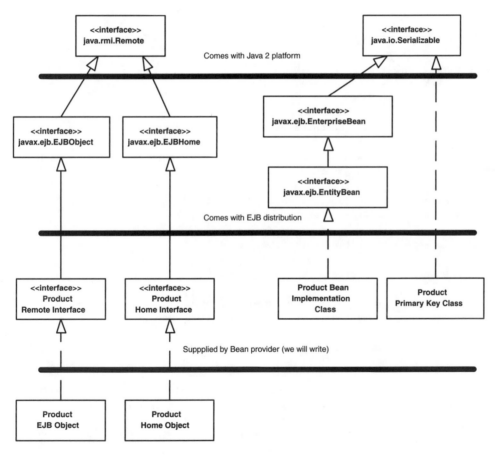

Figure 9.1 The object model for our product line.

Let's take a look at each of the files that we must create for our entity bean component.

Product.java

Our remote interface is specified by *Product.java*, shown in Source 9.1.

Our remote interface is very similar to Chapter 8's bank account remote interface. It has methods to modify the entity bean instance's fields and throws remote exceptions to indicate system-level errors.

ProductHome.java

Next, we have the product's home interface, *ProductHome.java*, presented in Source 9.2.

```java
package com.wiley.compBooks.roman.entity.product;

import javax.ejb.*;
import java.rmi.RemoteException;

/**
 * These are the public business methods of ProductBean.
 *
 * This interface is what clients operate on when they
 * interact with beans. The EJB Server vendor will
 * implement this interface; the implemented object instance
 * is called the EJB Object, which delegates invocations to
 * instances of the ProductBean class.
 */
public interface Product extends EJBObject {

    // Getter/setter methods for Entity Bean fields

    public String getName() throws RemoteException;
    public void setName(String name) throws RemoteException;

    public String getDescription() throws RemoteException;
    public void setDescription(String description) throws RemoteException;

    public double getBasePrice() throws RemoteException;
    public void setBasePrice(double price) throws RemoteException;

    public String getProductID() throws RemoteException;
}
```

Source 9.1 Product.java.

```java
package com.wiley.compBooks.roman.entity.product;

import javax.ejb.*;
import java.rmi.RemoteException;
import java.util.Enumeration;

/**
 * This is the home interface for Product.  This interface
 * is implemented by the EJB Server's glue-code tools.
 * The implemented object is called the Home Object and
 * serves as a factory for EJB Objects.
 *
 * One create() method is in this Home Interface, which
 * corresponds to the ejbCreate() method in the Product file.
 */
public interface ProductHome extends EJBHome {

    /*
     * This method creates the EJB Object.
     *
     * Notice that the Home Interface returns an EJB Object,
     * whereas the Bean returns void.  This is because the
     * EJB Container is responsible for generating the EJB
     * Object, whereas the Bean is responsible for
     * initialization.
     *
     * @param productID The number of the product (unique)
     * @param name The name of the product
     * @param description Product description
     * @param basePrice Base Price of product
     *
     * @return The newly created EJB Object.
     */
    Product create(String productID, String name, String description, double
        basePrice) throws CreateException, RemoteException;

    // Finder methods.  These are implemented by the
    // container.  You can customize the functionality of
    // these methods by using the EJB Container tools.

    public Product findByPrimaryKey(ProductPK key) throws FinderException,
        RemoteException;

    public Enumeration findByName(String name) throws FinderException,
        RemoteException;

    public Enumeration findByDescription(String description) throws
        FinderException, RemoteException;
```

Source 9.2 ProductHome.java (continues).

```
    public Enumeration findByBasePrice(double basePrice) throws
        FinderException, RemoteException;

    public Enumeration findExpensiveProducts(double minPrice) throws
        FinderException, RemoteException;

    public Enumeration findCheapProducts(double maxPrice) throws
        FinderException, RemoteException;

    public Enumeration findAllProducts() throws FinderException,
        RemoteException;
}
```

Source 9.2 ProductHome.java *(continued)*.

Our home interface defines a single create() method to create a new product in the database. It returns a Product EJB object so the client can manipulate the entity bean data and throws a *javax.ejb.CreateException* to indicate an application-level problem.

We also expose all sorts of finder methods to find existing products. Some of the finders return a single EJB object, while others return a *java.util.Enumeration* of multiple EJB objects. This is needed if the finder methods find more than one matching object. Note that *findByPrimaryKey()* should never return an enumeration because primary keys must be unique.

ProductPK.java

Our primary key class is defined by *ProductPK.java*, shown in Source 9.3.

As with our Bank Account, our primary key is a simple string. And as we've found out, there are restrictions for what our primary key can be. Our primary key fields are coming from the container-managed fields of the entity bean class, as is required with container-managed persistence. In particular, our primary key represents the ID string of a product (such as a product SKU number).

ProductBean.java

Next, we have our container-managed entity bean implementation, *ProductBean .java*, shown in Source 9.4.

This bean is more complex than our bank account example. We've defined many finder methods, and we have four persistent fields. Yet even though we've added all this complexity, our bean is less than 40 percent of the size of our Bank Account

```
package com.wiley.compBooks.roman.entity.product;

import java.io.Serializable;

/**
 * Primary Key class for our 'Product' Container-Managed
 * Entity Bean
 */
public class ProductPK implements java.io.Serializable {

    /*
     * Note that the primary key fields must be a
     * subset of the the container-managed Bean fields.
     * The fields we are marking as container-managed in
     * our Bean are productID, name, desc, and basePrice.
     * Therefore our PK fields need to be from that set.
     */
    public String productID;

    public ProductPK(String productID) {
        this.productID = productID;
    }

    public ProductPK() {
    }

    public String toString() {
        return productID.toString();
    }
}
```

Source 9.3   ProductPK.java.

bean. This is an amazing reduction in code complexity. And because our bean has no database code in it, we have reduced the chance for bugs in our bean that would be due to user error working with JDBC code. This is a huge savings in development and testing time.

We have four container-managed fields, all with public scope. They're public so that the container can manipulate them. Our *ejbCreate()* method simply sets our container-managed fields to the passed-in client parameters. The EJB container will extract those fields and set up the database data for us. Notice that our *ejbCreate()* method does not return a primary key because the EJB container does that for us.

The rest of our bean is just empty methods and comments. There's almost no logic at all. Our bean class is just data with some accessor methods.

```
package com.wiley.compBooks.roman.entity.product;

import java.sql.*;
import javax.naming.*;
import javax.ejb.*;
import java.util.*;
import java.rmi.RemoteException;

/**
 * Entity Bean that demonstrates Container-Managed persistence.
 *
 * This is a product that's persistent.  It has an ID #, a name,
 * a description, and a base price.
 */
public class ProductBean implements EntityBean {

    protected EntityContext ctx;

    // Container-managed state fields.  Note that they must
    // be public.
    public String productID;     // PK
    public String name;
    public String description;
    public double basePrice;

    public ProductBean() {
        System.out.println("New Product Entity Bean Java Object created by
            EJB Container.");
    }

    //
    // Business Logic Methods
    //

    // Simple getter/setter methods of Entity Bean fields.

    public String getName() throws RemoteException {
        System.out.println("getName() called.");
        return name;
    }

    public void setName(String name) throws RemoteException {
        System.out.println("getName() called.");
        this.name = name;
    }

    public String getDescription() throws RemoteException {
        System.out.println("getDescription() called.");
```

Source 9.4 ProductBean.java *(continues).*

```java
        return description;
    }

    public void setDescription(String description) throws RemoteException {
        System.out.println("setDescription() called.");
        this.description = description;
    }

    public double getBasePrice() throws RemoteException {
        System.out.println("getBasePrice() called.");
        return basePrice;
    }

    public void setBasePrice(double price) throws RemoteException {
        System.out.println("setBasePrice() called.");
        this.basePrice = price;
    }

    public String getProductID() {
        System.out.println("getProductID() called.");
        return productID;
    }

    //
    // EJB-required methods
    //

    /**
     * Called by Container.
     * Implementation can acquire needed resources.
     */
    public void ejbActivate() throws RemoteException {
        System.out.println("ejbActivate() called.");
    }

    /**
     * EJB Container calls this method right before it
     * removes the Entity Bean from the database.
     * Corresponds to when client calls home.remove().
     */
    public void ejbRemove() throws RemoteException {
        System.out.println("ejbRemove() called.");
    }

    /**
     * Called by Container.
     * Releases held resources for passivation.
     */
```

Source 9.4   ProductBean.java *(continues)*.

```
public void ejbPassivate() throws RemoteException {
    System.out.println("ejbPassivate () called.");
}


/**
 * Called from the Container.  Updates the entity bean
 * instance to reflect the current value stored in
 * the database.
 *
 * Because we're using Container-Managed Persistence, we
 * can leave this method blank.  The EJB Container will
 * automatically set our public fields to the correct values.
 */
public void ejbLoad() throws RemoteException {
    System.out.println("ejbLoad() called.");
}


/**
 * Called from the Container.  Updates the database to
 * reflect the current values of this in-memory Entity Bean
 * instance representation.
 *
 * Because we're using Container-Managed Persistence, we can
 * leave this method blank.  The EJB Container will
 * automatically save our public fields into the database.
 */
public void ejbStore() throws RemoteException {
    System.out.println("ejbStore() called.");
}


/**
 * Called by Container.  Associates this Bean instance with
 * a particular context.  Once done, we can query the
 * Context for environment info, such as Bean customizations
 * via properties.
 */
public void setEntityContext(EntityContext ctx) throws RemoteException {
    System.out.println("setEntityContext called");
    this.ctx = ctx;
}


/**
 * Called by Container.  Disassociates this Bean instance
 * with a particular context environment.
 */
public void unsetEntityContext() throws RemoteException {
```

Source 9.4 ProductBean.java *(continues)*.

```java
            System.out.println("unsetEntityContext called");
            this.ctx = null;
    }


    /**
     * Called after ejbCreate().  Now, the Bean can retrieve
     * its EJBObject from its context and pass it as a 'this'
     * argument.
     */
    public void ejbPostCreate(String productID, String name, String
        description, double basePrice) throws RemoteException {
        System.out.println("ejbPostCreate() called");
    }


    /**
     * This is the initialization method that corresponds to the
     * create() method in the Home Interface.
     *
     * When the client calls the Home Object's create() method,
     * the Home Object then calls this ejbCreate() method.
     *
     * NOTE: Since we're using Container-Managed persistence,
     * this method returns void.  With Bean-Managed Persistence,
     * we returned the PK.  This is because our Bean was
     * responsible for dealing with PKs and accessing
     * the database.  Now that we let the Container handle
     * persistence, the Container makes the Primary Key.
     *
     * We still need to initialize our Bean's fields with the
     * parameters passed from the client, so that the Container
     * can inspect our Bean and create the corresponding database
     * entries.
     */
    public void ejbCreate(String productID, String name, String description,
        double basePrice) throws CreateException, RemoteException {
        System.out.println("ejbCreate(" + productID + ", " + name + ", " +
        description + ", " + basePrice + ") called");

        this.productID = productID;
        this.name = name;
        this.description = description;
        this.basePrice = basePrice;
    }

    // No finder methods - they are implemented by Container
}
```

Source 9.4 ProductBean.java *(continued)*.

Client.java

Our client code is a simple suite of test cases to try out our bean, as shown in Source 9.5.

We perform a JNDI lookup to acquire the home object and create some entity bean data. We then try out a couple of finder methods. We can loop through the finders' returned numerations and call business methods on each EJB object. We then destroy all the EJB objects we created in a *finally{}* clause.

```java
package com.wiley.compBooks.roman.entity.product;

import javax.ejb.*;
import javax.naming.*;
import java.rmi.*;
import java.util.Enumeration;

/**
 * Client test application on a Container-Managed Entity Bean, Product.
 */
public class Client {

    public static void main(String[] args) {

        ProductHome home = null;

        try {
            /*
             * Get a reference to the Product Home Object - the
             * factory for Product EJB Objects
             */
            Context ctx = new InitialContext(System.getProperties());
            home = (ProductHome) ctx.lookup("ProductHome");

            /*
             * Use the factory to create the Product EJB Object
             */
            home.create("123-456-7890", "P5-350", "350 Mhz Pentium", 200);
            home.create("123-456-7891", "P5-400", "400 Mhz Pentium", 300);
            home.create("123-456-7892", "P5-450", "450 Mhz Pentium", 400);
            home.create("123-456-7893", "SD-64", "64 MB SDRAM", 50);
            home.create("123-456-7894", "SD-128", "128 MB SDRAM", 100);
            home.create("123-456-7895", "SD-256", "256 MB SDRAM", 200);

            /*
             * Find a Product, and print out its description
             */
```

Source 9.5 Client.java *(continues)*.

```
            Enumeration enum = home.findByName("SD-64");
            System.out.println("The following product descriptions match the
                product name SD-64:");
            while (enum.hasMoreElements()) {
                Product prod = (Product) enum.nextElement();
                System.out.println(prod.getDescription());
            }


            /*
             * Find all products that cost $200
             */
            System.out.println("Calling finder to find all products that cost
                $200");
            enum = home.findByBasePrice(200);

            while (enum.hasMoreElements()) {
                Product prod = (Product) enum.nextElement();
                System.out.println(prod.getDescription());
            }
        }
        catch (Exception e) {
            e.printStackTrace();
        }
        finally {
            if (home != null) {
            try {
                System.out.println("Destroying products..");

                /*
                 * Find all the products
                 */
                Enumeration enum = home.findAllProducts();
                while (enum.hasMoreElements()) {
                    try {
                        Product prod = (Product) enum.nextElement();
                        prod.remove();
                    }
                    catch (Exception e) {
                        e.printStackTrace();
                    }
                }
            }
            catch (Exception e) {
                e.printStackTrace();
            }
            }
        }
    }
}
```

Source 9.5   Client.java *(continued).*

The Deployment Descriptor

We now need to write our deployment descriptor. In addition to defining the standard entity bean fields, we now need to inform the container about our public container-managed fields. The deployment descriptor is shown in Table 9.2. Notice that we no longer have any JDBC application-specific properties because we've externalized all database activity to the container.

In addition to the deployment descriptor, we need to tell the container exactly how to perform persistent operations. This is one trade-off of container-managed persistence—you still need to declare persistent rules, rather than code them into your bean using JDBC or SQL/J.

If you're using a relational data store, you'll need to define exactly how your entity bean's public fields map to that database. Thus, we must define a series of object-relational mapping entries. These entries map entity bean fields to relational database column names. The EJB container (in this case, BEA WebLogic) will use this mapping when storing or retrieving our container-managed fields from the database. Note that this is very EJB container-specific! Some EJB containers will support object databases and thus will not have a mapping into a two-dimensional relational database. Consult your EJB container's documentation for more information. Our product line's persistent entries for BEA's WebLogic server are shown in Table 9.3.

We also need to specify the implementation of our home object's finder methods. This is also, unfortunately, proprietary for each EJB container. BEA WebLogic has a simple scripting language for this purpose. For example:

Table 9.2 Deployment Descriptor Settings for ProductBean

DEPLOYMENT DESCRIPTOR SETTING	VALUE
Bean home name	ProductHome
Enterprise bean class name	com.wiley.compBooks.roman.entity.product.ProductBean
Home interface class name	com.wiley.compBooks.roman.entity.product.ProductHome
Remote interface class name	com.wiley.compBooks.roman.entity.product.Product
Environment properties	<empty>
Re-entrant	false
Primary key class name	com.wiley.compBooks.roman.entity.product.ProductPK
Container-managed fields	productID, name, description, and basePrice

Table 9.3 Persistent Settings for ProductBean Assuming the BEA Weblogic Container

OBJECT/RELATIONAL SETTING (ENTITY BEAN FIELD = RELATIONAL COLUMN NAME)
productID=id
name=name
description=description
basePrice=basePrice

- "findByName(String name)" "(= name $name)" means to find all entity bean products whose container-managed field *name* matches the parameter "name" passed in by the client.

- "findCheapProducts(double maxPrice)" "(< basePrice $maxPrice)" means to find all products whose container-managed field *basePrice* is less than the *maxPrice* variable that the client specified.

- "findAllProducts()" "(= 1 1)" simply finds every product there is.

The complete script is shown in Table 9.4. The container will implement this logic, perhaps using JDBC or SQL/J. Whenever a client wants to execute a finder method on the home object, the container will automatically run the implemented JDBC or SQL/J code.

Running the Client Program

To run the client program, type a command similar to the following (depending on your EJB container Java Naming and Directory Interface, or JNDI, initialization parameters) shown on the next page:

Table 9.4 Finder Semantics for ProductBean Assuming the BEA Weblogic Container

FINDER SCRIPTING SYNTAX
"findByName(String name)" "(= name $name)"
"findByDescription(String description)" "(= description $description)"
"findByBasePrice(double basePrice)" "(= basePrice $basePrice)"
"findExpensiveProducts(double minPrice)" "(> basePrice $minPrice)"
"findCheapProducts(double maxPrice)" "(< basePrice $maxPrice)"
"findAllProducts()" "(= 1 1)"

```
java
-Djava.naming.factory.initial=weblogic.jndi.TengahInitialContextFactory
-Djava.naming.provider.url=t3://localhost:7001
com.wiley.compBooks.entity.Product.Client
```

The initialization parameters are required by JNDI to find the home object, as we learned in Chapter 4.

Server-Side Output

When you run the client, you should see something *similar* to the following on the server side. Note that your particular output may vary, due to variances in EJB container behavior.

```
New Product Entity Bean Java Object created by EJB Container.
setEntityContext called
ejbCreate(123-456-7890, P5-350, 350 Mhz Pentium, 200.0) called
ejbPostCreate() called
New Product Entity Bean Java Object created by EJB Container.
setEntityContext called
ejbCreate(123-456-7891, P5-400, 400 Mhz Pentium, 300.0) called
ejbPostCreate() called
New Product Entity Bean Java Object created by EJB Container.
setEntityContext called
ejbCreate(123-456-7892, P5-450, 450 Mhz Pentium, 400.0) called
ejbPostCreate() called
New Product Entity Bean Java Object created by EJB Container.
setEntityContext called
ejbCreate(123-456-7893, SD-64, 64 MB SDRAM, 50.0) called
ejbPostCreate() called
New Product Entity Bean Java Object created by EJB Container.
setEntityContext called
ejbCreate(123-456-7894, SD-128, 128 MB SDRAM, 100.0) called
ejbPostCreate() called
New Product Entity Bean Java Object created by EJB Container.
setEntityContext called
ejbCreate(123-456-7895, SD-256, 256 MB SDRAM, 200.0) called
ejbPostCreate() called
New Product Entity Bean Java Object created by EJB Container.
setEntityContext called
New Product Entity Bean Java Object created by EJB Container.
getDescription() called.
ejbStore() called.
New Product Entity Bean Java Object created by EJB Container.
getDescription() called.
ejbStore() called.
getDescription() called.
ejbStore() called.
New Product Entity Bean Java Object created by EJB Container.
```

```
ejbRemove() called.
ejbRemove() called.
ejbRemove() called.
ejbRemove() called.
ejbRemove() called.
ejbRemove() called.
```

We created a number of new products in our client code. For each new product, our EJB container created a dedicated bean instance. It didn't have to do this—it could have passivated/activated the same bean and switched context between clients. When creating a bean, our container first called *newInstance()*, followed by *setEntityContext()*, which got the bean into the pool. It then called *ejbCreate()*, set up the database data, bound the bean to an EJB object, and finally called *ejbPostCreate()*—all as expected. It then serviced a few business calls, instantiated a few new beans, and occasionally synchronized the beans with the underlying database.

Client-Side Output

For the client side, after creating some products, we performed a *find* for all products that cost $200. Indeed, multiple entity beans were returned in our enumeration, as is shown below:

```
The following product descriptions match the product name SD-64:
Product SD-64 has description 64 MB SDRAM
Calling finder to find all products that cost $200
350 Mhz Pentium
256 MB SDRAM
Destroying products..
```

Promises and Realities: Bean-Managed Persistence versus Container-Managed Persistence

Now that you've seen both bean-managed and container-managed persistent entity beans, you must be convinced that container-managed beans are the way to go. All that JDBC code was eliminated from our bean class, saving us significant development time.

However, the choice between container- and bean-managed persistence is not necessarily clear-cut. Both bean-managed and container-managed beans have virtues. Container-managed persistence may promise a lot, but its current manifestation fails to deliver on numerous counts, about which you must be informed. Let us look at three promises, and the realities of those promises, for container-managed persistence.

Promise: Container-Managed Persistence Reduces Code

If you tell the EJB container a couple of things about your bean, container-managed persistence can perform all data access logic for you. This reduces the size of your bean tremendously—no more JDBC code in your beans—which reduces overall development time.

Reality

Depending on your container, you still may need to write persistent code with container-managed beans. This could be going through a series of wizards to specify how your entity beans map to an underlying store. You also need to specify the logic behind your finder methods. The difference is that your data access logic is now specified declaratively, rather than being written in Java. This does significantly reduce your code size, however, and has the nice feature that you can migrate to new database schemas very quickly without changing any source code.

Another code benefit rarely mentioned is that your container can be very smart about how it caches entity bean state in memory. Advanced EJB containers ship with a shared object cache, which stores entity bean data in memory across transactions. Using a shared object cache, the container can avoid unnecessary ejbLoad/ejbStore calls, which increases transactional throughput exponentially. Note that you can cache entity bean state in memory using bean-managed persistence as well, but the burden of doing this falls on you.

Promise: Container-Managed Persistence Reduces Bugs

One benefit of container-managed persistence is that it eliminates many of the bugs that occur in a deployment—mostly due to buggy JDBC code. The problem with JDBC code is that it's not "type-safe." You can't detect whether it will work at compile time—your JDBC statements are simple strings that can be resolved only at runtime. By way of comparison, with container-managed persistence the EJB container has been written by a database professional whose sole job is to make sure the generated database calls are, in general, accurate. Plus, if you as a user have specified an error (perhaps you misnamed a container-managed field in the deployment descriptor), you *can* detect errors at compile time. The way you detect these errors is by running your EJB container tools, which, if they're any good, should use Java Reflection or the equivalent to figure out whether your deployment descriptor does indeed map to your container-managed fields. It can also check things such as whether your primary key fields are a subset of your container-managed fields.

Reality

While it may be true that user error is reduced at the database level, there are serious ramifications if there *is* some kind of bug. Because the container is performing your persistence for you, it becomes very tough to figure out what database operations the container is really doing. You may need to trace through container-generated code if it's available, decompile the container, or possibly wait on technical support lines, delaying a project.

In addition, some containers may not support mapping of complex field types to an underlying storage. For example, if your container-managed persistent entity bean class has a vector as a container-managed field, you may need to convert that vector into another form that the container can handle when mapping to storage. Most containers also do not support *relationships* between entity beans, a topic we'll revisit in Chapter 13.

In general, the vision of container-managed persistence reducing bugs is sound. Actual reduction in errors will improve as EJB container technology matures over the years. Until the EJB market matures, not all vendors will prioritize implementing complex mapping of data types to underlying storages, or correct relationship handling. Be sure to evaluate your container here to ensure it fits your application requirements.

Promise: Container-Managed Persistence Makes It Easy to Port to Different Databases

One nice thing about container-managed persistence is that you aren't hard-coding a particular database storage API into your beans, such as JDBC. Because you aren't issuing explicit relational database calls in your persistence layer, you can easily move into a different database, such as a different relational database, or even an object database or legacy storage.

Database independence is very important. EJB defines a market for beans to be purchased off-the-shelf, and those beans must be able to work with whatever target database the customer has. Given that enterprise beans represent intellectual property, they will most likely not ship with their source code. This means that if an entity bean uses bean-managed persistence, the customer cannot easily tweak the data access logic. For these vendors, container-managed persistence is the only alternative to shipping multiple versions of the same bean code.

Reality

Although it is true that container-managed persistence improves portability, portability is not perfect yet. For instance:

- There is no standard way to specify persistence semantics. Some containers will use property files, and some will use graphical wizards or some other proprietary scheme. As you saw earlier in this chapter, BEA's *WebLogic* has its own way of specifying how object-relational mapping and finder methods should be done. But what if you want to install your bean in a different container? You'll now need to respecify your persistent operations using the new container's tools. If you have a very complex object model at hand, this could become a hefty task. Hopefully, specifying persistence semantics will be standardized in an upcoming release of EJB, but it's not likely to happen until well into the year 2000.

- The problem gets even more out of hand if your entity beans do not map one-to-one to relational tables. Many EJB containers will not support the full functionality needed for a complicated O/R mapping, complicated finder methods involving interesting SQL JOIN operations, and so on. Be sure your target container handles your persistence needs.

In summary, know that container-managed persistence is an EJB feature that helps developers rapidly develop persistence code. Even today, almost every company I've dealt with uses container-managed persistence exclusively since it results in such great rapid application development. But also know that container-managed persistence is an evolving technology vision, and will improve over the years.

Resolving Your EJB Debugging Problems

As you're finding out, EJB is still in its infancy. EJB containers are not all that sophisticated at the moment, and they may have small weirdnesses to them. In addition, bugs may be introduced by users that are very difficult to debug. How do you debug with EJB?

Unfortunately, true debugging is a problem with EJB. Because your beans run under the hood of a container, you'd have to load the container itself into a debugger (WebLogic and Inprise, for example, support this). But for some containers, this is an impossible alternative because many containers are not even written in Java! They may be written in native code and use the Java Native Interface (JNI) to communicate with beans. For these situations, you may need to use the tried-and-true debugging method of logging.

An even more serious debugging problem occurs if exceptions are being thrown from the EJB container, rather than from your beans. This can happen for a number of reasons:

Your EJB container's generated classes are incorrect because your interfaces and classes haven't fully complied with the EJB specification. Your EJB container's tools should ship with compliance checkers to help resolve this. But know that not everything can be checked.

Your EJB container has a real bug. This is a definite possibility that you must be prepared to encounter. In the future, however, this should not happen very often because EJB containers that comply with the Java 2 Platform, Enterprise Edition must test their source code against Sun Microsystems' robust test suite.

There is a user error that occurs within the EJB container. For example, let's say that in the product line example we gave, you used the field "desc" rather than "description" to describe your products. Unfortunately, the keyword "desc" is an SQL reserved keyword. This means that your JDBC driver would throw an exception when trying to execute any database updates that involved the word "desc." These exceptions might be cryptic at best, depending on your JDBC driver. And when you try to figure out what JDBC code is acting up, you will run into a roadblock: With container-managed persistence, the JDBC code won't be available because your bean does not perform its own data access! What do you do in this situation?

When you're faced with grim situations such as this, contacting your EJB vendor is probably not going to be very helpful. If you are operating with a deadline, it may be too late by the time your vendor comes up with a solution. If you could only somehow get access to the JDBC code, you could try out the query yourself in Cloudscape or a similar program.

There are several options you can try here:

1. Some EJB containers support debugging environments, allowing you to step through your code in real time to pinpoint problems. This is something you should look for when choosing a container.

2. Check your database's logfile to view a snapshot of what is really happening.

3. Your EJB container tools may have an option to keep generated Java files, rather than delete them when compiling them into classes. You can do this with BEA's *WebLogic* with the *-keepgenerated* option to its deployer program. This is quite analogous to how you can use the *-keepgenerated* option to keep generated proxies with Java RMI's *rmic* compiler.

4. As a last resort, you may have to decompile the offending classes to see what's going on. A good decompiler is *Jad* by Pavel Kouznetsov (see the book's accompanying Web site for a link). Of course, decompiling may be illegal depending on your container's license agreement.

Summary

In this chapter, you learned how to write container-managed persistent entity beans. We saw how the bean instance callback methods differ between bean-managed persistence and container-managed persistence. We then went through an example modeling product line using container-managed persistent entity beans. Finally, we wrapped up with a discussion of the promises and realities of container-managed persistence.

Congratulations, you've reached the conclusion of Part II! You now understand the basics of writing Enterprise JavaBeans. From this point, you have several choices. You can dive right into EJB and start writing your own beans to get a better grip on developing them. Or you can join us for Part III, where we'll tackle more advanced concepts—including transaction theory and integrating EJB with CORBA. We promise you an intriguing ride.

## PART THREE

Advanced Enterprise JavaBeans Concepts

I f you've read up to this point, you should be quite familiar with the basics of Enterprise JavaBeans development. In Part III, we raise the bar by moving on to more advanced concepts. These include the following:

Transactions. Chapter 10 explains the basics of transaction theory, assuming you know nothing about transactions already. We'll relate transactions to EJB and explain the Java Transaction API (JTA). If you are performing any serious deployment, transaction knowledge is a must-have.

CORBA. Chapter 11 focuses on the *Common Object Request Broker Architecture* (or *CORBA*). CORBA is closely related to EJB, and it is a core technology in the Java 2 Platform, Enterprise Edition (J2EE). Understanding how CORBA and EJB relate is necessary when integrating with legacy systems.

These are extremely interesting middleware topics; indeed, many books have been written on their subjects alone. We will cover both these topics from an EJB perspective, relating them to the concepts we've explained thus far.

## CHAPTER 10

Transactions

I n Chapter 1, we first touched on the middleware services needed for robust, secure, scalable, and reliable server-side development. This includes resource pooling services, security services, remotability services, persistence services, and more. We then saw how component developers can leverage these services through EJB products without writing to complex middleware APIs. Component developers can harness these services automatically and implicitly from the underlying EJB architecture, yielding rapid server-side application development.

A key service that is required for robust server-side development is *transactions*. Transactions, when used properly, can make your mission-critical operations run predictably in an enterprise environment. Transactions are an advanced programming paradigm that allows you to write robust code. Transactions are also very useful constructs to use when performing persistent operations, such as updates to a database.

In the past, transactions have been difficult to use. Product developers needed to code directly to a transaction API. But with EJB, you can gain the benefits of transactions without performing any transaction programming.

In this chapter, we'll see some of the problems that transactions solve. We'll also see how transactions work and show how they're used in EJB. Because transactions are at the very core of EJB and are somewhat difficult to understand, we'll provide extensive background on the subject. To explain transactions properly, we'll occasionally get a bit theoretical. If the theory presented in this chapter piques your interest, there are many tomes written on transactions available for further reading. See the book's accompanying Web site for links to more information.

The Motivation for Transactions

We begin our discussion with a few motivational problems that transactions address.

Atomic Operations

Imagine that you'd like to perform multiple discrete operations, yet have them execute as one contiguous, large, *atomic* operation. Take the classic bank account example. When you transfer money from one bank account to another, you want to withdraw funds from one account and deposit those funds into the other account. Ideally, both operations will succeed. But if an error occurs, you'd like *both* operations to always fail—otherwise, you'll have incorrect funds in one of the accounts. You never want one operation to succeed and the other to fail because both operations are part of a single atomic transaction.

One simplistic way to handle this is to perform exception handling. You could use exceptions to write a banking module to transfer funds from one account to another, as in the following pseudo-code:

```
try {
    // Withdraw funds from account 1
}
catch (Exception e) {
    // If an error occurred, do not proceed.
return;
}
try {
    // Otherwise, deposit funds into account 2
}
catch (Exception e) {
    // If an error occurred, do not proceed,
    // and redeposit the funds back into account 1.
return;
}
```

This code tries to withdraw funds from account 1. If a problem occurs, then the application exits, and no permanent operations occur. Otherwise, we try to deposit the funds into account 2. If a problem occurs here, we redeposit the money back into account 1 and exit the application.

There are many problems with this approach:

- The code is bulky and unwieldy.
- We need to consider every possible problem that occurs at every step of the way and code error-handling routines to consider how to roll back our changes.

- Error-handling gets out of control if we perform more complex processes than a simple withdrawal and a deposit. It is easy to imagine, for example, a 10-step process that updates several financial records. We'd need to code error-handling routines for each step. In the case of a problem, we need to code facilities to undo each operation. This gets very tricky and error-prone to write.

- Testing this code is yet another challenge. You'd have to simulate logical problems as well as failures at many different levels.

Ideally, we would like a way to perform *both* operations in a single, large, atomic operation, with a guarantee that either both operations will either always succeed or both will always fail.

Network or Machine Failure

Let's extend our classic bank account example and assume our bank account logic is distributed across a multi-tier deployment. This may be necessary for security, scalability, and modularization reasons. In a multi-tier deployment, any client code that wants to use our bank account application must do so across the network via a remote method invocation. We show this in Figure 10.1.

Distributing our application across the network introduces failure and reliability concerns. For example, what happens if the network crashes during a banking operation? Typically, an exception will be generated and thrown back to the client code—but this exception is quite ambiguous in nature. The network may have failed *before* money was withdrawn from an account. It's also possible that the network failed *after* we withdrew the money. There's no way to distinguish between these two cases—all the client code sees is a network failure exception. Thus, we can never know for sure how much money is in the bank account.

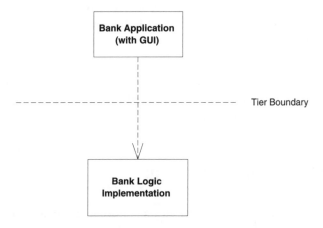

Figure 10.1 A distributed banking application.

In fact, the network may not be the only source of problems. Because we're dealing with bank account data, we're dealing with persistent information residing in a database. It's entirely feasible that the database itself could crash. The machine that the database is deployed on could also crash. If a crash occurs during a database write, the database could be in an inconsistent, corrupted state.

For a mission-critical enterprise application, none of these situations is acceptable. Mainframe systems and other highly available systems offer preventive measures to avoid system crashes. But in reality, nothing is perfect. Machines, processes, or networks will always fail. There needs to be a recovery process to handle these crashes.

Multiple Users Sharing Data

In any enterprise-level distributed system, you will see the familiar pattern of multiple clients connecting to multiple application servers, with those application servers maintaining some persistent data in a database. Let's assume these application servers all share the same database, as in Figure 10.2. Because each server is tied to the same database image, servers could potentially be modifying the *same* set of data records within that database.

For example, you might have written a tool to maintain your company's catalog of products in a database. Your catalog may contain product information that spans more than one database record. Information about a single product could span several database records or even tables.

It is conceivable that several people in your organization may need to use your tool simultaneously. But if two users modify the same product data simultaneously, their operations may become interleaved. Therefore, it is entirely possible that your database may contain product data that's been partially supplied by one tool and partially supplied by another tool. This is essentially corrupted data, and it is not acceptable in any serious deployment. The wrong data in a bank account could result in millions of dollars in loss to a bank or the bank's customers.

Thus, there needs to be a mechanism to deal with multiple users concurrently modifying data. We must guarantee that the many users concurrently updating data will not corrupt the data.

The Benefits of Transactions

The problems raised in the previous sections can lead to catastrophic errors. You can avoid these problems by properly using *transactions*.

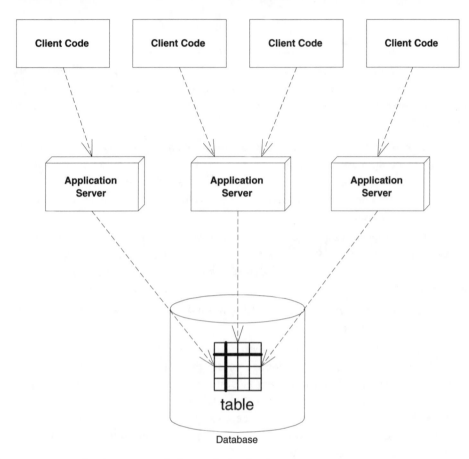

table

Database

Figure 10.2 Application servers tied to a single database.

A transaction is a series of operations that appear to execute as one large, atomic operation. Transactions guarantee an all-or-nothing value proposition: Either all of your operations will succeed, or none of them will. Transactions account for network or machine failure in a graceful, reliable way. Transactions allow multiple users to share the same data, and they guarantee that any set of data they update will be completely and wholly written, with no interleaving of updates from other clients.

By using transactions properly, you can enforce that multiuser interactions with databases (or other storages) occur independently. For example, if two clients are both reading and writing from the same database, they will be mutually exclusive if transactions are properly used. The database system will automatically perform the necessary concurrency control (i.e., locking) on the database to keep client threads from affecting each other.

Transaction Vocabulary

Before we get into the specifics of transactions, let's get some vocabulary down. There are several types of participants in a transaction: *transactional objects, transaction managers, resources,* and *resource managers.* Let's take a look at each of these parties in more detail.

A **transactional object** (or **transactional component**) is an application component, such as a banking component, that is involved in a transaction. This could be an enterprise bean, a Microsoft Transaction Server component, a CORBA component, and so on. These components perform operations that need to execute in a robust fashion, such as database interactions.

A **transaction manager** is responsible for managing the transactional operations of the transactional components. It manages the entire overhead of a transaction, running behind the scenes to coordinate things (similar to how a conductor coordinates a symphony).

A **resource** is a persistent storage from which you read or write. A resource could be a database, a message queue, or other storage.

A **resource manager** manages a resource. An example of a resource manager is a driver for a relational database, object database, message queue, or other store. Resource managers are responsible for managing all state that is permanent. The most popular interface for resource managers is the *X/Open XA* resource manager interface. Most database drivers support this interface. Because X/Open XA is the de facto standard for resource managers, a deployment with heterogeneous resource managers from different vendors can interoperate.

As you will find out, transactions offer far more than simply letting simultaneous users use the same persistent stores. By having your operations run within a transaction, you are effectively performing an advanced form of concurrency control and exception handling.

The ACID Properties

When you properly use transactions, your operations will always execute with a suite of four guarantees. These four guarantees are well-known as the *ACID properties* of transactions. The word ACID stands for *Atomicity, Consistency, Isolation,* and *Durability.* Here's the breakdown of each property:

Atomicity guarantees that many operations are bundled together and appear as one contiguous *unit of work.* In our banking example, when you transfer money from one bank account to another, you want to add funds to one account and remove funds from the other account, and you want both operations to occur or neither to occur. Atomicity guarantees that operations performed within a transaction undergo an *all-or-nothing paradigm*—either all the database updates are performed, or nothing happens if an error occurs at any time. Many different parties can participate in a transaction, such as an enterprise bean, a CORBA object, a servlet, and a database driver. These transaction participants can force the transaction to result in "nothing" happening for any reason. This is similar to a voting scheme—each transaction participant votes on whether the transaction should be successful, and if any vote "no" the transaction fails. If a transaction fails, all the partial database updates are automatically undone. In this way, you can think of transactions as a robust way of performing error handling.

Consistency guarantees that a transaction will leave the system's state to be *consistent* after a transaction completes. What is a consistent system state? A bank system state could be consistent if the rule "bank account balances must always be positive" is always followed. This is an example of an invariant set of rules that define a consistent system state. During the course of a transaction, these rules may be violated, resulting in a temporarily inconsistent state. For example, your enterprise bean component may temporarily make your account balance negative during a withdrawal. When the transaction completes, the state is consistent once again. That is, your bean never leaves your account at a negative balance. And even though your state can be made inconsistent temporarily, this is not a problem. Remember that transactions execute *atomically* as one, contiguous unit of work (from the Atomicity property above). Thus, to a third party, it appears as though the system's state is always consistent. Atomicity helps enforces that the system will *always* appear to be consistent.

Isolation protects concurrently executing transactions from seeing each other's incomplete results. Isolation allows multiple transactions to read or write to a database without knowing about each other because each transaction is *isolated* from the others. Without isolation, your application state may become inconsistent. This is very useful for multiple clients modifying a database at once. To each client, it appears as though he or she is the only client modifying the database at that time. The transaction system achieves Isolation by using low-level *synchronization protocols* on the underlying database data. This synchronization isolates the work of one transaction from another. During a transaction, locks on data are automatically assigned as necessary. If one transaction holds a lock on data, the lock prevents other concurrent transactions from interacting with that data until the lock is released. For example, if you write bank account data to a database, the transaction may obtain locks on the bank account record or table. The locks guarantee that, while the transaction is occurring, no other concurrent updates can interfere. This allows many users to modify the same set of database records simultaneously without concern for interleaving of database operations.

Durability guarantees that updates to managed resources, such as database records, survive failures. Some examples of failures are machines crashing, networks crashing, hard disks crashing, or power failures. Recoverable resources keep a transactional *log* for exactly this purpose. If the resource crashes, the permanent data can be reconstructed by reapplying the steps in the log.

Transactional Models

Now that you've seen the transaction value proposition, let's dive a bit deeper and explore how transactions work. We begin by taking a look at *transactional models*, which are the different ways you can perform transactions.

There are many different models for performing transactions. Each model adds its own complexity and features to your transactions. The two most popular models are *flat transactions* and *nested transactions*. We'll see what each of these models is in the following sections.

 To use a particular transaction model, your underlying transaction service must support it. And unfortunately, not all of the vendors who crafted the EJB specification currently implement nested transactions in their products. Hence, Enterprise JavaBeans mandates flat transactions but does not support nested transactions. Note that this may change in the future based on industry demands.

Flat Transactions

A *flat transaction* is the simplest transactional model to understand. A flat transaction is a series of operations that are performed atomically as a single *unit of work*. After a flat transaction begins, your application can perform any number of operations. Some of those operations may be persistent operations, and some may not. When you decide to end the transaction, there is always a binary result: either success or failure. A successful transaction is *committed*, while a failed transaction is *aborted*. When a transaction is committed, all of the persistent operations become permanent changes—that is, all of the updates to resources, such as databases, are made durable into permanent storage only if the transaction ends with a *commit*. If the transaction is aborted, none of the resource updates are made durable, and thus all changes are *rolled back*. When a transaction aborts, all persistent operations that your application may have performed are automatically undone by the underlying system. Your application can also be notified in case of an abort, so that your application can undo in-memory changes that occurred during the transaction.

This is the "all-or-nothing" proposition we described above. All-or-nothing means that you can withdraw from one bank account and deposit into another bank account, armed with the knowledge that these operations will either both succeed (commit) or both fail (roll back). The flat transaction process is outlined in Figure 10.3.

There are many reasons why a transaction might abort. As we've said, many components can be involved in a transaction, and any one component could suffer a problem that would cause an abortion. These problems include the following:

Invalid parameters passed to one of the components. For instance, a banking component may be called with a null argument, when it was expecting a bank account ID string.

An invariant system state was violated. For example, if a bank account has a negative balance, your banking component can force the transaction to abort, undoing all associated bank account operations.

Hardware or software failure. If the database that your component is using crashes, the transaction is rolled back, and all permanent changes are undone. Similarly, if there is a software failure (such as a distributed system where a JVM crashes) the transaction is rolled back as well.

Any of these problems can cause a transaction to abort. But when an abort occurs, how is the transactional state rolled back? That is the topic of the next section.

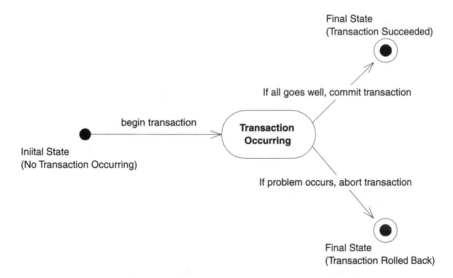

Figure 10.3 The flat transaction.

How Transactional State Is Rolled Back

Let's assume you're performing a flat transaction that includes operations on physical, permanent resources, such as databases. After the transaction begins, one of your business components requests a connection to a database. This database connection is automatically enlisted in the transaction in which your component is involved. Next, your component performs some persistent operations, such as database updates. But when this happens, your database's resource manager does not permanently apply the updates to the database—that is, your persistent operations are not yet durable and permanent. Rather, the resource manager waits until a *commit* statement has been issued. A commit is issued only when all your business components have finished performing all of the operations under that transaction—that is, a commit is issued only when the transaction is complete. If the resource is told to commit, it persists the data permanently. If the transaction aborts, the data is not persisted at all.

The take-away point from this discussion is that your business components typically do not perform any rollback of permanent state; if there's an *abort*, the resource (such as a database) does not make your database updates permanent. Your components don't have any "undo" logic for permanent data inside of them—rather, the underlying system does it for you behind the scenes. Your components control the transaction and tell the transaction to abort, but the persistent state rollback is performed for you automatically. Thus, when your business components perform operations under a transaction, each of your components should perform all persistent operations assuming that the transaction will complete properly.

Now that you've seen flat transactions, let's take a quick look at nested transactions.

Nested Transactions

We begin our nested transactions discussion with a motivational example. Let's say you need to write an application that can plan trips for a travel agency. You need to code your application to plan trips around the world, and your application must purchase the necessary travel tickets for the trip. Consider that your application performs the following operations:

1. Your application purchases a train ticket from Boston, USA to New York, USA.

2. Your application purchases a plane ticket from New York, USA to London, England.

3. Your application purchases a balloon ride ticket from London, England to Paris, France.

4. Your application finds out that there are no outgoing flights from France.

This is the famous *trip-planning problem*. If this sequence of bookings were performed under a flat transaction, your application would have only one option: to roll back the transaction. Thus, because there are no outgoing flights from France, your application has lost all of its bookings! But there may be a way to replace the balloon ride with another trip, allowing you to salvage the train ticket and plane ticket. Thus, a flat transaction is insufficient. The all-or-nothing proposition is shooting us in the foot, and we need a more robust transactional model.

A nested transaction solves this problem. A *nested transaction* allows you to embed atomic units of work within other units of work. The unit of work that is nested within another unit of work can roll back without forcing the entire transaction to roll back. Therefore, the larger unit can attempt to retry the embedded unit of work. If the embedded unit can be made to succeed, then the larger unit can succeed. If the embedded unit of work cannot be made to work, then it will ultimately force the entire unit to fail.

You can think of a nested transaction as a *tree* of transactions, all spawning off one *root-* or *top-level transaction*. The root transaction is the "main" transaction—for instance, in our trip-planning example, the root transaction is the overall process of booking tickets around the world. Every other transaction in the tree is called a *subtransaction*. The subtransactions can be flat or nested transactions. Figure 10.4 illustrates this concept.

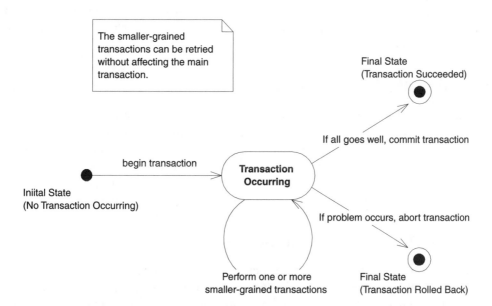

Figure 10.4 The nested transaction.

What's special about nested transactions is that subtransactions can independently roll back, without affecting higher transactions in the tree. That's a very powerful idea, and it solves our trip-planning problem: if each individual booking were a nested transaction, we could roll back any one booking without canceling all our other reservations. But in the end, if the nested transaction cannot be committed, the entire transaction will fail.

Other Transactional Models

This concludes our discussion of transactional models. There are other models as well, such as *chained transactions* and *sagas*, but we will not touch on these subjects here because the EJB specification does not support them. And because the EJB specification does not currently mandate support for nested transactions, we'll assume that our transactions are flat for the rest of this chapter.

Enlisting in Transactions with Enterprise JavaBeans

Let's apply what we've learned so far about transactions to the EJB world. If you'll recall, the EJB component is an enterprise bean. Enterprise beans expose the business logic methods that clients invoke to perform useful operations, such as depositing or withdrawing from a bank account.

Enterprise beans can be transactional in nature. This means enterprise beans can fully leverage the ACID properties to perform reliable, robust server-side operations. Thus, enterprise beans are ideal modules for performing mission-critical tasks.

Transaction Models Supported

Currently, Enterprise JavaBeans supports only one flavor of transactions—flat transactions. This may change in the future, if other transactional varieties, such as nested transactions, long-lived transactions, and chained transactions, become more popular with database vendors. Flat transactions are very simple to understand, are ubiquitous, and give us enough power to accomplish most business needs (EJB was built to address the needs of the business community).

Underlying Transaction System Abstraction

In EJB, your code never gets directly involved with the low-level transaction system. Your enterprise beans never interact with a transaction manager or a resource manager. You write your application logic at a much higher level, without regard for the specific underlying transaction system. The low-level transaction system is totally abstracted out by the EJB container, which runs behind the scenes. Your bean components are responsible for simply voting on whether a transaction should commit or abort. If things run smoothly, you should commit; otherwise, abort.

Declarative and Programmatic Transactions

Throughout this chapter, we've said that once a transaction begins, it ends with either commit or abort. The key piece of information we're lacking is *who* begins a transaction, and *who* issues either a commit or abort, and *when* each of these steps occurs. This is called *demarcating transactional boundaries*. As we will see, there are two ways for your enterprise beans to demarcate transactional boundaries—*programmatically* or *declaratively*.

Programmatic Transactions

Most existing systems demarcate transactional boundaries *programmatically*. When using programmatic transactions, you are responsible for programming transaction logic into your application code. That is, *you* are responsible for issuing a *begin* statement and either a *commit* or an *abort* statement.

For example, an EJB banking application might have an enterprise bean that acts as a bank teller. A teller bean would expose a method to transfer funds from one bank account to another. With programmatic transactions, the teller bean is responsible for issuing a *begin* statement to start the transaction, performing the transfer of funds, and then issuing either a *commit* or *abort* statement. This is the traditional way to perform transactions, and it is shown in Figure 10.5.

Declarative Transactions

Declarative transactions allow for components to *automatically* be enlisted in transactions. That is, your enterprise beans never explicitly issue a *begin*, *commit*, or *abort* statement. Rather, the EJB container performs it for you.

Let's take our bank teller example again, and assume some client code has called our teller bean to transfer funds from one account to another. With declarative transactions, the EJB container *intercepts* the request and starts up a transaction automatically on behalf of your bean. That is, the container issues the *begin* statement to the underlying transaction system to start the transaction. The container then delegates the invocation to your enterprise bean, which performs operations in the scope of that transaction. Your bean can do anything it wants to, such as perform logic, write to a database, send an asynchronous message, or call other enterprise beans. If a problem occurs, the bean can signal to the container that the transaction must abort. When the bean is done, it returns

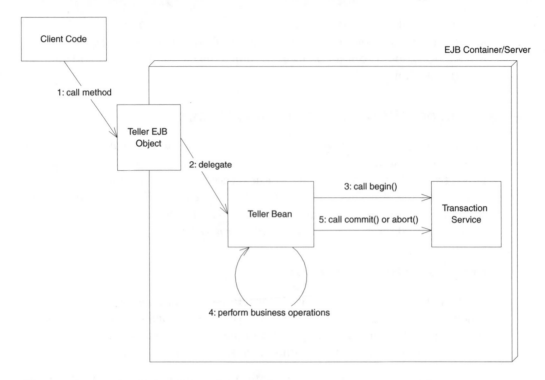

Figure 10.5 Beans with programmatic transactions.

control back to the container. The container then issues either a *commit* or *abort* statement to the underlying transaction system, depending on whether a problem occurred. This is a very simple model, and it is shown in Figure 10.6.

EJB declarative transactions add huge value to your deployments because your beans may not need to interact with any transaction API. In essence, your bean code and your client are not even really aware of transactions happening around them.

So how do you choose between declarative and programmatic transactions? EJB allows you to specify how your enterprise bean is enrolled in a transaction by setting a *transaction attribute* on your bean, as we will see in the following section.

Controlling How Your Enterprise Beans Are Enrolled in Transactions

A *transaction attribute* is a setting that you give to a bean to control how your bean is enlisted in transactions. You can specify that your bean should automatically be enlisted in transactions (declarative) or that your bean should control its own transactions (programmatic). You can specify a different transaction

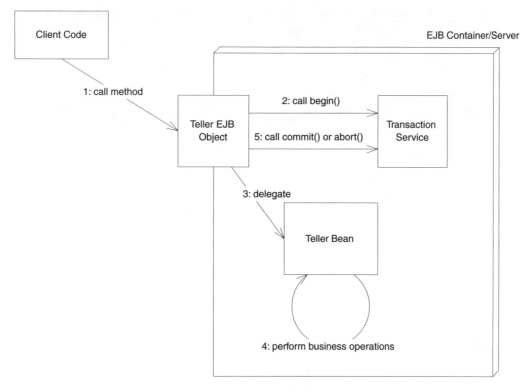

Figure 10.6 Beans with declarative transactions.

attribute on each bean in your system, regardless of how many beans are working together.

The transactional attribute is a required part of each bean's *deployment descriptor*. If you recall, a deployment descriptor ships with each bean and lists several properties that EJB containers use when interacting with beans. The container knows how transactions should be handled with a bean by reading that bean's transaction attribute from its deployment descriptor. You can specify transaction attributes for entire beans or for individual bean methods. If both are specified, then method-level attributes take precedence. The various settings for this attribute are listed below.

As a side note, the setting of properties on components in this manner is sometimes referred to as *attribute-based programming*. By the time you read this, there should be a number of available tools to assist you with defining your deployment descriptor's attributes. This includes tools that ship with Integrated Development Environments (IDEs), as well as tools that ship with application servers. For example, BEA's WebLogic application server comes with a deployment tool that allows you to graphically tune deployment descriptor settings. Figure 10.7 shows how we set a transaction attribute using BEA's WebLogic product.

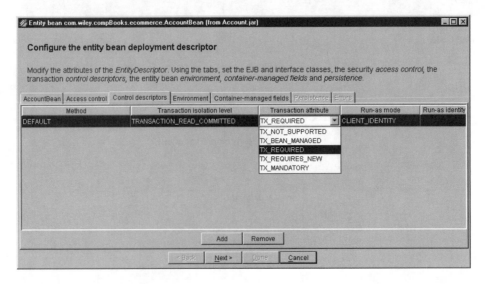

Figure 10.7 Setting a transaction attribute with BEA WebLogic.

EJB Transaction Attribute Values

Every enterprise bean must have a transaction attribute setting. The following are the possible values for the transaction attribute in the deployment descriptor.

TX_BEAN_MANAGED

If you set your bean to use the TX_BEAN_MANAGED attribute, then your bean *programmatically* controls its own transaction boundaries. Programming transaction control into your source code is the more traditional way of writing transactional code. When you use programmatic transactions, you issue the *begin*, *commit*, and *abort* statements through the *Java Transaction API (JTA)*, described later in this chapter.

The upside of programmatic (aka *bean-managed*) transactions is that your bean has full control over transactional boundaries. With declarative (aka *container-managed*) transactions, your entire bean method must either run under a transaction or not run under a transaction. Programmatic transactions, on the other hand, allow your bean to control transactions within it. For instance, you can use programmatic transactions to run a series of mini-transactions within a bean method.

In most cases, you will not need to use programmatic transactions, and you should avoid doing so if possible. The downside to using programmatic transactions is that you need to hard-code transactional logic into your application logic. In essence, you're mixing middleware service logic within your application logic.

Rather, you should strive to externalize middleware logic to the EJB container through declarative transactions. You'll find that with creative use of the available transaction attributes, you can solve most problems with automatic, implicit transactions. By having transactions automatically start up and end, you keep client code from misusing your beans. If you're a bean vendor, this will reduce a great number of headaches down the line.

Note that TX_BEAN_MANAGED beans must be *entirely* self-managed. Either your whole bean performs transactions programmatically, or none of it does. You can't mix transaction attributes on different methods on your bean when using TX_BEAN_MANAGED.

TX_NOT_SUPPORTED

If you set your bean to use TX_NOT_SUPPORTED, then your bean *cannot* be involved in a transaction at all. For example, assume we have two enterprise beans, A and B. Let's assume bean A begins a transaction and then calls bean B. If bean B is using the TX_NOT_SUPPORTED attribute, then the transaction that A started is suspended. None of B's operations are transactional, such as reads/writes to databases. When B completes, A's transaction is resumed.

You should use TX_NOT_SUPPORTED if you know for sure that your bean operations do not need the ACID properties. This should be used only if your beans are performing nonmission-critical operations, where you are not worried about isolating your bean's operations from other concurrent operations. An example here is an enterprise bean that performs rough reporting. If you have an e-commerce Web site, you might write a bean that routinely reports a rough average number of e-commerce purchases per hour by scanning a database. Because this is a low-priority operation and you don't need exact figures, TX_NOT_SUPPORTED is an ideal, low-overhead mode to use.

A Recurring Theme

Declarative transactions allow you to delegate transactional logic to the application server. This allows you to construct server-side component-based applications without writing to middleware APIs. Indeed, this has been a recurring theme of this book, and it is the EJB value proposition. As a component developer, you're responsible for setting properties on your components through the deployment descriptor, which inform the application server about the middleware services that you need. The middleware services you gain include persistence, security, transactions, transparent networking, and more. This empowers you to rapidly develop server-side applications from prewritten components, allowing you to easily flip property settings as necessary to tune components to your environment.

TX_REQUIRED

You should use the TX_REQUIRED mode if you want your bean to *always* run in a transaction. If there's a transaction already running, your bean joins in on that transaction. If there is no transaction running, the EJB container starts one for you.

For instance, let's say you write a credit card component that performs operations on credit cards, such as charging a credit card or refunding money on a credit card. Let's assume you ship the component with the TX_REQUIRED transaction attribute. You then sell that component to two customers:

Customer 1 deploys our component in its customer service center, using the component to refund money when an angry customer calls up. The customer writes some proprietary code to call your bean as necessary. When the client code calls your bean, the container will automatically start a transaction by calling *begin* and then delegating the call to your bean. When your method completes, the container will either issue a *commit* or *abort* statement, depending on whether a problem occurred.

Customer 2 uses our billing component as part of a complete workflow solution. The customer wants to use the credit card component to charge a user's credit card when a user purchases a product from a Web site. The customer then wants to submit an order to manufacture that product, which is handled by a separate component. Thus, the customer has two separate components running, but he or she would like both of them to run under the same transaction. If the credit card cannot be charged, the customer doesn't want the order to be submitted. If the order cannot be submitted, the customer doesn't want the credit card charged. Therefore, the customer produces his or her own workflow bean, which first calls our credit card charging bean and then calls the bean to generate a manufacturing order. The workflow bean is deployed with TX_REQUIRED, so a transaction automatically starts up. Because your credit card bean is also deployed with TX_REQUIRED, you *join* that transaction, rather than starting your own transaction. If the order submission component is also deployed with TX_REQUIRED, it will join the transaction as well. The container commits or aborts the transaction when the workflow bean is done.

Thus, TX_REQUIRED is a very flexible transaction attribute, and it allows you to start your own transaction or join existing ones, depending on the scenario.

TX_REQUIRES_NEW

You should use the TX_REQUIRES_NEW attribute if you always want a *new* transaction to begin when your bean is called. If there is a transaction already underway when your bean is called, that transaction is suspended during the bean invocation. The container then launches a new transaction and delegates the call to the bean. The bean performs its operations and eventually completes. The container then commits or aborts the transaction and finally resumes the old transaction. Of course, if there is no transaction currently running when your bean is called, there is nothing to suspend or resume.

TX_REQUIRES_NEW is useful if your bean needs the ACID properties of transactions but wants to run as a single unit of work without allowing other external logic to also run in the transaction.

TX_SUPPORTS

When a bean is called with TX_SUPPORTS, it runs only in a transaction if the client had one running already—it then joins that transaction. If the client does not have a transaction, the bean runs with no transaction at all.

TX_SUPPORTS is similar in nature to TX_REQUIRED, with the one exception that TX_REQUIRED enforces that a new transaction is started if one is not running already. Because TX_SUPPORTS will sometimes not run within a transaction, you should be careful when using this attribute. Mission-critical operations should be encapsulated with a stricter transaction attribute (such as TX_REQUIRED).

TX_MANDATORY

TX_MANDATORY mandates that a transaction *must be already running* when your bean method is called. If a transaction isn't already running, then the *javax.ejb.TransactionRequired* exception is thrown back to the caller.

TX_MANDATORY is a safe transaction attribute to use. It guarantees that your bean should run in a transaction. There is no way your bean can be called if there isn't a transaction already running. However, TX_MANDATORY relies on a third party to start the transaction before your bean is called. The container will *not* automatically start a transaction; rather, an exception is thrown back to the caller. This is the chief difference between TX_MANDATORY and TX_SUPPORTS. TX_MANDATORY is useful if your component is designed to run within a larger system, such as a workflow system, where your bean is only part of a larger suite of operations, and you want to mandate that the larger operations start a transaction before calling your bean.

Transactional Isolation

Now that you've seen how to enlist enterprise beans in transactions, let's discuss the "I" in ACID: Isolation. Isolation is the guarantee that concurrent users are isolated from one another, even if they are touching the same database data. Isolation is important to understand because it does not come for free. As we'll see, you can control how isolated your transactions are from one another. Choosing the right level of isolation is critical for the robustness and scalability of your deployment.

The underlying transaction system achieves isolation by performing *concurrency control* behind the scenes. We elaborate on this concept further in the following section.

The Need for Concurrency Control

Let's begin our isolation discussion with a motivational example. Imagine there are two instances of the same component executing concurrently, perhaps in two different processes or two different threads. Let's assume that the component wants to update a shared database using a database API such as JDBC or SQL/J. Each of the instances of the component performs the following steps:

1. Read an integer X from a database.
2. Add 10 to X.
3. Write the new value of X to the database.

If each these three steps executes together in an atomic operation, everything is fine. Neither instance can interfere with the other instance's operations. Remember, though, that the thread scheduling algorithm being used in the background does not guarantee this. If two instances are executing these three operations, the operations could be interleaved. The following order of operations is possible:

1. Instance A reads integer X from the database. The database now contains X = 0.
2. Instance B reads integer X from the database. The database now contains X = 0.
3. Instance A adds 10 to its copy of X and persists it to the database. The database now contains X = 10.
4. Instance B adds 10 to its copy of X and persists it to the database. The database now contains X = 10.

What happened here? Due to the interleaving of database operations, Instance B is working with a stale copy of X: the copy before Instance A performed a write. Thus, Instance A's operations have been lost! This famous problem is known as a *lost update*. It is a very serious situation—Instance B has been working with stale data and has overwritten Instance A's write. How can transactions avoid this scenario?

The solution to this problem is to use *locking* on the database to prevent the two components from reading data. By locking the data that your transaction is using, you guarantee that your transaction and only your transaction has access to that data until you release that lock. This prevents interleaving of sensitive data operations.

In our scenario, if our component acquired an exclusive lock before the transaction began and released that lock after the transaction, then there would be no interleaving possible:

1. Request a lock on X.

2. Read an integer X from a database.

3. Add 10 to X.

4. Write the new value of X to the database.

5. Release the lock on X.

If another component ran concurrently with ours, that component would have to wait until we relinquished our lock, which would give that component our fresh copy of X. We explore locking further in the "Isolation and Locking" sidebar.

Isolation and EJB

As an EJB component developer, you can control how isolated your transactions are from one another. You can enforce very strict isolation or allow very relaxed isolation. If you have very strict isolation, you can rest assured that each concurrent transaction will be isolated from all other transactions. But sometimes enforcing strict isolation is a hindrance rather than a benefit. Because isolation is achieved by acquiring locks on an underlying data storage, the locks can result in unacceptable performance degradation.

Thus, you need to be smart about how much isolation you really need. EJB offers you different *isolation levels* that give you this flexibility. Isolation levels allow you to specify concurrency control at a very high level. If you specify a very strict isolation level, then your transactions will be perfectly isolated from one another, at the expense of performance. If you specify a very loose isolation level, your transactions will not be isolated, but you will achieve higher concurrent transaction performance.

Transaction isolation levels are attached to beans just like the transaction attributes we described earlier—through the deployment descriptor. The EJB container knows how to inspect the deployment descriptor to apply the proper isolation levels to your beans. Figure 10.8 shows how we set a transaction isolation level using BEA's WebLogic deployment descriptor generation product. Transactions really can be as simple as point-and-click with EJB.

Isolation and Locking

During a transaction, a number of *locks* are acquired on the resource being updated. These locks are used to ensure isolation: that multiple clients all updating the same data set cannot interfere with each other. The locks are implicitly retrieved when you interact with resource managers—you do not have to worry about obtaining them yourself.

By intelligently acquiring locks on the resource being used, transactions guarantee a special property: *serializability*. Serializability means that a suite of concurrently executing transactions behaves as if the transactions were executing one after another (nonconcurrently). This is guaranteed no matter how scheduling of the transactions is performed.

The problem with locking is that it physically locks out other concurrent transactions from performing their database updates until you release your locks. This can lead to major performance problems. In addition, a *deadlock* scenario (not specific to databases, by the way) can arise. Deadlock causes the entire system to screech to a dead stop. An example of deadlock occurs when two concurrent transactions are both waiting for each other to release a lock.

To improve performance, transactions distinguish between two main types of locks: *read locks* and *write locks*. Read locks are nonexclusive, in that any number of concurrent transactions can acquire a read lock. In comparison, write locks are exclusive—only one transaction can hold a write lock at any time.

Locking exists in many circles: databases, Version Control Systems, and the Java language itself (through the *synchronized* keyword). And the problems experienced in locking are common to all arenas.

If you'd like to see more details about locking and transactions, check out *Principles of Databases Systems* by Jeffrey D. Ullman (Computer Science Press, 1980). This is a classic, theoretical book on databases that forms the basis for many database systems today.

This is the extent of our concurrency control discussion because frankly, as an EJB programmer, you shouldn't care about how concurrency control is performed. EJB abstracts concurrency control away from application developers via *isolation levels*.

There are four transaction isolation levels in EJB:

The TRANSACTION_READ_UNCOMMITTED mode does not offer any isolation guarantees but offers the highest performance.

The TRANSACTION_READ_COMMITTED mode solves the *dirty read* problem.

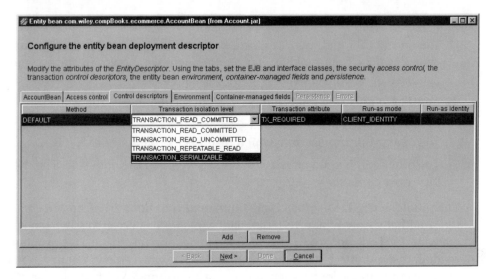

Figure 10.8 Setting a transaction isolation level with BEA WebLogic.

The TRANSACTION_REPEATABLE_READ mode solves the previous problem as well as the *unrepeatable read* problem.

The TRANSACTION_SERIALIZABLE mode solves the previous problems as well as the *phantom* problem.

It's important to understand why *dirty reads*, *unrepeatable reads*, and *phantoms* occur, or you won't be able to use transactions properly in EJB. This section is devoted to giving you the information you need to make an intelligent isolation level choice when programming with transactions.

 If you're a JDBC programmer, isolation levels may sound familiar. JDBC deals with transactions as well and has its own suite of isolation levels, which correspond exactly to the ones offered by EJB. (The one exception is the TRANSACTION_NONE isolation level in JDBC, which indicates that no transaction is supported. EJB does not allow this isolation level to be specified because the bean's transaction attribute should be set to TX_NOT_SUPPORTED for no transactions, and no isolation level should be specified.)

The Dirty Read Problem

A dirty read occurs when your application reads data from a database that has not been committed to permanent storage yet. Consider two instances of the same component performing the following:

1. You read integer X from the database. The database now contains X = 0.

2. You add 10 to X and save it to the database. The database now contains X = 10. You have not issued a *commit* statement yet, however, and so your database update has not been made permanent yet.

3. Another application reads integer X from the database. The value it reads in is X = 10.

4. You *abort* your transaction, which restores the database to X = 0.

5. The other application adds 10 to X and saves it to the database. The database now contains X = 20.

The problem here is the other application read your update before you committed. And because you aborted, the database data has erroneously been set to 20; your database update has been added in despite the abort! This problem of reading uncommitted data is a *dirty read*. (The word "dirty" occurs in many areas of computer science, such as caching algorithms. A dirty cache is a cache that is out of sync with the main source.)

The TRANSACTION_READ_UNCOMMITTED Mode

Dirty reads can occur if you use the weakest isolation level, called TRANSACTION_READ_UNCOMMITTED. With this isolation level, if your transaction is executing concurrently with another transaction, and the other transaction writes some data to the database *without* committing, your transaction will read that data in. This occurs regardless of the isolation level being used by the other transaction.

TRANSACTION_READ_UNCOMMITTED experiences the other transactional problems as well: unrepeatable reads and phantoms. We'll describe those problems in the pages to come.

When to Use TRANSACTION_READ_UNCOMMITTED

This isolation level is very dangerous to use in mission-critical systems with shared data being updated by concurrent transactions. It is totally inappropriate to use this mode in sensitive calculations, such as in a debit/credit banking transaction. For those scenarios, it's better to go with one of the stricter isolation levels we detail later.

This level is most appropriate if you know beforehand that an instance of your component will be running only when there are no other concurrent transactions. Hence, because there are no other transactions to be isolated from, this isolation level is adequate. But for most applications that use transactions, this isolation level is insufficient.

The advantage of this isolation level is performance. The underlying transaction system doesn't have to acquire any locks on shared data in this mode. This reduces the amount of time that you need to wait before executing, and it also reduces the time concurrent transactions waste waiting for you to finish.

TRANSACTION_READ_COMMITTED

The TRANSACTION_READ_COMMITTED isolation level is very similar to TRANSACTION_READ_UNCOMMITTED. The chief difference is that your code will read committed data only when running in TRANSACTION_READ_ COMMITTED mode. When you execute with this isolation level, you will *not* read data that has been written but is uncommitted. Hence, this isolation level solves the dirty read problem.

Note that this isolation level does not protect against the more advanced transactional problems, such as unrepeatable reads and phantoms.

When to Use TRANSACTION_READ_COMMITTED

This isolation level offers a step up in robustness from the TRANSACTION_ READ_UNCOMMITTED mode. You aren't going to be reading in data that has just been written but is uncommitted, which means that any data you read is going to be consistent data.

One great use for this mode is for programs that read data from a database to report values of the data. Because reporting tools aren't in general very mission-critical, taking a snapshot of committed data in a database makes sense.

When you run in TRANSACTION_READ_COMMITTED mode, the underlying concurrency control system needs to acquire additional locking. This makes performance slower than with TRANSACTION_READ_UNCOMMITTED. TRANSACTION_READ_COMMITTED is the default isolation level for most databases, such as Oracle or Microsoft SQL Server.

The Unrepeatable Read Problem

Our next concurrency control problem is an *Unrepeatable Read*. Unrepeatable reads occur when a component reads some data from a database, but upon re-reading the data, the data has been changed. This can arise when another concurrently executing transaction modifies the data being read. For example:

1. You read a data set X from the database.

2. Another application overwrites data set X with new values.

3. You reread the data set X from the database. The values have magically changed.

Again, by using transactional locks to lock out those other transactions from modifying the data, we can guarantee that unrepeatable reads will never occur.

TRANSACTION_REPEATABLE_READ

TRANSACTION_REPEATABLE_READ guarantees yet another property on top of TRANSACTION_READ_COMMITTED: Whenever you read committed data from a database, you will be able to reread the same data again at a later time, and the data will have the same values as the first time. Hence, your database reads are *repeatable*. In contrast, if you are using the TRANSACTION_READ_COMMITTED mode or a weaker mode, another concurrent transaction may commit data between your reads.

When to Use TRANSACTION_REPEATABLE_READ

Use TRANSACTION_REPEATABLE_READ when you need to update one or more data elements in a resource, such as one or more records in a relational database. You'll want to be able to read each of the rows that you're modifying and then be able to update each row, knowing that none of the rows are being modified by other concurrent transactions. If you choose to reread any of the rows at any time, you'd be guaranteed that the rows still have the same data.

The Phantom Problem

Finally, we have the phantom problem. A phantom is a *new* set of data that magically appears in a database between two database read operations. For example:

1. Your application queries the database using some criteria and retrieves a data set.

2. Another application inserts new data that would satisfy your query.

3. You perform the query again, and *new* sets of data have magically appeared.

The difference between the unrepeatable read problem and the phantom problem is that unrepeatable reads occur when existing data is changed, whereas phantoms occur when *new* data is inserted that didn't exist before. For example, if your transaction reads a relational record, then a concurrent transaction commits a new record to the database, a new *phantom record* appears that wasn't there before.

TRANSACTION_SERIALIZABLE

You can easily avoid phantoms (as well as the other problems described earlier) by utilizing the strictest isolation level: TRANSACTION_SERIALIZABLE. TRANSACTION_SERIALIZABLE guarantees that transactions execute serially with respect to each other, and it enforces the isolation ACID property to its fullest. This means that each transaction truly appears to be independent of the others.

When to Use TRANSACTION_SERIALIZABLE

Use TRANSACTION_SERIALIZABLE for mission-critical systems that absolutely must have perfect transactional isolation. You're guaranteed that no data will be read that has been uncommitted. You'll be able to reread the same data again and again. Plus, mysterious committed data will not show up in your database while you're operating due to concurrent transactions.

Use this isolation level with care because serializability does have its cost. If all of your operations execute in TRANSACTION_SERIALIZABLE mode, you will quickly see how fast your database performance grinds to a halt. (A personal note: Because transactional errors can be very difficult to detect, due to scheduling of processes, variable throughput, and other issues; I subscribe to the view that it's better to be safe than sorry.)

Transaction Isolation Summary

The various isolation levels and their effects are summarized in Table 10.1. You can specify these isolation levels for entire beans or for individual bean methods. If both are specified, then method-level attributes take precedence. One special rule, however, is that once a client invokes a bean's method, that bean becomes associated with a particular isolation level. This means that future invocations of other methods must use the same isolation level for that bean instance. Be wary of this restriction because if you accidentally invoke a method on a bean that has already been associated with a different isolation level, you will receive a Java RMI remote exception.

Now that we've concluded our discussion of isolation levels, we'll shift gears and talk about *distributed transactions*, which are transactions over a multi-tier deployment with several transaction participants.

Table 10.1 The Isolation Levels in EJB

ISOLATION LEVEL	DIRTY READS?	UNREPEATABLE READS?	PHANTOM READS?
TRANSACTION_READ_UNCOMMITTED	Yes	Yes	Yes
TRANSACTION_READ_COMMITTED	No	Yes	Yes
TRANSACTION_REPEATABLE_READ	No	No	Yes
TRANSACTION_SERIALIZABLE	No	No	No

Distributed Transactions

The most basic flat transaction occurs with a single application server tied to a single database. Depending on the functionality of your application server's transaction service, you may be able to perform *distributed flat transactions* as well. Distributed flat transactions obey the same rules as simple flat transactions— if one component on one machine aborts the transaction, the entire transaction is aborted. Distributed flat transactions can run across multiple application servers and databases. This means you can have components deployed in one application server running under the same transaction as other components deployed in another application server. This may be necessary if multiple machines are collaborating across a network to solve a business problem. Distributed flat transactions allow multiple application servers, *written by different vendors*, to collaborate under one transactional hood. While this may not be a reality today, the potential exists for such a scenario in the future, as we'll see a bit later.

Durability and the Two-Phase Commit Protocol

One important ACID property is durability. Durability guarantees that all resource updates that are committed are made permanent. Durability is easy to implement if you have one storage into which you are persisting. But what if multiple resource managers are involved? If one of your resources undergoes a catastrophic failure, such as a database crash, you need to have a recovery mechanism. How do transactions accomplish this?

One way would be to log all database operations before they actually happen, allowing you to recover from a crash by consulting the log and reapplying the updates. This is exactly how transactions guarantee durability. To accomplish this, transactions complete in two *phases*:

Phase One begins by sending a *before commit* message to all resources involved in the transaction. At this time, the resources involved in a transaction have a final chance to abort the transaction. If any resource involved decides to abort, the entire transaction is cancelled and no resource updates are performed. Otherwise, the transaction proceeds on course and cannot be stopped, unless a catastrophic failure occurs. To prevent catastrophic failures, all resource updates are written to a transactional log or journal. This journal is persistent, so it survives crashes and can be consulted after a crash to reapply all resource updates.

Phase Two occurs only if Phase One completed without an abort. At this time, all of the resource managers, which can all be located and controlled separately, perform the actual data updates.

The separation of transaction completion into two phases is called the *two-phase commit protocol* or *2PC*. The two-phase commit protocol is useful because it allows for many transaction managers and resource managers to participate in a transaction across a deployment. If any participant votes that the transaction should abort, all participants must roll back.

In the distributed two-phase commit, there is one master transaction manager called the *distributed transaction coordinator*. The transaction coordinator runs the show and coordinates operations between the other transaction managers across the network. The following steps occur in a distributed two-phase commit transaction:

1. The transaction coordinator sends a *prepare to commit* message to each transaction manager involved.

2. Each transaction manager may propagate this message to the resource managers that are tied to that transaction manager.

3. Each transaction manager reports back to the transaction coordinator. If everyone agrees to commit, then the commit operation that's about to happen is logged in case of a crash.

4. Finally, the transaction coordinator tells each transaction manager to commit. Each transaction manager in turn calls each resource manager, which makes all resource updates permanent and durable. If anything goes wrong, the log entry can be used to reapply this last step.

This process is shown in Figure 10.9.

The Transactional Communications Protocol and Transaction Contexts

A distributed two-phase commit transaction complicates matters because the transaction managers must all agree on a standard mechanism of communicating. Remember that each of the participants in a distributed transaction may have been written by a different vendor, such as a deployment with heterogeneous application servers. The communication mechanism used is called the *transactional communications protocol*. An example of such a protocol is the *Internet Inter-ORB Protocol (IIOP)*, which we describe in Chapter 11.

The most important piece of information sent over the transactional communications protocol is the *transaction context*. A transaction context is an object that holds information about the system's current transactional state. It is passed around between parties involved in transactions. By querying the transaction context, you can gain insight into whether you're in a transaction, what stage of a transaction you are at, and other useful data. In order for any component

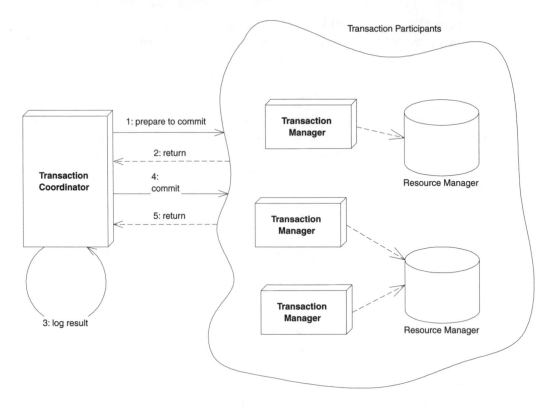

Figure 10.9   A distributed flat transaction using a two-phase commit protocol.

to be involved in a transaction, the current thread in which the component is executing must have a transaction context associated with it.

 The EJB 1.0 specification does not define a mechanism for transaction context propagation with the Java Remote Method Invocation (RMI) native protocol. This means that application servers from different vendors cannot participate in a distributed two-phase commit transaction because they will be unable to communicate in a standard way.

Fortunately, transaction context propagation is built in to CORBA's Object Transaction Service (OTS) and the Internet Inter-ORB Protocol (IIOP). Application servers that use these technologies should be interoperable and run in a distributed 2PC transaction. Sun is likely to standardize on a protocol that handles this as well, called *EJB/IIOP*. But until then, you can expect to see very little support for distributed two-phase commit transactions across heterogeneous application servers. For most users, this is acceptable because distributed 2PC has very poor performance and because most deployments will bet on a single application server vendor.

It's important to understand which communications protocol your application server uses. If you want to perform a distributed two-phase commit transaction, the transaction participants must agree on a standard protocol.

Programmatic Transactions in EJB

We wrap up this chapter with a discussion of how you can control transactions programmatically in EJB. Programmatic transactions allow for more advanced transaction control than declarative transactions, but they are trickier to use. To control transaction boundaries yourself, you must use the Java Transaction API (JTA). We begin by taking a look at how the JTA was established.

CORBA's Object Transaction Service (OTS)

When we described the ACID properties earlier in this chapter, we mentioned that many parties, such as an enterprise bean and a database driver, can participate in a transaction. This is really an extension to the basic ACID properties, and it's the primary reason that Object Management Group (OMG) developed a standardized *Object Transaction Service* (*OTS*) as an optional CORBA service. OTS improved on earlier transaction systems that didn't support multiple parties participating in a transaction.

OTS is a suite of well-defined interfaces that specify how transactions can run behind the scenes—interfaces that the transaction manager, the resource manager, and the transactional objects use to collaborate. OTS is decomposed into two parts: *CosTransactions* and *CosTSPortability*.

The *CosTransactions* interfaces are the basic interfaces that transactional objects/components, resources, resource managers, and transaction managers use to interoperate. These interfaces ensure that any combination of these parties is possible.

The *CosTSPortability* interface offers a portable way to perform transactions with many participants.

The inner workings of OTS are not relevant to the development of enterprise beans. As an EJB programmer, you should need to think only about writing your application, not about low-level transaction services. This is how EJB achieves rapid application development; you can write a distributed server-side application without understanding complex middleware APIs. EJB shields you from transaction services such as OTS.

The Java Transaction Service (JTS)

Sun realized that you, as an application developer, should not care about most of OTS. Only system-level vendors need to be concerned with the inner workings of OTS. Part of OTS is very applicable to you, however, because part of OTS allows you to demarcate transaction boundaries programmatically. Hence, Sun has split up OTS into two sub-APIs: the *Java Transaction Service (JTS)* and the *Java Transaction API (JTA)*.

The *Java Transaction Service (JTS)* is a Java mapping of CORBA OTS for system-level vendors. JTS defines the interfaces used by transaction managers and resource managers behind the scenes. It is used to have various vendors' products interoperate. It also defines various objects passed around and used by transaction managers and resource managers. As an application programmer, you should not care about most of OTS, and you should not care about JTS at all. What you should care about is the Java Transaction API (JTA), which allows you to programmatically control transaction boundaries.

The Java Transaction API (JTA)

The *Java Transaction API (JTA)* is a transaction API used by component and application developers. You can use the JTA in your client and bean code to programmatically control transactional boundaries. The JTA package is a standard Java extension, and hence the package will be automatically downloaded if needed.

You can do very useful things with the JTA, such as start a transaction inside your bean, call other beans that also are involved in a transaction, and control whether things commit or abort. Nonbeans can use the JTA as well—the client code that calls your beans can use the JTA to control transaction boundaries in a workflow scenario, where the client code is calling multiple beans and wishes each bean to participate in one transaction.

 If you use JTA to demarcate transaction boundaries in your client code, you must be careful. Once you've invoked a method on a bean and that bean is associated with a transaction, you can't call another method that would involve it in a different transaction (or no transaction). You first must complete the original transaction with a commit or an abort. If you try to do otherwise, your client code will receive a *java.rmi.RemoteException*.

JTA consists of two interfaces: one for X/Open XA resource managers (which we don't need to worry about) and one that we will use to support programmatic transaction control. The interface you use to programmatically control transactions is *javax.transaction.UserTransaction*.

javax.transaction.UserTransaction

The *javax.transaction.UserTransaction* interface (formerly called *javax.jts .UserTransaction*) allows you to programmatically control transactions. Here is what the *javax.transaction.UserTransaction* interface looks like:

```
package javax.transaction;

interface UserTransaction {
public static final int STATUS_ACTIVE;
public static final int STATUS_MARKED_ROLLBACK;
public static final int STATUS_PREPARED;
public static final int STATUS_COMMITTED;
public static final int STATUS_ROLLEDBACK;
public static final int STATUS_UNKNOWN;
public static final int STATUS_NO_TRANSACTION;
public static final int STATUS_PREPARING;
public static final int STATUS_COMMITTING;
public static final int STATUS_ROLLING_BACK;
public abstract void begin();
public abstract void commit();
public abstract void rollback();
public abstract void setRollbackOnly();
public abstract int getStatus();
public abstract void setTransactionTimeout(int);
}
```

As you can see, six methods are exposed by the *UserTransaction* interface. Three of them—*begin*, *commit*, and *rollback*—are used to begin a new transaction, commit a transaction permanently, and roll back a transaction in case some problem occurred, respectively. The constants for the JTA are summarized in Table 10.2, and the methods are in Table 10.3.

Table 10.2 The javax.transaction.UserTransaction Constants for Transactional Status

CONSTANT	MEANING
STATUS_ACTIVE	A transaction is currently happening and is active.
STATUS_NO_TRANSACTION	There is no transaction currently happening.
STATUS_MARKED_ROLLBACK	The current transaction will eventually abort because it's been marked for rollback. This could be because some party called *setRollbackOnly()*.
STATUS_PREPARING	The current transaction is preparing to be committed (during Phase One of the two-phase commit protocol).

continues

Table 10.2 (Continued)

CONSTANT	MEANING
STATUS_PREPARED	The current transaction has been prepared to be committed (Phase One is complete).
STATUS_COMMITTING	The current transaction is in the process of being committed right now (during Phase Two).
STATUS_COMMITTED	The current transaction has been committed (Phase Two is complete).
STATUS_ROLLING_BACK	The current transaction is in the process of rolling back.
STATUS_ROLLEDBACK	The current transaction has been rolled back.
STATUS_UNKNOWN	The status of the current transaction cannot be determined.

Table 10.3 The javax.transaction.UserTransaction Methods for Transactional Boundary Interaction

METHOD	DESCRIPTION
begin()	Begin a new transaction. This transaction becomes associated with the current thread.
commit()	Run the two-phase commit protocol on an existing transaction associated with the current thread. Each resource manager will make its updates durable.
getStatus()	Retrieve the status of the transaction associated with this thread.
rollback()	Force a rollback of the transaction associated with the current thread.
setRollbackOnly()	Call this to force the current transaction to roll back. This will eventually force the transaction to abort. One interesting use of this is to test out what your components will do, without having them perform any permanent resource updates.
setTransactionTimeout(int)	The *transaction timeout* is the maximum amount of time that a transaction can run before it's aborted. This is useful to avoid deadlock situations, when precious resources are being held by a transaction that is currently running.

Declarative versus Programmatic Transactions Example

We now show you how to write an enterprise bean in two equivalent ways: using programmatic (or bean-managed) transactions and using declarative (or container-managed) transactions. To illustrate this, we'll take our bank account example from Chapter 8. This bank account example has a method called *deposit()* that deposits funds into an account. We'll make this method transactional.

The following code illustrates a deposit method using declarative transactions:

```
/**
 * Deposits amt into account.
 */
public void deposit(double amt) throws AccountException {
    System.out.println("deposit(" + amt + ") called.");

    balance += amt;
}
```

A bean using the above method relies on the EJB container to demarcate transactional boundaries. Therefore, the bean should be deployed with a transaction attribute that provides this (such as TX_REQUIRED, TX_MANDATORY, or TX_REQUIRES_NEW).

The following code illustrates the same method using programmatic transactions:

```
/**
 * Deposits amt into account.
 */
public void deposit(double amt) throws AccountException {
    System.out.println("deposit(" + amt + ") called.");

    javax.transaction.UserTransaction userTran =
        ctx.getUserTransaction();
    userTran.begin();

    balance += amt;

    try {
        userTran.commit();
    }
    catch (Exception e) {
        throw new AccountException("Deposit failed because of " +
        e.toString());
    }
}
```

Here, we are controlling the transactional boundaries explicitly in code. Rather than relying on the EJB container to *begin* and *commit* transactions, we perform these steps by ourselves. A bean using the above method should be deployed with the TX_BEAN_MANAGED transaction attribute because the bean is performing its own transaction boundary demarcation.

Take a look at the size difference between the two sets of source code above. Bean-managed transactions clutter your source code because you need to write to a transaction API. Container-managed transactions allow you to elegantly write application code and externalize all transaction logic to the container. This is quite analogous to our discussion of container-managed persistence versus bean-managed persistence in Chapter 9.

How to Control Transactions from Client Code

We've seen using the Java Transaction API (JTA) from within a bean. But you can also use the JTA in client code that *calls* your beans. You might want to do this if you have a workflow bean that calls into several smaller beans to perform tasks. You can also use the JTA from Java servlets, stand-alone Java applications, or any other Java code.

In EJB 1.0, your beans can access the JTA *UserTransaction* interface by calling *getUserTransaction()* on your context object, as we illustrated in the previous example.

But how do you access the JTA *UserTransaction* interface from a servlet or other nonbean code? Unfortunately, there is no standardized way to do this in EJB 1.0. EJB 1.1, however, fixes this problem. In EJB 1.1, you can look up the JTA *UserTransaction* interface with the *Java Naming and Directory Interface* (*JNDI*). JNDI is a generic lookup facility to look up resources across a network, and it is fully described in Appendix B. The following code illustrates looking up the JTA *UserTransaction* interface from client code using JNDI and BEA's *WebLogic* server. The complete source code is in Part IV, when we use the JTA in an e-commerce deployment.

```
try {

    /*
     * 1: Set environment up.  You must set the JNDI Initial
     *    Context factory, the Provider URL, and any login
     *    names or passwords necessary to access JNDI.  See
     *    your application server product's documentation for
     *    details on their particular JNDI settings.
     */
    java.util.Properties env = ...
```

```
    /*
     * 2: Get the JNDI initial context
     */
    Context ctx = new InitialContext(env);

    /*
     * 3: Look up the JTA UserTransaction interface
     *    via JNDI
     */
    userTran = (javax.transaction.UserTransaction)
        ctx.lookup("javax.transaction.UserTransaction");

    /*
     * 4: Execute the transaction
     */
    userTran.begin();

    // perform business operations

    userTran.commit();
}
catch (Exception e) {
    // deal with any exceptions, including ones
    // indicating an abort.
}
```

When you demarcate transactional boundaries in client code, you should be *very* careful. You should always strive to keep your transactions as short in duration as possible. Longer-lived transactions result in multiuser performance grinding to a halt. If you need a very long transaction (that lasts for minutes, hours, or days) you should use a distributed locking mechanism, such as the CORBA locking service. Unfortunately, there is currently no distributed locking service equivalent in the Java 2 Platform, Enterprise Edition.

Designing Transactional Conversations in EJB

In this chapter we've seen that a transactional abort entails an automatic roll-back of database updates that were performed during the transaction. But database updates are only half of the picture. Your application code needs to consider the impacts of a failed transaction as well.

When a transaction aborts, your application code has several choices. You can abort your business process and throw an exception back to the client, or you can attempt to retry the transaction several times. But unfortunately, your application cannot sit in a loop retrying transactions forever, as that would yield horrible performance for concurrent threads of execution. If the transaction cannot eventually be made to succeed, you should consider aborting your business process.

For a stateless session bean, aborting a business process is a simple task—simply throw an exception back to the client. But for a stateful session bean, things are a bit trickier. Stateful session beans represent business processes that span multiple method calls and hence have in-memory *conversational state*. Tossing away that conversation and throwing an exception to the client could entail a significant amount of lost work.

Fortunately, a well-designed stateful session bean can salvage its conversations in the case of failed transactions. The key is to design your beans to be aware of changes to conversational state and to be smart enough to undo any of those changes in case of a transactional abort.

Because this process is highly application-specific, your application server cannot automate this task for you. Your application server *can* aid you in determining when a transaction failed, enabling you to take application-specific steps. If your session bean needs to be alerted to transaction status (such as failed transactions), your enterprise bean class can implement an optional interface called *javax.ejb.SessionSynchronization*, shown in the following code:

```
public interface javax.ejb.SessionSynchronization
{
    public void afterBegin();
    public void beforeCompletion();
    public void afterCompletion(boolean);
}
```

You should implement this interface in your enterprise bean class and define your own implementations of each of these methods. The container will call your methods automatically at the appropriate times during transactions, alerting you to important transactional events. This adds to the existing arsenal of alerts that your session beans receive already—life-cycle alerts via *ejbCreate()* and *ejbRemove()*, passivation alerts via *ejbActivate()* and *ejbPassivate()*, and now transactional alerts via *afterBegin()*, *beforeCompletion()*, and *afterCompletion()*.

Here's what each of the *SessionSynchronization* methods do:

afterBegin() is called by the container directly after a transaction begins.

beforeCompletion() is called by the container right before a transaction completes.

afterCompletion() is called by the container directly after a transaction completes.

The key method that is most important for rolling back conversations is *afterCompletion()*. The container calls your *afterCompletion()* method when a transaction completes either in a commit *or* an abort. You can figure out whether a commit or an abort happened by the Boolean parameter that gets passed to you in *afterCompletion()*—true indicates a successful commit, false indicates an abort. If an abort happened, you should roll back your conversational state to preserve your session bean's conversation.

Here's an example of *afterCompletion()* in action:

```
public class CountBean implements SessionBean, SessionSynchronization {

    private SessionContext ctx;
    public int val;

    public void ejbCreate(int val) throws CreateException {
        this.val = val;
    }

    public int count() {
        return ++val;
    }

    public void afterCompletion(boolean b) {
        if (b == false) --val;
    }

    public void afterBegin() {}
    public void beforeCompletion() {}
    public void ejbRemove() {}
    public void ejbActivate() {    }
    public void ejbPassivate() {}
    public void setSessionContext(SessionContext ctx) {}
}
```

This is a new version of our Count bean from Chapter 5. The conversational state is *val*, an integer that gets incremented whenever *count()* is called. The key method to notice is *afterCompletion()*—it rolls back our conversational state in case of a transactional abort. Note that we must make *count()* transactional in the deployment descriptor.

The other two methods in *SessionSynchronization*—both *afterBegin()* and *beforeCompletion()*—are useful for when your stateful session bean caches database data in memory during a transaction. You should use these methods as follows:

When the container calls *afterBegin()*, the transaction has just started. Thus, you should read in any database data you want to cache in your stateful session bean.

When the container calls *beforeCompletion()*, the transaction has ended. Write out any database data you've cached.

You can implement *SessionSynchronization only* if you're using a stateful session bean with declarative (container-managed) transactions. If your bean is using programmatic (bean-managed) transactions, you are already in control of the transaction because you issue the *begin()*, *commit()*, and *abort()* statements. Stateless session beans do not hold conversations and hence do not need these callbacks.

Summary

Whew! That's a lot of data to digest. You may want to come back and reread this chapter later to make sure you've grasped all the concepts. You should definitely return to this chapter frequently when you're creating transactional beans or when you're just wondering about transactions in general.

In this chapter, we learned about transactions and how they can make a server-side deployment robust. We saw the virtues of transactions, which are called the ACID properties. We then looked at different transactional models, including flat and nested transactions.

We then applied this transactional knowledge to EJB. We saw how both declarative and programmatic transactions were useful in EJB and when to use each. We saw the different transaction attributes that you can place on your beans. We then looked at transaction isolation levels and understood the problems that each level solves.

Finally, we learned about distributed transactions and the two-phase commit protocol. We wrapped up with explaining how programmatic transactions were performed in EJB, with an example of how a bean method could be written with either methodology, and ended with a look at writing transactional conversations.

Your efforts reading this chapter were well worth it because now you have a solid foundation in the importance and usefulness of transactions in EJB. You'll see some real-world examples using transactions in Part IV, when we perform a sophisticated e-commerce deployment using EJB.

## CHAPTER 11

CORBA and RMI-IIOP

E JB would not be complete without a way to integrate legacy systems. By itself, EJB gives you portable, enterprise-class server-side applications. These applications can be developed rapidly without the management overhead of having to construct a scalable, secure environment. Combining this with CORBA allows EJB customers to leverage legacy CORBA applications, as well as integrate with existing investments written in non-Java languages such as C++ and COBOL. Indeed, CORBA and EJB are very related—many of the concepts in Java 2 Platform, Enterprise Edition came from CORBA.

In this chapter, we'll learn the high-level concepts behind CORBA. We'll then see how Java RMI and CORBA can be combined via RMI-IIOP. Finally, we'll look at how to use RMI-IIOP and CORBA clients to access EJB systems.

 To understand this chapter, you must first understand Java RMI. If you are unfamiliar with this technology, please read Appendix A before reading this chapter.

What Is CORBA?

The *Common Object Request Broker Architecture (CORBA)* is a unifying standard for writing distributed object systems. The standard is completely neutral with respect to platform, language, and vendor. CORBA incorporates a host of technologies and is very broad in scope.

CORBA was invented by the Object Management Group (OMG), a consortium of companies that began in 1989. CORBA itself is simply a standard, just like

EJB. The CORBA specification is *implemented* by CORBA-compliant products, such as Inprise's *VisiBroker for Java*, Iona's *OrbixWeb*, and Sun Microsystem's *Java IDL*, just as the EJB specification is implemented by EJB-compliant products, such as BEA's *WebLogic*, IBM's *WebSphere*, and Oracle's *Oracle 8i* products.

CORBA as the Basis for EJB

Many of the concepts in EJB came out of CORBA. In a sense, you can think of EJB as CORBA with a new hat on. EJB and the Java 2 Platform, Enterprise Edition (J2EE) bring a Java-centric, component-based approach to traditional middleware programming—an architecture suitable for rapid application development. CORBA, on the other hand, offers a much broader suite of middleware features with which to work. This includes a time service, a distributed locking service, a relationship service, and more. To use CORBA's services, you need to program to complex middleware APIs, which increase the learning curve for CORBA programming. This is why EJB and J2EE are much more suitable for rapid application development than CORBA. And because EJB is officially being supported by the industry (there are 25+ vendors writing EJB products at this time), EJB will give you a much wider variety of tools to work with in the long run.

Regardless of this, CORBA is a very important technology and is quite useful for advanced middleware development, cross-language support, and legacy integration. In fact, most serious EJB products on the market are based on CORBA and use CORBA concepts behind the scenes.

Why Should I Care about CORBA?

To you, as an EJB application assembler or bean provider, CORBA is important for three reasons:

You can use CORBA for legacy integration. If you have an existing investment (such as a legacy banking application) you can leverage that investment today using CORBA. For example, let's say you have a banking application written in C++. CORBA gives you the ability to preserve and reuse it. You can wrap your existing investment as a CORBA object, allowing it to be called from any application. As we'll find out, CORBA is a language-neutral standard and allows code written in several languages to communicate. Thus CORBA is an ideal platform for code written in different languages to cooperate.

CORBA allows for advanced middleware development. Remember that EJB is not supposed to be an end-all to every problem. But if there is a middleware service that can be generalized, you're likely to find it standardized as a CORBA service. For those who need it, CORBA gives great functionality.

CORBA and EJB have hooks connecting them. Some EJB products will allow your enterprise beans to be called from two different kinds of clients: clients written to use the J2EE suite of APIs and clients written to use CORBA APIs. This means that code written in C++ or Smalltalk can call your enterprise beans.

Benefits of Using CORBA

Why would you want to use CORBA? There are many reasons:

CORBA is not controlled by one company. Because CORBA has been invented by a consortium of companies, there are many parties invested in CORBA's success. This also means that any changes to the CORBA specification are voted on jointly. This prevents CORBA from becoming a standard that's specific to one product or architecture (in the way that COM+, for example, is specific to MS Windows). And in reality, Enterprise JavaBeans is also the product of a consortium of companies, including IBM, Oracle, Sun, and others, which means that EJB is also not strictly controlled by one company.

CORBA is language-independent. When you use CORBA, you can invoke methods on objects written in other languages without programming in those languages. This allows for very easy legacy integration with languages such as COBOL. If you're writing your programs in Java, you can use CORBA as an alternative to the Java Native Interface for invoking objects written in native code such as C++.

CORBA provides optional value-added services. Vendors of CORBA products can add optional functionality to enhance deployments—common services that many objects will need, such as persistence, security, transactions, and events. Developers who use CORBA don't need to reinvent the wheel—they can leverage services written to a common standard by another vendor.

Drawbacks of CORBA

As usual, the world isn't perfect. Using CORBA has disadvantages as well as advantages:

CORBA is slow-moving. All standards committees are bureaucratic and slow to make decisions. This is because the standards committee itself is not driven by revenues, but rather by individual interests from participating companies. CORBA experiences benefits from not being owned by one company, but its openness is also a drawback. The cycle time for the OMG to adopt a new CORBA feature is on the order of years.

CORBA has a steep learning curve. As CORBA has evolved over the years, it's undergone "feature creep." More and more features have been added, which makes CORBA a robust standard but also increases the learning curve.

Indeed, the specifications that define the whole of CORBA are thousands of pages long and are quite challenging to master. The nice thing about CORBA is that you don't have to learn it all to use it—there are optional CORBA *services* that you can learn as you need them.

Products developed under CORBA may have incompatible features. It's great that CORBA is a unifying standard. Because no one company controls the standard, it levels the playing field for companies competing to build CORBA products. But there remain the problems of multivendor solutions. As with EJB products, if you mix and match CORBA products, you will inevitably run into assumptions that vendors have made but that are specific to their own products. This is the trade-off between a one-vendor solution, such as Microsoft, and an open standard, such as CORBA or EJB. The price of freedom is eternal vigilance.

Understanding How CORBA Works

Before we delve into CORBA/EJB interoperability, we'll cover the core CORBA fundamental concepts. This will lay the groundwork for us to discuss how CORBA and EJB are compatible.

Object Request Brokers

An *Object Request Broker* or *ORB* is a facilitator for objects on the network to communicate. ORBs are intermediaries between distributed objects. They enable disparate applications to communicate without being aware of the underlying communications mechanism. ORBs allow objects to call methods on each other, dynamically discover each other, and more. ORBs are responsible for finding objects to service method calls, handling parameter passing, and returning results. Whenever you have multiple objects interacting in a CORBA environment, ORBs facilitate the communications. This is shown in Figure 11.1.

There are numerous CORBA ORBs on the market. Some examples are Iona's *OrbixWeb*, Inprise's *VisiBroker*, and IBM's *ComponentBroker*. Each vendor offers various qualities of service that differentiate that vendor's product from those of other vendors in the marketplace.

The concept of an ORB is absolutely not specific to CORBA. Both Java RMI and Microsoft COM+ contain ORB functionality as well because both RMI and COM+ facilitate network communications and hence serve as object request brokers. For the rest of this chapter, however, we'll assume we're dealing with CORBA ORBs.

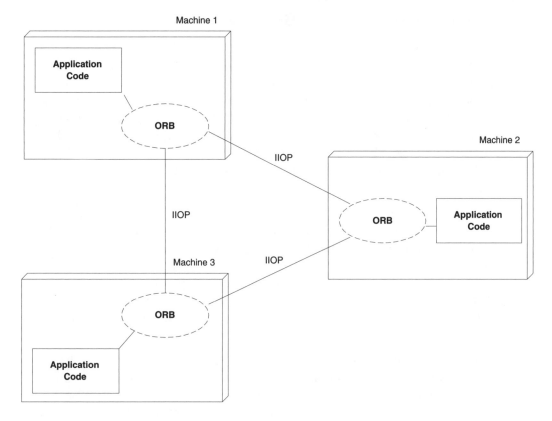

Figure 11.1 The ORB facilitates your networking needs.

What Is IIOP?

Throughout this book, we've seen EJB applications that communicate via the Java RMI API. Java RMI is a communications package for performing distributed computing in Java. Behind the scenes, Java RMI uses the *Java Remote Method Protocol* (*JRMP*) as the default protocol layer for communications.

The CORBA world, however, does not use JRMP. Rather, CORBA products use a different protocol called *IIOP* (*Internet Inter-ORB Protocol*). IIOP is the standard Internet protocol for CORBA. IIOP, just like JRMP, is used behind the scenes for distributed object communications. CORBA ORBs use IIOP to communicate with each other, as shown in Figure 11.1.

Object Implementations and Object References

CORBA provides a clean separation between an object's interface and its implementation. When you write a CORBA object implementation, that object is callable over the network by remote clients. Those clients deal with your CORBA object implementation's interface only—clients do not deal directly with your object implementation. This separation of interface from implementation is quite analogous to how distributed computing is performed in Java RMI. With both CORBA and Java RMI, clients are unaware of object implementation details— clients are concerned only with the interfaces to the object implementations that they are using.

In addition to interface/implementation separation, one of CORBA's goals is *location transparency* of distributed objects. Location transparency means that client code is unaware of where a real object implementation resides—perhaps it is local, perhaps remote. CORBA achieves location transparency with *object references*. An object reference is an identifier for a particular object implementation in CORBA. It uniquely identifies the object implementation across the network. An object reference automatically tracks the object implementation it represents behind-the-scenes.

Note that in theory, you should not need to worry yourself with the details of object references—you should just know that the ORB vendors use them internally in their ORBs to identify objects. In reality, each vendor's CORBA implementation deals with references in a slightly different way, and you have to know how to get an object reference from each type of ORB.

Object Adapters

A CORBA *object adapter* is a pluggable entity that assists in the following tasks:

- When an object is accessed, the object adapter is responsible for mapping an object reference onto an object implementation behind the scenes. When a client performs an invocation, the ORB, the object adapter, and the implementation object coordinate to figure out which implementation object should be called.

- If a client calls a method on an object implementation that is not in memory, the object adapter *activates* the object (or initializes it into memory) so it can service the client request. The converse is also true—object adapters also *deactivate* objects. Activation is a great help because it gives clients the illusion that server-side objects are always up and running, even though they are lazy-loaded (activated) into memory on the fly.

CORBA was designed to be flexible with object adapters. They are truly pluggable entities. You can have many different kinds of object adapters running in your system, with different kinds of behavior.

The first object adapter that the OMG introduced was the *Basic Object Adapter* or *BOA*. Very quickly, ORB vendors began to realize that the BOA was poorly defined and ambiguous in many cases (for example, the BOA did not define properly the mechanisms for activation and deactivation of objects). So what happened? ORB vendors began to write their own proprietary versions of the BOA, which are totally incompatible with each other. This severely hindered CORBA's portability.

The OMG realized this and decided to give up on the BOA (fixing it would be too difficult). Instead, a new *Portable Object Adapter* or *POA* was born. The POA is very flexible and defines a set of common services from which other object adapters can be derived. Hence, the POA is somewhat like a parent that defines rules for its children, so that each child adheres to the same rules, yielding portability.

Having the POA adds flexibility to CORBA. Object adapters can now be defined that are not only portable but have very different kinds of behavior. For example, different POA subobjects can have different policies for activating and deactivating objects. Each object adapter derived from the POA can have a policy that's applicable to certain objects in your system.

The POA makes a clear distinction between two kinds of object references in CORBA. A *transient object reference* is an object reference that is useful only for the lifetime of the client. While the client is still alive, the transient object reference is used to call the object implementation.

But what if the client wants to store an object reference persistently? It might be nice for clients to be able to get a reference to a CORBA object implementation, shut down, then start up and start calling methods again. The POA allows for this. The idea is to *stringify* the object reference (that is, convert the object reference into a human-readable string). Strings are easily sent around and saved to disk. You can later read the string back in and pass it to your object adapter to reconstruct the transient object reference. You can then start calling methods again. This is very handy because strings are human-readable, easily stored in a variety of media, and easily sent between parties.

Repositories

A *repository* is a service that stores information and can be queried for that information. Repositories are somewhat like databases (and, in fact, their implementation may indeed use a database).

In CORBA, there are two important repositories: an *Interface Repository* and an *Implementation Repository*. Let's take a look at these repositories and how they're used.

The Interface Repository

As we've mentioned, the ORB is responsible for facilitating distributed object communications. CORBA clients deal only with interfaces to object implementations. To help the ORB process the objects that clients work with, CORBA introduces the notion of an Interface Repository. An Interface Repository is a repository in which interface definitions are stored permanently. It's an aggregation facility for storing the interfaces that clients deal with.

The ORB itself makes extensive use of the Interface Repository internally. For example, the ORB uses the Interface Repository for performing type checking of signatures when performing invocations. It also uses it to help verify the correctness of inheritance, and it assists with interoperability between different ORB implementations.

As a CORBA client, you can also make use of the Interface Repository. For example, you can use it to manage how your interfaces are distributed and installed.

The Implementation Repository

Just as an Interface Repository stores interface definitions, an Implementation Repository stores the code that implements the logic defined by the interfaces. For example, an Implementation Repository might be a folder on a hard disk where class files are kept. Implementation Repositories do not have a well-defined interface to them (yet).

OMG's Interface Definition Language

The cornerstone of CORBA is the Object Management Group's *interface definition language (OMG IDL)*. OMG IDL is a language that CORBA uses to define the interfaces between clients and the objects they call. When you write a CORBA object implementation, that object implementation must have corresponding IDL that defines the interface for that object implementation. By programming with OMG IDL, you are forcing a clear distinction between interface and implementation—you can vary your implementation without changing the interface your clients use. The IDL concept is shown in Figure 11.2.

Another great benefit to OMG IDL is that it is a *language-neutral* interface for object implementations. You can write your IDL once and then define your object implementations in any language that CORBA supports, such as C++ or Smalltalk. And because IDL is language-neutral, client code that calls your object implementations can be written in any language that CORBA supports as well. Thus, IDL enables you to have a deployment mixing heterogeneous languages.

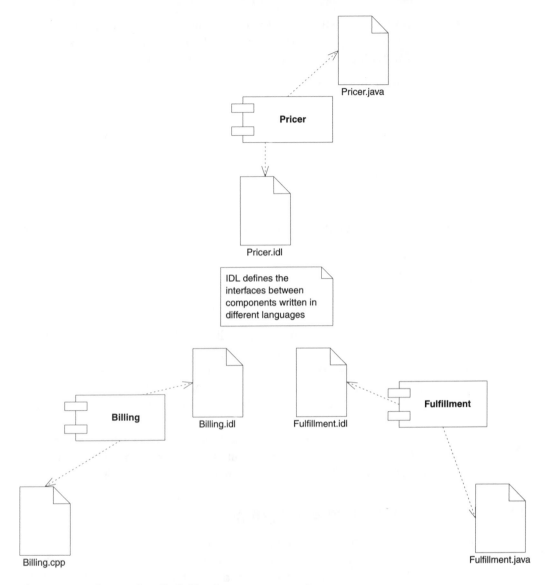

Figure 11.2 The Interface Definition Language concept.

IDL is also inherently *platform-neutral*, allowing clients and object implementations to be deployed in different platforms. For example, your clients can exist on a Windows NT box and be talking to business objects deployed on a Silicon Graphics IRIX box.

 OMG IDL is only one flavor of IDL. Microsoft has its own IDL as part of COM+. In this chapter, we'll assume we're using OMG IDL.

You should think of IDL as a "middleman" language—a common ground that is, in theory, independent of language change. IDL allows you to write a distributed application with the illusion that it's all written in one language.

Here is a sample snippet of IDL:

```
module com {
 module wiley {
  module compBooks {
   module roman {
    module corba {

     interface HelloWorld {
      string sayHello(in string myName);
     }


}}}}}
```

As you can see, IDL is very similar to C++ and Java.

There are many different types in IDL, including basic types (such as *short* and *float*) and constructed types (such as *struct* and *enumeration*). You'll find that if you know C++, learning to use OMG IDL is pretty straightforward. If you're a Java programmer, you should not have too much difficulty using IDL to define your object's interfaces either because Java's syntax is similar to C++.

 We only briefly describe IDL in this chapter. Most CORBA books will have a section explaining IDL fully. And if you're serious about CORBA, take a look at ftp://www .omg.org/pub/docs/formal/98-02-08.pdf, which details OMG IDL rigorously.

OMG IDL Maps to Concrete Languages

IDL is only a descriptive language in that it describes the interfaces to your objects. You cannot "execute" IDL. Neither your CORBA object implementations nor your CORBA clients ever see IDL. You program your clients and object implementations in whatever language you're using, such as Java or C++. But how, then, do you refer to CORBA objects? The answer is the OMG IDL *maps* to specific languages, such as Java or C++. If you go to the OMG Web site (www.omg.org), you'll see that there are specifications detailing how OMG IDL maps to various languages. For instance, there is an IDL-to-Java mapping specification that defines how IDL maps to Java. With the IDL-to-Java mapping, the *string* type in OMG IDL maps to the *java.lang.String* object in Java.

Thus, it's important to realize that, although IDL is a language, it is more of an abstraction because you never write client code or object implementations that use IDL files. Rather, you use IDL to define the interfaces to your objects and then *map* that IDL into your particular language using an *IDL compiler*. For example, an IDL-to-Java compiler would take as input an IDL file and generate Java interfaces for your object implementations. Once this is done, you can implement those interfaces in Java. You could then map the IDL to a different language, such as C++, by using an IDL-to-C++ compiler. This would allow you to write client code in C++ that calls your Java object implementations.

 For the sake of brevity, we do not cover the IDL-to-Java mapping here. You can download the complete IDL-to-Java mapping specification for free from ftp:// www.omg.org/pub/docs/formal/98-02-29.pdf.

Static Invocations

As we've said, the ORB facilitates client/server communications, simplifying client networking needs. But how does a client invoke a method on a remote CORBA object? The answer is via a local method call, which gets translated into a remote method call across the network. This is quite analogous to how networking is accomplished in Java RMI.

The conventional way of performing distributed computing in CORBA is to have the client invoke locally on a pregenerated *stub*. The stub is a proxy for the real object implementation, which exists elsewhere on the network. The stub is responsible for going through the client-side ORB runtime, which channels the request over the network via IIOP.

The receiving server-side ORB runtime receives the IIOP request, then calls a *skeleton* to handle the request. The server-side skeleton is a pregenerated file, just like the stub. The skeleton is responsible for delegating the invocation to the actual server-side CORBA object that will service the request. The skeleton is also responsible for coordinating with the object adapter (which we mentioned earlier in this chapter) to activate objects in case they don't exist already. This process is shown in Figure 11.3.

Both the stub and skeleton are pregenerated files. They are usually generated from the IDL file that defines the server-side CORBA object's method signatures. They need to be pregenerated for two reasons:

CORBA objects are inherently cross-language. This means you need to pregenerate the stubs and skeletons in the particular language you're using. You're free to use any language to which IDL maps.

Stubs and skeletons contain specific syntax about your particular CORBA object's method signatures. Thus you must generate them for each of your CORBA objects because each object will have different method

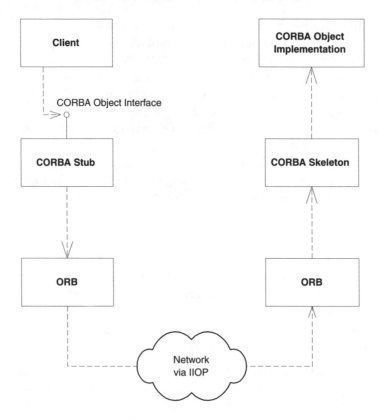

Figure 11.3 Calling a method in CORBA.

signatures. By generating them, you can simulate an environment where clients can invoke on proxies using the actual method signatures of the real object, located elsewhere.

The above invocation mechanism is called a *static invocation* because you're statically binding your client code to stubs at compile time.

Dynamic Invocations

There is another way for you to invoke on CORBA objects: *dynamically*. Dynamic invocations allow you to invoke on CORBA objects that might not be available when you write your client code. With dynamic invocations, your clients dynamically discover CORBA objects at runtime. This mechanism of invoking dynamically is CORBA's *Dynamic Invocation Interface*, or *DII*.

The DII is a very powerful idea, and it has a number of benefits, such as plugging in new objects without recompiling client code. Because everything is dynamically discovered at runtime, you don't need to pregenerate stubs and skeletons, as you do for static binding. And if you want your invocation to be asynchronous (that is, you perform the invocation, go off and do something else, and then come back later for the results), the DII can accommodate you.

There are also several drawbacks to dynamic invocations. For one, the runtime discovery of objects is a performance hit. When you precompile stubs and skeletons with static binding, you're performing all necessary "discovery" in a pre-processing step. When you are instead operating dynamically, you're making the ORB figure out which method to invoke, which slows things down.

 If you are a COM programmer, you will find that using dynamic invocations in CORBA through DII is much like using dynamic invocations in the COM world through COM's IDispatch interface. Similarly, static invocations in CORBA are much like the virtual function pointer table binding in COM.

CORBA's Many Services

In addition to enabling objects to communicate over the network, the Object Management Group has published a set of CORBA Object Services (known as *CORBAServices* or *COS*) that give your networked objects additional capabilities. These services are optionally provided by CORBA vendors. Most serious CORBA products will give you one or more services to aid development.

Let's take a look at a sampling of these services. There are many more services than we're listing here, and even more will surely be developed over time. As you'll notice, some of these services are very similar to those that EJB provides. Indeed, much of EJB was based on CORBA's services.

The Naming Service

The *CORBA Naming Service* (or *COS Naming*) is a CORBA service that allows you to look up CORBA objects by name. This allows you to identify the locations of objects across the network by a human-readable string.

COS Naming is a similar technology to the Java Naming and Directory Interface (JNDI), which we review in Appendix B. In fact, there is a service provider plugin for JNDI that allows JNDI clients to access CORBA Naming and Directory services. JNDI is much more robust than the CORBA Naming Service because JNDI can look up arbitrary resources on a network, not just CORBA objects.

The Event Service

The *CORBA Event Service* allows for asynchronous communications between CORBA objects. Asynchronous communications allow for parties to send or process events at their leisure. An object can send an event to another object without suspending (or *blocking*) the calling thread. Events support a much looser form of communication between objects: peer-to-peer rather than client-to-server. Using the CORBA Event Service, your objects can *subscribe* to certain types of events and be *notified* when an event of that type is generated.

The Object Transaction Service

CORBA's *Object Transaction Service* (*OTS*) enables CORBA objects to perform transactions. The Transaction Service is composed of two pieces: a low-level set of interfaces between transaction participants (such as a Resource Manager, a Transaction Manager, etc.), and a high-level interface for demarcating transactional boundaries.

The Concurrency Control Service

The *Concurrency Control Service* allows for multiple clients to concurrently interact with a resource. Clients concurrently access resources by obtaining *locks* on those resources. For example, I can request a read lock on an object, which does not allow any other client to write to the object while I hold the read lock. Other clients that also hold read locks can still interact with my object, however, because they're simply reading, not modifying the object. I can also request a write lock, which disallows any concurrent readers or writers. There are five different lock modes, allowing for a wide variety of interactions. The Concurrency Service works together with CORBA's Object Transaction Service.

The Security Service

The *CORBA Security Service* adds secure functionality to your CORBA system. The Security Service yields mechanisms to do the following:

- Identify and authenticate users and objects
- Perform authorization and access control, ensuring that clients are qualified to perform desired operations
- Enable confidentiality, ensuring that only authorized users can view object contents
- Create audit trails and perform other needed security functions

CORBA Components

As we go to press, several OMG participants have issued a revised specification for *CORBA Components*. This specification adds component features to CORBA objects, allowing them to function similarly to enterprise beans. This means that CORBA now has a proposal that allows for true components to be developed in the CORBA world.

If you browse through the specification (available at ftp://ftp.omg.org/pub/docs/orbos/98-12-02.pdf), you'll see that it's almost identical to Enterprise JavaBeans. This was done intentionally so that CORBA Components and enterprise beans can reside together. One goal of CORBA Components is to integrate with enterprise beans. Thus, it should be possible to do the following:

- Make a CORBA Component appear as though it were an enterprise bean
- Make an enterprise bean appear as though it were a CORBA Component

This will definitely be an interesting standard to keep an eye on as EJB and CORBA evolve. If you're curious, take a look at Chapter 11 of the CORBA Components specification, which details how CORBA Components and Enterprise JavaBeans can be mapped.

 We've just scratched the surface of CORBA's services here. A great reference for CORBA's services is *The CORBA Reference Guide* by Alan Pope (Addison-Wesley Publications, 1998, ISBN #0201633868). Take a look at this book if you want to understand CORBA's optional services at a high level but you don't want to read the formal OMG specifications.

RMI over IIOP

Now that you've seen the basics of CORBA theory, let's compare Java RMI to CORBA. RMI is an alternative mechanism for performing networking in Java, fully covered in Appendix A.

We'll first see why people use RMI and CORBA. Next, we'll look at the semantic differences that must be overcome in order to merge CORBA and RMI. Finally, we'll look at how the industry is merging RMI and CORBA with a standard known as *RMI over IIOP*. This standard is the key to EJB-CORBA compatibility.

The Need for RMI-CORBA Interoperability

RMI and CORBA are very similar technologies with slightly different goals. One technology is not better than the other—it all depends on what kind of development you're doing.

CORBA is a robust distributed object standard that allows for language interoperability. RMI, on the other hand, was built for very simple distributed object communications in Java. While RMI does not contain CORBA's cross-language support, it is well suited for pure Java development due to Java-specific features such as distributed garbage collection (see Appendix A).

While both RMI and CORBA are intended for distributed object communications, neither technology contains high-end middleware services, such as persistence or transactions. CORBA programmers can gain those middleware services by leveraging CORBA's optional services that we described earlier. RMI programmers can gain those middleware services by leveraging the Java 2 Platform, Enterprise Edition suite.

Unfortunately, although RMI and CORBA are similar in nature, they have historically been incompatible technologies. When you program code with Java RMI, you need to write your code to the RMI API. Similarly, when you program code with CORBA, you need to write your code to the CORBA API. This is terrible for code reuse: If you write code in either RMI or CORBA, you'll need to rewrite major pieces of your code if you want to switch networking technologies.

Ideally, we'd like a world where we could perform the following:

Combine client-side Java RMI with server-side CORBA. We should be able to write an object implementation to the CORBA API and write client code to the Java RMI API that calls that CORBA object. This is shown in Figure 11.4.

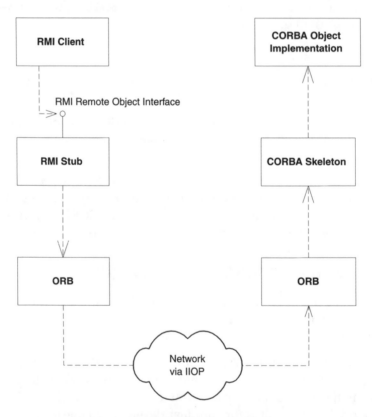

Figure 11.4 An RMI client calling a CORBA object implementation.

Combine client-side CORBA with server-side Java RMI. We should be able to write a remote object implementation with the RMI API and have a client written to the CORBA API call that object. This is shown in Figure 11.5.

Combining RMI with CORBA

What strategy should we use to combine the CORBA world with the Java RMI world? To begin to answer this, let's compare how CORBA and RMI work behind the scenes:

- Both CORBA (except in its dynamic communications mechanism) and RMI use pregenerated stubs and skeletons for performing network communications.

- Behind the scenes, CORBA uses IIOP as the protocol for performing client/server communications. This occurs beneath the stub/skeleton layer.

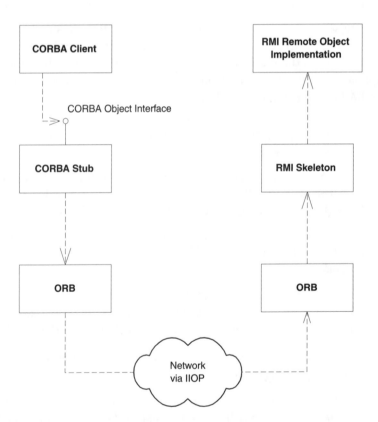

Figure 11.5 A CORBA client calling an RMI remote object implementation.

- Behind the scenes, Java RMI uses the Java Remote Method Protocol (JRMP) protocol for performing client/server communications. This occurs beneath the stub/skeleton layer as well.

Thus, CORBA and RMI are quite similar in how they perform remote invocations. They each have an API layer (stubs/skeletons) that uses either IIOP or JRMP as the wire protocol for transmitting data across the network.

The protocol being used is the key to interoperability of CORBA and RMI. RMI skeletons are always expecting a request to come in via the JRMP protocol, and CORBA skeletons are always expecting data to come in using the IIOP protocol. But this protocol layer should be totally pluggable. We should be able to, for example, switch out RMI's JRMP protocol and switch in the IIOP protocol. If we did this, we could perform the following procedure (see Figure 11.4):

1. An RMI client uses the RMI API and invokes a method on an RMI stub.

2. *The RMI stub contacts a local ORB, which uses IIOP as the protocol for server communication, rather than the standard JRMP protocol.*

3. On the server, an ORB is waiting to receive IIOP requests. With that ORB is the pure CORBA skeleton for our CORBA object implementation. The ORB receives the request. Because it's formatted using IIOP, the request appears as though it came from a CORBA client, when in fact it came from an RMI client using the IIOP protocol.

4. The ORB passes the request to the CORBA skeleton, which delegates the invocation to the CORBA object implementation. The object implementation services the invocation.

5. When the invocation is complete, the return results are passed back through the pure CORBA skeleton, which returns control to the ORB. The ORB sends the results back over IIOP as usual.

6. *A client-side ORB receives the return results via IIOP, and returns the results to the RMI client's stub. The stub then returns control to the RMI client code.*

This scenario is nice because it allows Java clients to use the RMI API to invoke methods on CORBA objects. What about CORBA clients invoking on RMI object implementations? This could be done as follows (see Figure 11.5):

1. A CORBA client invokes a method on a pure CORBA stub.

2. The IIOP protocol is used, as normal, as the wire-protocol over the network.

3. *On the receiving end, an ORB is waiting to receive requests formatted with IIOP. The ORB receives the request and calls a special RMI skeleton that knows how to accept the call from an ORB. (Notice that our RMI skeletons are receiving the request via IIOP, rather than the traditional JRMP protocol.)*

4. The RMI skeleton delegates the invocation to the RMI remote object implementation.

5. The RMI remote object implementation churns away and returns a result to the RMI skeleton.

6. *The RMI skeleton returns the result to the ORB. The ORB returns the data over the network using IIOP (again, our RMI remote objects return data over IIOP rather than over JRMP).*

7. The pure CORBA stub receives the result over IIOP and returns control to the CORBA client code.

So why is IIOP our protocol of choice, rather than JRMP? The reason is that IIOP is a much more robust protocol than JRMP (we'll see the specific benefits in the next section). IIOP is supported by numerous vendors in the industry and has been designed with interoperability of heterogeneous distributed objects in mind.

The scheme we've just presented is the basis for the unification of CORBA and RMI, and it is called *RMI over IIOP* (or *RMI-IIOP*). RMI over IIOP allows for CORBA clients, RMI clients, CORBA object implementations, and RMI object implementations to be mixed and matched. This accomplishes our goal of creating a bridge between RMI and CORBA. To keep things straight, you may want to refer back to these two scenarios as you read the rest of this chapter.

Benefits of RMI over IIOP

Let's now take a look at what we gain by using RMI over IIOP:

RMI and CORBA code achieve greater reusability. When performing simple networking of objects, you don't need to choose between RMI and CORBA anymore. You can develop portable client code in Java using either the RMI or CORBA APIs. You can also develop portable Java object implementations using either the RMI or CORBA APIs. RMI over IIOP lessens the impact of switching between the two.

Code written in almost any language can call RMI object implementations. RMI objects are now truly language-independent network citizens, and they can be invoked from clients written in any language to which CORBA maps. This allows you to plug RMI object implementation into an existing system. It also paves the way for the future, as existing RMI code can be leveraged as languages evolve. And with the COM/CORBA bridge, the possibility emerges for a COM-compliant object to connect with an RMI server.

RMI clients can now be integrated into legacy systems. Perhaps you have an existing investment written in C++, COBOL, or some other language that CORBA maps to, including C, C++, Java, SmallTalk, Ada, and COBOL. As we've mentioned, you can use straight CORBA to take these existing object implementations into the interoperable CORBA realm. Add RMI over IIOP, and you've got the simplicity of an RMI client, while still leveraging your existing investment.

IIOP gives RMI robust firewall navigation. One nice thing about using an industry standard protocol such as IIOP is that you gain all the support behind it. For example, as we mention in Appendix A, RMI has the ability to tunnel through firewalls. This is a very slow and arduous process, and it is really a security loophole. The CORBA community is making headway in developing an extensible way for distributed objects to communicate through firewalls. Special IIOP firewall proxies are being developed that will permit IIOP traffic to pass through. If you use the IIOP protocol, any RMI or CORBA code you write will have a natural way of navigating firewalls. Unfortunately, there is a severe limitation to the effectiveness of these proxies: You have to have the firewall proxy on both the client and the server systems. A company can't set up a business-to-consumer e-commerce site and expect an IIOP proxy to solve the firewall problem. If the client's system has a firewall, the client won't be able to send an IIOP call out through the net. For limited applications (such as intranet applications or Internet applications where they can control the client and server systems), IIOP proxies add value. Iona is an example of a vendor that provides such an IIOP proxy, called WonderWall. Inprise makes one too, called Gatekeeper. See the book's accompanying Web site for links to these products (www.wiley.com/compbooks/roman).

IIOP gives RMI a portable way to propagate contexts. Let's say your code is involved in a transaction or has security credentials associated with it. Most systems (including EJB) manifest transaction and security data in *contexts*. When you perform an invocation, you want this context information to be *propagated* automatically to the receiving system, so the object implementation can execute its business logic for you within the same contexts. We first introduced this concept of propagation in Chapter 10. With RMI, context propagation is done in a proprietary way, as RMI itself has no built-in way to accomplish propagation. This is a huge hindrance because as soon as propagation becomes proprietary, you cannot combine products from separate vendors. The IIOP protocol, and thus, RMI over IIOP, standardizes the way contexts are propagated. This is very important in the EJB world. In the past, you could have a mix of only CORBA-based EJB Servers working together because CORBA-based EJB servers are sharing transaction/context information in the same way (using IIOP). With RMI over IIOP, RMI-based EJB servers can be mixed with RMI-based or CORBA-based EJB servers because everyone is propagating context information using IIOP. This greatly improves EJB interoperability. (Note: The initial release of RMI/IIOP does *not* include support for propagation of service contexts. We hope this issue will be fixed in the next release.)

RMI object implementations can be invoked dynamically. Using CORBA's Dynamic Invocation Interface (DII), described earlier in this chapter, you can perform runtime discovery of RMI object implementations and perform dynamic invocations. This is not a huge benefit, though, because you can use Java Reflection to achieve similar results with straight RMI.

Problems That Arise When Combining RMI with IIOP

Everything we've said so far sounds very pretty. But is it really that easy for RMI and IIOP to work together? After all, these are two technologies that have been developed separately. Indeed, when you scratch the surface you'll find many semantic problems. Let's take a look at the difficulties that Sun Microsystems and the OMG are working hard together to resolve.

Differences in Parameter Passing Conventions

CORBA objects have traditionally been passed around the network by reference. This means that when a client receives a reference to a CORBA object, that CORBA object never moves from its remote host. Clients invoke on the original objects rather than on copies of the CORBA objects passed to them. Java Objects are also passed by reference in the Java language.

RMI is more robust than CORBA here. RMI does not mandate that all objects are passed by reference. With RMI, you can pass an object *by value*, which means that a copy of the object is sent, rather than a remote reference to the original object. This is accomplished through object serialization, as shown in Appendix A.

Needless to say, this is a huge semantic difference between RMI and CORBA.

Solution: The OMG Objects-by-Value Specification

Fortunately, the OMG has developed an *Objects-by-Value* specification (published in February 1998), which allows CORBA objects to be passed by value. A special *value type* was added to OMG IDL, which allows for objects to be identified as passed by copy, rather than by reference.

Value objects in CORBA work much like objects that are passed by value in Java RMI. As you'll see in Appendix A, the RMI parameter passing convention works as follows:

If the parameter is primitive or implements java.io.Serializable, it is passed by value. A copy of the parameter is sent to the target JVM.

If the parameter implements java.rmi.Remote, it is passed by reference. A remote stub is passed to the target JVM, which serves as a "cross-JVM" reference to an object.

CORBA's Objects-by-Value specification works very similarly. Objects-by-Value relies on a language (such as Java) to provide a mechanism (such as serialization) that will pack and unpack an object's state, so that it can be passed over the wire. In fact, Java serialization (or an equivalent) is used in the Java version of Objects-by-Value.

 To keep this discussion relevant to EJB, we've just touched on Objects-by-Value. The curious reader can download the complete Objects-by-Value specification free from ftp://ftp.omg.org/pub/docs/orbos/98-01-18.pdf.

The Objects-by-Value specification is quite useful. By introducing Objects-by-Value, RMI over IIOP can now support RMI's by-value parameter passing convention. In addition, straight CORBA programmers can use it to send objects over the wire, reducing potential network round trips in pure CORBA systems.

Other Semantic Differences between RMI and CORBA

Parameter passing conventions are not the only differences between RMI and CORBA. There are other semantic differences as well. Let's take a look at the major concerns:

Distributed garbage collection. RMI gives you an automatic way of cleaning up objects over the network with a distributed garbage collector (introduced in Appendix A). CORBA, on the other hand, has no such mechanism. Why? Because not every language that CORBA maps to even has the concept of asynchronous garbage collection.

Narrowing. When you receive an object using Java RMI, you can simply cast it into the desired object using a Java cast (as shown in the numerous examples in Appendix A). This is possible because RMI automatically downloads the appropriate stub for the object you're dealing with. CORBA, however, does not have a mechanism for automatic stub downloading.

Java RMI programmers don't want to learn OMG IDL. One of the niceties of Java RMI is that it's all Java, which means you don't need to learn a separate interface definition language (such as OMG IDL) to handle your networking needs. But with RMI over IIOP, you can mix CORBA clients with RMI server object implementations. Those CORBA clients are pure CORBA clients (with pure CORBA stubs), and they need to work with some IDL. That IDL needs to come from somewhere. Should we force Java RMI programmers to churn out an IDL file? If we make Java RMI coders learn OMG IDL, a large benefit of RMI has been lost.

Solution: The Java-to-IDL Mapping Specification

To resolve the semantic differences between RMI and CORBA, a separate OMG specification was made, called the *Java-to-IDL Mapping* specification. This document details all of the subtleties of combining the RMI API with the IIOP protocol. It addresses issues such as distributed garbage collection and inheritance, as well as the resolution of the differences between RMI and CORBA. In essence, the Java-to-IDL Mapping document is the complete specification for RMI over IIOP.

Note the difference between the Java-to-IDL Mapping and the IDL-to-Java Mapping. Both are OMG specifications, but each has a very different purpose. The Java-to-IDL Mapping is *not* simply a description of how the Java language syntactically maps to OMG IDL. It is a specification for how RMI and CORBA camps can be combined.

Here are some highlights of the Java-to-IDL Mapping goals:

- Java RMI and CORBA are semantically different. Trade-offs need to be made in several places to enable interoperability between the two technologies. Inevitably, some of the current Java RMI semantics are going to be unusable in the CORBA realm. Thus, the Java-to-IDL Mapping specification defines a *subset* of Java to which RMI programmers must now adhere. This subset is called *RMI/IDL*.

- RMI/IDL needs to be a strict subset of Java RMI, to avoid creating yet another networking dialect.

- RMI/IDL needs to support as large a subset of Java RMI as possible.

Let's take a look at how Java-to-IDL solves some of the semantic differences between RMI and CORBA:

Distributed garbage collection (DGC). RMI over IIOP does not propose to accomplish distributed garbage collection. And rightfully so—DGC is in general a very hard problem to solve. Instead, the Java-to-IDL specification mandates that RMI coders cannot rely on distributed garbage collection when using RMI over IIOP. This is an unfortunate consequence of combining RMI with CORBA. Some RMI features need to be removed when migrating to the RMI/IDL feature subset of RMI.

Narrowing. When using RMI over IIOP, you cannot simply cast an object you receive over the network. Rather, you must explicitly call a *narrowing* method that will convert the object into the desired type for you.

Java RMI programmers don't want to learn OMG IDL. One great benefit of Java RMI is that you don't need to learn a separate interface definition language to perform remote computing. We'd like to preserve this feature. Therefore, RMI over IIOP defines a mapping from RMI/IDL types to OMG IDL types. This mapping means that there is a well-defined way for Java language types used by RMI over IIOP to be automatically mapped into OMG IDL. Once we have this, a vendor can write a tool that automatically performs this mapping. Such a tool is called a *java-to-idl compiler*. It takes in code written in Java and spits out OMG IDL. This IDL can be used by CORBA clients when calling your RMI remote object implementations. The IDL can also be used by CORBA object implementations that your RMI clients call.

Java-to-IDL allows you to build complete distributed applications in Java and then use apps written in other languages to invoke on your distributed application. The Java-to-IDL mapping simplifies your network programming tremendously. No longer do you have to write IDL and then translate that into Java. Java-to-IDL compilers allow you to write your Java app as you normally would, yet they allow for CORBA interoperability by generating IDL for you. This is a great convenience—Java RMI programmers gain the benefits of CORBA/IIOP interoperability, such as cross-language support, at a very low cost.

Steps to Take for RMI and CORBA to Work Together: An Overview

Now that you've seen the theory of combining RMI with CORBA, let's see exactly what steps you need to take for interoperability.

 The RMI-IIOP bundle itself is downloadable from Sun's Web site. If you are going to be performing any RMI-IIOP programming, you may want to follow up by reading the documents included with this bundle, as well as the Java-to-IDL mapping specification. They give the complete set of changes to which RMI programmers must adapt in order to use RMI-IIOP. See the book's accompanying Web site for a link to the RMI-IIOP download.

RMI-IIOP Client with a CORBA Object Implementation

Our first scenario depicts an RMI-over-IIOP client with a CORBA object implementation. As with all RMI clients, an RMI-IIOP client needs to call methods on a remote interface. In addition, the CORBA object implementation that the RMI client calls must have accompanying OMG IDL. You'd like to avoid writing OMG IDL explicitly because RMI is about simple network programming.

To accomplish this, perform the following steps:

1. **Write your RMI remote interface.** You write the remote interface in Java as you'd normally do for any RMI program. The remote interface is RMI's client/server contract for distributed objects.

2. **Generate the needed client-side RMI over IIOP stubs.** The stubs will be used by the RMI-over-IIOP client to invoke on the CORBA object implementation. See the following section, "How Do I Generate Stubs and Skeletons?" for more details.

3. **Generate the OMG IDL.** When you define your CORBA object implementations, you're going to need IDL. This IDL must match your RMI remote interface if you want RMI clients to be able to invoke your CORBA object implementations. Rather than laboriously writing it yourself, you can automatically generate it through a Java-to-IDL compiler. The Java-to-IDL compiler takes in your RMI remote interface and spits out OMG IDL. Where do you get a Java-to-IDL compiler? There's one that ships free with RMI-IIOP. In fact, it's built into the *rmic* tool. Simply call *rmic* with the *–idl* switch to generate IDL from your Java code.

4. **Generate the needed server-side CORBA files.** You're going to need some helper code, such as skeletons for your CORBA object implementations. And remember that this helper code can be in any CORBA-compliant language in which you choose to implement your CORBA object implementations. This is where the IDL you generated in step 3 comes into play. When you define your CORBA object implementations, you can use any

How Do I Generate Stubs and Skeletons?

In Appendix A, you learned that the RMI compiler (*rmic*) is a tool for generating stubs and skeletons with RMI. Now, with RMI over IIOP, *rmic* has been bolstered with additional functionality to generate IIOP stubs and skeletons. The new RMI compiler generates two styles of stubs and skeletons:

It generates normal JRMP stubs and skeletons. This is the default behavior of *rmic*.

It also can generate IIOP stubs and skeletons. Use the –iiop flag to tell rmic you want IIOP stubs/skeletons.

The JRMP stubs and skeletons are only useful for creating a pure RMI client/server solution that uses JRMP. The IIOP stubs and skeletons are useful in the following three scenarios:

- If you have an RMI client with a CORBA object implementation, you need an IIOP stub so that your RMI client can invoke on the CORBA object over IIOP.

- If you have a CORBA client with an RMI object implementation, you need an IIOP skeleton so that your RMI object implementation can receive invocations from the CORBA client over IIOP.

- If you have an RMI client with an RMI object implementation and you want to use the IIOP protocol rather than JRMP, you need both IIOP stubs and skeletons. This allows you to take advantage of the robustness of the IIOP protocol with straight RMI programs.

Once you've done these steps, you've got all the files you need for an RMI client to invoke on a CORBA object implementation.

language to which IDL maps. You then use an IDL-to-Java compiler to take in your IDL and produce network management code in the language in which you're implementing your objects. For example, if you use Java, you'll need an IDL-to-Java compiler. There's a free IDL-to-Java compiler called *idlj* that ships with RMI-IIOP. There are docs about idlj that come with RMI-IIOP, as well as a complete specification on the OMG Web site. Most major ORB vendors that support Java include an IDL-to-Java tool with their products as well.

5. **Write the client and the server.** You can now write your RMI client and your CORBA object implementations.

CORBA Client with an RMI-IIOP Object Implementation

The second scenario depicts a CORBA client with an RMI-over-IIOP object implementation. You're going to need an RMI remote interface again for your RMI remote objects. You're also going to need OMG IDL so that the CORBA client can invoke on your RMI remote objects. Again, you'd like to avoid writing OMG IDL explicitly because RMI is about simple network programming.

To accomplish this, you perform the following steps:

1. **Write your RMI remote interface.** You write the remote interface in Java as you normally would for any RMI program. The remote interface is RMI's client/server contract for distributed objects.

2. **Generate the needed server-side RMI over IIOP skeletons.** The skeletons will be used to receive invocations and delegate them to your RMI remote object implementations. You generate the skeletons via *rmic*, as explained in the previous section.

3. **Generate the OMG IDL.** When you define your CORBA clients, you're going to need IDL. This IDL must match your RMI remote interface if you want CORBA clients to call your RMI object implementations. Rather than laboriously writing it yourself, you can automatically generate it through a Java-to-IDL compiler. The Java-to-IDL compiler takes in your RMI remote interface and spits out OMG IDL, as described in the previous section.

4. **Generate the needed client-side CORBA files.** As in the previous section, you need to generate helper code, such as stubs for your CORBA clients. Thus, you need to generate these network plumbing classes from the IDL with an IDL compiler, such as an IDL-to-Java compiler (as described in the previous section).

5. **Write the client and the server.** You can now write your CORBA client and your RMI object implementations.

Now you've seen both scenarios—an RMI client with a CORBA object implementation, and a CORBA client with an RMI object implementation. If you define your

Table 11.1 Combinations Possible Using RMI-IIOP

CLIENT	SERVER
RMI client with RMI-IIOP stub	RMI server with RMI-IIOP skeleton
RMI client with RMI-IIOP stub	CORBA object implementation
CORBA client	RMI server with RMI-IIOP skeleton
CORBA client	CORBA object implementation

interfaces the same way in each scenario, you should be able to mix and match RMI clients, RMI object implementations, CORBA clients, and CORBA object implementations. Table 11.1 shows the RMI-IIOP combinations that are possible.

The RMI-IIOP API

We've looked at the big picture of RMI-IIOP. But how does RMI programming itself change? After all, there's no more distributed garbage collection with RMI-IIOP. In this section, we'll take a look at what changes for you, as an RMI programmer.

Choosing an ORB

As we've discussed, RMI-IIOP clients must have a local ORB to talk to, which knows how to communicate with other ORBs via IIOP. RMI-IIOP servers must have a local ORB for the same reason.

For RMI over IIOP to work, the ORB vendor you're using must do the followiing:

■ Implement the Java-to-IDL mapping specification

■ Implement the CORBA Objects-by-Value specification

Sun Microsystems has written its own CORBA ORB, called *Java IDL*, which is a free reference implementation of CORBA. Java IDL is currently the only ORB that can be used with RMI-IIOP because it implements both specifications listed above.

Note that Java IDL does not provide the full range of features defined by CORBA. For example, Java IDL does not define an Interface Repository. This means runtime checking of parameters when performing dynamic invocations is impossible.

Java IDL ships as part of Java 2 (formerly JDK 1.2). See the book's accompanying Web site for links to resources on this product.

As you'll see, two new packages are needed when we introduce RMI over IIOP:

javax.rmi. There are differences in programming style between RMI and CORBA, such as narrowing of objects. *javax.rmi* addresses these issues. *javax.rmi* defines a unified RMI API that is portable between RMI and CORBA object implementations. As an RMI-over-IIOP programmer, you deal with the *javax.rmi* package directly, so it's important to understand how it works. We'll explain this package shortly.

javax.rmi.CORBA. This is an internal package that RMI over IIOP uses. If you ever want to define your own version of RMI over IIOP, or if you want to use another vendor's, this package ensures portability. As an RMI-over-IIOP programmer, you don't need to concern yourself with this package (thus we do not cover it here). Refer to the Java-to-IDL mapping specification if you want the details.

javax.rmi

The *javax.rmi* package is the new RMI API that you must use with RMI-IIOP. It defines one new class, called *javax.rmi.PortableRemoteObject*:

```
public abstract class javax.rmi.PortableRemoteObject {
  public static void exportObject(java.rmi.Remote obj);
  public static void unexportObject(java.rmi.Remote obj);
  public static java.rmi.Remote toStub(java.rmi.Remote obj);
  public static Object narrow(Object narrowFrom, Class narrowTo);
  public static void connect(java.rmi.Remote unconnected, java.rmi.Remote
      connected);
}
```

This class is the new alternative to *java.rmi.UnicastRemoteObject*, which we cover in Appendix A. While *UnicastRemoteObject* will work with JRMP, *Portable-RemoteObject* will work with both the JRMP and IIOP protocols. As with *UnicastRemoteObject*, your remote objects can inherit from the *javax.rmi .PortableRemoteObject* class, or you can call the static methods on this class to export yourself as a remote object.

Let's take a look at the methods this class exposes:

exportObject. Call this to register your remote objects as server objects. This makes your objects available to be called remotely. Note that the default constructor for *PortableRemoteObject* automatically exports your remote objects for you. Thus, if your remote object extends *PortableRemoteObject*, by calling *super()* you will automatically export your object. This is the same behavior we saw with *UnicastRemoteObject* in Appendix A.

unexportObject. With Java RMI, your objects are cleaned up automatically if clients drop their references or if clients time out. Because your remote objects are no longer automatically garbage collected, you need to manually unregister your remote objects so they will be available for garbage collection. This is accomplished via the *unexportObject()* method.

toStub. This method transforms a previously exported remote object into a stub. You can treat the stub as a true proxy, passing it around and invoking on it. The stub will delegate calls to the real object. Before you use the stub, however, you must call the *connect()* method, described next.

connect. This method makes a remote object ready for remote communication. Normally this method is automatically called for you when you pass remote objects over the network as parameters. If you manually generate a stub via the *toStub()* method, however, you must call *connect()* yourself.

narrow. As we've described, RMI and CORBA have different mechanisms for coercing received remote objects into user-defined objects. With RMI, when you receive a remote object over the network, you simply cast it into the desired object. With RMI-IIOP, you must call this *narrow()* method instead. You pass *narrow()* the object you've received and the class to which you wish to cast it. It returns the resultant object or throws an exception if the narrow is not possible.

Bootstrapping with RMI over IIOP

How do RMI-over-IIOP clients find an object over the network? Normally with Java RMI, you bind objects to an RMI registry, which serves as a registry for all your exported remote objects. Clients can then look up objects by using RMI's *Naming.lookup()* facilities. *Naming.lookup()* knows how to contact a remote RMI registry, which is listening at a well-defined port. This is fully described in Appendix A.

Naming.lookup() has several disadvantages. For one, it does not lend itself well to enterprise deployments because you must hard-code the location of the target machines in which your remote objects live. The more serious problem is that *Naming.lookup()* finds RMI remote objects via the RMI registry, but it cannot find CORBA object implementations. We'd like RMI-over-IIOP clients to be able to call CORBA object implementations as well as RMI remote objects. That's one of the goals of RMI over IIOP: to provide a standard API to access both RMI and CORBA objects.

In Appendix B, we detail the Java Naming and Directory Interface (JNDI) as a mechanism for binding, and later finding, resources on a network. Appendix B shows how JNDI is a generic lookup service for any kind of resource, such as a printer or a computer. JNDI provides a standard API, with several "service providers" plugging into a Service Provider Interface (SPI). These service providers could be LDAP providers, Novell NDS providers, or others.

Of particular importance to RMI over IIOP is the RMI Registry service provider. The RMI Registry service provider allows you to reference RMI remote objects through JNDI (see Appendix B for a hands-on example of this). JNDI is a much better solution for bootstrapping than the normal RMI's *Naming.lookup()* convention because clients are not hard-coding the addresses of machines. Rather, you bind your remote object locations to a well-known directory tree, such as an LDAP server.

Recall from earlier in this chapter that CORBA has its own built-in naming service, called the CORBA Naming Service (or *COS Naming*). COS Naming is the standard way CORBA clients look up remote CORBA objects. But again, this is simply looking up an arbitrary resource over the network—the resource just happens to be CORBA objects rather than printers or RMI objects. Therefore, COS Naming is a perfect fit for JNDI. JNDI has a CORBA Naming Service provider, called the *COS Naming service provider*. The COS Naming service provider allows you to look up CORBA objects over the network using JNDI.

JNDI is thus a perfect fit for RMI over IIOP. RMI-over-IIOP clients need to be able to access both CORBA object implementations and RMI remote objects using the same API, so that we no longer have two different camps for network computing in Java. We can unite these camps by providing a standard way to look up either CORBA or RMI objects using JNDI as follows:

- RMI over IIOP clients cannot use RMI's *Naming.lookup()* facility. Clients must use JNDI. This unified lookup API gives us a single interface to both RMI remote objects and CORBA object implementations.

- By plugging in JNDI's CORBA Naming Service service provider, our RMI-over-IIOP clients will be able to access CORBA object implementations.

- By plugging in JNDI's RMI Registry service provider, our RMI-over-IIOP clients will be able to access RMI remote objects.

This last bit finally gets us exactly what we want—being able to mix CORBA clients and server objects with RMI clients and server objects, without recompiling code. The good news for you is that your EJB server should abstract most of this away from you, and that it can handle the steps of generating the appropriate stubs, skeletons, and IDL. Most likely, though, if you are writing client code that uses JNDI, you will be responsible for choosing the correct JNDI service provider.

The Big Picture: CORBA and EJB Together

In this section, we'll assume you've understood how RMI-IIOP bridges RMI and CORBA, and we'll apply these concepts to EJB. Before we get into the technical details, you should note how EJB and CORBA re being positioned relative to one another.

As you know, EJB is useful for server-side component development, sporting features such as networking, threading, transactions, persistence, security, and a well-defined server-side component model. CORBA, on the other hand, is more of the *enabling technology* that resides beneath the EJB level. Most serious EJB server vendors will be layering their EJB products *on top of* an existing CORBA infrastructure, and RMI-IIOP allows just this to happen.

So if anyone tells you that CORBA is dying, they're simply wrong—CORBA is really the physical basis for EJB. CORBA ORBs are a natural fit for brokering method requests across the network. CORBA's persistent Interoperable Object References (IORs) make a great foundation for EJB object handles. And in the future, CORBA OTS and IIOP will hopefully be used as well to guarantee on-the-wire transaction interoperability.

Benefits of CORBA/EJB Interoperability

Although CORBA/EJB interoperability is still in its infancy, the vision is solid, and there are several benefits that we hope will come from it. For one, CORBA clients written in any language (that OMG IDL maps to) should be able to call your enterprise beans. This can happen only if everyone agrees to use RMI-IIOP. Sun Microsystems has realized this, and has defined RMI-IIOP as the de-facto communications API in EJB 1.1 (see Appendix D). This means vendors will no longer be able to use other communications APIs, such as the vanilla RMI API we've seen throughout this book with BEA's *WebLogic*. Thus, when vendors ship their EJB 1.1 products, you should be able to connect an RMI-IIOP client and a CORBA client to the same enterprise bean. We'll demonstrate how to do this shortly.

Another benefit of CORBA/EJB interoperability is at the transaction level. Clients should be able to mix calls to both CORBA objects and enterprise beans under the hood of the same transaction. Similarly, you should be able to construct a distributed transaction that spans heterogeneous EJB servers. For this to happen, vendors not only need to agree to use IIOP, but they also need to agree on how to propagate transaction contexts across the network, and CORBA's Object Transaction Service specifies exactly this. To answer this need, Sun Microsystems has promised to release a new standard called *EJB/IIOP* which will yield on-the-wire transaction interoperability. This will hopefully be part of EJB 2.0, due out well into the year 2000.

What You Don't Get from Corba-ejb Interoperability

Lastly, I want to make it clear that there is one benefit that you do *not* get out of EJB-CORBA interoperability. CORBA-EJB interoperability is for connecting a

CORBA *client* to an enterprise bean written in *Java*. You *cannot* write your enterprise beans in any language but Java. If you want to write your server-side components using another language, you have four choices:

1. Write your components in the language of your choice, and wrap them in an EJB layer. This works very well for existing investments. Your enterprise beans should use CORBA APIs to delegate to your non-Java code. Note that you cannot use the Java Native Interface (JNI), as native methods are banned from EJB.

2. If you have a fairly hairy existing investment with its own middleware issues, you could write a J2EE Connector (see Chapter 1) to bridge this investment into the EJB world. But you'll have to wait until Sun finalizes the Connector specification in EJB 2.0.

3. Use Microsoft's COM+ architecture, a language-neutral standard for distributed server-side components. If you do this you'll be completely departing from EJB. COM+ has its own ups and downs, and is a completely separate debate (a debate, by the way, in which I've participated. See the book's accompanying Web site at *www.wiley.com/compbooks/roman* for a transcript).

4. Wait and see what happens with the CORBA Components specification.

CORBA/EJB Interoperability Scenarios

Now that we've whetted your appetite, let's illustrate how to tie together CORBA clients with EJB systems. There are two types of Enterprise JavaBeans clients: Java RMI-IIOP based clients and CORBA-based clients. There are also two types of EJB servers: CORBA-based EJB servers and proprietary EJB servers. Both of these servers use the RMI-IIOP API. The real difference is the communications they use *beneath* the API.

A CORBA-based EJB server ships with a CORBA Object Request Broker (ORB). The server exposes its objects, such as EJB objects and home objects, as CORBA objects. It accomplishes this by generating RMI-IIOP skeletons for all server-side objects. Thus you can write client code using either the CORBA API or the RMI-IIOP API. The ORBs deployed on the clients and servers communicate via IIOP. This is shown in Figures 11.6 and 11.7.

A proprietary EJB server does not ship with a CORBA ORB. Rather, it has its own proprietary communications architecture. The proprietary EJB server must still allow clients to call methods using RMI-IIOP API, because that is mandated as of EJB 1.1. However, the implementation of RMI-IIOP does not use an ORB, and IIOP is not used as the transport protocol, which means CORBA clients cannot call your enterprise beans. This is shown in Figure 11.8.

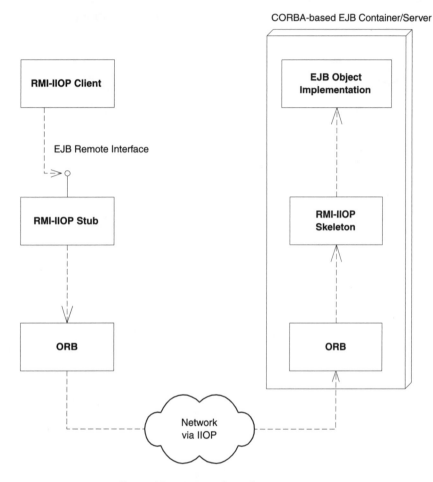

Figure 11.6   Java RMI-IIOP client with a CORBA-based EJB server.

Example Code

Now let's write some sample code to illustrate both RMI-IIOP EJB clients and CORBA EJB clients. These examples have been tested with an early access release of Inprise Corporation's *Inprise Application Server*. The key thing to notice about both these examples is that we'll access the exact same enterprise bean from both RMI-IIOP and CORBA without modifying the bean.

RMI-IIOP EJB Client Example

First, let's see how to write an RMI-IIOP client to access an EJB system. This example uses the "Hello, World!" session bean we developed in Chapter 4. We'll use the following:

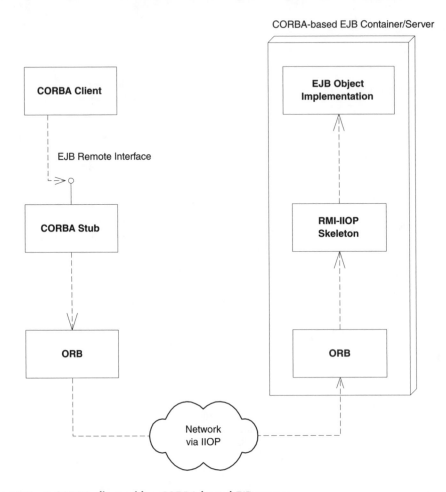

Figure 11.7 A CORBA client with a CORBA-based EJB server.

- JNDI to look up the home object
- JTA to demarcate transaction boundaries

Source 11.1 shows the code, which is relatively self-documenting.

The key thing to notice in Source 11.1 is we're using the RMI-IIOP *Portable-RemoteObject.narrow()* method to help cast returned remote objects.

CORBA EJB Client Example

Next, let's take that exact same "Hello, World!" session bean and access it from a CORBA client. We'll use the following:

- COS Naming to look up the home object

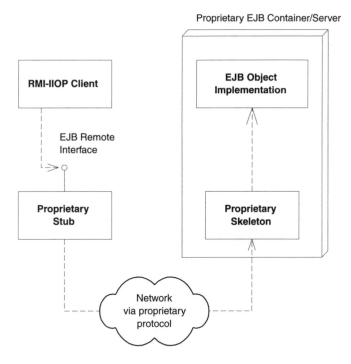

Proprietary EJB Container/Server

Figure 11.8 A Java RMI-IIOP client with a proprietary EJB server.

- OTS to demarcate transaction boundaries
- The Java language to write our CORBA client

Source 11.2 shows the implementation.

```
package com.wiley.compBooks.roman.corba.helloworld;

import javax.ejb.*;
import javax.naming.*;
import javax.rmi.*;
import java.util.Properties;
import javax.transaction.UserTransaction;

/**
 * This class is an example of client code that invokes
 * methods on a simple stateless session bean.
 */
public class RMIClient {
```

Source 11.1 Example RMI-IIOP EJB client *(continues)*

```
public static void main(String[] args) {

    try {
        /*
         * Get System properties for JNDI initialization
         */
        Properties props = System.getProperties();

        /*
         * Use JNDI to look up the home object
         */
        Context ctx = new InitialContext(props);
        HelloHome home = (HelloHome)
            javax.rmi.PortableRemoteObject.narrow(
                ctx.lookup("HelloHome"),
                HelloHome.class);

        /*
         * Use JNDI to look up the JTA
         * UserTransaction interface
         */
        UserTransaction userTran = (UserTransaction)
            ctx.lookup("javax.transaction.UserTransaction");

        /*
         * Start the transaction
         */
        userTran.begin();

        /*
         * Use the home object to create the Hello EJB Object
         */
        Hello hello = home.create();

        /*
         * Call the hello() method, and print it
         */
        System.out.println(hello.hello());

        /*
         * Done with EJB Object, so remove it
         */
        hello.remove();

        /*
         * Commit the transaction
         */
        userTran.commit();
```

Source 11.1 Example RMI-IIOP EJB client *(continues)*

```
            } catch (Exception e) {
                e.printStackTrace();
            }
        }
    }
}
```

Source 11.1 Example RMI-IIOP EJB client *(continued)*.

```
package com.wiley.compBooks.roman.corba.helloworld;

import java.util.*;
import org.omg.CosNaming.*;
import org.omg.CosTransactions.*;

public class CORBAClient {

    public static void main(String[] args) throws Exception {

        /*
         * Initialize the ORB.
         *
         * A more portable way to do this is:
         *
         *   Properties p = new Properties();
         *   p.put("org.omg.CORBA.ORBClass", <..ORB class..>);
         *   org.omg.CORBA.ORB orb = org.omg.CORBA.ORB.init(args, p);
         */
        org.omg.CORBA.ORB orb = com.inprise.ejb.Global.orb();

        /*
         * Get a reference to a naming context
         */
        NamingContext context = NamingContextHelper.narrow
            (orb.resolve_initial_references("NameService"));

        /*
         * Look up the home object using COS Naming
         */
        NameComponent[] names = { new NameComponent("HelloHome", "") };
        HelloHome helloHome = HelloHomeHelper.narrow
            (context.resolve(names));

        /*
         * Get the CORBA OTS Current interface for
         * controlling transactions
         */
```

Source 11.2 Example CORBA EJB client *(continues)*.

```
Current currentTX = CurrentHelper.narrow
    (orb.resolve_initial_references("TransactionCurrent"));

/*
 * Begin the transaction
 */
currentTX.begin();

/*
 * Use the home object to create an EJB object
 */
Hello hello = helloHome.create();

/*
 * Call a business method
 */
System.out.println(hello.hello());

/*
 * Remove the EJB object
 */
hello.remove();

/*
 * Commit the transaction
 */
currentTX.commit(true);
    }
}
```

Source 11.2   Example CORBA EJB client *(continued)*.

As you can see, CORBA clients are a bit more complex than RMI-IIOP clients. We first need to initialize the ORB before beginning any CORBA operations. Next, we get a reference to a naming context via COS Naming, which we use to look up home objects. Once we've retrieved the home object, calling methods on enterprise beans is syntactically similar to Java RMI. We also get a reference to the OTS *Current* interface, which is used to demarcate transactional boundaries (analogous to the JTA *UserTransaction* interface we retrieved in Source 11.1). The *begin()* and *commit()* calls have the same semantic meaning as their JTA equivalents.

Summary

In this chapter, you've experienced a whirlwind tour of CORBA and IIOP. We've displayed CORBA's advantages and the reasons why CORBA is a useful technology. We then delved into the inner workings of CORBA and explored its architecture. We also glanced at CORBA's services and touched on the IDL-to-Java mapping.

We then compared RMI to CORBA and reasoned why the two worlds need cohesion. We designed the requirements for RMI-IIOP interoperability and dived into several scenarios illustrating RMI and CORBA working in unison. We wrapped up our discussion of RMI-IIOP by illustrating the steps necessary for you to write RMI-IIOP code, and we examined the details of the *javax.rmi* package.

In the last section of this chapter, we caught a glimpse of the future: EJB and CORBA interoperability. Although it wasn't possible at the time of this writing, by the time you read this, EJB and CORBA should be showing their first signs of coexisting in deployments.

For more information about the topics in this chapter, see these resources:

The OMG Home Page: www.omg.org. This is the home of the Object Management Group, a consortium of companies that invented CORBA and IIOP. You can download the CORBA-related specifications here.

Client/Server Programming with Java and CORBA by Robert Orfali and Dan Harkey (John Wiley & Sons, 1998, ISBN 047124578X). This book is great for those new to CORBA, with an emphasis on broad exposure to CORBA concepts, rather than depth of examples.

Java Programming with CORBA by Andreas Vogel and Keith Duddy (John Wiley & Sons, 1998, ISBN 0471-24765-0). This book goes into a bit more depth and explores concepts such as security and events in CORBA.

Programming with VisiBroker by Doug Pedrick, Jonathan Weedon, Jon Goldberg, and Erik Bleifield (John Wiley & Sons, 1998, ISBN 0471-23901-1). This book is extremely useful for programmers using Inprise's *VisiBroker for Java* CORBA-compliant product.

Sun Microsystems' RMI-IIOP package. The book's accompanying Web site includes a link to download the RMI-IIOP package from the Sun Web site. The RMI-IIOP download comes with two complete examples of RMI-IIOP, which illustrate converting an existing RMI application to use IIOP rather than JRMP as the protocol, and interoperability between RMI clients/servers and CORBA clients/servers. I encourage you to try out RMI-IIOP for yourself by playing with the examples included with the download.

## PART FOUR

J2EE in the Real World: A Sophisticated E-Commerce Deployment

The previous sections of this book provided you with insight into the concepts behind EJB, and you've seen a number of relatively straightforward examples of EJB in use. Now we're going to bolster our basic knowledge with some practical applications. You'll get to put everything you've learned together in a sophisticated real-world e-commerce deployment.

We'll take the basics that we learned about session beans and entity beans and combine them. You'll see how every different kind of bean has its own role in a sophisticated object model. Our deployment will make use of the following:

- Stateful session seans
- Stateless session beans
- Bean-managed persistent entity beans
- Container-managed persistent entity beans

In total, we'll have *nine* different enterprise beans working together. This should prove to you that the Java 2 Platform, Enterprise Edition (J2EE) has the potential for serious work.

The transaction concepts you learned in Chapter 10 will come into practice in this section. Our deployment will make use of both client-demarcated and declarative transactions. If you're itching to see how transactions can be used in the EJB world, the e-commerce solution we put together will demonstrate just that.

Once we've designed our object model, we'll put it all together with a Web-based graphical user interface. Here's your chance to get up to speed with how to tie a Web-based GUI to an EJB system. Specifically, we'll learn about how to write a GUI layer on top of enterprise beans with *Java servlets* in a Web-based Internet deployment.

When our deployment is complete, we'll examine tuning and optimizing it in several ways, including surveying mechanisms to generate globally unique primary keys for entity beans, lazy-loading enterprise beans for enhanced performance, and more.

Inventing this e-commerce solution will be a blast. You'll get a chance to use J2EE to solve real-world problems. And if you have e-commerce needs, you can leverage the code from this example as a basis for your own deployments. We'll put the basic framework together, leaving room for extensibility. At the end of our discussion, we'll look at future enhancements you may want to make.

## CHAPTER 12

J2EE in the Real World: Designing an E-Commerce Object Model

Jasmine's Computer Parts, Inc. is a fictitious manufacturing company that makes a wide variety of computer equipment, including motherboards, processors, and memory. Jasmine, the company's owner, has been selling her products using direct mail catalogs, as well as a network of distributors and resellers.

Jasmine wants to lower the cost of doing business by selling her computer parts directly to the end customer, through an e-commerce Web-based sales model. Jasmine has given us a high-level description of the functionality of the e-commerce solution. She'd like the following features in the system we provide for her:

User authentication. Registered users would first log in to the Web site to access the complete catalog. Only registered users should be able to browse and purchase from her online store.

An online catalog. Users should be able to browse her complete product line on the Web and view details of each product.

Online quote generation. While browsing the catalog, a user should be able to pick and choose the products he or she wants. The user should then be able to view the current shopping basket (we'll call this a *quote*). The user should be able to, for example, change quantities of items he or she has already picked out.

Specialized pricing functionality. Users who order items in bulk should get a percentage discount. For example, if I order five memory modules, I might get a 10 percent discount on that memory. In addition, registered users who frequent the store often should get additional discounts.

Order generation. Once the user is happy with his or her selections and has committed to ordering the products, a permanent order should be generated. A separate fulfillment application (which we won't write) would use the data in the orders to manufacture the products and ship them. The user would be able to return to the Web site later to view the status of current orders.

Billing functionality. Once the user has placed the order, we should bill it to him or her. If the user does not have enough funds to pay, the order should be cancelled.

This is definitely going to be a full-featured deployment! Over the next several chapters, we will implement these requirements. By the time we're done, you should have a solid understanding of how you can use EJB and the Java 2 Platform, Enterprise Edition for e-commerce solutions. We kick things off in this chapter by designing a high-level object model for our deployment.

A Preview of the Final Product

To give Jasmine an idea of what the final product should be like, our sales team has put together a series of screenshots. The screenshots show what the e-commerce system will look like when an end user hits the Web site.

Figure 12.1 shows a user logging into the system initially. Our authentication will be through login names and passwords.

When the user has been recognized, he or she is presented with a Web storefront. The Web storefront is the main page for Jasmine's online store. This is shown in Figure 12.2. From the Web storefront, the user can jump to the catalog of products that Jasmine offers, shown in Figure 12.3. If the user wants to view

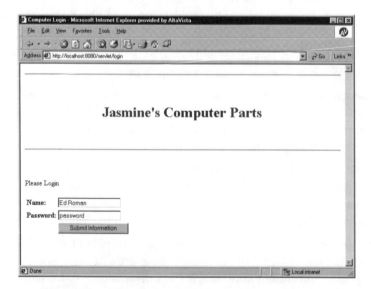

Figure 12.1 A user logging into Jasmine's Computer Parts.

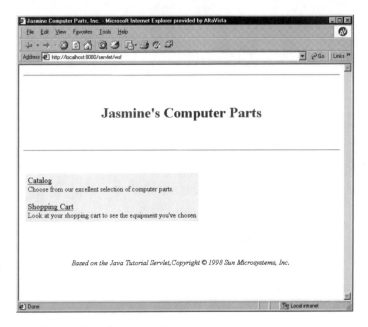

Figure 12.2   The Web storefront for our online store.

details about a product, he or she can check out the product detail screen, shown in Figure 12.4. The user can also add the product to the current shopping cart, or *quote*. A quote is a temporary selection of products that the user has made.

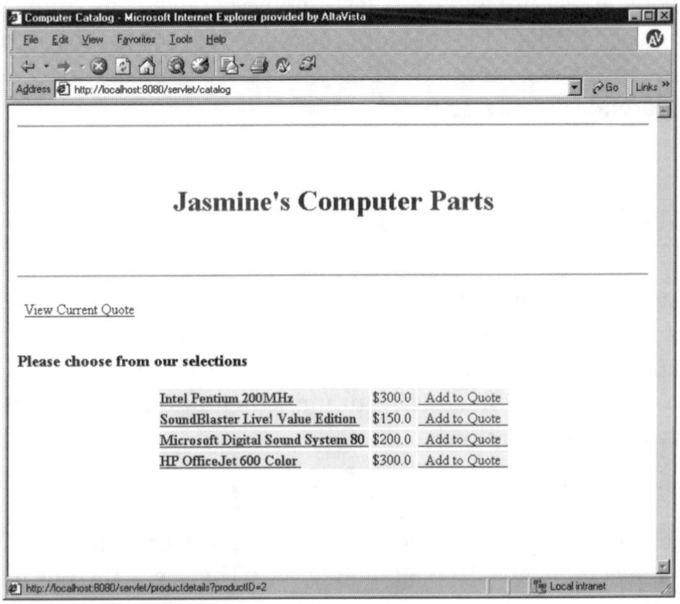

Figure 12.3   Browsing the online catalog.

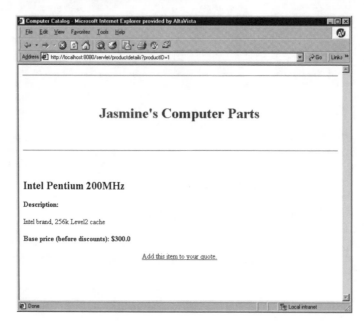

Figure 12.4 Viewing a particular product.

Quotes are temporary because the user has not committed to purchasing the goods yet.

Once the user has made his or her choices, the user can view a quote for the current selections (and make any last-minute changes), as shown in Figure 12.5. When the user clicks the button to purchase the selection, he or she is billed and a new order is generated. Finally, the user is given the order number for future reference (Figure 12.6).

Scoping the Technical Requirements

While meeting Jasmine's requirements, we'd like to develop an extensible infrastructure that she can add to in the future. That means making the right abstractions to loosen the coupling between our components. Ideally, Jasmine should be able to plug in a different implementation of any part of the system with very few modifications.

Our deployment will be partitioned into three tiers:

The business logic tier will consist of multiple Enterprise JavaBeans, running under the hood of an EJB container/server. These will be reusable components

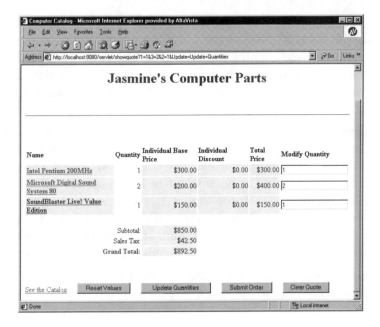

Figure 12.5   Viewing and modifying a quote.

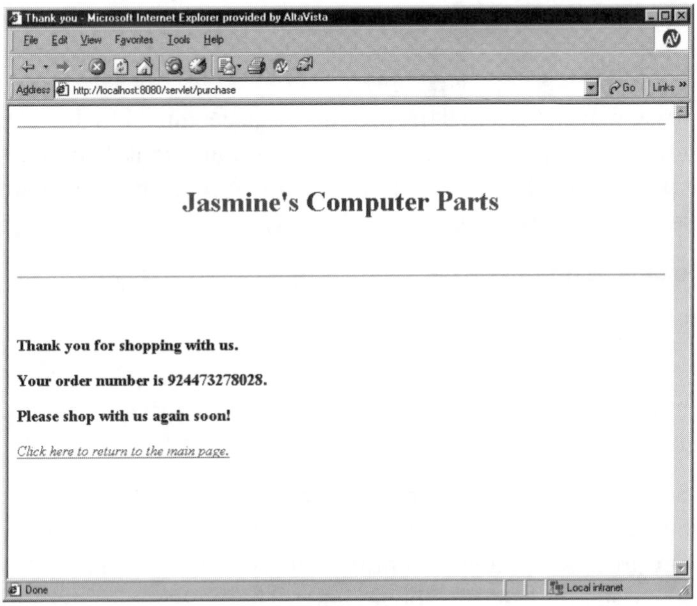

Figure 12.6   Making a purchase.

that are independent of any user interface logic. We should be able to, for example, take our business tier and port it to a different presentation tier (such as an independent laptop) with no modifications. Our business tier will be made up of persistent entity bean objects that represent data being modified, as well as session beans to provide application rules for interacting with that data.

The presentation tier will involve one or more Web servers, each responsible for interacting with the end user. The presentation tier displays the requested information in HTML to the end user; it also reads in and interprets the user's selections and makes invocations to the business tier's enterprise beans. The implementation of the presentation tier will use Java *servlets*—networked objects that know how to interact with a user on a specific protocol. We'll see how servlets work a bit later. And, of course, our choice of using servlets could easily be replaced with a different presentation package.

The data tier is where our permanent data stores reside. The databases aggregate all persistent information related to the e-commerce site.

Object Model for the Business Logic Tier

Let's begin designing our EJB object model. To fulfill Jasmine's requirements, we make abstractions in our business's object model.

Products

First, we will need to model the products that Jasmine is selling. A product could be a motherboard, a monitor, or any other component. Products should be persistent parts of the deployment that last forever. Our product abstractions should represent the following data:

- The unique product ID
- The product name
- A description of the product
- The base price of the product (indicating the price of the product, with no discounts or taxes applied)

Jasmine should be able to add and delete products from the system using a maintenance tool. Because products are permanent, persistent parts of the system, they are best modeled as entity beans. Our Product entity bean should have methods to get and set the above fields.

In fact, in Chapter 9, we wrote this exact bean to illustrate container-managed persistent entity beans. That Product bean fits this purpose quite well, and we'll reuse it in our deployment.

Customers

Next, we need to represent information about Jasmine's customers. A customer represents an end user—perhaps an individual or a corporation that purchases goods from our Web site. Our Customer abstraction contains the following data:

- Customer ID
- The customer's name (also used as the customer's login name for our Web site)
- The customer's address
- The customer's password (used to verify the customer's identify)

 There are many ways new Customers, Products, and so on could be added to the system. Jasmine could have users log in through a separate Web site and input their name, address information, password, and other profile data. We could also develop a custom maintenance tool (stand-alone or Web-based) for adding new Products. To keep this example simple, we'll manually insert direct database data, but feel free to extend this for your purposes.

Quotes

Next, we need to keep track of the selections a customer has made while navigating our catalog. Essentially, we need the abstraction of a "shopping cart," which is a temporary selection of goods and their prices. We'll call this shopping cart a *quote* because a shopping cart embodies a price quote on goods. As the user traverses the Web site, he or she adds or removes goods from the quote.

Each customer who's logged in should have his or her own temporary and separate quote in which to work. Therefore, our quotes will need to hold client-specific state in them. They should not be persistent because the user can always cancel the quote.

This naturally lends itself to the stateful session bean paradigm. Each Quote stateful session bean will hold conversational state about the user's current quote. It will allow us to treat the entire quote as one coarse-grained object. A new Quote would need to be generated every time a user logged in. Each Quote bean will contain the following information:

- The Customer (entity bean) who we authenticated at the login screen. We need to store Customer information so that we know who to bill, what discounts to apply, and where to ship the manufactured products.
- The products and quantities that the Customer currently has selected. This data is best represented in its own separate bean, called a *Quote Line Item*, described later.

- The subtotal for the quote, taking into account all the prices of the products the user wants, as well as any discounts the user gets.
- The taxes charged. This is added to the subtotal for the final grand total.

In addition to this data, the Quote beans will be smart and will know how to generate a permanent Order from themselves. We describe Orders a bit later.

Our deployment uses an enterprise bean, called a Quote bean, to store the user's current shopping cart information. One alternative to this is to keep the user's current selections at the presentation tier (i.e., at the Web server), to reduce the number of round trips between tiers. You can accomplish this by using regular JavaBeans in the Web server to hold the shopping cart data.

Quote Line Items

As the user navigates the Web site, he or she will be adding products to the Quote. For convenience of manipulation, we'd like to separate a Quote into individual line items, where each line item represents data pertaining to a single product the user has currently selected. A Quote has a 1:N relationship with its constituent line items.

Quote Line Items contain the following data:

- The ID of the line item
- The Product (entity bean) that the user wants to buy
- The quantity of that Product
- Any discounts the customer gets from the base price of the Product

Again, since a Quote Line Item is specific to one customer and is not persistent, it is best modeled as a stateful session bean.

Pricers

Because Jasmine wants customized pricing, we need the concept of a Pricer— a component that takes a Quote as input and calculates the price of that Quote based on a set of pricing rules. A pricing rule might be "Customer X gets a 5 percent discount" or "If you purchase 10 motherboards you get a 15 percent discount." These pricing rules could be read in from a database or set via properties.

Our Pricer will take a Quote as input and compute the subtotal (before taxes) of that Quote. It figures out the subtotal by computing a discount for each Quote line item in that bean and subtracting the discounts from the total price.

Our Pricer will work on any Quote and holds no client-specific state—once the Pricer has computed a price on a Quote, it is available to perform another computation on a different Quote. It is also not a persistent object (it would not make sense to save a Pricer because a Pricer simply performs logic, and holds no state). This means our Pricer fits into the EJB world best as a stateless session bean.

Orders

Next, we need to model a permanent order for goods. We'll define an Order abstraction for this purpose. An Order is a Quote that has been converted into a work request. An Order represents a real business action that needs to take place, such as the production of goods. Generating an Order and billing a Customer go hand-in-hand.

An Order contains the following information:

- The ID of this Order (which the user can use to check on order status)
- The Customer (entity bean) for which this Order is generated (used for shipping address information)
- The products and quantities that should be ordered (as with Quotes, best represented as separate information—contained in *Order line items*, described later)
- The subtotal and taxes on the order
- The date the order was placed

Orders are permanent, persistent objects. You want an Order's state to be around if your deployment crashes for any reason because an Order means money. Therefore, Orders are best depicted as entity beans. In comparison, Quotes are not permanent—they represent temporary interactions with the customer. You don't want to write a Quote's data to a database during a customer interaction, but you do want to keep track of the user's information—hence the stateful session bean is best applied for Quotes.

Our notion of an Order can be easily extended to include order status, such as "Manufacturing" or "Shipping", and other order fulfillment information. It would also be interesting to e-mail the order status to the end user, using the *JavaMail* API. Since we do not fulfill orders, we leave this as an exercise to the reader.

Order Line Items

For convenience of manipulation, we break up our notion of an Order into individual line items, where each line-item represents data pertaining to a single product the user has ordered. An Order has a 1:N relationship with its constituent line items. Our Order Line Item abstraction contains the following data:

- The ID of this Order Line Item

- The Product that this Order Line Item represents (used by manufacturing to reveal which product to make)
- The quantity of the Product that should be manufactured
- The discount that the customer received on this Product

Because Order Line Items are permanent, persistent objects, they are best represented as entity beans.

Bank Accounts

Next, Jasmine needs functionality to bill a customer, such as by charging a credit card account or mailing an invoice. In a real deployment, you will need to use such mechanisms. But for illustrative purposes, we'll rely on withdrawing directly from the customer's bank account. In Chapter 8, we developed an entity bean for just such a purpose—a Bank Account entity bean. A Bank Account

---

EJB Design Strategies

Session Beans as a Facade to Entity Beans

One problem with multi-tier development is that you need to be aware of network round-trip issues. When Java servlets (or other client code) call enterprise beans across the network, a potential bottleneck could ensue. For example, if a servlet had to call across the network for every get/set method on an entity bean, the network would be flooded in no time.

To keep performance high, you should design your system to minimize the number of network round trips. One way to do this is to use session beans to perform bulk operations on entity beans. Rather than going across the network for every get/set method on an entity bean, your client code (such as Java servlet code) should call a session bean that performs a bulk operation on behalf of that servlet.

For example, our Bank Teller session bean serves as a wrapper for our Bank Account entity bean. The Bank Teller performs bulk operations on Bank Accounts. For example, our Bank Teller can transfer funds from one Bank Account to another. A transfer operation involves two Bank Account entity beans, yet it can be done in one network call by a Bank Teller session bean.

The design pattern of a session bean wrapping an entity bean is a common one that you will see in many EJB deployments. Not only does it minimize network round trips, but it promotes reuse of your entity beans. You can design your entity beans to be very simple and then wrap them with session beans whose logic can change and be customized. This results in high reuse of entity beans, which is necessary because they model permanent data that should not be changed often.

represents a user's permanent, persistent Bank Account information. This is data such as the following:

- The Bank Account number
- The name of the Bank Account holder
- The current balance of the Bank Account

We'll reuse this Bank Account entity bean in our e-commerce deployment.

Bank Account Tellers

Finally, our last Enterprise JavaBean is a Bank Account Teller. A Teller represents a "virtual person" with whom you interact to modify a bank account. For example, our Teller will be able to transfer funds from one Bank Account (entity bean) to another.

Our Teller is not itself a persistent object—the notion of "saving" a Teller to disk means nothing. Our Teller will be a generic, stateless object, and it will be reusable for multiple clients. Therefore, it fits into the EJB world as a stateless session bean.

Business Logic Tier Object Model Summary

This completes our object model design for our business logic tier. The static relationships between our enterprise beans are depicted in Figure 12.7.

Object Model for the Presentation Tier

Our next task is to design our presentation tier, which displays the graphical user interface to the end user. For our presentation tier, we will use a few Java servlets to interact with a client over HTTP.

What Are Servlets?

A servlet is a module that runs within a request/response–oriented server. A *request* is a call from a client, perhaps remotely located. Requests contain data that the client wants to send to the server. A *response* is data that the server wants to return to the client to answer the request. A servlet is a Java object that takes a request as input, parses its data, performs some logic, and then issues a response back to the client. This is shown in Figure 12.8.

Servlets work on the same concept as CGI scripts. A CGI script is a program that takes data from standard input, performs some logic, and then sends data to standard output. It doesn't matter what language you write a CGI script in,

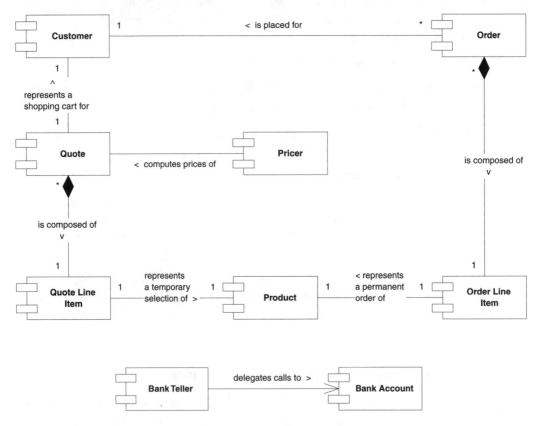

Figure 12.7 Component diagram of our e-commerce enterprise beans.

so long as it follows this convention of reading data from standard input and writing data to standard output. This is shown in Figure 12.9.

The problem with CGI is that your server must restart the CGI script every time a new request is issued. This means every time a client communicates, your server needs to begin a new process. Starting and stopping processes are expensive operations.

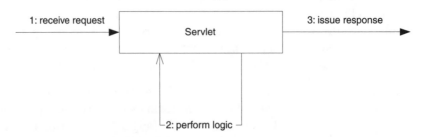

Figure 12.8 The basic servlet paradigm.

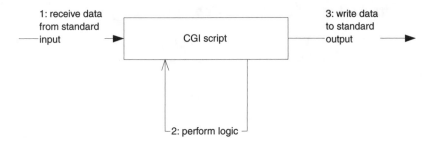

Figure 12.9 CGI scripts.

This is where servlets have an edge over CGI. Servlets are Java objects that function the same way as CGI scripts—taking in data (a request), performing some logic, and writing out data (a response). The difference between CGI and servlets is that CGI scripts must be restarted for every request, where servlets are pooled and reused over and over again to service many requests. This means you don't have to restart a process every time a new request comes over the network. This greatly enhances performance. Servlets are pooled by an external manager called a *servlet engine* in the same way that enterprise beans are pooled by an EJB container.

Web servers are a specific type of server that communicates with clients using the HTTP protocol. A Web server is responsible for accepting HTTP requests and sending back HTTP responses. An HTTP servlet is a servlet that works using the HTTP protocol. This is shown in Figure 12.10. Note that you can define other types of servlets as well—the concept of servlets is protocol-independent.

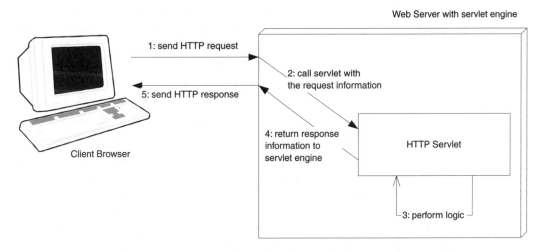

Figure 12.10 HTTP servlets.

Servlets in Our E-Commerce Deployment

Our e-commerce deployment will make extensive use of servlets for our presentation tier. To fulfill Jasmine's requirements, we'll define the following servlets.

A Login servlet. The Login servlet will be the first servlet the user deals with when going to Jasmine's Web site. It's responsible for reading in the user's name and then retrieving the appropriate Customer entity bean that matches that name. It then compares the user's submitted password with the permanent password stored with the Customer entity bean.

If the passwords match, a new shopping cart (or quote) needs to be created for that user. Hence, a Quote stateful session bean is started on behalf of this customer. The Customer information is stored in the Quote so that the Quote will contain the user's billing and shipping information. As the user navigates the store, the Quote will serve as a shopping cart to which the user can add and remove products.

If the passwords don't match, an error is displayed and the user is given another chance to enter a password.

A Web Storefront servlet. Once the user gets through the Login servlet, he or she will be redirected to the Web Storefront, which is the main page for Jasmine's store. This is the main navigation page for Jasmine's store. It links to the Catalog servlet and the View Quote servlet.

A Catalog servlet. To start adding products to the Quote, the user can browse the list of products available by going to the catalog servlet. He or she can also view details of a particular product, in which case the Catalog servlet will direct the user to the Product Detail servlet, described later.

A Product Base servlet. Many of our servlets need to work with Product entity beans. It would be very inefficient to have each servlet communicate across the tier boundary every time a Product needed to be found. Therefore, we cache our entire product line in a Product Base servlet. The Product Base servlet *never* interacts directly with the user. It's simply a servlet that other servlets can call when they need to retrieve Products.

A Product Detail servlet. When the user wants information about a particular product in the catalog, the Product Detail servlet shows that information. From this screen, the user can add the Product to his or her Quote.

A Quote View servlet. The user is able to view and modify the Quote at any time by going to a separate page, manifested by the Quote View servlet. The user can view each of his or her selections from this page, as well as change the desired quantities of the selected products. Every time the user changes something, our Quote View servlet recalculates the price of the Quote by calling the Pricer stateless session bean.

A Purchasing servlet. Finally, when the user is happy, he or she can convert the Quote stateful session bean into an Order entity bean. When generating the Order, this Purchasing servlet contacts a Bank Teller stateless session bean to transfer funds to Jasmine's account. The user is then shown his or her Order Number, which is extracted from the Order bean.

Presentation Tier Object Model Summary

This completes our object model design for our presentation tier. The flow of control for our servlets is depicted in Figure 12.11.

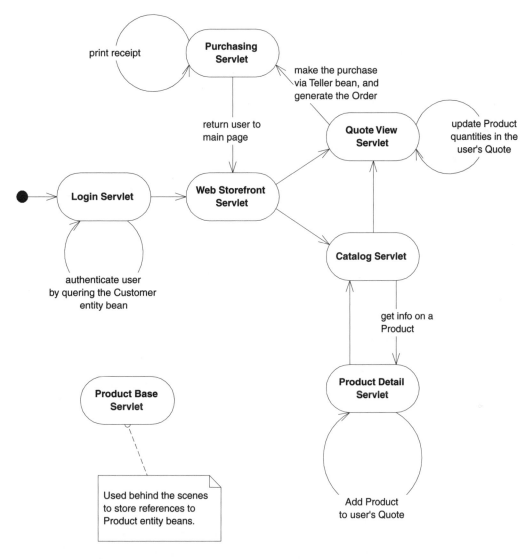

Figure 12.11   State diagram for our e-commerce servlets.

Summary

In this chapter, we've painted a picture of how our e-commerce system should behave. Now that we've made the proper abstractions, our components should fall into place very easily. By performing this high-level analysis, we can be confident that our final product will be extensible and reusable for some time to come.

## CHAPTER 13

J2EE in the Real World:
Implementing Our E-Commerce
Entity Beans

I n the previous chapter, we discussed the high-level requirements and object model for an e-commerce deployment for Jasmine's Computer Parts. In this chapter, we'll tackle the entity beans that make up our object model. These entity beans represent the *core* of Jasmine's business—Customers, Products, Orders, and Line Items. These are unlikely to change or evolve much over time because they are fundamental components of a retail business. By way of comparison, the session beans that we'll design in the next chapter are likely to change more often in the long run because they contain evolving logic.

The great news here is that we've already implemented *two* of the entity beans we'll need in our e-commerce system:

- We'll reuse the Bank Account entity bean (from Chapter 8) for recording monetary data. Our session beans in the next chapter will use the Bank Account to bill the client once he or she has submitted an Order.

- The Product entity bean (from Chapter 9) will come in handy for describing Jasmine's product line. We'll reuse this bean here.

We'll also design three new entity beans: a Customer entity bean, an Order Line Item entity bean, and an Order entity bean. The motivation for designing these beans is in Chapter 12.

This chapter (as well as the next two) will be very code-intensive because we are getting into the guts of our e-commerce deployment. Feel free to flip back to the previous chapter at any time to remind yourself of the high-level relationships in our object model. When you're ready, read on about our new entity beans—starting with the Customer bean.

The Customer Entity Bean

Our Customer entity bean is useful for describing a user who wants to purchase goods from our online store. This Customer bean could easily be generalized to be a generic "Person" bean as well, representing anyone, not just a Customer.

Why do we need to encapsulate customer information?

1. We'll need to track information such as the customer name, so that our Pricer session bean can calculate customer-specific discounts.

2. Our login screen will use Customer beans to authenticate users by checking the user's permanent password.

3. We could also use the Customer's address information to ship an order once it's been placed.

Specifically, our Customer will model the following data:

- Customer ID
- The customer's name (also functions as the customer's login name to our Web site)
- The customer's address
- The customer's password (used to verify the customer's identity)

For brevity, we're going to assume that Customers are created via direct database inserts. A simple maintenance utility could easily be written to add new Customers via a GUI as well.

Customer.java

Let's first look at our remote interface, *Customer.java*. This is the interface that clients of the Customer bean will be dealing with. Our EJB container will generate an EJB object that implements this interface. The code is shown in Source 13.1.

Our interface is fairly straightforward—we simply expose methods to get and set the fields of our Customer's data.

CustomerBean.java

Our bean implementation is contained in *CustomerBean.java*, shown in Source 13.2.

To keep the code simple, we're using container-managed persistence for our Customer bean. Hence, many of the EJB required methods have been left empty because the container will perform the persistent operations for us. We also don't implement any finder methods—that is delegated to the container as well. Thus,

```
package com.wiley.compBooks.ecommerce;

import javax.ejb.*;
import java.util.Vector;
import java.rmi.RemoteException;

/**
 * These are the business logic methods exposed publicly by Customerbean.
 *
 * This interface is what clients operate on when they interact with
 * beans. The EJB Server vendor will implement this interface; the
 * implemented object is called the EJB object, which delegates
 * invocations to the actual bean.
 */
public interface Customer extends EJBObject {

    // Getter/setter methods for entity bean fields

    public String getName() throws RemoteException;
    public void setName(String name) throws RemoteException;

    public String getPassword() throws RemoteException;
    public void setPassword(String password) throws RemoteException;

    public String getAddress() throws RemoteException;
    public void setAddress(String address) throws RemoteException;

}
```

Source 13.1 Customer.java.

```
package com.wiley.compBooks.ecommerce;

import java.sql.*;
import javax.naming.*;
import javax.ejb.*;
import java.util.*;
import java.rmi.RemoteException;

/**
 * This container-managed persistent entity bean represents
 * a customer record.
 */
public class CustomerBean implements EntityBean {
```

Source 13.2 CustomerBean.java *(continues)*.

```
protected EntityContext ctx;

//----------------------------------------------------------
// Begin Container-Managed fields
//----------------------------------------------------------

/*
 * The customer's identification number.  It's also our
 * Primary Key.
 */
public String customerID;

/*
 * The customer name
 */
public String name;

/*
 * The customer address
 */
public String address;

/*
 * The user's password for this customer record
 */
public String password;

//----------------------------------------------------------
// End Container-Managed fields
//----------------------------------------------------------

public CustomerBean() {
    System.out.println(
        "New Customer Entity Bean Java Object created by EJB Container.");
}

//----------------------------------------------------------
// Begin business methods
//----------------------------------------------------------

public String getName() throws RemoteException {
    System.out.println("getName() called.");
    return name;
}

public void setName(String name) throws RemoteException {
    System.out.println("setName() called.");
    this.name = name;
}
```

Source 13.2 CustomerBean.java *(continues)*.

```
public String getPassword() throws RemoteException {
    System.out.println("getPassword() called.");
    return password;
}

public void setPassword(String password) throws RemoteException {
    System.out.println("setPassword() called.");
    this.password = password;
}

public String getAddress() throws RemoteException {
    System.out.println("getAddress() called.");
    return address;
}

public void setAddress(String address) throws RemoteException {
    System.out.println("setAddress() called.");
    this.address = address;
}

//--------------------------------------------------------
// End public business methods
//--------------------------------------------------------

//--------------------------------------------------------
// Begin EJB-Required methods.  The methods below are called
// by the Container, and never called by client code.
//--------------------------------------------------------

/**
 * Associates this Bean instance with a particular context.
 * Once done, we can query the Context for environment info,
 * such as Bean customizations via properties.
 */
public void setEntityContext(EntityContext ctx) throws RemoteException {
    System.out.println("setEntityContext called");
    this.ctx = ctx;
}

/**
 * Disassociates this Bean instance with a particular
 * context environment.
 */
public void unsetEntityContext() throws RemoteException {
    System.out.println("unsetEntityContext called");
    this.ctx = null;
}
```

Source 13.2 CustomerBean.java *(continues).*

```java
/**
 * Called directly after activating this bean instance.
 * You should acquire needed resources in this method.
 */
public void ejbActivate() throws RemoteException {
    System.out.println("ejbActivate() called.");
}

/**
 * Called directly before passivating this bean instance.
 * Release any resources you acquired in ejbActivate() in
 * this method.
 */
public void ejbPassivate() throws RemoteException {
    System.out.println("ejbPassivate () called.");
}

/**
 * Updates the database to reflect the current values of
 * this object.
 *
 * Since we're using Container-Managed Persistence, the
 * Container will automatically save our public container-
 * managed fields into the database.  We should perform
 * any necessary pre-processing here.
 */
public void ejbStore() throws RemoteException {
    System.out.println("ejbStore() called.");
}

/**
 * Updates this object to reflect any changes to the
 * database data.
 *
 * Since we're using Container-Managed Persistence, the
 * EJB Container will automatically set our public fields
 * to the correct values.  We then do post-processing
 * here.
 */
public void ejbLoad() throws RemoteException {
    System.out.println("ejbLoad() called.");
}

/**
 * Called when new database data is created.
 *
 * When the client calls the Home Object's create()
```

Source 13.2 CustomerBean.java *(continues)*.

```
           * method, the Home Object then calls this
           * ejbCreate() method.
           *
           * We need to initialize our Bean's container-managed
           * fields with the parameters passed from the client,
           * so that the Container can inspect our Bean and create
           * the corresponding database entries.
           */
          public void ejbCreate(String customerID, String name, String address,
              String password) throws CreateException, RemoteException {
              System.out.println("ejbCreate(" + customerID + ", " + name + ", " +
              address + ") called");

              this.customerID = customerID;
              this.name = name;
              this.address = address;
              this.password = password;
          }


          /**
           * The Container calls this after ejbCreate().  At this
           * point, the bean instance is associated with
           * its own EJB Object.  You can get a reference to that
           * EJB Object by querying the context.  You'd use that
           * EJB Object reference when calling an external module,
           * and you'd like to pass a reference to yourself.
           */
          public void ejbPostCreate(String customerID, String name, String address,
              String password) throws RemoteException {
              System.out.println("ejbPostCreate() called");
          }


          /**
           * Called before the container removes entity bean data
           * from the database.  Corresponds to when client calls
           * home.remove().
           */
          public void ejbRemove() throws RemoteException {
              System.out.println("ejbRemove() called.");
          }


          // No finder methods - they are implemented by Container

          //---------------------------------------------------------
          // End EJB required methods
          //---------------------------------------------------------
      }
```

Source 13.2   CustomerBean.java *(continued)*.

our entity bean is left with an *ejbCreate()* initializer, some empty EJB required methods, and some get/set methods.

As you can imagine, writing these get and set methods for entity beans such as this could become very tedious. Filling in the EJB required methods could also be a burden. In the future, Integrated Development Environments (IDEs), such as Inprise's *JBuilder* or Symantec's *Visual Cafe*, may provide facilities for automatically writing a husk of an entity bean for you, saving you time and allowing you to concentrate on the real infrastructure you're developing.

CustomerHome.java

Our home interface defines mechanisms for creating and instantiating our Customer EJB objects, and it is depicted in Source 13.3. The class for the home object that implements this interface will be created automatically by the EJB container.

The home interface's *create()* is used by client code to create a new customer. When *create()* is called, the container delegates the call to the bean implementation's *ejbCreate()* method, which initializes things. Once the container sets up the database data, the *create()* method returns a new EJB object to the client code.

We also have a number of customized finder methods for locating existing customers, based on certain attributes such as the customer name and the customer's address. We also have a way to find all customers—in this case, an *Enumeration* is returned (which will change to a *Collection* in Java 2).

```
package com.wiley.compBooks.ecommerce;

import javax.ejb.*;
import java.rmi.RemoteException;
import java.util.Enumeration;

/**
 * This is the home interface for Customer.  This interface is
 * implemented by the EJB Server's glue-code tools - the
 * implemented object is called the Home Object and serves as
 * a factory for EJB Objects.
 *
 * One create() method is in this Home Interface, which
 * corresponds to the ejbCreate() method in the Customer file.
 */
public interface CustomerHome extends EJBHome {
```

Source 13.3 CustomerHome.java *(continues)*.

```
/*
 * This method creates the EJB Object.
 *
 * Notice that the Home Interface returns an EJB Object,
 * whereas the Bean returns void.  This is because the
 * EJB Container is responsible for generating the EJB
 * Object, whereas the Bean is responsible for
 * initialization.
 *
 * @param customerID The globally unique Customer ID.
 *             This serves as our primary key.
 * @param name The full name of the Customer.  This
 *             parameter should match the bank account
 *             record name.
 * @param address The Customer's address.
 * @param password The Customer's password.
 *
 * @return The newly created EJB Object.
 */
Customer create(String customerID, String customerName, String address,
    String password) throws CreateException, RemoteException;

// Finder methods.  These are implemented by the
// Container.  The functionality of these methods can
// be customized by using the EJB Container tools.

public Customer findByPrimaryKey(CustomerPK key) throws FinderException,
    RemoteException;

public Enumeration findByName(String name) throws FinderException,
    RemoteException;

public Enumeration findByAddress(String address) throws FinderException,
    RemoteException;

public Enumeration findAllCustomers() throws FinderException,
    RemoteException;
}
```

Source 13.3   CustomerHome.java *(continued)*.

CustomerPK.java

The primary key class for our customers is a simple *String* for the Customer ID. This is the same Customer ID we defined in *CustomerBean.java*. This ID must be globally unique for all Customer bean instances. It is the responsibility of the creator of the Customer to assign the Customer a unique primary key when

```
package com.wiley.compBooks.ecommerce;

import java.io.Serializable;

/**
 * Primary Key class for our Customer container-managed
 * persistent entity bean
 */
public class CustomerPK implements java.io.Serializable {

    /*
     * Note that the primary key fields must be a
     * subset of the the container-managed Bean
     * fields.  The fields we are marking as
     * container-managed in our Bean are customerID,
     * name, and address.  Therefore our PK fields
     * need to be from that set.
     */
    public String customerID;

    public CustomerPK(String customerID) {
        this.customerID = customerID;
    }

    public CustomerPK() {
    }

    public String toString() {
        return customerID.toString();
    }

    public int hashCode() {
        return customerID.hashCode();
    }

    public boolean equals(Object cust) {
        return ((CustomerPK)cust).customerID.equals(customerID);
    }
}
```

Source 13.4 CustomerPK.java.

the Customer is created via its home interface. The code for our primary key is shown in Source 13.4.

The Deployment Descriptor

Finally, we have our Customer's deployment descriptor. We use the deployment descriptor to declaratively specify attributes about our bean, such as persistence, security, and transaction attributes. The EJB container will inspect the deployment descriptor at runtime and will use the information to manage the bean. Our deployment descriptor is shown in Table 13.1.

Notice that we've enumerated the five public container-managed entity bean fields we defined in our bean. This is necessary so the container will know which fields it should manage when performing persistent operations, such as an *ejbStore()* or an *ejbLoad()*.

There are also two transaction-oriented deployment descriptor settings in this example. First is a transaction attribute, which describes how our bean should be enlisted in transactions. If you'll recall, the possible settings here are the following:

TX_BEAN_MANAGED. The bean explicitly conducts transactions itself. This means you need to program transactional logic for demarcating transactional boundaries in the bean itself. This is the "traditional" (yet cumbersome) way of performing transactions in other middleware systems.

TX_NOT_SUPPORTED. The bean cannot participate in a transaction. Any current transactions are suspended during the invocation and then resumed afterward.

TX_REQUIRED. If a transaction is already going, the bean will join it. If not, the bean runs in its own new transaction.

Table 13.1 Deployment Descriptor Settings for CustomerBean

DEPLOYMENT DESCRIPTOR SETTING	VALUE
Bean home name	Ecommerce.CustomerHome
Enterprise bean class name	com.wiley.compBooks.ecommerce.CustomerBean
Home interface class name	com.wiley.compBooks.ecommerce.CustomerHome
Remote interface class name	com.wiley.compBooks.ecommerce.Customer
Environment properties	<empty>
Re-entrant	false
Primary key class name	com.wiley.compBooks.ecommerce.CustomerPK
Container-managed fields	customerID, name, address, and password
Transaction isolation level	TRANSACTION_READ_UNCOMMITTED
Transaction attribute	TX_SUPPORTS
Run-as mode	CLIENT_IDENTITY

TX_REQUIRES_NEW. A new transaction must always occur during an invocation.

TX_SUPPORTS. If a transaction is already going, the bean will join it. If not, no transaction occurs.

TX_MANDATORY. If a transaction is already going, the bean will join it. If not, an exception is thrown.

We don't anticipate that concurrent clients will manipulate instances of our Customer bean. Typically a Customer will be created once and only once, updates are rare, and it is unlikely that two concurrent users will simultaneously modify the same customer record. Therefore, we set a transaction mode of TX_SUPPORTS and an isolation level of TRANSACTION_READ_UNCOMMITTED. Of course, if this situation changes in the future, we can upgrade the deployment descriptor's isolation level to suit any new needs.

 In EJB 1.0, there is a small bug that prevents you from setting the TX_SUPPORTS transaction attribute. This bug applies only to TX_SUPPORTS, not the other attributes. This bug will also be fixed in future releases of EJB. For now, the workaround is to use a different isolation level, such as TX_REQUIRED.

Next, we have a security setting to have our bean run as the identity of the client. Since our bean will not be performing any secure operations, this mode is acceptable.

We also define a set of relationships between the container-managed fields and our underlying relational database. This step will vary from container to container because the EJB specification does not define how to map fields to an underlying data source. The field mapping is shown for the BEA WebLogic container in Table 13.2.

We also enumerate the logic of the finder methods that the container should implement. Again, this is also EJB container-specific and is shown for the BEA WebLogic container in Table 13.3.

Table 13.2 Persistent Settings for Our Customer Bean Assuming the BEA WebLogic Container

OBJECT/RELATIONAL SETTING (ENTITY BEAN FIELD = RELATIONAL COLUMN NAME)
customerID=id
name=name
address=address
password=password

Table 13.3 Finder Semantics for Customer Bean Assuming the BEA WebLogic Container

FINDER SCRIPTING SYNTAX
"findByName(String name)" "(= name $name)"
"findByAddress(String address)" "(= address $address)"
"findAllCustomers()" "(= 1 1)"

The Order Line Item Entity Bean

Our next entity bean is a bean that models a line item of an order. If you recall from Chapter 12, an Order is a permanent record for goods purchased. Clients who connect to our Web site perform the following steps to create an Order:

1. Browse the catalog, adding Products to the user's temporary Quote stateful session bean.

2. View the Quote on a separate screen, making any last-minute changes. Each distinct Product, along with the quantity of that Product that the user wants, is represented as a Quote Line Item.

3. Generate an Order from the Quote. Every Quote Line Item is converted into a permanent Order Line Item, which is a signal to manufacture goods.

Our Order Line Item entity bean contains information for a particular Product ordered. Why have Order Line Items, rather than simply aggregating Products in the Order entity bean? The answer is convenience of manipulation. With line items, our Pricer bean can compute discounts on a per-Product basis. The user also should be able to add and delete whole line items via the Web GUI we create. An order processing utility can inspect the line items one by one once they're generated.

Our Line Items will model the following information:

■ The ID of this Order Line Item. This must be globally unique, and it will be our primary key.

■ The product that this Order Line Item represents. A manufacturing utility program can use this information to reveal which product to construct.

■ The quantity of the product that should be manufactured.

■ The discount that the Customer received on this Product. This is calculated with an external Pricer session bean, which we show in the following chapter.

More data, such as a separate billing address, could always be added later as needed.

OrderLineItem.java

Our remote interface is detailed in *OrderLineItem.java*, shown in Source 13.5.

The remote interface exposes methods to get and set the various fields we've identified. Most of the fields, such as the product, the discount, and the quantity, are settable. There are two exceptions:

- There is no setter method for our line item's unique ID because the ID is a permanent part of our line item, which is set on initialization.

- The base price of the product is not settable—it's extracted automatically from the Product bean.

```java
package com.wiley.compBooks.ecommerce;

import javax.ejb.*;
import java.rmi.RemoteException;

/**
 * These are the business logic methods exposed pubicly
 * by OrderLineItemBean.
 *
 * This interface is what clients operate on when they
 * interact with beans. The container vendor will
 * implement this interface; the implementation object
 * is called the EJB Object, which delegates
 * invocations to the actual bean.
 */
public interface OrderLineItem extends EJBObject {

    // Getter/setter methods for Entity Bean fields

    public Product getProduct() throws RemoteException;
    public void setProduct(Product product) throws RemoteException;

    public double getBasePrice() throws RemoteException;

    public double getDiscount() throws RemoteException;
    public void setDiscount(double discount) throws RemoteException;

    public int getQuantity() throws RemoteException;
    public void setQuantity(int quantity) throws RemoteException;
}
```

Source 13.5 OrderLineItem.java

OrderLineItemBean.java

The implementation of our line-item is in *OrderLineItemBean.java*, shown in Source 13.6.

Most of this bean is fairly standard. We have a number of container-managed fields, such as the quantity and discount. They are initialized upon *ejbCreate()* and are automatically saved to and loaded from the database by the container. As with most container-managed persistent entity beans, our EJB-required methods have fairly trivial implementations.

Notice also that this is our first bean that has a relationship with other entity beans. But this is not as easy as it sounds, and it raises many issues. We examine this further in the following section.

```
package com.wiley.compBooks.ecommerce;

import java.sql.*;
import javax.naming.*;
import javax.ejb.*;
import java.util.*;
import java.rmi.RemoteException;
import javax.naming.*;

/**
 * This is a container-managed persistent entity bean.  It
 * represents an order line item.  A line item is an order
 * for a quantity of a single product.  Many line items
 * together form an entire order.
 */
public class OrderLineItemBean implements EntityBean {

    protected EntityContext ctx;

    //--------------------------------------------------
    // Begin Container-Managed fields
    //--------------------------------------------------

    /*
     * The id number of this line item.  This is our
     * primary key as well.
     */
    public String orderLineItemID;
```

Source 13.6 OrderLineItemBean.java *(continues)*.

```
/*
 * These fields are:
 * - The product that has been purchased.
 * - The order that this line item is part of.
 *
 * Product information is encapsulated in a separate
 * enterprise bean, called ProductBean, with an EJB
 * Object called Product.
 *
 * Order information is encapsulated in a separate
 * enterprise bean, called OrderBean, with an EJB
 * Object called Order.
 *
 * Unfortunately, EJB 1.0 does not mandate that
 * Containers persist references to EJB Objects.
 * We must persist these fields as serializable
 * primary keys, rather than as EJB Objects.  Yet
 * we still want to work with EJB Objects so that
 * we can call methods on them.  Hence, we must
 * keep two sets of fields:
 *
 * - The productPK field is our Product's Primary
 *   Key, and the orderPK field is our Order's
 *   Primary Key.  These are persistable
 *   container-managed fields.
 *
 * - The product field is our Product's EJB Object,
 *   and the order field is our Order's EJB Object.
 *   These are not persistent container-managed
 *   fields, but rather are there for convenience,
 *   so we can call methods on them.
 *
 */
public String productPK;
public String orderPK;
protected Product product;
protected Order order;

/*
 * The quantity of goods that should be ordered
 */
public int quantity;

/*
 * The discount that this specific Customer gets
 */
public double discount;
```

Source 13.6 OrderLineItemBean.java *(continues).*

```
    //--------------------------------------------------
    // End Container-Managed fields
    //--------------------------------------------------


    //--------------------------------------------------
    // Begin business methods
    //--------------------------------------------------

    public OrderLineItemBean() {
        System.out.println("New OrderLineItem Entity Bean Java Object " +
        "created by EJB Container.");
    }

    public Product getProduct() throws RemoteException {
        System.out.println("OrderLineItem.getProduct() called.");
        return product;
    }

    public void setProduct(Product product) throws RemoteException {
        System.out.println("OrderLineItem.setProduct() called.");
        this.product = product;
    }

    public int getQuantity() throws RemoteException {
        System.out.println("OrderLineItem.getQuantity() called.");
        return quantity;
    }

    public void setQuantity(int quantity) throws RemoteException {
        System.out.println("OrderLineItem.setQuantity() called.");
        this.quantity = quantity;
    }

    /**
     * Returns the base price.  The base price is the
     * product's price times the quantity ordered.  This
     * figure does not take discounts into consideration.
     */
    public double getBasePrice() throws RemoteException {
        System.out.println("OrderLineItem.getBasePrice() called.");
        return quantity * product.getBasePrice();
    }

    /**
     * Returns the discount that the customer gets on
     * this order.
     *
```

Source 13.6 OrderLineItemBean.java *(continues)*.

```
 * Note: The discount is a whole number, not
 *       a percentage discount.
 */
public double getDiscount() throws RemoteException {
    System.out.println("OrderLineItem.getDiscount() called.");
    return discount;
}

/**
 * Sets the discount that the customer gets on
 * this order.
 *
 * Note: The discount is a whole number, not
 *       a percentage discount.
 */
public void setDiscount(double discount) throws RemoteException {
    System.out.println("OrderLineItem.setDiscount() called.");
    this.discount = discount;
}

//-------------------------------------------------
// End business methods
//-------------------------------------------------


//-------------------------------------------------
// Begin EJB-required methods.  The methods below
// are called by the Container, and never called
// by client code.
//-------------------------------------------------


/**
 * Associates this Bean instance with a particular
 * context.  Once done, we can query the Context
 * for environment info, such as Bean
 * customizations via properties.
 */
public void setEntityContext(EntityContext ctx) throws RemoteException {
    System.out.println("OrderLineItem.setEntityContext called");
    this.ctx = ctx;
}

/**
 * Disassociates this Bean instance with a
 * particular context environment.
 */
public void unsetEntityContext() throws RemoteException {
    System.out.println("OrderLineItem.unsetEntityContext called");
    this.ctx = null;
}
```

Source 13.6 OrderLineItemBean.java *(continues)*.

```
/**
 * Called directly after activating this bean
 * instance.  You should acquire needed
 * resources in this method.
 */
public void ejbActivate() throws RemoteException {
    System.out.println("OrderLineItem.ejbActivate() called.");
}


/**
 * Called directly before passivating this bean
 * instance.  Release any resources you acquired
 * in ejbActivate() in this method.
 */
public void ejbPassivate() throws RemoteException {
    System.out.println("OrderLineItem.ejbPassivate () called.");
}


/**
 * Updates the database to reflect the current
 * values of this object.
 *
 * Since we're using Container-Managed
 * Persistence, the Container will automatically
 * save our public container-managed fields into
 * the database.  We should perform any
 * necessary pre-processing here.
 */
public void ejbStore() throws RemoteException {
    System.out.println("OrderLineItem.ejbStore() called.");

    /*
     * Since the container persists primary keys only, we must
     * convert our references to EJB Objects into primary keys.
     */
    productPK = ((ProductPK)product.getPrimaryKey()).productID;
    orderPK = ((OrderPK)order.getPrimaryKey()).orderID;
}


/**
 * Updates this object to reflect any changes to
 * the database data.
 *
 * Since we're using Container-Managed
 * Persistence, the Container will automatically
 * set our public fields to the correct values.
 * We then do post-processing here.
 */
```

Source 13.6 OrderLineItemBean.java *(continues)*.

```java
public void ejbLoad() throws RemoteException {
    System.out.println("OrderLineItem.ejbLoad() called.");

    /*
     * Since the container persists primary keys only, we must
     * convert the loaded primary keys into EJB Objects.
     */
    try {
        /*
         * Form JNDI initial context.
         *
         * Note: We rely on the environment properties
         * that the bean was deployed with for any
         * necessary initialization parameters.
         */
        Context initCtx = new InitialContext(ctx.getEnvironment());

        /*
         * Lookup home objects via JNDI
         */
        ProductHome productHome = (ProductHome)
            initCtx.lookup("Ecommerce.ProductHome");
        OrderHome orderHome = (OrderHome)
            initCtx.lookup("Ecommerce.OrderHome");

        /*
         * Find the EJB Objects based upon their primary keys
         */
        product = productHome.findByPrimaryKey(new ProductPK(productPK));
        order = orderHome.findByPrimaryKey(new OrderPK(orderPK));
    }
    catch (Exception e) {
        throw new RemoteException(e.toString());
    }
}

/**
 * Called when new database data is created.
 *
 * When the client calls the Home Object's
 * create() method, the Home Object then calls
 * this ejbCreate() method.
 *
 * We need to initialize our Bean's container-
 * managed fields with the parameters passed
 * from the client, so that the Container can
 * inspect our Bean and create the corresponding
 * database entries.
 */
```

Source 13.6 OrderLineItemBean.java *(continues).*

```java
    public void ejbCreate(String orderLineItemID, Order order,
        Product product, int quantity, double discount) throws
        CreateException, RemoteException {
        System.out.println("OrderLineItem.ejbCreate(" + orderLineItemID + ", "
            + product.getName() + ", " + quantity + ") called");

        this.orderLineItemID = orderLineItemID;

        this.product = product;
        productPK = ((ProductPK)product.getPrimaryKey()).productID;

        this.order  = order;
        orderPK = ((OrderPK)order.getPrimaryKey()).orderID;

        this.quantity = quantity;
        this.discount = discount;
    }

    /**
     * The Container calls this after ejbCreate().
     * At this point in time, the bean instance is
     * associated with its own EJB Object.  You can
     * get a reference to that EJB Object by querying
     * the context.  You'd use that EJB Object
     * reference when calling an external module, and
     * you'd like to pass a reference to yourself.
     */
    public void ejbPostCreate(String orderLineItemID, Order order,
        Product product, int quantity, double discount) throws
        CreateException, RemoteException {
        System.out.println("OrderLineItem.ejbPostCreate() called");
    }

    /**
     * Called before the container removes entity
     * bean data from the database.  Corresponds to
     * when client calls home.remove().
     */
    public void ejbRemove() throws RemoteException {
        System.out.println("OrderLineItem.ejbRemove() called.");

        // NOTE: We do not remove the Product because the Product
        // can be reused over and over again for different line
        // items.  Similarly, we do not remove the Order because
        // deleting a single line item should not delete an
        // entire Order.
    }

    // No finder methods - they are implemented by Container
```

Source 13.6   OrderLineItemBean.java *(continues).*

```
    //-------------------------------------------------
    // End EJB-required methods
    //-------------------------------------------------
}
```

Source 13.6 OrderLineItemBean.java *(continued).*

Handling Entity Bean References

The careful reader will notice that our Order Line Item bean makes use of our Product entity bean from Chapter 9. But our bean keeps two different pieces of information: a reference to a Product EJB object and that Product's primary key. Why do we have both?

Let's say you have an entity bean called *FooBean*, which references an EJB object of a separate entity bean called *Bar*:

```
public class FooBean implements EntityBean {
    public Bar bar;
    // ...
}
```

The field bar is a container-managed entity bean field. In EJB 1.0, an EJB container performing container-managed persistence is not required to transparently persist this reference.

This restriction has implications on our code. In our Order Line Item code, we reference a Product entity bean EJB object. We need to work with the EJB object because we need to call methods on our Product. An example of this is in the *getBasePrice()* method:

```
return quantity * product.getBasePrice();
```

But when our container persists our Order Line Item, we want to persist the Product reference as well. Because this is not transparent in EJB, we need to have the following code in *ejbStore()*:

```
productPK = ((ProductPK)product.getPrimaryKey()).productID;
```

This converts the EJB object into its primary key, which is a container-managed field and will be persisted.

We also need to perform the opposite steps in *ejbLoad()* by converting the primary key back into an EJB object:

```
Context initCtx = new InitialContext(ctx.getEnvironment());
ProductHome productHome =
    (ProductHome)initCtx.lookup("Ecommerce.ProductHome");
product = productHome.findByPrimaryKey(new OrderPK(orderPK));
```

This performs JNDI initialization and then looks up the EJB object based on the primary key that the container retrieved from the database.

In general, when your bean references another entity bean, you as a bean developer must construct and reconstruct your references in the following ways:

1. In the bean's *ejbStore()* implementation, you must convert the EJB object into a primary key and let the EJB container persist the primary key.

2. In the bean's *ejbLoad()* implementation, the bean developer must perform JNDI initialization, find a home object, and then perform a *findByPrimaryKey()* to reconstruct the EJB object reference.

A related issue arises in our bean's *ejbRemove()* method. *ejbRemove()* is called on behalf of a client who wishes to remove this entity bean from the database. But our entity bean is holding a reference to a Product bean as well—should we remove the Product? The answer is no. Products are created once and are reusable over and over again in many quotes in a read-only fashion. It makes no sense to delete the Product when we remove this Order Line Item. This is the concept of *aggregation* in the *Unified Modeling Language* (*UML*): Deleting the owner object does not delete the subobject. *Composition* is the opposite: Deleting the owner object deletes all subobjects. We need to programmatically hard-code these relationships into our Java code.

Needless to say, this does not promote rapid application development very well. Performing steps such as converting and unconverting primary keys, manually deleting subobjects, and more are quite cumbersome and can easily be taken care of by the container, assuming you supply properties that go with your beans that describe your needs. And there is good news—some EJB containers transparently handle relationships between beans for you. But unfortunately, this is currently a proprietary feature that only some EJB container vendors provide. This leaves your beans as nonportable and increases your affinity to a single application server vendor. The EJB 2.0 specification promises to mandate standard relationship services. This will be a welcome addition, as almost any large-scale deployment needs this functionality.

OrderLineItemHome.java

Our home interface defines ways to create and find our Order Line Items. The code is in *OrderLineItem.java*, listed in Source 13.7.

We define one simple create method for creating a new Order Line Item and the required *findbyPrimaryKey()* method to look up existing line items by their ID.

```java
package com.wiley.compBooks.ecommerce;

import javax.ejb.*;
import java.rmi.RemoteException;
import java.util.Enumeration;

/**
 * This is the home interface for OrderLineItem.  The
 * container implements this interface; the
 * implementation object is called the Home Object
 * and serves as a factory for EJB Objects.
 */
public interface OrderLineItemHome extends EJBHome {

    /*
     * This method creates the EJB Object.
     *
     * Notice that the Home Interface returns an EJB
     * Object, whereas the Bean returns void.  This is
     * because the EJB Container is responsible for
     * generating the EJB Object, whereas the Bean is
     * responsible for initialization.
     *
     * @param orderLineItemID The line item's unique ID
     * @param product The product this line item represents
     * @param quantity The quantity of product in this line item
     * @param discount The discount the customer receives
     *
     * @return The newly created EJB Object.
     */
    public OrderLineItem create(String orderLineItemID, Order order,
        Product product, int quantity, double discount) throws
        CreateException, RemoteException;

    /*
     * Finder methods.  Locate existing entity bean data.
     */
    public OrderLineItem findByPrimaryKey(OrderLineItemPK key) throws
        FinderException, RemoteException;

    public Enumeration findByOrder(String orderID) throws FinderException,
RemoteException;
}
```

Source 13.7 OrderLineItemHome.java.

OrderLineItemPK.java

Finally, we have the primary key class for our Order Line Item, as shown in Source 13.8.

Our primary key class's public fields must come from the container-managed fields of the bean. We select the ID of the order to encompass our primary key.

```java
package com.wiley.compBooks.ecommerce;

import java.io.Serializable;

/**
 * Primary Key class for our OrderLineItem
 * Container-Managed Persistent Entity Bean
 */
public class OrderLineItemPK implements java.io.Serializable {

  /*
   * These are the primary key fields.  They must be a
   * subset of the bean's container-managed Bean fields.
   */
  public String orderLineItemID;


  public OrderLineItemPK(String orderLineItemID) {
     this.orderLineItemID = orderLineItemID;
  }

  public OrderLineItemPK() {
  }

  public String toString() {
     return orderLineItemID.toString();
  }

  public int hashCode()
  {
     return orderLineItemID.hashCode();
  }

  public boolean equals(Object oli)
  {
     return ((OrderLineItemPK)oli).orderLineItemID.equals(orderLineItemID);
  }
}
```

Source 13.8 OrderLineItemPK.java.

The Deployment Descriptor

Our deployment descriptor will be inspected by the EJB container to discover information about our bean. It's shown in Table 13.4.

Orders are mission-critical placements for goods, and they may be modified in a multiuser situation (consider a fulfillment application running concurrently with our e-commerce deployment). To ensure safety, we use the TRANSACTION_ SERIALIZABLE isolation level.

Next, we define a mapping for our container-managed fields to an underlying data store—currently a step that varies for each container. The field mapping is shown for the BEA WebLogic container in Table 13.5.

Table 13.4 Deployment Descriptor Settings for OrderLineItemBean

DEPLOYMENT DESCRIPTOR SETTING	VALUE
Bean home name	Ecommerce.OrderLineItemHome
Enterprise bean class name	com.wiley.compBooks.ecommerce.OrderLineItemBean
Home interface class name	com.wiley.compBooks.ecommerce.OrderLineItemHome
Remote interface class name	com.wiley.compBooks.ecommerce.OrderLineItem
Environment properties	see Table 13.7
Re-entrant	false
Primary key class name	com.wiley.compBooks.ecommerce.OrderLineItemPK
Container-managed fields	orderLineItemID, productPK, quantity, and discount
Transaction isolation level	TRANSACTION_SERIALIZABLE
Transaction attribute	TX_REQUIRED
Run-as mode	CLIENT_IDENTITY

Table 13.5 Persistent Settings for Our OrderLineItem Bean Assuming the BEA WebLogic Container

OBJECT/RELATIONAL SETTING (ENTITY BEAN FIELD = RELATIONAL COLUMN NAME)
orderLineItemID=id
productPK=productPK
quantity=quantity
discount=discount

Table 13.6 Finder Semantics for OrderLineItem Bean Assuming the BEA WebLogic Container

FINDER SCRIPTING SYNTAX
"findByOrder(java.lang.String orderID)"
"(= orderID $orderID)"

Table 13.7 Environment Properties for OrderLineItemBean

ENVIRONMENT PROPERTY SETTING	VALUE
java.naming.factory.initial	"weblogic.jndi.TengahInitialContextFactory"
java.naming.provider.url	"t3://localhost:7001"

We also enumerate the logic of the finder methods that the container should implement. Again, this is also EJB container–specific and is shown for the BEA WebLogic container in Table 13.6.

We also use a number of environment properties. They are shown in Table 13.7. Recall that our bean's *ejbLoad()* method uses JNDI to reconstruct the referenced Product EJB object from its stored primary key. The environment properties are needed to perform this JNDI initialization.

The Order Entity Bean

Our last entity bean models an entire Order work request. Our Orders will contain the following information:

- The unique ID of the Order
- The Customer who placed the Order, so we know who to bill and where to ship our Order
- The subtotal, taxes, and price of the Order
- The date that the Order was placed

Let's dive into the implementation and see how our Order bean works.

Order.java

Order.java, shown in Source 13.9, is our Order's remote interface. It consists of a few get/set methods on the Order's data fields.

```
package com.wiley.compBooks.ecommerce;

import javax.ejb.*;
import java.rmi.RemoteException;
import java.util.*;

/**
 * These are the business logic methods exposed publicly
 * by OrderBean.
 *
 * This interface is what clients operate on when they
 * interact with beans. The container vendor will implement
 * this interface; the implementation object is called the
 * EJB Object, which delegates invocations to the actual bean.
 */
public interface Order extends EJBObject {

    /**
     * Returns the set of Order Line Items that compose
     * this Order.  Each Line Item represents a specific
     * product and quantity ordered.
     */
    public Enumeration getLineItems() throws RemoteException;

    /**
     * Returns the customer address set by setCustomer()
     */
    public Customer getCustomer() throws RemoteException;

    /**
     * Returns the subtotal price that has been previously
     * set by setSubtotal().
     */
    public double getSubtotal() throws RemoteException;

    /**
     * Sets the subtotal price.  The subtotal should be
     * externally calculated from the line item base
     * prices and adjusted based on customer discounts.
     */
    public void setSubtotal(double subTotal) throws RemoteException;

    /**
     * Returns the taxes for this Order.
     */
    public double getTaxes() throws RemoteException;
```

Source 13.9 Order.java *(continues)*.

```
    /**
     * Sets the taxes for this Order.
     */
    public void setTaxes(double taxes) throws RemoteException;

    /**
     * Returns the total price.  Total Price is computed from:
     * 1) Subtotal price
     * 2) Tax
     */
    public double getTotalPrice() throws RemoteException;

    /**
     * Retrieves the date this was ordered on.  Date is set
     * automatically when new Order is created.
     */
    public Date getDate() throws RemoteException;
}
```

Source 13.9 Order.java *(continued)*.

The date for the order will automatically be set on order creation, so there is no method to set the date. The total price is calculated from each line item, so that is not mutable by clients either.

OrderBean.java

Our Order's implementation is in *OrderBean.java*, shown in Source 13.10.

The bean code should be fairly self-explanatory. Our *ejbCreate()* method is called when a new order is created. *ejbCreate()* initializes the bean's fields to the passed-in values. For example, we set the date field to be the current date. The container will persist our container-managed fields to the database for us after *ejbCreate()*.

Notice how we're using a *java.sql.Timestamp* for our date field. This is the JDBC analog to a date. We use this so that our dates will map well to a relational database date field. If you'd like to work with a regular *java.util.Date*, you can simply modify the *ejbLoad()* and *ejbStore()* methods to convert and unconvert from a *java.sql.Timestamp* to a *java.util.Date*.

As with the Order Line Item example, our bean is referencing external entity beans—specifically, we reference a Customer bean. Because we can't persist EJB object references, our *ejbStore()* method must convert the EJB objects into primary keys in preparation for the container to save the fields. Our *ejbLoad()* method must do the opposite—convert the container-loaded primary keys back into EJB objects so we can use them again.

```
package com.wiley.compBooks.ecommerce;

import java.util.*;
import java.io.*;
import java.rmi.*;

import javax.naming.*;
import javax.ejb.*;

/**
 * This is a container-managed persistent entity bean that
 * represents an order placed for goods.
 *
 * Note: This Bean could easily be extended to include other
 * things, such as:
 * - Shipping charges
 * - Shipping address vs. Billing address
 * - A date that this order is scheduled to be completed/shipped.
 * - Status information about the order.  This could be set by a
 *   Fulfillment component to different status levels, such as
 *   "manufacturing" or "shipping" or "delivered".
 */
public class OrderBean implements EntityBean {

    protected EntityContext ctx;

    //----------------------------------------------------------
    // Begin Container-Managed fields
    //----------------------------------------------------------

    /*
     * This order's identification number.  It's also our
     * Primary Key.
     */
    public String orderID;

    /*
     * The Customer who placed this Order.  Customer
     * information is encapsulated in a separate bean,
     * called CustomerBean, with an EJB Object called
     * Customer.
     *
     * Unfortunately, EJB 1.0 does not mandate that
     * Containers persist references to EJB Objects.  We
     * must persist this Customer field as a serializable
     * primary key, rather than an EJB Object.  Yet we
     * still want to work with an EJB Object so that we can
     * call methods on it.  Hence, we must keep two fields:
```

Source 13.10 OrderBean.java *(continues)*.

```
 *
 * - The customerPK field is our Customer's Primary Key,
 *   and is a persistable container-managed field.
 *
 * - The customer field is our Customer's EJB Object.
 *   It is not a persistent container-managed field, but
 *   rather is there for convenience, so we can call
 *   methods on it.
 *
 */
protected Customer customer;
public String customerPK;

/*
 * The date this order was placed.
 */
public java.sql.Timestamp date;

/*
 * The order subtotal.
 */
public double subTotal;

/*
 * The taxes incurred.
 */
public double taxes;

//---------------------------------------------------------
// End Container-Managed fields
//---------------------------------------------------------


//---------------------------------------------------------
// Begin business methods
//---------------------------------------------------------

public Enumeration getLineItems() throws RemoteException {
    OrderLineItemHome home = null;
    try {
        Context initCtx = new InitialContext(ctx.getEnvironment());
        home = (OrderLineItemHome)
            initCtx.lookup("Ecommerce.OrderLineItemHome");
        return home.findByOrder(orderID);
    } catch (Exception e) {
        throw new ServerException("Lookup failed", e);
    }
}
```

Source 13.10 OrderBean.java *(continues)*.

```java
    public Customer getCustomer() throws RemoteException {
        return customer;
    }

    public double getSubtotal() throws RemoteException {
        return subTotal;
    }

    public void setSubtotal(double subTotal) throws RemoteException {
        this.subTotal = subTotal;
    }

    public double getTaxes() throws RemoteException {
        return taxes;
    }

    public void setTaxes(double taxes) throws RemoteException {
        this.taxes = taxes;
    }

    public double getTotalPrice() throws RemoteException {
        return subTotal - taxes;
    }

    public java.sql.Timestamp getDate() throws RemoteException {
        return date;
    }

    //---------------------------------------------------------
    // End public business methods
    //---------------------------------------------------------


    //---------------------------------------------------------
    // Begin EJB-Required methods.  The methods below are
    // called by the Container and are never called by client
    // code.
    //---------------------------------------------------------

    /**
     * Associates this Bean instance with a particular context.
     * Once done, we can query the Context for environment
     * info, such as Bean customizations via properties.
     */
    public void setEntityContext(EntityContext ctx) throws RemoteException {
        System.out.println("Order.setEntityContext called");
        this.ctx = ctx;
    }
```

Source 13.10 OrderBean.java *(continues)*.

```java
/**
 * Disassociates this Bean instance with a particular
 * context environment.
 */
public void unsetEntityContext() throws RemoteException {
    System.out.println("Order.unsetEntityContext called");
    this.ctx = null;
}


/**
 * Called directly after activating this bean instance.
 * You should acquire needed resources in this method.
 */
public void ejbActivate() throws RemoteException {
    System.out.println("Order.ejbActivate() called.");
}


/**
 * Called directly before passivating this bean instance.
 * Release any resources you acquired in ejbActivate() in
 * this method.
 */
public void ejbPassivate() throws RemoteException {
    System.out.println("Order.ejbPassivate () called.");
}


/**
 * Updates the database to reflect the current values of
 * this object.
 *
 * Since we're using Container-Managed Persistence, the
 * Container will automatically save our public container-
 * managed fields into the database.  We should perform any
 * necessary preprocessing here.
 */
public void ejbStore() throws RemoteException {
    System.out.println("Order.ejbStore() called.");

    /*
     * Since the container persists primary keys only,
     * we must convert our references to EJB Objects
     * into primary keys.
     */
    customerPK = ((CustomerPK)customer.getPrimaryKey()).customerID;
}

/**
 * Updates this object to reflect any changes to the
```

Source 13.10 OrderBean.java *(continues)*.

```
    * database data.
    *
    * Since we're using Container-Managed Persistence, the EJB
    * Container will automatically set our public fields to
    * the correct values.  We then do post-processing here.
    */
public void ejbLoad() throws RemoteException {
    System.out.println("Order.ejbLoad() called.");

    /*
     * Since the container persists primary keys only,
     * we must convert the loaded primary key info for
     * our Customer into an EJB Object.
     */
    try {
        /*
         * Form JNDI initial context.
         *
         * Note: We rely on the environment properties
         * that the bean was deployed with for any
         * necessary initialization parameters.
         */
        Context initCtx = new InitialContext(ctx.getEnvironment());

        /*
         * Lookup home object via JNDI
         */
        CustomerHome home = (CustomerHome)
            initCtx.lookup("Ecommerce.CustomerHome");

        /*
         * Find the EJB Object based on its primary key
         */
        customer = home.findByPrimaryKey(new CustomerPK(customerPK));
    }
    catch (Exception e) {
        throw new RemoteException(e.toString());
    }
}

/**
 * Called when new database data is created.
 *
 * When the client calls the Home Object's create() method,
 * the Home Object then calls this ejbCreate() method.
 *
 * We need to initialize our Bean's container-managed
 * fields with the parameters passed from the client, so
 * that the Container can inspect our Bean and create the
```

Source 13.10 OrderBean.java *(continues).*

```
     * corresponding database entries.
     */
    public void ejbCreate(String orderID, Customer c) throws CreateException,
        RemoteException {
        System.out.println("Order.ejbCreate(" + orderID + ") called");

        this.orderID = orderID;

        this.customer = c;
        this.customerPK = ((CustomerPK)customer.getPrimaryKey()).customerID;

        this.date = new java.sql.Timestamp(System.currentTimeMillis());
        this.subTotal = 0;
        this.taxes = 0;
    }


    /**
     * The Container calls this after ejbCreate().  At this
     * point in time, the bean instance is associated with its
     * own EJB Object.  You can get a reference to that
     * EJB Object by querying the context.  You'd use that
     * EJB Object reference when calling an external module,
     * and you'd like to pass a reference to yourself.
     */
    public void ejbPostCreate(String orderLineItemID, Customer c) throws
        CreateException, RemoteException {
        System.out.println("Order.ejbPostCreate() called");
    }


    /**
     * Called before the container removes entity bean data
     * from the database.  Corresponds to when client calls
     * home.remove().
     */
    public void ejbRemove() throws RemoteException, RemoveException {
        System.out.println("Order.ejbRemove() called.");

        Enumeration e = getLineItems();
        while (e.hasMoreElements()) {
            OrderLineItem li = (OrderLineItem) e.nextElement();
            li.remove();
        }
    }

    // No finder methods - they are implemented by Container


    //---------------------------------------------------------
    // End EJB required methods
    //---------------------------------------------------------
}
```

Source 13.10   OrderBean.java *(continued)*.

OrderHome.java

Our home interface is used to create new Orders and find existing Orders. The code is in *OrderHome.java*, presented in Source 13.11.

In addition to a *create()* and *findByPrimaryKey()* method, our entity bean defines several custom finder methods. This will give clients several useful ways to find existing Orders.

```java
package com.wiley.compBooks.ecommerce;

import javax.ejb.*;
import java.rmi.RemoteException;
import java.util.Enumeration;
import java.util.Date;

/**
 * This is the home interface for Order.  This interface
 * is implemented by the EJB Server's glue-code tools -
 * the implemented object is called the Home Object and
 * serves as a factory for EJB Objects.
 *
 * One create() method is in this Home Interface, which
 * corresponds to the ejbCreate() method in the Order file.
 */
public interface OrderHome extends EJBHome {

    /*
     * This method creates the EJB Object.
     *
     * Notice that the Home Interface returns an
     * EJB Object, whereas the Bean returns void.
     * This is because the EJB Container is responsible
     * for generating the EJB Object, whereas the Bean
     * is responsible for initialization.
     *
     * @param orderID The unique ID of this order
     * @param c The customer who owns this order
     *
     * @return The newly created EJB Object.
     */
    public Order create(String orderID, Customer c) throws CreateException,
        RemoteException;

    // Finder methods, implemented by Container due to
    // Container-Managed Persistence
```

Source 13.11 OrderHome.java *(continues)*.

```
    public Order findByPrimaryKey(OrderPK key) throws FinderException,
        RemoteException;
    public Enumeration findByCustomerKey(CustomerPK key) throws
        FinderException, RemoteException;
    public Enumeration findByDate(java.sql.Timestamp date) throws
        FinderException, RemoteException;
    public Enumeration findAllOrders() throws FinderException,
        RemoteException;
}
```

Source 13.11 OrderHome.java *(continued)*.

OrderPK.java

Our primary key class, *OrderPK.java*, is straightforward. It exposes the Order ID as the single primary key field. The code is shown in Source 13.12.

```
package com.wiley.compBooks.ecommerce;

import java.io.Serializable;

/**
 * Primary Key class for our Order Container-
 * Managed Persistent Entity Bean
 */
public class OrderPK implements java.io.Serializable {

  /*
   * Note that the primary key fields must be a subset of
   * the container-managed Bean fields.
   */
  public String orderID;

  public OrderPK(String orderID) {
    this.orderID = orderID;
  }

  public OrderPK() {
  }

  public String toString() {
    return orderID.toString();
  }
```

Source 13.12 OrderPK.java *(continues)*.

```
   public int hashCode()
   {
      return orderID.hashCode();
   }

   public boolean equals(Object order)
   {
      return ((OrderPK)order).orderID.equals(orderID);
   }
}
```

Source 13.12   OrderPK.java *(continued)*.

OrderException.java

Finally, we define a custom exception class, *OrderException.java*. These exceptions are thrown from several of our bean's methods. The code is displayed in Source 13.13.

The Deployment Descriptor

We present our Order entity bean's deployment descriptor in Table 13.8.

```
package com.wiley.compBooks.ecommerce;

/**
 * Exceptions thrown by Order
 */
public class OrderException extends Exception {

    public OrderException() {
        super();
    }

    public OrderException(Exception e) {
        super(e.toString());
    }

    public OrderException(String s) {
        super(s);
    }
}
```

Source 13.13   OrderException.java.

Table 13.8 Deployment Descriptor Settings for Order Bean

DEPLOYMENT DESCRIPTOR SETTING	VALUE
Bean home name	Ecommerce.OrderHome
Enterprise bean class name	com.wiley.compBooks.ecommerce.OrderBean
Home interface class name	com.wiley.compBooks.ecommerce.OrderHome
Remote interface class name	com.wiley.compBooks.ecommerce.Order
Environment properties	see Table 13.11
Re-entrant	false
Primary key class name	com.wiley.compBooks.ecommerce.OrderPK
Container-managed fields	orderID, customerPK, lineItemPKs, date, subTotal, and taxes
Transaction isolation level	TRANSACTION_SERIALIZABLE
Transaction attribute	TX_REQUIRED
Run-as mode	CLIENT_IDENTITY

As with order line items, orders represent mission-critical data that must be preserved in a multiuser situation. We use the TRANSACTION_SERIALIZABLE isolation level to enforce this.

Next, we define a mapping for our container-managed fields to an underlying data store—currently a step that varies for each container. The field mapping is shown for the BEA WebLogic container in Table 13.9.

Table 13.9 Persistent Settings for Our Order Bean Assuming the BEA WebLogic Container

OBJECT/RELATIONAL SETTING (ENTITY BEAN FIELD = RELATIONAL COLUMN NAME)
orderID =id
customerPK=customerPK
lineItemPKs=lineItemPKs
date=orderDate
subTotal=orderSubTotal
taxes=orderTaxes

Table 13.10   Finder Semantics for Order Bean Assuming the BEA WebLogic Container

FINDER SCRIPTING SYNTAX
"findByCustomerKey(com.wiley.compBooks.ecommerce.CustomerPK key)" "(= customerPK $key)"
"findByDate(java.util.Date date)" "(= date $date)"
"findAllOrders()" "(= 1 1)"

Table 13.11   Environment Properties for OrderLineItemBean

ENVIRONMENT PROPERTY SETTING	VALUE
java.naming.factory.initial	"weblogic.jndi.TengahInitialContextFactory"
java.naming.provider.url	"t3://localhost:7001"

We also enumerate the logic of the finder methods that the container should implement. Again, this is also EJB container–specific, and it is shown for the BEA WebLogic container in Table 13.10.

We also use a number of environment properties. They are shown in Table 13.11. As with our Order Line Items, these environment property settings are necessary for JNDI initialization in our bean's *ejbLoad()* method, when transforming primary keys into EJB objects.

Summary

This concludes our e-commerce deployment's entity beans. You've now been exposed to some of the hairy issues that arise when performing a real deployment with EJB, such as how to use multiple entity beans together and dealing with the limitations of entity bean relationships.

We continue with our EJB coding in the next chapter, defining our business logic session beans. This includes a Quote bean acting as a shopping cart, a Quote Line Item bean, a Pricing engine bean, and a Bank Teller bean.

J2EE in the Real World: Implementing Our E-Commerce Session Beans

I n Chapter 12, we designed an object model for a real e-commerce solution using EJB. In this chapter, we're going to implement our e-commerce deployment's session beans. Whereas entity beans model data, our session beans will contain business logic that performs the necessary algorithms and strategies. In general, every serious EJB deployment will have a combination of beans such as this.

We'll present four new session beans in this chapter. If you need a refresher on the motivation behind creating these beans, or if you need to see the big picture for our deployment, refer to Chapter 12.

A Quote Line Item session bean. When the user navigates our Web site, he or she will choose certain products and add them to the shopping cart, or *Quote*. A Quote is composed of many line items, where each line item has information about a single product that the user wants. The user is free to add or remove line items from the Quote until he or she is satisfied and wants to buy the selections. Once the user clicks the purchase button, the Quote Line Items become line items for a permanent order. Thus, a Quote Line Item is temporary and in-memory only and is well modeled as a stateful session bean. The bean's state is the product and quantity being quoted.

A Quote session bean. A Quote represents the user's shopping cart and stores each of the user's Quote Line Items. A Quote is also a stateful session bean.

A Pricer session bean. Our Pricer bean will be responsible for taking a Quote bean as input, and computing its price. The price is calculated based on a set of pricing rules, such as a discount for a particular customer. Our Pricer bean serves as a simple method provider of business logic, and it is well-modeled as a stateless session bean because it retains no state after computing a price.

EJB Design Strategies

When Should I Wrap Entity Beans with Session Beans?

As we mentioned in Chapter 12, a useful EJB paradigm is to keep your functional objects in session beans and have them transactionally manipulate entity beans that reside in an underlying store.

Working with this paradigm has many benefits. For example:

- If you cache your transactional functionality in a session bean (as we'll see later in this chapter), you eliminate the need for your client code (such as servlets) to have any transaction know-how. This greatly reduces usage errors.

- Because clients don't need to have any explicit transaction calls, client programming is simplified. You can perform transactions declaratively, rather than programmatically, by deploying a session bean whose transactions are managed by the application server.

- By wrapping entity beans with session beans, you reduce round trips between the client and the beans. If your presentation tier is making numerous transactional calls to the business logic tier, your application's performance is going to grind to a halt.

However, you shouldn't *always* wrap entities with sessions. If you have a simple deployment where you are in control of the operational environment, wrapping entities with sessions may be an unnecessary layer of indirection. An example of when you'd want to call entity beans directly is an e-commerce deployment where servlets and enterprise beans are running in the same application server. Because they're in the same address space, there are no network round trips to deal with, so performance is high. Unfortunately, if you're in the market of selling beans, you can't always choose your deployment environment.

We'll see more design strategies, such as the one at the end of Chapter 15, when we've completed our e-commerce system. For now, let's begin writing our session beans.

A Teller bean. If you'll recall, in Chapter 8 we design a Bank Account entity bean. In this chapter, we'll write a Bank Teller session bean, which wraps that Bank Account entity bean. The Teller serves as a convenience class for performing bulk bank account operations (such as a transfer of funds from one account to another). You'll see this familiar paradigm of wrapping entity beans with session beans frequently in the EJB world. It makes a lot of sense—rather than calling across the network frequently when accessing entity beans, you can design a session bean to perform bulk entity bean updates for you.

The Quote Line Item Stateful Session Bean

Our first session bean is a Quote Line Item. As the user goes through the catalog, he or she will pick out different Products and add them to the Quote bean (described later in this chapter). Quotes are made up of Quote Line Items, where each line item contains information about a single product and quantity. More specifically, a line item contains the following data:

- The ID of this line item
- The Product (entity bean) that the user wants to buy
- The quantity of that Product
- Any discounts the customer gets from the base price of the Product

Because a Quote Line Item is specific to one customer and is not persistent, it is best modeled as a stateful session bean. Let's begin our implementation.

QuoteLineItem.java

The first source code that we'll generate is our bean's remote interface. The remote interface is the interface that clients operate on to call methods on our bean. The code is in *QuoteLineItem.java*, shown in Source 14.1.

This is a straightforward remote interface, exposing simple get/set methods to modify the session bean's internal state. Of note, the *getProduct()* method returns the Product entity bean that this line-item represents. There is no *setProduct()* method—our bean implementation's *ejbCreate()* method will handle that.

```
package com.wiley.compBooks.ecommerce;

import javax.ejb.*;
import java.rmi.RemoteException;

/**
 * These are the business logic methods exposed publicly
 * by QuoteLineItemBean.
 *
 * This interface is what clients operate on when they
 * interact with beans. The container vendor will implement
 * this interface; the implementation object is called the
```

Source 14.1 QuoteLineItem.java *(continues)*.

```
 * EJB Object, which delegates invocations to the actual
 * bean.
 */
    public interface QuoteLineItem extends EJBObject {

    // Getter/setter methods for Entity Bean fields

    public Product getProduct() throws RemoteException;

    public double getBasePrice() throws RemoteException;

    public double getDiscount() throws RemoteException;
    public void setDiscount(double discount) throws RemoteException;

    public int getQuantity() throws RemoteException;
    public void setQuantity(int quantity) throws RemoteException;
}
```

Source 14.1 QuoteLineItem.java *(continued)*.

QuoteLineItemBean.java

Next, we'll write our core bean's implementation. The code is in *QuoteLineItemBean .java*, shown in Source 14.2.

Our session bean does not contain much logic—indeed, most of our bean is made up of get/set methods, comments, and empty methods that EJB requires. Our bean's state is the product that this line-item represents, the product quantity desired, and the discount that the customer receives. Notice that our session bean references the Product entity bean we created in Chapter 9. It uses that bean to identify the product associated with this line item.

Our session bean has no unique identifier or primary key. No session beans have primary keys because session beans are not permanent, identifiable, persistent, locatable objects, as entity beans are.

```
package com.wiley.compBooks.ecommerce;

import java.sql.*;
import javax.naming.*;
import javax.ejb.*;
import java.util.*;
import java.rmi.RemoteException;
import javax.naming.*;
```

Source 14.2 QuoteLineItemBean.java *(continues)*.

```
/**
 *
 * This stateful session bean represents an individual
 * line item, which is part of a quote that a customer is
 * working on.  A quote is a set of products that the
 * customer is interested in but has not committed to buying
 * yet.  You can think of this bean as a shopping cart - as the
 * customer surfs our e-commerce Web site, the quote stores all
 * the products and quantities he or she is interested in.
 *
 * A quote consists of a series of line items.  Each line item
 * represents one particular product the customer wants, as
 * well as a quantity for that product.  This bean models a
 * line item.
 *
 * The distinction between a quote and an order is that a quote
 * is only temporary and in-memory (hence a stateful session
 * bean), whereas an order is a persistent record (hence an
 * entity bean).  This quote bean is smart enough to know how
 * to transform itself into an order (via the purchase() method).
 */
public class QuoteLineItemBean implements SessionBean {

    protected SessionContext ctx;

    //------------------------------------------------------------
    // Begin Stateful Session Bean Conversational State fields
    //
    // (Conversational state is non-transient, and is
    // perserved during passivation and activation)
    //------------------------------------------------------------

    /*
     * The product that this line item represents.
     */
    private Product product;

    /*
     * The quantity of the product desired
     */
    private int quantity;

    /*
     * Any discount the customer gets
     */
    private double discount;

    //------------------------------------------------------------
    // End Stateful Session Bean Conversational State fields
    //------------------------------------------------------------
```

Source 14.2   QuoteLineItemBean.java *(continues)*.

```java
public QuoteLineItemBean() {
    System.out.println(
        "New QuoteLineItem Session Bean created by EJB Container.");
}

//-------------------------------------------------------------
// Begin public business methods
//-------------------------------------------------------------

// Simple getter/setter methods of Session Bean fields.

public Product getProduct() throws RemoteException {
    System.out.println("QuoteLineItem.getProduct() called.");
    return product;
}

/**
 * Returns the base price.  The base price is the
 * product's price times the quantity ordered.  This
 * figure does not take discounts into consideration.
 */
public double getBasePrice() throws RemoteException {
    System.out.println("QuoteLineItem.getBasePrice() called.");
    return quantity * product.getBasePrice();
}

/**
 * Returns the discount that the customer gets on this
 * order.
 *
 * Note: The discount is a whole number, not a percentage
 *       discount.
 */
public double getDiscount() throws RemoteException {
    System.out.println("QuoteLineItem.getDiscount() called.");
    return discount;
}

/**
 * Sets the discount that the customer gets on this order.
 *
 * Note: The discount is a whole number, not a percentage
 *       discount.
 */
public void setDiscount(double discount) throws RemoteException {
    System.out.println("QuoteLineItem.setDiscount() called.");
    this.discount = discount;
}
```

Source 14.2 QuoteLineItemBean.java *(continues)*.

```java
    public int getQuantity() throws RemoteException {
        System.out.println("QuoteLineItem.getQuantity() called.");
        return quantity;
    }

    public void setQuantity(int quantity) throws RemoteException {
        System.out.println("QuoteLineItem.setQuantity() called.");
        this.quantity = quantity;
    }

    //-----------------------------------------------------------
    // End public business methods
    //-----------------------------------------------------------


    //-----------------------------------------------------------
    // Begin EJB-required methods.  The methods below are
    // called by the Container and are never called by client
    // code.
    //-----------------------------------------------------------

    /**
     * Associates this Bean instance with a particular context.
     */
    public void setSessionContext(SessionContext ctx) throws RemoteException {
        System.out.println("QuoteLineItem.setSessionContext called");
        this.ctx = ctx;
    }

    /**
     * The container calls this method directly after
     * activating this instance.  You should acquire any
     * needed resources.
     */
    public void ejbActivate() throws RemoteException {
        System.out.println("QuoteLineItem.ejbActivate() called.");
    }

    /**
     * The container calls this method directly before
     * passivating this instance.  You should release
     * resources acquired during ejbActivate().
     */
    public void ejbPassivate() throws RemoteException {
        System.out.println("QuoteLineItem.ejbPassivate () called.");
    }

    /**
     * This is the initialization method that corresponds
```

Source 14.2 QuoteLineItemBean.java *(continues)*.

```
          * to the create() method in the Home Interface.
          *
          * When the client calls the Home Object's create()
          * method, the Home Object then calls this ejbCreate()
          * method.
          */
         public void ejbCreate(Product product) throws CreateException,
             RemoteException {
             System.out.println("QuoteLineItem.ejbCreate(" + product.getName() +
             ") called");

             this.product = product;
             this.quantity = 1;
             this.discount = 0;
         }


         /**
          * Removes this quote line-item, and hence all
          * client-specific state.
          */
         public void ejbRemove() throws RemoteException {
             System.out.println("QuoteLineItem.ejbRemove() called.");
         }


         //-----------------------------------------------------------
         // End EJB-required methods.
         //-----------------------------------------------------------
     }
```

Source 14.2   QuoteLineItemBean.java *(continued)*.

QuoteLineItemHome.java

Next, we'll write our bean's home interface. Clients will call the home interface to create and destroy Quote Line Item EJB objects. The code is in *QuoteLineItemHome.java*, shown in Source 14.3.

Our home interface has a single create method—*create()*—that creates a new quoted line item for a specific product.

The Deployment Descriptor

Finally, we have a deployment descriptor for our Quote Line Item, shown in Table 14.1.

The most important entries in Table 14.1 are the transaction isolation level and the transaction attribute. When deciding on the proper isolation level for this

```
package com.wiley.compBooks.ecommerce;

import javax.ejb.*;
import java.rmi.RemoteException;
import java.util.Enumeration;

/**
 * This is the home interface for QuoteLineItem.  This interface
 * is implemented by the EJB Server's glue-code tools - the
 * implemented object is called the Home Object and serves as a
 * factory for EJB Objects.
 *
 * One create() method is in this Home Interface, which
 * corresponds to the ejbCreate() method in the QuoteLineItem
 * file.
 */
public interface QuoteLineItemHome extends EJBHome {

    /*
     * This method creates the EJB Object.
     *
     * Notice that the Home Interface returns an EJB Object,
     * whereas  the Bean returns void.  This is because the
     * EJB Container is responsible for generating the
     * EJB Object, whereas the Bean is responsible for
     * initialization.
     *
     * @param product Product Entity Bean for this line item
     *
     * @return The newly created EJB Object.
     */
    public QuoteLineItem create(Product product) throws CreateException,
        RemoteException;
}
```

Source 14.3 QuoteLineItemHome.java.

bean, we recall that Quote Line Items are temporary, in-memory session beans. We do not perform any persistent operations at all, and we do not anticipate any concurrency issues. This leads us to choose the weakest isolation level—TRANSACTION_READ_COMMITTED—that will give us the highest performance. We also choose to support transactions but not require them, as we are not performing any operations that require a transaction. For our security run-as mode, we are not performing any secure operations, so we'll leave the bean to run as the client identity.

Table 14.1 Deployment Descriptor Settings for QuoteLineItemBean

DEPLOYMENT DESCRIPTOR SETTING	VALUE
Bean home name	Ecommerce.QuoteLineItemHome
Enterprise bean class name	com.wiley.compBooks.ecommerce.QuoteLineItemBean
Home interface class name	com.wiley.compBooks.ecommerce.QuoteLineItemHome
Remote interface class name	com.wiley.compBooks.ecommerce.QuoteLineItem
Environment properties	<empty>
Re-entrant	false
Stateful or stateless	STATEFUL_SESSION
Session timeout	15 minutes
Transaction isolation level	TRANSACTION_READ_UNCOMMITTED
Transaction attribute	TX_SUPPORTS
Run-as mode	CLIENT_IDENTITY

The Quote Stateful Session Bean

The Quote Line Item bean we have just written represents a single product the user is interested in purchasing. The next session bean we'll write is the complement of this—a Quote bean. A quote acts as a shopping cart, holding many product selections the user has made. As the user traverses the Web site, he or she adds or removes goods from the quote. Our Quote bean will use the Quote Line Item bean we just made to represent each product the user wants.

Each customer who's logged in should have his or her own temporary and separate quote to work in. Therefore, our quotes will need to hold client-specific state in them. They should not be persistent because the user can always cancel the quote. These requirements naturally lend themselves to the stateful session bean paradigm.

Our Quote bean will contain the following information:

- The Customer (entity bean), who we authenticated at the login screen. We need to store the Customer so that we know who to bill, what discounts to apply, and where to ship the manufactured products.

- We will be able to locate the individual Quote Line Items, each of which hold information about a quantity for a single product.

- The subtotal for the quote, which is computed from the prices and quantities of the products, as well as any discounts the customer gets.

- The taxes charged. This is added to the subtotal for the final grand total.

In addition to this data, our Quote bean will be smart and will know how to generate a permanent Order from itself.

Quote.java

We begin our quote bean implementation by designing our remote interface, which is the interface that clients use when calling methods on our bean. The code is in *Quote.java*, shown in Source 14.4.

```java
package com.wiley.compBooks.ecommerce;

import javax.ejb.*;
import java.rmi.RemoteException;
import java.util.*;

/**
 * These are the business logic methods exposed publicly
 * by QuoteBean.
 *
 * This interface is what clients operate on when they
 * interact with beans. The container vendor will
 * implement this interface; the implementation object
 * is called the EJB Object, which delegates invocations
 * to the actual bean.
 */
public interface Quote extends EJBObject {

    /**
     * Returns the # of items in the quote
     */
    public int getNumberOfItems() throws RemoteException;

    /**
     * Returns the line items.  Each line item
     * represents a quantity of a single product.
     */
    public Vector getLineItems() throws RemoteException;
```

Source 14.4 Quote.java *(continues)*.

```
    /**
     * Adds a product to the quote.
     */
    public void addProduct(Product prod) throws RemoteException;

    /**
     * Call to adjust the quantity of a product.
     * If the quantity is 0, the product is removed.
     *
     * @exception QuoteException thrown if Product doesn't exist.
     */
    public void setProductQuantity(Product prod, int quantity) throws
        RemoteException;

    /**
     * Empties the quote
     */
    public void clear() throws RemoteException;

    /**
     * Returns the customer we're quoting.
     */
    public Customer getCustomer() throws RemoteException;

    /**
     * Returns the subtotal price which has been
     * previously set by setSubtotal().
     */
    public double getSubtotal() throws RemoteException;

    /**
     * Sets the subtotal price.
     *
     * Our external pricer bean is responsible for
     * calculating the subtotal.  It calculates it
     * based on customer discounts (and can be
     * extended to include other rules as well).
     */
    public void setSubtotal(double subTotal) throws RemoteException;

    /**
     * Returns the taxes for this Quote.
     */
    public double getTaxes() throws RemoteException;

    /**
     * Sets the taxes for this Quote.
     */
    public void setTaxes(double taxes) throws RemoteException;
```

Source 14.4 Quote.java *(continues)*.

```
    /**
     * Returns the total price.  Total Price is computed from:
     * 1) Subtotal price
     * 2) Tax
     */
    public double getTotalPrice() throws RemoteException;

    /**
     * Converts this temporary quote into a
     * permanent, persistent order.  When the
     * user clicks the "Purchase" button on the
     * Web site, a servlet will call this method.
     *
     * @throw QuoteException thrown if no items in quote
     */
    public Order purchase() throws RemoteException, QuoteException;
}
```

Source 14.4   Quote.java *(continued)*.

Other than the standard get/set methods, we have a *clear()* method to wipe the quote clean. This *clear()* method does *not* eliminate the Customer associated with the quote because the Customer can still add items to the quote even after clearing it via the Web user interface.

We've got one other interesting method as well—*purchase()*. Purchase takes this quote and magically converts it into a persistent Order. We'll see how this is accomplished in our bean's implementation.

QuoteBean.java

We now define our quote bean's core business logic implementation in *QuoteBean .java*. Take a look at it in Source 14.5. Although it's quite lengthy, it contains some interesting methods, which we explain later.

```
package com.wiley.compBooks.ecommerce;

import javax.naming.*;
import javax.ejb.*;
import java.util.*;
import java.rmi.RemoteException;
import javax.naming.*;
```

Source 14.5   QuoteBean.java *(continues)*.

```
/**
 *
 * This stateful session bean represents a quote that
 * a customer is working on.  A quote is a set of
 * products that the customer is interested in but has
 * not committed to buying yet.  You can think of this
 * bean as a shopping cart - as the customer surfs our
 * e-commerce Web site, this bean stores all the
 * products and quantities he or she is interested in.
 *
 * A quote consists of a series of line items.  Each
 * line item represents one particular product the
 * customer wants, as well as a quantity for that
 * product.
 *
 * The distinction between a quote and an order is that
 * a quote is only temporary and in-memory (hence a
 * stateful session bean), whereas an order is a
 * persistent record (hence an entity bean).  This
 * quote bean is smart enough to know how to transform
 * itself into an order (via the purchase() method).
 *
 * This bean could easily be extended to include other
 * things, such as:
 * - Shipping charges.
 * - Comments or special instructions the user gives.
 */
public class QuoteBean implements SessionBean {

    private SessionContext ctx;

    //-------------------------------------------------
    // Begin Stateful Session Bean Conversational State
    // fields
    //
    // (Conversational state is non-transient, and
    // is perserved during passivation and activation)
    //-------------------------------------------------

    /*
     * The customer this quote belongs to.
     */
    private Customer customer;

    /*
     * The line items that constitute this quote
     */
    private Vector lineItems;
```

Source 14.5 QuoteBean.java (continues).

```
/*
 * The subtotal (price before taxes) of the goods
 */
private double subTotal;

/*
 * The taxes on the goods
 */
private double taxes;

//---------------------------------------------------
// End Stateful Session Bean Conversational State
// fields
//---------------------------------------------------


/*
 * These are home objects that we need to find/
 * create EJB Objects.
 *
 * The home objects are not client specific and
 * are not part of the conversational state on
 * behalf of a single client.  Hence they are
 * marked as transient.
 */
private transient QuoteLineItemHome qliHome;
private transient OrderLineItemHome oliHome;
private transient OrderHome orderHome;

public QuoteBean() {
    System.out.println(
        "New Quote Stateful Session Bean created by EJB Container.");
}


//---------------------------------------------------
// Begin internal methods
//---------------------------------------------------


/**
 * For internal use only.  Finds a Home Object
 * using JNDI.
 *
 * Usage example:
 *   findHome("Ecommerce.QuoteLineItemHome")
 */
private EJBHome findHome(String homeName) throws Exception {

    /*
     * Get a reference to the Home Object
```

Source 14.5 QuoteBean.java (continues).

```
        * via JNDI.
        *
        * We rely on app-specific properties
        * to define the Initial Context
        * params which JNDI needs.
        */
       Context initCtx = new InitialContext(ctx.getEnvironment());
       EJBHome home = (EJBHome) initCtx.lookup(homeName);
       return home;
   }


   /**
    * For internal use only.  Generates a unique ID.
    *
    * When we convert this temporary quote into a
    * permanent order, we need to generate unique
    * IDs for the primary keys of the data we create.
    *
    * This is a poor-man's implementation that uses
    * the current system time.  A real deployment
    * should use a more robust method.
    */
   private long uniqueID = System.currentTimeMillis();
   private String makeUniqueID() {
       return Long.toString(uniqueID++);
   }


   /**
    * For internal use only.  Finds a line-item
    * based on a product.
    *
    * @return The matching line item, or null if
    *  not found
    */
   private QuoteLineItem findLineItem(Product prod) throws RemoteException {

       /*
        * Loop through all Line Items
        */
       Enumeration e = lineItems.elements();
       while (e.hasMoreElements()) {
           QuoteLineItem li = (QuoteLineItem) e.nextElement();

           /*
            * Get the Product EJB Object
            * from the line item.
            */
           Product oldProd = li.getProduct();
```

Source 14.5 QuoteBean.java *(continues)*.

```
            /*
             * If the Products match (via
             * EJB Object equivalency) then
             * we've found our Line Item.
             */
            if (oldProd.isIdentical(prod)) {
                return li;
            }
        }

        return null;
    }


    //-------------------------------------------------
    // End internal methods
    //-------------------------------------------------


    //-------------------------------------------------
    // Begin public business methods
    //-------------------------------------------------


    /**
     * Returns the # of items in the quote
     */
    public int getNumberOfItems() throws RemoteException {
        return lineItems.size();
    }


    /**
     * Returns the line items.  Each line item
     * represents a quantity of a single product.
     */
    public Vector getLineItems() throws RemoteException {
        return lineItems;
    }


    /**
     * Adds a product to the quote.
     */
    public void addProduct(Product prod) throws RemoteException,
        QuoteException {

        /*
         * See if a line-item exists for this product already..
         */
        QuoteLineItem li = findLineItem(prod);
```

Source 14.5   QuoteBean.java *(continues)*.

```
        /*
         * If it exists, simply increase the quantity.
         */
        if (li != null) {
            li.setQuantity(li.getQuantity() + 1);
            return;
        }

        /*
         * Otherwise, we need to make a new Quote
         * Line Item.  Use the Quote Line Item
         * Home Object to create a new Quote Line
         * Item EJB Object.
         */
        try {
            li = qliHome.create(prod);
            lineItems.addElement(li);
        }
        catch (CreateException e) {
            throw new QuoteException("Could not create line item: " +
            e.toString());
        }
    }

    /**
     * Call to adjust the quantity of a product.
     * If the quantity is 0, the product is removed.
     *
     * @exception QuoteException thrown if Product
     * doesn't exist.
     */
    public void setProductQuantity(Product prod, int quantity) throws
        QuoteException, RemoteException {
        QuoteLineItem li = findLineItem(prod);
        if (li != null) {
            if (quantity > 0) {
                li.setQuantity(quantity);
            }
            else {
                lineItems.removeElement(findLineItem(prod));
            }

            return;
        }

        throw new QuoteException("No such Product in Quote!");
    }
```

Source 14.5 QuoteBean.java (continues).

```java
    /**
     * Empties the quote
     */
    public void clear() throws RemoteException {
        /*
         * Remove each Quote Line Item
         * EJB Object
         */
        for (int i=0; i < lineItems.size(); i++) {
            QuoteLineItem li = (QuoteLineItem) lineItems.elementAt(i);
            try {
                li.remove();
            }
            catch (Exception e) {
                e.printStackTrace();
            }
        }

        /*
         * Reset quote fields
         */
        lineItems = new Vector();
        taxes = 0;
        subTotal = 0;
    }

    /**
     * Returns the customer we're quoting.
     */
    public Customer getCustomer() throws RemoteException {
        return customer;
    }

    /**
     * Returns the subtotal price that has been
     * previously set by setSubtotal().
     */
    public double getSubtotal() throws RemoteException {
        return subTotal;
    }

    /**
     * Sets the subtotal price.
     *
     * Our external pricer bean is responsible for
     * calculating the subtotal.  It calculates it
     * based on customer discounts (and can be
     * extended to include other rules as well).
     */
```

Source 14.5 QuoteBean.java *(continues)*.

```java
public void setSubtotal(double subTotal) throws RemoteException {
    this.subTotal = subTotal;
}

/**
 * Returns the taxes computed for this Quote.
 */
public double getTaxes() throws RemoteException {
    return taxes;
}

/**
 * Sets the taxes for this Quote.
 */
public void setTaxes(double taxes) throws RemoteException {
    this.taxes = taxes;
}

/**
 * Returns the total price.  Total Price
 * is computed from:
 *  1) Subtotal price
 *  2) Tax
 */
public double getTotalPrice() throws RemoteException {
    return subTotal + taxes;
}

/**
 * Converts this temporary quote into a
 * permanent, persistent order.  When the
 * user clicks the "Purchase" button on the
 * Web site, a servlet will call this method.
 *
 * @throw QuoteException thrown if no items in quote
 */
public Order purchase() throws RemoteException, QuoteException {

    /*
     * Find home objects via JNDI, so we
     * can create an order and its
     * constituent order line items.
     */
    try {
        if (oliHome == null)
            oliHome = (OrderLineItemHome)
                findHome("Ecommerce.OrderLineItemHome");
```

Source 14.5   QuoteBean.java *(continues)*.

```
        if (orderHome == null)
            orderHome = (OrderHome) findHome("Ecommerce.OrderHome");
    }
    catch (Exception e) {
        throw new RemoteException(e.toString());
    }

    /*
     * Make a unique ID for the order
     */
    String orderID = makeUniqueID();

    /*
     * Make a new persistent Order.
     */
    Order order = null;
    try {
        order = orderHome.create(orderID, customer);
        order.setSubtotal(subTotal);
        order.setTaxes(taxes);
    }
    catch (Exception e) {
        e.printStackTrace();
        throw new QuoteException("Error generating an order: " +
            e.toString());
    }

    /*
     * Convert each of our quote's line
     * items into permanent, persistent
     * order line items.
     */
    try {
        Vector orderLineItems = new Vector();

        /*
         * For each quote line item...
         */
        for (int i=0; i < lineItems.size(); i++) {

            /*
             * Extract the fields from
             * the Quote Line Item...
             */
            QuoteLineItem qli =
              (QuoteLineItem) lineItems.elementAt(i);
            Product prod = qli.getProduct();
            int quantity = qli.getQuantity();
            double discount = qli.getDiscount();
```

Source 14.5 QuoteBean.java *(continues)*.

```
                  /*
                   * And shove the fields into
                   * a new Order Line Item.
                   */
                  String id = makeUniqueID();
                  OrderLineItem oli = oliHome.create(id, order, prod, quantity,
                      discount);
              }
          }
          catch (Exception e) {
              e.printStackTrace();
              throw new QuoteException("Error generating an order line items: "
                  + e.toString());
          }

          return order;
      }

      //-------------------------------------------------
      // End public business methods
      //-------------------------------------------------


      //-------------------------------------------------
      // Begin EJB-Required methods.  The methods below
      // are called by the Container, and never called by
      // client code.
      //-------------------------------------------------


      /**
       * Associates this Bean instance with a particular
       * context.
       */
      public void setSessionContext(SessionContext ctx) throws RemoteException {
          System.out.println("Quote.setSessionContext called");
          this.ctx = ctx;

          /*
           * Get the QuoteLineItemHome Home Object
           * so we can create Line Items.
           */
          try {
              this.qliHome = (QuoteLineItemHome)
                  findHome("Ecommerce.QuoteLineItemHome");
          }
          catch (Exception e) {
              throw new RemoteException(
                  "Could not retrieve Quote Line Item Home Object: " +
                  e.toString());
          }
      }
```

Source 14.5 QuoteBean.java *(continues)*.

```java
/**
 * The container calls this method directly after
 * activating this instance.  You should acquire
 * any needed resources.
 */
public void ejbActivate() throws RemoteException {
    System.out.println("Quote.ejbActivate() called.");
}


/**
 * The container calls this method directly before
 * passivating this instance.  You should release
 * resources acquired during ejbActivate().
 */
public void ejbPassivate() throws RemoteException {
    System.out.println("Quote.ejbPassivate() called.");
}


/**
 * This is the initialization method that
 * corresponds to the create() method in the
 * Home Interface.
 *
 * When the client calls the Home Object's
 * create() method, the Home Object then calls
 * this ejbCreate() method.
 */
public void ejbCreate(Customer customer) throws CreateException,
    RemoteException {
    System.out.println("Quote.ejbCreate(" + customer + ") called");

    this.customer = customer;
    this.lineItems = new Vector();
    this.subTotal = 0;
    this.taxes = 0;
}


/**
 * Removes this quote, and hence all client-
 * specific state.
 *
 * In our example, there is really no way for
 * the client to 'abort' the quote, so the EJB
 * Container will call this when the Session
 * times out.
 */
public void ejbRemove() throws RemoteException {
    System.out.println("Quote.ejbRemove() called.");
```

Source 14.5 QuoteBean.java *(continues)*.

```
        /*
         * Remove all the Line Items that are
         * part of the quote.  We want to remove
         * the Line Items because an Quote is
         * made up of unique Line Items, which
         * other quotes cannot use.
         *
         * (For you UML fans, this is
         *  Composition, rather than
         *  Aggregation).
         */
        Enumeration e = lineItems.elements();
        while (e.hasMoreElements()) {
            try {
                QuoteLineItem li = (QuoteLineItem) e.nextElement();
                li.remove();
            }
            catch (Exception ex) {
                // Ignore exceptions. EJB Container may
                // have removed the Line Items already
                // due to Session timeout.
            }
        }

        /*
         * Don't remove the Customer, since the
         * Customer can be re-used over and over
         * again in different Quotes.
         *
         * (For you UML fans, this is
         *  Aggregation, rather than
         *  Composition).
         */
    }

    //--------------------------------------------------
    // End EJB-Required methods
    //--------------------------------------------------
}
```

Source 14.5 QuoteBean.java *(continued)*.

The first thing to notice is our three transient Home Object fields. These fields will not be persisted as part of the conversational state. The fields are as follows:

- A Quote Line Item Home Object for creating new Quote Line Items. We need to create a Quote Line Item whenever the client adds a Product to our Quote for which we don't already have a Line Item. If we already have a Line Item, we'll increase that Line Item's quantity.

■ An Order Line Item Home Object for transforming the Quote Line Items into permanent Order Line Items in the *purchase()* method.

■ An Order Home Object for transforming the Quote into a permanent Order in the *purchase()* method.

When our bean is context switched in via *ejbActivate()*, these three fields will not be set by the container. We must manually refind the Home Objects. This is done via the private *findHome()* method—a convenience method we write that will find a generic Home Object for us.

As with the Order entity bean, when our Quote is removed via *ejbRemove()*, all the line items are removed. This same process happens when the Quote's *clear()* method is called to clear out the quote. Note that we don't remove the Customer referenced by the Quote because the Customer can be reused over and over again for many different quotes.

QuoteHome.java

Next, we'll write the home interface used to create new quotes or find existing quotes. Our home interface is in *QuoteHome.java*, and it is shown in Source 14.6.

```
package com.wiley.compBooks.ecommerce;

import javax.ejb.*;
import java.rmi.RemoteException;
import java.util.Enumeration;
import java.util.Date;

/**
 * This is the home interface for Quote.  This interface
 * is implemented by the EJB Server's glue-code tools -
 * the implemented object is called the Home Object and
 * serves as a factory for EJB Objects.
 *
 * One create() method is in this Home Interface, which
 * corresponds to the ejbCreate() method in the Quote file.
 */
public interface QuoteHome extends EJBHome {

    /*
     * This method creates the EJB Object.
     *
     * Notice that the Home Interface returns an
     * EJB Object, whereas the Bean returns void.
     * This is because the EJB Container is responsible
```

Source 14.6 QuoteHome.java *(continues)*.

```
    * for generating the EJB Object, whereas the Bean
    * is responsible for initialization.
    *
    * @param customer The Customer for this Quote
    *
    * @return The newly created EJB Object.
    */
   public Quote create(Customer customer) throws CreateException,
       RemoteException;
}
```

Source 14.6 QuoteHome.java *(continued)*.

Our home interface exposes a single method to create a new Quote EJB Object. It takes a customer as a parameter because the quote (aka shopping cart) needs to be associated with a particular customer. Our login servlet will call this *create()* method when the user first logs in, and that quote will stay with the user throughout his or her visit to our store.

QuoteException.java

Finally, we have a custom exception class, *QuoteException.java*, for indicating problems that occur in our Quote bean. The code is in Source 14.7.

```
package com.wiley.compBooks.ecommerce;

/**
 * Exceptions thrown by Quote
 */
public class QuoteException extends Exception {

    public QuoteException() {
        super();
    }

    public QuoteException(Exception e) {
        super(e.toString());
    }

    public QuoteException(String s) {
        super(s);
    }
}
```

Source 14.7 QuoteException.java.

Table 14.2 Deployment Descriptor Settings for QuoteBean

DEPLOYMENT DESCRIPTOR SETTING	VALUE
Bean home name	Ecommerce.QuoteHome
Enterprise bean class name	com.wiley.compBooks.ecommerce.QuoteBean
Home interface class name	com.wiley.compBooks.ecommerce.QuoteHome
Remote interface class name	com.wiley.compBooks.ecommerce.Quote
Environment properties	<empty>
Re-entrant	false
Stateful or stateless	STATEFUL_SESSION
Session timeout	15 minutes
Transaction isolation level	TRANSACTION_READ_UNCOMMITTED
Transaction attribute	TX_SUPPORTS
Run-as mode	CLIENT_IDENTITY

The Deployment Descriptor

Now that we've written our bean code, we need to specify our bean's declarative properties in a deployment descriptor. The descriptor values are in Table 14.2.

As with our Quote Line Item bean, we do not perform any persistent operations, and we do not anticipate any concurrency issues. Hence we have no need for transactional support. Hence, we use the weakest isolation level, TRANSACTION_READ_UNCOMMITTED, and support transactions if they are already occurring but do not require transactions.

The Pricer Stateless Session Bean

One of the requirements that we laid out for our e-commerce architecture in Chapter 12 is support for customized pricing. A customized price is a specialized price computed from discounts, bulk purchases, and other factors.

The best way to have pricing behavior in an extensible manner is to externalize the entire pricing logic into its own enterprise bean. Thus, we have the concept of a Pricer—a component that takes a price quote as input and calculates the price of that quote based on a set of *pricing rules*. A pricing rule might be "Customer

X gets a 5% discount" or "If you purchase 10 motherboards you get a 15% discount." These pricing rules could be read in from a database, or set via properties.

Internally, our Pricer will take a Quote stateful session bean as input and compute the subtotal (before taxes) of that Quote. It figures out the subtotal by computing a discount for each Quote Line Item and subtracting the discounts from the total price.

Our Pricer bean is a business logic provider—it will work on any Quote, and it holds no client-specific state. It is not a persistent object (it would not make sense to save a Pricer because a Pricer simply performs logic and holds no state). This means our Pricer fits into the EJB world best as a stateless session bean.

Let's take a look at the implementation.

Pricer.java

First, we'll design our Pricer's remote interface, shown in Source 14.8 as *Pricer.java*.

We have one business method—*price()*—that takes a Quote and prices it. *price()* will set the individual pricing fields of the Quote for us. Therefore, it returns nothing.

```java
package com.wiley.compBooks.ecommerce;

import javax.ejb.*;
import java.rmi.RemoteException;
import java.rmi.Remote;

/**
 * These are the business logic methods exposed publicly
 * by PricerBean.
 *
 * This interface is what clients operate on when they
 * interact with beans. The container vendor will
 * implement this interface; the implementation object is
 * called the EJB Object, which delegates invocations to
 * the actual bean.
 */
public interface Pricer extends EJBObject {

    /**
     * Computes the price of a set of goods
     */
    public void price(Quote quote) throws RemoteException, PricerException;
}
```

Source 14.8 Pricer.java.

PricerBean.java

Next, we'll write the implementation of our Pricer's business rules. The code for the bean implementation is in *PricerBean.java*, depicted in Source 14.9.

Because our bean holds no state whatsoever, most of our EJB required methods are blank. We have one public business logic method—*price()*—which computes the price of a quote. *price()* calls two private helper methods, *priceSubtotal()* and *priceTaxes()*.

```java
package com.wiley.compBooks.ecommerce;

import javax.ejb.*;
import java.rmi.RemoteException;
import java.util.*;

/**
 * Stateless Session Bean that computes prices based
 * on a set of pricing rules.  The pricing rules are
 * deployed with the bean as environment properties.
 */
public class PricerBean implements SessionBean {

    // Constants used for reading properties
    public static final String ENV_DISCOUNT = "DISCOUNT_";
    public static final String ENV_TAX_RATE = "TAX_RATE";

    /*
     * Although this is a stateless session bean, we
     * do have state - the session context.  Remember
     * that stateless session beans can store state; they
     * just can't store state on behalf of particular
     * clients.
     */
    private SessionContext ctx;

    //-----------------------------------------------------
    // Begin business methods
    //-----------------------------------------------------

    /**
     * Computes the total price of a quote.  This includes
     * subtotal and taxes.  Sets the appropriate quote
     * fields.  We expose this coarse-grained method to
     * avoid network round trips for pricing individual
     * parts of a quote.
     */
```

Source 14.9   PricerBean.java *(continues)*.

```java
public void price(Quote quote) throws PricerException, RemoteException {
    priceSubtotal(quote);
    priceTaxes(quote);
}

/**
 * Computes the subtotal price for a set of products the
 * customer is interested in.  The subtotal takes into
 * account the price of each product the customer wants,
 * the quantity of each product, and any discounts the
 * customer gets.  However, the subtotal ignores taxes.
 *
 * @param quote All the data needed to compute the
 * subtotal is in this parameter.
 */
private void priceSubtotal(Quote quote) throws PricerException,
    RemoteException {
    System.out.println("PricerBean.priceSubtotal() called");

    /*
     * Customers with certain names get discounts.
     * The discount rules are stored in the
     * environment properties that the bean is
     * deployed with.
     *
     * Get the name of this customer.
     */
    Customer customer = quote.getCustomer();
    String customerName = customer.getName();

    double percentDiscount = 0;
    try {
      for (int i=0; ; i++) {

        /*
         * Get the next discount equation from
         * the environment properties.  A
         * discount equation has the form
         * "<name>=<% discount>".  For example,
         * "Ed Roman=50" means that the
         * Customer whose name is "Ed Roman"
         * gets a 50% discount.
         */
        String discount = (String) ctx.getEnvironment().get(ENV_DISCOUNT
            + i);

        /*
         * Break the equation up into
```

Source 14.9 PricerBean.java *(continues)*.

```
                    * customer name, discount
                    */
                   StringTokenizer tokens = new StringTokenizer(discount, "=",
                       false);
                   String discountCustomerName = tokens.nextToken();
                   percentDiscount =
                       Double.valueOf(tokens.nextToken()).doubleValue();

                   /*
                    * If this discount applies to this
                    * customer, then stop.  Otherwise,
                    * move on to the next discount
                    * equation.
                    */
                   if (!discountCustomerName.equals(customerName)) {
                       continue;
                   }

                   System.out.println("Pricer.priceSubtotal(): " + customerName +
                       " gets a " + percentDiscount + "% discount.");
               }
           }
           catch (Exception e) {
               System.out.println("Pricer.priceSubtotal(): " + customerName +
                   " doesn't get a discount.");
           }

           /*
            * Now we know how much discount to apply.  The
            * next step is to apply the discount to each
            * product the customer is interested in.
            *
            * We need to get the price and quantity of each
            * product the customer* wants.  The quote object
            * stores this information in individual quote
            * line items.  Each line item has price and
            * quantity information for a single product.
            */

           /*
            * First, get the Line Items contained within the
            * Quote.
            */
           Enumeration lineItems = quote.getLineItems().elements();

           /*
            * Compute the subtotal
            */
```

Source 14.9 PricerBean.java *(continues)*.

```
        double subTotal = 0;
        try {
            /*
             * For each line item...
             */
            while (lineItems.hasMoreElements()) {
                QuoteLineItem li = (QuoteLineItem) lineItems.nextElement();

                /*
                 * Get the price of the line item...
                 */
                double basePrice = li.getBasePrice();

                /*
                 * Set the discount for this line item...
                 */
                li.setDiscount(basePrice * percentDiscount);

                /*
                 * Apply the discount...
                 */
                double aggregatePrice =
                basePrice - (basePrice * percentDiscount);

                /*
                 * And add the price to the subtotal.
                 */
                subTotal += aggregatePrice;
            }

            quote.setSubtotal(subTotal);
        }
        catch (Exception e) {
            throw new PricerException(e.toString());
        }
    }

    /**
     * Computes the taxes on a quote.
     * Since the taxes are based on the subtotal, we assume
     * that the subtotal has already been calculated.
     */
    private void priceTaxes(Quote quote) throws PricerException,
        RemoteException {
        System.out.println("PricerBean.priceTaxes() called");

        Properties props = ctx.getEnvironment();
```

Source 14.9 PricerBean.java *(continues)*.

```
        /*
         * Compute the taxes
         */
        String taxRateStr = (String) ctx.getEnvironment().get(ENV_TAX_RATE);
        double taxRate = Double.valueOf(taxRateStr).doubleValue();
        double subTotal = quote.getSubtotal();

        quote.setTaxes(taxRate * subTotal);
    }

    //-----------------------------------------------------
    // End business methods
    //-----------------------------------------------------


    //-----------------------------------------------------
    // Begin EJB-required methods.  The methods below are
    // called by the Container, and never called by client
    // code.
    //-----------------------------------------------------

    public void ejbCreate() throws RemoteException {
        System.out.println("ejbCreate() called.");
    }

    public void ejbRemove() {
        System.out.println("ejbRemove() called.");
    }

    public void ejbActivate() {
        System.out.println("ejbActivate() called.");
    }

    public void ejbPassivate() {
        System.out.println("ejbPassivate() called.");
    }

    public void setSessionContext(SessionContext ctx) {
        System.out.println("setSessionContext() called");
        this.ctx = ctx;
    }

    //-----------------------------------------------------
    // End EJB-required methods
    //-----------------------------------------------------
}
```

Source 14.9 PricerBean.java *(continued)*.

PricerBean.priceSubtotal()

Our Pricer bean performs only one kind of discount—a *customer-specific discount*. These are discounts a preferred customer receives, such as a percentage discount on the entire Quote.

The correlation between discounts and customers is data-driven via the bean's deployed environment properties. You can use the properties file to customize the bean's pricing rules.

The customer-specific discount is computed in the following way:

1. Retrieve the customer's name from the Customer object.
2. Read all the customer-specific discounts from the environment properties.
3. If a discount applies to this Customer, reduce the price based on that discount.

PricerBean.priceTaxes()

Once we've got the subtotal, we compute the tax on that subtotal. The tax rate is customizable and is also set in the bean's deployed environment properties. We read the tax rate in and apply it to the subtotal, yielding the tax amount. This tax amount is set on the Quote.

Once we've set the taxes, the *price()* method is finished. We could easily add more steps as well, such as pricing the shipping.

PricerHome.java

Next, we'll write our Pricer bean's home interface. The home interface is used by clients as a factory for Pricer EJB objects. The code is in *PricerHome.java*, shown in Source 14.10.

The simple *create()* method makes a new Pricer EJB Object. As with all stateless session beans, there can be only one *create()* method, which takes no parameters.

PricerException.java

Our last Java class for our Pricer bean is a custom exception class, which is used by our bean when throwing bean-specific application-level exceptions. The code is in *PricerException.java*, shown in Source 14.11.

```java
package com.wiley.compBooks.ecommerce;

import javax.ejb.*;
import java.rmi.RemoteException;

/**
 * This is the home interface for Pricer.  The
 * container implements this interface; the
 * implementation object is called the Home Object
 * and serves as a factory for EJB Objects.
 */
public interface PricerHome extends EJBHome {

   /*
    * This method creates the EJB Object.
    *
    * @return The newly created EJB Object.
    */
  Pricer create() throws RemoteException, CreateException;
}
```

Source 14.10 PricerHome.java.

```java
package com.wiley.compBooks.ecommerce;

/**
 * Exceptions thrown by Pricer
 */
public class PricerException extends Exception {

    public PricerException() {
        super();
    }

    public PricerException(Exception e) {
        super(e.toString());
    }

    public PricerException(String s) {
        super(s);
    }
}
```

Source 14.11 PricerException.java.

The Deployment Descriptor

Now that we've written our Pricer bean code, we need to declare properties about our bean in a deployment descriptor. The container will inspect the deployment descriptor and use its values to determine the proper ways to manage our bean. The deployment descriptor is shown in Table 14.3.

Because our Pricer is working with nonpersistent quote objects, and because the quote objects should not be shared between users, we can afford to use the simple TX_SUPPORTS attribute, which will attach our bean to an optional existing transaction in which the client may be running. We support the weakest isolation level as well—TRANSACTION_READ_UNCOMMITTED.

Our Pricer's pricing rules are customizable by the environment properties. Some sample properties are listed in Table 14.4. Our customer-specific discounts are simple equations. For example, the setting "Ed Roman=50" indicates that Ed Roman should get a 50% discount.

The tax rate property is a simple float. Our example shows that all users pay a 5% tax on their orders.

By externalizing these rules into property files, we as bean providers can reuse this pricing bean for other customers. A more robust pricer might make use of

Table 14.3 Deployment Descriptor Settings for PricerBean

DEPLOYMENT DESCRIPTOR SETTING	VALUE
Bean home name	Ecommerce.PricerHome
Enterprise bean class name	com.wiley.compBooks.ecommerce.PricerBean
Home interface class name	com.wiley.compBooks.ecommerce.PricerHome
Remote interface class name	com.wiley.compBooks.ecommerce.Pricer
Environment properties	<empty>
Re-entrant	false
Stateful or stateless	STATELESS_SESSION
Session timeout	15 minutes
Transaction isolation level	TRANSACTION_READ_UNCOMMITTED
Transaction attribute	TX_SUPPORTS
Run-as mode	CLIENT_IDENTITY

Table 14.4 Environment Properties for PricerBean

ENVIRONMENT PROPERTY SETTING	VALUE
DISCOUNT_1	"Ed Roman=50"
DISCOUNT_2	"James Kao=30"
DISCOUNT_3	"Jonah Probell=20"
TAX_RATE	"0.05"

a database as well, providing advanced pricing functionality and a user interface for manipulating pricing rules.

The Bank Teller Stateless Session Bean

Our final e-commerce bean is a Bank Teller, used for billing the customer after an Order has been generated. A teller represents a "virtual person" with whom you interact to modify a bank account. For example, our Teller will be able to transfer funds from one Bank Account (entity bean) to another.

Our Teller itself is not a persistent object—the notion of "saving" a Teller to disk means nothing. Our Tellers will be stateless method providers, and they will be reusable for multiple clients. Therefore, our Teller fits into the EJB world as a stateless session bean.

The Teller makes extensive interactions with the Bank Account bean described in Chapter 8. At this time, you may want to revisit that chapter to refresh your memory.

Billing Mechanisms

As EJB matures and bean providers become more abundant, you may see billing mechanisms similar to our Teller bean begin to surface. Most likely, they will be in the form of credit card beans that know how to interface with an American Express or VISA system elsewhere.

Because our structure is very modular, we could easily change our deployment to use a different billing system. For example, rather than store the user's bank account information, we'd need to code the user's credit card number in the Customer entity bean. That will allow us to save the user from having to reenter his or her credit card information each time he or she uses our site.

Teller.java

First, we'll write our Teller's remote interface—the interface client code uses to interact with our teller bean. The code is *Teller.java*, shown in Source 14.12.

Notice that almost every Teller method takes an account number as a parameter. This is because our Teller is stateless—it can operate on *any* existing bank account. We also have provided functionality to look up a bank account number if the user has lost it. Of course, in the real world a bank would impose some security restrictions, to verify the user's identity.

```java
package com.wiley.compBooks.ecommerce;

import javax.ejb.*;
import java.rmi.RemoteException;
import java.rmi.Remote;

/**
 * These are the business logic methods exposed publicly
 * by TellerBean.
 *
 * This interface is what clients operate on when they
 * interact with beans. The container vendor will implement
 * this interface; the implementation object is called the
 * EJB Object, which delegates invocations to the actual bean.
 */
public interface Teller extends EJBObject {

    /**
     * Looks up an account number (if you forgot it)
     *
     * @param name Your full name
     */
    public String lookupAccountNumber(String name) throws RemoteException,
        TellerException;

    /**
     * Creates a new account with a starting deposit.
     *
     * @param name Your full name
     * @param initialDeposit The initial starting balance you
     *                       want to deposit.
     *
     * @return Your new account number
     */
```

Source 14.12 Teller.java *(continues)*.

```java
    public String createNewAccount(String yourName, double initialDeposit)
      throws RemoteException, TellerException;

    /**
     * Closes your account.
     *
     * @return The funds left in your account are returned to
     *         you.
     */
    public double closeAccount(String accountNum) throws RemoteException,
    TellerException;

    /**
     * Gets your current balance for an account.
     *
     * @param accountNum the account number string.
     */
    public double getBalance(String accountNum) throws RemoteException,
    TellerException;

    /**
     * Switches names on an account.
     */
    public void changeNames(String accountNum, String newName) throws
    RemoteException, TellerException;

    /**
     * Transfers funds from accountNum1 to accountNum2
     */
    public void transfer(String accountNum1, String accountNum2, double funds)
    throws RemoteException, TellerException;

    /**
     * Withdraws from your account.
     *
     * @exception TellerException thrown if you have
     *            insufficient funds.
     * @return Your withdrawn funds.
     */
    public double withdraw(String accountNum, double funds) throws
    RemoteException, TellerException;

    /**
     * Deposits into your account.
     */
    public void deposit(String accountNum, double funds) throws
    RemoteException, TellerException;
}
```

Source 14.12 Teller.java *(continued)*.

TellerHome.java

Next, we'll write our bank teller's home interface, used by client code as a factory for bank teller EJB objects. The code is in *TellerHome.java*, shown in Source 14.13.

As with all stateless session beans, you cannot customize a bean with *create()* because the bean will not remember your state for the next invocation. Therefore we expose one *create()* method that takes no parameters and returns a new EJB Object.

TellerBean.java

Next, we'll write our teller bean's implementation. The code is in *TellerBean.java*, shown in Source 14.14.

Our Teller bean has a number of interesting facets. For one, we need to store a private home object for creating and finding Bank Account entity beans for us

```
package com.wiley.compBooks.ecommerce;

import javax.ejb.*;
import java.rmi.RemoteException;

/**
 * This is the home interface for TellerBean.  This
 * interface is implemented by the EJB Server's glue-
 * code tools - the implemented object is called the
 * Home Object and serves as a factory for EJB Objects.
 *
 * One create() method is in this Home Interface, which
 * corresponds to the ejbCreate() method in the
 * TellerBean file.
 */
public interface TellerHome extends EJBHome {

    /*
     * This method creates the EJB Object.
     *
     * @return The newly created EJB Object.
     */
    Teller create() throws RemoteException, CreateException;
}
```

Source 14.13 TellerHome.java.

```
package com.wiley.compBooks.ecommerce;

import javax.ejb.*;
import java.rmi.*;
import java.util.*;
import javax.naming.*;

/**
 * Stateless Session Bean that acts as a bank teller,
 * operating a bank.  Behind the scenes, this Teller
 * Bean interacts with the Account entity bean.
 */
public class TellerBean implements SessionBean {

    /*
     * Although this is a stateless session bean,
     * we do have state - the session context, and
     * a home object used to find/create accounts.
     * Remember that stateless session beans can
     * store state, they just can't store state on
     * behalf of particular clients.
     */
    private AccountHome home;
    private SessionContext ctx;

    //-----------------------------------------------
    // Begin internal methods
    //-----------------------------------------------

    /**
     * Finds the Home Object for Bank Accounts.
     */
    private void findHome() throws Exception {
        try {
            /*
             * Get properties from the
             * Session Context.
             */
            Properties props = ctx.getEnvironment();

            /*
             * Get a reference to the AccountHome
             * Object via JNDI.  We need the
             * Account's Home Object to create
             * Accounts.
             *
             * We rely on app-specific properties
             * to define the Initial Context params
```

Source 14.14   TellerBean.java *(continues)*.

```
                    * which JNDI needs.
                    */
                Context initCtx = new InitialContext(props);
                home = (AccountHome) initCtx.lookup("Ecommerce.AccountHome");
            }
        catch (Exception e) {
            e.printStackTrace();
            throw e;
        }
    }


    //------------------------------------------------
    // End internal methods
    //------------------------------------------------


    //------------------------------------------------
    // Begin business methods
    //------------------------------------------------


    /**
     * Private helper method.  Finds an Account Entity
     * Bean based upon its ID.
     */
    private Account findAccountByNumber(String accountID) throws
      TellerException, RemoteException {
        try {
            /*
             * Construct a Primary Key from the
             * passed accountID, and call the
             * Entity Bean Home's default finder
             * method.
             */
            return home.findByPrimaryKey(new AccountPK(accountID));
        }
        catch (FinderException e) {
            e.printStackTrace();
            throw new TellerException(e.toString());
        }
    }


    /**
     * Private helper method.  Finds an Account Entity
     * Bean based on its owner's name.
     */
    private Account findAccountByOwnerName(String name) throws
      TellerException, RemoteException {
        try {
            /*
             * Call our Entity's custom finder
```

Source 14.14 TellerBean.java *(continues)*.

```
             * method that finds by name.
             */
            return home.findByOwnerName(name);
        }
        catch (FinderException e) {
            e.printStackTrace();
            throw new TellerException(e.toString());
        }
    }

    /**
     * Looks up an account number based on your name
     * (perhaps you forgot it).
     *
     * @exception TellerException thrown if error occurs,
     *            such as a name not found.
     * @param name Your full name
     */
    public String lookupAccountNumber(String name) throws RemoteException,
      TellerException {

        /*
         * Get the Account Entity Bean
         */
        Account account = findAccountByOwnerName(name);

        /*
         * Return the value of the getAccountID()
         * accessor method on our Entity Bean.
         */
        return ((AccountPK)account.getPrimaryKey()).accountID;
    }

    /**
     * Creates a new account with a starting deposit.
     *
     * @param name Your full name
     * @param initialDeposit The initial starting balance
     *        you want to deposit.
     *
     * @return Your new account number
     */
    public String createNewAccount(String name, double initialDeposit) throws
      RemoteException, TellerException {
        /*
         * Generate a unique Bank Account Number.  This
         * is a hard problem to solve, in general, with
         * EJB.  We'll see the issues at hand in Chapter
         * 15.  For now, we'll punt and use the System
```

Source 14.14 TellerBean.java (continues).

```
     * Clock to create a unique identifier.  However,
     * note that this will cause our bank account to
     * fail if two accounts are created in the same
     * millisecond.
     */
    String accountNum = Long.toString(System.currentTimeMillis());

    try {
        /*
         * Create a new Account Entity Bean
         */
        Account account = home.create(accountNum, name);

        /*
         * Start the account off with an initial deposit
         */
        account.deposit(initialDeposit);

        /*
         * Return the new account number
         */
        return accountNum;
    }
    catch (CreateException e) {
        e.printStackTrace();
        throw new TellerException("Could not create account: " +
            e.toString());
    }
}

/**
 * Closes your account.
 *
 * @return The funds left in your account are
 *         returned to you.
 */
public double closeAccount(String accountNum) throws RemoteException,
  TellerException {

    /*
     * Find the correct Account Entity Bean
     */
    Account account = findAccountByNumber(accountNum);

    /*
     * Withdraw all the funds from the Entity
     */
    double balance = account.getBalance();
```

Source 14.14 TellerBean.java *(continues)*.

```
        /*
         * Close the account by removing the Entity Bean
         */
        try {
            account.remove();
        }
        catch (RemoveException e) {
            e.printStackTrace();
            throw new TellerException("Could not close account: " +
                e.toString());
        }

        /*
         * Return the remaining funds
         */
        return balance;
    }

    /**
     * Gets your current balance for the account
     * numbered accountNum.
     */
    public double getBalance(String accountNum) throws RemoteException,
      TellerException {

        /*
         * Find the correct Account Entity Bean
         */
        Account account = findAccountByNumber(accountNum);

        /*
         * Get the Entity Bean's balance, and return it
         */
        return account.getBalance();
    }

    /**
     * Switches names on an account.
     */
    public void changeNames(String accountNum, String newName) throws
      RemoteException, TellerException {

        /*
         * Find the correct Account Entity Bean
         */
        Account account = findAccountByNumber(accountNum);

        /*
         * Change the Entity Bean's owner name field
```

Source 14.14 TellerBean.java *(continues)*.

```
        */
      account.setOwnerName(newName);
}


/**
 * Transfers funds from accountNum1 to accountNum2
 */
public void transfer(String accountNum1, String accountNum2, double
   funds) throws RemoteException, TellerException {

    /*
     * Withdraw from account #1 into account #2.
     */
    withdraw(accountNum1, funds);
    deposit(accountNum2, funds);
}


/**
 * Withdraws from your account.
 *
 * @exception TellerException thrown if you have
 *            insufficient funds.
 * @return Your withdrawn funds.
 */
public double withdraw(String accountNum, double amt) throws
   RemoteException, TellerException {

    /*
     * Find the correct Account Entity Bean
     */
    Account account = findAccountByNumber(accountNum);

    /*
     * Withdraw from it
     */
    try {
        return account.withdraw(amt);
    }
    catch (AccountException e) {
        e.printStackTrace();
        throw new TellerException(e);
    }
}

/**
 * Deposits into your account.
 */
public void deposit(String accountNum, double funds) throws
   RemoteException, TellerException {
```

Source 14.14 TellerBean.java *(continues)*.

```
        /*
         * Find the correct Account Entity Bean
         */
        Account account = findAccountByNumber(accountNum);

        /*
         * Deposit into it
         */
        account.deposit(funds);
    }


    //-----------------------------------------------
    // End business methods
    //-----------------------------------------------


    //-----------------------------------------------
    // Begin EJB-required methods.  The methods below
    // are called by the Container and never called
    // by client code.
    //-----------------------------------------------

    public void ejbCreate() throws RemoteException {
        System.out.println("ejbCreate() called.");

        /*
         * Retrieve Home Object for Bank Accounts.
         * If failure, throw a system-level error.
         */
        try {
            findHome();
        }
        catch (Exception e) {
            throw new RemoteException(e.toString());
        }
    }

    public void ejbRemove() {
        System.out.println("ejbRemove() called.");
    }

    public void ejbActivate() {
        System.out.println("ejbActivate() called.");
    }

    public void ejbPassivate() {
        System.out.println("ejbPassivate() called.");
    }
```

Source 14.14 TellerBean.java *(continues)*.

```
    public void setSessionContext(SessionContext ctx) {
        System.out.println("setSessionContext called");
        this.ctx = ctx;
    }


    //-------------------------------------------------
    // End EJB-required methods
    //-------------------------------------------------
}
```

Source 14.14   TellerBean.java *(continued)*.

to work with. Because we're stateless, our bean will never be passivated/activated; it will simply be destroyed when the container's working set is too large. Therefore we don't need to reconstruct the home object on passivation/activation.

Most of the application logic methods involve an initial step of finding the correct Bank Account based on the account number passed into the method. We then delegate calls to the Bank Account object.

Notice our implementation of *transfer()*—it withdraws from one bank account and deposits into another. This is the classic debit-credit problem, which needs a transaction to run securely. If we don't run in a transaction, we might withdraw but not deposit, or we might be in an unknown state. Therefore we'll make sure that this method (as well as the other methods in the bean—they are also critical because we're dealing with money) run in a transaction.

TellerException.java

Our final Java file is a custom exception class, *TellerException.java*, shown in Source 14.15. We use it to report any problems occurring with bank account operations.

The Deployment Descriptor

Now that we've written our Teller bean code, we'll specify the system-level properties on our component by writing a deployment descriptor. The container will inspect the deployment descriptor at runtime to gain information about managing our bean. The deployment descriptor values are shown in Table 14.5.

Our Bank Account needs to run in a transactionally safe mode. Therefore, we require all transactions to run in a transaction via TX_REQUIRED. We also impose the toughest transaction isolation mode—TRANSACTION_SERIALIZABLE. This is necessary because we're performing both read and write operations on

```
package com.wiley.compBooks.ecommerce;

/**
 * Exceptions thrown by Tellers
 */
public class TellerException extends Exception {

    public TellerException() {
        super();
    }

    public TellerException(Exception e) {
        super(e.toString());
    }

    public TellerException(String s) {
        super(s);
    }
}
```

Source 14.15 TellerException.java.

Bank Accounts from our Teller, and because monetary issues are so important to get right. These transaction settings should be applied to our Bank Account bean as well.

Table 14.5 Deployment Descriptor Settings for TellerBean

DEPLOYMENT DESCRIPTOR SETTING	VALUE
Bean home name	TellerHome
Enterprise bean class name	com.wiley.compBooks.entity.Teller.TellerBean
Home interface class name	com.wiley.compBooks.entity.Teller.TellerHome
Remote interface class name	com.wiley.compBooks.entity.Teller.Teller
Environment properties	<empty>
Session timeout	15 minutes
Transaction attribute	TX_REQUIRED
Transaction isolation level	TRANSACTION_SERIALIZABLE
Run-as mode	CLIENT_IDENTITY

Summary

In this chapter, we've written the session beans for our e-commerce deployment. This completes the work we need to do for our business logic tier. In the next chapter, we'll complete our deployment by writing a few Java servlets that make up our presentation tier.

## CHAPTER 15

J2EE in the Real World: Combining Servlets with Enterprise JavaBeans

I n this chapter, you will learn how to tie Java servlets to Enterprise JavaBeans. We'll illustrate these concepts by adding a servlet layer to the e-commerce EJB system we've been developing.

By reading this chapter, you'll see how servlets work, how to partition the servlets into manageable entities, how to tie servlets to enterprise beans, and how to control transactions from servlets. Additionally, we'll look at how to optimize and tune our e-commerce deployment, and we will discuss EJB design strategies.

The Role of Servlets in an EJB Deployment

In the Web-based world, Sun Microsystems promotes two choices for rendering a user interface to browser-based clients: Java applets or thin Java Server Pages / servlets. Applets are interesting because they can be fully functional Java programs (assuming you digitally sign them). Due to their download time, however, large applets are starting to die off in favor of a thin-client scenario. Some applet enthusiasts may argue that HTML does not give the breadth of GUI features needed in a complex interface. But with the advent of DHTML, XML, and other thin-client advances, the GUI functionality of thin clients begins to look very appealing. This is especially true for a business application such as our e-commerce deployment—we shouldn't need anything more than what the flavors of HTML can provide.

There are other benefits of thin-client deployments as well. In a thick-client scenario, RMI's JRMP or IIOP (see Chapter 11) is the transport protocol used.

In a corporate firewall environment, these transports need to tunnel through firewalls to facilitate client/server communication (firewall tunneling is briefly mentioned in Appendix A). Unfortunately, firewall tunneling is very slow because you're performing remote procedure calls over HTTP, a protocol that requires a new connection to be made on every data transfer. Thus, although JRMP and IIOP both tunnel through firewalls, they are inefficient for serious use.

To facilitate a Web-based user interface, we have chosen to use servlets in our deployment. Servlets are networked modules that run within a request/response-oriented server. A request is a call from a client, perhaps remotely located. Requests contain data that the client wants to send to the server. A response is data that the server wants to return to the client to answer the request. A servlet is a Java object that takes a request as input, parses its data, performs some logic, and then issues a response to the client.

Servlets, on the other hand, serve as an HTTP-aware middle layer that resides on the server side. They know how to communicate with both the client, in HTTP, and your enterprise beans, via RMI or IIOP. This makes servlets the ideal technology for Web-based GUI development.

Alternatives to Servlets

There are other mechanisms for Web-based communications as well. For example, both Microsoft's Active Server Pages (ASP) and Sun's Java Server Pages (JSP) provide a script-like environment for performing GUI operations. (JSP is designed as a cross-platform solution; ASP is not, although there are cross-platform implementations that are unsupported by Microsoft.) What advantages do these technologies have over servlets?

To answer this question, let's take a deeper look at how servlets work. Servlets are compiled Java classes—they are not script. When a servlet wants to write HTML back to the client, it must make a method call, such as:

```
response.write("<B>Hi there</B>");
```

In ASP or JSP, you'd put the HTML directly into the script file itself:

```
<B>Hi there</B>
```

With servlets, you have the annoyance of having to code in a *response.write()* whenever you want to send some UI text to the client. With JSP, you simply write the UI directly into the script; however, with JSP, you need to perform extra dancing steps to do any Java operations. Thus, ASP and JSP are very well suited for look-and-feel-centric applications that rely heavily on GUI work, whereas servlets are well suited for logic-centric applications. That is, if your servlet's primary purpose is to dump a UI to the client, it's better modeled as JSP, whereas if your servlet performs computations or other overhead, it's best left as a servlet. In reality, JSP script pages are *compiled* into a Java servlet and then executed, so you're really dealing with the same underlying technology in either scenario.

The great thing about externalizing look-and-feel into JSP is that a Web designer can later modify the script's look and feel without knowing how to write or compile Java programs. This is great for an IT department, and it allows end users to easily customize the flavor of their Web sites. This effectively reduces the maintenance cost of your Web pages.

In the end, most deployments will have a combination of both servlets and JSP:

The logic part of your application should be in servlets or in a combination of servlets and JavaBeans. Note that these are regular JavaBeans—*not* Enterprise JavaBeans (we touch on the differences between JavaBeans and Enterprise JavaBeans in Chapter 1). You can use JavaBeans as a cache for your Enterprise JavaBeans, reducing network round trips.

The look-and-feel part of your application should be externalized into JSP to allow the end user to easily change it. Your JSP could call into the servlets or JavaBeans for performing logic operations.

Unfortunately, JSP currently cannot talk to Enterprise Beans, only to JavaBeans and servlets. Sun Microsystems is promising that the new version of JSP will correct this. For our deployment, we'll stick with straight Java servlets.

Implementing Our Servlets

In Chapter 12, we first designed our servlet architecture. We design a total of seven different servlets composing our presentation tier:

A Login servlet for handling user login

A Web Storefront servlet for presenting the initial main page

Thin-Client Resources

Lots of data is already available on servlets. Rather than repeat what's already been said, we'll concentrate on how our e-commerce servlets are used in an EJB environment. We'll assume that you understand servlet basics. If you're new to this arena, check out the book's accompanying Web site, where we list links to several resources on learning Java servlets. From here on, we'll assume you already have a grasp on servlet basics.

A **Catalog servlet** for browsing the available products

A **Product Base servlet** for containing all the available products

A **Product Detail servlet** for displaying the specifics of a particular product

A **Quote View servlet** for final quantity modifications before ordering the products

A **Purchasing servlet** for completing the transaction when an order has been generated

Let's take a look at the servlets in more detail.

The Login Servlet

The login servlet will be the first servlet the user deals with when going to Jasmine's Web site. It's responsible for reading in the user's name and password, then retrieving the Customer entity bean that matches that name.

If the passwords match, a new Quote stateful session bean is started on behalf of this customer. The customer information is stored in the Quote so that the quote will be associated with a specific customer—used for billing and shipping information. As the user navigates the store, the Quote will serve as a cache that the user can add products to and remove products from.

If the passwords don't match, an error is displayed and the user is given another chance to enter his or her information.

We'll perform all the authentication through querying the fields on existing customer entity beans. This is a fairly secure means of authentication. If we're worried that someone will intercept the client's password over the Internet, we could impose encryption via the Secure Socket Layer (SSL) when sending the password over HTTP.

Let's take a look at the implementation. It resides in *LoginServlet.java*, shown in Source 15.1.

There are three important methods in our Login servlet: *init()*, *doGet()*, and *writeForm()*.

init() is called automatically by the underlying servlet engine when it kicks our servlet into memory. *init()* is called only once, and it performs one-time initialization that is not client-specific. In our *init()*, we perform JNDI initialization and use JNDI to look up a couple of home objects. We store these home objects in local variables, so we can use them over and over again when any client connects and calls our *doGet()* method.

doGet() is responsible for processing page hits from users. If the user is connecting for the first time (i.e., if there are no form results coming back to us),

```java
package com.wiley.compBooks.ecommerce;

import java.io.*;
import java.util.*;
import javax.servlet.*;
import javax.servlet.http.*;
import javax.naming.*;

/**
 * This is the very first servlet the client deals with.
 * It's a Login authentication servlet.  It asks the user
 * for his or her name and password, and it verifies that data
 * against the Customer entity beans stored in a database.
 * If the user authenticates properly, a new Quote is saved
 * in his or her HttpSession object, and the user can begin to add
 * items to the quote and shop around.
 */
public class LoginServlet extends HttpServlet {

  /*
   * Customer home object for authenticating user
   */
  private CustomerHome customerHome;

  /*
   * Quote home object for creating a new quote when
   * the user logs in.
   */
  private QuoteHome quoteHome;

  /**
   * The servlet engine calls this method once to
   * initialize a servlet instance.
   *
   * In the body of this method, we acquire all the
   * EJB home objects we'll need later.
   */
  public void init(ServletConfig config) throws ServletException {

    super.init(config);

    try {
        /*
         * Get the JNDI initialization parameters.
         * We externalize these settings to the
         * servlet properties file to allow end
         * users to dynamically reconfigure their
         * environment without recompilation.
         */
```

Source 15.1 LoginServlet.java *(continues)*.

```
        String initCtxFactory =
            getInitParameter(Context.INITIAL_CONTEXT_FACTORY);
        String providerURL = getInitParameter(Context.PROVIDER_URL);

        /*
         * Add the JNDI init parameters to a
         * properties object.
         */
          Properties env = new Properties();
        env.put(Context.INITIAL_CONTEXT_FACTORY, initCtxFactory);
        env.put(Context.PROVIDER_URL, providerURL);

        /*
         * Get the initial JNDI context using the above
         * startup params.
         */
          Context ctx = new InitialContext(env);

        /*
         * Look up the Home Objects we need via JNDI
         */
        customerHome = (CustomerHome) ctx.lookup("Ecommerce.CustomerHome");
        quoteHome = (QuoteHome) ctx.lookup("Ecommerce.QuoteHome");
    }
    catch (Exception e) {
        log(e);
        throw new ServletException(e.toString());
    }
}

/**
 * Writes the Login Screen (private use only)
 *
 * @param showError true means show an error b/c client
 *          was not authenticated last time.
 */
private void writeForm(HttpServletResponse response, boolean showError)
    throws IOException {
    /*
     * Now, we write the response.  Set content-type
     * header, indicating that we will be writing in
     * HTML.
     */
    response.setContentType("text/html");
    PrintWriter out = response.getWriter();

    out.println(
        "<html>" +
        "<head><title> Computer Login </title></head>" +
```

Source 15.1 LoginServlet.java *(continues)*.

```
            "<body  bgcolor=\"#ffffff\">" +
            "<center>" +
            "<hr> <br>  " +
            "<h1>" +
            "<font size=\"+3\" color=\"red\">Jasmine's </font>" +
            "<font size=\"+3\" color=\"purple\">Computer </font>" +
            "<font size=\"+3\" color=\"green\">Parts</font>" +
            "</h1>" +
            "</center>" +
            "<br>   <hr> <br>  ");

        /*
         * Print out the total and the form for the user.
         */
        out.println(
            "<p>Please Login<p>" +

            "<form action=\"" +
            response.encodeUrl("/servlet/login") +
            "\" method=\"get\">" +

            "<table>" +
            "<tr>" +
            "<td><strong>Name:</strong></td>" +
            "<td><input type=\"text\" name=\"Login\"" +
            "value=\"Ed Roman\" size=\"19\"></td>" +
            "</tr>" +

            "<tr>" +
            "<td><strong>Password:</strong></td>" +
            "<td>" +
            "<input type=\"text\" name=\"Password\" " +
            "value=\"password\" size=\"19\"></td>" +
            "</tr>" +

            "<tr>" +
            "<td></td>" +
            "<td><input type=\"submit\"" +
            "value=\"Submit Information\"></td>" +
            "</tr>" +
            "</table>" +
            "</form>");

        if (showError == true) {
            out.println(
                "<p><strong>Could not log in!" +
                " Please try again.</strong><p>");
        }
```

Source 15.1 LoginServlet.java *(continues)*.

```
        out.println("</body></html>");
        out.close();
}


/**
 * The servlet engine calls this method when the user's
 * desktop browser sends an HTTP GET request.
 */
public void doGet (HttpServletRequest request, HttpServletResponse
    response) throws ServletException, IOException {

    /*
     * Set up the user's HttpSession
     */
    HttpSession session = request.getSession(true);

    /*
     * Retrieve the login name / password from the
     * URL string.
     */
    String loginName = request.getParameter("Login");
    String password = request.getParameter("Password");

    /*
     * If user has not tried to log in yet, present
     * him with the login screen.
     */
    if ( (loginName == null) || (password == null) ) {
      writeForm(response, false);
    }

    /*
     * Otherwise, the user has been to this screen
     * already and has entered some information.
     * Verify that information.
     */
    else {
        /*
         * Find all Customer Entity Beans which
         * match the loginname
         */
        Enumeration customers = null;
        try {
            customers = customerHome.findByName(loginName);
        }
        catch (Exception e) {
            log(e);
            throw new ServletException(e.toString());
        }
```

Source 15.1 LoginServlet.java *(continues)*.

```
          /*
           * For each customer, check if the passwords
           * match.
           */
          while (customers.hasMoreElements()) {
              Customer c = (Customer) customers.nextElement();

              /*
               * Do a little sanity check to make
               * sure the customer has a password.
               */
              String verifiedPassword = c.getPassword();
              if (verifiedPassword == null) {
                  System.err.println("Error: Customer " + c.getName() +
                      " does not have a password registered.");
                  break;
              }

              /*
               * If the passwords match, make a new
               * Quote session bean and add it to
               * the user's HttpSession object.  When
               * the user navigates to other servlets,
               * the other servlets can access the
               * HttpSession to get the user's Quote.
               */
              if (verifiedPassword.equals(password)) {
                  try {
                      Quote quote = quoteHome.create(c);
                      session.putValue("quote", quote);

                      /*
                       * Call the welcome screen servlet
                       */
                      response.sendRedirect(response.encodeUrl("/servlet/wsf"));
                      return;
                  }
                  catch (ClassCastException e) {
                      log(e);
                      throw new ServletException(e.toString());
                  }
                  catch (Exception e) {
                      log(e);
                      throw new ServletException(e.toString());
                  }
              }
          }
```

Source 15.1 LoginServlet.java *(continues)*.

```
      /*
       * If there was no match, the user is
       * not authenticated.  Present another
       * login screen to the user, with an error
       * message indicating that he or she is not
       * authenticated.
       */
      writeForm(response, true);
  }
}

private void log(Exception e) {
    getServletConfig().getServletContext().log(e, "");
}

public String getServletInfo() {
  return "The Login servlet verifies a user.";
}
}
```

Source 15.1   LoginServlet.java *(continued)*.

we simply print the form out. This is what the *writeForm()* method does. The *writeForm()* method prints out some HTML to the client, along with a couple of input tags. The input tags will look like text input boxes to the end user, as shown in Figure 15.1.

When the user enters data into the input boxes and submits them, our *doGet()* method will be called again, only this time, we'll have a username and password parameter passed back to us from the client. We extract the parameters from the request and then perform an EJB *find()* on the Customer home object, which we saved from *init()*. The finder method will return all Customers whose names match the input text. We then query the password on each of the returned EJB objects. If the passwords match, the user is authenticated. Otherwise, we print out the form again, only this time indicating an error message as well.

If the client is authenticated, we use the Quote home object to create a new Quote EJB object for this user. We then store the Quote in the user's servlet session. This is a per-client presentation tier stateful cache that we can exploit to store the current Quote. When the user connects again later, no matter which servlet he or she hits, we can extract the current Quote from the servlet session. Thus, all of our servlets will be nonclient-specific, being able to service any client. They'll figure out which client browser is connecting to the Web server by querying the Quote stateful session bean, stored in the servlet session.

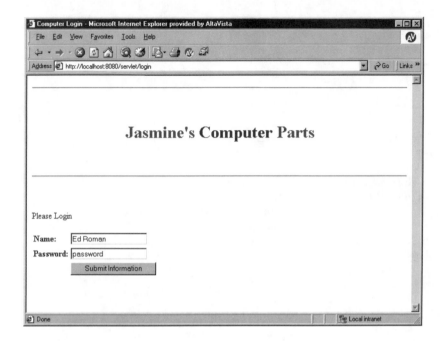

Figure 15.1 The login screen.

Once the user has been authenticated and his or her Quote has been created, we direct the user to the next servlet—the Web Storefront.

 For clarity, this chapter's servlets perform a great deal of string concatenation when writing HTML. Each concatenation results in an expensive method call. In a performance-intensive deployment, you'd want to use a *StringBuffer* instead, as follows:

```
StringBuffer buf = new StringBuffer();
buf.append("<html>");
buf.append("<head>...
...
out.println(buf.toString());
```

The Web Storefront Servlet

Once the user gets through the Login servlet, he or she will be redirected to the Web Storefront (*WebStorefrontServlet.java*), which is the main page for our store. Our Web Storefront is quite simple, and it is shown in Source 15.2.

Notice that we have no *init()* method to initialize the servlet when it's first loaded into memory. This is because there's no state initialization that our servlets need when they're processing service calls from the client.

```
package com.wiley.compBooks.ecommerce;

import java.io.*;
import javax.servlet.*;
import javax.servlet.http.*;

/**
 * This servlet displays the main page for our
 * e-commerce site.
 *
 * By the time this servlet is called, the user has
 * logged in (via the Login servlet) and has a shopping
 * cart started (i.e., Quote bean). Because this servlet
 * is pooled and reused for different user requests,
 * the servlet code does not store any information
 * specific to any user.  Rather, we store a reference
 * to the user's Quote in the user's HttpSession object,
 * which is globally accessible to all servlets.
 */
public class WebStorefrontServlet extends HttpServlet {

    /**
     * Called by servlet engine to service a request
     */
    public void service (HttpServletRequest request,
                         HttpServletResponse response)
        throws ServletException, IOException
    {
    /*
     * Get the user's session, and from that get the
     * user's current quote.
     */
    HttpSession session = request.getSession(false);
    if (session == null) {
        /*
         * Redirect user to login page if
         * there's no session.
         */
        response.sendRedirect(response.encodeUrl("/servlet/login"));
        return;
    }

    Object obj = session.getValue("quote");
    if (obj == null) {
        /*
         * Redirect user to login page if
         * there's no session.
         */
```

Source 15.2 WebStorefrontServlet.java *(continues)*.

```
            response.sendRedirect(response.encodeUrl("/servlet/login"));
            return;
        }
        Quote quote = (Quote) obj;

        /*
         * Now, we write the response.  Set content-type
         * header, indicating that we will be writing in
         * HTML.
         */
        response.setContentType("text/html");
        PrintWriter out = response.getWriter();

        /*
         * Then write the data of the response.  Start
         * with the header.
         */
            out.println(
            "<html>" +
            "<head><title>Jasmine Computer Parts, Inc.</title></head>" +

            "<body bgcolor=\"#FFFFFF\">" +
            "<center>" +
            "<hr> <br>  " +
            "<h1>" +
            "<font size=\"+3\" color=\"red\">Jasmine's </font> " +
            "<font size=\"+3\" color=\"purple\">Computer </font> " +
            "<font size=\"+3\" color=\"green\">Parts </font>" +
            "</h1>" +
            "</center>" +
            "<br>   <hr> <br>  ");

        /*
         * Write the main body of our Web page
         */
            out.println(
            "<table border=0 cellspacing=5 cellpadding=5>" +
            "<tr>" +
            "<td valign=\"TOP\" bgcolor=\"#FFFFAA\">" +
            "<p><font size=\"+1\"><a href=\"" +
            response.encodeUrl("/servlet/catalog") +
            "\">Catalog</a></font><br>" +
            "Choose from our excellent selection of computer parts." +

            "<p><font size=\"+1\"><a href=\"" +
            response.encodeUrl("/servlet/showquote") +
            "\">Shopping Cart</a></font><br>" +
            "Look at your shopping cart to see the equipment " +
```

Source 15.2 WebStorefrontServlet.java *(continues)*.

```
            "you've chosen" +

            "</td>" +
            "</tr>" +
            "</table>" +

            "<br>  " +
            "<br>  " +
            "<br>  " +
            "<center><em>" +
            "Based on the Java Tutorial Servlet," +
            "Copyright &copy; 1998 Sun Microsystems, Inc." +
            "</em></center>" +
            "</body>" +
            "</html>");
            out.close();
    }

    public String getServletInfo() {
        return "The WebStorefront servlet returns the main web page " +
        "for Jasmine's Computer Parts.";
    }
}
```

Source 15.2 WebStorefrontServlet.java *(continued)*.

When the user connects, we first check to see if he or she has a current Quote going, by extracting the Quote from the user's servlet session. If the user has no Quote, we redirect the user back to the Login screen for authentication. Otherwise, we simply print out the main storefront page, which contains links to other servlets. The Web Storefront screen is shown in Figure 15.2.

The Online Catalog Servlet

To start adding products to his or her Quote, the user can browse the list of products available by going to the catalog Web page, which is a Java servlet, *CatalogServlet.java*, shown in Source 15.3. From the catalog, the user can add products to his or her Quote. He or she can also view details of a particular product, in which case the Catalog servlet will direct the user to the Product Detail servlet, described later.

Like the Web Storefront, our Catalog servlet will kick the user back to the Login servlet if he or she has no Quote going. Otherwise, the Catalog prints out the current list of products available. The Catalog screen is shown in Figure 15.3.

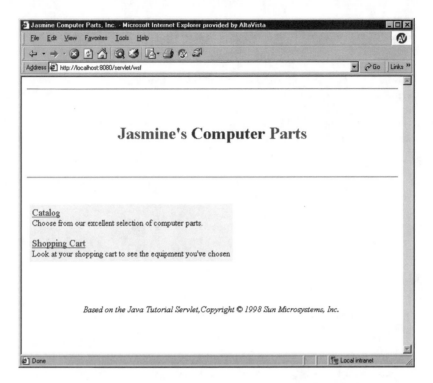

Figure 15.2   The Web Storefront screen.

```
package com.wiley.compBooks.ecommerce;

import java.io.*;
import java.util.*;
import javax.servlet.*;
import javax.servlet.http.*;

/**
 * This servlet displays a catalog of products to
 * the end user.
 *
 * By the time this servlet is called, the user has
 * logged in (via the Login servlet) and has a shopping
 * cart started (i.e., Quote bean). Because this servlet is
 * pooled and reused for different user requests, the
 * servlet code does not store any information specific to
 * any user.  Rather, we store a reference to the user's
 * Quote in the user's HttpSession object, which is
 * globally accessible to all servlets.
 */
```

Source 15.3   CatalogServlet.java *(continues)*.

```java
public class CatalogServlet extends HttpServlet {

  /**
   * The servlet engine calls this method when the user's
   * desktop browser sends an HTTP GET request.
   */
  public void doGet (HttpServletRequest request, HttpServletResponse
    response) throws ServletException, IOException {

    /*
     * Get the user's HttpSession, and from that get
     * the user's current quote.
     */
    HttpSession session = request.getSession(false);
    if (session == null) {
        /*
         * Redirect user to login page if he
         * doesn't have a session.
         */
        response.sendRedirect(response.encodeUrl("/servlet/login"));
        return;
    }

    Object obj = session.getValue("quote");
    if (obj == null) {
        /*
         * Redirect user to login page if he
         * doesn't have a session.
         */
        response.sendRedirect(response.encodeUrl("/servlet/login"));
        return;
    }
    Quote quote = (Quote) obj;

    /*
     * Now, we write the response.  Set content-type
     * header, indicating that we will be writing in HTML.
     */
    response.setContentType("text/html");
    PrintWriter out = response.getWriter();

    /*
     * Then write the response.  Start with the header.
     */
    out.println(
        "<html>" +
        "<head><title> Computer Catalog </title></head>" +
```

Source 15.3 CatalogServlet.java *(continues)*.

```
                "<body  bgcolor=\"#ffffff\">" +
                "<center>" +
                "<hr> <br>  " +
                "<h1>" +
                "<font size=\"+3\" color=\"red\">Jasmine's </font>" +
                "<font size=\"+3\" color=\"purple\">Computer </font>" +
                "<font size=\"+3\" color=\"green\">Parts</font>" +
                "</h1>" +
                "</center>" +
                "<br>   <hr> <br>  ");

        /*
         * Get our ProductBase servlet that contains
         * all the available products.
         */
        ProductBaseServlet productBase = (ProductBaseServlet)
            getServletConfig().getServletContext().getServlet("productbase");

        /*
         * If user wants to purchase something (via
         * the URL parameter 'Buy'), add the desired
         * product to the quote.
         */
        String productIDToAdd = request.getParameter("Buy");
        if (productIDToAdd != null) {

            /*
             * Convert the product ID into a Product.
             */
            Product product = null;
            try {
            product = productBase.getProduct(productIDToAdd);
            }
            catch (Exception e) {
            throw new ServletException(e.toString());
            }

            /*
             * Add the product to the quote
             */
            quote.addProduct(product);
            out.println(
            "<p><h3>" +
            "<font color=\"#ff0000\">" +
            "<i>" + product.getName() + "</i> "+
            "has been added to your quote.</font></h3>");
        }
```

Source 15.3 CatalogServlet.java *(continues)*.

```
    /*
     * Give the option of viewing the current quote.
     * Also give option to purchase the selections
     * made.
     */
    out.println(
        "<a href=\"" +
        response.encodeUrl("/servlet/showquote") +
        "\"> View Current Quote</a></th>");

    /*
     * Show the catalog
     */
    out.println(
        "<br>  " +
        "<h3>Please choose from our selections</h3>" +
        "<center> <table>");

    /*
     * Print out info on each product in the catalog
     */
    Vector products = productBase.getAllProducts();
    for(int i=0; i < products.size(); i++) {
        Product prod = (Product) products.elementAt(i);
        String productID = ((ProductPK)prod.getPrimaryKey()).productID;

        out.println(
            "<tr>" +
            "<td bgcolor=\"#ffffaa\">" +
            "<a href=\"" +
            response.encodeUrl("/servlet/productdetails" +
            "?productID=" + productID) +
            "\"> <strong>" + prod.getName() +
            "  </strong></a>" +
            "</td>" +

            "<td bgcolor=\"#ffffaa\">" +
            "$" + prod.getBasePrice() + "  " +
            "</td>" +

            "<td bgcolor=\"#ffffaa\">" +
            "<a href=\"" +
            response.encodeUrl("/servlet/catalog?Buy=" + productID)
            + "\">   Add to Quote  </a>" +
            "</td>" +
            "</tr>");
    }
```

Source 15.3 CatalogServlet.java *(continues)*.

```
out.println("</table></center></body></html>");
out.close();
}

public String getServletInfo() {
return "The Catalog servlet adds products to the user's " +
      "quote and prints the catalog.";


}
}
```

Source 15.3 CatalogServlet.java *(continued)*.

The Catalog servlet gets its list of products via a different servlet, the Product Base servlet (described later). We cache the list of products in the Product Base servlet for efficiency. Our catalog prints out a URL link to add each product to the user's current shopping cart (Quote). If the user clicks on the link, the Web browser will return the Product ID to the Catalog servlet as a URL parameter. When the Catalog servlet is called with a Product ID, the servlet first extracts the ID from the request. It then uses the Product Base servlet to convert the

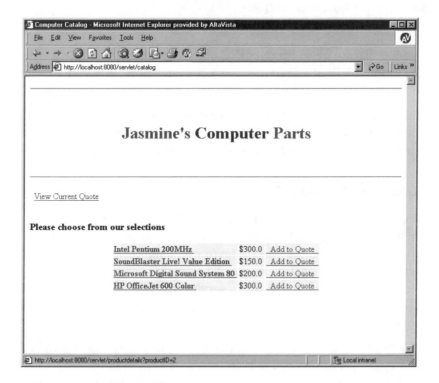

Figure 15.3 The Catalog screen.

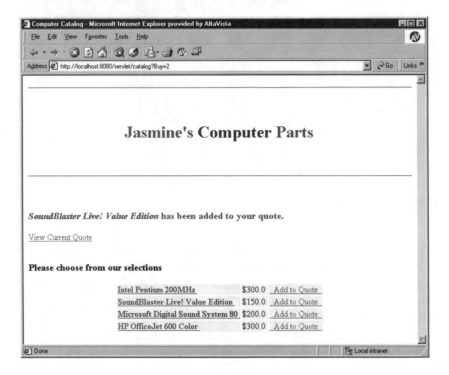

Figure 15.4 Adding a Product to the Quote.

Product ID into a real Product EJB object. Finally, the Catalog servlet then adds the Product EJB object to the user's current Quote. Adding a Product is shown in Figure 15.4.

The user can also navigate to several other servlets from the catalog, such as the Product Detail servlet for viewing the details of a particular product. In this case, the product ID to be viewed is passed as a parameter to that servlet.

The Product Base Servlet

Many of our servlets need to work with Product entity beans. It would be very inefficient, though, to have each servlet communicate across the tier boundary every time a Product needed to be found. Therefore, we cache our entire product line in a Product Base servlet. The Product Base servlet *never* interacts directly with the user. It's simply a servlet that other servlets can call when they need to retrieve Products. The code is in *ProductBaseServlet.java*, shown in Source 15.4.

Our Product Base servlet is responsible for holding all the Product EJB objects that exist. Therefore, it needs to look them all up in its *init()* method. *init()* performs JNDI initialization, locates the Product home object, and then finds

```java
package com.wiley.compBooks.ecommerce;

import java.io.*;
import java.util.*;
import javax.servlet.*;
import javax.naming.*;

/**
 * This servlet stores the list of products that the
 * user can purchase.
 *
 * This Generic Servlet is a helper servlet called by
 * other servlets.  There is no user interface logic
 * in this servlet because this servlet is never called
 * directly from clients.
 */
public class ProductBaseServlet extends GenericServlet {

  // Vector of Product EJB Objects
  private Vector products;

  /**
   * The servlet engine calls this method once to
   * initialize a servlet instance.
   *
   * In the body of this method, we need to acquire the
   * EJB Product Home Object.  We then acquire all the
   * products.
   */
  public void init(ServletConfig config) throws ServletException {

    super.init(config);

    try {
        /*
         * Get the deployed properties from the
         * config object.  We externalize the JNDI
         * initialization params to the servlet
         * properties file to allow end users to
         * dynamically reconfigure their environment
         * without recompilation.
         */
        String initCtxFactory =
            getInitParameter(Context.INITIAL_CONTEXT_FACTORY);
        String providerURL = getInitParameter(Context.PROVIDER_URL);

        /*
         * Add the JNDI init parameters to a
```

Source 15.4 ProductBaseServlet.java *(continues)*.

```
         * properties object.
         */
        Properties env = new Properties();
        env.put(Context.INITIAL_CONTEXT_FACTORY, initCtxFactory);
        env.put(Context.PROVIDER_URL, providerURL);

        /*
         * Get the initial JNDI context using the
         * above startup params.
         */
            Context ctx = new InitialContext(env);

        /*
         * Look up the Product Home Object.
         */
        ProductHome productHome = (ProductHome)
            ctx.lookup("Ecommerce.ProductHome");

        /*
         * Get all the products.
         */
        Enumeration e = productHome.findAllProducts();
        this.products = new Vector();
        while (e.hasMoreElements()) {
            this.products.addElement(e.nextElement());
        }
    }
  catch (Exception e) {
            e.printStackTrace();
  }
}

public void service(ServletRequest req, ServletResponse res) throws
  ServletException, IOException {

  throw new UnavailableException(this,
      "This servlet does not accept client requests.");

}

/**
 * Retrieves a product based upon it's product id.
 * Called by other servlets.
 * @return null if no match.
 */
public Product getProduct(String productID) throws Exception {
  ProductPK pk = new ProductPK(productID);
    for (int i=0; i < products.size(); i++) {
```

Source 15.4   ProductBaseServlet.java *(continues)*.

```
            Product prod = (Product) products.elementAt(i);
            if (prod.getPrimaryKey().equals(pk)) {
                return prod;
            }
        }

        return null;
    }

    public Vector getAllProducts() {
        return products;
    }

    public int getNumberOfProducts() {
        return products.size();
    }

    public String getServletInfo() {
        return "The ProductBase servlet contains all the products." +
            "It is called by other servlets, not directly by a user.";
    }
}
```

Source 15.4   ProductBaseServlet.java *(continued)*.

all the Products via the *findAllProducts()* custom finder method on the Product home interface.

Other servlets can access the products available via the *getAllProducts()*, *getNumberOfProducts()*, and *getProduct()* methods. If an HTTP client attempts to connect to our servlet, our *service()* method will throw an exception—thin clients should never be calling this servlet directly.

The Product Detail Servlet

The Product Detail servlet (*ProductDetailServlet.java*) is responsible for displaying the page to the user enumerating the low-level details of a particular Product. The user can add a Product to his or her Quote from here as well. The code is shown in Source 15.5.

Our Product Detail servlet always expects a URL parameter passed to it—the parameter is the particular product ID that should be detailed. It then retrieves the Product EJB object corresponding to that ID by calling the Product Base servlet. Finally, it prints out the Product's details by calling the get methods on the Product. The user can add this Product to his or her Quote as well—if so, the user will be redirected back to the Catalog.

```
package com.wiley.compBooks.ecommerce;

import java.io.*;
import javax.servlet.*;
import javax.servlet.http.*;

/**
 * This servlet displays detailed information about a
 * particular product in the catalog.
 *
 * By the time this servlet is called, the user has
 * logged in (via the Login servlet) and has a shopping
 * cart started (i.e., Quote bean). Because this servlet is
 * pooled and reused for different user requests, the
 * servlet code does not store any information specific
 * to any user.  Rather, we store a reference to the
 * user's Quote in the user's HttpSession object, which
 * is globally accessible to all servlets.
 */
public class ProductDetailServlet extends HttpServlet {

  /**
   * The servlet engine calls this method when the user's
   * desktop browser sends an HTTP GET request.
   */
  public void doGet (HttpServletRequest request, HttpServletResponse
    response) throws ServletException, IOException {

    /*
     * Get the user's HttpSession, and from that get
     * the user's current quote.
     */
    try {
        HttpSession session = request.getSession(false);
        Quote quote = (Quote) session.getValue(session.getId());
    }
    catch (Exception e) {
        throw new ServletException(
            "Error: You don't have a current quote going.  Re-login.");
    }

    /*
     * Now, we write the response.  Set content-type
     * header, indicating that we will be writing in HTML.
     */
    response.setContentType("text/html");
    PrintWriter out = response.getWriter();
```

Source 15.5 ProductDetailServlet.java *(continues)*.

```
/*
 * Then write the response.  Start with the header.
 */
out.println(
    "<html>" +
    "<head><title> Computer Catalog </title></head>" +

    "<body  bgcolor=\"#ffffff\">" +
    "<center>" +
    "<hr> <br>  " +
    "<h1>" +
    "<font size=\"+3\" color=\"red\">Jasmine's </font>" +
    "<font size=\"+3\" color=\"purple\">Computer </font>" +
    "<font size=\"+3\" color=\"green\">Parts</font>" +
    "</h1>" +
    "</center>" +
    "<br>   <hr> <br>  ");


/*
 * Get our ProductBase Servlet which contains all
 * the available products.
 */
ProductBaseServlet productBase = (ProductBaseServlet)
    getServletConfig().getServletContext().getServlet("productbase");

/*
 * To print out the product information, we first
 * must figure out which product to show.  We
 * assume that the product ID has been passed to us
 * as a URL parameter, called "productID".
 */
String productID = request.getParameter("productID");
if (productID != null) {

    /*
     * Retrieve the product from the ProductBase
     * servlet, keyed on product ID.
     */
    Product product = null;
    try {
        product = productBase.getProduct(productID);
    }
    catch (Exception e) {
        throw new ServletException(e.toString());
    }
```

Source 15.5   ProductDetailServlet.java *(continues)*.

```
        /*
         * Print out the information obtained
         */
        out.println(
            "<h2>" + product.getName() + "</h2>" +

            "<h4>Description: </h4>" + product.getDescription() +

            "<h4>Base price (before discounts): $" +
            product.getBasePrice() + "</h4>" +

            "<center>" +
            "<p><a href=\"" +
            response.encodeUrl("/servlet/catalog?Buy=" +
            productID) +
            "\"> Add this item to your quote.</a></p>" +
            "</center>");
    }

    out.println("</body></html>");
    out.close();
  }

  public String getServletInfo() {
    return "The ProductDetail servlet returns information about" +
        "any product that is available from the catalog.";
  }
}
```

Source 15.5   ProductDetailServlet.java *(continued)*.

The Quote Viewing Servlet

The user is able to view and modify his or her Quote at any time by going to a separate page, manifested by the Quote View servlet in *ShowQuoteServlet.java*. The user can view each individual Quote Line Item stateful session bean that constitutes the Quote. The user can also change the desired quantities of the selected Products. Every time the user changes something, our Quote View servlet recalculates the price of the Quote by calling the Pricer stateless session bean. The code is rather involved, and it is shown in Source 15.6.

Let's see exactly what this code is doing.

The *init()* method grabs a Pricer EJB object for performing pricing operations. It does this via JNDI, calling *create()* on the Pricer's home object.

```
package com.wiley.compBooks.ecommerce;

import java.io.*;
import java.util.*;
import java.text.*;
import javax.servlet.*;
import javax.servlet.http.*;
import javax.naming.*;

/**
 * This servlet allows the user to view and modify his or her
 * current selections.
 *
 * By the time this servlet is called, the user has
 * logged in (via the Login servlet) and has a shopping
 * cart started (i.e., Quote bean). Because this servlet is
 * pooled and reused for different user requests, the
 * servlet code does not store any information specific
 * to any user.  Rather, we store a reference to the user's
 * Quote in the user's HttpSession object, which is globally
 * accessible to all servlets.
 */
public class ShowQuoteServlet extends HttpServlet {

  // Pricer EJB Object for pricing the quote
  private Pricer pricer;

  /**
   * The servlet engine calls this method once to initialize
   * a servlet instance.
   *
   * In the body of this method, we need to acquire a Pricer
   * EJB Object for pricing the quotes.
   */
  public void init(ServletConfig config) throws ServletException {

    /*
     * Call parent to store the config object, so that
     * getServletConfig() can return it.
     */
    super.init(config);

    try {
        /*
         * Get the JNDI initialization parameters.
         * We externalize these settings to the
         * servlet properties file to allow end-users
```

Source 15.6 ShowQuoteServlet.java *(continues)*.

```
         * to dynamically reconfigure their
         * environment without recompilation.
         */
        String initCtxFactory =
            getInitParameter(Context.INITIAL_CONTEXT_FACTORY);
        String providerURL = getInitParameter(Context.PROVIDER_URL);

        /*
         * Add the JNDI init parameters to a
         * properties object.
         */
        Properties env = new Properties();
        env.put(Context.INITIAL_CONTEXT_FACTORY, initCtxFactory);
        env.put(Context.PROVIDER_URL, providerURL);

        /*
         * Get the initial context using the above
         * startup params.
         */
          Context ctx = new InitialContext(env);

        /*
         * Look up the Home Object.
         */
        PricerHome pricerHome = (PricerHome)
            ctx.lookup("Ecommerce.PricerHome");

        /*
         * Create a Pricer EJB Object.
         */
        pricer = pricerHome.create();
    }
    catch (Exception e) {
        log(e);
        throw new ServletException(e.toString());
    }
}


/**
 * The servlet engine calls this method when the user's
 * desktop browser sends an HTTP GET request.
 */
public void doGet (HttpServletRequest request, HttpServletResponse
    response) throws ServletException, IOException {

    /*
     * Get the user's HttpSession, and from that get
```

Source 15.6 ShowQuoteServlet.java *(continues).*

```
  * the user's current quote.
  */
HttpSession session = request.getSession(false);
if (session == null) {
    /*
     * Redirect user to login page if no session
     */
    response.sendRedirect(response.encodeUrl("/servlet/login"));
    return;
}

Object obj = session.getValue("quote");
if (obj == null) {
    /*
     * Redirect user to login page if no session
     */
    response.sendRedirect(response.encodeUrl("/servlet/login"));
    return;
}
Quote quote = (Quote) obj;

/*
 * If the user clicked the 'Order' button, he
 * wants to purchase his selections.  We forward
 * the user to the servlet that handles purchasing.
 */
if (request.getParameter("Order") != null) {
    response.sendRedirect(response.encodeUrl("/servlet/purchase"));
    return;
}

/*
 * Now, we write the response.  Set content-type
 * header, indicating that we will be writing in
 * HTML.
 */
response.setContentType("text/html");
PrintWriter out = response.getWriter();

/*
 * Then write the data of the response.
 * Start with the header.
 */
out.println(
    "<html>" +
    "<head><title> Computer Catalog </title></head>" +

    "<body  bgcolor=\"#ffffff\">" +
```

Source 15.6 ShowQuoteServlet.java *(continues).*

```
                "<center>" +
                "<hr> <br>  " +
                "<h1>" +
                "<font size=\"+3\" color=\"red\">Jasmine's </font>" +
                "<font size=\"+3\" color=\"purple\">Computer </font>" +
                "<font size=\"+3\" color=\"green\">Parts</font>" +
                "</h1>" +
                "</center>" +
                "<br>   <hr> <br>  ");

        /*
         * Get our ProductBase Servlet which contains
         * all the available products.
         */
        ProductBaseServlet productBase = (ProductBaseServlet)
            getServletConfig().getServletContext().getServlet("productbase");

    /*
     * Next, we need to figure out what button the user
     * clicked, if any.  These come to us as form
     * parameters.  We need to loop through each
     * parameter and interpret it.
     */
    Enumeration paramNames = request.getParameterNames();
    while (paramNames.hasMoreElements()) {
      String paramName = (String) paramNames.nextElement();
      String paramValue = request.getParameter(paramName);

      /*
       * If user clicked 'Update' button, then the user
       * wants to change the quantities of each product
       * he is ordering.  We'll process those quantities
       * below.
       */
      if (paramName.equals("Update")) {
      }

      /*
       * If the user wants to clear the form
       */
      else if (paramName.equals("Clear")) {

        quote.clear();

        out.println(
            "<font color=\"#ff0000\" size=\"+2\">" +
            "<strong>You just cleared your quote!" +
            "</strong> <br>  <br> </font>");
```

Source 15.6 ShowQuoteServlet.java *(continues).*

```
        break;
    }

    /*
     * If the parameter represents a quantity
     * of a particular product the user is interested
     * in, then we should update that product's
     * quantity to reflect this new value.
     */
    else {
        /*
         * Convert the quantity to int format
         */
        int quantity = 0;
        try {
            quantity = Integer.parseInt(paramValue);
        }
        catch (NumberFormatException e) {
            throw new ServletException("Bad parameter to servlet: " +
            paramName + ", " + paramValue);
        }

        /*
         * Use the ProductBase servlet to convert the
         * product ID into a Product.
         */
        Product product = null;
        try {
            product = productBase.getProduct(paramName);
        }
        catch (Exception e) {
            throw new ServletException(e.toString());
        }

        /*
         * Set the new quantity.
         */
        try {
            quote.setProductQuantity(product, quantity);
        }
        catch (Exception e) {
            throw new ServletException(e.toString());
        }
    }
}

/*
 * Recalculate all totals based upon new quantities
```

Source 15.6   ShowQuoteServlet.java *(continues).*

```
    */
    try {
        pricer.price(quote);
    }
    catch (Exception e) {
        log(e);
        throw new ServletException(e.toString());
    }

    /*
     * Otherwise, show the current quote again
     */
    int num = quote.getNumberOfItems();
    if (num > 0) {

        out.println(
            "<form action=\"" +
            response.encodeUrl("/servlet/showquote") +
            "\" method=\"get\">" +

            "<table>" +
            "<tr>" +
            "<th align=left> Name </TH>" +
            "<th align=left> Quantity </TH>" +
            "<th align=left> Individual Base Price </TH>" +
            "<th align=left> Individual Discount </TH>" +
            "<th align=left><strong> Total Price </strong></TH>" +
            "<th align=left>Modify Quantity</TH>" +
            "</tr>");

        /*
         * Print each line item in the quote
         */
        Vector lineItems = quote.getLineItems();
        for (int i=0; i < lineItems.size(); i++) {
            QuoteLineItem li = (QuoteLineItem) lineItems.elementAt(i);
            int quantity     = li.getQuantity();
            double discount  = li.getDiscount();
            Product product  = li.getProduct();
            String productID =
                ((ProductPK)product.getPrimaryKey()).productID;
            double basePrice = product.getBasePrice();

            out.println(
                "<tr>" +

                "<td bgcolor=\"#ffffaa\">" +
                "<strong><a href=\"" +
```

Source 15.6 ShowQuoteServlet.java *(continues)*.

```
                    response.encodeUrl(
                        "/servlet/productdetails?productID=" +
                        productID) +
                    "\">" + product.getName() + "</a></strong>" +
                    "</td>" +

                    "<td align=\"right\" bgcolor=\"#ffffff\">" +
                    li.getQuantity() +
                    "</td>" +

                    "<td bgcolor=\"#ffffaa\" align=\"right\">" +
                    format(basePrice) +
                    "</td>" +

                    "<td bgcolor=\"#ffffaa\" align=\"right\">" +
                    format(discount) +
                    "</td>" +

                    "<td bgcolor=\"#ffffaa\" align=\"right\">" +
                    format((basePrice - discount) * quantity) +
                    "</td>" +

                    "<td><input type=\"text\" name=\"" + productID +
                    "\" value=\"" + quantity + "\">" +
                    "</td>" +

                    "</td></tr>");
        }

        /*
         * Print the total at the bottom of the table
         */
        out.println(
            "<tr><td colspan=\"5\" bgcolor=\"#ffffff\">" +
            "<br></td></tr>" +

            "<tr>" +
            "<td colspan=\"2\" align=\"right\"" +
            "bgcolor=\"#ffffff\">" +
            "Subtotal:</td>" +
            "<td bgcolor=\"#ffffaa\" align=\"right\">" +
            format(quote.getSubtotal()) + "</td>" +
            "</td><td><br></td></tr>" +

            "<tr>" +
            "<td colspan=\"2\" align=\"right\"" +
            "bgcolor=\"#ffffff\">" +
            "Sales Tax:</td>" +
```

Source 15.6 ShowQuoteServlet.java *(continues)*.

```java
            "<td bgcolor=\"#ffffaa\" align=\"right\">" +
            format(quote.getTaxes()) + "</td>" +
            "</td><td><br></td></tr>" +

            "<tr>" +
            "<td colspan=\"2\" align=\"right\"" +
            "bgcolor=\"ffffff\">" +
            "<font color=\"ff0000\">" +
            "<strong>Grand Total:</strong></font></td>" +
            "<td bgcolor=\"ffffaa\" align=\"right\">" +
            format(quote.getTotalPrice()) + "</td>" +
            "</td><td><br></td></tr>" +
            "</table>");

        /*
         * Print out links and buttons for user feedback.
         * When the user clicks a button to perform an
         * action (such as submitting an order), this
         * servlet will be called again with a parameter
         * instructing the servlet about what to do.  We
         * processed those parameters at the beginning of
         * this method.
         */
        out.println("<p>   <p><a href=\"" +
            response.encodeUrl("/servlet/catalog") +
            "\">See the Catalog</a>      " +

            "<input type=\"reset\"" +
            "value=\"Reset Values\">      " +

            "<input type=\"submit\" name=\"Update\"" +
            "value=\"Update Quantities\">      " +

            "<input type=\"submit\" name=\"Order\"" +
            "value=\"Submit Order\">      " +

            "<input type=\"submit\" name=\"Clear\"" +
            "value=\"Clear Quote\">      ");
    }

    /*
     * If there are no products, print out that the
     * quote is empty.
     */
    else {

        out.println(
            "<font size=\"+2\">" +
```

Source 15.6 ShowQuoteServlet.java *(continues)*.

```
              "Your quote is empty.</font>" +
              "<br>   <br>" +
              "<center><a href=\"" +
              response.encodeUrl("/servlet/catalog") +
              "\">Back to the Catalog</a> </center>");
    }

    out.println("</body> </html>");
    out.close();
    }


    /**
     * Currency localization formatting
     */
    private String format(double d) {
        NumberFormat nf = NumberFormat.getCurrencyInstance();
        return nf.format(d);
    }


    private void log(Exception e) {
        getServletConfig().getServletContext().log(e, "");
    }


    public String getServletInfo() {
        return "The ShowQuote servlet returns information about" +
               "the products that the user is in the process of ordering.";
    }
}
```

Source 15.6 ShowQuoteServlet.java *(continued).*

Next, our *doGet()* method is responsible for showing the quote to the user and handling any requests for modifications to the quote. The simplest case is when the user first connects to this servlet—we just print out the user's current Quote, by retrieving each Quote Line Item from the Quote and displaying it to the end user. This is shown in Figure 15.5.

The user can update the quantities of his or her quote by changing the text box values, then pressing the Update button. When this happens, extra HTTP parameters are passed back to the servlet. The name of each HTTP parameter is a Product ID, and the value of each HTTP parameter is the new desired quantity. When the servlet is called with these parameters, our servlet parses each parameter and in turn updates the quantities on the quote. It then tells our Pricer EJB object to price the entire quote, yielding the new values (with possibly new discounts). We then redisplay the Quote to the user.

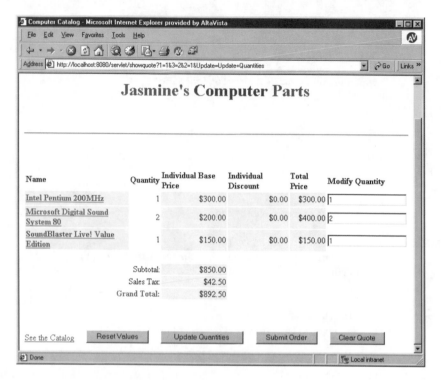

Figure 15.5   Viewing the initial quote.

The user can also clear the quote by pressing the Clear button. When this happens, an HTTP parameter is passed back to our servlet called "Clear." If we see the "Clear" parameter, we call the Quote's *clear()* method, which empties all the Quote Line Items. Note that the user can still shop around because the Quote is still in the servlet session and the Quote is still associated with that Customer. Clearing the quote is shown in Figure 15.6.

The Purchasing Servlet

Finally, when the user is happy, he or she can turn the shopping cart into a permanent order and get charged for the order by clicking the Submit button. When this happens we need to convert the Quote stateful session bean into an Order entity bean. Fortunately, we designed the Quote bean to be smart enough to convert itself into an order automatically. Our servlet needs to contact a Bank Teller to bill the customer. Once the transaction is complete, we display the user's Order number (you can extend this example to allow users to query the status of orders by submitting their Order number).

The code for *PurchaseServlet.java* is shown in Source 15.7.

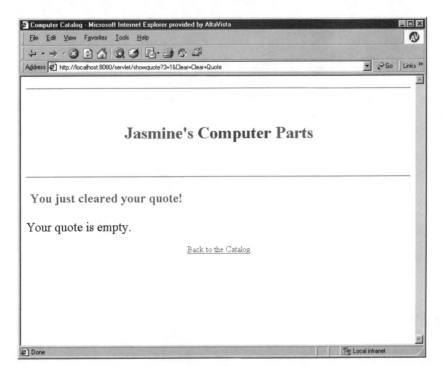

Figure 15.6 Clearing the quote.

```
package com.wiley.compBooks.ecommerce;

import java.io.*;
import java.util.*;
import java.text.*;
import javax.servlet.*;
import javax.servlet.http.*;
import javax.naming.*;

/**
 * This servlet performs an actual purchase of goods, printing
 * out a receipt.
 *
 * By the time this servlet is called, the user has logged in (via the
 * Login servlet) and has a shopping cart started (i.e., Quote bean).
 * Because this servlet is pooled and reused for different user
 * requests, the servlet code does not store any information specific
 * to any user.  Rather, we store a reference to the user's Quote in
 * the user's HttpSession object, which is globally accessible to all
```

Source 15.7 PurchaseServlet.java *(continues).*

```
  * servlets.
  */
public class PurchaseServlet extends HttpServlet {

  // Bank Teller EJB Object for performing bank transactions
  private Teller teller;

  /*
    * Our purchase servlet needs to conduct a transaction.  When
    * a purchase is made, an order needs to be submitted and
    * the customer needs to be billed.  If either of these
    * operations fails, both should fail.  Therefore, we run both
    * operations together under a flat transaction.  For a servlet
    * to begin and end a transaction, it must use the Java
    * Transaction API (JTA), as described in Chapter 10.  The JTA
    * UserTransaction interface is used for exactly this purpose.
    * The EJB server must make this interface available to us
    * via JNDI.  We'll look it up using JNDI in the init() method.
    */
  private javax.transaction.UserTransaction userTran;

  /**
    * The servlet engine calls this method once to initialize a
    * servlet instance.
    *
    * In the body of this method, we need to acquire a Pricer
    * EJB Object for pricing the quotes, as well as the JTA
    * UserTransaction interface, used for demarcating
    * transactional boundaries.
    */
  public void init(ServletConfig config) throws ServletException {

    super.init(config);

    try {
        /*
          * Get the JNDI initialization parameters.  We
          * externalize these settings to the servlet properties
          * file to allow end users to dynamically reconfigure
          * their environment without recompilation.
          */
        String initCtxFactory =
            getInitParameter(Context.INITIAL_CONTEXT_FACTORY);
        String providerURL = getInitParameter(Context.PROVIDER_URL);

        /*
          * Add the JNDI init parameters to a properties object
          */
```

Source 15.7 PurchaseServlet.java *(continues).*

```
            Properties env = new Properties();
            env.put(Context.INITIAL_CONTEXT_FACTORY, initCtxFactory);
            env.put(Context.PROVIDER_URL, providerURL);

            /*
             * Get the initial context using the above startup params
             */
            Context ctx = new InitialContext(env);

            /*
             * Look up the Home Object
             */
            TellerHome tellerHome = (TellerHome)
                ctx.lookup("Ecommerce.TellerHome");

            /*
             * Create a Pricer EJB Object
             */
            teller = tellerHome.create();

            /*
             * Look up the JTA UserTransaction interface via JNDI
             */
            userTran = (javax.transaction.UserTransaction)
                ctx.lookup("javax.transaction.UserTransaction");
        }
        catch (Exception e) {
            log(e);
            throw new ServletException(e.toString());
        }
    }

    /**
     * The servlet engine calls this method when the user's
     * desktop browser sends an HTTP GET request.
     */
    public void doGet (HttpServletRequest request, HttpServletResponse
        response) throws ServletException, IOException {

        /*
         * Get the user's HttpSession and from that get the user's
         * current quote.
         */
        HttpSession session = request.getSession(false);
        if (session == null) {
            /*
             * Redirect user to login page if no session
             */
```

Source 15.7   PurchaseServlet.java *(continues)*.

```
            response.sendRedirect(response.encodeUrl("/servlet/login"));
            return;
    }

    Object obj = session.getValue("quote");
    if (obj == null) {
        /*
         * Redirect user to login page if no session
         */
        response.sendRedirect(response.encodeUrl("/servlet/login"));
        return;
    }
    Quote quote = (Quote) obj;

    /*
     * Now, we write the response.  Set content-type
     * header, indicating that we will be writing in
     * HTML.
     */
    response.setContentType("text/html");
    PrintWriter out = response.getWriter();

    /*
     * Then write the data of the response.  Start with the header.
     */
    out.println(
        "<html>" +
        "<head><title> Thank you </title></head>" +

        "<body  bgcolor=\"#ffffff\">" +
        "<center>" +
        "<hr> <br>  " +
        "<h1>" +
        "<font size=\"+3\" color=\"red\">Jasmine's </font>" +
        "<font size=\"+3\" color=\"purple\">Computer </font>" +
        "<font size=\"+3\" color=\"green\">Parts</font>" +
        "</h1>" +
        "</center>" +
        "<br>   <hr> <br>  ");

    Order order = null;
    try {
        /*
         * Begin a new user transaction.  We require a
         * transaction here so that we can charge the
         * user and generate the order atomically.
         */
        userTran.begin();
```

Source 15.7 PurchaseServlet.java *(continues)*.

```
        /*
         * First, turn the quote into an order
         */
        order = quote.purchase();

        /*
         * Next, charge the user
         */
        Customer customer = order.getCustomer();
        String custAcctNum = teller.lookupAccountNumber(customer.getName());
        String storeAcctNum = teller.lookupAccountNumber("Jasmine");
        teller.transfer(custAcctNum, storeAcctNum, quote.getTotalPrice());

        /*
         * Finally, commit the transaction
         */
        userTran.commit();
    }
    catch (Exception e) {
        try {
            log(e);
            userTran.rollback();
            throw new ServletException(e.toString());
        }
        catch (Exception ex) {
            log(ex);
            throw new ServletException(e.toString() +
                " ** Rollback failed ** : " + ex.toString());
        }
    }

    /*
     * Payment received -- clear the quote
     */
    quote.clear();

    /*
     * Then write the response
     */
    out.println(
        "<h3>Thank you for shopping with us. " +
        "<p>Your order number is " + ((OrderPK)order.getPrimaryKey()).orderID
        + "." + "<p>Please shop with us again soon!</h3>" +

        "<p><i><a href=\"" + response.encodeUrl("/servlet/wsf") +
        "\">Click here to return to the main page.</a></i>" +

        "</body></html>");
```

Source 15.7 PurchaseServlet.java *(continues)*.

```
        out.close();
    }

    private void log(Exception e) {
        getServletConfig().getServletContext().log(e, "");
    }

    public String getServletInfo() {
        return "This servlet performs an actual purchase, prints out " +
        "a receipt, and returns the user to the Web storefront.";
    }
}
```

Source 15.7   PurchaseServlet.java *(continued)*.

The most interesting aspect of the code in Source 15.7 is that it shows how to perform a transaction programmatically from a servlet. When the user purchases his or her goods, we'd like to both submit an order to manufacture the goods and bill the customer for the cost of the goods. We'd like these operations to either both succeed or both fail, but never have one succeed without the other. Therefore, we perform the operations as a single transactional atomic operation. To do this, we need to *begin* and *end* a transaction from a servlet. You can do this by accessing the Java Transaction API (JTA)'s *UserTransaction* interface. The *UserTransaction* interface allows you to demarcate transactional boundaries in your Java code, such as this example shows. To get access to the *UserTransaction* interface, we look it up via JNDI. See Chapter 10 for a complete description of the *UserTransaction* interface.

The other interesting thing to notice about our code is that we keep the user's cleared Quote around even after the Order has been generated, so the user can continue to shop in the store.

This completes the servlets for our e-commerce deployment. The receipt screen is shown in Figure 15.7.

The Servlet Properties

The final ingredient in our presentation tier is our servlet's properties file. This is read in by the servlet engine, and it associates servlets with common names that can be referenced in a thin-client browser. For example, we call the Login servlet "login" and the Web Storefront servlet "wsf"; those will be part of the URL the end user needs to type into his browser (such as "http://localhost:8080/ servlet/wsf").

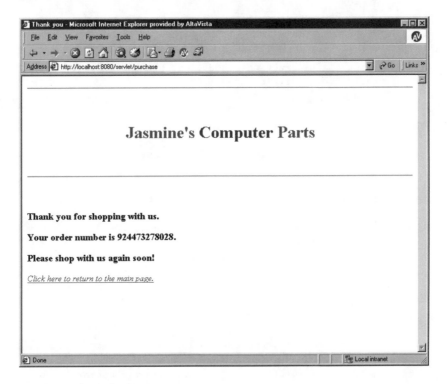

Figure 15.7   The final purchasing screen.

Our properties file also lists a number of JNDI initialization parameters. Our servlets will use these parameters to connect to the home objects for the enterprise beans they use. In general, you should externalize properties such as these to properties files so that you don't need to recompile your servlets if you change EJB container/server or if you change where your beans are located when they're deployed. This is exactly analogous to how we externalized JNDI parameters to our EJB properties files when our enterprise beans looked up other enterprise beans using JNDI.

The code for *servlet.properties* is in Source 15.8.

```
# Used by Servletrunner.
# This file contains the properties for the Ecommerce GUI servlets.

#
# The servlet that manages list of products available
#
```

Source 15.8   servlet.properties *(continues)*.

```
servlet.login.code=com.wiley.compBooks.ecommerce.LoginServlet
servlet.login.initArgs=\
 java.naming.factory.initial=weblogic.jndi.TengahInitialContextFactory,\
 java.naming.provider.url=t3://localhost:7001


#
# Web Storefront to our entire online-store
#
servlet.wsf.code=com.wiley.compBooks.ecommerce.WebStorefrontServlet


#
# The servlet that manages list of products available
#
servlet.productbase.code=com.wiley.compBooks.ecommerce.ProductBaseServlet
servlet.productbase.initArgs=\
 java.naming.factory.initial=weblogic.jndi.TengahInitialContextFactory,\
 java.naming.provider.url=t3://localhost:7001


#
# View all the products in the store
#
servlet.catalog.code=com.wiley.compBooks.ecommerce.CatalogServlet
servlet.catalog.initArgs=\
 java.naming.factory.initial=weblogic.jndi.TengahInitialContextFactory,\
 java.naming.provider.url=t3://localhost:7001


#
# Show information about a specific product
#
servlet.productdetails.code=com.wiley.compBooks.ecommerce.ProductDetailServlet


#
# See the current quote
#
servlet.showquote.code=com.wiley.compBooks.ecommerce.ShowQuoteServlet
servlet.showquote.initArgs=\
 java.naming.factory.initial=weblogic.jndi.TengahInitialContextFactory,\
 java.naming.provider.url=t3://localhost:7001


#
# Purchase the quote
#
servlet.purchase.code=com.wiley.compBooks.ecommerce.PurchaseServlet
servlet.purchase.initArgs=\
 java.naming.factory.initial=weblogic.jndi.TengahInitialContextFactory,\
 java.naming.provider.url=t3://localhost:7001
```

Source 15.8 servlet.properties *(continued)*.

Running the Complete E-Commerce System

We're finally ready to go! Running our e-commerce system involves several steps. Let's walk through the procedure together.

Starting the Business Logic Tier

First, we'll start the business logic tier, which contains our enterprise beans defined in the previous chapters. To do this, we need to start one or more EJB servers. It doesn't matter whether we do this before or after the presentation tier because the presentation tier won't reference the business logic tier until we try to connect with a client. To start up the BEA WebLogic server we tested against, we ran the *t3server* program. See your EJB server documentation for details on starting your server.

Starting the Presentation Tier

Next, we'll start up our presentation tier—one or more Web servers. For simplicity, we'll use Sun's basic free servlet engine, *servletrunner*, to manage our servlets. In a real deployment, you'd probably want to use the Java Web Server or some other advanced Web server. Note that you may need to import your *servlet.properties* file into other Web servers in some other manner because each Web server handles properties differently.

The arguments you pass to *servletrunner* are very important. You must pass an *absolute path* name to *servletrunner* when you tell it where your servlet classes are located. For example, on my machine, I run *servletrunner* as follows:

```
servletrunner -d f:\book\9\ecommerce\gui-classes -s
f:\book\9\ecommerce\servlet.properties
```

The *-d* parameter references where the servlet classes reside, and the *-s* parameter directs *servletrunner* to the correct *servlet.properties* file. Depending on where you install the servlets, your parameters will vary.

Starting the Thin Client

Finally, we start up our thin-client browser, such as Microsoft Internet Explorer or Netscape Navigator. Because servletrunner listens at port 8080 by default, we direct our Web browser to:

```
http://localhost:8080/servlet/login
```

This will cause servletrunner to automatically load the Login servlet, initialize it, and have it service our HTTP request.

Have fun trying out the e-commerce deployment—you've earned it. There are many ways you can extend this deployment as well. For example:

- Play around with different settings in the Pricer rules, and see how that affects your discounts in the view quote screen.

- Try adding a Web-based maintenance utility for importing new Products and Customers.

- Generalize the Pricer to use database-based pricing rules, rather than properties files. Make some new advanced pricing rules that take into account bundling of different kinds of products.

- Add shipping charges to orders.

- Write a fulfillment utility for setting Order status. You'd have to add a new "order status" field to the Order entity bean.

- Add functionality to view existing orders. This could enable users to view how their orders are progressing (whether the order is still being manufactured, being shipped, been delivered, etc.).

- Add a mechanism to associate more details with each product, such as a picture of the product.

- Write a credit card billing system to allow credit-card purchases. Add a credit card number field to the Customer Bean.

- Write a maintenance utility to add new Customers or Products.

There are a plethora of ways you can go with this—and we encourage you to do so. Only by programming with EJB will you truly understand its limitations and virtues.

Optimizations and Design Strategies

Now that we've seen our e-commerce example in action, let's go over a few ways we can tune and optimize it to make it more robust. We'll also look at a few general EJB design strategies that you can apply in your EJB projects.

Unique Primary Key Generation

In our Quote bean designed in Chapter 14, we used a primary key generator via *System.currentTimeMillis()*. This generates a long integer based on the number of milliseconds that have passed since 1970—a quick and dirty way to get unique values.

However, this has a serious limitation. If two concurrent users create primary keys in the same millisecond, we may have a uniqueness collision. And remember, primary keys must be unique values within the database. How can we solve this problem?

One mechanism is to have a singleton object responsible for creating all primary keys. The singleton would ensure that all primary keys are unique because it governs primary key generation. All clients who wish to create a new primary key would have to go through this singleton, even if it involves a network round trip. In fact, this singleton could simply call *System.currentTimeMillis()*. The only restriction is that we'd need to ensure that only one client was ever calling this singleton at any given time. We could easily do this by making a method such as:

```
public abstract class uniqueGen {

    private static long uniqueID = System.currentTimeMillis();

        public static synchronized long getUnique() {
            return uniqueID++;
        }
}
```

Because the method is synchronized, only one client can ever be executing within the method at once. Since we increment the static variable *uniqueID* on each method call, each client will get a monotonically increasing value, guaranteeing unique primary keys. If the program crashes, the *uniqueID* field will be reinitialized to the current time, which is always greater than any previously generated primary key values, guaranteeing that no collisions will occur. The downside to this algorithm is that it does *not* guarantee uniqueness across multiple servers because each server has its own *uniqueGen* singleton. Two instances of *uniqueGen* on two different servers could generate the same primary key.

And, unfortunately, we can't make a singleton enterprise bean either. The EJB 1.0 specification disallows static variables, which eliminates any possibility of a singleton bean. But singletons are a very important and useful design pattern. How do we use singletons in EJB?

The answer is to use JNDI. In Appendix B, we learn how to bind a networked Java object to a directory. Using that mechanism, we can have a singleton object be bound and available at a well-known JNDI tree location. All clients who need to generate Primary Keys would reference this singleton across machine boundaries. The trade-off here is that any Primary Key generation involves a JNDI lookup and a possible network call, which is expensive.

Another alternative is to use the database itself to create Primary Keys. Many databases have their own (proprietary) way of having a unique counter. You can use this to your advantage, by hard-coding a hook to your database's proprietary unique counting mechanism and using that for Primary Key generation. The problem here is your code is nonportable, unless you use properties files to customize the particular database's counter mechanism. But there's another, even larger problem as well—to ensure that two concurrent clients each get a unique counter, you need to serialize all calls to the database counter by making each client run in a transaction, using the TRANSACTION_SERIALIZABLE isolation level. This makes your system grind to a halt because serializable transactions are very, very expensive.

Perhaps the best way to create unique primary keys is to use a globally unique identifier algorithm, such as GUIDs. There are many native algorithms available that take into account things like the current time and your net card's NIC address to ensure that the chance of two generated IDs colliding is almost zero.

Reducing Network Round Trips: Lazy-Loading Beans

One way in which our code is not optimized is that a bean's *ejbLoad()* call forces the bean to load of all its referenced subbeans, all at the same time. This could be a huge waste of resources because the client may never call a method that uses those subbeans.

A better way to approach this is to *lazy-load* beans. Lazy-loading is just-in-time loading of beans, and it reduces the large one-time hit of initially loading an entire graph of subbeans. A future version of EJB may standardize how this is done— perhaps via a deployment descriptor setting on container-managed fields.

For now, you can get lazy-loading functionality by adding a proxy layer of indirection between your beans and your subbeans. This proxy layer is responsible for loading beans dynamically as needed. Thus, instead of loading your subbeans in *ejbLoad()*, you load proxies, and the proxies load the real beans as needed when they're referenced.

A fellow by the name of Rickard Oberg has developed such a proxy package. He calls it *SmartProxies*—intelligent proxies that perform lazy-loading of the real objects, plus a host of other nifty features. The idea is to load the proxies, rather than the real enterprise beans, in your *ejbLoad()* operations. When a client wants to use the real object, the smart proxy will load it dynamically.

Rickard Oberg has some other useful tools available as well. His home page is referenced from the book's Web site (www.wiley.com/compbooks/roman).

Identifying Entity Bean Synchronization Needs

There is one final optimization we can apply to our e-commerce example. In Part II, when we first introduced entity beans, we described how a single entity bean instance can be reused to represent many different database instances of entity bean data. For example, an instance of a bank account entity bean can be reused by the container to represent different bank accounts. When a container wants to load new data into an entity bean instance, it must *passivate* the entity bean instance and call *ejbStore()* to write the instance's state to the database.

Unfortunately, *ejbStore()* is a heavyweight operation because it involves database work. Is it really necessary to call this method? After all, the entity bean instance's state may not need to be written to disk if it hasn't changed. Having to call *ejbStore()* for unmodified entity beans seems like a waste of effort.

Some EJB product vendors have worked around this and made vendor-specific ways of identifying whether an entity bean needs to be persisted. The idea is to associate your entity bean with a dirty flag and persist to the database only if your entity bean is "dirty"—that is, if your bean has been modified. BEA's WebLogic server does this—its EJB container first calls a bean method called *isDirty()*. If your Bean indicates that it's dirty, the container will save the bean state to the database and call *ejbStore()*. Otherwise, it skips this operation, saving precious database bandwidth.

Unfortunately, EJB 1.0 does not standardize a way to perform *isDirty()*. A future version of EJB may change this. For now, you'll have to go with a vendor-specific solution if you want this optimization.

Entity Bean versus Session Bean Design

Our e-commerce example has several session beans and entity beans in action together. As you've learned, session beans encapsulate a business task, such as computing the price of a quote. Changing a pricing algorithm should not affect client code because all pricing logic is encapsulated in a session bean, which resides on the business logic tier. Session beans also handle your transactional needs, reducing the need for clients to be aware of transaction behavior.

Entity beans, on the other hand, are useful for modeling persistent data and the business logic associated with that data. You *must* strive to keep the business logic in entity beans very simple because the more complex your business logic gets, and the more your entity beans are coupled to other parts of your system, the less reusable your entity beans become.

Try to have the scope of your business logic encapsulate everything the entity bean itself needs, but no more. For example, it would probably be wrong for you to perform any heavy interactions with other beans in your entity beans. Of course, because entity beans can reference other, smaller grained entity beans, you will need to perform some bean-bean interactions. But keep this logic straightforward, and have it revolve around the data itself. Keep the task-oriented application logic in session beans, where it can evolve over time. This will yield a highly extensible architecture.

As we've seen with the Teller bean example, ideally you should encapsulate all access to entity beans with a session bean facade. The session beans can perform bulk operations on the entity beans, reducing network latency.

Fine-Grained versus Coarse-Grained Entity Beans

One bottleneck with our deployment is that we make many cross-tier boundary calls. For example, when we display the Quote to the user, our servlets need to retrieve each Quote Line Item's data, and they do so by calling our Quote Line Item enterprise beans. Each call is a cross-tier boundary call, which could result in network lockup—especially if several Web servers are concurrently performing similar tasks.

We've already reduced network round trips somewhat by having our session beans be caches for entity beans. Sometimes, though, that is not enough. One way you could boost the performance of this example is to provide *aggregate* entity bean get and set methods, which get/set many fields at once. Performing these coarse-grained operations will reduce the network load between your tiers tremendously.

In addition, you may want to cache some enterprise bean data in presentation tier objects. For example, you could supplement our Quote bean with a presentation-tier shopping cart that holds all the shopping cart data. A perfect way to do this is to cache your data in regular JavaBeans. This reduces the frequency of calling the business logic tier. Of course, the more you do this, the more your presentation tier starts looking like a business logic tier, which increases coupling between the tiers and lessens the extensibility of your deployment—so be careful with how far you take this notion.

In general, it's acceptable to have fine-grained entity beans such as line-items, so long as you limit over-the-wire interactions with these fine-grained beans. My recommended approach is to interact with fine-grained entity beans through a façade of session beans or larger-grained entity beans.

Finding a Large Number of Entity Beans

When our Product Base servlet searched for every Product sold on the Web site, the returned entity beans could potentially represent millions of records in an underlying database. The database, as well as the network, could easily become bogged down because of this. If our client does not need all the entity beans, this could be wasted effort. What alternatives are there to reduce the clog?

One way to perform all retrieval of these entity beans is to define specialized finder methods. For example, a method such as

```
findBeansMatching(String criteria, int numToReturn)
```

could yield at most *numToReturn* matches, which is highly useful for displaying discrete chunks of data. The trade-off here is overall database load. Databases are designed to handle batch operations very well. Single individual queries cannot be optimized as well. Therefore, if you need to scan through all the entity beans in the database, your overall database usage has increased.

Another question you should be asking yourself is if you really need a finder method at all. Remember that every time a finder method is called, an EJB object is constructed for every element in the returned *Enumeration* (or *Collection* in Java 2). Instead, having a session bean perform these queries for you directly at the database level may improve performance. Once you've found the Primary Keys for the entity beans you're looking for, you can construct EJB objects for only those beans via a *findByPrimaryKey()* on the found keys.

Summary

In this chapter, we've finally completed our e-commerce deployment. We began the chapter by writing our e-commerce servlets, and we showed how they tied in with enterprise beans. We then executed the deployment and looked at ways to extend it. Finally, we covered some broad performance tuning tips that apply not only to this deployment, but to almost any other EJB deployment as well. If you've made it this far, then congratulations because you now have a real-world e-commerce deployment using EJB under your belt!

Introduction to Appendices

I n this final section of the book, we describe several ancillary topics to EJB programming. Specifically:

Java Remote Method Invocation (RMI). Appendix A kicks things off by exploring Java RMI. Here you'll gain a solid foundation in RMI, at both the conceptual and programmatic levels. You'll also see how RMI is used in the EJB world and how it compares with CORBA.

The Java Naming and Directory Interface (JNDI). Appendix B then continues by investigating the JNDI, a standard Java extension package for performing naming and directory operations. We'll learn the concepts, how to program with JNDI, and how JNDI relates to EJB.

The Extensible Markup Language (XML). Appendix C is a brief introduction to XML. XML is a very complementary technology to J2EE, as it provides a universal standard for structuring content in electronic documents. Several J2EE APIs depend on XML, including EJB 1.1 and Java Server Pages (JSPs).

The EJB 1.1 Specification. Appendix D surveys the new EJB 1.1 specification. EJB 1.1 increases code portability, defines the roles of EJB development more crisply, and leverages XML.

Making an EJB Purchase Decision. Appendix E is an overview of making an EJB purchase decision. It reviews common criteria that you should be taking into account when shopping for EJB products.

EJB API and Diagram Reference. Finally, Appendix F is a quick reference for programmers to use during EJB development. It includes diagrams illustrating what's really going on in an EJB system, a guide to the core EJB API, and a transaction reference.

Understanding Java Remote Method Invocation (RMI)

J ava Remote Method Invocation (RMI) is the Java language's native mechanism for performing simple, powerful networking. RMI allows you to write distributed objects in Java, enabling objects to communicate in memory, across Java Virtual Machines, and across physical devices.

RMI is an alternative to using CORBA, the Object Management Group's distributed object architecture. How do the two compare? It's becoming tougher and tougher to draw the line. In fact, neither RMI nor CORBA is clearly a superior technology.

Historically, RMI has had several distinct advantages over CORBA. For example, RMI provides almost seamless, simple, transparent integration into the Java language itself. The overhead cost of developing an application that uses RMI is very low. RMI's strength lies in ease of use, and it has had great appeal to software developers who want to focus on the business logic of their code and leave the networking to RMI.

By way of comparison, CORBA has historically been well suited for enterprise applications. CORBA provides a cross-platform, cross-language architecture. CORBA also provides a full suite of enterprise features, such as transactions, security, and persistence. The Internet Inter-Orb Protocol (IIOP), a robust protocol for distributed object communications, is used behind the scenes in CORBA.

Note that both these trade-offs are historical. The differences between RMI and CORBA are beginning to disappear because both RMI and CORBA are learning from each other. Many of the services specific to CORBA are becoming available with RMI coupled with the Java 2 Platform, Enterprise Edition. Similarly, the ease of use of RMI is becoming available in CORBA. In essence, the two camps are converging. We'll look at exactly how later in this appendix and also in Chapter 11.

This appendix examines the benefits and drawbacks of RMI and details the architecture and logic behind it. We also compare RMI with CORBA, and we examine how RMI and EJB relate. After reading this, you will be able to write your own distributed object applications based on the RMI standard.

Remote Method Invocations

A *remote procedure call (RPC)* is a procedural invocation from a process on one machine to a process on another machine. RPCs enable traditional procedures to reside on multiple machines, yet still remain in communication. They are a simple way to perform cross-process or cross-machine networking.

A *remote method invocation* in Java takes the RPC concept one step further and allows for distributed *object* communications. RMI allows you to invoke methods on objects remotely, not merely procedures. You can build your networked code as full objects. This yields the benefits of an object-oriented programming, such as inheritance, encapsulation, and polymorphism.

Remote method invocations are by no means simple. Below are just some of the issues that arise:

Marshalling and unmarshalling. Remote method invocations (as well as RPCs) allow you to pass parameters, including Java primitives and Java objects, over the network. But what if the target machine represents data differently than the way you represent data? For example, what happens if one machine uses a different binary standard to represent numbers? The problem becomes even more apparent when you start talking about objects. What happens if you send an object reference over the wire? That pointer is not usable on the other machine because that machine's memory layout is completely different from yours. *Marshalling* and *unmarshalling* is the process of massaging parameters so that they are usable on the machine being invoked on remotely. It is the packaging and unpackaging of parameters so that they are usable in two heterogeneous environments. As we shall see, this is taken care of for you by Java and RMI.

Parameter passing conventions. There are two major ways to pass parameters when calling a method: *pass-by-value* and *pass-by-reference*, as shown in Figure A.1. When you pass by value, you pass a copy of your data so that the target method is using a copy, rather than the original data. Any changes to the argument are reflected only in the copy, not the original. Pass-by-reference,

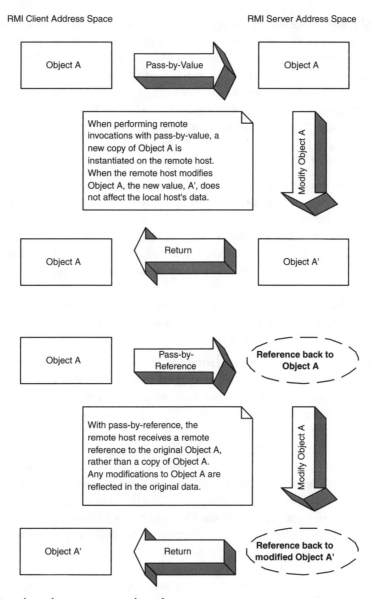

RMI Client Address Space

RMI Server Address Space

Object A

Pass-by-Value

Object A

When performing remote invocations with pass-by-value, a new copy of Object A is instantiated on the remote host. When the remote host modifies Object A, the new value, A', does not affect the local host's data.

Modify Object A

Object A

Return

Object A'

Object A

Pass-by-Reference

Reference back to Object A

With pass-by-reference, the remote host receives a remote reference to the original Object A, rather than a copy of Object A. Any modifications to Object A are reflected in the original data.

Modify Object A

Object A'

Return

Reference back to modified Object A'

Figure A.1 Pass-by-value versus pass-by-reference.

on the other hand, does not make a copy. With pass-by-reference, any modifications to parameters made by the remote host affect the original data. The flexibility of both the pass-by-reference and pass-by-value models are advantageous to have, and RMI supports both. We'll see how in the pages to come.

Distributed garbage collection. The Java language itself has built-in garbage collection of objects. Garbage collection allows users to create objects at will, and it leaves the destruction of objects to the underlying Java Virtual Machine. But in a distributed object system, things become more complicated. An object residing on a remote host might have a reference (called a *remote reference*) to a local object. Thus, the remote host has a reference that actually refers to an object across the network, rather than a local object. But how does garbage collection work then? After all, a JVM's garbage collector runs within that JVM and does not take into account object references from remote hosts. Because of this, a *distributed garbage collector* is needed to track remote hosts that reference local objects.

Network or machine instability. With a single JVM application, a crash of the JVM brings the entire application down. But consider a distributed object application, which has many JVMs working together to solve a business problem. In this scenario, a crash of a single JVM should not cause the distributed object system to grind to a halt. To enforce this, remote method invocations need a standardized way of handling a JVM crash, a machine crash, or network instability. When some code performs a remote invocation, the code should be informed of any problems encountered during the operation. RMI performs this for you, abstracting out any JVM, machine, or network problems from your code.

Downloadable implementations. Remote method invocations allow you to pass whole Java objects as parameters to methods invoked over the network. This means, for example, that you can pass a *java.lang.String* over the network as a parameter to a method. If you pass an entire Java object to a target machine, what you're really passing is that object's data to the target machine. In our String example, this could be the String's character buffer. But objects also contain code, and that code might not be available on the target machine. For example, String objects have a method called *length()* that returns the length of the String. This logic, as well as the other logic surrounding objects, is stored in *.class* files in Java. The target machine needs those class files so that it can construct the code portion of the objects you send as parameters to methods over the network. RMI allows for these class files to be automatically downloaded behind the scenes, relieving you of this dogmatic chore. This also means RMI is a very dynamic system, allowing for different object implementations to come in over the wire.

Security. We mentioned that RMI contains built-in dynamic class loading. This allows object implementations to arrive from remote, and possibly hostile, sources. Java applets are perfect examples because they are downloaded on the fly and could be malicious. A security mechanism needs be in place to restrict possibly hostile implementations and grant system-level access only to authenticated implementations. RMI has such support.

Activation. You'd like to be able to invoke methods on remote objects, even if they are not in memory yet. If you invoke a method on a remote object that is not in memory yet, RMI contains measures to automatically fault the object into memory so that it can service method calls. This is called *remote object activation*.

As you can see, there's a lot involved in performing remote method invocations. RMI contains measures to handle many of these nasty networking issues for you. This reduces the total time spent dealing with the distribution of your application, allowing you to focus on the core functionality.

RMI is the Java language's native remote method invocation service. It ships with the Java 2 platform, and it is required for any 1.1-compatible Java Runtime Environment. It is built entirely in Java and is therefore highly cross-platform. This is a big win for RMI—you can write your networking code once and run it in any recent Java Runtime Environment. Contrast this with proprietary, platform-dependent RPC libraries, and you can see some real value in RMI.

 Java RMI has historically *not* been supported by Microsoft. If you wanted to use Microsoft's Java environment, you needed to download an RMI add-on, available at **ftp://ftp.microsoft.com/developr/msdn/unsup-ed/rmi.zip**. A recent court order, however, has required Microsoft to support Java RMI in future versions of its product. Make sure the environment you're developing with does indeed support RMI.

RMI Architecture

In RMI, any object whose methods can be invoked from another Java VM is called a *remote object*. Remote objects are networked objects, which expose methods that can be invoked by remote clients. The physical locations of remote objects and the clients that invoke them are not important. For example, it's possible for a client running in the same address space as a remote object to invoke a method on that object. It's also possible for a client across the Internet to do the same thing. To the remote object, both invocations appear to be the same.

RMI and Interface versus Implementation

In Chapter 1, we discussed one of object-oriented design's great programming practices—the separation of the interface of code from its implementation.

The interface defines the exposed information about an object, such as the names of its methods and what parameters those methods take. It's what the client works with. The interface masks the implementation from the viewpoint of clients of the object, so clients deal only with the end result: the methods the object exposes.

The implementation is the core programming logic that an object provides. It has some very specific algorithms, logic, and data.

By separating interface from implementation, you can vary an object's proprietary logic without changing any client code. For example, you can plug in a different algorithm that performs the same task more efficiently.

RMI makes extensive use of this concept. All networking code you write is applied to interfaces, *not* implementations. In fact, you *must* use this paradigm in RMI—you do not have a choice. It is impossible to perform a remote invocation directly on an object implementation. You can operate solely on the interface to that object's class.

To designate that your object can be invoked on remotely, your class must implement the interface *java.rmi.Remote*. You must perform this by creating your own custom interface extending *java.rmi.Remote*. That interface should have within it a copy of each method your remote object exposes.

For example, the following code snippet is a valid remote interface:

```
public interface IMyRemoteInterface extends java.rmi.Remote {
    public void foo() throws java.rmi.RemoteException;
}
```

Your remote object implementation (that is, the networked object) implements this interface. Client code that wants to call methods on your remote object must operate on *IMyRemoteInterface*.

An additional restriction of RMI is that each method must also throw a *java.rmi.RemoteException*. A *java.rmi.RemoteException* is thrown when there is a problem with the network, such as a machine crashing or the network dying. Your remote objects can throw their own regular exceptions in addition to the required *java.rmi.RemoteException*.

Stubs and Skeletons

One of the benefits of RMI is an almost illusionary, transparent networking. You can invoke methods on remote objects just as you would invoke a method on any other Java object. In fact, RMI completely masks whether the object you're invoking on is local or remote. This is called *local/remote transparency*.

But local/remote transparency is not as easy as it sounds. To mask the fact that you're invoking on an object residing on a remote host, RMI needs to somehow simulate a local object that you can invoke on. This local object is called a *stub*, and it is responsible for accepting method calls locally and *delegating* those method calls to their actual object implementations, which are possibly located across the network. This effectively makes every remote invocation appear to be a local invocation. You can think of a stub as a placeholder for an object that knows how to look over the network for the real object. Because you invoke on local stubs, all the nasty networking issues are hidden behind the scenes.

Stubs are only half of the picture. We'd like the remote objects themselves—the objects that are being invoked on from remote hosts—to not worry about networking issues as well. Just as a client invokes on a stub that is local to that client, your remote object needs to accept calls from a *skeleton* that is local to that remote object. Skeletons are responsible for receiving calls over the network (perhaps from a stub) and delegating that call to the remote object implementation. This is shown in Figure A.2.

One of the more interesting responsibilities of stubs and skeletons is the marshalling and unmarshalling of parameters. RMI relies on a technology called *object serialization* to assist with this, which we'll learn about a bit later.

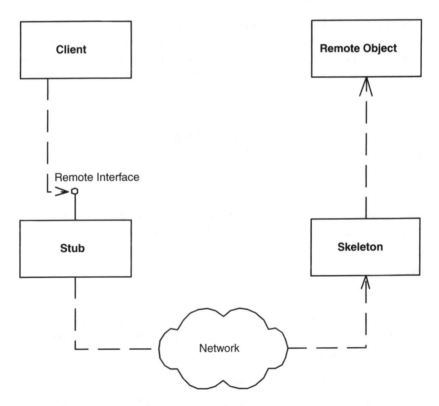

Figure A.2   Stubs and skeletons.

Bootstrapping and the RMI Registry

For a client and a server to start talking, they need some way to connect. Acquiring this connection is known as *bootstrapping*. How does RMI accomplish bootstrapping?

RMI provides an entity known as the *RMI Registry* for this purpose. When you want to make an object remotely accessible, you register it with the registry. You give the registry a name for the object during this registration. From then on, the Registry will route all incoming requests for that name to your object. You can think of the RMI Registry as a giant hashtable that maps names to objects.

The RMI Registry accomplishes this task by sitting at a well-known network port and listening for incoming connections. When a remote client wants to access an object registered with a particular registry, the client issues a request over the network to the registry. The Registry reads the request, looks up the name of the remote object requested, and returns the stub for that remote object to the client. This is shown in Figure A.3.

You can have as many RMI registries as you want on a machine, but only one Registry per VM. And, of course, only one Registry can be bound to a specific port. There are thousands of ports for you to choose from, though, so that's no problem. If you don't specify a port, RMI uses port 1099 by default. Remember that both your client and server must agree on which port the Registry sits at, or they will never find each other.

There are two ways to start the RMI Registry. You can launch it as a stand-alone program by typing

```
rmiregistry
```

from a command prompt. You can also start a registry from inside your Java program by accessing the *java.rmi.Registry* class.

RMI URLs

An *RMI URL* is a Java String that is used to locate a remote object on another Java Virtual Machine. It looks very similar to other types of URLs, such as http://www.java.sun.com or ftp://ftp.microsoft.com. RMI enforces the following conventions for URLs:

1. The URL must begin with the text `rmi://`.
2. Next, you may specify the target machine where the Java Virtual Machine is located—for example, `rmi://foobar.baz.com/`. If you don't specify a target machine, RMI defaults to the local host.

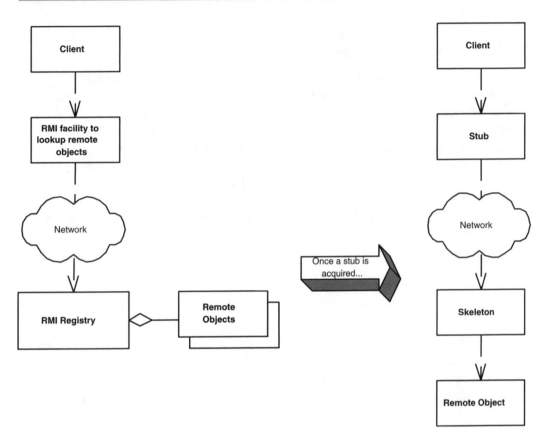

Figure A.3 Bootstrapping with the RMI Registry.

3. Finally, append the name of the remote object to which you wish to acquire a remote reference. For example, if your remote object is bound as the name "myObject", you can reference it from any machine in the world with the RMI URL `rmi://foobar.baz.com/myObject`.

Looking Up a Remote Object

So far, our discussion has touched the following concepts:

- An RMI Registry is a remote object used by clients for bootstrapping, or initially connecting, to your remote objects. Remote objects register themselves with the registry, which clients connect to at a well-known port.

- RMI URLs are used to identify the locations of objects over the network.

How do clients use these two abstractions to actually connect to remote objects? This is what the *java.rmi.Naming* class is used for. When a client wants to acquire a reference to a remote object, he or she goes through *java.rmi.Naming*.

RMI URLs versus JNDI

RMI URLs are great for identifying object locations across the network, but they are fairly inflexible for enterprise computing. You need to hard-code RMI URLs into your Java code (or provide them in properties files). If the locations of your distributed objects change, you must change and possibly redeploy each client of those distributed objects. In essence, there is no location transparency of distributed objects.

A much more flexible system of looking up distributed objects is to use naming and directory services through the Java Naming and Directory Interface (JNDI). Naming and directory services allow for your client code to escape hard-coding the locations of distributed objects, yielding a much more robust deployment. We'll study how that's done in Appendix B.

java.rmi.Naming is responsible for connecting to RMI registries for the purposes of finding remote objects.

The most important method that *java.rmi.Naming* exposes is the *lookup()* method, which takes an RMI URL, connects to an RMI registry on a target JVM, and returns a *java.lang.Object* representing the remote object. The returned object is actually the remote stub, and it can be cast into your remote object's interface type.

RMIC—The RMI Compiler

The stubs and skeletons we described earlier provide a screen to block networking issues and make it appear as if things are happening locally. Both stubs and skeletons must implement your custom remote objects' interfaces. Because of

Skeletons in the Java 2 Platform

The RMI runtime in Java 2 contains generic code that will perform the function of skeletons for you. Hence, skeleton generation is optional in Java 2. Stubs, on the other hand, are still required to be generated for each remote object.

This makes sense because a skeleton is responsible for delegating invocations to a remote object. It doesn't matter to what interface the skeleton code conforms. A stub, on the other hand, is accessed directly by your client code and hence must implement your remote object's remote interface. This gives clients the illusion that they are invoking on a local object implementation.

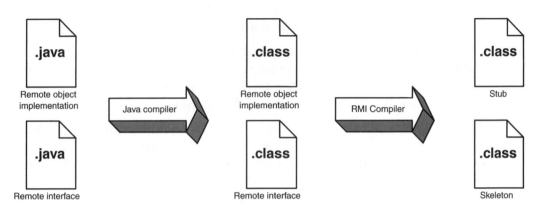

Figure A.4   Generating stubs and skeletons with RMIC.

this, no two stubs or skeletons are the same, and they must be generated anew for each remote object class that you create. Fortunately, Sun ships a tool to perform this generation for you. The name of the tool is *rmic*, the RMI compiler. It takes as input your remote object implementation (the class that implements your remote interface), and it creates a stub and skeleton for that remote object. This is shown in Figure A.4. The stub mimics each method exposed by the remote object, copying the method signatures exactly, so clients can call that stub locally as if the remote object itself were there.

Object Serialization and Parameter Passing

This next section discusses how parameters are passed in Java RMI. We also explore the power of *object serialization* and how it assists in parameter passing and object marshalling/unmarshalling.

Passing by Value

When invoking a method using RMI, all parameters to the remote method are passed by *value*. This means that all parameters are copied from one machine

---

Taking a Look at the Generated Proxy Code

You can use the *-keepgenerated* option of *rmic* to see the generated stub (or "proxy") code. This is useful if you want to learn how RMI works internally. It's also great if you want to rewrite your own stub/skeleton layer of RMI. You can use these generated proxies as a basis for your code.

to the other when the target method is invoked.

Passing objects by value is in stark contrast with the Java programming language, which uses a pass-by-reference calling convention for an object's state. In Java, when calling a method normally with an Object parameter, the reference to the object is copied, but the actual object's data is not.

There's a big problem with passing by value. If you're trying to pass an object over the network and that object contains references to other objects, how are those references resolved on the target machine? A memory address on one machine does not map to the same memory address on another machine. Also, the referenced object may not even exist on the target machine. How do we get around this?

Object Serialization

Java introduces the concept of *object serialization* to handle this problem. *Serialization* is the conversion of a Java object into a bit-blob representation of that object. Once in bit-blob form, the object can be sent anywhere—onto your hard disk or across the network. When you're ready to use the object again, you must *deserialize* the bit-blob back into a Java object. Then it's magically usable again.

The Java language handles the low-level details of serialization. In most cases, you don't need to worry about any of it. In order to tell Java that your object is serializable, your object must implement the *java.lang.Serializable* interface. That's all there is to it—take this one simple step, and let Java handle the rest. *java.lang.Serializable* defines no methods at all—it's simply a *marker interface* that identifies your object as something that can be serialized and deserialized.

How Objects Are Serialized

Once your objects implement *java.lang.Serializable*, they can be serialized into a stream of data. The serialization process is accomplished automatically by Java Serialization. You can provide your own custom serialization by implementing the *writeObject()* method on your object. This might be useful if, for example, you'd like to perform some sort of compression on your data before your object is converted into a bit-blob.

Similarly, deserialization is also automatic in most cases. If you want to, you can provide your own deserialization method as well. This method is called *readObject()*, and it is called automatically whenever your object is deserialized. This might be useful if, for example, you'd like to decompress your object's data during the deserialization process.

This process is shown in Figure A.5.

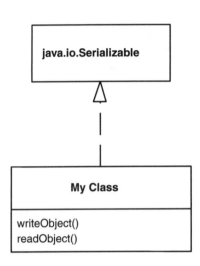

writeObject() is responsible for saving the state of the class.

readObject() is responsible for restoring the state of the class.

These two methods will be called automatically when an object instance is being serialized or deserialized.

If you choose not to define these methods, then the default serialization mechanisms will be applied. The default mechanisms are good enough for most situations.

Figure A.5   The Java serialization process.

Rules for Serialization

Java serialization has the following rules regarding member variables held in serialized objects:

- Any basic primitive type (int, char, etc.) is automatically serialized with the object and is available when deserialized.
- Java Objects can be included with the serialized bit-blob or not; it's your choice. The way you make your choice is as follows:
  - Objects marked with the transient keyword are not serialized with the object and are not available when deserialized.
  - Any object that is *not* marked with the transient keyword must implement *java.lang.Serializable*. These objects are converted to bit-blob format along with the original object. If your Java objects neither are transient nor implement *java.lang.Serializable*, a *NotSerializableException* is thrown when *writeObject()* is called.

Thus, when you serialize an object, you also serialize all nontransient subobjects as well. This means you also serialize all nontransient sub-subobjects (the objects referenced from the subobjects). This is repeated recursively for every object until the entire reference graph of objects is serialized. This recursion is

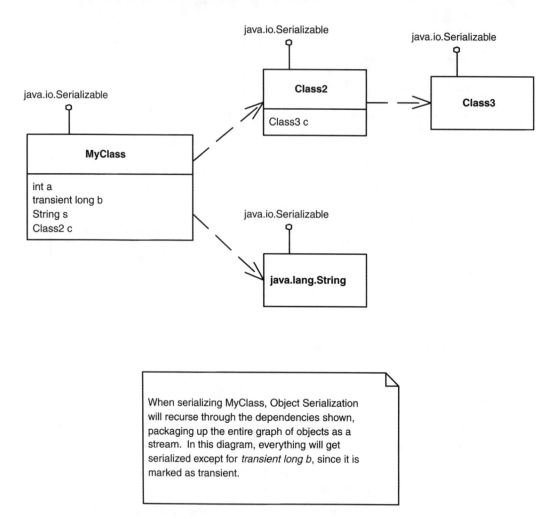

Figure A.6   Object serialization.

handled automatically by Java serialization, as shown in Figure A.6. You simply need to make sure that each of your member objects implements the *java.lang. Serializable* interface.

What Should You Make Transient?

How do you know which member variables should be marked transient and which should not? Here are some good reasons why you would want to mark an object as transient:

- The object is very large. Large objects may not be suitable for serialization because operations you do with the serialized blob may be very intensive.

Examples here include saving the blob to disk or transporting the blob across the network.

■ The object represents a resource that cannot be reconstructed on the target machine. Some examples of such resources are database connections and sockets.

■ The object represents sensitive information that you do not want to pass in a serialized stream.

Note that object serialization is not free—it is a very heavyweight operation for large graphs of objects. Make sure you take this into account when designing your distributed object application.

Uses of Object Serialization

Object serialization is the mechanism used when passing parameters by value using RMI. When you pass an argument using RMI, RMI checks whether your object is serializable. If it is, it serializes the object and sends it over the network. The recipient takes the object and deserializes it, making it available for use. When the object is deserialized, all of its references to other objects are automatically reconstructed because those objects referred to were also part of the bit-blob. There's no danger of a reference being invalid after an invocation because references are dynamically reconstructed in real time. This is shown in Figure A.7.

Thus, object serialization assists Java RMI with the marshalling (packaging) of parameters and the unmarshalling (unpackaging) of parameters. But serialization has a wide variety of other purposes as well. For instance, object serialization provides an instant file format for your objects. All you need to do is serialize them and write the serialized bit-blob to disk. It's a quick and easy way to make your state persistent. For more information about Object Serialization, please see the book's accompanying Web site.

How RMI Simulates Pass by Reference

As we've said, Java RMI relies on Object Serialization for passing parameters via remote method invocations. The scenario we've described is *pass by value*, where an entire graph of objects is serialized into a bit-blob, sent across the network, and then deserialized on the target machine.

But passing parameters by value can lead to inefficiencies. What if your referenced graph of objects is very large? What if you have lots of state to send across the network? The ensuing network lag from performing the invocation may be unacceptable.

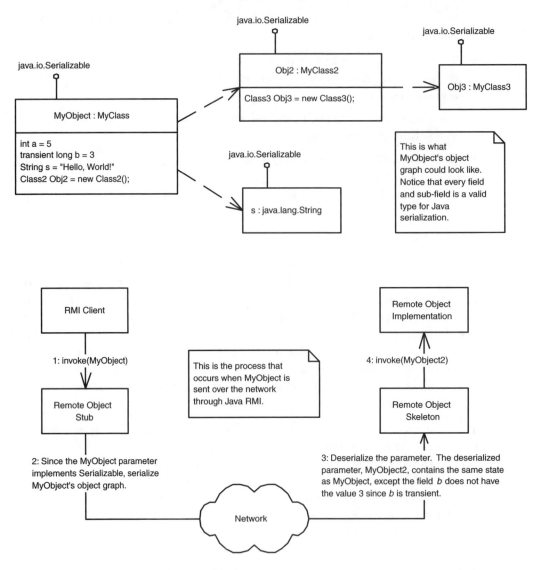

Figure A.7 Java RMI and Object Serialization.

Because of this, there is another way to pass arguments. RMI simulates a pass-by-reference convention, which means the arguments are not copied over. Rather, the remote method works with the original object.

If you want a parameter by reference, the parameter itself must be a remote object—that is, an object that is callable remotely. Let's consider the scenario where a remote host acquires a reference to this remote object, perhaps as a parameter to one of its own methods. That remote host can then invoke operations on this remote object, the operations will occur on the local host, rather than on the remote host. That is, the operation is itself a remote method invocation that runs over the network.

But what is actually passed as a parameter when passing a remote object by reference? After all, we are not copying that remote object over the network. Yet the remote host still needs some object on which to operate. The answer is to pass that remote object's stub object, as shown in Figure A.8. Stubs are network-aware references to remote objects. Just as in regular Java you have references to objects, in RMI you have remote references to objects. *java.rmi.RemoteStub* objects are the manifestation of those remote references. These are the exact same stubs we described earlier that are generated by the *rmic* tool.

Java RMI simulates pass by reference only if the object parameter being passed is itself a remote object and is callable from remote hosts. In this case, the stub for the remote object is passed, rather than the object itself being serialized.

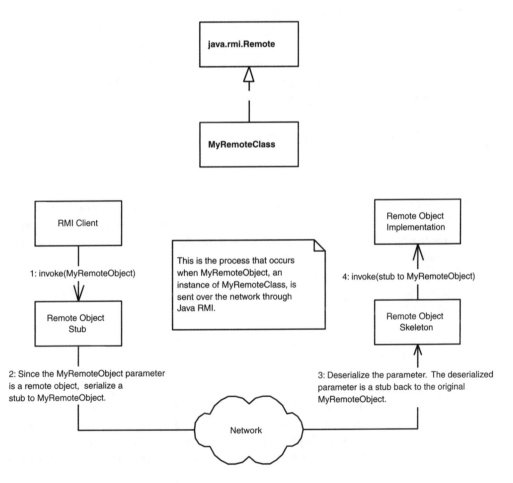

Figure A.8 Pass by reference with Java RMI.

Because Java RMI stubs are also serializable, they are passable over the network as a bit-blob. This is why earlier we said that *all* parameters in Java RMI are passed by-value. Thus, Java RMI only *simulates* pass by reference by passing a serializable stub, rather than serializing the original object. By making your parameters remote objects, you can effectively avoid the network lag in passing large objects.

In summary, we have the following rules for passing objects using Java RMI:

- All Java basic primitives are passed by value when calling methods remotely. This means copies are made of the parameters. Any changes to the data on the remote host are not reflected in the original data.

- If you want to pass an object over the network by value, it must implement *java.lang.Serializable*. Anything referenced from within that object must follow the rules for Java Serialization. Again, any changes to the data on the remote host are not reflected in the original data.

- If you want to pass an object over the network by reference, it must be a remote object, and it must implement *java.rmi.Remote*. A stub for the remote object will be serialized and passed to the remote host. The remote host can then use that stub to invoke callbacks on your remote object. There is only one copy of the data at any time, which means that all hosts are updating the same data.

Exporting Your Remote Objects

To make your object a remote object available to be invoked on by remote hosts, your remote class must perform *one* of the following steps:

Extend the class *java.rmi.server.UnicastRemoteObject*. *UnicastRemoteObject* is a base class from which you can derive your remote objects. When your remote object is constructed, it will automatically call the *UnicastRemoteObject*'s constructor, which will make the object available to be called remotely. You can see this by looking at the code for *UnicastRemoteObject* constructor, included with the Java 2 platform (formerly known as JDK Java Development Kit 1.2):

```
protected UnicastRemoteObject() throws RemoteException {
exportObject((Remote)this);
}
```

Don't extend *java.rmi.server.UnicastRemoteObject*. Perhaps your objects are inheriting implementation from another class. In this case, because Java does not allow for multiple implementation inheritance, you cannot extend *UnicastRemoteObject*. If you do this, you must manually export your object

Is *UnicastRemoteObject* My Only Choice?

If you want your objects to become remote objects, you have several options besides using *java.rmi.server.UnicastRemoteObject*.

1. You can extend *java.rmi.activation.Activatable,* which allows your objects to be kicked into memory when needed (called "activation"). For more information about activation, see the book's accompanying Web site.

2. You can also extend *javax.rmi.PortableRemoteObject,* which allows you to use the Internet Inter-ORB Protocol, a robust protocol for distributed object communications. This is very handy for CORBA interoperability. For more information, see Chapter 11.

so that it is available to be invoked on by remote hosts. To export your object, call *java.rmi.server.UnicastRemoteObject.exportObject()*.

A Simple Example

We now present a simple example illustrating the basics of RMI. In this example, a remote object exposes one method, *flip()*. *flip()* takes an integer as a parameter and negates it, returning the result. You can't get much simpler than this.

The IFlip Interface

First, we must create a remote interface containing every method that our remote object will expose to remote hosts. This interface must extend *java.rmi.Remote*. The code is shown in Source A.1.

```
package com.wiley.compBooks.roman.rmi.flip;

import java.rmi.Remote;
import java.rmi.RemoteException;

/**
 * The remote interface for the remote object.  Remote hosts use this
 * remote interface to perform any operations on the remote object.
 */
public interface IFlip extends Remote {
    public int flip(int i) throws RemoteException;
}
```

Source A.1 IFlip.java.

The Flip Class

Now let's create the remote object class. This class implements the IFlip interface, and it is shown in Source A.2.

We have a quick *main()* program that starts things up. First, we start an RMI Registry (if needed). We then construct our remote object. In our remote object constructor, we export our remote object and bind it to an RMI registry. Once the remote object's constructor is complete, this object will be available forever for any Virtual Machine to invoke on, by contacting the RMI registry listening at the specified port.

```java
package com.wiley.compBooks.roman.rmi.flip;

import java.rmi.*;
import java.rmi.registry.*;
import java.rmi.server.*;

/**
 * The remote object that performs the integer negation.
 * Notice that we extend UnicastRemoteObject, which will
 * automatically export our remote object for us.
 */
public class Flip extends UnicastRemoteObject implements IFlip {

    /**
     * Our main() method starts things up
     */
    public static void main(String args[]) throws Exception {

        /*
         * If the user called this program incorrectly,
         * report an error
         */
        if (args.length != 2) {
            System.err.println("Syntax: Flip <true|false> <port>");
            System.err.println();
            System.err.println("true demarcates to start RMI Registry, " +
                "false demarcates to bind to existing one.");
            System.err.println("port is the port # for RMI Registry.");
            System.exit(-1);
        }

        /*
         * If desired, start RMI Registry at specified port.
         */
```

Source A.2 Flip.java *(continues)*.

```
        int port = new Integer(args[1]).intValue();
        Registry reg = null;
        if (args[0].equals("true")) {
            reg = LocateRegistry.createRegistry(port);
            System.out.println("Successfully created registry.");
        }

        /*
         * Otherwise, acquire a reference to an existing
         * registry which the user may have started up.
         */
        else {
            reg = LocateRegistry.getRegistry(port);
            System.out.println("Connected to existing registry.");
        }

        /*
         * Start up our Flip remote object.  It will
         * auto-bind itself to the RMI Registry.
         */
        Flip flip = new Flip(reg);
    }

    /*
     * Our remote object's constructor performs RMI Initialization.
     */
    public Flip(Registry reg) throws Exception, RemoteException {

        /*
         * Since we extend UnicastRemoteObject, the super
         * class will export our remote object here.
         */
        super();

        /*
         * Bind our Flip remote object to the RMI registry
         */
        reg.rebind("Flip", this);
        System.out.println("Flip object bound.");
    }

    /*
     * Our single business logic method, flip(), is callable over
     * the network.  Notice that it throws a RemoteException,
     * which is required for all remote methods.
     */
    public int flip(int i) throws RemoteException {
        return i * -1;
    }
}
```

Source A.2 Flip.java *(continued).*

The Client

Finally, let's take a look at the client code calling the remote object. First, we perform a lookup on the remote host's RMI registry. This lookup returns a remote stub for the remote object we'd like to invoke upon. Next, our client simply calls the remote object's *flip()* method, which flips the value of 5 to –5 and prints the result. Note that the client operates on the IFlip interface rather than on Flip itself, as RMI dictates. The code is depicted in Source A.3.

```
package com.wiley.compBooks.roman.rmi.flip;

import java.rmi.Remote;
import java.rmi.RemoteException;
import java.rmi.Naming;

public class FlipClient {

    public static void main (String[] args) {

        IFlip flip = null;

        /*
         * Do some parameter checking..
         */
        if (args.length != 2) {
            System.err.println(
                "Usage: Flip <hostname of Flip remote object> <port>");
            System.exit(-1);
        }

        /*
         * Set the security manager (required because we may
         * be downloading implementation)
         */
        try {
            System.setSecurityManager(new java.rmi.RMISecurityManager());
        }
        catch (java.rmi.RMISecurityException exc) {
            System.err.println("Security violation " + exc.toString());
            System.exit(-1);
        }

        /*
         * Get a handle to a remote Flip object.
         */
```

Source A.3 FlipClient.java *(continues).*

```
        try {
            /*
             * We use an RMI URL to locate the remote object.
             * We construct the RMI URL from the
             * parameters passed from the end user.
             */
            String targetMachine = "rmi://" + args[0] + ":" + args[1] +
                "/Flip";
            System.out.println("Attempting to contact " + targetMachine);

            /*
             * Get the object from the remote RMI Registry
             */
            Remote remoteObject = Naming.lookup(targetMachine);

            /*
             * Perform a quick check to make sure the object
             * is of the expected IFlip interface type.
             */
            if (remoteObject instanceof IFlip) {
                flip = (IFlip) remoteObject;
            }
            else {
                throw new Exception(
                    "Bad object returned from remote machine");
            }
        }
        catch (Exception e) {
            System.err.println("Error in lookup() " + e.toString());
            System.exit(-1);
        }

        /*
         * Print the result of flipping 5.  We're actually
         * invoking on a stub here, which delegates across the
         * network to the real object.
         */
        try {
            System.err.println(flip.flip(5));
        }
        catch (RemoteException e) {
            System.err.println("Remote error: " + e.toString());
        }
    }
}
```

Source A.3   FlipClient.java *(continued)*.

Compiling the Program

We compile the program using the normal java compiler, *javac*. The additional step we need is to generate the stub (and optionally skeleton) using rmic:

```
rmic com.wiley.compBooks.roman.rmi.flip.Flip
```

This generates the stub and skeleton files, *Flip_Stub.class* and *Flip_Skeleton.class*.

Running the Program

To start the server, we type:

```
rmiregistry 1000
java com.wiley.compBooks.roman.rmi.flip.Flip false 1000
```

The first line starts a new RMI Registry at port 1000. The second line starts up our Flip server, which binds to the RMI Registry we started at port 1000.

Finally, we run the client program:

```
java com.wiley.compBooks.roman.rmi.flip.FlipClient localhost 1000
```

When running the client, we need to specify the target machine where the Flip server is running. We use `localhost` to denote that the client and server are on the same machine. We also need to specify the port (1000) at which it should look for the RMI Registry that contains an entry for our Flip object.

The following is the output of the server:

```
Connected to existing registry.
Flip object bound.
```

And the following is the output of the client:

```
Attempting to contact rmi://localhost:1000/Flip
-5
```

As you can see, the remote object correctly negated 5 to –5. This completes our basic example.

Dealing with Remote Exceptions

When designing object models with RMI, you usually want to have as much of your code decoupled from RMI as possible. Ideally, you want to separate your business logic from your networking code as much as possible. This is very difficult to do with RMI because of all those annoying RemoteExceptions being thrown, which you need to wrap try..catch blocks around (see our previous example). How can you effectively separate the two?

One common design pattern with RMI is to construct a "gateway" remote object that is dependent on RMI. Once a client has acquired a handle to the gateway remote object, the gateway can serve as a conduit into an entire suite of objects running within a JVM. All method invocations can happen through the gateway. When the gateway receives a request, it *delegates* calls to other local objects on its machine—those objects providing the business logic. In the simplest case, only one reference to one remote object on another machine is needed in order to access that machine's functionality. This technique also reduces the number of times you need to form that initial RMI connection. We depict this in Figure A.9.

Of course, you can never fully separate your application from the network. Somewhere, at some point, you'll need to deal with Remote Exceptions being thrown due to networking issues. Some may consider this a limitation of RMI because the network is not entirely "seamless," because Remote Exceptions force you to differentiate a local method from a remote method. But in some ways, this is an advantage of RMI as well. Interlacing your code with Remote Exceptions forces you to think about the network and encourages distributed object developers to consider issues such as the network failing, the size of parameters going across the network, and more.

RMI's Remote Exception limitations

As we've said, Remote Exceptions are useful for detecting nasty networking issues, such as application death, machine crashes, and network failures. But how robust are Remote Exceptions for detecting problems in enterprise-class deployments?

Let's investigate this matter by using RMI as a communications mechanism for performing banking operations. Banking operations are a perfect example because they are mission-critical. Any errors in a bank statement could result in millions in lost funds.

We'll implement a bank operator as a distributed object based on the RMI standard. One of the methods our banking operator exposes is withdraw(), which is used for withdrawing money. Seems simple enough, right?

Wrong. There is a serious danger in doing this. Let's say you call withdraw() remotely, but the network dies at some point:

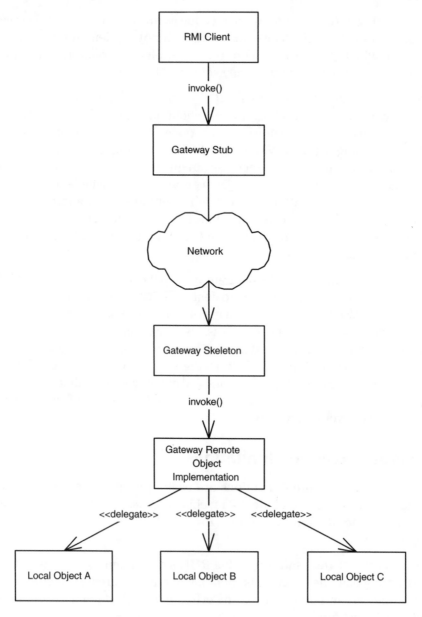

Figure A.9 Using gateway objects to mask RMI from your business objects.

- If the network dies *before* the method was invoked, then the money will not be withdrawn.
- If the network dies *after* the method was invoked, then the money will be withdrawn.

As you can see, these two scenarios produce drastically different results. There are other problematic scenarios as well, such as processes crashing or databases crashing. How can you deal with this in your RMI code? The blunt answer is that with straight RMI, you can't do this in any clean way. You will never know for sure if your method finished properly.

These types of problems are really what *transactions* were made to assist with. If a networking problem happens during a transaction, the transaction will be rolled back, undoing any changes (such as a withdrawal) that may have happened. In this sense, transactions are acting as a sophisticated form of exception handling. Similarly, if a database crashes, transactions guarantee that the database will be in a consistent state.

Because of this, and because of the host of other middleware necessary, RMI by itself is not sufficient for enterprise-class deployments. But RMI does have its purpose in the Java 2 Platform, Enterprise Edition (J2EE)—as a networking technology that allow for distributed objects to communicate, which complements the other Enterprise Java APIs.

RMI Tips

The following are helpful hints for using RMI:

- Design your remote interface and object interface separately.
- To minimize the number of objects you register with the RMI Registry, you can register one object and have that object be a factory for other objects you need. Clients contact the RMI Registry once, get a handle to the remote factory, and have the factory generate the objects you really want. Because the factory generates the real objects, they don't clutter up the RMI Registry. For more details about factories, see the link provided on this book's Web site.
- You can debug your RMI programs by using RMI's built-in logging facility. You can turn on logging by setting *java.rmi.logCalls=true* as a system property when launching your VM.
- If you need to cross a firewall with RMI, this is also possible, as described in the accompanying sidebar.

Advanced RMI

So far, in this chapter we've touched the basics of RMI. Let's move on to some advanced issues. Specifically, we'll show you how to do the following:

RMI and Firewalls

A *firewall* is a barrier that controls network traffic for the purposes of security. Although necessary for a secure intranet, a firewall can be a real hassle to deal with when you start talking about distributed computing. Many corporate intranets will let users through the firewall only to browse the Web, which happens at port 80. And that port is reserved for Web traffic.

It would seem that firewalls make it impossible to do any form of client/server communication—a pretty harsh restriction. Imagine if you code a Java applet to be downloaded by clients who are sitting behind their corporate intranet firewalls. If your applet needs any communication with your central server, you're out of luck.

Out of luck, that is, unless you could somehow get the use of port 80. What if you sent all client/server traffic as regular HTTP requests/responses? This blatant hack is exactly how RMI really solves the firewall problem. RMI passes through firewalls by simulating an RMI Registry listening at port 80. It wraps all transported data in Web tags, so that they look like normal Web communications. The masking of a request as an HTTP request on port 80 is known as *HTTP tunneling* through firewalls. By tunneling through and pretending that you're doing normal HTTP communications, you can reach your target RMI Registry.

To use this tunneling, a Web server must be deployed on the same machine on which the target RMI Registry sits. That Web server acts as a *router*—it takes requests that come in at port 80 (which the firewall permits) and routes them to the actual port where the RMI Registry sits on that machine. This is accomplished by a CGI script included with the Sun's Java 2 platform. By this mechanism, clients can get through their firewalls because their firewalls think they are making normal HTTP port 80 communications. RMI accomplishes this transparently—you don't need to worry about these details. All you need to do is install the java-rmi.cgi script included with the JDK.

Note that firewalls will not allow any incoming connections from outside the firewall to be established. This means that if you're behind a firewall, you can't start an RMI Registry to listen for incoming connections. You must initiate all connections—external VMs may not make remote invocations to your machine, due to the firewall's blockade.

For more information on this subject, see the link provided on this book's Web site.

1. Take RMI to a bit more depth by building a simple message queuing product on top of RMI

2. Throw exceptions across the network using RMI

3. Pass objects by value as well as by reference

4. Exploit RMI's distributed garbage collector

We'll explain these concepts in hands-on examples.

RMI Example: A Message Queue for Distributed Logging

Traditionally, when software components communicate, they do so in a *synchronous* manner. That is, when component A invokes a method on component B, component B executes immediately. Component A must block (that is, wait) until component B is done. This is shown in Figure A.10.

In many scenarios (especially server-side development), however, it is nice to have components communicate in an *asynchronous* manner. This means component B does not execute immediately. It also means component A does not block. How is this accomplished?

One way is to get a third party involved. The third party acts as a storage for *deferred invocations*. Each invocation component A makes is stored as a message

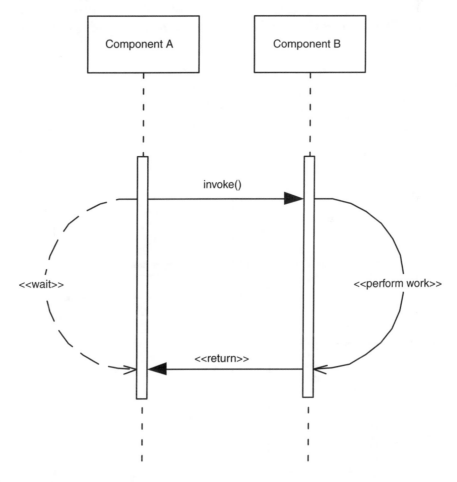

Figure A.10 Synchronous communication.

in this third party's internal queue. The queue is used to keep an ordering of the messages. When component B wants to service the invocation, it contacts the third party and reads the message off the queue. Component A is a producer of data for the queue, and component B is a consumer of data. By using this networked queue of data, we can have distributed components service requests at their leisure, in an asynchronous manner.

This technology is called *Message Queueing*. A *Message Queue* is the queued storage that stores messages from distributed objects across the enterprise. They are responsible for accepting new messages as they arrive and delivering others as they are requested. Message Queues can also have their messages be transactional in nature, gaining all the benefits of transactions that we listed in Chapter 10. Message Queues are shown in Figure A.11.

Message Queues fall under the general software heading of *Message-Oriented Middleware (MOM)*. There are a number of MOM vendors on the market, including IBM, Microsoft, and BEA Systems. In the Java world, you can accomplish

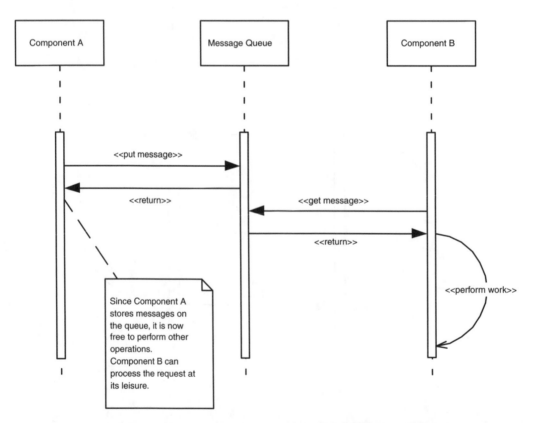

Figure A.11 Asynchronous communication using Message Queues.

MOM tasks by using the *Java Messaging Service* (*JMS*). JMS is a high-level API for using different MOM products.

In this example, we'll be developing our own stripped-down Message Queue using Java RMI. The Message Queue we develop will be useful for illustrating asynchronous networked producer-consumer relationships, as well as giving you hands-on experience with RMI.

The Channel Class

The Message Queue we create will be useful for a variety of domains. It is possible that several different sets of components would want to use the Message Queue at the same time, but for different purposes. For example, one set of components might want to use the Message Queue as a distributed logging facility. One or more *logging components* could store objects on the queue that represented information to be logged. Other *listener components* could take messages off the queue, logging the information in some way—say, one listener could represent the logs in a UI, while another could log it to a text file.

Thus, for a generic logging mechanism, we need some concept of differentiating messages on our queue. We provide this functionality with the concept of a *channel*. A channel represents a particular queue that one or more components are using. This is shown in Figure A.12. If two sets of components are using different channels, they won't interfere with each other. You send and receive data

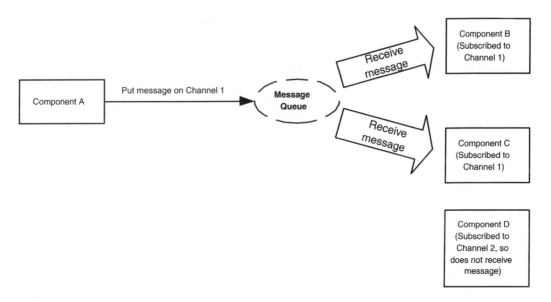

Figure A.12   Different channels in our Message Queue.

on only the channel you're using, much as if it were a TV channel or radio frequency that you were tuning in. The code for the Channel class is shown in Source A.4.

```java
package com.wiley.compBooks.roman.rmi.mq;

import java.util.Random;

/**
 * Abstraction representing a channel for sending messages.
 * Running Java code can make as many copies of this as necessary,
 * so that multiple distributed objects can communicate on the
 * same channel.
 */
public class Channel implements java.io.Serializable {

    // A single, static randomizer for channel id generation
    private static Random rand = new Random(System.currentTimeMillis());

    private String id, name;

    /**
     * Creates a new Channel.
     *
     * @param name The name of the channel.
     */
    public Channel(String name) {

        this.name = name;

        /*
         * Create a new, random identifier for this channel
         */
        this.id = String.valueOf(rand.nextInt());
    }

    /**
     * Because we use Channels as elements of a hashtable, we
     * hash based on the channel id.  We don't hash based on
     * the Channel name because that may not be unique.
     */
    public int hashCode() {
        return id.hashCode();
    }

    public boolean equals(Object obj) {
        return id.equals(obj.toString());
    }
```

Source A.4   Channel.java *(continues)*.

```
    public String toString() {
        return id;
    }

    /**
     * Returns the channel name.
     */
    public String getName() {
        return name;
    }
}
```

Source A.4   Channel.java *(continued)*.

The IMessageQueue Interface

The Message Queue itself will be structured as follows. The Message Queue class, *MessageQueue*, is accessed by RMI clients using its remote interface, *IMessageQueue. IMessageQueue* exposes methods to (for example) put and get messages on internal queues representing specific channels. All Message Queue operations happen through this interface. The code for *IMessageQueue* is shown in Source A.5.

Notice that each method throws a RemoteException, as required by RMI.

```
package com.wiley.compBooks.roman.rmi.mq;

import java.rmi.Remote;
import java.rmi.RemoteException;
import java.io.InputStream;

/**
 * Remote Interface for the Message Queue.  Clients should use
 * this API for communicating with the Message Queue.
 */
public interface IMessageQueue extends Remote {

    /**
     * Initializes a channel for a particular client.  Our
     * MessageQueue will initialize an internal queue for
     * storing messages on that channel.
     *
     * @param name The name of the channel to create.
     *
```

Source A.5   IMessageQueue.java *(continues)*.

```
         * @return The newly created channel
         */
        public Channel createChannel(String name) throws MessageQueueException,
            RemoteException;

        /**
         * Call to close channel
         */
        public void destroyChannel(Channel channel) throws MessageQueueException,
            RemoteException;

        /**
         * Waits for the next message to occur in this channel,
         * and returns that message.
         */
        public Object getMessage(Channel channel, long timeout) throws
            MessageQueueException, RemoteException;

        /**
         * Puts a message on the queue of a particular channel.
         */
        public void putMessage(Channel channel, Object message) throws
            MessageQueueException, RemoteException;
    }
```

Source A.5   IMessageQueue.java *(continued)*.

The MessageQueueException Exception

If you noticed in the preceding code, each method on the *IMessageQueue* interface also threw a *MessageQueueException*. This is an application-level exception, and it is meant to denote logical problems, such as invalid channels. We'll reserve the *java.rmi.RemoteExceptions* for Java RMI to indicate networking problems. This is a good design philosophy that you should follow when writing your RMI programs (in fact, EJB enforces the separation of application-level and system-level exceptions, which we describe in Chapter 4).

Our exception simply extends the normal *java.lang.Exception* class. The code for this command is detailed in Source A.6.

The MessageQueue Class

Internally, our MessageQueue class uses a hashtable for storing messages. Each hashtable entry represents one channel. Thus, we use channel identifiers as hash values for the hashtable. The value of each hash entry is a queue—to store messages for that particular channel. Thus, we're using a hashtable of queues. This

```
package com.wiley.compBooks.roman.rmi.mq;

/**
 * Exceptions thrown by MessageQueue
 */
public class MessageQueueException extends Exception {

    public MessageQueueException() {
        super();
    }

    public MessageQueueException(Exception e) {
        super(e.toString());
    }

    public MessageQueueException(String s) {
        super(s);
    }
}
```

Source A.6   MessageQueueException.java.

enables us to have as many channels as we want, with a message queue for each channel. This is illustrated in Figure A.13.

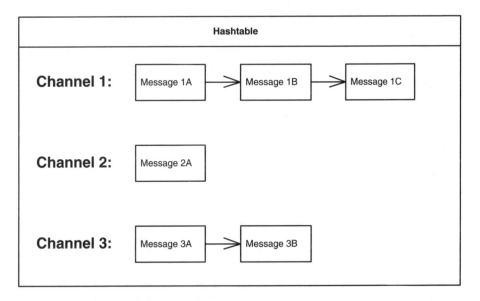

Figure A.13   Our Message Queue architecture.

The actual channel identifiers are abstracted out by the Channel class. You create a new Channel by calling the *createChannel* method on *IMessageQueue*. You can pass these Channels around, *clone()* them, and so on. The Channel object implements *java.io.Serializable*, so you pass it around by value. By giving each client the same Channel object, you can have many clients all sharing the same channel.

The following procedure shows how the Message Queue can be typically used:

1. Start up the *MessageQueue* remote object server. *MessageQueue* registers itself with the local RMI registry.

2. Your client looks up the *IMessageQueue* object over the network using the RMI lookup facilities.

3. Your client calls *IMessageQueue.createChannel()* to create a new channel and queue for storing messages. This returns a Channel object.

4. Your client can then give the Channel object to any other party, such as another process that wants to send or receive messages on the same channel.

5. Anyone who owns a Channel object can send messages by calling *IMessageQueue.putMessage()* with the correct Channel. The messages can be any Java objects. Anyone who wants to receive messages can similarly call *IMessageQueue.getMessage()*.

6. After everyone's done using the Message Queue, the channel can be destroyed by calling *IMessageQueue.destroyChannel()*.

One interesting thing about our Message Queue is that we don't dictate what kinds of objects are passed. All we say is that each object has to be a *java.lang.Object*. This means that both *java.io.Serializable* messages and java.rmi.Remote messages are possible, for both pass-by-value and pass-by-reference semantics. If the client tries to store non-RMI-safe objects, a *java.rmi.RemoteException* will automatically be thrown.

The basic idea of a Message Queue brings up a very basic Computer Science problem called the *readers/writers problem*: What if someone tries to read a message when there are no messages on the queue?

We have two possibilities here. We can either throw an exception if there is no data available, or we can wait for data to become available. The problem with throwing an exception is that client code needs to continuously poll the message queue for any available messages. This is definitely not a scalable solution.

Therefore, we'll enforce that any clients who request messages are suspended until a message has arrived. To do this, we use Java's built-in threading support. When a client asks for a message, if the queue is empty we *wait()* the thread, suspending the client. This means that both the client's thread and the remote

Threads and Transactions

Our message queue synchronizes all operations to *putMessage()* and *getMessage()* messages on channel queues. This effectively makes each *put* and *get* a critical section, and it ensures that every *put* and *get* operation is atomic with respect to other threads.

If you've read the transactions chapter of this book (Chapter 10), you may recognize how analogous this is to performing atomic transactions. This is no accident—transactions and object synchronization are highly related.

calling thread are effectively suspended. When someone puts a new message on the queue, we call *notifyAll()*, which wakes up any clients that we called *wait()* on.

Of course, strictly speaking, we should also consider the opposite half of the readers/writers problem: What happens if the queue overflows when there are too many messages on it? We'll make sure to implement our queue to be theoretically unlimited in length, so we don't have to worry about that situation. The code for MessageQueue is given in Source A.7.

```
package com.wiley.compBooks.roman.rmi.mq;

import java.util.*;
import java.io.*;
import java.rmi.*;
import java.rmi.registry.*;
import java.rmi.server.*;
import com.objectspace.jgl.Queue;

/**
 * MessageQueue is a generic Buffer for passing information.
 * The MessageQueue is a Hashtable, where each hash entry
 * represents a "channel" that someone wishes to listen to.
 * Each hash entry is a queue of messages for that channel.
 * Listening threads are suspended until messages arrive.
 * This allows networked applications to take advantage of
 * event-driven networked programming but have events occur
 * synchronously.
 */
public class MessageQueue extends UnicastRemoteObject implements
    IMessageQueue {
```

Source A.7 MessageQueue.java *(continues)*.

```
/**
 * main() creates the Message Queue.
 */
public static void main(String args[]) {
    if (args.length != 1) {
        System.err.println(
            "Usage: MessageQueue <port to bind RMI Registry to>");
            System.exit(-1);
    }

    try {
        MessageQueue queue = new MessageQueue(Integer.parseInt(args[0]));
    }
    catch (Exception e) {
        System.err.println(e);
    }
}


/*
 * Hashtable for storing channel queues of messages
 */
private Hashtable dataHash = new Hashtable();

/**
 * Initialization.
 *
 * @param port Port to register MessageQueue at.
 */
public MessageQueue(int port) throws Exception, RemoteException {
        super();

        System.out.println("");
        System.out.println("MessageQueue starting up...");

        /*
         * Set the security manager
         */
        try {
            System.setSecurityManager(
                new java.rmi.RMISecurityManager());
        }
        catch (java.rmi.RMISecurityException e) {
                throw new Exception("Security violation " +
                e.toString ());
        }

        /*
         * Start up an RMI Registry at designated port
```

Source A.7 MessageQueue.java *(continues)*.

```java
            */
            Registry reg = LocateRegistry.createRegistry(port);

            /*
             * Bind our Message Queue object to the registry
             */
            reg.rebind("MessageQueue", this);

        System.out.println("MessageQueue now in ready mode.");
    }

    /**
     * Creates a new channel (queue) for a particular client.
     *
     * @return The new channel
     */
    public Channel createChannel(String name) throws MessageQueueException {
        try {
            Channel channel = new Channel(name);

            /*
             * Create the queue for the channel, and store it
             * in the hashtable.
             */
            Queue queue = new Queue();
            dataHash.remove(channel);
            dataHash.put(channel, queue);

            System.out.println("Channel " + channel.getName() + " created.");

            return channel;
        }
        catch (Exception e) {
            throw new MessageQueueException(e);
        }
    }
    /**
     * Call to close channel
     */
    public void destroyChannel(Channel channel) throws MessageQueueException {
        System.out.println("Channel " + channel.getName() +
        " is now closed.");

        try {
            /*
             * Take the channel off the hashtable
             */
            Object obj = dataHash.remove(channel);
```

Source A.7   MessageQueue.java *(continues)*.

```
            /*
             * Signal any threads that were
             * waiting on that channel
             */
            if (obj instanceof Queue) {
                Queue queue = (Queue) obj;
                synchronized (queue) {
                    queue.notifyAll();
                }
            }
        }
    catch (Exception e) {
        throw new MessageQueueException(e);
    }
}

/**
 * Gets a message off the queue.  Blocks until one arrives.
 *
 * @param channel Channel name to get messages from
 * @param timeout How long to block for max
 *
 * @return the next message, or null if time out
 */
public Object getMessage(Channel channel, long timeout) throws
    MessageQueueException {

    try {
        /*
         * Get the right queue off the hashtable
         */
        Queue queue = Channel2Queue(channel);

        /*
         * Wait around until someone has a message for me.
         *
         * We synchronize threads in case other clients
         * are trying to read/write to the channel.  By
         * synchronizing, they each have to wait their turn.
         *
         * We synchronize on the queue object rather than the
         * entire class, so that other channels aren't
         * affected by our activity.
         */
        synchronized (queue) {
            if (queue.isEmpty()) {
                queue.wait(timeout);
            }
```

Source A.7 MessageQueue.java *(continues).*

```java
                /*
                 * In case channel was destroyed..
                 */
                if (queue.isEmpty()) {
                    return null;
                }
            }

            /*
             * Pop the message off the queue, and return it.
             */
            return queue.pop();
        }
        catch (Exception e) {
            throw new MessageQueueException(e);
        }
    }


/**
 * Puts a message onto the queue for a certain channel.
 *
 * @param channel Channel to put message on.
 * @param message Message to put on the channel.
 */
public void putMessage(Channel channel, Object message) throws
    MessageQueueException {

    try {
        // Get the queue for this channel
        Queue queue = Channel2Queue(channel);

        /*
         * Stick the message in the queue.
         *
         * We synchronize threads in case other clients
         * are trying to read/write to the channel.  By
         * synchronizing, they each have to wait their turn.
         *
         * We synchronize on the queue object rather than the
         * entire class, so that other channels aren't
         * affected by our activity.
         */
        synchronized (queue) {

            /*
             * Push the message onto the queue.
             */
            queue.push(message);
```

Source A.7 MessageQueue.java *(continues)*.

```
                    /*
                     * There's a new message, so signal
                     * any waiting threads.  Of course, if
                     * multiple threads are waiting, only one
                     * of them will acquire the new lock
                     * because they're all waiting inside of
                     * critical sections.
                     */
                    queue.notifyAll();
                }
            }
        catch (Exception e) {
            throw new MessageQueueException(e);
        }
    }


    /*
     * Gets a queue based upon a channel.  Used internally.
     *
     * @param channel The channel for the queue you want to get
     */
    private Queue Channel2Queue(Channel channel) throws Exception {

        /*
         * Get the queue off the hashtable and return it.
         */
        Object obj = dataHash.get(channel);
        if (obj instanceof Queue) {
            return (Queue) obj;
        }
        else {
            throw new Exception("Error: No such channel: " +
                channel.getName() + ".");
        }
    }
}
```

Source A.7   MessageQueue.java *(continued)*.

The QueueClient Class

Finally, we write a sample piece of code that uses the Message Queue, embodied in the QueueClient class. The client code starts up three threads: Two threads write to a channel, and the third reads data from the channel. This is shown in Source A.8.

Objectspace's JGL and the Java Collections Framework

If you noticed, we used Objectspace's Generic Collections Library (JGL) 3.1.0 for our Message Queue's internal queue. JGL is an example of a *collections framework*. A collections framework is useful for representing and manipulating collections, or groups of objects, in a very object-oriented fashion.

Collections frameworks have three main notions:

- The interface to a collection of objects
- Specific data structure implementations of interfaces
- Specific algorithms that can be applied to a collection

For example, by using the JGL, you can create a data structure such as a queue and then apply an iterator to iterate over the items in the queue. But just as easily, you could apply an iterator to a stack instead. You could also apply a sorting algorithm on a doubly linked list structure. The possibilities are endless.

In fact, you get a free collections framework built into the Java 2 platform: the Java Collections Framework. Java Collections have the advantage that they're very easy to understand and use. But JGL is much more powerful. In fact, we could have implemented our entire Message Queue very simply by combining Objectspace's powerful networking technology, Voyager, with JGL.

This book's Web site provides links for more information about both JGL and Java Collections.

```java
package com.wiley.compBooks.roman.rmi.mq;

import java.rmi.Remote;
import java.rmi.RemoteException;
import java.rmi.Naming;

public class QueueClient extends Thread {

    public static void main (String[] args) {

        IMessageQueue queue = null;

        if (args.length != 2) {
            System.err.println("Usage: Queue <hostname of MessageQueue" +
                " remote object> <port to connect to>");
            System.exit(-1);
        }
```

Source A.8   QueueClient.java *(continues)*.

```
        /*
         * Set the security manager
         */
        try {
            System.setSecurityManager(new java.rmi.RMISecurityManager());
        }
        catch (java.rmi.RMISecurityException exc) {
            System.err.println("Security violation " + exc.toString());
            System.exit(-1);
        }


        /*
         * Get a handle to a remote MessageQueue object.
         * We name this handle as an RMI URL.
         */
        try {
            String targetMachine = "rmi://" + args[0] + ":" + args[1] +
                "/MessageQueue";
            System.out.println("Attempting to contact " + targetMachine);

            /*
             * Get the object from the remote RMI Registry
             */
            Remote remoteObject = Naming.lookup(targetMachine);

            /*
             * Perform a quick check to make sure the object
             * is of the expected IMessageQueue interface type
             */
            if (remoteObject instanceof IMessageQueue) {
                queue = (IMessageQueue) remoteObject;
            }
            else {
                throw new Exception(
                    "Bad object returned from remote machine");
            }
        }
        catch (Exception e) {
            System.err.println("Error in lookup() " + e.toString());
            System.exit(-1);
        }

        try {
            /*
             * Create a channel on the queue
             */
            Channel channel = queue.createChannel("Log");
```

Source A.8 QueueClient.java *(continues)*.

```
            /*
             * Start up two senders and a logger.  The senders
             * will send messages to the queue, and the logger
             * will receive messages from the queue.
             */
            QueueClient sender1 = new QueueClient(queue, channel, true,
                "Sender #1", 333);
            QueueClient sender2 = new QueueClient(queue, channel, true,
                "Sender #2", 1000);
            QueueClient logger = new QueueClient(queue, channel, false,
                "Logger", 0);

            /*
             * Let the clients run for 10 seconds, then kill
             * the channel.
             */
            Thread.sleep(10000);
            queue.destroyChannel(channel);
        }
        catch (Exception e) {
            System.err.println(e.toString());
        }
}

/*
 * Per-client local variables
 */
private Channel channel;
private boolean sendMessages;
private IMessageQueue queue;
private String name;
private int delay;

/**
 * Starts up a client to hit the queue.
 *
 * @param queue The queue to use.
 * @param channel The channel to communicate on the queue
 * @param sendMessages
 *              TRUE: Send messages to the channel.
 *              FALSE: Receive messages from the channel.
 * @param name The name of this client.
 * @param delay If sending, delay between sending messages
 */
public QueueClient(IMessageQueue queue, Channel channel, boolean
    sendMessages, String name, int delay) {
    this.channel = channel;
    this.sendMessages = sendMessages;
```

Source A.8 QueueClient.java *(continues)*.

```
        this.queue = queue;
        this.name = name;
        this.delay = delay;

        /*
         * Start the client thread up
         */
        start();
    }


    /**
     * This method actually starts the client.  This is
     * automatically called from the constructor.
     */
    public void run() {
        try {

            /*
             * If I'm a sender, then send messages to the queue.
             * The message content is the name of this client,
             * plus an incrementing variable.
             */
            if (sendMessages) {

                int i = 0;

                while (true) {
                    /*
                     * Remember that strings are auto-
                     * converted to Objects by the compiler!
                     */
                    queue.putMessage(channel, name + ": " + i++);
                    sleep(delay);
                }
            }

            /*
             * Otherwise, retrieve and log messages from
             * the queue
             */
            else {
                while (true) {
                    String msg = (String) queue.getMessage(channel, 5000);
                    if (msg != null) System.out.println(msg);
                }
            }
        }
```

Source A.8 QueueClient.java *(continues)*.

```
        catch (Exception e) {
           System.err.println(e);
        }
    }
}
```

Source A.8   QueueClient.java *(continued)*.

Compiling the Program

We compile the Message Queue using the normal javac compiler, and we then generate stubs/skeletons using rmic as follows:

```
rmic -d classes com.wiley.compBooks.MessageQueue.MessageQueue
```

This generates the needed *MessageQueue_stub.class* and *MessageQueue_skel.class* proxies.

Running the Program

To start the Message Queue, we type:

```
java com.wiley.compBooks.MessageQueue.MessageQueue 5000
```

Here, 5000 is the port at which the RMI Registry is running.

Next, we need to run the Message Queue client program:

```
java com.wiley.compBooks.MessageQueue.QueueClient localhost 5000
```

When running the client, we need to specify the target machine where the Message Queue is running. In this example, `localhost` is the name of the (local) Message Queue server machine. We also need to specify the port (5000) at which it should look for the Message Queue object's RMI registry.

The following is the output of the Message Queue:

```
MessageQueue starting up...
MessageQueue now in ready mode.
Channel Log created.
Channel Log is now closed.
```

Here is what the client program reports:

```
Attempting to contact rmi://foobar:5000/MessageQueue
security properties not found. using defaults.
```

```
Sender #1: 0
Sender #2: 0
Sender #1: 1
Sender #1: 2
Sender #2: 1
Sender #1: 3
Sender #1: 4
Sender #1: 5
Sender #2: 2
Sender #1: 6
Sender #1: 7
Sender #1: 8
Sender #2: 3
Sender #1: 9
Sender #1: 10
Sender #1: 11
Sender #2: 4
Sender #1: 12
Sender #1: 13
Sender #1: 14
Sender #2: 5
Sender #1: 15
Sender #1: 16
Sender #1: 17
Sender #2: 6
Sender #1: 18
Sender #1: 19
Sender #1: 20
Sender #2: 7
Sender #1: 21
Sender #1: 22
Sender #1: 23
Sender #2: 8
Sender #1: 24
Sender #1: 25
Sender #1: 26
Sender #2: 9
Sender #1: 27
Sender #1: 28
com.wiley.compBooks.MessageQueue.MessageQueueException:
java.lang.Exception: Error: No such channel: Log.
com.wiley.compBooks.MessageQueue.MessageQueueException:
java.lang.Exception: Error: No such channel: Log.
com.wiley.compBooks.MessageQueue.MessageQueueException:
java.lang.Exception: Error: No such channel: Log.
```

What's happened here? First, the client program created a channel on the Message Queue called "Log." It then started three clients of the queue: Sender #1, Sender #2, and the Logger. The Senders each counted up from 0, and they put that number on the Message Queue, along with the Sender's identifier. The messages sent were *java.lang.String* objects, which implement *java.lang.Serializable* and thus are passed by value. The Logger kept reading the messages off the queue and printing out the results. That is why the two senders' messages are interleaved.

After 10 seconds, the main program closed the channel. That's why there are three exceptions at the end—each client could no longer use the channel because it was destroyed. This is the desired functionality; it illustrates how RMI can throw exceptions over the network.

RMI Example: Exploiting Distributed Garbage Collection

Let's continue our advanced RMI discussion with a final illustrative example.

One problem with our MessageQueue example is that the channel queues are stored in a permanent hashtable. The queues stored in the hashtable could become a memory leak if the end users never destroy the channels. We need a way to automatically clean things up.

To avoid memory leaks, we're going to augment our Message Queue with some cleanup routines. Rather than hard-coding our own way of detecting clients who disconnect, we're going to leverage RMI's built-in *Distributed Garbage Collection (DGC)* in a very interesting way.

Distributed Garbage Collection

RMI can automatically clean up objects over the network using DGC. This is done through *leases*. What is an RMI lease? A lease is a temporary holding on an object. If you rent an apartment, you have to renew your lease every year or your landlord will kick you out. The same thing is true with RMI. Whenever a client acquires a remote reference to a remote object, that client automatically starts sending *pings* back to the server the remote object is on. RMI does this automatically whenever a client acquires a *RemoteStub* to a remote object. If no pings come for awhile, that *RemoteStub's* lease has expired. On the server, there's a low-priority thread that runs routinely and cleans up any objects whose leases have expired.

In most scenarios involving remote objects, eventually there will be a point when there are no more remote references to a particular remote object—because either clients have dropped their remote references or the lease has expired. There is a way to detect this with RMI—by implementing the java.rmi.Unreferenced interface. This interface defines one method: public void *unreferenced()*. This method is called whenever the remote object has no more *RemoteStub* references to it. That is, *unreferenced()* will get called as soon as all clients' *RemoteStub* objects are garbage collected or as soon as leases expire on all clients that may have held *RemoteStub* objects but crashed. This is exactly what we want.

If you're using Java RMI-IIOP (a standard Java extension we cover in Chapter 11), you cannot rely on distributed garbage collection. RMI-IIOP does not support it to remain compatible with languages that support only synchronous destruction.

Reimplementing the Channel Class

We're going to modify our Message Queue so that a queue is automatically destroyed if no more clients hold references to the Channel object for that queue. The basic steps are as follows:

1. Modify the Channel object so that it is now a fully fledged remote object, not just a simple serializable object. Channel objects will no longer be passed by value; they'll be passed by reference. This means clients will acquire *RemoteStub* objects rather than copies of Channel objects. When a client receives a stub, the distributed garbage collector will start tracking that client, and it will monitor for when the client drops its Channel reference or disconnects.

2. Make the Channel object implement the *java.rmi.Unreferenced* interface. When no more remote references to the Channel exist, DGC will automatically call the *unreferenced()* method.

3. Implement *unreferenced()* to clear the message queue from the main hashtable. That way, when all clients disconnect from a channel, we'll destroy that channel's queue, eliminating memory leaks.

The bulk of the modified code is shown in Source A.9.

Notice that we are also implementing a new IChannel interface, which is the RMI Remote Interface for Channels. This is needed because Channel objects are no longer serializable.

A few other classes have changed as well, but in minor ways. To keep this appendix as brief as possible, the details have been omitted from the text. See the CD-ROM or Web site for the full code.

Compiling and Running the Program

We compile the program in a similar way, except that we now need to generate stubs/skeletons for the Channel class as well. We do this in the same manner as we generated stubs/skeletons for our message queue in the previous example.

The DGC uses 10 minutes as the default timeout for leases. To shorten this, you can set the *java.rmi.dgc.leaseValue* to the desired number of milliseconds (e.g., by calling java—*Djava.rmi.dgc.leaseValue=2000* for 2 seconds). If you want to see the Distributed Garbage Collector in action, set *java.rmi.logCalls=true*.

```
package com.wiley.compBooks.roman.rmi.mqdgc;

import java.util.Random;
import java.rmi.*;
import java.rmi.server.*;

/**
 * Abstraction representing a channel for sending messages.  There
 * is only one copy of this Channel object, and multiple stubs for
 * the channel can be generated and passed around from client to
 * client.  When all the stubs have been garbage collected, this
 * original Channel object will be collected via the Distributed
 * Garbage Collector.  This will force the Channel object to free
 * the associated queue of messages in the Message Queue - see the
 * finalize() method below.
 */
public class Channel extends UnicastRemoteObject implements IChannel,
Unreferenced {

    .
    .
    .


    public void unreferenced() {
        try {
            System.out.println("Channel.unreferenced() called.");
            queue.destroyChannel(this);
        }
        catch (Exception e) {
            System.err.println(e);
        }
    }

    .
    .
    .


}
```

Source A.9 MessageQueue.java.

The following is the log for the Message Queue:

```
MessageQueue starting up...
MessageQueue now in ready mode.
Channel Log created.

<Many minutes later, after all clients disconnected...>
```

```
Channel.unreferenced() called.
Channel Log is now closed.
```

As you can see, even though we never directly destroyed the channel's queue, the Channel object destroyed its own queue when all remote clients disconnected. When trying this example out, be patient because the DGC often takes a very, very long time before calling *unreferenced()*.

RMI, CORBA, and EJB

Let's conclude our RMI discussion with a few thoughts on how RMI, CORBA, and EJB are related.

RMI or CORBA?

Historically, developers have had to decide between RMI as a simple networking package and CORBA as a heavyweight networking technology that provides additional enterprise-level services. But, as we mentioned earlier in this chapter, the times are changing.

When you combine RMI with some of the other Java APIs, the benefits of CORBA begin to dwindle. For example, the Java Naming and Directory Interface provides naming and directory services, which are related to CORBA's Naming Service. The Java Transaction API and Java Transaction Service can be used to perform robust transactions, which are related to CORBA's Object Transaction Service. Security, MOM support, persistence, and more are all provided in the Java 2 Platform, Enterprise Edition. You can even achieve some semblance of cross-language interoperability by combining RMI with the Java Native Interface (JNI), called RMI/JNI. You can also perform relational database operations over the network by combining Java Database Connectivity (JDBC) with RMI, called RMI/JDBC.

CORBA, on the other hand, is becoming easier and easier to use. CORBA provides a breadth of functionality, which in the past has been very tough to use because you had to learn a separate Interface Definition Language (IDL). Now there are automatic tools that will generate IDL for you. Sun's *Java IDL* product, for example, can read a standard remote interface definition and generate IDL automatically. And with the new CORBA Components proposal, it may be possible to provide many of CORBA's services automatically, providing a rich server-side component architecture for developers.

For these reasons, Sun endorses both RMI and CORBA. There is no clear "winner" in networking technology. As both technologies mature, you'll start to see many of CORBA's services reflected in the Java 2 Platform, Enterprise Edition (J2EE), as well as the ease-of-use of the J2EE in CORBA. The advantage that the J2EE has right now is industry momentum. Many vendors are embracing the J2EE (in fact, most of those vendors are CORBA vendors). If you want to learn more about CORBA and RMI, please refer to Chapter 11.

RMI and EJB

RMI is an essential part of EJB. In EJB, many distributed objects use RMI as the standard API for networking.

EJB Objects

In EJB, your enterprise beans must be made available for remote clients to invoke. This is achieved by using Java RMI.

Note that enterprise beans are not full-fledged remote objects. That is, your beans do not extend *UnicastRemoteObject*. Rather, your beans are wrapped in an RMI-aware shell, called an *EJB object*. EJB objects are the remote objects clients invoke. When a client calls an EJB object, that object delegates the remote call to your bean. This is shown in Figure A.14.

As a bean developer, you need to write the interface to your bean's EJB object. This interface is called the *remote interface*, and it is exactly the same concept as the remote interface that we have been discussing this entire chapter. This remote interface duplicates every method signature that your beans have. That's how things appear seamless to clients—they invoke on the EJB object as if it were the bean itself.

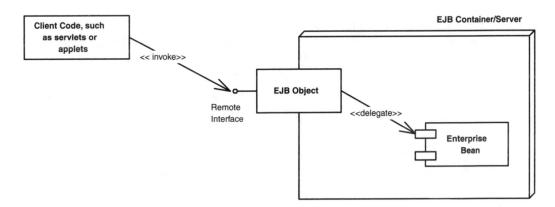

Figure A.14   RMI and EJBObjects.

Here are some characteristics about remote interfaces in EJB:

- An EJB remote interface derives (indirectly) from *java.rmi.Remote*.

- Each method in an EJB remote interface must throw a *java.rmi* *.RemoteException*.

- Each of the remote interface's methods must accept parameters that are valid types for Java RMI. This means your parameters need to be primitives, serializable, or remote objects. This also means that by using the techniques described in this appendix, you can control the pass-by-value or pass-by-reference parameter semantics to your beans.

The EJB object implements the remote interface. But you don't need to write the EJB object—it is automatically generated for you by the EJB container's tools. This is because the EJB object must contain proprietary logic for dealing with transactions, interact with the container in a proprietary way, possibly implement fault tolerance if your bean crashes, and perform other operations that involve the container. That is why you should think of the EJB object as being part of the container itself. The EJB object masks these hairy details from the average bean developer.

The EJB object your clients use can be either the actual EJB object or a *RemoteStub* to an EJB object that is located elsewhere on the network. Your client code doesn't care because it's invoking on the EJB object's interface, which both the object and the stub implement. Thus, EJB local/remote transparency is achieved through RMI.

Home Objects

In EJB, a *home object* is a factory for creating EJB objects. You look up the Home Object using the *Java Naming and Directory Interface (JNDI)*, which is described in Appendix B. Once you have a home object, you call it using Java RMI.

The home object's interface (called the *home interface*) is also a Java RMI remote interface, and it obeys the rules for Java RMI. It must throw remote exceptions, implement *java.rmi.Remote*, and accept serializable parameters. As with EJB objects, home objects are proprietary to each container. Thus, the home object's implementation is generated by the EJB container vendor's tools.

Clients of home objects always deal with the home interface, just as clients of EJB objects always deal with remote interfaces. And as with EJB objects, a reference to a home object could be the actual home object or a *RemoteStub* to the real home object located elsewhere on the network. This is shown in Figure A.15.

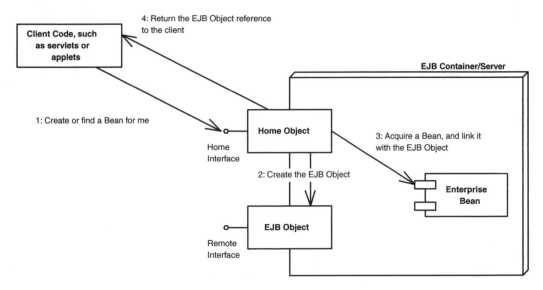

Figure A.15   RMI and home objects.

Summary

In this chapter, you've learned how Java RMI adds distributed object computing power to your Java applications. We've looked at RMI's architecture, comparing it to traditional RPCs. We examined stubs and skeletons, the RMI registry, the RMI compiler, and we've looked at the two ways parameters were passed in RMI. We also took a brief tour of object serialization.

To make things more concrete, we then went through several RMI examples. First, we looked at a simple networked application that flipped a number to its inverse. We then took RMI a step further, and we implemented a useful Message Queue utility. Our last and most advanced RMI example stepped through how to exploit Distributed Garbage Collection for cleanup of state.

Finally, we wrapped up by discussing how RMI, CORBA, and EJB relate. You've taken a big step here and learned an important part of the Java 2 Platform, Enterprise Edition. The next appendix covers another essential concept: naming and directory services.

Understanding the Java Naming and Directory Interface (JNDI)

T he *Java Naming and Directory Interface* (JNDI) is an essential component of the Java 2 Platform, Enterprise Edition (J2EE). JNDI adds value to your enterprise deployments by providing a standard interface for locating users, machines, networks, objects, and services. For example, you can use the JNDI to locate a printer on your corporate Intranet. You can also use it to locate a Java object or to connect with a database. In EJB, JNDI is used extensively for the purposes of locating objects across an enterprise deployment.

This appendix will explore the various facets of JNDI, including why it was created, what it's useful for, and how to use it. After reading this appendix, you'll be armed with knowledge about naming, directories and how they are accessed from Java. You'll also see how JNDI is used in the EJB world.

We'll begin with a quick overview of naming and directories. From there, we'll go into the specifics of the JNDI package, and we will walk through several examples. Finally, we'll wrap up with thoughts on how EJB and JNDI are used together.

You'll notice that this appendix goes into a lot of detail about JNDI, especially for an EJB book. And rightfully so! JNDI is a vital part of J2EE, and it is used in EJB, RMI, JDBC, and more. It is the standard way of looking things up over the network. Because JNDI is so ubiquitous in J2EE, it's important that you acquire a solid foundation in this technology.

Naming and Directory Services

To understand JNDI, we must first understand the concept of naming and directory services.

A naming service is analogous to a telephone operator. When you want to call up someone over the phone and you don't know that person's phone number, you can call your telephone company's information service operator to *look up* the person you want to talk with. You supply the telephone operator with the *name* of the person. The operator then looks up the phone number of the person you want to speak with and can dial the number for you, connecting you to that person.

A *naming service* is an entity that performs the following tasks:

- It associates names with objects. We call this *binding* names to objects. This is very similar to a telephone company's associating a person's name with a specific residence's telephone number.

- It provides a facility to find an object based on a name. We call this looking up or searching for an object. This is similar to a telephone operator finding a person's telephone number based on that person's name and connecting the two people together.

Naming services are everywhere in computing. When you want to locate a machine on the network, the *Domain Name System (DNS)* is used to translate a machine name to an IP address. If you look up "wiley.com" on the Internet, the name "wiley.com" is translated into the object (which happens to be a String) 199.171.201.14 by the DNS.

Another example of naming occurs in file systems. When you access a file on your hard disk, you supply a name for the file such as "c:\autoexec.bat" or "/etc/fstab." How is this name translated into an actual file of data? A File System Naming Service can be consulted to provide this functionality.

In general, a naming service can be used to find any kind of generic object, like a file handle on your hard drive or a printer located across the network. But one type of object is of particular importance: a *directory object* (or *directory entry*). A directory object is different from a generic object because you can store *attributes* with directory objects. These attributes can be used for a wide variety of purposes.

For example, you can use a directory object to represent a user in your company. You can store information about that user, such as the user's password, as attributes in the directory object. If you have an application that requires authentication, you can store a user's login name and password in directory object attributes. When a client connects to your application, the client supplies a login name and password, which you can compare with the login name and password that are stored as a directory object's attributes. If the data matches, the user is authenticated. If the data doesn't match, your application can return an error. You can also store other attributes, too, besides a login name and password, such as a user's e-mail address, phone number, and postal address.

A *directory service* is a naming service that has been extended and enhanced to provide directory object operations for manipulating attributes. A directory is a system of directory objects, all connected. Some examples of directory products are Netscape Directory Server and Microsoft's Active Directory. Your company probably uses a directory to store internal company information—locations of computers, current printer status, personnel data, and so on.

What does a directory look like internally? The directory's contents—the set of connected directory objects—usually forms a hierarchical tree-like structure. Why would you want a tree-like structure? Well, a tree's form suggests the way a real-world company is organized. For example, the *root* (or top node) of your directory tree can represent your entire company. One branch off the root could represent people in the company, while another branch could represent network services. Each branch could have subtrees that decrease in granularity more and more, until you are at individual user objects, printer objects, machine objects, and the like. This is illustrated in Figure B.1.

Information about how a directory is organized is contained in *metadata*. Directory metadata defines the structure of your directory. It defines the *schema* of how your directory is laid out. Metadata supplies a set of rules about your directory, such as restrictions on tree branches, restrictions on attributes, and more. This is analogous to how a telephone book might restrict information about a person's home address to include a zip code. Usually, you can modify a directory's metadata usually by playing with the administrative tools that ship with the directory product.

All in all, directories are not very different from databases. A database can store arbitrary data, just like a directory. Databases provide query operations to look up items in a database, just like directories. You can think of a directory as a scaled-down, simplified database. In fact, most directories are implemented by a database behind the scenes.

Problems with Naming and Directories

There are many popular naming and directory products out today. Directory vendors differentiate their product lines by offering different types of services. Unfortunately, this leads to different naming and directory standards. And each directory standard has a different protocol for accessing the directory. For example, directories based on the *Lightweight Directory Access Protocol* (*LDAP*)

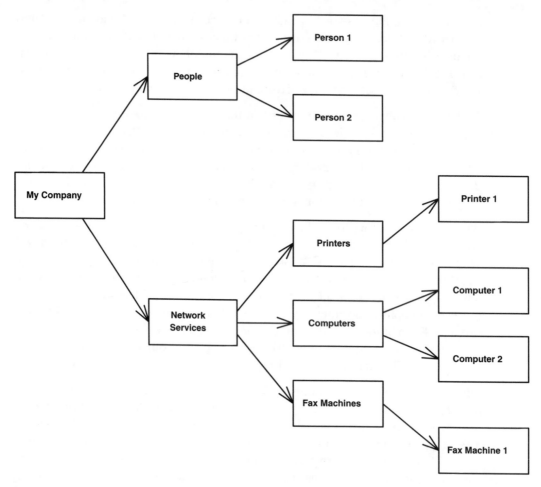

Figure B.1 A hierarchical directory structure.

are accessed differently than those based on the *Network Information System* (*NIS*) or Novell's *Network Directory System* (*NDS*).

This means that if you want to switch directory vendors, you need to rewrite all of your client code that accesses the directory. It also means you need to download a new library, learn a new API, and test new code each time you use a different directory.

Initially, LDAP was meant to resolve this problem by becoming *the* ubiquitous protocol for directories. LDAP is very straightforward and is being adopted quickly by the industry—IBM's Lotus Notes and Microsoft's Active Directory both are LDAP-based. However, not all directory products are LDAP-based.

Enter JNDI

The Java Naming and Directory Interface (JNDI) is a system for Java-based clients to interact with naming and directory systems. JNDI is a *bridge* over naming and directory services—a beast that provides one common interface to disparate directories. Users who need to access an LDAP directory use the same API as users who want to access an NIS directory or Novell's directory. All directory operations are done through the JNDI interface, providing a common framework.

If you use the JNDI, you have to download only one package and learn only one interface to access directories. And JNDI is a standard Java extension, which means it is officially endorsed and supported by Sun Microsystems.

In theory, by using the JNDI you should be able to replace the underlying directory without affecting the client code very much. This is useful if your company one day decides to switch directories, such as from an LDAP directory to an NDS directory. Rather than rewriting all of your directory-based applications, JNDI allows your code to be portable between directory services. This minimizes overhead headaches.

Benefits of JNDI

The following surveys the advantages that JNDI has to offer:

- JNDI is a unified system to access all sorts of directory service information, such as security credentials, phone numbers, electronic and postal mail addresses, application preferences, network addresses, machine configurations, and more.

- JNDI is a single API to access different directories with different protocols.

- JNDI insulates the application from protocol and implementation details.

- JNDI is extensible. Future providers of directories can plug in their particular directory services to JNDI without affecting your client code.

- Using JNDI, you can read and write whole Java objects from directories. This is a very powerful idea, which we'll illustrate in the discussion that follows.

- You can link different types of directories, such as an LDAP directory with an NDS directory, and have the combination appear to be one large, federated directory. The federated directory appears to be one contiguous directory to the client.

- JNDI is supported by Sun Microsystems, and it is a standard Java extension. Standard Java extensions can be automatically downloaded from a URL if they aren't present in a particular Java 2 platform installation.

JNDI Overview

Now that you've seen the motivation for the JNDI, let's look at the architecture and API details.

JNDI Architecture

JNDI is made up of two halves: *the client API* and the *Service Provider Interface* (*SPI*). The client API allows Java code to perform directory operations. This API is uniform for all types of directories. The client API is probably what you will be spending the most time using.

The JNDI SPI is an interface to which naming and directory service vendors can plug in. The SPI is the converse of the API: While the API allows clients to code to a single, unified interface, the SPI allows naming and directory service vendors to fit their particular proprietary protocols into the system, as shown in Figure B.2. This allows for client code to leverage proprietary naming and directory services in Java while maintaining a high level of code portability.

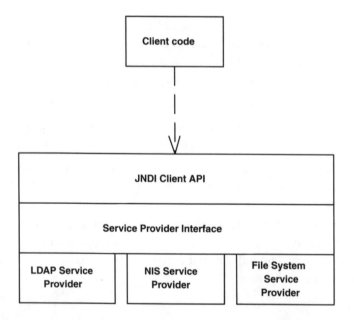

Figure B.2 JNDI architecture.

JNDI's architecture is somewhat like the Java Database Connectivity package (JDBC):

- In JDBC, there is one uniform client API for performing database operations. In JNDI, naming and directory service clients invoke a unified API for performing naming and directory operations.

- In JDBC, relational database vendors provide JDBC drivers to access their particular databases. In JNDI, directory vendors provide *service providers* to access their specific directories. These providers are aware of specific directory protocols, and they plug in to the JNDI SPI.

For example, Sun Microsystems gives away an LDAP service provider for free. The LDAP service provider knows how to map a JNDI client API operation into an LDAP operation. It then executes the LDAP operation on an LDAP directory, using the specific LDAP protocol.

Available Service Providers

At the time of this writing, there are nine service providers for JNDI. Anyone can write a service provider—and new ones will probably have emerged by the time you read this.

Note that a service provider may not support every operation JNDI's client API exposes. Each service provider ships with documentation that details the JNDI supported functions, as well as any specifics about the service provider. When you choose your service provider, see the included documentation for further details.

LDAP

The Lightweight Directory Access Protocol (LDAP), invented at the University of Michigan, was originally intended to be a ubiquitous protocol for accessing directory services. Indeed, many directory services use LDAP as their standard protocol. JNDI's value-add over basic LDAP is as follows:

- JNDI is Java-based and provides Java clients with access to LDAP-based directories. Instead of using a custom LDAP package in Java, you can use Sun Microsystem's LDAP service provider, which is available free of charge.

- JNDI allows you to bind Java objects to directory structures (which we'll see a bit later).

- The JNDI vision is to allow you to use other directory protocols besides LDAP.

Because LDAP is the most popular directory protocol, we'll use LDAP in some of the examples later in this appendix. The LDAP service provider from Sun

Microsystems is very robust, and it can perform authentication of users, establish secure socket connections, and more.

NIS

The Network Information Service (NIS) is used by Sun's Solaris operating system, as well as other UNIX operating systems, to store information about users, machines, and network services. The NIS protocol does not support all of the operations that write to a directory, so this service provider is an example of a service provider that does not completely support the JNDI client API operations.

Novell NDS

Novell Directory Services (NDS) is a distributed database that stores information about hardware and software resources on a network. NDS gives developers, users, and administrators global access to all network resources through a single login and a single point of network administration. It also provides a flexible directory database schema, network security, and a robust development environment. Novell is famous for its directory products, and it has been a major proponent of JNDI.

SLP

The Service Location Protocol (SLP) provides a scalable framework for the discovery and selection of network services, minimizing the need for static configuration within network-based applications. SLP is an Internet Standard protocol that can be used for a variety of purposes, such as discovering DHCP servers, DNS servers, Novell NDS servers, and more.

CORBA COS Naming

The CORBA standard (described in Chapter 11) contains a specification for an optional naming service in CORBA. CORBA's naming service is called the *Object Naming Service*, or *COS Naming*. COS Naming allows CORBA client programs to look up CORBA objects over a multi-tier deployment or across enterprises.

Typically, if you are a CORBA programmer, you would access CORBA's COS Naming facilities through a CORBA implementation that includes the COS Naming service. Sun Microsystem's CORBA implementation, Java IDL, is an example of a CORBA implementation that provides the COS Naming service.

Sun Microsystems also provides a free service provider for JNDI that knows how to talk with CORBA's COS Naming Service. This service provider plugs into JNDI just like any other service provider, such as the LDAP service provider. The

CORBA COS Naming service provider allows JNDI clients to access CORBA naming and directory services through the JNDI client API. It does this by wrapping the CORBA COS Naming package and delegating to it.

So why would you use JNDI rather than Java IDL (or some other CORBA implementation) to access CORBA's COS Naming facilities? Well, if you're a CORBA programmer and you use Java IDL, you restrict yourself to looking up only CORBA object references. COS Naming was intended to look up only CORBA objects, and not to serve as a general naming and directory service utility. For example, you could not use COS Naming to look up someone's username and password in an LDAP directory structure. But by using JNDI, your client code can use the COS Naming provider for looking up CORBA objects, yet still use the same JNDI client API as a general-purpose naming and directory interface by plugging in other providers.

JNDI is the future path for looking up CORBA objects from other naming services such as LDAP. We will also be able to bind other kinds of objects to COS Naming as well. In RMI over IIOP (described in Chapter 11), JNDI can be used to bind RMI remote objects into the COS Naming Service.

File System

The File System service provider gives you access to a file system through the JNDI client API. You can use the File System service provider to browse a hard disk, for example, using JNDI operations. Clients can also store Java objects in the file system using JNDI. In a sense, when you use the File System service provider, your file system itself is acting as a naming and directory service. We will demonstrate how to use this service provider later in this appendix.

RMI Registry

The RMI Registry service provider allows you to bind a whole RMI Registry into a directory (see Appendix A for an RMI tutorial). The idea here is to bind your RMI remote objects to a local RMI registry, then bind that registry to a directory via JNDI. Clients can access your remote objects via JNDI rather than looking up objects in your RMI registry. This allows multiple server machines to publish their remote objects within a robust directory system, centralizing the location of business objects. When clients use the regular RMI bootstrapping mechanism, they are connecting to individual servers that may, in fact, be down at the time. With the centralized directory system, clients can instead use JNDI to find a list of available RMI registries. We'll explain more about how the RMI Registry service provider works, along with a complete example, later in this chapter.

BEA's WebLogic Naming Service

BEA Systems, Inc. is an EJB container/server vendor that bundles a proprietary directory service with their product. Their directory service is fault-tolerant, providing a high level of availability. They also supply an integrated naming service that ties together with the Enterprise Java services, such as RMI, JDBC, EJB, and event services. Finally, their product ships with tools for building custom naming and directory providers.

To access their naming and directory service, they provide a JNDI service provider. BEA's JNDI package actually implements the entire JNDI specification published by Sun Microsystems. BEA provides more than just a service provider—WebLogic JNDI is involved in all levels of directory operations, and it is a total replacement for Sun Microsystems's reference implementation of JNDI.

Why would you use WebLogic's JNDI? For one, WebLogic JNDI uses WebLogic's own custom socket implementation, which multiplexes many types of traffic (for example, JDBC traffic mixed with JNDI traffic) all on one socket. This optimization leads to enhanced performance.

More importantly, WebLogic's implementation of the JNDI specification is a distributed implementation of JNDI. It is distributed in the sense that its JNDI implementation can *delegate* to a JNDI service provider that is located on a different machine across a network. This means the WebLogic service provider is acting as a proxy for the real service provider, such as an LDAP service provider or an NDS service provider. This distributed JNDI implementation is especially useful if your JNDI client is a Java applet. Java applets have security restrictions that prevent them from running native code (unless they are digitally signed). And unfortunately, JNDI service providers often contain native code, such as a service provider that may access the Windows NT registry. Because JNDI service providers may contain native code, they cannot run within the context of an unsigned Java applet. WebLogic's delegation method allows service providers to be located on a secure machine and still be usable by clients that are not secure.

Because BEA has actually shipped a complete JNDI implementation, it is more than just a service provider. Note that this is merely an example of a JNDI implementation; the playing ground is open for other vendors to do the same.

Understanding the Concepts behind JNDI Programming

Before we embark on a JNDI example, let's lay a foundation of the concepts behind JNDI. We begin with naming concepts.

Naming Concepts

As we have said, a naming service is an entity that associates names with objects. You can use these names to later find the object based on that name.

Atomic, Compound, and Composite Names

There are several kinds of names in JNDI:

- An *atomic name* is a simple, basic, indivisible component of a name. For example, in the string */etc/fstab*, *etc* and *fstab* are atomic names.

- A *compound name* is zero or more atomic names put together. In the previous example, the entire string */etc/fstab* is a compound name.

Bindings, Contexts, and Subcontexts

A *binding* is an association of a name with an object. For example, the filename *autoexec.bat* in the Windows file system has a binding to the file data on your hard disk. Your *c:\windows* folder is a name that is bound to a folder on your hard drive. Note that a compound name such as */usr/people/ed/.cshrc* consists of multiple bindings, one to *usr*, one to *people*, one to *ed*, and one to *.cshrc*. Bindings are illustrated in Figure B.3.

A *context* is an object that contains zero or more bindings. Each binding has a distinct atomic name. So, for example, in the UNIX file system, let's consider a folder named */etc* that contains files named *mtab* and *exports*. In JNDI, the */etc* folder is a context containing bindings with atomic names *mtab* and *exports*. Each of the *mtab* and *exports* atomic names is bound to a file on the hard disk. Figure B.4 illustrates this concept.

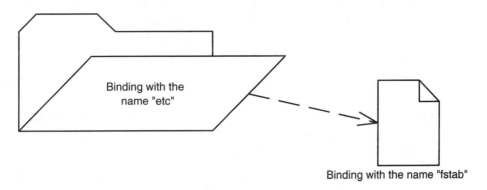

Binding with the name "etc"

Binding with the name "fstab"

Figure B.3   Bindings.

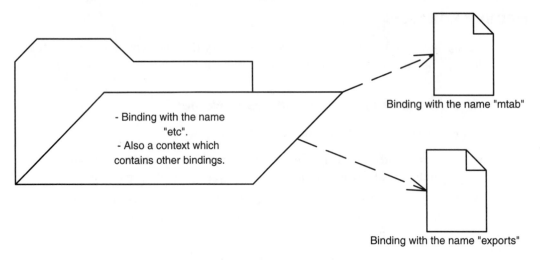

- Binding with the name
"etc".
- Also a context which
contains other bindings.

Binding with the name "mtab"

Binding with the name "exports"

Figure B.4   Contexts.

To expand this further, consider a folder named */usr* with subfolders */usr/people*, */usr/bin*, and */usr/local*. Here, the */usr* folder is a context that contains the *people*, *bin*, and *local* atomic names. Each of these atomic names is bound to a subfolder. In JNDI terms, these subfolders are called *subcontexts*. Each subcontext is a full-fledged context in its own right, and it can contain more name-object bindings, such as other files or other folders. Figure B.5 depicts subcontexts.

Naming Systems, Namespaces, and Composite Names

A *naming system* is a connected set of contexts. For example, a branch of an LDAP tree could be considered a naming system, as could a folder tree in a file system. Unfortunately, naming systems each have a different syntax for accessing contexts. For example, in an LDAP tree, a compound name is identified by a string such as "cn=Ed Roman, ou=People, o=Middleware-Company.com, c=us", whereas a file system compound name might look like "c:\java\lib\classes.zip." Keep this in mind, as we will revisit this issue a bit later.

Within a naming system, a *namespace* is all the names contained within that naming system. Your hard drive's entire collection of filenames and directories or folders is your hard drive file system's namespace; the set of all names in an LDAP directory's tree is an LDAP server's namespace. Naming systems and namespaces are shown in Figure B.6.

A *composite name* is a name that spans multiple naming systems. For example, on the Web, the URL *http://java.sun.com/products/ejb/index.html* is composed from the following namespaces:

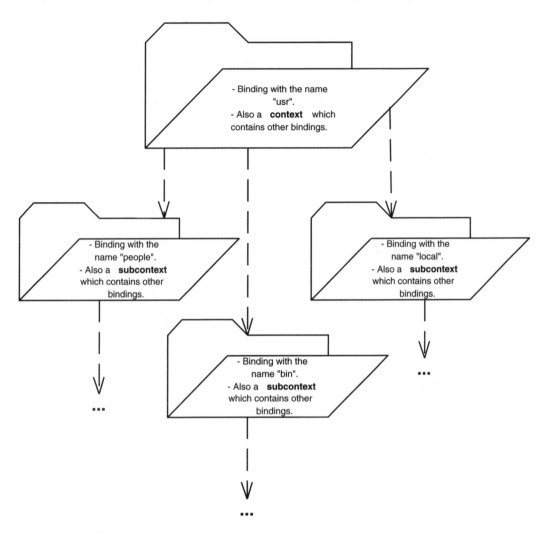

Figure B.5 Subcontexts.

- *http* comes from the *URL scheme-id* namespace. You can use other scheme-ids, such as ftp and telnet. This namespace defines the protocol you use to communicate.

- *java.sun.com* uses the Domain Name Service (DNS) to translate machine names into IP addresses.

- *products* and *ejb* and *index.html* are from the file system namespace on the Web server machine.

By linking multiple naming systems like the URL above, we can arrive at a unified *composite namespace* (also called a *federated namespace*) containing all

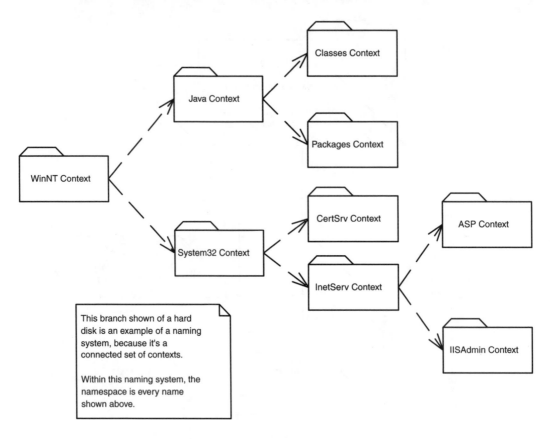

Figure B.6 Naming systems and namespaces.

the bindings of each naming system. Composite namespaces are illustrated in Figure B.7.

Initial Context Factories

One question commonly asked is, if you are to traverse a composite namespace, how do you know which naming system to look into first? For example, which namespace do you first look in when traversing the string *http://www.trilogy.com/products/products.asp*?

The starting point of exploring a namespace is called an *initial context*. An initial context simply is the first context you happen to use. An initial context is a starting point for performing all naming and directory operations.

To acquire an initial context, you use an *initial context factory*. An initial context factory is responsible for churning out initial contexts. Initial context factories are provided by specific JNDI service providers. For example, there is an

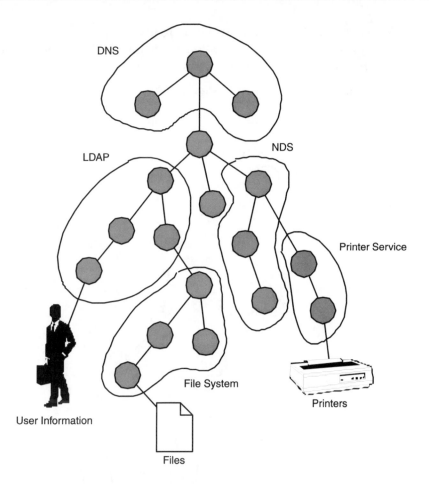

DNS

LDAP

NDS

Printer Service

User Information

File System

Printers

Files

Figure B.7 A composite (federated) namespace.

LDAP initial context factory, as well as a File System initial context factory. These initial context factories know the specific semantics of a particular directory structure. They know how to acquire an arbitrary context that you can use as an initial starting context for traversing a directory structure.

Initial context factories are used for *bootstrapping*, or jump starting, your naming and directory service operations. This is quite similar to Java RMI. In RMI, you use the RMI naming facility to locate an RMI registry, which serves as a bootstrapping mechanism for identifying an initial remote object (see Appendix A). In JNDI, you use an initial context factory as a bootstrapping mechanism for identifying an initial naming system.

When you acquire an initial context, you must supply the necessary information for JNDI to acquire that initial context. For example, you could pass the IP address of the LDAP directory you want to use, the port number that the LDAP directory accepts, the starting location within the LDAP tree, and the username/password necessary to use the LDAP server.

Initial contexts are illustrated in Figure B.8.

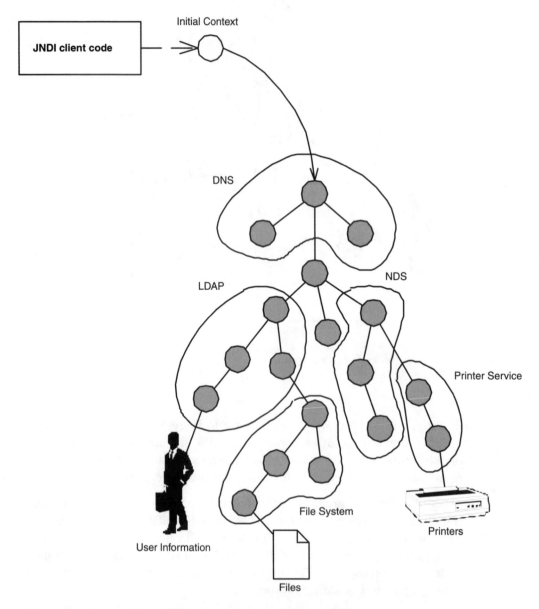

Figure B.8   A composite (federated) namespace with an initial context.

Directory Concepts

Let's now briefly touch on directory concepts. From our naming concepts, we learned that a context is an object that contains one or more bindings. An example of a context is a folder. A folder can contain names bound to files and other subfolders.

A *directory context* (or *directory object*) is a particular type of context that has *attributes* associated with it. Directory contexts are just like regular contexts. Both contexts and directory contexts can contain name-object bindings, just as a file folder contains files and subfolders. The value-add of directory contexts is that they can store other *attributes* as well. Going with our file system analogy, a directory attribute is similar to *permissions* on a folder. Permissions can be, for example, read-only permission to a folder or read-write permissions. These are natural attributes that go along with the folder. If you think of a context as a folder, think of a directory context as a folder with permissions. For example, you could use a directory context's attributes to store usernames and passwords of users in your business.

Programming with JNDI

Now that you've seen the concepts behind JNDI, let's put our theory into concrete use. This section will explain the details of the JNDI API, and it will show several examples of JNDI in action.

Setting Up the Required Software

To try out the examples in this appendix, you need the following software installed:

- The Java Development Kit version 1.1.2 or higher.
- The JNDI Java extension package. Alternatively, you can use another implementation of JNDI, such as BEA's *WebLogic*.
- Service providers for the particular directory you are using. We'll be using the LDAP, File System, and RMI Registry providers in this appendix, so you'll need to download them from the Sun Microsystems Web site.
- If you'd like to try out the LDAP service provider, you'll need to download an LDAP-compatible directory server. The University of Michigan provides a free one. America Online also provides an LDAP directory server (previously named the Netscape Directory Server), which is much easier to use than the University of Michigan's. Be forewarned that configuring an LDAP server is not trivial. If you're in a hurry, you may want to bypass this step.

For links to these products and more, see the book's accompanying Web site. For tips and tricks in setting up LDAP servers, see the free JNDI tutorial on Sun Microsystems' Web site.

The JNDI Packages

There are three core packages in JNDI:

The naming package, *javax.naming*, is used for accessing a naming service. As we first mentioned in this appendix, naming services associate names with objects and provide facilities for finding objects based on their names. We will cover the *javax.naming* package extensively.

The directory package, *javax.naming.directory*, is used for accessing naming services as well as directory services. The directory package extends the naming package. You can perform all naming service operations with the directory package. The directory package adds the ability to manipulate attributes associated with objects. While this is an important subject, we do not cover *javax.naming.directory* here because Enterprise JavaBeans does not depend on it.

The service provider interface (SPI), *javax.naming.spi*, is an interface to which service providers can plug in. We don't cover the SPI in this book because it is intended for naming and directory service vendors.

Basic JNDI Steps

The following steps are necessary whenever you perform any JNDI operations:

1. Identify what service provider you are using. If you're connecting to an LDAP service provider, you need to specify the LDAP Initial Context Factory.

2. Specify any ancillary information that the service provider may need. This is usually information the service provider needs to start up. Examples are the location of an LDAP directory on a network, usernames and passwords (for the LDAP service provider), or the location of a starting folder on your hard drive (for the File System service provider).

3. Acquire an initial context. To refresh your memory, a naming context is like a folder on a file system. Contexts store name-object bindings. For example, if you have a Windows NT machine, your *c:\winnt* folder can be thought of as a context. The *c:\winnt* folder contains a collection of names bound to objects, such as the name *jview.exe* that is bound to a file on a hard disk. The *c:\winnt* context might also contain the name *system32* that is bound to a subfolder, or in JNDI terms, a subcontext. Thus, your initial context could be *c:\winnt*, or it might also be *c:\winnt\system32*.

But your initial context could not be *c:\winnt\jview.exe* because *jview.exe* is not a context. The initial context can also be a directory context. Directory contexts are naming contexts that can also store attributes, just as a folder can have permissions.

The following code snippet illustrates setting your environment properties and acquiring an initial context. The code is listed in Source B.1.

The code first chooses an initial context factory. The initial context factory will bootstrap us and acquire an initial context for us to begin navigating a directory structure. Remember, initial context factories are necessary so that JNDI knows what kind of directory structure we're first using, such as an LDAP directory. In this example, we'll use the File System service provider, which is very

```java
package com.wiley.compBooks.roman.jndi.initctx;

import java.util.Properties;

/**
 * Illustrates how to acquire a JNDI initial context
 */
public class InitCtx {

    public static void main(String args[]) {

        try {
            Properties env = new Properties();

            env.put(javax.naming.Context.INITIAL_CONTEXT_FACTORY,
                    "com.sun.jndi.fscontext.RefFSContextFactory");

            env.put(javax.naming.Context.PROVIDER_URL,
                    "file:c:\\");

            javax.naming.Context ctx =
                new javax.naming.InitialContext(env);

            System.out.println("Success!");
        }
        catch (javax.naming.NamingException e) {
            e.printStackTrace();
        }
    }
}
```

Source B.1   InitCtx.java.

easy to use because you don't need to install and configure a complex directory product.

Following the initial context factory, we then identify the starting point on the file system that we want to begin navigating: specifically, the *c:* folder. This starting point is structured in the form of a Uniform Resource Locator (URL), and in JNDI it is called the *provider URL* because it's a URL that the service provider accepts for bootstrapping.

Finally, we acquire an initial context to that folder. Normally at this point, you can begin to execute JNDI operations, such as binding data to directory trees, searching a directory tree, and so on. Our program simply terminates. Thus, you now know the basic first three steps for all JNDI programs.

Ideally, you should not couple the JNDI initialization settings with your Java code. A much better design model is to pass properties to your Java program. That way, you can change the location, type, and parameters of your JNDI provider in a declarative rather than programmatic fashion. This saves you from recompiling your Java code and enables non-Java savvy users to customize your products without modifying source code. This source code may not even be available if you ship your products only as *.class* files.

Exploring the javax.naming Package

Now that you've got your feet wet by learning how to connect to JNDI, let's take a more in-depth look at the various classes and interfaces of JNDI, so that we can move on to more interesting applications.

Tables B.1 and B.2 enumerate the more interesting interfaces and classes found in *javax.naming*. You'll notice that many of the interface and class names correspond to the concepts we discussed earlier, such as a Name, a Binding, and a Context.

Table B.1   Selected Interfaces from the javax.naming Package

INTERFACE	DESCRIPTION
Context	A naming context that contains name-object bindings. Exposes methods to bind, rebind, and unbind a name to an object. Also can create/destroy subcontexts, list the names currently bound to objects, look up an object based on a name, and more.
Name	Rather than working with raw Strings, JNDI abstracts the notion of a Name, such as */etc/fstab* or *cn=Ed Roman, ou=People*. A Name can be atomic or compound, as defined by the class that implements the name. Exposes methods to manipulate the name.

INTERFACE	DESCRIPTION
NameParser	A NameParser assists in constructing a particular Name object. NameParsers know the specific syntax that an underlying directory structure uses. For example, an LDAP NameParser knows how an LDAP string is constructed, whereas a File System NameParser knows how to format a File System string. As we mentioned earlier in this chapter, naming conventions differ from directory to directory. NameParsers insulate you from these differences.
NamingEnumeration	NamingEnumerations are used to enumerate the list of objects returned by list and search operations exposed by Context objects.

Table B.2 Selected Classes from the javax.naming Package

CLASS	DESCRIPTION
NameClassPair and Binding	These classes are used to associate a name with an object. A NameClassPair associates a JNDI Name object with a Java class, and it is a fairly weak kind of association because a NameClassPair associates only a Name with a class.
	A JNDI Binding extends NameClassPair. Bindings associate a Name with a class as well as a specific object instance. This is the "binding" concept we have been referring to in this chapter.
CompositeName	A composite name is a name that spans more than one namespace, as when an LDAP namespace is combined with a file system namespace. If your composite name is not encapsulated within a CompositeName object, you can use a java.util.String instead. To indicate different namespaces within a composite name String, separate them with a "/" character.
CompoundName	A CompoundName is zero or more atomic names put together, such as /etc/fstab. Each of the atomic names in a compound name must be from the same namespace (for example, there can be no mixing and matching of DNS with file system names). You can pass a special java.util.Properties object to the CompoundName constructor to help specify the syntax of the naming system you are using.
InitialContext	To perform any naming operations, you first need an InitialContext. Because an initial context is a special kind of context, the InitialContext class implements the Context interface. You pass the constructor of InitialContext information about where the directory is, security information, etc., so that it can bootstrap. Once you've got the initial context, you can start traversing the directory structure, perform lookup operations, and bind objects. Initial contexts are generated from Initial Context Factories (*javax.spi.InitialContextFactory*) such as the LDAP Initial Context Factory.

continues

Table B.2 *Continued*

CLASS	DESCRIPTION
LinkRef	A LinkRef is a link that can span possibly multiple namespaces. A LinkRef is a symbolic link within a directory structure. By using LinkRef, you can link one part of a directory to another, just as a symbolic link in UNIX (or a shortcut, in Windows) is a link from one part of a file system to another.

Example: An Interactive Browser

Now that you've taken a rough look at the *javax.naming* concepts and API, let's put JNDI to use. This example will put some common naming operations together to create an *interactive browser*. Our browser will be able to peruse any kind of directory structure because it is entirely based on the unified JNDI client API. This example will illustrate a practical JNDI application using both the File System service provider and the LDAP service provider. Specifically, this utility will provide functionality to traverse a directory structure, add and remove folders (contexts), get a folder (context) listing, and view a file (the latter is possible with the File System service provider only). This interactive browser will use familiar UNIX commands to traverse a file system, including the following:

cd to change folders (contexts)

ls to get a listing of subcontexts

mv to rename a context

cat to view a file

You can use this utility to browse your own hard disk, for example, or to browse an LDAP directory.

The code is shown in Source B.2. Although it is fairly self-explanatory, we'll take a look at some key pieces in detail.

Browser.java starts off by creating a class and initializing some variables:

```
ctx = new InitialContext(System.getProperties());
parser = ctx.getNameParser("");
currName = parser.parse("");
```

We create the Initial Context based on System properties passed in with the *-D* interpreter switch. This means that we aren't specifying a particular service provider. The System properties need to define the Initial Context Factory to identify the service provider, the Provider URL, and any other parameters such as authentication information needed by the service provider.

```java
package com.wiley.compBooks.roman.jndi.browser;

import javax.naming.*;
import java.io.*;
import java.util.*;

/**
 * Interactive directory structure browser.
 */
public class Browser {

    /**
     * Main() is just a wrapper that starts the directory browsing.
     */
    public static void main (String[] args) {
        try {
            new Browser().browse();
        }
        catch (Exception e) {
            System.err.println(e);
            e.printStackTrace();
        }
    }

    // Initial Context
    protected Context ctx;

    // This JNDI Name object is used to track the current
    // context (folder) we're in as we traverse the directory tree
    protected Name currName;

    // We use a NameParser to generate Name objects for us.
    // A NameParser knows how to construct a Name using
    // a proprietary service provider syntax, such as
    // "c:\winnt" for the File System service provider, or
    // "cn=Ed Roman, ou=People, o=Airius.com" for the LDAP
    // service provider.
    protected NameParser parser;

    /*
     * Constructor called from main().  Initializes things.
     */
    public Browser() throws Exception {
        /*
         * 1) Create the initial context.  Parameters are
         *    supplied in the System properties.
         */
        ctx = new InitialContext(System.getProperties());
```

Source B.2 Browser.java *(continues).*

```
        /*
         * 2) Get the NameParser from the service provider.
         */
        parser = ctx.getNameParser("");

        /*
         * 3) Use the NameParser to create the initial location
         *    of where we are in the directory structure.  Because
         *    the NameParser is service provider specific, the
         *    resulting Name object will be formatted to a
         *    specific directory syntax.
         */
        currName = parser.parse("");
    }

    /**
     * Call to begin browsing the file system directory structure.
     * This method isn't important, it just interacts with the user.
     */
    public void browse() {

        /*
         * Start reading input from standard input
         */
        String line = null, command = null, args = null;
        StringTokenizer tokens = null;
        BufferedReader reader =
            new BufferedReader(new InputStreamReader(System.in));

        while (true) {

            /*
             * Print prompt, read next input line,
             * and get command
             */
            try {
                System.out.println();
                System.out.print(currName + "> ");
                line = reader.readLine();
                System.out.println();
                tokens =
                    new StringTokenizer(line, " ", false);

                // Get command.  e.g. "cd" in "cd .."
                command = tokens.nextToken();

                // Get arguments.  e.g. ".." in "cd .."
                if (tokens.hasMoreElements()) {
```

Source B.2 Browser.java *(continues).*

```
                args = line.substring(
                  command.length()+1,
                  line.length());
            }
        }
        catch (Exception e) {
            continue;
        }

        /*
         * Do case analysis based on command.  Call
         * the corresponding JNDI function.
         */
        try {
            if (command.equals("ls")) {
                ls();
            }
            else if (command.equals("mv")) {
                /*
                 * Figure out the name of the
                 * context the user is trying
                 * to rename (mv)
                 */
                String oldStr = null,
                       newStr = null;
                try {
                    StringTokenizer argtokens = new StringTokenizer(args,
                        " ", false);
                    oldStr = argtokens.nextToken();
                    newStr = argtokens.nextToken();
                }
                catch (Exception e) {
                    throw new Exception("Syntax: mv <old context>
                        <new context>");
                }

                mv(oldStr, newStr);
            }
            else if (command.equals("cd")) {
                cd(args);
            }
            else if (command.equals("mkdir")) {
                mkdir(args);
            }
            else if (command.equals("rmdir")) {
                rmdir(args);
            }
```

Source B.2 Browser.java *(continues)*.

```
            else if (command.equals("cat")) {
                cat(args);
            }
            else if (command.equals("quit")) {
                System.exit(0);
            }
            else {
                System.out.println("Syntax:
                    [ls|mv|cd|mkdir|rmdir|cat|quit] [args...]");
            }
        }
        catch (Exception e) {
            e.printStackTrace();
        }
    }
}


/**
 * Lists the contents of the current context (folder)
 */
private void ls() throws Exception {
    // Get an enumeration of Names bound to this context
    NamingEnumeration e = ctx.list(currName);

    // Each enumeration element is a NameClassPair.
    // Print the Name part.
    while (e.hasMore()) {
        NameClassPair p = (NameClassPair) e.next();
        System.out.println(p.getName());
    }
}


/**
 * Navigate the directory structure
 */
private void cd(String newLoc) throws Exception {
    if (newLoc == null) {
        throw new Exception("You must specify a folder");
    }

    // Save the old Name, in case the user tries to cd
    // into a bad folder.
    Name oldName = (Name) currName.clone();

    try {
        /*
         * If the user typed "cd ..", pop up one
         * directory by removing the last element from
```

Source B.2 Browser.java *(continues)*.

```
               * the Name.
               */
           if (newLoc.equals("..")) {
               if (currName.size() > 0) {
                   currName.remove(currName.size()-1);
               }
               else {
                   System.out.println(
                    "Already at top level.");
               }
           }

           /*
            * Otherwise, the user typed "cd <folder>".  Go
            * deeper into the directory structure.
            *
            * Note that we use "addAll()" which will add every
            * atomic folder name into the total name.  This means
            * when we type "cd .." later, we will only traverse
            * down one folder.
            */
           else {
               currName.addAll(parser.parse(newLoc));
           }

           /*
            * Confirm our traversal by trying to do a lookup()
            * operation after we've popped out a directory.  If
            * lookup() fails, we need to restore the directory
            * Name to what it was, and throw an exception.
            */
           ctx.lookup(currName);
       }
       catch (Exception e) {
           currName = oldName;
           throw new Exception("Cannot traverse to desired directory: " +
               e.toString());
       }
   }

   /**
    * Renames (moves) one context to a new name.
    *
    * @param oldStr the old context
    * @param newStr the new context
    */
   private void mv(String oldStr, String newStr) throws Exception {
```

Source B.2 Browser.java *(continues)*.

```
        /*
         * Navigate to the current context (folder)
         */
        Context currCtx = (Context) ctx.lookup(currName);

        /*
         * Rename the subcontext
         */
        currCtx.rename(oldStr, newStr);
    }

    /**
     * Makes a subfolder (subcontext)
     */
    private void mkdir(String str) throws Exception {
        Context currCtx = (Context) ctx.lookup(currName);
        currCtx.createSubcontext(str);
    }

    /**
     * Removes a subfolder (subcontext)
     */
    private void rmdir(String str) throws Exception {
        Context currCtx = (Context) ctx.lookup(currName);
        currCtx.destroySubcontext(str);
    }

    /**
     * displays a file (specific to File System service provider)
     */
    private void cat(String fileStr) throws Exception {

        /*
         * Append the filename to the folder string
         */
        Name fileName = (Name) currName.clone();
        fileName.addAll(parser.parse(fileStr));

        /*
         * Use JNDI to get a File Object reference
         */
        File f = (File) ctx.lookup(fileName);

        /*
         * Print out file contents
         */
        FileReader fin = new FileReader(f);
        Writer out = new PrintWriter(System.out);
```

Source B.2 Browser.java *(continues)*.

```
            char[] buf = new char[512];
            int howmany;
            while ((howmany = fin.read(buf)) >= 0) {
                out.write(buf, 0, howmany);
            }
        out.flush();
        fin.close();
    }
}
```

Source B.2   Browser.java *(continued)*.

We then acquire a NameParser object and use it to create the *currName* object, which is of type Name. *currName* identifies where we are in the directory structure, such as */usr/bin*. Objects of type Name can be either compound or composite names—the Name interface abstracts that out.

Why do we use NameParser to create *currName*? Can't we create Name objects directly, by using, for example, the CompoundName object constructor? Well, remember that CompoundName objects can be composed of more than one atomic name—*/usr/bin* has two atomic names. CompoundName objects also expose methods such as *add()*, which will add other names to lengthen the total compound name. But if we're going to construct a compound name from individual atomic names, we're going to need to specify the particular naming convention for the service provider being used. For example, in the LDAP string *cn=Ed Roman, ou=People, o=Middleware-Company.com*, the string *cn=Ed Roman* is an atomic name, but the comma "," is a separator character that is specific to LDAP. The File System service provider, in comparison, might have a compound name such as */usr/bin*, where a different separator character, "/", demarcates the atomic name boundaries.

To achieve service provider independence, we acquire a NameParser object from the Initial Context, which knows how to take a *java.lang.String* and convert it into a *Name*. Once we've got the Name, we can pass it around without knowing what particular directory structure is being used. For example, let's compare running the *cd* operation on a file system versus an LDAP directory. Here's the result of navigating a file system:

```
java -Djava.naming.factory.initial =
    com.sun.jndi.fscontext.RefFSContextFactory
    -Djava.naming.provider.url =
    file:c:\ com.wiley.compBooks.Browser.Browser

> ls
```

```
AUTOEXEC.BAT
COMMAND.COM
Program Files
WINNT

> cd Program Files

Program Files> ls

Accessories
Internet Explorer
Java Plug-in 1.1
Microsoft Visual Studio
MSMQ
NetMeetingNT
winamp

Program Files> cd winamp

Program Files\winamp> ls

maps
pics
Plugins
Skins
tabs
winamp.ini
winamp.m3u

Program Files\winamp> cat winamp.ini

[3Dfx Squiggle]
Screen_x=50527560
Screen_y=50527580

Program Files\winamp> cd ..

Program Files\winamp> cd ..


Program Files> cd ..


> quit
```

And here's the result of navigating an LDAP tree:

```
java -Djava.naming.factory.initial =
     com.sun.jndi.ldap.LdapCtxFactory
     -Djava.naming.provider.url =
     ldap://louvre:389/o=Airius.com
```

```
            com.wiley.compBooks.Browser.Browser

    > ls

    ou=Groups
    ou=People
    ou=Special Users
    ou=Netscape Servers

    > cd ou=Groups

    ou=Groups> ls

    cn=Directory Administrators
    cn=Accounting Managers
    cn=HR Managers
    cn=QA Managers
    cn=PD Managers

    ou=Groups> cd cn=Directory Administrators

    cn=Directory Administrators,ou=Groups> cd ..

    ou=Groups> cd ..

    > quit
```

Notice that in the File System example, we recursed into the subfolder Program Files/winamp, while in the LDAP tree, we recursed into cn=Directory Administrators, ou=Groups. The LDAP string is in the reverse order! But that's OK, because this is the LDAP convention. When we perform our *cd ..* operation, the LDAP service provider correctly removes the cn=Directory Administrators atomic name because the LDAP service provider is smart enough to know that LDAP strings are in reverse order. Our client code, however, was never aware of it. We simply added the next context on. This is the power of JNDI in action, separating us from the specific directory protocol being used.

Next, let's take a look at some of the directory operations we implemented. The *cd* method is fairly straightforward: It modifies the *currName* object based on where the user wants to go. It then checks to make sure the updated currName is a valid subcontext by performing a *Naming.lookup()* operation, which will throw an exception if *currName* is not a valid context. The *ls* method has the following body:

```
    // Get an enumeration of Names bound to this context
    NamingEnumeration e = ctx.list(currName);

    // Each enumeration element is a NameClassPair.
    // Print the Name part.
```

```
while (e.hasMore()) {
    NameClassPair p = (NameClassPair) e.next();
    System.out.println(p.getName());
}
```

With *ls*, we first performed a *list()* operation, which returns all of the bound objects (including subcontexts) in the current context. The returned results are a set of NameClassPair objects, which identify the Name of the bound object and the class of the object to which the Name is bound. By printing out the Names, we get the desired functionality of *ls*. Notice that we used *list()*, as opposed to its cousin method, *listBindings(). listBindings()* is a less efficient method that returns the bound objects themselves, not just their classes.

mkdir, *rmdir*, and *mv* are also straightforward. The one interesting case is *cat*. *cat* works only with the File System service provider. It retrieves a whole bound object (not just its class). The File System service provider's specific implementation returns a *File* object, which can be treated like any regular Java File object. That is why we can print out the File object—it was located and returned

Does JNDI Truly Bridge Arbitrary Naming and Directory Services?

JNDI is wonderful because you can now access different directories through one standard API. But does it truly bridge naming and directory services, allowing your client code to remain constant if you switch directories? The answer, unfortunately, is no. The JNDI API is a standard interface for you to work with, separating you from proprietary APIs and protocols. Each directory, though, must be navigated according to a different syntax. How can we then keep our client code static?

There is no easy answer to this. As it stands, JNDI cannot eliminate fully your client code changes if you switch to a different directory. But by using a few tricks, you can minimize these client code changes.

Let's say you want to reference a directory entry deep within a tree. If you specify the entry using a long string such as "cn=Ed Roman, ou=People, o=wiley.com, c=us", you are committing to a specific syntax (here, LDAP's). If you switch from LDAP, you will need to use a different syntax. How can you avoid this problem?

Well, one technique you can use is to acquire a list of all contexts at every level of the directory tree. Instead of identifying an absolute location, such as "cn=Ed Roman, ou=People, o=wiley.com, c=us", you can start at the root node ("o=wiley.com, c=us") and get a list of all subcontexts. From there, you can choose the context "People" and get a list of all subcontexts there. Then you will finally arrive at the "Ed Roman" object. This eliminates the need for directory-specific syntax. Unfortunately, it is a costly technique because you need to access the directory many times (once at each level of the tree)

to us through the File System naming service. This illustrates what JNDI can do—you can store many different kinds of objects using JNDI, and you can use it as a generic lookup service for your objects.

One take-away point from this example is that we were able to plug in the LDAP provider with *zero* code changes. Slap on a JFC/Swing UI, and you've got a Windows NT explorer written in JNDI that can work with any kind of directory protocol, not just a file system. Now that we've written this browser, we can use it to debug any JNDI code you write or to see how objects are bound in the other examples in this appendix.

Advanced JNDI: Combining JNDI with JDBC

With EJB, you can use *Java Database Connectivity (JDBC)* operations from inside your beans to perform relational database access operations. JDBC is essentially a portable Java-based interface to relational databases. In fact, JDBC and JNDI are much alike.

---

rather than just once. You also need to perform list operations, which are expensive, especially if the list is long. In reality, if you want an efficient client, this scheme is not practical.

You can also keep your client code as portable as possible between directories, by keeping the directory syntax-specific section of your client code as small and mutable as possible, preferably by using properties files. But the real answer to this problem is to use Name objects rather than Strings. Name objects can be constructed with directory-specific syntax from NameParser objects that know a particular service provider's convention. Always use Name objects—they enable JNDI to be a closer to a true common directory API.

Of course, JNDI will never truly be able to bridge all naming and directory service technologies because of unsupported methods in certain service providers. If you want to use the qualities of service that a certain directory vendor uses to distinguish itself from other directory services, you may need to write directory-specific code. This is an unfortunate consequence of the nature of a competitive industry. It is also true with EJB—by using proprietary features that certain EJB container or server vendors provide, you are tying yourself to those vendors.

Realistically, this is the best that any kind of software that provides a common API bridge over arbitrary technologies is going to do. You have to remember that these directory protocols were invented totally independently. Just the mere existence of JNDI is a huge win. To address the needs of directory service vendors, JNDI encompasses a subset of the union of features that all vendors provide. And while the JNDI cannot possibly cover everything, the bases that it does cover are the most important ones. You can reap many benefits with the intelligent use of JNDI.

JNDI. Vendors of directory services provide service providers to access their particular directory. The service providers know the particular semantics and protocol the directory service uses. JNDI provides a high-level client API that is independent of any particular directory service protocol.

JDBC. Vendors of databases, as well as third parties, provide *drivers* that know how to access a particular database. The driver knows the access method for interacting with the desired database. For example, Oracle provides database drivers to access its Oracle database. JDBC provides a high-level client API that is independent of any particular database access method.

JDBC is based on the *Open Database Connectivity* (*ODBC*) standard. ODBC is a relational database API that is language-independent. JDBC represents the Java language bindings of ODBC. Both Sun and Microsoft provide JDBC-ODBC drivers, which can connect any JDBC data source to an ODBC data source. You can also use JDBC to connect to a database directly (circumventing ODBC drivers) with a native JDBC driver that does not use the JDBC-ODBC bridge. Thus, JDBC is a unifying API for accessing any kind of relational database, whether ODBC-based or not.

If you're new to JDBC, you can get ramped up by going through the JDBC tutorial. This is a free service provided by Sun Microsystems. See http://java.sun.com/ docs/books/tutorial/jdbc/index.html. The new JDBC 2.0 standard extension documentation is available at http://java.sun.com/products/jdbc/html/.

Although JDBC by itself is great for accessing relational databases, it is hardly a complete API for the enterprise. The problem with JDBC is that you need to hard-code the location of your database (i.e., the machine name and port at which your database resides). You also have to hard-code the data source's configuration parameters, as well as the particular JDBC driver being used. This impedes maintenance of a multi-tier solution. If you want to switch data sources, there is no automatic way for each of your machines to become aware of the new database. You have to manually administer each machine and change the database driver and parameters.

To alleviate this problem, our example is going to make use of JNDI to store a JDBC data source object in a well-known JNDI tree location.

What Is a JDBC DataSource?

JDBC programmers who have not worked with the new JDBC 2.0 specification, may be unfamiliar with JDBC DataSource objects. A JDBC DataSource is an entity that doles out database connections. You are responsible for asking the

DataSource for a connection to a database and then releasing that connection when you are done.

The JDBC DataSource is the evolution of the classic JDBC *DriverManager*. The chief differences between the two are these:

1. JDBC DataSources can automatically pool and reuse database connections for multiple clients. This is absolutely necessary for portable database connection pooling in an Enterprise JavaBeans environment.

2. DataSource objects can be stored in a JNDI tree. Java clients who wish to access a database via JDBC will acquire this DataSource from the well-known JNDI location. If the database vendor or location changes, we need to change only the single DataSource object stored in the JNDI tree. The new DataSource will automatically be used by clients when they request the DataSource. This is shown in Figure B.9.

Storing Java Objects in Directories

To store our JDBC DataSource, we'll need to learn how JNDI allows you to store Java objects in directories. Using JNDI, you can instantiate a Java object, serialize the instance into a bitstream (see Appendix A for an explanation of serialization),

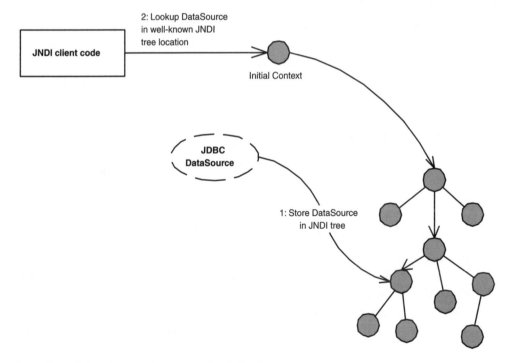

Figure B.9 Using JNDI to store a JDBC DataSource.

and store the serialized object into a directory structure using JNDI. Later, another piece of code elsewhere on the network can retrieve and deserialize the object from the directory, load the class, and then finally use the object.

There are two ways to store a Java object in a directory using JNDI:

Store your serialized Java object as a whole directory context. When you store a Java object in a JNDI tree, JNDI takes care of the implementation details for you. How is the actual serialized data represented in the JNDI tree? Well, because each JNDI service provider may store data differently, the actual mechanism of storing serialized Java objects is service provider-dependent. If you're curious, see the book's accompanying Web site for the LDAP scheme of storing objects.

Store your serialized Java object as a directory context attribute. As we learned previously, a directory context can contain attributes, such as username and password strings. Why not store your Java object as an attribute of a directory context? You can do this if you like.

Under certain circumstances, you may not want to store a whole Java object in a JNDI tree at all. Instead, you can store a compact *JNDI reference* that knows how to construct the real object. This concept is explained later in this chapter.

Implementing Our JNDI-JDBC Code

This example will use Java serialization to bind a JDBC DataSource to a JNDI tree. Note that this implementation is only illustrative, and it is not in any way prescriptive. You may encounter JDBC vendors that use other mechanisms rather than serialized objects to store their JDBC DataSources in a JNDI tree as well.

TestDataSource.java

To illustrate binding a JDBC DataSource object to a directory structure, we needed to invent our own test pseudo-DataSource, shown in the code below. We'll simply implement the methods required for a JDBC DataSource and provide no implementation. Note that most of the methods are simply required methods of the parent DataSource interface. The code is shown in Source B.3.

The key point to notice about TestDataSource is that it implements *java.io .Serializable*. This means any service provider (such as the LDAP service provider) that knows how to store serialized objects will automatically do so when the service provider encounters our DataSource. When a Java client later tries to retrieve the DataSource, the service provider will automatically deserialize the object.

```java
package com.wiley.compBooks.roman.jndi.jdbc;

import java.sql.*;
import javax.sql.*;
import javax.naming.*;
import java.io.*;

/**
 * Dummy class for a JDBC 2.0 DataSource.
 *
 * We implement Serializable so we can be stored in a JNDI tree
 * that supports storage of Serialized objects.  LDAP is one example.
 */
public class TestDataSource implements DataSource, Serializable {

    private String loc, name;
    private int port;
    private int loginTimeout = 0;
    private PrintWriter logWriter;

    public void setDatabaseServer(String loc) {
        this.loc = loc;
    }

    public String getDatabaseServer() {
        return loc;
    }

    public void setDatabaseName(String name) {
        this.name = name;
    }

    public String getDatabaseName() {
        return name;
    }

    public void setDatabasePort(int port) {
        this.port = port;
    }

    public int getDatabasePort() {
        return port;
    }

    public Connection getConnection() {
        return null;
    }
```

Source B.3 TestDataSource.java *(continues)*.

```
    public Connection getConnection(String username, String pass) {
        return null;
    }

    public void setLoginTimeout(int seconds) {
        this.loginTimeout = seconds;
    }

    public int getLoginTimeout() {
        return 0;
    }

    public void setLogWriter(PrintWriter out) {
        logWriter = out;
    }

    public java.io.PrintWriter getLogWriter() {
        return logWriter;
    }
}
```

Source B.3   TestDataSource.java *(continued)*.

Client.java

To test our DataSource, we've written a small client application. It performs the following tasks:

- Sets up a DataSource with database-specific parameters
- Binds the DataSource to a JNDI tree
- Retrieves the DataSource from the JNDI tree and then uses it

The code is shown in Source B.4.

```
package com.wiley.compBooks.roman.jndi.jdbc;

import java.sql.*;
import javax.sql.*;
import javax.naming.*;
import java.io.*;
import java.util.*;
```

Source B.4   Client.java *(continues)*.

```java
/**
 * Demonstration client using JDBC via JNDI
 */
public class Client {

    /**
     * Binds a JDBC 2.0 DataSource to a JNDI tree, then retrieves it
     */
    public static void main (String[] args) {
        try {
            /*
             * Instantiate our fictitious DataSource
             */
            TestDataSource source = new TestDataSource();

            /*
             * Set up the database machine name
             */
            source.setDatabaseServer("edro.middleware-company.com");

            /*
             * Set up the database machine port
             */
            source.setDatabasePort(1521);

            /*
             * Set up the image name of the database
             */
            source.setDatabaseName("MyDB");

            /*
             * Retrieve a JNDI initial context from the System
             * properties.
             */
            Context ctx =
             new InitialContext(System.getProperties());

            /*
             * Bind the DataSource to a JNDI tree under the
             * node "dn=MyDB"
             */
            ctx.rebind("dn=MyDB", source);

            /*
             * Release the old reference to the data source.
```

Source B.4 Client.java *(continues)*.

```
                        * Retrieve a new reference from the JNDI tree
                        */
                       source = null;
                       source = (TestDataSource) ctx.lookup("dn=MyDB");

                       /*
                        * Make sure the retrieved object has our set fields
                        */
                       System.out.println("DataSource returned, bound to " +
                           source.getDatabaseServer() + ":" + source.getDatabasePort() +
                           ":" + source.getDatabaseName());

                       /*
                        * Request a database connection.  Specify my
                        * authentication to ensure that I can use it.
                        */
                       Connection con =
                           source.getConnection("login", "pass");
               }
               catch (Exception e) {
                   e.printStackTrace();
               }
           }
       }
```

Source B.4   Client.java *(continued)*.

The following is the output after running the client program:

```
java -Djava.naming.factory.initial=com.sun.jndi.ldap.LdapCtxFactory
-Djava.naming.provider.url=ldap://louvre:389/o=Airius.com
com.wiley.compBooks.jndi.jdbc.Client

security properties not found. using defaults.

DataSource returned, bound to edro.middleware-company.com:1521:MyDB
```

The program successfully deserialized the stored information for our client's use. Now let's try running it with the File System service provider:

```
java
-Djava.naming.factory.initial=com.sun.jndi.fscontext.RefFSContextFactory
-D java.naming.provider.url=file:c:\
com.wiley.compBooks.jndi.jdbc.Client

javax.naming.OperationNotSupportedException: Can only bind References or
Referenceable objects
```

This exception is expected, because the File System service provider happens not to be able to store *serializable* objects.

Advanced JNDI: Combining JNDI with EJB

EJB uses the Java Naming and Directory Interface extensively. It is used for naming and locating many goodies in the EJB world. The EJB container vendor can choose to exploit JNDI for storing any kind of information. For example, a value-add of an EJB container might be a mechanism for monitoring a deployment, such as what machines are up, what machines are down, and how many beans are in memory. Using JNDI, this monitoring information can be stored in a directory tree and then displayed on a centralized GUI on a system administrator's machine. Containers can use JNDI to store resources used by the container and many other kinds of information—the possibilities are endless.

JNDI and EJB Home Objects

The greatest use of JNDI—at least for EJB clients—is to acquire a reference to a *home object*. If you'll recall from Chapter 3, a home object is a factory that creates beans, or a locator that finds beans somewhere in a database.

In the real world, a home object is simply an RMI remote object because it implements *java.rmi.Remote* (described in Appendix A). Remote objects are networked objects whose methods can be called from clients residing on remote hosts.

When you write EJB client code, you use the JNDI API to locate home objects over the network. Home objects are bound to a well-known directory location so that clients know where to look for them.

As an example, here is a segment of the "Hello, World!" example shown in Chapter 4:

```
/*
 * Get System properties for JNDI initialization
 */
Properties props = System.getProperties();

/*
 * Get a reference to the HelloHome Object - the
 * factory for Hello EJB Objects
 */
Context ctx = new InitialContext(props);
HelloHome home = (HelloHome) ctx.lookup("HelloHome");
```

As you can see, to acquire a reference to a home object using EJB, you use the basic JNDI steps we've learned in this chapter, including the following:

- Declaratively specifying environment properties using properties files or System properties. These properties detail the JNDI service provider used in your deployment, the initial context URL, the security settings you need to access a directory tree, and more.

- Creating an initial context factory using those environment properties.

- Using JNDI to look up an object stored in a directory tree.

When you perform a JNDI *lookup()* for a home object, a typical EJB container might use JNDI to return a Java RMI remote stub. The remote stub is a proxy for the actual home object, which is located elsewhere (perhaps on the EJB Server machine). Once the client has the stub, he or she can invoke remote methods on the home object through the remote stub proxy. And remember, because Java RMI remote stubs are in themselves serializable objects and can be passed over the network, they can be stored in a JNDI tree.

The EJB container could also use referenceable objects and object factories to store objects, which the curious reader can learn about in the following sidebar. There is yet a third mechanism: The EJB container could use the RMI registry JNDI service provider as an assistance to locating remote objects. The RMI registry service provider is very useful in many scenarios, which we'll learn about shortly.

Other Uses of JNDI

The new EJB 1.1 specification has extended the use of JNDI to several other technologies as well, including the following:

- Using JNDI to acquire a reference to the Java Transaction API (JTA) *UserTransaction* interface

- Using JNDI to connect to resource factories, such as JDBC drivers or Java Message Service (JMS) drivers

- Using JNDI for beans to look up other beans

See Appendix D for more information about the new changes in EJB 1.1.

Advanced JNDI: Combining JNDI with Java RMI

As you learned in Appendix A, finding networked objects using Java RMI is not a pretty picture. When you make a remote object available to be invoked on by remote hosts, you register that object with an RMI registry. When a client wants

JNDI References and Object Factories

As we showed in the JDBC example, you can use JNDI to store a Java object in a directory structure by serializing that object, thus storing a copy of the object's original state. But sometimes this is infeasible, perhaps because the Java object is particularly large. Or perhaps the Java object is a database connection or network connection and has nonserializable state. Some types of directories do not even support storage of Java objects. Thus, an alternative mechanism for storing Java objects is needed.

This is where *JNDI references* come into play. JNDI references are like handles to objects. When you store a reference into a directory, you're effectively storing a handle to an object, rather than the whole object itself. The JNDI reference that you store is a compact representation that provides enough information to construct the real object. Note that while JNDI references are powerful, every JNDI service provider does not support them.

Storing Java objects in a JNDI tree via serialization versus using JNDI references has many parallels in Java RMI. When you program with Java RMI, you can pass parameters to remote methods in one of two ways: by serializing the object (pass by value) or by giving the client a remote stub, or proxy, for the actual Java object (pass by reference). Storing a serialized Java object in a directory via JNDI is similar to RMI parameter serialization, while storing JNDI references is similar to passing remote stubs via Java RMI.

Complementing JNDI references are *object factories*. Object factories are pieces of Java code that know how to reconstruct Java objects from a JNDI reference. For example, an object factory for printers might know how to establish a printer connection based on printer location information stored in a JNDI reference retrieved from a directory structure. You are empowered as a JNDI programmer to specify exactly how the object factory reconstructs objects because you can write your own object factories.

We briefly describe the classes and interfaces related to JNDI references and object factories in Table B.3. If you're interested in learning more, see the JNDI Tutorial on the Sun Microsystems home page link on the book's Web site, where the topic is covered in full.

Table B.3   JNDI Interfaces and Classes Used for Storing Referenceable Objects

CLASS OR INTERFACE	DESCRIPTION
Interface javax.naming.Referenceable	A class should implement this interface if you want JNDI to store a JNDI Reference, rather than a serialized object, when instances of the class are bound to a directory. You should implement the getReference method that generates a Reference to yourself—this is called when you are about to be stored.

continued

Table B.3 *Continued*

CLASS OR INTERFACE	DESCRIPTION
class javax.naming.Reference	A JNDI Reference is a placeholder for an actual object that is located outside of the JNDI directory tree being parsed. You should store references when you don't want to serialize and store your Java objects directly, which stores copies of Java objects. You also can use references when an object is not the correct manifestation of the information you want to store in a directory. The Reference class contains two pieces of information: the object factory used to create the real object that the Reference represents and a set of RefAddr objects (described later).
class javax.naming.RefAddr class javax.naming.BinaryRefAddr class javax.naming.StringRefAddra	These objects represent *location information* about JNDI Reference. Location information can be any kind of information the corresponding object factory needs to create the actual object. The RefAddr class is the abstract base class. BinaryRefAddr and StringRefAddr extend it. For example, you can store the hostname of a machine on which the actual object is located in a StringRefAddr. You can serialize an object's handle and store it as a BinaryRefAddr.
Interface javax.naming.spi.ObjectFactory	An ObjectFactory is responsible for creating object instances from a given Reference. When you retrieve a referenceable object from a JNDI tree, an ObjectFactory is called to actually construct the object behind-the-scenes for you.

EJB Design Strategies

JNDI, EJB, and the Singleton Design Pattern

A *singleton* is a very useful design pattern in software engineering. In a nutshell, a singleton is a single instantiation of a class with one global point of access. Normally, you would create a singleton in Java by using the *static* keyword when defining a class. However, one restriction of EJB is that you cannot use static fields in your beans. This precludes the use of the singleton design pattern. But we'd still like to use singletons—how can we?

The answer is JNDI. You can use JNDI to store arbitrary objects to simulate the singleton pattern. If all your objects know of a single, well-known place in a JNDI tree where a particular object is stored, they can effectively treat the object as a single instance. You could perform this by binding a serializable RMI remote stub to a single object in a JNDI tree. Any client code that accessed the JNDI tree would get a copy of that remote stub, and each copy would point back to the same object.

to connect to that remote object, the client needs to hard-code the location of that RMI registry. If that machine changes or if it goes down, your clients need to be redeployed. This is definitely not a suitable situation for a scalable, enterprise-class deployment.

JNDI's RMI registry service provider can alleviate this situation. The RMI registry service provider allows you to bind RMI remote objects, or an entire RMI registry's worth of remote objects, to a JNDI tree. When a client wants to acquire a reference to a remote object, it goes through JNDI rather than connecting through standard means via an RMI *naming.lookup()*.

The RMI registry service provider's advantage is that it enables clients to be unaware of where exactly your remote objects are located. No physical names of machines are ever used when looking up remote objects. With the RMI registry service provider, you specify a well-known location in a JNDI tree that is the binding point for your remote objects. Clients simply connect to this well-known location via JNDI, rather than hard-coding a specific machine name and going through the RMI *naming.lookup()*. If a machine goes down, another machine can replace the old machine's remote objects with a new one in the JNDI tree, yielding a level of fault-tolerance to your deployment. Note that this level of fault-tolerance relies on remote objects being *activatable*, or loaded when needed.

In the EJB world, EJB containers may use the RMI Registry service provider behind the scenes. The service provider allows home objects to be stored and accessed, with clients unaware of their real locations. The RMI Registry service provider is ideally suited for locating EJB Objects.

Let's take the familiar RMI Flip example we used in Appendix A and convert it to use JNDI.

IFlip.java

First we must define our RMI remote interface, *IFlip.java*. IFlip is the remote interface for our remote object, which is defined in *Flip.java*. Client code performs all invocations on the IFlip interface because RMI separates interface from implementation.

The IFlip remote interface hasn't changed since we introduced it in Appendix A. It's shown in Source B.5.

Flip.java

Our remote object, *Flip.java*, is the networked RMI object that implements the remote interface. Flip has changed a bit. It still binds itself to an RMI registry, but now it has an additional method for then binding the RMI registry to a JNDI tree, named *JNDIbind()*. Source B.6 details the code.

```
package com.wiley.compBooks.roman.jndi.rmi;

import java.rmi.Remote;
import java.rmi.RemoteException;

/**
 * The interface for the Remote Object that must be invoked on
 */
public interface IFlip extends Remote {
    public int flip(int i) throws Exception, RemoteException;
}
```

Source B.5 IFlip.java.

```
package com.wiley.compBooks.roman.jndi.rmi;

import java.util.*;
import java.rmi.*;
import java.rmi.registry.*;
import java.rmi.server.*;
import javax.naming.*;

/**
 * Demonstration Remote Object that is bound to an RMI Registry.
 * We then bind the RMI Registry to a JNDI tree.  The System
 * properties must specify the JNDI Initial Context parameters.
 */
public class Flip extends UnicastRemoteObject implements IFlip {

    public static void main(String args[]) throws Exception {
        if (args.length != 4) {
            System.err.println(
                "Syntax: Flip <true|false> <host> <port> <dir>");
            System.err.println();
            System.err.println("true demarcates to start RMI Registry," +
                " false demarcates to bind to existing one.");
            System.err.println("host is the host for RMI Registry.");
            System.err.println("port is the port # for RMI Registry.");
            System.err.println(
                "dir should specify the location of a directory structure.");
            System.exit(-1);
        }

        String host = args[1];
        int port = new Integer(args[2]).intValue();
        Registry reg = null;
```

Source B.6 Flip.java *(continues)*.

```
        /*
         * If desired, start RMI Registry at specified port
         */
        if (args[0].equals("true")) {
            reg = LocateRegistry.createRegistry(port);
            System.out.println("Connected to existing registry.");
        }

        /*
         * Otherwise, bind to an existing registry
         */
        else {
            reg = LocateRegistry.getRegistry(host, port);
            System.out.println("Successfully created registry.");
        }

        /*
         * Start up our Flip object.  It will auto-bind to reg.
         */
        Flip flip = new Flip(reg);

        /*
         * Now bind all the objects in the RMI Registry to a JNDI tree
         */
        flip.JNDIbind("rmi://" + host + ":" + port, args[3]);
    }

    /**
     * Constructor performs RMI Initialization, binds object to reg,
     * and binds reg to JNDI tree.
     */
    public Flip(Registry reg) throws Exception {

        super();

        /*
         * Bind our Flip object to the RMI Registry
         */
        reg.rebind("Flip", this);
        System.out.println("Flip object bound.");
    }

    /**
     * Binds RMI Registry's objects to JNDI tree
     */
    protected void JNDIbind(String RMIURL, String dir) throws Exception {

        Properties env = new Properties();
```

Source B.6 Flip.java *(continues).*

```
        env.put(Context.INITIAL_CONTEXT_FACTORY,
            "com.sun.jndi.rmi.registry.RegistryContextFactory");
        env.put(Context.PROVIDER_URL, RMIURL);

        /*
         * Obtain an initial context
         * (should use RMI Registry service provider).
         */
        Context ctx = new InitialContext(env);

        /*
         * Now use our initial context to look up a _different_
         * directory structure (the example in the book uses
         * LDAP).  This will return a context to that other
         * directory structure.  We can then bind Remote Objects
         * or whole RMI Registries to that context.
         */
        Context otherCtx = (Context) ctx.lookup(dir);

        /*
         * Bind the Context containing RMI Registry info to a
         * JNDI tree.
         */
        otherCtx.rebind("cn=Flip", this);

        System.out.println("Successfully bound object to JNDI tree.");
    }

    public int flip(int i) throws Exception, RemoteException {
        return i * -1;
    }
}
```

Source B.6   Flip.java *(continued)*.

Notice what *JNDIbind()* does. It first sets up some environment variables, and it acquires an Initial Context using the RMI Registry service provider. This Initial Context is then used to perform a *lookup()* operation on a different directory structure. That is, we're using the RMI Registry service provider's Initial Context as a springboard to get a handle to an LDAP context. Once we have the LDAP context, we bind our RMI registry to it. The information bound will be used when future clients try to look up the RMI registry later and retrieve the remote objects from it.

FlipClient.java

Next, we have the client code that wants to use the remote Flip object. Our client has hardly changed, except that now instead of connecting via RMI's *naming.lookup()*, it retrieves the remote object via JNDI. The code is listed in Source B.7.

```java
package com.wiley.compBooks.roman.jndi.rmi;

import java.util.*;
import java.rmi.*;
import javax.naming.*;

public class FlipClient implements Remote {

    public static void main (String[] args) {

        IFlip flip = null;

        /*
         * Set the security manager
         */
        try {
            System.setSecurityManager(new java.rmi.RMISecurityManager());
        }
        catch (java.rmi.RMISecurityException exc) {
            System.err.println("Security violation " + exc.toString());
            System.exit(-1);
        }

        /*
         * Get a handle to a remote Flip object.  We do this via
         * a JNDI lookup, using the RMI Registry service provider.
         */
        try {
            /*
             * Get initial context
             */
            Context ctx = new InitialContext(System.getProperties());

            /*
             * Get the object from RMI Registry bound to JNDI
             * tree.  The RMI Registry service provider
             * automatically looks into the registry that is
```

Source B.7 FlipClient.java *(continues)*.

```
         * bound to this JNDI entry.  It then returns the
         * correct object.
         */
        Remote remoteObject = (Remote) ctx.lookup("cn=Flip");

        /*
         * Perform a quick check to make sure the object is
         * of the expected IFlip interface type
         */
        if (remoteObject instanceof IFlip) {
            flip = (IFlip) remoteObject;
        }
        else {
            throw new Exception(
                "Bad object returned from remote machine");
        }
    }
    catch (Exception e) {
        System.err.println("Error: " + e.toString());
        System.exit(-1);
    }

    /*
     * Print the result of flipping 5.
     */
    try {
        System.err.println(flip.flip(5));
    }
    catch (RemoteException e) {
        System.err.println("Remote error: " + e.toString());
    }
    catch (Exception e) {
        System.err.println("Logical Error: " + e.toString());
    }
  }
}
```

Source B.7 FlipClient.java *(continued)*.

Only a few lines have changed. The line that used to be:

```
Remote remoteObject = Naming.lookup(targetMachine);
```

Has now evolved into:

```
Context ctx = new InitialContext(System.getProperties());
Remote remoteObject = (Remote) ctx.lookup("cn=Flip");
```

The difference is that now we don't hard-code the targetMachine variable.

Running the Example

First, let's run the Flip server. This will register the Flip Remote Object with the RMI Registry, then bind it to an LDAP directory:

```
java com.wiley.compBooks.jndi.rmi.Flip.Flip true edro 1099 ldap://
louvre:389/o=Airius.com
Connected to existing registry.
Flip object bound.
Successfully bound object to JNDI tree.
```

Now, let's run the FlipClient. This will connect to the LDAP server, retrieve the Remote Object and compute the inverse of "5":

```
java -Djava.naming.factory.initial=com.sun.jndi.ldap.LdapCtxFactory -
Djava.naming.provider.url=ldap://louvre:389/o=Airius.com
com.wiley.compBooks.jndi.rmi.Flip.FlipClient
-5
```

Notice that the client code is using the LDAP Context Factory and is unaware of the RMI Registry service provider being used behind the scenes.

In summary, every operation in RMI naming has been cloned in JNDI. JNDI generalizes RMI naming and is able to find arbitrary resources. This is why JNDI is the preferred naming mechanism for enterprise-level deployments.

Summary

In this appendix, you have acquired a breadth of understanding about JNDI. You are now aware of the many intricacies of the JNDI API, and you have seen the File System, LDAP and RMI registry service providers in action. This will give you a solid foundation for using JNDI with EJB, and it will pave the way for you to do serious development with JNDI in the future.

We started this appendix with the basics of naming and directory concepts. You learned about everything from an atomic name to a federated namespace. We then examined the specifics of *javax.naming*, and we wrote an interactive example that browsed a directory structure.

We then approached JNDI from the EJB perspective. We saw how it was possible to bind serializable Java objects to a JNDI tree while learning a little about how JDBC and JNDI could be used together for robust database access.

Finally, we then saw how JNDI and EJB relate and the many uses JNDI could have in an EJB environment. We concluded with a hands-on example of JNDI as a lookup mechanism for RMI remote objects, which demonstrated the RMI Registry service provider in action.

By reading this appendix, you should have a solid understanding for how naming and directory concepts can be applied globally in an enterprise. Ideally, all Java-based naming operations, whether they involve remote objects, printers, JDBC resources, physical machines, enterprise beans, or Web pages, should use JNDI. Interested readers who want to learn more about JNDI should consult the following references:

The JNDI Tutorial. This tutorial is one of many tutorials available for free on the Sun Microsystems Web site. The JNDI Tutorial is very broad in scope, and it will address almost all of your JNDI needs.

The JNDI Specification. The specification defines the core of JNDI. This is a bit more technical, but it should not be tough now that you've read this appendix.

JNDI is leveraged even further in the EJB 1.1 specification, including home objects, resource factories, and references to enterprise beans. We cover EJB 1.1 in Appendix D.

Understanding the Extensible Markup Language (XML)

This appendix takes a look at the *Extensible Markup Language (XML)*—a superb structured document format standard that businesses are using to exchange business data. XML complements EJB nicely as well; in fact, the EJB 1.1 specification uses XML as a document format for deployment descriptors.

By reading this appendix, you will learn the following:

- Why businesses need XML
- The core concepts behind XML programming
- How EJB and XML are related (which we'll expand upon in Appendix D, covering EJB 1.1)

XML is an extremely important technology for the Internet, and it is destined to become the de-facto standard for structuring document content. If you already know XML, feel free to skip to the second half of this appendix, where we discuss how XML and EJB are related. Otherwise, read on, and we will explain XML from the ground-up.

 This appendix explains enough XML for you to begin programming with EJB 1.1. For a full tour of XML, see the book's accompanying Web site for links to external resources.

Business Needs for XML

We begin by studying the needs of the business community that make XML such a useful standard. Why is XML important? What business problems does it solve? Why did we need to create XML rather than use existing technology? Those are the questions we will answer in this section.

Electronic Commerce

The business need for a standard such as XML has arisen with the advent of electronic commerce (also called e-commerce, e-business, or your favorite buzzword). When most people hear the word "electronic commerce", they usually think of Web storefronts that you can visit to purchase goods electronically. This is called business-to-consumer e-commerce because a business is conducting a transaction with a consumer. Examples of business-to-consumer Web sites are Amazon.com (www.amazon.com), Buy.com (www.buy.com), and carOrder.com (www.carOrder.com).

But e-commerce extends beyond simply the business-to-consumer model. For instance, an online auction house such as eBay (www.ebay.com) facilitates transactions between consumers by hosting auctions. This is called consumer-to-consumer e-commerce because goods are exchanging hands between consumers.

A business may also sell goods to other businesses and take consumers out of the picture altogether. This economic model is called business-to-business e-commerce, and is where most of the money changes hands by far, because every business needs to conduct inter-business transactions to survive. Manufacturers need to buy parts from suppliers. Resellers need to buy products from manufacturers. And all corporations need to buy office supplies and furniture. Geographically distributed companies, conglomerates and even whole industries (such as aerospace) rely on communication, and the ability to distribute manufacturing activities gives some companies an essential economic advantage. Business-to-business e-commerce is the single largest financial impact the Internet is making on the world economy, and has been estimated to be 20 times as large as the other Internet economic models. As we will see, business-to-business e-commerce is where XML has the largest impact as well.

Inadequacies with Existing Technology

The challenge for businesses to conduct affairs electronically is for businesses to understand each other's data, such as products, customers, and financial data. With a paper-based system, a human being always intervened and could make logical guesses about ambiguous data. With electronic business, however, computer programs need to receive accurate, structured data, or millions of dollars could be lost due to incorrect transactions.

Thus, a structured data document standard is needed that businesses can use to share information. This document standard should be simple enough for anyone to use elegantly, yet be powerful enough to represent any business data. A computer program should be able to read an electronic document structured in this language and figure out the semantic details of the document based on its structure. For example, an application should be able to query a digital purchase order document and determine what product and quantity the purchase order is for.

Let's take a look at the existing technology standards and examine why they are inadequate for our needs.

VANs and EDI

Electronic business is not a new concept. Companies have already been doing it for years in a very proprietary way. Before the Internet hit mainstream, two corporations would conduct business electronically using a third-party vendor's *value-added network (VAN),* or private network that links companies together. The largest four VAN vendors are General Electric Information Services, IBM Global Information Network, Sterling Commerce, Inc., and Harbinger Corporation.

The standard for conducting business over VANs is called *Electronic Data Exchange (EDI),* a standard for facilitating the electronic exchange of data. EDI has traditionally been used over VANs although it is been extended to run over the Internet as well. EDI has widespread use in multiple vertical industries, from the business sector (transferring business documents) to the educational sector (transferring student records, transcripts, and test scores).

The problems with VANs and EDI are as follows:

- VANs using EDI are a very expensive subscription service, and charge businesses outrageous per transaction fees.

- VANs are a challenge to link to other businesses that are already on the Internet.

- VANs are designed for batch-mode processing (rather than just-in-time processing, which is necessary for efficient transactions).

- Within industries, large companies typically define a set of EDI templates that lock other companies into proprietary standards for data exchange.

- EDI is an outdated, cumbersome, and non-extensible format for transferring data.

Note that there is definitely a lot to be said about VANs and EDI. Many businesses run quite smoothly on these technologies today, as VANs using EDI are quite reliable and secure. Many corporations are also very concerned about gambling their businesses on anything new. Due to these factors, plus the slow rate of technology adoption, the EDI market is growing rapidly as we speak. In the long run, though, VANs and EDI are likely to die off in favor of newer technology evolutions.

What would you do to replace VANs and EDI with an Internet-based model? First you would need to replace the proprietary VAN networks with an Internet link. That's simply a hardware problem. The larger issue is replacing or enhancing EDI with an efficient, modern, structured data document standard that business can use to exchange information. As we will see, XML is that standard, and it is what early adopting businesses are tackling as an integration method, even as we speak.

SGML

The Standard Generalized Markup Language (SGML) is a *meta-markup language*—you can use a meta-markup language to design your own markup language (such as XML or HTML). SGML provides a mechanism to add structure to your documents, and has a great track record of successful deployments of applications, especially in the publishing realm. But, unfortunately, SGML has never become mainstream, largely because of its complexity. SGML is quite powerful, and it could easily be used to represent business data. Its power comes at the cost of ease of use, as SGML is a bit too powerful for everyday business applications. The ramp-up curve for programming with SGML is particularly steep, and the high cost of leveraging SGML is very prohibitive. Few people use SGML in its raw form, but everyone uses implementations of SGML, such as HTML and XML.

HTML

The *HyperText Markup Language (HTML)* is the predominant standard for Web documents. HTML is an application of SGML that is intended for multimedia presentation of information over the Internet.

HTML is an inappropriate markup language for electronic data, primarily because HTML was designed around the use of GUI tags, rather than business data content. HTML is great for displaying documents to end users, but it is very poor for defining other structure in a document. For example, consider the following HTML snippet:

```
<B>John Doe</B>
<I>The Doe Corporation</I>
```

Here, The <B> and <I> tags tell the client-side browser to represent the associated text in **bold** and *italics*, respectively. However, the structure ends there. The browser has no way of structuring the semantic meaning of the text within the document. For example, by glancing at this code, there's no way we can automatically identify that the string "John Doe" is the name of a person. Nor can a computer program discern that "The Doe Corporation" is the name of a company. Note that there are clunky ways around this (for example, you could add ID attributes).

Similary, HTML is not extensible. If a business needs to add new tags to accommodate its needs, that business will run into a wall with HTML. This is because HTML is a markup language, but is not a meta-markup language.

XML

The Extensible Markup Language (XML) is a universal standard for structuring content in electronic documents. XML is extensible, enabling businesses to add new structure to their documents as needed. The XML standard does not suffer the version control problems of other markup languages such as HTML because it has no predefined tags. Rather, with XML you define your own tags for your business needs. XML is a meta-markup language because you can define your own markup language which is self-describing. This makes XML the ideal document format for transferring business data electronically, and it has a wide variety of other applications as well.

Benefits of XML

From a business perspective, XML is compelling because it allows businesses to structure data in an elegant, extensible way. But XML has other benefits as well:

XML is simple and easy to use. The raw XML language does not contain specific tags for vertical markets. Learning to use XML is straightforward and does not require much ramp-up time.

XML is an open, Internet-standard. The Worldwide Web Consortium (W3C) recommended the XML 1.0 standard in February 1998. No single commercial company controls the standard, which means that everyone's interests are taken into account.

XML is human-readable. An XML document can be stored as a simple text file, yet it can represent complex business data. If you want to inspect or modify an XML document, you can simply edit the text file. This is a huge benefit over binary data formats that cannot be easily viewed or modified, such as serialized Java objects (see Appendix A for more on Java object serialization).

XML compresses very well. Because an XML document can be stored as a flat text file, it gains the advantage of very high compression rates. This makes XML well suited for massive document storage, and it also makes XML useful as an on-the-wire data format.

XML has massive industry support behind it. Microsoft, IBM, Sun Microsystems, Oracle Corporation, webMethods, SAP, and many others are jumping on the XML bandwagon.

XML has great tools available. There are already numerous XML tools and other XML applications available for download or purchase. These include XML viewers, high-performance XML parsers, XML JavaBean toolkits, XML-based databases, XML browsers, XML search engines, XML file utilities, and much more. See the book's accompanying Web site for links to XML resources.

XML is the basis for other standards. Already there are companies using XML as a foundation for standards in other technologies and industries. For example, WebMethods has defined an interface definition language for the Web using XML. Sun Microsystems has used XML within its EJB and JSP specifications. By learning XML, you will be prepared to understand these new topics as well.

XML brings new power to content searches. Once you add structure to your data using XML, it is quite straightforward to search your documents for specific information. For example, let's say you're building a repository of historical information. Using XML, you can specify that the string *George Washington* represents a United States president. Once you've built up your historical information repository, you can search that repository for all documents that contain information about United States presidents. Note that this is unlikely to happen on a large-scale (such as searching the Internet for XML tags) because of schema differences between companies.

XML is self-describing. An XML document can contain all the information needed for a program to interpret it. This makes XML highly useful for communicating data between applications because an application can discover information about a document at runtime, without preconceived knowledge of the document's format.

XML uses Unicode, rather than ASCII. This makes XML highly suitable for international electronic commerce.

XML allows for the use of URLs. This makes XML ideal for Internet usage (SGML does not support URLs).

XML Compared to EDI

While EDI is a useful format for structuring business data, it is also a fixed format. EDI does not have the flexibility that XML offers because it does not let you define rules for your business data. XML is a language that can be used to define message formats, whereas EDI defines a bunch of message formats that are used to conduct specific business-to-business transactions. Just as HTML has limited success as a Web markup language because it isn't extensible, EDI has limited success in conducting business-to-business transactions because the predefined transactions aren't extensible. XML's extensibility is its big win over EDI.

It should also be noted that endeavors are underway to unite XML and EDI. For instance, The *XML/EDI* Group is working on *XML/EDI*, a standard that allows XML to express EDI, and also allows for EDI to be transported across the Internet rather than through traditional VANs. This opens up new potential for EDI, as XML brings widespread industry support with it. See the book's accompanying Web site for links to XML/EDI resources.

XML Compared to SGML

XML is an application profile of SGML, meaning XML is a subset of SGML. The advantage that XML has over SGML is simplicity—it will not take you long at all to understand how XML works, yet XML is powerful enough to format any business's data. XML packages the most important aspects of SGML into an easy-to-use document format that you can use to format data transferred over the Internet, using conventional Internet protocols such as HTTP.

XML Compared to HTML

HTML is also an application profile of SGML. Whereas HTML serves as a markup language that defines static tags such as *<B>* and *<I>*, XML is a meta-markup language that you can use to define your own markup language. You can invent your own tags that represent business data in XML, and you can use the tags to represent semantic information about your business data. The power that XML has over HTML is XML documents can contain tags that relate business semantics, and not just format semantics.

XML Concepts

Now that you've seen the XML value proposition, let's take a quick technical tour of XML concepts. The best way to learn XML is by example, and so that is how we will begin. Source C.1 shows a sample XML document.

Let's dissect this document and reveal how XML works.

```
<?xml version="1.0"?>

<library>
    <book isbn="0451524934">
        <title>1984</title>
        <author>George Orwell</author>
        <pages>268</pages>
        <softcover/>
    </book>

    <book isbn="0201634465">
        <title>Essential COM</title>
        <author>Don Box</author>
        <pages>440</pages>
        <description>
            Microsoft COM explained for developers.
        </description>
        <softcover/>
    </book>

    <book isbn="0316769487">
        <title>The Catcher in The Rye</title>
        <author>J. D. Salinger</author>
        <pages>214</pages>
        <hardcover/>
    </book>
</library>
```

Source C.1 An XML document.

Prolog

Every XML document begins with a *prolog*, or a header statement introducing the document. The prolog in our example above is:

```
<?xml version="1.0"?>
```

This identifies that our document uses version 1.0 of XML (which is the only version of XML right now). There are some other interesting things you can put in the prolog as well, such as your text encoding type or whether the document is a *stand-alone* document that does not have any dependencies on external markup declarations.

XML Elements

An *XML element* is the basic building block for defining structured data. The following is an example of an XML element:

```
<title>Essential COM</title>
```

A typical XML element begins with a starting tag (such as *<title>*), has some data (such as *Essential COM*), and is followed by an ending tag (such as *</title>*).

XML elements are useful for structuring your document content. For instance, consider the following flat text file snippet:

```
0201634465
Essential COM
Don Box
440
Microsoft COM explained for developers.
```

There is no way for a computer program to discern what's what in this document. What does 440 stand for? Is it the number of pages, or is it an area code for a phone number? There is no way for a computer program to know this. However, if you mark up the text with XML:

```
<book isbn="0201634465">
    <title>Essential COM</title>
    <author>Don Box</author>
    <pages>440</pages>
    <description>
        Microsoft COM explained for developers.
    </description>
    <softcover/>
</book>
```

Suddenly there is a wealth of knowledge that a computer program can discern from the document. A computer program can read this document in, and then you can query the program for the title, the author, or the number of pages because the computer program can parse that information from the document. This is why it's important to mark up your documents' text into elements.

The more fine-grained your XML elements are, the finer your document searches and queries can be. For example, if you write an XML financial news article, you could mark up your news article with tags such as *<stockPriceIncrease>* and *<marketCapitalization>*. You could then search all news articles for stock price increases that were greater than 50 percent or search for all news articles about companies with a market capitalization over $30 billion.

Attributes

An element can have *attributes* associated with it that provide extra information with the element. For example, consider the following XML snippet:

```
<book isbn="0316769487">
    <title>The Catcher in The Rye</title>
    <author>J. D. Salinger</author>
    <pages>214</pages>
    <hardcover/>
</book>
```

The *book* element has one attribute whose name is *isbn* and whose value is *0316769487*.

HTML programmers will recognize attributes right away, as HTML uses attributes extensively for setting GUI tag parameters. For instance, consider the following HTML snippet:

```
<a href="http://www.amazon.com">
Click here for Amazon.com
</a>
```

This is an HTML anchor tag that links one document to another. It is syntactically almost identical to our book snippet above. The HTML document, though, makes sense only when rendered in a graphical Web browser because the text refers to clicking on a link. The XML document, on the other hand, describes semantic information about the document—specifically, the book's ISBN—and it can be queried at a later date.

You can also have XML elements that are empty and that stand alone. For example, the *<hardcover/>* element in the previous XML snippet is an empty element. Empty elements are single tags, rather than a pair of beginning and ending tags. They are useful for conveying element structure without text or subelements. Empty elements need to look like *<hardcover/>* instead of *<hardcover>* to keep things unambiguous.

The Root Element

A special type of element in a document is the document's *root element*. The root element is the main element tags that wrap the entire document. In our library example, the *<library>* and *</library>* tags denote the root element.

A root element is a requirement in any XML document because it demarcates the beginning and ending of each document. If there were no root, it would be impossible to know whether you've reached the end of a document. Remember that XML documents can be streamed over a slow network, rather than simply read in from files. Without an ending root element tag, a program receiving an

XML document would never know whether it has received the entire document, and it would never know if it should close the network connection.

XML Entities

An *XML entity* is a nickname for something else. XML entities allow you to type a brief keyword in your XML document, which when parsed results in something different. The following code illustrates this.

```
five is &lt; ten.
```

When the above line is parsed (by an *XML parser* that we'll explain in a bit), the resulting text is:

```
five is < ten.
```

The reason you need to use the *<* entity is because the less-than sign, <, is used to begin tags, such as *<library>*. It would be ambiguous if you could use < in your text because programs that read in your XML documents would not be able to determine what was a tag and what was regular content.

CDATA Sections

A *CDATA section* is a portion of your document that should be interpreted literally (similar to the HTML *<PRE>* tag). For example, consider the following XML:

```
five is < ten.
```

The above is not legal XML because there is a less-than sign that the XML parser is mistakenly interpreting as a tag. The following code is legal:

```
<![CDATA[
five is < ten.
]]>
```

It's legal because we've declared that the text inside the CDATA section should be interpreted literally and should not be scanned for tags. CDATA sections are useful for long text sections with lots of symbols such as < and & that a program would normally interpret as markup. You cannot apply styling or format to CDATA sections.

Well-Formed Documents

An XML document is *well-formed* if it meets the well-formed criteria of the XML specification. Well-formed documents follow the syntactic rules of XML, such as properly nesting tags. An XML parser must check whether your document is well formed so that it can parse your document. For example, the following XML document is well formed:

```
<?xml version="1.0" standalone="yes"?>
<food>Banana</food>
```

This document is not well-formed:

```
<?xml version="1.0" standalone="yes"?>
<food>Banana
```

The above example is not well-formed because the *<food>* tag doesn't have a matching *</food>* end tag.

Similarly, this document is well formed:

```
<?xml version="1.0" standalone="yes"?>
<food>
<name>Banana</name><color>yellow</color>
</food>
```

This document is not:

```
<?xml version="1.0" standalone="yes"?>
<food>
<name>Banana<color></name>yellow</color>
</food>
```

This example is not well-formed because two tags overlap and are not properly nested.

XML Parsers

An XML parser is a program that reads in an XML document and verifies whether it is well formed. Several companies make XML parsers, such as IBM, DataChannel, Oracle Corporation, and Sun Microsystems. Most XML parsers are libraries, rather than stand-alone applications, so that you can call an XML parser programmatically from another application.

XML DTDs

Earlier in this chapter, we mentioned that XML is a *meta-markup language* because it allows you to define your own markup language with your own tags. We've done this already in the previous section when we constructed a document with a root element of *<library>* that contained many *<book>* elements. But we could have used any tag names at all, such as *<booklist>* instead of *<library>*

or *<novel>* instead of *<book>*. This means the next guy who writes an XML document might use completely different tags as well. How do we understand his XML then?

 It's very useful to have an XML parser as a stand-alone program so that you can verify whether your documents are well formed. IBM's XML parser for Java (called *XML4J*) ships with a sample application that you can use from the command line to verify that your XML files are well formed. Assuming your CLASSPATH references IBM's XML parser and XML samples .jar files, type:

```
java sax.SAXWriter <filenames...>
```

to verify that your XML documents are well formed.

The answer is to use a *document type definition (DTD)*. A DTD specifies rules about constructing XML documents. DTDs limit the tags you can use in your XML documents, and they also impose rules about how and when you use tags. For example, we might write a DTD that specifies all books must have *<author>* and *<title>* tags—no more, no less.

DTDs limit how flexible you can make your XML documents. This is a good feature because it restricts people to a very well defined set of common structures. Common structures are necessary for two programs to be able to parse and understand exchanged information written in XML. Agreed structures are absolutely necessary when heterogeneous organizations exchange business data because each company needs to understand the other company's information.

DTDs can be embedded within XML files, or they can ship separately. Because they are embeddable, XML is a self-describing language.

Valid Documents

An XML document is *valid* if it satisfies the structural rules laid out in its corresponding DTD. Do not confuse *validity* with the *well-formedness* concept we learned in the previous section. A well-formed document is syntactically correct according to the XML specification (for example, all tags are nested, not overlapped). A document is valid if it is well-formed *and* it satisfies the constraints imposed by the DTD, such as every *book* element contains *title* and *author* elements.

XML Validating Parsers

An *XML validating parser* is a program that checks that an XML document is valid according to its DTD. XML validating parsers are more powerful than plain vanilla XML parsers because they can check whether a document is valid. An XML parser that does not check validity is called a *nonvalidating XML parser*.

 It's also very useful to have an XML validating parser as a stand-alone program so that you can verify whether your documents are well formed as well as valid. IBM's XML parser for Java (called *XML4J*) ships with a sample application that you can use from the command line to verify that your XML files are well formed and valid. Assuming your CLASSPATH references IBM's XML parser and XML samples .jar files, type:

```
java sax.SAXWriter -p com.ibm.xml.parsers.ValidatingSAXParser
<filenames...>
```

to verify that your XML documents are well formed and valid. Note that you must include your DTD embedded within your XML file when using this program.

Understanding DTDs

Let's make our DTD knowledge a bit more concrete with an example, shown in Source C.2.

This simple DTD illustrates many of the core DTD concepts. The XML library file we introduced earlier is well formed and valid with respect to this DTD, so feel free to refer back to Source C.1 as we break apart this DTD and explain it.

The Document Type Declaration

Our DTD begins with some header information indicating the XML version number:

```
<?xml version="1.0" standalone="yes"?>
```

Our DTD then introduces a *document type declaration* as follows:

```
<!DOCTYPE library [
...
]>
```

The document type declaration is very, very different from the document type definition (DTD). The declaration does not introduce any semantic rules; rather, it declares the type of the document and points to the DTD in which its rules are declared. We use the word *library* in our document type declaration to identify the *root element* for our document.

```
<?xml version="1.0" standalone="yes"?>

<!DOCTYPE library [

<!ELEMENT library (book*)>

<!ELEMENT book (title, author+, pages, description?, (hardcover | softcover))>

<!ELEMENT author (#PCDATA)>

<!ELEMENT title (#PCDATA)>

<!ELEMENT pages (#PCDATA)>

<!ELEMENT description (#PCDATA)>

<!ELEMENT hardcover EMPTY>

<!ELEMENT softcover EMPTY>

<!ATTLIST book isbn CDATA #REQUIRED>
]>
```

Source C.2   A Sample XML DTD.

Element Type Declarations

The first line of grammar in our DTD is:

```
<!ELEMENT library (book*)>
```

This is an *element type declaration* because it declares rules about an element—the *<library>* element. This rule says that all libraries contain zero or more book elements (the * stands for zero or more). Indeed, if you look at Source C.1, you'll see that our XML file contains zero or more books (it actually contains three books).

The next line of our DTD is:

```
<!ELEMENT book (title, author+, pages, description?, (hardcover |
softcover))>
```

This line defines rules for the *<book>* element. The rules are shown in Table C.1.

As you can see from Source C.1, the rules in Table C.1 were adhered to in our XML document. We have no books with more than one title, and every book is either a hardcover or a softcover.

Table C.1   Rules for the *<book>* Element

RULE	MEANING
title	All books must have *exactly one* title.
author+	All books must have *at least one* author.
pages	All books must have *exactly one* number of pages.
description?	All books *may have zero or one* descriptions.
(hardcover | softcover)	All books must be *either* a softcover or hardcover, *but not both*.

#PCDATA

The next few lines in our DTD are:

```
<!ELEMENT author (#PCDATA)>

<!ELEMENT title (#PCDATA)>

<!ELEMENT pages (#PCDATA)>

<!ELEMENT description (#PCDATA)>
```

These rules specify that the *<author>*, *<title>*, *<pages>*, and *<description>* elements contain normal character data, such as words, sentences, or paragraphs of text. In a DTD, parsable character data is identified with the word *#PCDATA*. For example, one of our books contains the following text:

```
<author>J. D. Salinger</author>
```

The text *J. D. Salinger* is normal character text, and it is valid *#PCDATA* for this *<author>* element.

Empty Elements

The next few lines of our DTD are:

```
<!ELEMENT hardcover EMPTY>

<!ELEMENT softcover EMPTY>
```

These lines specify *empty elements*, such as *<hardcover/>* and *<softcover/>*. If you'll recall, an empty element is an element with a single tag that has no text or subelements. From Source C.1, you can see that each of our books contains either a *<hardcover/>* or *<softcover/>* element.

Attributes

The final rule in our DTD is:

```
<!ATTLIST book isbn CDATA #REQUIRED>
```

This is an *attribute list declaration*. It declares rules for the *isbn* attribute within the *<book>* element. For example, take the following snippet from Source C.1:

```
<book isbn="0451524934">
    <title>1984</title>
    <author>George Orwell</author>
    <pages>268</pages>
    <softcover/>
</book>
```

The *isbn* attribute above has the value *0451524934*. The attribute list declaration specifies that all books must have an *isbn* attribute. The word *CDATA* means that the *isbn* attribute's value must be plain text. The word *#REQUIRED* means that all books must have an *isbn* attribute. A book without an *isbn* attribute makes the XML document invalid (but still well formed).

There are other settings we could have used as well. The *#IMPLIED* keyword would make the *isbn* attribute optional, but not mandatory, for all books to have. We also could have supplied a default *isbn* value that all books get if they don't have an *isbn* attribute.

XML Summary

This completes our quick tour of XML. We hope you've found XML to be a lot simpler than you may have imagined. Note that we've only scratched the surface of XML; if you want more information on advanced XML topics, see the book's accompanying Web site for links to external resources.

XML and EJB

Now that you've seen the basic XML concepts, let's apply our knowledge to the EJB space. We'll see how XML is used in the EJB deployment descriptor, and we'll also examine XML as an on-the-wire data format for transferring enterprise information.

XML Deployment Descriptors

As we've seen throughout the coding examples in this book, an EJB *deployment descriptor* provides declarative information about your enterprise beans, such as your transaction requirements, your security requirements, your persistent fields, and so on. Deployment descriptors are crucial parts of the EJB specification because they allow you to gain middleware services from the EJB container without directly programming to middleware APIs. Rather, the container *inspects* your deployment descriptor and applies middleware services to your beans as you've declared.

EJB 1.0 Deployment Descriptors

In EJB 1.0, deployment descriptors are serializable Java objects that have been saved to disk. To create a deployment descriptor in EJB 1.0, you need a program that is capable of creating a serializable Java object. For example, BEA's *WebLogic* server currently ships with a *DDCreator* tool that can manufacture a deployment descriptor for you. To use this tool, you first must create a text file that lists your deployment descriptor settings. You then pass this text file to the *DDCreator* tool, and it manufactures a serializable deployment descriptor for you. Note that this is not the only current way to create a deployment descriptor—several vendors (including BEA) provide graphical tools that let you visually create deployment descriptors as well. Once you've created the deployment descriptor, you bundle it with your bean class in an Ejb-jar file, which is a deployable component you can import into an EJB container/server.

The disadvantage of serializable deployment descriptors is that they are tough to maintain. You need a graphical front end to create your deployment descriptor because you cannot work with the serializable bit-blob directly in a text editor.

EJB 1.1 Deployment Descriptors

We've seen that XML is an elegant, simple language you can use to add structure to a document. XML can be used to describe your data, so that another party can query your documents to ascertain information. EJB leverages XML for exactly this purpose: to describe your enterprise beans.

EJB 1.1 completely departs from serializable deployment descriptors. As a bean developer writing to the J2EE platform using EJB 1.1, you must create your declarative bean settings in an XML document. You cannot use serialized deployment descriptors anymore (they are deprecated), but rather, you include an XML document with your enterprise bean classes. All EJB 1.1-compliant containers must accept a deployment descriptor written in XML, and they cannot accept a serialized Java object. We cover the EJB 1.1 XML DTD in Appendix D.

XML as an On-The-Wire Data Format

XML is also applicable to EJB as an on-the-wire data format for sending enterprise information between heterogeneous applications. As we've seen throughout this book, EJB defines a component model for developing robust server-side components—modules that perform tasks such as billing a customer, paying a salary, or fulfilling an order. The EJB paradigm enables corporations to assemble applications from existing prewritten components that solve most of the business problem already.

As good as this sounds, assembling applications from disparate components is not all roses. The problem with assembling heterogeneous components is getting them all to work together. For example, let's say you purchase a bean that computes prices (as we wrote in Part IV), and you combine it with some home-grown entity beans, such as an Order bean and a Product bean. Let's assume we also use a Billing component from a different vendor. How do you get these components to work together? None were created with the knowledge of the others.

There is no easy answer to this problem. EJB defines standard interfaces for components to be deployable in any container, but EJB cannot specify how domain-specific components interact. For example, EJB cannot specify the de facto bean to represent a Product or an Order because each corporation models these differently in its existing information systems.

Unfortunately, you're always going to need to write some workflow component that maps to each vendor's proprietary API and object model. The only way you can get around mapping to APIs is if a standards committee decides on an official object model for a problem domain, such as standardizing on what a purchase order looks like. Problem domains such as pricing are very open and customizable, which makes this a very large challenge to overcome.

There's a second problem with having these components work together: data mapping. How does the billing component understand the data computed by the pricing component? Sure, you might be able to call the billing component's API, but it won't magically know how to deal with the data passed to it. The data was formatted by another vendor's component. You're going to need to write an adapter object that bridges the gap between the two formats. If you purchase components from n vendors, you're going to be spending all your time writing adapter code. This is quite mindless and boring.

XML has the potential to help with data mapping. Rather than application components sending proprietary data, components could interoperate by passing XML documents as parameters. Because the data is formatted in XML, each component could inspect the XML document to determine what data it received.

XML must overcome several challenges before it reaches this level. One hurdle is performance. Parsing XML documents takes time, and sending XML documents over the wire takes even longer. For high-performance enterprise applications, using XML at runtime for routine operations is very costly. The performance barrier is slowly becoming a more trivial concern, however, as XML parsers become higher performing and as people begin to use text compression to send XML documents over the wire.

The larger issue that must be overcome before XML is extensively used as an on-the-wire document format is that every participant component must agree on a standard representation, or DTD, for exchanged data. This is a trivial problem when the components are written by a single vendor because that vendor can simply invent a DTD and include it with its components. This becomes a monstrous problem, though, when integrating heterogeneous vendors' components. For a large number of corporations to agree on document structure for data, a standards body would need to specify a suite of standard DTDs that all enterprise applications used within their industries (two organizations attempting to do this on a widespread basis currently are *XML.org* and Microsoft's *BizTalk.org*). Once industry-standard DTDs are developed, everyone needs to agree to use these DTDs in enterprise applications. Indeed, human competition very much precludes this possibility from gaining widespread adoption, as companies attempt to bend XML for their own business needs, resulting in vendor-specific standards. The need for e-business is there, and so hope remains.

Summary

In this appendix, you've been introduced to the Extensible Markup Language (XML). We began with a look at the business's need for XML to conduct business-to-business e-commerce, and we saw why existing technologies (such as EDI, HTML, and SGML) are insufficient for this purpose. Next, we dove into XML programming, and we quickly got up to speed with writing XML documents, including understanding DTDs. Finally, we applied our XML knowledge to EJB, examining XML both for specifying deployment descriptor structure and for on-the-wire data format.

This chapter has only scratched the surface of XML. There is a wealth of more information to learn, such as the following:

The Extensible Linking Language (*XLL*). XLL allows you to link and address parts of XML documents together, similar to how HTML pages have hyperlinks to one another. XLL is divided into two parts: *XLinks* for creating a link from one XML document to another and *XPointers* for one XML document to address parts within another document.

Extensible Stylesheet Language (*XSL*). XSL allows you to add a GUI presentation to your XML documents. You can apply the GUI rules in an XSL document to an XML document to result in a document that has GUI formatting tags in it, such as the HTML *<B>* and *<I>*.

The Document Object Model (DOM). The DOM is a platform-neutral, language-neutral interface for programs to access, manipulate, and update content, structure, and styles of documents. The DOM defines a tree-like structure for representing an HTML or XML document in memory using objects. You can use the DOM as an API for manipulating an XML document programmatically.

The Simple API for XML (*SAX*). SAX is similar to the DOM, in that it allows you to manipulate XML documents programmatically. The big win SAX has over DOM is that SAX is an event-based interface. SAX allows you to query XML documents from a program without loading that entire XML document into memory. This is necessary for performance reasons, especially if the XML document is particularly huge.

I encourage you to learn as much as you can about this emerging standard, as it will play a key role in Internet applications. For links to this information and much more, please visit the book's accompanying Web site at www.wiley.com/compbooks/roman.

Understanding EJB 1.1

I n this appendix, you'll learn about the major improvements Sun Microsystems has introduced in the EJB 1.1 specification. We've held up production of this book to get you this late-breaking information, and it was definitely worth it. EJB 1.1 addresses many of the problems we've raised throughout this book, and it is a major step forward toward bean portability. By late 1999, the first EJB 1.1-based application servers should arrive on the market. This chapter will fill you in on the major details and paradigm shifts necessary to begin programming with EJB 1.1.

Note that we'll spend minimal time refreshing you on the basics, and so you should have a solid understanding of EJB 1.0 as well as XML (see Appendix C) before reading this appendix.

 This appendix has been written to the third EJB 1.1 public draft. Sun Microsystems may have added minor changes since this appendix was written. Similarly, the code in this chapter is untested, since actual EJB 1.1 products were not available at the time of this writing. Be sure to check the book's accompanying Web site at www.wiley.com/compbooks/roman for any updates to this technology (you should probably do this right now).

Portable Deployment Descriptors

In Appendix C, we saw that XML is an elegant, simple language you can use to add structure to a document. EJB 1.1 leverages XML to describe your enterprise beans. All EJB 1.1-compliant containers must accept deployment descriptors written in XML, and cannot accept serialized Java objects. Sun will provide a tool that aids converting an EJB 1.0 deployment descriptor to EJB 1.1, as well as validating an EJB 1.1 deployment descriptor.

One Deployment Descriptor Per Ejb-Jar File

With EJB 1.0, you need to write a separate deployment descriptor for each enterprise bean. This has changed in EJB 1.1. With EJB 1.1 you write one deployment descriptor *for each ejb-jar file*. Your single deployment descriptor contains information for *all* the beans in the ejb-jar file. This has an interesting side effect: since there is only one deployment descriptor, there is no need for a manifest file that points to all the deployment descriptors within an ejb-jar file. In EJB 1.1, you simply include an XML deployment descriptor, and it must be named *META-INF/ejb-jar.xml*; manifests no longer exist.

EJB 1.1 XML Deployment Descriptor Example

To get you going, let's convert an EJB 1.0-style deployment descriptor into EJB 1.1. We'll start off very simple, and grow our deployment descriptor as we learn more about EJB 1.1 throughout this chapter.

Table D.1 gives an EJB 1.0-style deployment descriptor for an Employee bean.

Source D.1 shows the new EJB 1.1 XML deployment descriptor, which we've commented for clarity.

The deployment descriptor is fairly self-explanatory. One interesting part is the *<assembly-descriptor>* element at the end. The assembly descriptor is where you can add security and transaction information, and we'll see it in action a bit later. These values may very well change when your bean is actually deployed.

Table D.1   EJB 1.0 Serialized Deployment Descriptor Settings for our Product Entity Bean

DEPLOYMENT DESCRIPTOR SETTING	VALUE
Bean Home Name (for client JNDI lookups)	EmployeeHome
Enterprise Bean Class Name	EmployeeBean
Home Interface Class Name	EmployeeHome
Remote Interface Class Name	Employee
Re-entrant	false
Primary Key Class Name	EmployeePK
Container-managed fields	employeeID, name, email

```
<!--
This statement must be included with every EJB 1.1 deployment descriptor.  It
refers to the EJB 1.1 document type definition (DTD).  Unfortunately, Sun has
yet to provide a URL for the SYSTEM id.
-->
<!DOCTYPE ejb-jar PUBLIC "-//Sun Microsystems Inc.//DTD Enterprise JavaBeans
1.1//EN" SYSTEM "TBD">


<!--
This is the required root element of all EJB 1.1 deployment descriptors.
-->
<ejb-jar>

    <!--
    This describes the purpose of this ejb-jar file, and the beans within it.
    If you're writing beans for others to use or maintain, the description
    element is a great place to put special instructions.
    -->
    <description>
    This ejb-jar file contains an assembled Employee entity bean.  No special
    instructions.
    </description>

    <!--
    Within this element, we can declare one or more enterprise beans.
    -->
    <enterprise-beans>

        <!--
        Enterprise bean type: "session" for session bean,
        "entity" for entity bean.
        -->
        <entity>

            <!--
            The description for this bean.
            -->
            <description>
                This bean represents internal employees.
            </description>

            <!--
            This is a unique identifier for this bean.
            -->
            <ejb-name>Employee</ejb-name>

            <!--
            The home interface class.
```

Source D.1 A trivial EJB 1.1 XML deployment descriptor *(continues)*.

```
    -->
    <home>EmployeeHome</home>

    <!--
    The remote interface class.
    -->
    <remote>Employee</remote>

    <!--
    The enterprise bean class.
    -->
    <ejb-class>EmployeeBean</ejb-class>

    <!--
    The primary key class.
    -->
    <prim-key-class>EmployeePK</prim-key-class>

    <!--
    Persistence type: "Container" for container-managed-persistence,
    "Bean" for bean-managed persistence.
    -->
    <persistence-type>Bean</persistence-type>

    <!--
    Whether or not the bean is re-entrant.
    -->
    <reentrant>False</reentrant>

    <!--
    The container-managed persistent fields.  You also can put
    optional <description> elements for each cmp-field.
    -->
    <cmp-field>
        <field-name>employeeID</field-name>
    </cmp-field>

    <cmp-field>
        <field-name>name</field-name>
    </cmp-field>

    <cmp-field>
        <field-name>email</field-name>
    </cmp-field>

    </entity>

</enterprise-beans>
```

Source D.1 A trivial EJB 1.1 XML deployment descriptor *(continues)*.

```
<!--
Application assembly information, such as security roles,
method permissions, and transaction attributes.
-->
<assembly-descriptor>
</assembly-descriptor>

</ejb-jar>
```

Source D.1 A trivial EJB 1.1 XML deployment descriptor *(continued)*.

This brings us to an interesting point: one advantage of XML deployment descriptors is they *evolve over time*. When an enterprise bean is first created, the bean provider constructs an XML deployment descriptor and ships it with the bean. Then when an application assembler purchases the bean, he can modify the deployment descriptor for his particular needs. The application assembler can change the enterprise bean's name, environment properties, description fields, security roles, method permissions, transaction attributes, and more simply by modifying the deployment descriptor.

Now that we've had a taste of EJB and XML, let's take a look at some of the other features in EJB 1.1.

Entity Bean Support Mandated

In EJB 1.0, containers could optionally support entity bean components. It's been over a year since EJB 1.0, and people are beginning to realize the need for persistent components. Thus, Sun Microsystems has mandated that EJB 1.1 containers must support entity beans. This is great news for you because your entity beans should be able to run in any EJB 1.1-compliant application server.

RMI-IIOP API Standardized

In EJB 1.0, each container had a different API for accessing networked objects. Some containers used plain vanilla Java RMI, some used a flavor of RMI-IIOP, and some had proprietary APIs. The EJB 1.1 specification, along with the Java 2 Platform, Enterprise Edition, enforces that containers *must* use Java RMI-IIOP. Sun will enforce this via a compatibility test suite that all containers must pass.

The key API difference between Java RMI and RMI-IIOP is that you need to use *PortableRemoteObject.narrow()* whenever you want to cast any remote object into a more specific type. For example, whenever you receive a home object or EJB object and need to cast it into a more specific type, you need to use *PortableRemoteObject.narrow()*. In EJB 1.0, containers did this in a totally nonportable way. For instance, consider the following snippet of code used with the EJB 1.0-compliant BEA *WebLogic* server, which uses plain vanilla Java RMI:

```
// 1: Get handle
javax.ejb.Handle handle = <retrieve from disk or elsewhere>

// 2: Get EJB object from handle
javax.ejb.EJBObject genericEJBObject = handle.getEJBObject();

// 3: Cast EJB object to our specific remote interface type
Employee emp = (Employee) genericEJBObject;
```

This is invalid when using RMI-IIOP because RMI-IIOP does not support directly casting remote objects. With RMI-IIOP you need to use a helper function to cast the returned object for you. The following code illustrates portable EJB 1.1 casting.

```
// 1: Get handle
javax.ejb.Handle handle = <retrieve from disk or elsewhere>

// 2: Get EJB object from handle
javax.ejb.EJBObject genericEJBObject = handle.getEJBObject();

// 3: Cast EJB object to our specific remote interface type
Employee emp = (Employee)
    javax.rmi.PortableRemoteObject.narrow(
        genericEJBObject, Employee.class);
```

There are some other differences with using RMI-IIOP as well, such as lack of distributed garbage collection, but this is the only key API difference. See Chapter 11 for more details on RMI-IIOP.

 Although you use Java RMI-IIOP as an API, your container does *not* need to use IIOP as transport protocol. Containers can use JRMP (Java RMI's native protocol) or a proprietary protocol for network communications. In the future, Sun Microsystems will likely mandate that IIOP is used as the de facto protocol, allowing for true transaction and security on-the-wire interoperability.

Everything JNDI

We saw the value proposition of JNDI in Appendix B—JNDI is a universal lookup API for resources across a deployment, such as printers, computers, or networks.

EJB 1.0 used JNDI to look up home objects from client code. EJB 1.1 takes JNDI to the extreme, leveraging it to look up many types of resources:

- Enterprise bean home objects from client code
- Enterprise bean home objects from within a bean
- Resource factories (such as JDBC drivers or JMS drivers)
- Environment properties
- The Java Transaction API (JTA) *UserTransaction* interface

This is wonderful news for you because you need to learn only a single API—JNDI—to look up any resource. When you look up EJB 1.1 resources using JNDI, you always follow these steps:

First, acquire a JNDI initial context. The initial context is a starting point for locating resources via JNDI. See Appendix B for more details.

Next, use the initial context to look up the desired resource. The resource could be a home object, a resource factory, the JTA, or environment properties.

If the resource is a remote object, you must cast it RMI-IIOP style. To cast a remote object into a more specific type, you need to use the RMI-IIOP *PortableRemoteObject.narrow()* method.

We now give examples of how to look up each of these resources.

How to Look Up Home Objects from Client Code

Whenever a client wants to use enterprise beans, it needs to first acquire the bean's home object. It then uses the home object to create EJB objects. The client can then call business methods on the EJB objects, which delegate calls to the enterprise bean instances.

The following code shows how to look up home objects using BEA's *WebLogic* in EJB 1.0. Note that this API may be different for other EJB 1.0 containers.

```
// Get System properties for JNDI initialization
Properties props = System.getProperties();

// Get the initial context
Context ctx = new InitialContext(props);

// look up the home object
EmployeeHome home = (EmployeeHome) ctx.lookup("EmployeeHome");

// start creating EJB objects...
Employee emp = home.create();
```

By way of comparison, all EJB 1.1 containers must support JNDI in conjunction with RMI-IIOP style casts, as shown below.

```
// Get System properties for JNDI initialization
Properties props = System.getProperties();

// Get the initial context
Context ctx = new InitialContext(props);

// look up the home object
EmployeeHome home = (EmployeeHome)
    javax.rmi.PortableRemoteObject.narrow(
        ctx.lookup("EmployeeHome"), EmployeeHome.class);

// start creating EJB objects...
Employee emp = home.create();
```

The key difference here is that every EJB 1.1 container must use RMI-IIOP style casting via *PortableRemoteObject.narrow()*.

How to Look Up Home Objects from within a Bean

For your enterprise bean to use other enterprise beans, you need to locate the other enterprise beans' home objects via JNDI. In EJB 1.0, this was handled quite poorly. Remember that to use JNDI, you first need to supply *initialization parameters* such as the JNDI service provider you're using, which differs from container to container. But if you're a bean provider, how do you know what JNDI service provider to use? After all, you're writing reusable components that should run in any container, and each container has its own JNDI service provider. The EJB 1.0 hack solution to this is to externalize all JNDI initialization settings to the environment properties that your bean reads in at runtime (see Chapter 6).

For example, let's say our Employee bean uses an Address bean for storing the employee's address. The following code illustrates the EJB 1.0 way of looking up an Address home from within an Employee bean:

```
// Retrieve the JNDI initialization paramters from
// the bean's environment
Properties props = sessionContext.getEnvironment();

// Obtain a JNDI initial context with the properties
Context ctx = new InitialContext(props);

// Look up the home interface
AddressHome home = (AddressHome) ctx.lookup("AddressHome");
```

EJB 1.1 makes things right. In EJB 1.1, you don't need to supply *any* JNDI initialization parameters. Rather, you simply acquire a *default* JNDI initial context.

The container sets the default JNDI initial context before your bean ever runs. Thus, you can write a bean that runs in any container's JNDI implementation because you don't need to provide JNDI initialization parameters, as shown in the following code example.

```
// Obtain the DEFAULT JNDI initial context by calling the
// no-argument constructor
Context initCtx = new InitialContext();

// Look up the home interface
Object result = initCtx.lookup(
"java:comp/env/ejb/AddressHome");

// Convert the result to the proper type, RMI-IIOP style
AddressHome home = (AddressHome)
    javax.rmi.PortableRemoteObject.narrow(
        result, AddressHome.class);
```

The EJB 1.1 code above is much more portable than the EJB 1.0 code because nobody ever needs to supply container-specific JNDI initialization parameters. Notice also that we look up home objects in *java:comp/env/ejb*. This is the suggested (but not required) location for home objects in EJB 1.1.

Understanding EJB References

One problem with EJB 1.0 is no structured way to refer to home objects. When a bean provider writes some EJB 1.0 client code that calls a home object, what JNDI location should he use? What if that JNDI location changes upon deployment, perhaps because the deployment is spread out across multiple domain boundaries? Unfortunately, the bean provider's code will break if the JNDI location changes. And if bean provider's code ships as *.class* files only, there is no way to modify the original source code.

EJB 1.1 resolves this situation with *EJB references*. An EJB reference is a deployment descriptor entry that says enterprise bean A uses enterprise bean B. When enterprise bean A is finally deployed, the deployer sees the EJB reference to enterprise bean B, and makes sure that enterprise bean B is available at the correct JNDI location. If enterprise bean B is located in a different enterprise domain, the deployer can add symbolic links within the JNDI tree using JNDI *LinkRef*, described in Appendix B.

Source D.2 illustrates a sample deployment descriptor using EJB references.

Programming with EJB references are straightforward. Our Employee bean is using an Address bean, so inside the Employee bean we simply list all the necessary information about the Address bean in an EJB reference. The deployer then knows that our Employee bean uses exactly one other enterprise bean—

```
...
<enterprise-beans>

    <entity>

        <ejb-name>EmployeeEJB</ejb-name>
        <ejb-class>EmployeeBean</ejb-class>
        ...

        <!--
        This is an EJB reference.  It says that Employee uses Address.
        -->
        <ejb-ref>
            <description>
                This is a reference from an Employee bean to an Address bean.
                The Address bean holds the employee's address.
            </description>

            <!--
                The JNDI location that Employee uses to look up Address.  We
                declare it so the deployer knows to bind the Address home in
                java:comp/env/ejb/Address.
            -->
            <ejb-ref-name>ejb/Address</ejb-ref-name>

            <!--
            Address is an Entity bean.
            -->
            <ejb-ref-type>Entity</ejb-ref-type>

            <!--
            The Address home interface class.
            -->
            <home>AddressHome</home>

            <!--
            The Address remote interface class.
            -->
            <remote>Address</remote>

            <!--
            (Optional) the Address ejb-name.
            -->
            <ejb-link>AddressEJB</ejb-link>
        </ejb-ref>
    </entity>
```

Source D.2 Declaring an EJB Reference within an EJB 1.1 Deployment Descriptor *(continues)*.

```
<!--
Here, we define our Address bean.  Notice we use the "AddressEJB" ejb-
name.  This is the same "AddressEJB" that the above ejb-link element uses.
-->
<entity>
    <ejb-name>AddressEJB</ejb-name>
    <ejb-class>AddressBean</ejb-class>
    <home>AddressHome</home>
    <remote>Address</remote>
    ...
</entity>

</enterprise-beans>
...
```

Source D.2   Declaring an EJB Reference within an EJB 1.1 Deployment Descriptor *(continued)*.

Address—and no other. This is useful information for the deployer, because the deployer now knows which class files Employee depends on, and what JNDI location needs to be bound. Similarly, the container's tools can easily inspect the deployment descriptor and verify that the deployer has done his job.

Finally, note that while the above example declares the Address bean within our deployment descriptor, we didn't have to do this. The Address bean could have been in its own ejb-jar file with its own deployment descriptor.

How to Look Up Resource Factories

A *resource factory* is a provider of resources, such as a JDBC driver or a JMS driver. You can use resource factories from within your beans to acquire resources such as database connections. For example, a typical bean-managed persistent entity bean uses the JDBC 1.0 *DriverManager* resource factory to acquire *javax.sql.Connection* database connection resources, used to read to and write from a database.

EJB 1.0 does not specify how to obtain references to resource factories, and this has led to nonportable code. For example, the following illustrates how to obtain a JDBC connection from within a bean using BEA *WebLogic* (for a full example, see Chapter 8):

```
Properties env = entityContext.getEnvironment();
String jdbcURL = (String) env.get(JDBC_URL);
javax.sql.Connection conn =
    javax.sql.DriverManager.getConnection(jdbcURL, env);
```

This code has many problems and is highly nonportable, for the following reasons:

JDBC version problems. We're using a JDBC 1.0 *DriverManager* class, but the target-deployed environment may support JDBC 1.0, or it may support JDBC 2.0's *DataSource* class. As a bean provider, you may not be aware of the eventual deployment environment or application server being used, especially if you are selling beans on the market.

JDBC 1.0 does not support connection pooling. Every EJB container has the liberty to perform connection pooling differently with proprietary APIs. This makes your bean code non-portable across application servers.

Acquiring a reference to a resource factory is not portable. EJB 1.0 does not specify how resource factories such as JDBC drivers should be obtained or initialized.

EJB 1.1 and J2EE address each of these issues.

JDBC versions have been standardized. J2EE requires that all J2EE-compliant products support the JDBC 2.0 standard extension's *javax.sql.DataSource* resource factory. This means if you're developing with J2EE, you can rest assured that your JDBC code will run in any J2EE-compliant product.

Connection pooling is portable. JDBC 2.0 specifies standard interfaces for connection pooling, further enhancing your code portability. Connection pooling happens completely behind the scenes, and your bean code is oblivious to it.

Acquiring a reference to a resource factory is portable. EJB 1.1 mandates that you use JNDI to look up resource factories, which makes your bean code portable across application servers.

The following code illustrates how to look up a JDBC 2.0 *DataSource* via JNDI from within an EJB 1.1 bean method:

```
// obtain the initial JNDI context
Context initCtx = new InitialContext();

// perform JNDI lookup to obtain resource factory
javax.sql.DataSource ds = (javax.sql.DataSource)
    initCtx.lookup("java:comp/env/jdbc/EmployeeDB");
```

Notice that we're using *java:comp/env/jdbc* for the JNDI location of our JDBC 2.0 driver. This is the EJB 1.1 suggested location for your JDBC resources. You must specify your resource factory's JNDI location in the deployment descriptor. When your bean is deployed, the deployer will bind a real resource factory to that JNDI location. The corresponding deployment descriptor is shown in Source D.3.

```
...
<enterprise-beans>

    <entity>

        <ejb-name>EmployeeEJB</ejb-name>
        <ejb-class>EmployeeBean</ejb-class>
        ...

        <!--
        This element indicates a resource factory reference
        -->
        <resource-ref>

            <description>
            This is a reference to a JDBC 2.0 driver used within the Employee
            bean.
            </description>

            <!--
            The JNDI location that Employee uses to look up the JDBC driver.
            We declare it so the deployer knows to bind the JDBC driver in
            java:comp/env/jdbc/EmployeeDB.
            -->
            <res-ref-name>jdbc/EmployeeDB</res-ref-name>

            <!--
            The resource factory class
            -->
            <res-type>javax.sql.DataSource</res-type>

            <!--
            Security for accessing the resource factory.  Can either be
            "Container" or "Application".
            -->
            <res-auth>Container</res-auth>
        </resource-ref>

    </entity>
</enterprise-beans>
...
```

Source D.3 Declaring a Resource Factory Reference within an EJB 1.1 Deployment Descriptor.

Source D.3 is fairly self-explanatory, save for the *res-auth* entry. The following section has more details on this element.

Security with External Resources

When you acquire a connection to a database or other resource, that resource may require authorization. For example, you may need to specify a username and password when obtaining a JDBC connection. EJB 1.1 gives you two choices for authenticating yourself to a resource:

Perform the authentication yourself in the bean code. You should call the resource factory with the appropriate sign-on information, such as a login name and password. In this case, you should set the deployment descriptor's *res-auth* element to *Application*.

Let the deployer handle authentication for you. The deployer specifies all sign-on information in the deployment descriptor. In this case, you should set the deployment descriptor's *res-auth* element to *Container*.

The second choice is the most useful, especially when you are writing beans for resale or reuse by other companies, because only the deployer will know what sign-on credentials are needed to access a particular resource.

How to Look Up Environment Properties

Your bean's environment properties are application-specific properties that your beans read in at runtime. In EJB 1.0, you read in your environment properties by querying your session context or entity context object, as shown below:

```
// 1: Get the environment properties from the context
Properties props = sessionContext.getProperties();

// 2: Retrieve the desired environment property
Integer myInteger = (Integer) props.get("myInteger");
```

Again, EJB 1.1 uses the unified JNDI API to look up deployed resources, including environment properties. The following code illustrates this.

```
// 1: Acquire the initial context
Context initCtx = new InitialContext();

// 2: Use the initial context to look up
//    the environment properties
Integer myInteger = (Integer)
initCtx.lookup("java:comp/env/myInteger");
```

Notice that we look up environment properties under the JNDI name *java:comp/env*. All EJB 1.1 environment properties *must* be in this naming context or in a subcontext of it. An example using a subcontext example is:

```
// 1: Acquire the initial context
Context initCtx = new InitialContext();
```

```
// 2: Use the initial context to look up
//    the environment properties
String companyName = (String)
initCtx.lookup("java:comp/env/EmployeeProps/companyName");
```

For a container to make your environment properties available under the correct JNDI names, you must specify your environment properties in an EJB 1.1 deployment descriptor. An example is shown in Source D.4.

```
...
<enterprise-beans>

    <entity>

        <ejb-name>EmployeeEJB</ejb-name>
        <ejb-class>EmployeeBean</ejb-class>
        ...

        <!--
        This element contains a single environment property.  The property is
        only accessible from the EmployeeBean.
        -->
        <env-entry>

            <description>
            The company name for this employee.
            </description>

            <!--
            The JNDI location that Employee uses to look up the environment
            property.  We declare it so the container knows to bind the
            property in java:comp/env/EmployeeProps/companyName.
            -->
            <env-entry-name>EmployeeProps/companyName</env-entry-name>

            <!--
            The type for this environment property
            -->
            <env-entry-type>java.lang.String</env-entry-type>

            <!--
            The environment property value
            -->
            <env-entry-value>MyCompany</env-entry-value>
        </env-entry>
    </entity>
</enterprise-beans>
...
```

Source D.4   Declaring Environment Properties within an EJB 1.1 Deployment Descriptor.

How to Look Up the JTA UserTransaction Interface

The Java Transaction API (JTA) *UserTransaction* interface is used to explicitly issue *begin, commit,* and *abort* statements in your code, rather than allowing the container to do it for you. In EJB 1.0, session beans could gain access to the Java Transaction API (JTA) via the *SessionContext* interface as follows:

```
public class MySessionBean implements javax.ejb.SessionBean {

    SessionContext ctx;
    ...

    public void someMethod() {
        UserTransaction utx = ctx.getUserTransaction();
        utx.begin();
        // perform logic
        utx.commit();
    }

    ...
}
```

In EJB 1.1, the equivalent way to perform this is via JNDI:

```
public class MySessionBean implements javax.ejb.SessionBean {

    SessionContext ctx;
    ...

    public void someMethod() {
        Context initCtx = new InitialContext();
        UserTransaction utx = (UserTransaction)
     initCtx.lookup("java:comp/UserTransaction");
        utx.begin();
        // perform logic
        utx.commit();
    }

    ...
}
```

For the above code to work, your EJB 1.1 container is required to bind a *UserTransaction* interface in *java:comp/UserTransaction*. Client code that wants to use the JTA (such as purchasing servlet we wrote in Chapter 15) can look up the JTA in a similar fashion.

Bean References Done Right

As we saw in Chapter 13, many EJB 1.0 containers do not correctly maintain a bean's state during passivation/activation or during persistent operations. This has been massively improved in EJB 1.1. The EJB 1.1 specification mandates that containers maintain references correctly, assuming your bean's state adheres to rules that we describe below.

Passivation and Activation Improvements

If you'll recall from Chapter 5, a container can *passivate* your bean at any time, swapping its state out to disk to save system resources. Later on, the container can *acitvate* your bean so that it can service method calls once again.

In EJB 1.0, many containers did not correctly maintain your bean's state for you during passivation/activation. Often times, your bean's internal fields would be left blank, or exceptions would be thrown during the passivation/activation process. In EJB 1.1, your container *must* maintain your bean's state, assuming your state fits into the following categories:

- Serializable types
- EJB object references
- Home object references
- Session context references
- Environment naming contexts used for JNDI lookup

For example, let's say you have the following stateful session bean code:

```
public class MySessionBean implements javax.ejb.SessionBean
{
    // State variables
    private Long myLong;
    private MySessionBeanRemoteInterface ejbObject;
    private MySessionBeanHomeInterface homeObject;
    private javax.ejb.SessionContext mySessionContext;
    private javax.naming.Context envContext;

    // EJB-required methods (fill in as necessary)
    public void setSessionContext(SessionContext ctx) {}
    public void ejbCreate() {}
    public void ejbPassivate() {}
    public void ejbActivate() {}
    public void ejbRemove() {}
```

```
    // Business methods
    ...
}
```

The container must retain the values of the above member variables across passivation and activation operations. And because vendors must pass Sun Microsystems' J2EE test suite, Sun has a mechanism of enforcing these rules. This is wonderful news for bean developers.

Persistence Improvements

In Chapter 9, we saw how to write entity beans whose persistent operations are completely handled by the container (called *container-managed persistence*). With container-managed persistence, your container is responsible for saving and loading your bean's in-memory state fields to an underlying storage.

Unfortunately, many EJB 1.0 containers have a very restricted set of types that it will persist. For example, if you have an entity bean A that contains a reference to an entity bean B's EJB object, many containers will not persist that EJB object reference properly. This is horrible because any complex EJB deployment will have many interesting relationships between entity beans.

EJB 1.1 improves this situation immensely. An EJB 1.1-based container must be able to persist the following:

- Serializable types
- EJB object references
- Home object references

For example, let's say you have the following entity bean code:

```
public class MyEntityBean implements javax.ejb.EntityBean
{
    // Container-Managed fields
    public String myString;
    public MyOtherEntityBeanRemoteInterface ejbObject;
    public MyOtherEntityBeanHomeInterface homeObject;

    // EJB-required methods (fill in as necessary)
    public void setEntityContext(EntityContext ctx) {}
    public void unsetEntityContext() {}
    public void ejbCreate() {}
    public void ejbPassivate() {}
    public void ejbActivate() {}
    public void ejbRemove() {}
    public void ejbStore() {}
    public void ejbLoad() {}
```

```
    // Business methods
    ...
  }
```

The container must be able to persist each of the above container-managed field types to storage. Again, this is great news for you because you now have a flexible arsenal of types you can safely define as your container-managed fields. This also means you can have systems of entity beans referring to other entity beans in a complex hierarchy, and your container will maintain persistent relationships for you.

 Containers are *not* responsible for persisting entity context references or environment naming contexts used for JNDI lookups. You would never want to store these persistently as container-managed fields because they contain runtime EJB-specific information, and they do not represent persistent business data.

Transactions Clarified and Enhanced

Transactions have undergone significant changes in EJB 1.1. Let's take a look at these changes.

Entity Beans Must Use Container-Managed Transactions

As we saw in Chapter 10, there are two ways for enterprise beans to perform transactions: declaratively or programmatically. With programmatic transactions, you must program to a transaction API to begin, commit, and abort transactions. With declarative transactions, the container calls a transaction service for you based upon your deployment descriptor settings, saving you the hassle of dealing with transaction APIs.

With EJB 1.1, only session beans can perform transactions programmatically. Entity beans *must* use declarative transactions.

Changes in Declarative Transactions

In Chapter 10, we learned about transactional *isolation levels*—used to control transactional concurrency. Transactional isolation can range from no isolation at all (the maximum concurrency with the least isolation) through full serializable isolation (lock-step operations with the highest isolation).

In EJB 1.0, there were two ways to use isolation levels:

If your bean is managing transactions, you specify isolation levels with your resource manager API (such as JDBC).

If your container is managing transactions, you declare your isolation levels in your deployment descriptor. The container then fulfills your isolation requirements at runtime.

In EJB 1.1, things have changed quite a bit.

If your bean is managing transactions, you specify isolation levels with your resource manager API (such as JDBC).

If your container is managing transactions, there is no way to specify isolation levels in the deployment descriptor. You need to either use resource manager APIs (such as JDBC), or rely on your container's tools to specify isolation. Thus, isolation has been completely removed from the deployment descriptor.

In this new change, EJB 1.1 has added a bit of flexibility to isolation. If you're using different resource managers within a single transaction, each resource manager can have a different isolation level, yet all run together under a single transaction. Note that any particular resource manager running under a transaction usually requires a single isolation level for the duration of that transaction. Note that there are some drawbacks to this new model as well, as described in the following sidebar.

Finally, note that although you cannot specify transaction isolation in the EJB 1.1 deployment descriptor, you *can* specify *transaction attributes* on bean methods. For example, you can mandate that a bean always runs in a transaction, or that a bean never runs in a transaction. Source D.5 demonstrates this.

```
<assembly-descriptor>

    <!--
    This demonstrates setting a transaction attribute on every method on the
    bean class.
    -->
    <container-transaction>

        <method>
            <ejb-name>Employee</ejb-name>
            <method-name>*</method-name>
        </method>

        <!--
        Transaction attribute.  Can be "NotSupported",
        "Supports", "Required", "RequiresNew",
        "Mandatory", or "Never".
        -->
```

Source D.5 Declaring Transaction Attributes within an EJB 1.1 Deployment Descriptor *(continues).*

```
                <trans-attribute>Required</trans-attribute>

        </container-transaction>

        <!--
        You can also set transaction attributes on individual methods.
        -->
        <container-transaction>

            <method>
                <ejb-name>Employee</ejb-name>
                <method-name>setName</method-name>
            </method>

            <trans-attribute>Required</trans-attribute>

        </container-transaction>

        <!--
        You can even set different transaction attributes on methods with the
        same name that take different parameters.
        -->
        <container-transaction>

            <method>
                <ejb-name>Employee</ejb-name>
                <method-name>setName</method-name>
                <method-param>String</method-param>
            </method>

            <trans-attribute>Required</trans-attribute>

        </container-transaction>

</assembly-descriptor>
```

Source D.5 Declaring Transaction Attributes within an EJB 1.1 Deployment Descriptor *(continued)*.

Security Updates

Next, let's examine the major changes to security in EJB 1.1.

Security Context Propagation Changes

In Chapter 6, we showed you how to control the *propagation* of *security contexts* in an EJB system. For example, let's say a client is authenticated, and has

Isolation in EJB 1.1

Unfortunately with the isolation changes in EJB 1.1, there is no longer any way to specify isolation for container-managed transactional beans in a portable way. This means if you have written an application, you cannot ship that application with built-in isolation. The deployer now needs to know about transaction isolation when he uses the container's tools, and the deployer might not know a whole lot about your application's transactional behavior. This approach is also somewhat error prone, because the bean provider and application assembler need to informally communicate isolation requirements to the deployer, rather than specifying it declaratively in the deployment descriptor.

When I queried Sun on this matter, I got the following response from Mark Hapner, co-author of the EJB specification:

"Isolation was removed because the vendor community found that implementing isolation at the component level was too difficult. Some felt that isolation at the transaction level was the proper solution; however, no consensus was reached on a specific replacement semantics.

This is a difficult problem that unfortunately has no clear solution at this time. We will be examining it again in the context of EJB 2.0 and possibly by then a solution will emerge.

At present, enterprise beans can use JDBC isolation facilities (since databases differ in the isolation facilities they provide, over reliance on this can lead to portability problems) as well as any deployment time isolation control provided by EJB containers. EJB 1.1 does not require that containers provide any specific isolation control.

The best strategy is to develop EJBs that are as tolerant of isolation differences as possible. This is the typical technique used by many optimistic concurrency libraries that have been layered over JDBC and ODBC."

associated security credentials. That client calls bean A, which calls bean B. Should the client's security credentials be sent to bean B, or should bean B receive a different principal? By controlling security context propagation, you can specify the exact semantics of credentials streaming from method to method in a distributed system.

In EJB 1.0, you could control security context propagation via the *runAsMode* and *runAsIdentity* deployment descriptor settings. *runAsMode* controls whether your bean runs as the client identity, as the system identity, or as an identity specified in *runAsIdentity*.

In EJB 1.1, there are no facilities for controlling security context propagation. This has been left as a container-specific feature, and you need to use container-specific tools to specify propagation semantics.

Java 2 Security Model Updates

EJB 1.1 has been updated to reflect security changes in the Java 2 platform. The most significant change is that *java.security.Identity* has been deprecated in Java 2 in favor of the new *java.security.Principal*.

If you'll recall from Chapter 6, an *EJBContext* allows bean developers to access security information at runtime. The EJB 1.0 *EJBContext* relied on *java.security .Identity*, as shown below:

```
public interface javax.ejb.EJBContext
{
    ...
    public java.security.Identity getCallerIdentity();
    public boolean isCallerInRole(java.security.Identity);
    ...
}
```

These methods have been updated to reflect the Java 2 security model as follows:

```
public interface javax.ejb.EJBContext
{
    ...
    public java.security.Principal getCallerPrincipal();
    public boolean isCallerInRole(String roleName);
    ...
}
```

Notice that *isCallerInRole()* now takes a *String* rather than an *Identity*. As we're about to see, you define this String in the deployment descriptor under the *role-name* element. This eliminates the need to provide a custom implementation of *java.security.Identity* as shown in Chapter 6.

Step by Step: Adding Programmatic Security to an EJB 1.1 System

When programming with EJB 1.1 security, you must define the necessary *security policies* for your beans. An example of a security policy is, "only bank administrators may delete bank accounts." You can hard-code security policies into the bean code itself (programmatic security), or you can define method permissions in the deployment descriptor (declarative security). This example shows how to use programmatic security; the next example shows declarative security.

Step 1: Write the Programmatic Security Logic

First, you need to hard-code the security logic into your bean code. Source D.6 demonstrates this.

```
public class EmployeeBean implements EntityBean {

    private EntityContext ctx;

    ...

    public void foo() throws SecurityException {
        /*
         * If the caller is not in the 'sysadmins'
         * security role, throw an exception.
         */
        if (!ctx.isCallerInRole("sysadmins")) {
            throw new SecurityException(...);
        }

        // else, perform operation
        ...
    }
}
```

Source D.6 Programmatic Security Logic in EJB 1.1.

Step 2: Declare the Abstract Security Roles Your Bean Uses

Next, you must declare all the security roles that your bean code uses, such as a *sysadmins* role, in your deployment descriptor. This signals to others (such as application assemblers and deployers) that your bean requires a *sysadmins* security role. That is important information for them to have, because they need to fulfill that role. See Source D.7 for an example deployment descriptor.

```
...
<enterprise-beans>

    <entity>

        <ejb-name>EmployeeEJB</ejb-name>
        <ejb-class>EmployeeBean</ejb-class>
        ...

        <!--
        This declares that our bean code relies on
        the sysadmins role; we must declare it here
```

Source D.7 Declaring a Bean's Required Security Roles within an EJB 1.1 Deployment Descriptor *(continues)*.

```
               to inform the application assembler and deployer.
               -->
               <security-role-ref>

                   <description>
                   This security role should be assigned to the
                   sysadmins who are responsible for modifying
                   employees in the database.
                   </description>

                   <role-name>sysadmins</role-name>

               </security-role-ref>

           ...
       </entity>

       ...

   </enterprise-beans>
   ...
```

Source D.7   Declaring a Bean's Required Security Roles within an EJB 1.1 Deployment Descriptor *(continued)*.

Step 3: Declare the Actual Security Roles

Once you've written your bean, you can ship it for resale, build it into an application, or make it a part of your company's internal library of beans. The consumer of your bean might be combining beans from all sorts of sources, and each source may have declared security roles a bit differently. For example, we used the string *sysadmins* in our bean above, but another bean provider might use the string *administrators*, or have completely different security roles.

The consumer of your bean is responsible for generating the *real* security roles that the final application will use. Source D.8 shows this.

```
<assembly-descriptor>

    ...

    <!--
    This is an example of a real security role used in
    the final application.
```

Source D.8   Declaring Actual Security Roles within an EJB 1.1 Deployment Descriptor *(continues)*.

```
    -->
    <security-role>

        <description>
        This role is for personnel authorized to perform
        employee administration.
        </description>

        <role-name>admins</role-name>
    </security-role>

    ...
</assembly-descriptor>
```

Source D.8 Declaring Actual Security Roles within an EJB 1.1 Deployment Descriptor *(continued)*.

Step 4: Map Principals to the Actual Roles

Next, the consumer of your bean scans through your deployment descriptor for the security roles you've declared with *security-role-ref* elements (as shown in Step 2). He then maps those abstract roles to real security roles, as shown in Source D.9.

```
...
<enterprise-beans>

    <entity>

        <ejb-name>EmployeeEJB</ejb-name>
        <ejb-class>EmployeeBean</ejb-class>
        ...

        <security-role-ref>

            <description>
            This security role should be assigned to the
            sysadmins who are responsible for modifying
            employees in the database.
            </description>

            <role-name>sysadmins</role-name>
            <!--
            Here the application assembler is linking the
```

Source D.9 Mapping Actual Roles to Abstract Roles within an EJB 1.1 Deployment Descriptor *(continues)*.

```
            security-role-ref, called "sysadmins", to a
            real security-role, called "admins".
            -->
                  <role-link>admins</role-link>

      </security-role-ref>

      ...
    </entity>

  ...

</enterprise-beans>
...
```

Source D.9 Mapping Actual Roles to Abstract Roles within an EJB 1.1 Deployment Descriptor *(continued).*

Once you've completed your application, you can deploy it in a wide variety of scenarios. For example, if you write a banking application, you could deploy that same application at different branches of that bank, because you haven't hard-coded any specific principals into your application. The deployer of your application is responsible for mapping principals to the roles you've declared. This mapping is called a *security policy descriptor*, and is a fancy term for the statement, "every container handles mapping roles to principals differently." The bottom line: your deployer looks at your security roles, and assigns principals to them using proprietary container APIs and tools.

Step by Step: Adding Declarative Security to an EJB 1.1 System

This example shows how to add declarative security to an EJB 1.1 system. The process is much simpler because there are no security role strings hard-coded in your bean logic, and hence there are no *security-role-refs* that we need to deal with.

Step 1: Declare Method Permissions

First, you need to declare permissions on the bean methods that you want to secure. Source D.10 demonstrates this.

Step 2: Declare Security Roles

Declaring security roles is the same as for programmatic security. See the previous example.

```
...
<assembly-descriptor>

    ...

    <!--
    This demonstrates allowing a role "sysadmins" to call every method on the
    bean class.
    -->
    <method-permission>
        <role-name>sysadmins</role-name>

        <method>
            <ejb-name>Employee</ejb-name>
            <method-name>*</method-name>
            </method>
    </method-permission>

    <!--
    This demonstrates allowing a role "roleA" to only call methods "foo" and
    "bar".
    -->
    <method-permission>
        <role-name>roleA</role-name>

        <method>
            <ejb-name>Employee</ejb-name>
            <method-name>foo</method-name>
        </method>

        <method>
            <ejb-name>Employee</ejb-name>
            <method-name>bar</method-name>
        </method>
    </method-permission>

    <!--
    This demonstrates allowing a role "roleB" to only call method "bar" that
    takes a parameter "String".
    -->
    <method-permission>
        <role-name>roleB</role-name>

        <method>
            <ejb-name>Employee</ejb-name>
```

Source D.10 Declaring a Bean's Required Security Roles within an EJB 1.1 Deployment Descriptor *(continues)*.

```
                <method-name>bar</method-name>
                <method-params>String</method-params>
            </method>
        </method-permission>

    ...

</assembly-descriptor>
...
```

Source D.10   Declaring a Bean's Required Security Roles within an EJB 1.1 Deployment
Descriptor *(continued)*.

Step 3: Map Abstract Roles to Actual Roles

The consumer of your bean now has the liberty to change around your declared
security roles as necessary. If they want to change a security role, they can simply change the assembly descriptor from Source D.10 into Source D.11.

Step 4: Map Principals to the Actual Roles

Again, mapping principals to actual roles is a container-specific process.

```
<assembly-descriptor>

    ...

    <method-permission>
        <role-name>admins</role-name>

        <method>
            <ejb-name>Employee</ejb-name>
            <method-name>*</method-name>
        </method>
    </method-permission>

    ...

</assembly-descriptor>
...
```

Source D.11   Mapping Actual Roles to Abstract Roles within an EJB 1.1 Deployment Descriptor.

New Home Handles

In Chapter 6, we showed you how to use *EJB object handles*—references to EJB objects that can be persisted and re-used later (the equivalent of CORBA interoperable object references). EJB 1.1 adds a new kind of handle—an *EJB home handle*. EJB home handles are simply persistent references to home objects, rather than persistent references to EJB objects. Home handles are useful because you can acquire a reference to a home object, persist it, and then use it again later without knowledge of the home object's JNDI location.

The following code shows how to use home handles.

```
// First, get the EJB home handle from the home object.
javax.ejb.HomeHandle homeHandle = myHomeObject.getHomeHandle();

// Next, serialize the home handle, and then save it in
// permanent storage.
ObjectOutputStream stream = ...;
stream.writeObject(homeHandle);

// time passes...

// When we want to use the home object again,
// deserialize the home handle
ObjectInputStream stream = ...;
javax.ejb.HomeHandle homeHandle =
 (HomeHandle) stream.readObject();

// Convert the home object handle into a home object
MyHomeInterface myHomeObject = (MyHomeInterface)
    javax.rmi.PortableRemoteObject.narrow(
        homeHandle.getHomeObject(), MyHomeInterface.class);

// Resume using the home object
myHomeObject.create();
```

Other Important Changes in EJB 1.1

Here are the rest of the major changes in EJB 1.1.

Finder methods can return collections. If you recall from Chapters 7, 8, and 9, an entity bean *finder method* locates existing entity bean data in an underlying storage. Finder methods can return more than one result, such as when you want to find all employees that are in the same department. In EJB 1.0, a finder method returns multiple results as a *java.util.Enumeration*. EJB 1.1

has synched with Java 2, and allows you to return *java.util.Collection* classes as well.

New ejb-client jar file. One common question deployers ask is, "which classes do I need to deploy with my *client* applications that call enterprise beans?" EJB 1.1 allows you to specify the exact classes you need with an *ejb-client JAR file*. An ejb-client JAR file is an archive of classes that must be deployed for any clients of a particular ejb-jar file. You specify the name of the ejb-client JAR file in your XML deployment descriptor, as shown in Source D.12.

Primary key class creation can be deferred until deployment time. When you're developing beans, you occasionally might not know which primary key should be associated with one of your container-managed persistent entity beans. This is especially true if you're shipping a bean for others to use, and each deployed environment may have a different underlying storage, and each storage may require a different primary key structure. If you're in this situation, EJB 1.1 allows you to *defer* the creation of the primary key class until deployment time. The deployer will then need to create the appropriate primary key class. See the EJB 1.1 specification for more details here.

javax.ejb.deployment deprecated. EJB 1.0 defines a package called *javax.ejb .deployment*. You use these APIs to access serializable deployment descriptors in-memory. You could write a small Java program that generated deployment descriptors using this package. Don't worry about understanding this package—since EJB 1.1 deployment descriptors are XML documents rather than serialized Java objects, EJB 1.1 completely deprecates *javax.ejb.deployment*.

```
...
<ejb-jar>

    <enterprise-beans>
    ...
    </enterprise-beans>

    <!--
    This is an optional instruction to the deployer that he must make the
    EmployeeClient.jar file accessible to clients of these beans.  If this
    instruction does not exist, the deployer must make the entire ejb-jar
    file accessible to clients.
    -->
    <ejb-client-jar>EmployeeClient.jar</ejb-client-jar>

</ejb-jar>
```

Source D.12 Declaring an ejb-client JAR file within an EJB 1.1 Deployment Descriptor.

For More Information

For the complete (and final) EJB 1.1 DTD, see the EJB 1.1 specification, linked from this book's accompanying Web site at www.wiley.com/compBooks/roman. There is also a comprehensive sample deployment descriptor in the EJB 1.1 specification. You can use it as a template for your own deployment descriptors.

Beyond EJB 1.1

On December 8, 1998, at the Java Business Expo in New York City, Sun Microsystems announced a roadmap for the future of EJB. The road ahead is segmented into three phases:

Phase One is represented by the EJB 1.1 specification, which is rolling out as this book goes to press. It focuses on stabilizing the application servers that vendors create. The enhancements to the specification is mostly issue clarifications and bug fixes. It "improves" security, but certainly doesn't eliminate the issue. It replaces serialized deployment descriptors with XML. It does not address heterogeneous EJB servers and interoperability, nor does it define an event service based on JMS. Entity bean support has become mandatory in EJB 1.1.

Phase Two is represented by the EJB 2.0 specification, which should roll out in late 2000. EJB 2.0 promises some enhancements to provide vendors with more sophisticated legacy integration. It will define a standard framework for existing enterprise information system connectors. In other words, if 3rd party enterprise software developers (such as SAP) were to integrate with EJB, they would only have to build one connector, and that connector could run in any EJB server. EJB 2.0 also promises support for relationships between entity beans, handling such things as cascading deletes (what happens if you delete an entity bean that refers to another entity bean?). Finally, EJB 2.0 will have JMS support for asynchronous communications.

Phase Three will standardize the mapping between a specific deployment scenario and EJB. The goal is to allow developers to create applications built upon the Java 2 Platform, Enterprise Edition without binding themselves to the specifics of an underlying proprietary technology, such as a database, transaction server, or directory server. This release should enable true portability and interoperability across multivendor implementations.

The roadmap for EJB appears in Table D.2. Note that Sun will likely take a bit longer than what we see in this chart.

Table D.2 The Future of EJB

PHASE	ADVANCEMENT	DATE
Phase One (EJB 1.1)	Specification available for public review	Q1 '99
	Phase One Specification finalized	Q2 '99
	Reference implementation available as a technology preview	Q2 '99
	Beta reference implementation available	Q3 '99
	Final reference implementation available	Q4 '99
Phase Two (EJB 2.0)	Phase Two Specification finalized	Q1 '00
Phase Three	Phase Three Specification finalized	Q4 '00

Summary

In this appendix, we've seen the new features in EJB 1.1. Although EJB 1.1 is a minor update from EJB 1.0, it is a very important update because it allows you to write very portable enterprise bean code. This, along with the Java 2 Platform, Enterprise Edition, provides for a stable, robust development platform for the enterprise.

Making a Purchase Decision

Throughout this book, we've explained the concepts behind EJB programming, and put the concepts to practice in concrete examples. But perhaps an even more daunting task than learning about EJB is choosing from the legion of container/ server product vendors out there—and currently there are 27 such products. For the uninformed, this is a very harrowing task. Fortunately, as EJB matures, the industry will begin to consolidate and larger players will emerge from the pack. But until then, what should you be looking for when choosing an EJB product? That is the focus of this appendix.

To best make use of this appendix, first ask yourself which application server features are most important to you in your deployment, including specific features that you need (such as support for a particular database). Once you've gotten the requirements down, you can assign weights to each feature. For example, if transparent fail-over is important in your deployment, you might rank it a 7 out of 10. Once you've weighted each feature, you can begin evaluating application server products, and create a scorecard for each product.

EJB Specification Compliance

Perhaps the most important issue to think about when choosing an EJB container/server product is compatibility. When you make your purchase decision, you need to write code and purchase beans that are compatible with your container/server product. If down the line you decide to switch to a different vendor's product, the transition will surely not be free, and will always require some migration headaches. While the EJB standard defines the interfaces that should make products compatible, every vendor's product will realistically differ from the next in some semantic ways, which will impact your deployment. Ideally, you want to make the right choice the first time you make the purchase.

Unfortunately, there is currently no way to verify whether a product truly is compatible with EJB 1.0. There is no "EJB 1.0-compliant" brand that Sun Microsystems issues to container/server products, because there is no process to verify that a container/server is indeed compatible with EJB 1.0.

With the advent of the Java 2 Platform, Enterprise Edition (J2EE), things are changing. Sun plans to release a compatibility test suite with J2EE, and this test suite verifies that a particular vendor's product is indeed compatible with the J2EE specifications, including the new EJB 1.1 specification. What this means to you is that you will be able to verify compatibility by looking for a J2EE seal of approval which Sun Microsystems stamps on J2EE-compliant products. This seal should significantly reduce compatibility problems between application server products, and should be the first thing you check when you purchase J2EE software.

But until J2EE-compliant products begin to emerge (unlikely to happen until early 2000), your best bet is to read magazine articles and white papers to deduce whether a vendor's application server does indeed implement the EJB specification accurately. This is a necessary step you must take, because otherwise, you may be gambling on a proprietary distributed object framework. If you eventually decide to migrate your software to a different vendor's application server, your porting costs will be significantly reduced if you have written portable enterprise beans.

Entity Bean Support

As you've seen from the entity bean chapters in Part II, and from the e-commerce deployment in Part IV, entity beans are a crucial part of any significant EJB deployment. Entity beans provide an object view into a database or other storage, allowing you to interact with business data at an object-level granularity.

The EJB 1.0 specification does not mandate that container/server products support entity beans—rather, products only need to support session beans. In EJB 1.1, which is part of the Java 2 Platform, Enterprise Edition, every EJB container/server must support entity beans.

When choosing whether entity bean is support is necessary, ask yourself whether your server-side deployment really needs the functionality of entity beans. If you're using a design based on objects, then entity beans are a natural mechanism to map your persistent entities to permanent storage, while session beans map to your process entities. If you're using traditional procedural design methodologies, rather than object design methodologies, you won't miss entities quite as much.

You can count on entity beans to be supported in future versions of every serious EJB server product. Most multi-tier deployments will have a wide variety of both entity and session beans, yielding a rich object model that represents underlying business entities as well as processes, respectively.

Persistence

If you are modeling your persistent data as entity beans, you need to choose a persistence mechanism. Should you persist your objects yourself (using bean-managed persistence), or hand off persistence to the EJB container/server (container-managed persistence)? Once you make this decision, you need to choose an EJB container/server product that supports your persistence method of choice. Let's review the tradeoffs between the two persistence models that we first presented at the end of Chapter 9.

Bean-Managed Persistence

Bean-managed persistence is your best bet if you have a legacy system, since you need to control how data is persisted to that legacy system. Bean-managed persistence is also useful if you have very complex relationships between your persistent data. For example, if you're persisting your objects into multiple tables of a relational database, some EJB containers may not be able to handle this mapping. Performing the persistence yourself via JDBC makes your beans portable to any EJB container that supports entity beans.

Unfortunately, as we saw in Part II, crafting a bean-managed persistence layer into your entity beans requires many man-hours to build and maintain compared to leveraging container-managed persistence. You'll also find that much of your bean-managed persistence code is buggy and unwieldy, since database operations are represented as strings that cannot be validated at compile time. Additionally, bean-managed persistent entity beans are tied to a particular database schema, and if the schema changes, you will probably need to modify the code of the application.

Container-Managed Persistence

Container-managed persistence is useful if you are looking to very quickly develop an application that does not rely on a complex legacy system. If you are building a system from the ground-up with EJB, container-managed persistence will save you significant time and effort because the container handles all the data mapping for you, and your debugging time should be reduced because there is no unwieldy JDBC code to test. And since your code contains no data access logic, your application code is completely independent of the underlying database schema.

Additionally, some EJB containers will be providing APIs for plugging in third-party persistence modules, such as a module that persists your entity beans to an object database rather than a relational database. There are other possibilities as well, such as persisting to a file, persisting to a relational database using a simple object-relational mapping, persisting to a relational database using a complex object-relational mapping, or persisting using user-defined persistence routine (which may implement persistence through a legacy application).

There is a downside to container-managed persistence: It is very difficult to port your entity beans between EJB containers. As we saw in Part II, entity bean persistence is not portable across container products—each vendor performs it differently. This greatly increases your switching cost when porting beans between application servers. Some EJB servers do not support complex mappings of entities to databases (mappings that span multiple tables or databases). Ultimately, a future version of the EJB specification should standardize on a persistence service, but until that happens, my advice is to tie yourself to one container vendor that supports complex mapping to databases, and only port to a different vendor if absolutely necessary.

Choosing a CORBA-based versus an RMI-based EJB Product

In Chapter 11, you saw how enterprise beans can be deployed in either Java RMI-based EJB servers or CORBA-based EJB servers. The Java RMI-based servers communicate using JRMP or IIOP as the protocol, whereas the CORBA-based servers communicate via IIOP.

CORBA-based EJB servers have a single advantage over Java RMI-based EJB servers: legacy integration. If you have an existing deployment written in another language that is CORBA-compatible, such as C++ or COBOL, then CORBA can help you to reuse that existing code base in an EJB environment. Since CORBA-based EJB products bundle ORBs with their application servers, you are in a natural situation to build on your existing investments.

Usage of RMI-IIOP API

Whether your EJB server is CORBA-based or RMI-based, it should *always* support the Java RMI-IIOP API. RMI-IIOP is the de facto API to call enterprise beans, and is the only API you should be using if you want to write portable client code. Make sure your vendor supports RMI-IIOP.

Accessibility of JTA via JNDI

When you want to control transactions from clients, you must look up the Java Transaction API (JTA) *UserTransaction* interface via the Java Naming and Directory Interface (JNDI). Some EJB server vendors have proprietary APIs, which again make your client code not portable. Be sure your EJB server supports accessing JTA via JNDI.

Protocol Issues

Another question you should ask your container vendor is what protocol they use behind the scenes. If it's a CORBA-based EJB server, it most likely uses IIOP as the transport layer. If it's a Java RMI-based EJB server, it may use IIOP, JRMP, or a proprietary protocol. And as we saw in Chapter 11, IIOP is an industry-standard protocol, is much more robust than JRMP, and offers a host of features that JRMP cannot match. For example, if you separate the tiers of your deployment with a firewall (to protect your secure data), the firewall navigation support of IIOP becomes quite handy. IIOP also offers the ability to combine heterogeneous EJB servers in a single distributed transaction, and supports propagation of security information between application servers.

Integrated Tier Support

Throughout this book, we've concentrated on EJB as a server-side component model. But for many deployments, a client-side GUI will also be tied to that back-end system. In particular, e-commerce and other related initiatives will need a mechanism for tying Web components written with Java servlets, JavaBeans, or Java Server Pages (see Part IV for concrete examples of servlets communicating with enterprise beans).

As we mentioned in Chapter 1, it is advantageous to logically (as well as physically) partition your deployment into one or more tiers. For example, a typical three-tier deployment consists of a presentation tier for GUI-related activity, a business logic tier for business rules and processes, and a data tier for durable storage. By separating tiers into different processes or physical machines, each tier can scale independently of the others. Having multiple tiers also enables you to protect sensitive data behind a firewall. The downside to separating your deployment into tiers is twofold: There are more machines to maintain, and performance deteriorates due to distributed objects communicating between tiers over the network.

To sidestep these problems, some EJB container/server products will offer the ability to represent multiple tiers as one. For example, with the *Oracle 8i* database, your application server and bean logic run *within* the database itself—a new alternative to traditional stored procedures. This minimizes roundtrips between business components and the data layer. Other products (such as IBM's *WebSphere*) offer the ability to run GUI components (such as Java servlets or JSP scripts) in the same Java Virtual Machine as your enterprise beans. The result of these innovations is a high-performance, low-maintenance deployment.

In-Memory Data Cache

If you are using entity beans (and most deployments will), you should be aware that entity bean performance is not equal between application servers. Some application servers work in a "pass-through" mode, which means that any entity bean operations are "passed through" to the database, resulting in a low-level database transaction. Other vendors implement smart caching of entity beans, allowing some operations to occur in memory rather than at the database level. For example, if you're merely reading the same data over and over again from an underlying storage, you should not need to hit the database on every method call.

The difference between pass-through and caching application servers is tremendous. Persistence Software, an EJB container vendor, has published a white paper contrasting the two, and the results are staggering: The caching application server had a 60-fold performance increase over the pass-through application server. See the book's accompanying Web site for links to this white paper and other resources.

Scalability

Your EJB server should scale linearly with the amount of resources thrown at it. If you add extra machines with equal power (memory, processor power, disk space, and network bandwidth), then the number of concurrent users your server-side deployment can support, and the number of transactions your system can execute per second, should increase linearly. Be sure to ask your EJB server vendor for case studies and customer references to back up their scalability story.

High Availability

High availability is critical for server-side deployments. You want the highest level of confidence that your EJB server won't come down, and there are a number of things to look for to increase your confidence. For one, your EJB server vendor should have compelling numbers indicating the availability of their product, backed up by existing customers. Secondly, realize that your EJB server is only as available as the operating system and hardware that it's deployed on. Be sure to ask your EJB server vendor what operating systems and hardware configurations they support.

Security

A typical EJB deployment leverages predefined security lists that are already available in existing systems. For example, an IT shop may store access control lists of users in a Lotus Notes LDAP server; you may need to use these lists in your EJB deployments. Many EJB products will offer aid and assistance with importing and exporting ACLs from existing deployments, so that you won't have create your own solutions from scratch, saving you time when deploying EJB products. Some systems can even tap into existing security systems—they get the user and authorization information from the existing security service. Be sure to ask your EJB container/server vendor about these features.

IDE Integration

An essential component of any development is an easy-to-use *Integrated Development Environment (IDE)*, such as Inprise's *JBuilder*, Symantec's *Visual Cafe*, or IBM's *VisualAge for Java*. IDEs can assist in code management, automate programming tasks, and aid in debugging.

Some EJB container/server vendors are IDE vendors as well (such as IBM, Inprise, and Sun Microsystems). This duality allows them to seamlessly integrate their container/server product with their IDE. The end result is compelling: The IDE can aid in coding, debugging, and deploying your beans by working together with the application server. Other EJB container/server vendors who do not have their own IDE are forming strategic alliances with IDE vendors to gain a competitive edge in the marketplace.

Intelligent Load Balancing

A common deployment scenario involves a heterogeneous set of machines, all working together to provide an n-tier solution. Each machine may have different resources to offer, such as more memory or a greater number of processors. We'd like to leverage these resources as much as possible in our deployments.

The traditional way to service requests is to *load-balance* requests in an even, distributed fashion between machines, using a round-robin scheme. This method has the advantage of simplicity, and it works well for a homogenous set of application servers. But when heterogeneous resources are involved, even distribution does not make best use of the resources—intelligent load balancing does.

An intelligent *active load-balancer* tracks information about the load of each application server providing services. As a machine becomes bogged down, the load-balancer intelligently routes requests to other machines as needed. This maximizes your available resources.

Yet another option is *weighted round-robin*, which assigns weights to different machines based upon their capacity. This typically works better than an active load-sensitive balancer because it's a much more lightweight implementation.

Secant and IBM are examples of vendors that provide these high-end load-balancing schemes.

Stateless Transparent Fail-over

When your application server crashes, there should be a transparent re-routing of all requests to a different application server. The natural place to put this process is in intelligent client-side proxies, which intercept all network-related problems and retry methods on alternative application servers, or in the object request broker runtime. Transparent fail-over is fairly easy to implement if you restrict the client to invoke only on a stateless server, and assume that all transactional resource updates can be rolled back.

Clustering

A more advanced level of transparent fail-over is stateful transparent fail-over or clustering. With clustering, your application server is replicating conversational state across servers. If an application server crashes, another server can pick up the pieces since it has replicated state. If your application server supports clustering both for Web components (servlets, JSP scripts) as well as clustering for enterprise beans, then you can completely eliminate single points of failure from your deployment, ensuring uninterrupted business processes.

Clean Shutdown

What happens when you want to take down an application server for maintenance? Perhaps you want to reboot the machine the application server is installed on, upgrade the application server, or install software on the machine. But if you simply kill the process, any connected clients' work would be lost, potentially resulting in financial errors or other catastrophes.

This leads to another area of value that EJB products can provide: a clean way to shut the application server down without having a gross impact on clients. For example, the EJB application server may simply have a routine that refuses connections from new clients, and allows for all existing clients to gracefully disconnect.

Real-time Deployment

Starting up and shutting down an EJB application server is usually a fairly heavyweight operation. If you're debugging an EJB application, having to restart the EJB application server each time you regenerate your beans is a hassle. Having to shut down an application server in order to deploy new beans has an even greater impact, since that application server cannot service clients when it is down.

An enhanced value that some EJB products can provide above and beyond the EJB specification is a mechanism for deploying enterprise beans in real time. This means the ability to deploy and re-deploy beans without shutting down a running application server.

Distributed Transactions

In Chapter 10, we examined transactions in depth, and noted how multiple processes on different physical machines could participate in one large transaction. This is known as a *distributed transaction*, and it is a fairly heavyweight operation. It necessitates the use of the *distributed two-phase commit protocol*, a reliable but cumbersome dance that transaction participants must take part in for a distributed transaction to succeed.

If you require distributed transactions, make sure your EJB server supports them. For a two-phase commit transaction to work, you also need to have the same transaction service deployed on all participant machines, or have interoperable transaction services (which don't exist yet). Note that very few percent of deployed transactional systems actually employ distributed transactions today.

Existing Enterprise System Integration

Integration with existing enterprise information systems (such as ERP systems) will not be portable until EJB 2.0 and the EJB connector specification. With EJB connectors, the legacy vendor will ship a connector that runs in any application server product. But until then, you may want to look to your application server vendor for some help. Netscape's application server, for instance, provides integration aid for both SAP and Peoplesoft ERP systems.

Asynchronous Messaging Support

Although neither EJB 1.0 nor EJB 1.1 support asynchronous messaging via the Java Message Service (JMS), asynchronous communications are still necessary for many scalable multi-tier deployments. With asynchronous messaging, you can subscribe to distributed messaging events, have guaranteed message delivery, and perform non-blocking operations. If your distributed system architecture requires asynchronous messaging, then that should be part of your selection criteria for choosing an application server product.

Integration with Bean Providers

Already there are a few bean providers spawning in the EJB marketplace, such as The Theory Center, recently aquired by BEA Systems, Inc. (www.beasys.com), and Xenosys (www.livebiz.com). These bean providers give you prebuilt components that you can customize and re-use in your own deployments, saving you development time.

If you plan on using a third-party bean provider's product, you should ask your application server vendor if they have a partnership with that bean provider. If they don't, then the beans will most likely not run in your vendor's product due to portability issues.

Specialized Services

There are numerous other features that EJB vendors provide to differentiate their products. Some of these features do not impact your code at all. For instance, your bean code should always remain the same no matter what load-balancing scheme your application server uses. Other features may require explicit coding on your part, such as ERP integration. When choosing a product, ask yourself how much explicit coding you would need to write to a particular vendor's proprietary API. The more of these APIs you use, the less portable your EJB code becomes.

Some examples of special features offered in EJB products are:

- BEA's *WebLogic* has an optimized mechanism for pooling and reusing sockets in their own custom RMI implementation.

- Oracle's *Oracle 8i* EJB Application Server runs on Oracle's own JVM, which adds enhanced garbage collection and native compilation.

- IBM's *WebSphere* application server adds systems management integration to professional monitoring tools, such as Tivoli and Computer Associates monitoring tools. IBM also has a well-defined migration path for CICS customers to move to EJB.

As you can see, the emergence of these services becomes one of the chief advantages of EJB as a competitive playing field that encourages vendors to provide unique qualities of service.

Non-Technical Criteria

There are a host of non-technical criteria that you should consider as well, such as:

Reputable vendor. Does the vendor have a brand name and a history of distributed transaction processing systems? How large is the firm? How many years have they been in operation?

High-quality technical support available after hours. If a crisis situation ensues in the middle of the night, will your vendor be available to resolve problems?

Verifiable customer success stories. Look for large, well-known (ideally Fortune 500) companies implementing solutions with the vendor's product. Don't hesitate to ask tough questions to get beyond the marketing hype.

Training and consulting services available. The company should have their own internal training and consulting services or should have partnerships with other firms to provide those services to you. Be sure that the vendor's training/consulting department is adequately staffed to provide the care you need, and that the vendor is not overburdened with other projects.

Free evaluation copy. Any deserving vendor should let you evaluate their product free-of-charge for either a limited time period, or as a stripped-down product version. Otherwise, rule that vendor out immediately.

Summary

In this appendix, you've surveyed the criteria for making an EJB application server purchase decision. The EJB specifications (as well as the products that implement it) are evolving rapidly. The features offered in the marketplace are likely to change over time. For the latest information about EJB products and news, check out the following resources:

Online white papers. Some research firms offer white paper reviews they have performed on EJB products. See the book's accompanying Web site for links to these white papers.

The Sun Microsystems Web site. The EJB homepage has an *EJB Directory* of current EJB products with links to vendor information. This directory is likely to evolve greatly over time. For a link to this, see the book's accompanying Web site at *www.wiley.com/compbooks/roman*.

Magazine article reviews. Some Java-based, printed magazines offer comparisons of EJB products as well. Examples here include Java Report, Java Developer's Journal, and JavaPro.

Third-party Web sites. Examples here include www.develop.com, www.jc100.com, and www.builder.com. See the book's accompanying Web site for links to these and other sites.

EJB Quick Reference Guide

T his appendix is a quick reference for programmers to use during EJB development. In the first section of this appendix, you'll find diagrams illustrating what's really going on in an EJB system. These diagrams were taken directly from the EJB specification; I've condensed the diagrams and commented them to clarify their meaning. You'll also find summaries and explanations of each method in the EJB architecture, as well as a transaction reference.

Session Bean Diagrams

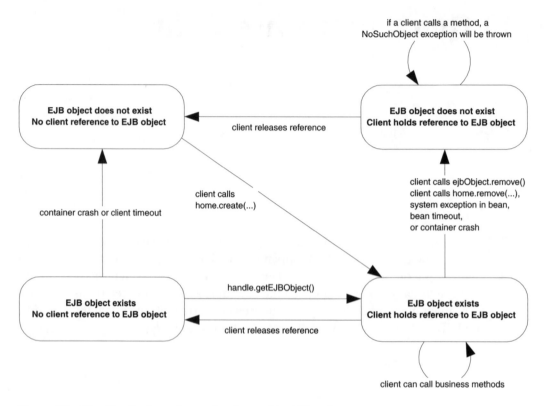

Figure F.1   The client's view of a session bean object lifecycle.

Stateless Session Bean Diagrams

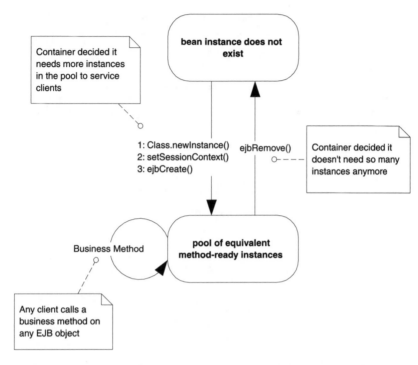

Figure F.2 The lifecycle of a stateless session bean. Each method call shown is an invocation from the container to the bean instance.

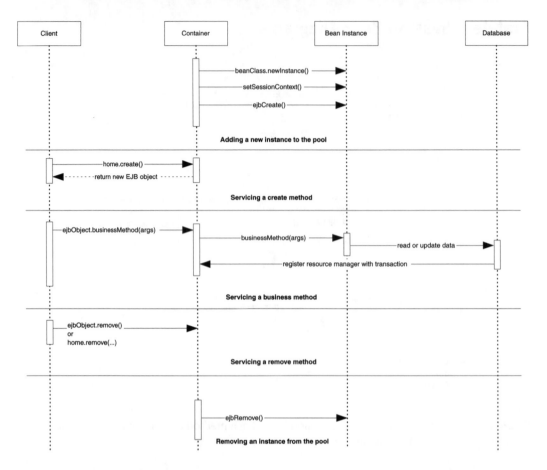

Figure F.3 Sequence diagram for stateless session beans. For simplicity, the Container object represents all container subsystems, including EJB objects, home objects, transaction services, and so on.

Stateful Session Bean Diagrams

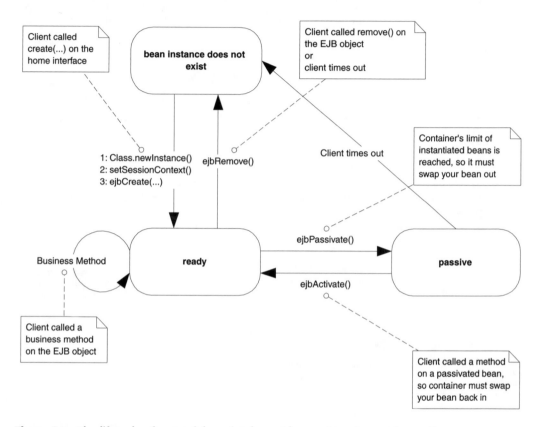

Figure F.4 The lifecycle of a stateful session bean (does not implement *javax.ejb* .*SessionSynchronization*). Each method call shown is an invocation from the container to the bean instance.

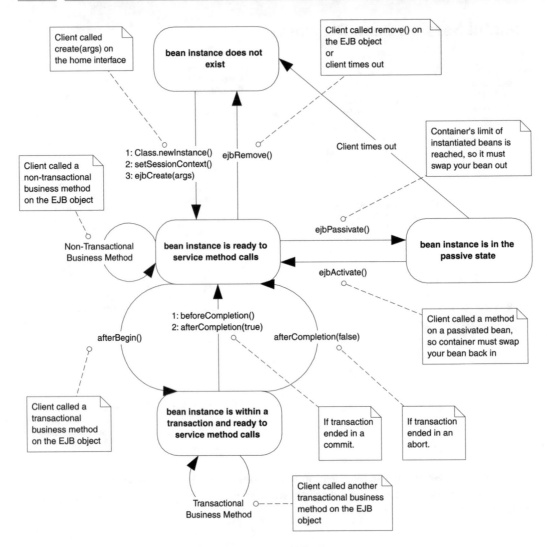

Figure F.5 The lifecycle of a stateful session bean (implements *javax.ejb.SessionSynchronization*). Each method call shown is an invocation from the container to the bean instance.

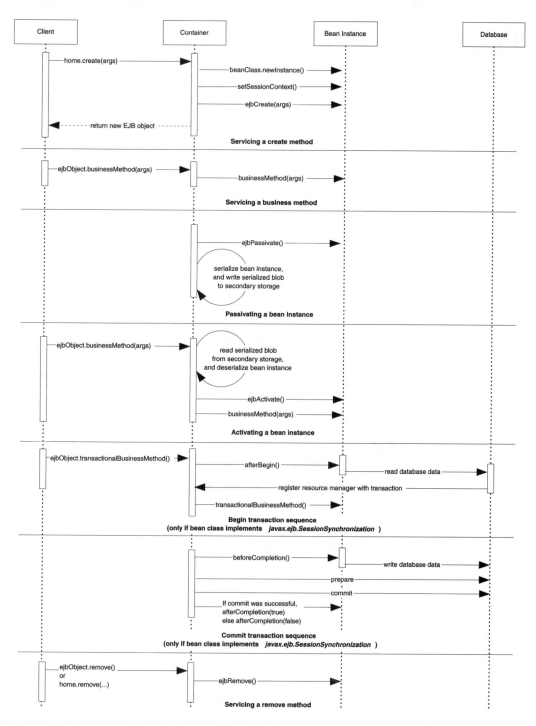

Figure F.6 Sequence diagram for stateful session beans. For simplicity, the Container object represents all container subsystems, including EJB objects, home objects, transaction services, and so on.

Entity Bean Diagrams

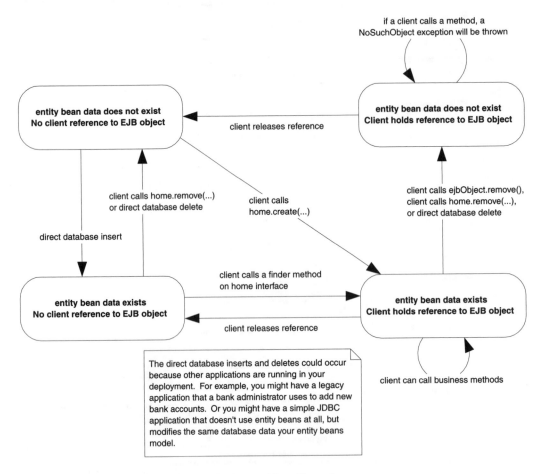

Figure F.7 The client's view of an entity bean object life cycle.

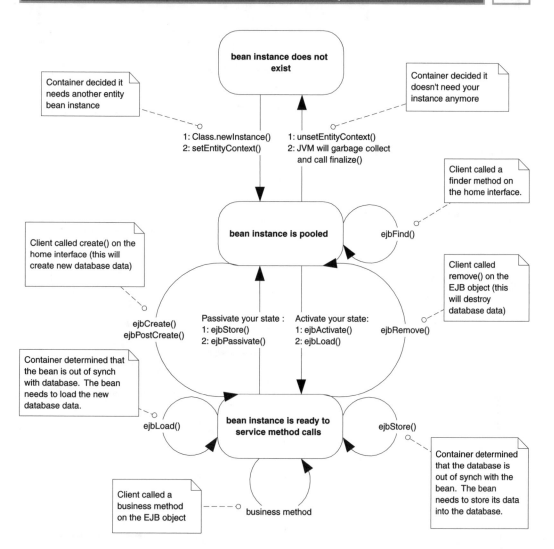

Figure F.8 The life cycle of an entity bean. Each method call shown is an invocation from the container to the bean instance.

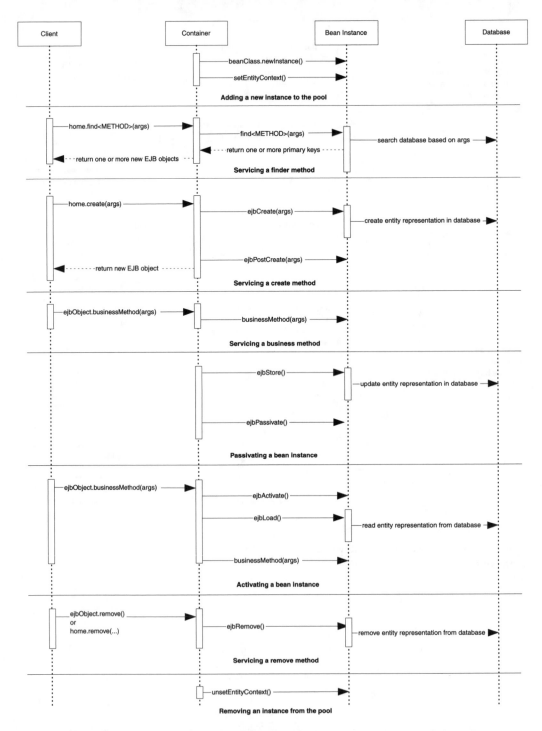

Figure F.9 Sequence diagram for bean-managed persistent entity beans. For simplicity, the Container object represents all container subsystems, including EJB objects, home objects, transaction services, and so on.

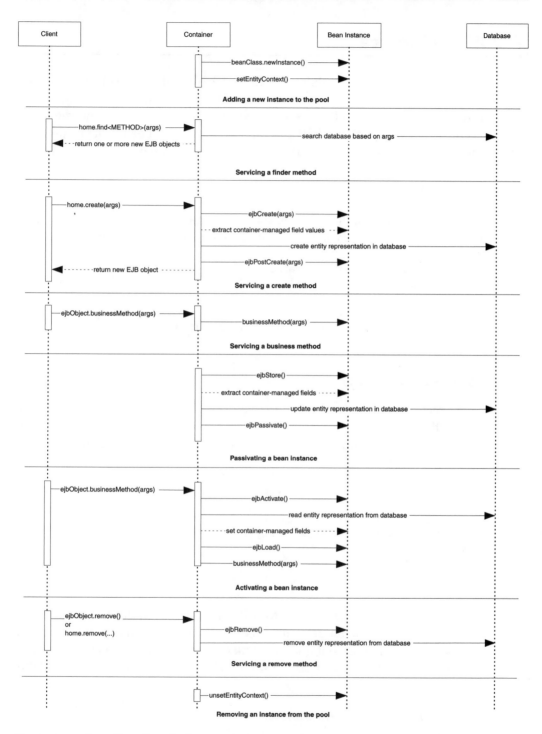

Figure F.10 Sequence diagram for container-managed persistent entity beans. For simplicity, the Container object represents all container subsystems, including EJB objects, home objects, transaction services, and so on.

EJB API Reference

The following section explains the Enterprise JavaBeans API, which is the *javax.ejb* package. This API is the essence of EJB, and defines the specific signature contracts between clients, enterprise beans, and containers. This reference is consistent with both the EJB 1.0 standard that we've been using throughout the book, as well as the new EJB 1.1 standard we outlined in Appendix D.

CreateException

This exception type indicates failure to create an enterprise bean. You should throw this exception in your home interface's *create(...)* methods.

```
public class javax.ejb.CreateException
    extends java.lang.Exception
{
    public CreateException();
    public CreateException(java.lang.String);
}
```

DuplicateKeyException

This exception type indicates failure to create an entity bean because an entity bean with the same primary key already exists. This is a subclass of *CreateException* and is thrown in an entity bean home interface's *create(...)* methods.

```
public class javax.ejb.DuplicateKeyException
    extends javax.ejb.CreateException
{
    public DuplicateKeyException();
    public DuplicateKeyException(java.lang.String);
}
```

EJBContext

Your bean can use an EJB context to perform callbacks to the container. These callbacks help your bean determine its current transactional status, security status, and more. Your container must make an EJB context available to your enterprise bean at runtime. Both *SessionContext* and *EntityContext* extend this interface.

```
public interface javax.ejb.EJBContext
{
    public javax.ejb.EJBHome getEJBHome();
```

```
/*
 * This method has changed in EJB 1.1.  You should
 * use JNDI instead.  See Appendix D.
 */
public java.util.Properties getEnvironment();

/*
 * This method has changed in EJB 1.1.  You should
 * use getCallerPrincipal() instead.  See Appendix D.
 */
public java.security.Identity getCallerIdentity();

/* This method has changed in EJB 1.1.  You should
 * use isCallerInRole(java.lang.String) instead.
 * See Appendix D.
 */
public boolean isCallerInRole(java.security.Identity);

/*
 * This method has changed in EJB 1.1.  You should
 * use JNDI instead.  See Appendix D.
 */
public javax.jts.UserTransaction getUserTransaction()
    throws IllegalStateException;

public void setRollbackOnly();
public boolean getRollbackOnly();
}
```

Table F.1   javax.ejb.EJBContext

METHOD	DESCRIPTION	USEFULNESS
getHome()	Returns a reference to your bean's own home object.	Useful when your bean needs to create, destroy, or find EJB objects of its own bean class.
getEnvironment()	Returns your bean's deployed environment properties.	Call to access deployed environment properties. Allows users to customize your beans via properties.
getCallerIdentity()	Returns the caller's security identity.	Useful for programmatic security within your bean. For example, you can use the caller's distinguished name as a key to unlock secured information in a database.

continues

Table F.1 *(Continued)*

METHOD	DESCRIPTION	USEFULNESS
isCallerInRole()	Tests if a bean's caller is in a particular security role (a group authorized to perform operations).	Useful for querying whether the authenticated client is authorized to perform an operation.
setRollbackOnly()	Marks the current transaction such that the only outcome of the transaction is a rollback.	Call this method to force a transaction to abort and roll back.
getRollbackOnly()	Returns a Boolean indicating whether the current transaction has been marked for rollback.	If the current transaction is going to abort, you may be able to bypass logic in your bean, saving valuable computation time.
getUserTransaction() *Note: This method is only supported for bean-managed transactions.*	Returns the *javax.transaction .UserTransaction* interface.	Controlling transactions explicitly in your bean.

EJBException

Your enterprise bean class should throw this exception to indicate an unexpected error, such as a failure to open a database connection, or a JNDI exception. Your container will treat this exception as a serious problem, and may take action such as logging the event or paging a system administrator, depending upon your container's policy. The container will then throw a *java.rmi.RemoteException* back to the client code.

```
public class javax.ejb.EJBException
    extends java.lang.Exception
{
    public javax.ejb.EJBException();
    public javax.ejb.EJBException(java.lang.String);
    public javax.ejb.EJBException(java.lang.Exception);
    public java.lang.Exception getCausedByException();
}
```

EJBHome

Clients create, find, and remove EJB objects through home interfaces. All home interfaces extend *javax.ejb.EJBHome*. The container will implement the methods in *javax.ejb.EJBHome* when it implements your home interface as a concrete home object.

```
public interface javax.ejb.EJBHome
    extends java.rmi.Remote
{
    public EJBMetaData getEJBMetaData()
        throws java.rmi.RemoteException;

    public void remove(Handle handle)
        throws java.rmi.RemoteException,
            javax.ejb.RemoveException;

    public void remove(Object primaryKey)
        throws java.rmi.RemoteException,
            javax.ejb.RemoveException;

    /*
     * This method applies to EJB 1.1 only.  It retrieves
     * a home handle, which is a persistent reference to
     * a home object.  See Appendix D.
     */
    public javax.ejb.HomeHandle getHomeHandle()
}
```

Table F.2   javax.ejb.EJBHome *(these methods are called by clients)*

METHOD	EXPLANATION
getEJBMetaData()	Returns metadata about the enterprise bean you're working with. Useful if your client code is written in a scripting language, or if you're writing EJB development tools.
remove()	This method destroys an EJB object based upon an EJB object handle or primary key you pass in.
	Note: For entity beans, remove() also deletes the bean from the underlying persistent store.

EJBMetaData

This interface encapsulates metadata about an enterprise bean. Metadata is not very useful for typical client code, but it more suited towards clients that need to dynamically discover information about an enterprise bean, such as scripting languages or EJB development tools. Your client code can retrieve this metadata by calling *homeObject.getEJBMetaData()*. The client code will get back a serializable implementation of *javax.ejb.EJBMetaData*.

```
public interface javax.ejb.EJBMetaData
{
    public javax.ejb.EJBHome getEJBHome();
```

```
public java.lang.Class getHomeInterfaceClass();
public java.lang.Class getPrimaryKeyClass();
public java.lang.Class getRemoteInterfaceClass();
public boolean isSession();

// EJB 1.1 only
public boolean isStatelessSession();
}
```

EJBObject

A client accesses a bean through an EJB object, which implements a remote interface. Your remote interface must implement *javax.ejb.EJBObject*. The container will implement the methods in *javax.ejb.EJBObject* when it implements your remote interface as a concrete EJB object.

```
public interface javax.ejb.EJBObject
    extends java.rmi.Remote
{
    public javax.ejb.EJBHome getEJBHome()
        throws java.rmi.RemoteException;

    public java.lang.Object getPrimaryKey()
        throws java.rmi.RemoteException;

    public void remove()
        throws java.rmi.RemoteException,
      javax.ejb.RemoveException;

    public javax.ejb.Handle getHandle()
        throws java.rmi.RemoteException;

    public boolean isIdentical(javax.ejb.EJBObject)
        throws java.rmi.RemoteException;
}
```

Table F.3   javax.ejb.EJBObject

METHOD	EXPLANATION
getEJBHome()	Gets the home object for this EJB object.
getPrimaryKey()	Returns the primary key for this EJB object. A primary key is only used for entity beans (see Chapters 7-9).
remove()	Destroys this EJB object. When your client code is done using an EJB object, you should call this method. The system resources for the EJB object can then be reclaimed.
	Note: For entity beans, remove() also deletes the bean from the underlying persistent store.

METHOD	EXPLANATION
getHandle()	Acquires a *handle* for this EJB object. An EJB handle is a persistent reference to an EJB object that the client can stow away somewhere. Later on, the client can use the handle to re-acquire the EJB object and start using it again.
isIdentical()	Tests whether two EJB objects are identical.

EnterpriseBean

This interface serves as a *marker* interface; implementing this interface indicates that your class is indeed an enterprise bean class. You should not implement this interface; rather, implement either *javax.ejb.EntityBean* or *javax.ejb.SessionBean*, which both extend this interface.

```
public interface javax.ejb.EnterpriseBean
    extends java.io.Serializable
{
}
```

EntityBean

To write an entity bean class, your class must implement the *javax.ejb.EntityBean* interface. This interface defines a few required methods that you must fill in. These are management methods that the EJB container calls to alert your bean to life cycle events. Clients of your bean will never call these methods because these methods are not made available to clients via the EJB object.

```
public interface javax.ejb.EntityBean
    implements javax.ejb.EnterpriseBean
{
    public void setEntityContext(javax.ejb.EntityContext);
    public void unsetEntityContext();
    public void ejbRemove();
    public void ejbActivate();
    public void ejbPassivate();
    public void ejbLoad();
    public void ejbStore();
}
```

In EJB 1.0, each of these methods can throw a *java.rmi.RemoteException*. However, this doesn't make complete sense, since an entity bean is not an RMI remote object. Thus, in EJB 1.1, this has changed to *javax.ejb.EJBException*.

Table F.4 Required methods for Entity Bean classes.

METHOD	DESCRIPTION	TYPICAL IMPLEMENTATION (BEAN-MANAGED PERSISTENT ENTITIES)	TYPICAL IMPLEMENTATION (CONTAINER-MANAGED PERSISTENT ENTITIES)
setEntityContext (EntityContext ctx)	Associates your bean with an entity context. You can query the entity context about your current transactional state, your current security state, and more.	Store the context away in a member variable so the context can be queried later.	Store the context away in a member variable so the context can be queried later.
ejbFind() Note: You only use ejbFind() methods with bean-managed persistent entity beans.	Finds an existing entity bean in storage. You can have many different finder methods, which all perform different operations.	Search through a data store using a storage API such as JDBC or SQL/J. For example, you might perform a relational query such as "SELECT id FROM accounts WHERE balance > 0". Return the resulting primary key set.	Do not implement these methods for container-managed persistent entity beans. The EJB container will handle all issues relating to finding data for you. Use your container tools to describe your finder method needs.
ejbCreate(...)	Initializes a bean for a particular client, and creates underlying database data. Each ejbCreate() method you define gives clients a different way to create your entity beans.	Validate the client's initialization parameters. Explicitly create the database representation of the data via a storage API such as JDBC or SQL/J.	Validate the client's initialization parameters. Set your container-managed fields to the parameters passed in. The container will then extract these values from your bean and create the database data for you
ejbPostCreate(...)	Your bean class must define ejbPostCreate() for each one ejbCreate(). Each pair must accept the same parameters. The container calls ejbPostCreate() right after ejbCreate().	Perform any initialization you need to that requires a reference to your own EJB object, such as passing your bean's EJB object reference to other beans. You can get your EJB object via entityContext. getEJBObject().	Perform any initialization you need to that requires a reference to your own EJB object, such as passing your bean's EJB object reference to other beans. You can get your EJB object via entityContext. getEJBObject().

Method		
ejbPassivate()	Called immediately before your bean is passivated (swapped out to disk because there are too many beans instantiated).	Release any resources your bean may be holding.
ejbStore()	Called when the container needs to update the database with your bean's state. The current transactional state dictates when this method is called. This method is also called during passivation, directly before *ejbPassivate()*.	Explicitly update the database representation of the data via a storage API such as JDBC. Typically, you'll write a number of your member variable's fields out to disk.	*Do not update the database in this method.* Rather, the EJB container will update the database for you automatically right *after* calling your *ejbStore()* method. It does this by extracting your container-managed fields and writing them to the database. Thus, you should prepare your container-managed fields to be written to the database, such as compressing fields.
ejbLoad()	Called when the container needs to update your bean with the database's state. The current transactional state dictates when this method is called. This method is also called during activation, directly before *ejbActivate()*.	First, your bean instance must figure out what data it should load. Call the *getPrimaryKey()* method on the entity context; that will tell your bean what data it should be loading. Next, read database data into your bean via a storage API such as JDBC or SQL/J.	*Do not read data from the database in this method.* Rather, the EJB container will read in data from the database for you automatically right *before* calling your *ejbLoad()* method. It does this by setting your container-managed fields to the data it reads from the database. Thus, you should perform any necessary post-load operations, such as decompressing fields.
ejbActivate()	Called immediately before your bean is activated (swapped in from disk because a client needs your bean).	Acquire any resources your bean needs, such as those released during *ejbPassivate()*.	Acquire any resources your bean needs, such as those released during *ejbPassivate()*.

continues

Table F.4 *(Continued)*

METHOD	DESCRIPTION	TYPICAL IMPLEMENTATION (BEAN-MANAGED PERSISTENT ENTITIES)	TYPICAL IMPLEMENTATION (CONTAINER-MANAGED PERSISTENT ENTITIES)
ejbRemove()	To destroy an entity bean's data in a database, the client must call *remove()* on the EJB object or home object. This method causes the container to issue an *ejbRemove()* call on the bean. *ejbRemove()* is a required method of all beans, and takes no parameters. *Note: ejbRemove() does not mean the in-memory entity bean instance is going to be destroyed—ejbRemove() only destroys database data. The bean instance can be recycled to handle different database data, such as a bank account bean representing different bank accounts.*	First, figure out what data you should be destroying via *getPrimaryKey()* on the *EntityContext*. Then explicitly delete the database representation of the data via a storage API such as JDBC or SQL/J.	*Do not destroy database data in this method.* Rather, simply perform any operations that must be done before the data in the database is destroyed. The EJB container will destroy the data for you right after *ejbRemove()* is called.
unsetEntityContext()	Called right before your entity bean instance is destroyed (when the container wants to reduce the pool size).	Release any resources you allocated during *setEntityContext()*, and get ready to be garbage collected.	Release any resources you allocated during *setEntityContext()*, and get ready to be garbage collected.

EntityContext

An *entity context* is a specific EJB context used only for entity beans.

```
public interface javax.ejb.EntityContext implements
    javax.ejb.EJBContext
{
    public javax.ejb.EJBObject getEJBObject()
        throws IllegalStateException;

    public java.lang.Object getPrimaryKey();
        throws IllegalStateException;
}
```

Table F.5   javax.ejb.EntityContext

METHOD	DESCRIPTION	USEFULNESS
getEJBObject()	Returns a reference to your bean's own EJB object.	Useful if your bean needs to call another bean, and you want to pass a reference to yourself.
getPrimaryKey()	Retrieves the primary key that is currently associated with this entity bean instance.	Call to determine what database data your instance is associated with. You need to use this in *ejbLoad()* to determine what database data to load and in *ejbRemove()* to determine what database data to remove.

FinderException

This exception indicates a failure to locate an existing entity bean. You should throw this method from your home interface's finder methods.

```
public class javax.ejb.FinderException
    extends java.lang.Exception
{
    public javax.ejb.FinderException();
    public javax.ejb.FinderException(java.lang.String);
}
```

Handle

An EJB object handle is a persistent reference to an EJB object. Handles allow you to disconnect from your EJB server, shut your application down, and later resume your application while preserving the conversational state in the beans you've been working with. Home handles are also useful when your client code needs to store a reference to an EJB object in stable storage and re-connect to that EJB object later.

```
public interface javax.ejb.Handle
{
    public javax.ejb.EJBObject getEJBObject();
}
```

HomeHandle

Just as an EJB object handle is a persistent reference to an EJB object, a home handle is a persistent reference to a home object. Home handles are useful when your client code needs to store a reference to a home object in stable storage and re-connect to that home object later. They also allow you to circumvent JNDI lookups when re-connecting to a home object. Home handles were introduced in EJB 1.1.

```
public interface javax.ejb.Handle
{
    public javax.ejb.EJBObject getEJBObject();
}
```

NoSuchEntityException

Your entity bean class should throw this exception to indicate that the database data corresponding to the in-memory entity bean instance has been removed. You can throw this exception from any of your entity bean class' business methods, and from your *ejbStore* and *ejbLoad* methods. This exception was introduced in EJB 1.1.

```
public class javax.ejb.NoSuchEntityException
    extends javax.ejb.EJBException
{
    public javax.ejb.NoSuchEntityException();
    public javax.ejb.NoSuchEntityException(Exception);
    public javax.ejb.NoSuchEntityException(String);
}
```

ObjectNotFoundException

When you're writing finder methods in your entity bean's home interface, you should throw this exception to indicate that the specified EJB object was not found. You should only use this exception when your finder method is returning a single EJB object. If you're returning more than one EJB object, a null collection is returned instead.

```
public class javax.ejb.ObjectNotFoundException
    extends javax.ejb.FinderException
{
    public javax.ejb.ObjectNotFoundException();
    public javax.ejb.ObjectNotFoundException(java.lang.String);
}
```

RemoveException

Your enterprise bean should throw this exception when an error occurrs during *ejbRemove()*. The container will rethrow this exception back to the client. This is considered a normal, run-of-the-mill application-level exception and does not indicate a systems-level problem. When your client code receives this exception, you do not know for sure whether the entity bean has been removed or not.

```
public class javax.ejb.RemoveException
    extends java.lang.Exception
{
    public javax.ejb.RemoveException();
    public javax.ejb.RemoveException(java.lang.String);
}
```

SessionBean

To write a session bean class, your class must implement the *javax.ejb.SessionBean* interface. This interface defines a few required methods that you must fill in. These are management methods that the EJB container calls to alert your bean about life cycle events. Clients of your bean will never call these methods because these methods are not made available to clients via the EJB object.

```
public interface javax.ejb.SessionBean
    extends javax.ejb.EnterpriseBean
{
    public void setSessionContext(SessionContext ctx);
    public void ejbPassivate();
    public void ejbActivate();
    public void ejbRemove();
}
```

In EJB 1.0, each of these methods can throw a *java.rmi.RemoteException*. However, this doesn't make complete sense since a session bean is not an RMI remote object. Thus, in EJB 1.1, this has changed to *javax.ejb.EJBException*.

Table F.6 Required methods for Session Bean classes.

METHOD	DESCRIPTION	TYPICAL IMPLEMENTATION
setSessionContext (SessionContext ctx)	Associates your bean with a session context. Your bean can query the context about its current transactional state, its current security state, and more.	Store the context away in a member variable so the context can be queried later.
ejbCreate(...)	Initializes your session bean. You can define several *ejbCreate(...)* methods, and each can take different arguments. You must provide at least one *ejbCreate()* method in your session bean.	Perform any initialization your bean needs, such as setting member variables to the argument values passed in.
ejbPassivate()	Called immediately before your bean is passivated (swapped out to disk because there are too many beans instantiated). Does not apply to stateless session beans.	Release any resources your bean may be holding.
ejbActivate()	Called immediately before your bean is activated (swapped in from disk because a client needs your bean). Does not apply to stateless session beans.	Acquire any resources your bean needs, such as those released during *ejbPassivate()*.
ejbRemove()	Called by the container immediately before your bean is removed from memory.	Prepare your bean for destruction. Free all resources you may have allocated.

SessionContext

A *session context* is a specific EJB context used only for session beans.

```
public interface javax.ejb.SessionContext
    extends javax.ejb.EJBContext
{
    public javax.ejb.EJBObject getEJBObject()
        throws IllegalStateException;
}
```

Table F.7   javax.ejb.SessionContext

METHOD	DESCRIPTION	USEFULNESS
getEJBObject()	Returns a reference to your bean's own EJB object.	Useful if your bean needs to call another bean, and you want to pass a reference to yourself.

SessionSynchronization

If your stateful session bean is caching database data in memory, or if it needs to rollback in-memory conversational state upon a transaction abort, you should implement this interface. The container will call each of the methods in this interface automatically at the appropriate times during transactions, alerting you to important transactional events.

```
public interface javax.ejb.SessionSynchronization
{
    public void afterBegin();
    public void beforeCompletion();
    public void afterCompletion(boolean);
}
```

In EJB 1.0, each of these methods can throw a *java.rmi.RemoteException*. However, this doesn't make complete sense, since a session bean is not an RMI remote object. Thus, in EJB 1.1, this has changed to *javax.ejb.EJBException*.

Table F.8   javax.ejb.SessionSynchronization

METHOD	DESCRIPTION
afterBegin()	Called by the container directly after a transaction begins. You should read in any database data you want to cache in your stateful session bean during the transaction.
beforeCompletion()	Called by the container right before a transaction completes. Write out any database data you've cached during the transaction.
afterCompletion(boolean)	Called by the container when a transaction completes either in a commit *or* an abort—true indicates a successful commit, false indicates an abort. If an abort happened, you should roll back your conversational state to preserve your session bean's conversation.

Transaction Reference

Table F.9 Transaction Attributes

CONSTANT	MEANING
TX_BEAN_MANAGED	Your bean *programmatically* controls its own transaction boundaries via the JTA.
TX_NOT_SUPPORTED	Your bean *cannot* be involved in a transaction at all. When a bean method is called, any existing transaction is suspended.
TX_REQUIRED	Your bean must *always* run in a transaction. If there's already a transaction running, your bean joins in on that transaction. If there is no transaction running, the EJB container starts one for you.
TX_REQUIRES_NEW	Your bean must always run in a *new* transaction. Any current transaction is suspended.
TX_SUPPORTS	If a transaction is already underway, your bean will join that transaction. Otherwise, the bean runs with no transaction at all.
TX_MANDATORY	Mandates that a transaction *must be already running* when your bean method is called, else a *javax.ejb.TransactionRequired* exception is thrown back to the caller.

Table F.10 Transaction Isolation Levels

ISOLATION LEVEL	DIRTY READS?	UNREPEATABLE READS?	PHANTOM READS?
TRANSACTION_READ_UNCOMMITTED	Yes	Yes	Yes
TRANSACTION_READ_COMMITTED	No	Yes	Yes
TRANSACTION_REPEATABLE_READ	No	No	Yes
TRANSACTION_SERIALIZABLE	No	No	No

Table F.11 The *javax.transaction.UserTransaction* Constants for Transactional Status

CONSTANT	MEANING
STATUS_ACTIVE	A transaction is currently happening and is active.
STATUS_NO_TRANSACTION	There is no transaction currently happening.

CONSTANT	MEANING
STATUS_MARKED_ROLLBACK	The current transaction will eventually abort because it's been marked for rollback. This could be because some party called *setRollbackOnly()*.
STATUS_PREPARING	The current transaction is preparing to be committed (during Phase One of the two-phase commit protocol).
STATUS_PREPARED	The current transaction has been prepared to be committed (Phase One is complete).
STATUS_COMMITTING	The current transaction is in the process of being committed right now (during Phase Two).
STATUS_COMMITTED	The current transaction has been committed (Phase Two is complete).
STATUS_ROLLING_BACK	The current transaction is in the process of rolling back.
STATUS_ROLLEDBACK	The current transaction has been rolled back.
STATUS_UNKNOWN	The status of the current transaction cannot be determined.

Table F.12   The javax.transaction.UserTransaction Methods for Transactional Boundary Demarcation

METHOD	DESCRIPTION
begin()	Begin a new transaction. This transaction becomes associated with the current thread.
commit()	Run the two-phase commit protocol on an existing transaction associated with the current thread. Each resource manager will make its updates durable.
getStatus()	Retrieve the status of the transaction associated with this thread.
rollback()	Force a rollback of the transaction associated with the current thread.
setRollbackOnly()	Call this to force the current transaction to rollback. This will eventually force the transaction to abort. One interesting use of this is to test out what your components will do, without having them perform any permanent resource updates.
setTransactionTimeout(int)	The *transaction timeout* is the maximum amount of time that a transaction can run before it's aborted. This is useful to avoid deadlock situations, when precious resources are being held by a transaction that is currently running.

Page references followed by italic *t* indicate material in tables.

Using the CD-ROM

Your system must meet the following requirements.

Platform/Processor/Operating System

Windows NT (recommended), Windows 95/98, or UNIX

RAM

64 MB

Hard Drive Space

400 MB

Peripherals

Internet connection for downloading necessary packages, and for source code updates

Installation Notes

Insert the CD-ROM into your computer. Then refer to the README file on the CD-ROM's root directory.

TO ENSURE SUCCESS, YOU MUST FOLLOW THE README INSTRUCTIONS EXACTLY.